WORLD MOUNTAIN RANGES
THE SWISS ALPS

WORLD MOUNTAIN RANGES
THE SWISS ALPS

by Kev Reynolds

JUNIPER HOUSE, MURLEY MOSS,
OXENHOLME ROAD, KENDAL, CUMBRIA LA9 7RL
www.cicerone.co.uk

© Kev Reynolds 2012
ISBN 978 1 85284 465 3
Reprinted 2021 (with updates)
Printed by KHL Printing, Singapore
A catalogue record for this book is available from the British Library.
All photographs are by the author unless otherwise stated.

For my wife whose love, support and patience – and company on so many mountain trips – has made the writing of this book such a joy.

Updates to this Guide

While every effort is made by our authors to ensure the accuracy of guidebooks as they go to print, changes can occur during the lifetime of an edition. Any updates that we know of for this guide will be on the Cicerone website (www.cicerone.co.uk/465/updates), so please check before planning your trip. We also advise that you check information about such things as transport, accommodation and shops locally. Even rights of way can be altered over time. We are always grateful for information about any discrepancies between a guidebook and the facts on the ground, sent by email to updates@cicerone.co.uk or by post to Cicerone, Juniper House, Murley Moss, Oxenholme Road, Kendal, LA9 7RL.

Register your book: To sign up to receive free updates, special offers and GPX files where available, register your book at www.cicerone.co.uk.

Warning

Every mountain walk has its dangers, and those described in this guidebook are no exception. All who walk or climb in the mountains should recognise this and take responsibility for themselves and their companions along the way. The author and publisher have made every effort to ensure that the information contained in this guide was correct when it went to press, but, except for any liability that cannot be excluded by law, they cannot accept responsibility for any loss, injury or inconvenience sustained by any person using this book.

Front cover: No mountain captures the essence of the Swiss Alps better than the Matterhorn
Frontispiece: The lovely Märjelensee reflects mountains on the far side of the Aletschgletscher (Chapter 5:10)

CONTENTS

Overview Map 7

INTRODUCTION 11
About this Book 11
The Mountain Ranges 12

PRACTICALITIES 16
When to Go 16
Weather 18
Getting There 18
Getting Around 20
Accommodation 21
Mountain Huts 22
Maps and Guidebooks 24
Health Considerations 28

THE MOUNTAINS 31
Mountain Activities 33
Safety Dos and Don'ts 41
Mountain Rescue 42
Plant and Animal Life 43
Environmental Ethics 46
Information at a Glance 48

CHAPTER 1: CHABLAIS ALPS 49
1:1   Val de Morgins 53
1:2   Val d'Illiez 54
1:3   Vallon de Susanfe 64
1:4   Rhône Valley Approaches 66
1:5   Vallée du Trient 67
Access, Bases, Maps and Guides 80

CHAPTER 2: PENNINE ALPS 81
2:1   Val Ferret 86
2:2   Val d'Entremont 96
2:3   Val de Bagnes 103
2:4   Val de Nendaz 115
2:5   Val d'Hérémence 116
2:6   Val d'Hérens 120
2:7   Val de Moiry 132
2:8   Val d'Anniviers 137
2:9   Turtmanntal 146
2:10   Mattertal 149
2:11   Saastal 168
2:12   Simplon Pass 179
Access, Bases, Maps and Guides 181

CHAPTER 3: LEPONTINE AND ADULA ALPS 183
3:1   Simplon Pass East 189
3:2   Binntal 191

3:3	Val Bedretto	194
3:4	Valle Leventina	200
3:5	Val Verzasca	205
3:6	Valle Maggia and its Tributaries	211
3:7	Valle di Blenio	217
3:8	Vals Calanca and Mesolcina	224
3:9	The Northern Valleys	229
	Access, Bases, Maps and Guides	237

CHAPTER 4: BERNINA, BREGAGLIA AND ALBULA ALPS 239

4:1	Val Madris and the Averstal	244
4:2	Engadine Valley: Left Bank	248
4:3	Val Bregaglia	256
4:4	The Bernina Alps	270
4:5	The Swiss National Park	285
	Access, Bases, Maps and Guides	289

CHAPTER 5: BERNESE ALPS 291

5:1	Alpes Vaudoises	296
5:2	Les Diablerets to the Rawil Pass	301
5:3	The Wildstrubel Massif	306
5:4	Kandersteg and the Gemmipass	308
5:5	Blüemlisalp and the Gasterntal	310
5:6	The Kiental	313
5:7	Lauterbrunnen Valley	316
5:8	Grindelwald and the Lütschental	325
5:9	Haslital and Grimsel Pass	336
5:10	The Southern Valleys	341
	Access, Bases, Maps and Guides	351

CHAPTER 6: CENTRAL SWISS ALPS 353

6:1	Uri Alps: Dammastock Group	359
6:2	North of the Sustenpass: Titlis Group	369
6:3	Glarner Alps	378
	Access, Bases, Maps and Guides	401

CHAPTER 7: SILVRETTA AND RÄTIKON ALPS 403

7:1	Silvretta Alps: Lower Engadine	408
7:2	Silvretta Alps: Prättigau	413
7:3	Rätikon Alps	420
7:4	The Alpstein Massif	429
	Access, Bases, Maps and Guides	435

APPENDIX A	Glossary of Alpine Terms	437
APPENDIX B	Selective Bibliography	439
APPENDIX C	Index of Maps	440
APPENDIX D	The Swiss 4000m Peaks	442

INDEX 449

OVERVIEW MAP

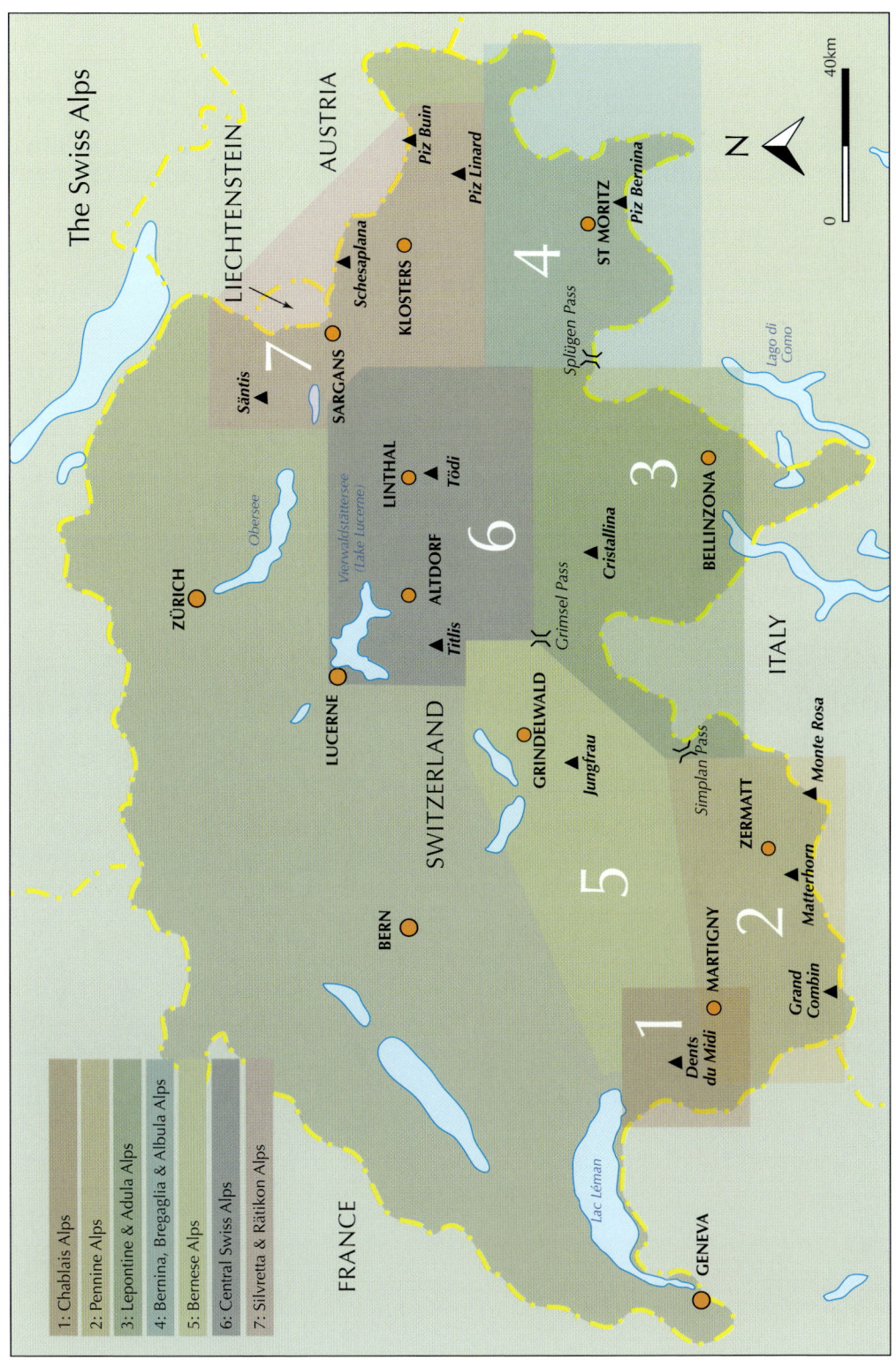

Acknowledgements

It has taken six years to write this book, but in truth research began four decades before any words were written, for I first went to the Swiss Alps in the mid-1960s, fell in love with the mountains and their valleys, found work there, and have since been back scores of times in all seasons, on writing and photographic assignments, leading mountain holidays, researching guidebooks and devising hut-to-hut routes. This, then, has been a labour of love. But none of it would have been possible without the infinite patience of my wife whose support has been crucial at every stage.

I am also indebted to Ernst Sondheimer, good friend and one-time editor of the *Alpine Journal*, for his encouragement and valuable advice, to Roland Hiss whose knowledge of so many alpine regions of Switzerland is almost encyclopaedic, and with whom I've had some memorable mountain days, and to the many friends who have shared numerous Swiss trails and/or summits: Brian and Aileen Evans, Nigel Fry, Richard Moon, Alan Payne, Derek Roberts, John Robertson, Trevor Smith, Alan and Morna Whitlock, Janette Whittle, and Jonathan and Lesley Williams. My daughters, Claudia and Ilsa, cut their mountain teeth in the Swiss Alps, as did my grandsons, and my hope is that they will come to enjoy as many rewarding mountain days there as I have. I'm also fortunate in having the friendship of numerous folk in Switzerland, and their hospitality and company in the mountains has been greatly valued; among them Myrta and Jörg Dössegger, Hedy and the late Marcel Fux, Marc Jones and Diane Sifis, Lisbeth Spielmann, Silvia Linder and Alexandre and Monique Luczy.

My thanks too, to Switzerland Tourism for generous assistance over many years, and to Jonathan Williams at Cicerone who has been incredibly patient as one deadline after another drifted by before he caught sight of this manuscript. And finally, my sincere gratitude to my editor, Andrea Grimshaw, and to the production team in Milnthorpe for working their magic once more to create the attractive book you hold in your hands. Their combined skill, talent and friendship are greatly valued.

Kev Reynolds

Northeast of the Titlis the Engelbergtal is flanked by the Spannort peaks (Chapter 6:2)

INTRODUCTION

Up there in the sky, to which only clouds belong and birds and the last trembling colours of pure light, they stood fast and hard; not moving as do the things of the sky ... These, the great Alps, seen thus, link one in some way to one's immortality.

Hilaire Belloc, *The Path to Rome*

After the Mont Blanc range the Swiss Alps contain the highest and most spectacular mountains in Western Europe, as well as the longest glacier, the greatest number of 4000m summits, and numerous other peaks on which the foundations of alpinism were forged. The 1786 ascent of Mont Blanc by Paccard and Balmat may have signalled the beginnings of alpine interest and activity under a veil of scientific enquiry, but in the same decade the Benedictine monk Father Placidus à Spescha was busy climbing and exploring the Glarner and Adula Alps with an undisguised passion for mountains and mountaineering that is now shared by tens of thousands of visitors who flock to Switzerland in summer and winter alike.

With their rich variety of massifs, their snowpeaks and immense rock faces, their glaciers, lakes and waterfalls, their forests, flower meadows and pastures, the Swiss Alps may justifiably claim to be the quintessential Alps, a love of which is not confined simply to those who walk, climb or ski among them, but also shared by the frail and elderly and those content simply to sit and gaze in wonder. Yet thanks to its mountains, more than a century after Leslie Stephen coined the phrase, Switzerland remains for many the playground of Europe.

The Alps are without question the best known of all the world's mountains, and those that tower over the valleys of Switzerland count among the most easily recognised by both connoisseur and layman alike. The Matterhorn instantly comes to mind, but it is not the only one, for Eiger, Mönch and Jungfrau are symbolic of the Oberland, and the graceful buttresses of Piz Palü in the Bernina range, for example, are depicted on calendar and chocolate box with as much frequency as the proverbial edelweiss and flower-hung chalet. Yet familiarity with such mountains should not breed contempt, for the beauty of the Swiss Alps remains a perennial gift for all to admire.

Mountains make up over 60 per cent of this small landlocked country. With an area of just 41,285 square kilometres, small it may be, but if it were rolled out flat it would be enormous! The landscape, being at once abrupt, dramatic and sublime, is what makes Switzerland so appealing, and while the Pennine and Bernese Alps remain the principal focus of attention for the general tourist as well as for climber, skier and hillwalker, elsewhere the Bernina, Uri and Glarner Alps, the Lepontines, Adula, Silvretta and Rätikon – to name but a few – host a great number of compelling summits that remain unknown to all but a relative handful of enthusiasts.

ABOUT THIS BOOK

This book sets out to redress the balance, to introduce those who have not yet found them to some of the unfamiliar and largely unsung mountains and valleys, while still giving due regard to the giants that dominate the landscape at Zermatt, Grindelwald or Pontresina. It's a handy resource for the active hillwalker, trekker, climber and ski tourer; a guide and gazetteer to the peaks, passes and valleys, providing sufficient background information to help anyone planning a visit to make the most of their time there. Questions such as 'Where to walk, climb or ski?', 'What multi-day treks are available and where do they go?', 'Where are the mountain huts, what are their facilities, which peaks do they serve?', and 'Where are the most suitable valley bases?' – all these and more are addressed in detail.

This book does not give detailed route directions but information is given about all the guides

◀ *The Ried glacier hangs above the tiny village of Gasenried (Chapter 2:10)*

THE SWISS ALPS – INTRODUCTION

Val Morteratsch, the original route to Piz Bernina (Chapter 4:4)

and maps available for every region under review. The aim of this volume is not to lead step by step, but to inspire, to entertain and to inform; to show the first-time visitor – and those who have already discovered one or two of its districts – what the Swiss Alps have to offer. The emphasis is on activity; the intention to help the reader gain a quality experience with every visit. In truth the outdoor enthusiast is spoilt for choice, but armed with this guide, it should be possible to make that choice a better informed one.

Throughout this guide, the following symbols are used to indicate different activities:

- walks and multi-day tours
- climbs
- *via ferrata/klettersteig* routes
- summits for all
- highlight routes of special appeal

Dozens of individual valleys are described, together with the mountains that wall them, with recommendations given for their finest walks, treks and climbs. As such recommendations are purely subjective readers may well take issue with some of the suggestions. That is just how it should be.

Working eastwards across the country, this guide is divided into seven chapters, each devoted to a specific range or group of connecting ranges.

THE MOUNTAIN RANGES

1: Chablais Alps

A small area located south of the Lake of Geneva (Lac Léman) in Canton Valais, its most emblematic peaks are those of the Dents du Midi. No summit exceeds 3200m, and there's very little permanent snow and ice, but plenty of rock routes can be found in the lower-to-medium grades. There are lots of good walking opportunities, including multi-day hut-to-hut routes, and downhill skiing is popular around Champéry and Morgins. Despite its close proximity to the Mont Blanc range, the Chablais district has some surprisingly little-trod corners where activists may experience a degree of solitude unknown in several other regions of the Swiss Alps.

2: Pennine Alps

Extending along the Swiss-Italian border from the edge of the Mont Blanc massif to the Simplon Pass, the Pennines boast the largest concentration of 4000m summits in the Alps, including Monte Rosa, Matterhorn, Weisshorn, Dent Blanche and the Dom. Snow and ice climbs abound, and while the ordinary rock routes are not technically difficult, the length of many climbs, and the exposure and sometimes questionable quality of the rock, tends to raise the standard of seriousness. Ski mountaineering is popular, with classic tours like the Haute Route (Mont Blanc to the Matterhorn) being a major attraction. Some of Switzerland's busiest downhill ski resorts are found here (Verbier, Zermatt, Saas Fee), but there are also many seemingly timeless villages and unspoilt valleys. In summer day walks and hut-to-hut tours make the Pennine Alps a veritable mecca for mountain walkers of all persuasions.

3: Lepontine and Adula Alps

The Lepontine Alps of Canton Ticino (Tessin) rise northeast of the Pennine range between the Simplon Pass and the Lukmanier, where the Adula Alps then continue the line as far as the Splügen Pass. The Lepontines gather round surprisingly remote valleys – perfect for walkers, but less rewarding for the ambitious climber. Glaciers are in short supply and the rock is not always reliable. However, a good number of its peaks would repay a visit by scramblers and first-season alpinists. The highest Adula summit is the 3402m Rheinwaldhorn, while Monte Leone (3553m) and the Ofenhorn (3235m) in the western Lepontines have much to commend them. There are no major resorts, but charming and unspoilt villages provide low-key accommodation in a romantic setting, and the whole area is suffused with the warmth and light of Italy.

4: Bernina, Bregaglia and Albula Alps

In the far southeastern corner of the country these three diverse groups are linked by the Bregaglia and Engadine valleys. In the Bernina massif stands the easternmost 4000m summit (Piz Bernina) among an attractive group of snow- and ice-clad peaks where several classic, traditional routes await the

The evening alpenglow on the Grand Combin (Chapter 2:3)

THE SWISS ALPS – INTRODUCTION

The Grosser Aletschgletscher in the Bernese Alps is the longest glacier in the Alps (Chapter 5:10)

visiting mountaineer. Pontresina is the main centre here. The neighbouring Bregaglia is renowned for its quality granite, and in particular the 800m northeast face of Piz Badile. Carrying the Swiss-Italian border, the Bregaglia is a rock climber's playground *par excellence*. By contrast the Albula Alps, which spread along the Engadine's left flank, have several relatively unknown peaks that form a backdrop to good walking country. Above Zuoz and Madulain the 3418m Piz Kesch is the Albula's best known summit. Switzerland's only national park is located on the opposite bank of the Engadine, while some of the country's most celebrated downhill ski runs are found above St Moritz.

5: Bernese Alps

North of the Rhône valley the Bernese Alps may be slightly lower than the neighbouring Pennines, but they can certainly equal them with opportunities for climber, walker and skier. The western half of the range (St Maurice to the Gemmipass) offers plenty of scope for walkers, and mostly low-altitude climbing up to and slightly above 3000m. The main peaks are Les Diablerets (3210m), Wildhorn (3257m) and Wildstrubel (3243m), the latter renowned for its Plaine Morte glacier. East of the Gemmipass will be found a cluster of 4000m summits, with the imposing 4273m Finsteraarhorn being the highest of them all. Others include the Schreckhorn, Fiescherhorn, Mönch and Jungfrau, while the Eiger falls short by just 30m. Quality rock climbs can be found in most districts, but glaciers are also a major feature. The Grosser Aletschgletscher is the largest in the Alps, but it's just one of several ice sheets that fill the heart of the range. Not surprisingly ski touring is popular, while Wengen, Mürren and Grindelwald, among others, gather winter crowds for downhill skiing. In summer several excellent hut-to-hut walking tours can be made.

6: Central Swiss Alps

Divided by major road passes, the Alps of Central and Eastern Switzerland are extremely diverse. Immediately to the east of the Bernese Alps, the Dammastock group dominates the neatly contained Urner Oberland, shared between Cantons Bern and Uri. High-standard, but low-altitude rock climbs abound on walls flanking the Göschenertal, the 2981m Salbitschijen being prominent among them. Snow and ice climbs are found at the head of the valley, also above the Furkapass and west of the Susten. North of the Sustenpass the Titlis (3238m) is

THE MOUNTAIN RANGES

the main focus of attention for visitors to Engelberg. But elsewhere in this group the Gross and Klein Spannort and Uri-Rotstock each have their own unique appeal. Comparatively easy climbs are the order of the day, although hard routes exist on the massive East Face of the Titlis. Walking is the main activity. On the east side of the Reuss valley the Glarner Alps are subdivided by charming valleys little known to outsiders. A few glaciers and snowfields remain among the highest peaks, but this is a range of mostly easy summits. Best known is the 3614m Tödi, first climbed in 1824, but others with considerable appeal include the Grosse Windgällen, Oberalpstock and Clariden. Ski ascents are not uncommon, and mountain walkers are rewarded with countless opportunities.

7: Silvretta and Rätikon Alps

In the far east of Switzerland these connecting groups share borders with Austria and Liechtenstein, but while the Silvretta is mostly a range of crystalline rock, with small glaciers and snowfields, the Rätikon is limestone and almost completely ice-free. To the northwest the Alpstein massif has the famous 2502m Säntis as its symbolic crown. Low-altitude but high-quality rock climbs can be enjoyed on the nearby Altmann and multi-turreted Kreuzberge. But the best climbing is to be had among the Rätikon's big walls – Sulzfluh and Kirchlispitzen especially. Reminiscent of the Dolomites, this narrow range bursts from a chaos of boulder and scree, with magnificent rock gardens at their feet. Highest of the Rätikon peaks, the 2964m Schesaplana marks the Swiss-Austrian border. By the normal route it is an easy ascent, while a small glacier is draped on its northwest (Austrian) flank. Larger glaciers remain on the north side of the Silvretta group, where traditional-style ascents and spring ski tours are common. But the range comes into its own for the mountain walker in summer, when tempting hut-to-hut circuits are easy to plan and challenging to put into practice.

The Rätikon is a natural rock garden. Here alpenroses flower below the Kirchlispitzen crags (Chapter 7:3)

PRACTICALITIES

En route to the Carschina Hut in the Rätikon Alps (Chapter 7:3)

WHEN TO GO

No season is out of bounds to the lover of mountains, but success in any outdoor activity will largely depend on conditions under foot. So far as general tourist interest is concerned, the months of May and November are off-season in almost every alpine district, when accommodation and facilities are severely limited. Many high road passes are closed by snow from November until June, although tunnels have been created beneath some of the highest to allow year-round travel.

Ski touring/Ski mountaineering takes place between March and the end of May. In popular districts mountain huts will often be manned for a few weeks in order to serve the touring parties who enjoy what is undoubtedly one of the most demanding but rewarding of all mountain pursuits. Naturally an awareness of potential avalanche danger is a prerequisite of all participants.

The precise period for **hut-to-hut trekking** will depend on the specific route and the height of passes that need to be crossed, but from early July until the end of September these should be snow-free and safe to attempt. As a general rule, the most popular huts are manned from July until late September – but check first as there are numerous variations.

Walking and **climbing/mountaineering** take place at varying altitudes between June and the end of September or early October, although given the right conditions, the keenest of participants will make the most of every opportunity no matter what the calendar says. However, July is the optimum month for mountaineering, when the glaciers should still retain some snow cover but the highest ridges are usually bare and dry. The weather is often fairly settled, although a heatwave can bring major rockfalls as the glue of permafrost melts. Global warming has resulted in several recent heatwave summers, ruling out any predictability for

WHEN TO GO

good conditions on snow and ice faces outside the late winter months.

Winter mountaineering must be the most masochistic of pursuits, sometimes played out in appalling conditions, and those who wish to have any new route recognised will follow the International Mountaineering and Climbing Federation (UIAA) ruling that gives the period for alpine winter ascents to be from 21 December until 20 March inclusive.

Downhill skiing usually begins a week or two before Christmas and continues until Easter, although the altitude of the chosen resort, and snow conditions at the time, will have a major impact on facilities available. The best time for **snowshoeing** usually runs from January until April, but whenever there's sufficient snowfall it could be worth getting the snowshoes out. The Alps in winter are at their busiest during the Christmas/New Year period, and in February.

National public holidays are listed below, during which virtually all public offices and shops in Switzerland are closed.

- 1 January – New Year's Day
- March/April – Good Friday and Easter Monday
- May – Ascension Day (40 days after Easter)
- May/June – Whit Monday (7 weeks after Easter)
- 1 August – Swiss National Day
- 25 December – Christmas Day
- 26 December – St Stephen's Day (Boxing Day)

In addition several cantons have their own special holidays, and many local cultural events and festivals take place in specific towns and valleys throughout the year.

High season prices in hotels, restaurants and some shops are often considerably greater than in the low season. In summer the high season in most mountain resorts covers July and August, when pressure on accommodation (including mountain

The Mönch, as seen from Mettlenalp (Chapter 5:7)

huts) is at its greatest. The winter high season coincides with the ski season, although there are fluctuations. For example, prices are highest over Christmas and the New Year, and in February, while January and March are often less crowded and less expensive.

WEATHER

Mountains create their own weather patterns, so there's no surprise to find that Switzerland is home to a variety of local and regional microclimates. For instance, a storm may be isolated on the Matterhorn without affecting the nearby Ober Gabelhorn, and what may appear from Alpiglen to be an innocent cloud on the Eiger could, in fact, be launching a blizzard on the mountain. The north side of the Bernese Alps is notoriously wet, while the Rhône valley which divides those mountains from the Pennine Alps to the south is one of the driest in the country. The Rochers de Naye overlooking Lac Léman in Vaud has 257cm of annual precipitation, while Staldenried, less than 75km away at the junction of the Mattertal and Saastal in Canton Valais, has only 53cm.

Projecting into Italy Canton Ticino, whose mountains belong to the Lepontine and Adula Alps, enjoys the most settled weather, with a Mediterranean climate giving consistently hot and sunny days in summer and comparatively mild winters. Lying in the rain shadow of the Bernese Alps, the Pennine Alps of neighbouring Valais are among the driest.

Although occurring with some frequency in summer, storms in the Bernina and Bregaglia Alps are generally less dangerous than those experienced in the Bernese Alps where they often arrive with little warning and sometimes last for many hours, or even days. At high altitudes bad weather is not only physically uncomfortable for climbers caught mid-route, but rocks can rapidly cover with snow, ice or *verglas* to turn an otherwise straightforward climb into a real epic. Mist and cloud can also make glacier crossing a hazardous exercise.

The Swiss Alps are affected by unusual seasonal winds; the *bise* comes from the north and can be bitterly cold, even in summer, with night frosts and generally settled weather providing good climbing conditions. The *föhn* is a very different wind. This blows from the south or southwest with hot air being sucked from the Mediterranean or even the Sahara. As the air is forced to rise over the Alps, it cools and rain or snow falls on the south side of the mountains, with floods sometimes resulting. Having shed its moisture the *föhn* is then funnelled through the northern valleys, drying and warming as it does. Snow cover diminishes, and conditions for climbing are bad.

Out of the high mountains, most of the country has a Central European climate with temperatures ranging from 20° to 30°C in summer, and around –2° to 6°C in winter.

Weather reports

Hut wardens and local tourist offices often display a daily weather forecast, with an outlook for up to five days. Daily forecasts in German, French or Italian are also obtained by calling 162 (premium rates apply), or checking www.meteoschweiz.ch, where once again information is in German, French or Italian only. Weather reports, forecasts and satellite images can be seen on the Switzerland Tourism website: www.myswitzerland.com.

GETTING THERE

Switzerland is easy to reach from the UK by road, rail and air. The French motorway system enables drivers to reach the Swiss border within a day's journey from southern England. By rail, high-speed trains link London with Paris, and Paris with Geneva, Lausanne and Bern, while more than 50 flights a day operate between UK airports and Geneva, Basel and Zürich. When reading the following section please note that travel information is notoriously susceptible to change; ferry services, and train and air schedules may be abandoned or altered overnight, and airlines go out of business with little advance warning. When planning a trip it is advisable to check carefully the current situation either with your local travel agent, or on the internet.

By road

This is probably the most expensive way to reach the Swiss Alps, but is the obvious choice of walkers and climbers who fill their car with camping equipment, climbing gear and food, and for those who plan to visit several different regions.

GETTING THERE

Walkers below Cabane d'Arpitetta with the Moming glacier ahead in the Val d'Anniviers (Chapter 2:8)

Cross-Channel car ferries currently operated by P&O (www.poferries.com) and Sea France (www.seafrance.com) sail many times daily between Dover and Calais, while Eurotunnel (www.eurotunnel.com) runs frequent car-carrying trains through the Channel Tunnel from Folkestone to Calais in 40–45 minutes.

The distance from Calais to the Swiss border is about 850km, with fast toll-paying motorways (*autoroutes*) for much of that distance. However, on reaching the Jura mountains the motorways run out and slower roads continue through bottleneck towns and villages. On arrival at the Swiss border it is advisable to purchase a *vignette* (current cost CHF40) which enables you to drive on Swiss motorways. (Be caught driving on a motorway without one and you'll face a hefty fine.) Note that the minimum driving age in Switzerland is 18, third-party insurance is compulsory, seat belts must be used, and it is a legal requirement to carry a warning triangle and the vehicle's registration documents.

The national speed limit is 120kph (75mph) on motorways, 80kph (50mph) on main roads, 50kph (30mph) in urban areas, and 30kph (18mph) in residential streets. Numerous speed cameras and radar traps are ready to catch speeding motorists, with on-the-spot fines for the guilty driver. Note also that parking can be prohibitively expensive in both town and country.

By train

Taking the train is perhaps the most relaxing way to go, as well as being the most environmentally friendly. It also compares well with air travel, for the journey time of high-speed trains between London and Bern is not all that different from the actual door-to-door time taken by air passengers.

Eurostar (www.eurostar.com) operates a high-speed rail service from London St Pancras through the Channel Tunnel direct to the Gare du Nord in Paris in 2½hrs. Eurostar trains also depart from Ebbsfleet (near the M25/M2) and Ashford (by the M20) in Kent; both stations have plenty of long-term parking available.

The rail journey from Paris to Switzerland continues via TGV from the Gare de l'Est (next to Gare du Nord) to Basel and Zürich (4hrs 25mins); or from the Gare de Lyon to Geneva (3hrs 25mins), Lausanne (3hrs 50mins) and Bern (4hrs 35mins).

Timetable information for rail journeys between London and any station in Switzerland is available from www.rail.ch.

19

The Swiss Alps – Practicalities

By air
Major Swiss airports are located at Basel, Geneva and Zürich, with smaller regional airports at Bern, Lugano and Sion. Friedrichshafen (Germany) and Milan Malpensa in Italy are also close enough and with good transport links, to offer alternative options.

The majority of scheduled flights from a variety of UK airports are operated by British Airways (www.ba.com) and the Swiss national carrier, Swiss International Airlines – known simply as Swiss (www.swiss.com) – with BMI (www.bmi.com), and EasyJet (www.easyjet.com) following behind. Aer Lingus (www.aerlingus.com), Ryanair (www.ryanair.com) and Swiss all have flights from Dublin. Flight time from London to Basel, Geneva or Zürich is around 1½hrs, but 2–3hrs from the north of England, Scotland and Ireland.

Visitors flying to Geneva or Zürich can take advantage of a **Fly-Rail Baggage Transfer Scheme** which enables 'nothing to declare' baggage with a green customs label attached to be checked in at the departure airport, and delivered directly to the railway station of a nominated Swiss resort. There's no waiting at the arrival airport's carousel, nor the hassle of manhandling baggage from carousel to train. The scheme is straightforward and convenient, is also available for the homeward journey, and currently costs CHF20. For full details see www.rail.ch/baggage.

Online booking agents
Useful websites to consult are:
www.cheapflights.com
www.skyscanner.net
www.ebookers.com
Flight tickets can also be arranged through the Switzerland Travel Centre, the commercial arm of the national tourist office. Go to www.stc.co.uk.

GETTING AROUND

Switzerland's integrated public transport network is legendary. The term 'user-friendly' could have been coined with Swiss railways in mind, for trains are almost religiously punctual, clean and comfortable. Timetables are devised in conjunction with those of the postbus service which operates on routes not covered by trains. In some areas private or regional bus operators have taken over former postbus routes, but virtually every valley in the country can be reached by some form of public

The Saint Bernard Express, a good example of local transport

transport. At the end of each chapter in this guide, outline details of access by bus or train are given.

A number of different travel passes are available, each of which offers value for money when travelling around the country (see www.swisstravelsystem.com). The most popular is the **Swiss Pass** which gives free unlimited travel on 4, 8, 15, 22 or 30 consecutive days on virtually every train, boat and bus in Switzerland. It can also be used to gain discounts of at least 25% on most cable cars and funiculars. The **Swiss Flexi Pass** gives the same advantages as the Swiss Pass, but on 3, 4, 5 or 6 days within a month. These two passes can be purchased from major railway stations within the country on production of a foreign passport, or from the Switzerland Travel Centre in London (www.stc.co.uk). Two or more people travelling together (up to a maximum of five) qualify for a 15% discount on the cost of the Swiss Pass and Swiss Flexi Pass.

If you plan to use a single valley base from which to go walking, climbing or skiing and do not anticipate any intermediate journeys by public transport, the **Swiss Transfer Ticket** could be worth having. It can only be purchased outside Switzerland (see www.swisstravelsystem.com), and gives one free journey from the airport of arrival to anywhere in the country and back again within one month. The **Swiss Card** has similar validity to the Transfer Ticket, but it also allows the holder to buy ordinary train and bus tickets at a 50% discount.

A **regional pass** is another option for moving within one specific area, providing five days of free travel in a 15-day period. And finally, the local **guest card** given to visitors staying in a resort for a few days will often grant free travel on local buses, and sometimes reduced fares on cable cars and funiculars.

ACCOMMODATION

Finding accommodation should not be a problem except perhaps during the high season (Christmas/New Year; February; July and August). The range and quality of hotels, mountain inns and hostels is uniformly high and not as expensive as reputation might suggest. (Mountain huts are dealt with

Left *The Suls-Lobhorn Hut; simple accommodation in a matchless setting*
Right *Berghaus Obersteinberg, a typical mountain inn rich with atmosphere. Both huts are high above the Lauterbrunnen valley*

in a separate section below.) Of course, opulent 4 or 5-star **hotels** are not cheap, but it's not unusual to find a good quality en-suite room in a 2-star establishment costing no more than a b&b in the UK. And the standard of service will be high. Apart from hotels at the two extreme ends of the pricing scale breakfast is usually included in the cost of a room, and half-board (which includes an evening meal) is often available.

The umbrella term **mountain inn**, covers a range of low-key, sometimes simple or rustic establishments, variously described as a *berghaus*, *berggasthaus*, *berggasthof* or *berghotel*. Invariably situated in a spectacular location, and often accessible only on foot, some of these are converted farmhouses, many have no en-suite facilities and a few do not even have electricity in the guest rooms. What most of them do have in abundance is atmosphere – creaking floors, pine panelled walls, and a history.

For those on a very tight budget, note that in many resorts low-cost **dormitory accommodation** is available; some hotels and mountain inns have a *touristenlager* set aside, while it's not unusual to find a cable car station having a dormitory or two within or close to the main building. Such facilities may not be immediately obvious or advertised. Enquire at the local tourist office for details. Dormitories may be listed under *touristenlager*, *massenlager*, *matratzenlager*, *dortoir* or *dormitorio*. Communal washrooms with showers are the norm, and meals are usually available.

Switzerland has 70-odd **youth hostels** affiliated to Hostelling International (see www.youthhostel.ch) that also provide budget accommodation. Despite the name there is no upper age limit for users, and although it is a membership-based organisation, non-members can stay by paying an extra CHF6 on top of the normal overnight fee. Small dormitory rooms are standard.

A group of independent, less formal hostels has spread across Switzerland under the heading of **Swiss Backpackers** (www.swissbackpackers.ch). A number of these are located in cities and large towns, but as many exist in mountain resorts. No membership is required, and facilities on offer are similar to those of youth hostels, with self-catering kitchens and/or low-cost restaurants.

The **Naturfreunde** organisation also has a chain of traditional buildings in alpine regions that are a cross between backpackers' hostels and mountain inns, offering a warm welcome to all. Meals are usually on offer, but self-catering facilities are also provided. See www.nfh.ch for details.

Self-catering chalets and apartments can be found in all major resorts and many smaller mountain villages too, and these can be cost-effective for small groups of friends and families based in one place for a week or more. Again, tourist offices can provide a list of properties.

Wild camping is officially banned throughout Switzerland, but approved **campsites** will be found in major mountain resorts. Facilities are not always of a high standard, although the majority are well equipped and efficiently run, and sites are classified from 1-star to 5-star, which should provide a clue as to what to expect. A number of sites are fully subscribed in July and August, so booking ahead is recommended. Check with the tourist office of your chosen resort for details.

Flexible **holiday packages** that provide both accommodation and travel can be useful for outdoor activists content with a base in a specific resort. 'Lakes and Mountains' specialists such as Crystal (www.crystalholidays.co.uk), Inghams (www.inghams.co.uk), Kuoni (www.kuoni.co.uk) and Thomson (www.thomsonlakes.co.uk) all have a range of competitively priced deals in a number of Swiss resorts.

MOUNTAIN HUTS

Climbers, mountaineers, ski tourers, trekkers and keen hillwalkers too will no doubt make use of mountain huts at some time in their alpine careers. Known variously as a *cabane*, *camona*, *chamanna*, *hütte*, *refuge* or *rifugio*, Switzerland has plenty to choose from. The latest Swiss Alpine Club (www.sac-cas.ch) hut book gives details of more than 350, most of which belong to individual clubs affiliated to the SAC, but many others included are either privately owned or belong to other organisations, yet are open to all comers. The majority are staffed during the high summer season; some have part-time wardens in residence at weekends or when booked in advance by a group; a few are unmanned, and a small handful are little more than simple bivouac shelters with minimal facilities. For up-to-date information on all SAC huts check www.schweizer.huetten.ch or www.alpesonline.ch.

Zmutt, a traditional alp hamlet above Zermatt

Communal dormitories of varying size are common to all. While bedding such as pillows, mattresses, blankets or duvets is provided, users should bring their own thin sleeping bag liner for reasons of hygiene. Toilet and washing facilities vary widely. At lower altitudes many washrooms have hot and cold running water; some have showers and indoor flush toilets, while facilities in general are more limited and basic the higher you go. Bivouacking is not allowed within 400m of a hut.

At staffed huts a full meals service is usually available, with alcoholic drinks as well as a range of hot and cold beverages and a limited variety of snacks for sale. A continental-style breakfast is the norm, but a substantial three- or even four-course evening meal can be expected. Vegetarian meals may be provided if sufficient advanced warning is given. Meal times are usually fixed, with a schedule of breakfast timings (eg 4.00am–7.00am) for climbers arranged according to their chosen route. On occasion a warden will leave out a thermos of hot drink and a plate of breakfast food for those planning an even earlier departure. Given the difficulty and cost of provisioning mountain huts, the price of food and drinks will almost certainly be higher than in the valleys. To keep costs down, some parties carry tea bags and/or coffee sachets and make their own drinks with hot water bought from the warden, others bring snack food from the valley to eat during the day.

There are no self-catering facilities in staffed huts, and personal cooking stoves are not allowed inside or immediately outside the building. Simple food brought to the hut may be prepared on a climber's behalf by the warden for a small charge, but this can be really inconvenient, especially during the busy main season.

Reductions of up to 50% on overnight fees at SAC huts are given to members of other affiliated European alpine clubs, and to BMC members (www.thebmc.co.uk) who have pre-purchased a reciprocal rights card. Anyone planning to spend six nights or more in SAC huts will find membership of an alpine club to be financially beneficial. Note that membership of the UK branch of the Austrian Alpine Club (www.aacuk.org.uk) is one of the cheapest to join, with benefits including free mountain rescue insurance. (See also www.swiss-sport.ch/sac-cas for details of the Swiss Alpine Club.)

23

As a matter of courtesy reservations should be made in advance at all manned huts in order to help the staff plan their catering arrangements. A telephone call is usually all that's expected, and most tourist office staff and hut wardens are happy to phone ahead for you. A frosty welcome may greet climbers who arrive unannounced, other than in an emergency. Should you be forced to abandon your plans, you are expected to call the warden to cancel your reservation.

Outside the staffed period a 'winter room' is usually left unlocked. Bunks with blankets are all that should then be expected, although some winter rooms also have a wood-burning stove, a supply of firewood and an axe. Parties must take their own food and stove to bivouac huts, but crockery and cookware are provided.

Hut conventions

To book a place in a mountain hut, telephone in advance. Phone numbers are normally listed in area guidebooks, otherwise check at the nearest tourist office. Hut wardens will usually phone ahead on your behalf. In the high season, it may be necessary to book several weeks ahead for huts serving the most popular routes.

On arrival leave boots, ice axe, crampons, trekking poles or skis in the boot room/ski room or porch, and select a pair of hut shoes or clogs usually provided for indoor wear. Sometimes rucksacks are not allowed beyond the boot room, in such cases a basket will be provided. Leave your sack in the porch, place essentials in the basket and take this inside with you. As John Barry advises: 'Keep tabs on your gear, in the early morning scramble it is all too easy for someone to mistakenly take your axe – especially if it is a better model than their own – and it is not unknown for boots to walk away on the wrong feet' (*Alpine Climbing*).

Locate the warden to announce your arrival and to book whatever meals are required.

Once a room has been allocated (some wardens specify a particular bunk to use), make your bed using the sleeping bag liner carried for the purpose, and keep a torch handy as the room may not be lit when you need to go there in the dark.

It is customary to pay for services (overnight fee and meals) before going to bed. Cash payments are normal, although at a number of huts it is possible to pay with a credit card (check first).

Lights out and silence in dormitories is usually expected from 10.00pm.

MAPS AND GUIDEBOOKS

Maps

Swiss cartography is world class, with national survey maps published by the Federal Office of Topography (www.swisstopo.ch) covering the whole country with sheets of several different scales: 1:25,000, 1:50,000, 1:100,000 and 1:200,000.

The Monte Moro Pass (2868m) at the head of the Saas valley with its gilded Madonna (Chapter 2:11)

Maps and Guidebooks

The 1:50,000 series, which is perfectly adequate for the majority of walkers, mountaineers and ski tourers, includes a set of maps with major walking routes marked. These *Wanderkarten* are distinguished by the letter T given after the individual sheet number, while sheets marked with ski touring routes (*Skitourenkarten*) are distinguished by the letter S. National survey maps detailed at the end of each chapter in this book are listed with the prefix LS (*Landeskarten der Schweiz*).

The complete 1:25,000 series (more than 230 separate sheets) is also available on eight CD-ROM discs under the heading Swiss Map 25.

Independent publisher Kümmerly & Frey (www.swisstravelcenter.ch) also produces a series of maps for walkers at a scale of 1:60,000. As with LS maps, these *Wanderkarten* have major walking routes and mountain huts prominently marked, and the clearly defined contours and artistic use of shading produce an instant representation of ridge, spur and valley. Again, details of relevant sheets are given at the end of each chapter.

> **MAP AVAILABILITY**
>
> Recommended maps are available in the UK from the following outlets:
> - **Cordee** www.cordee.co.uk
> - **Edward Stanford Ltd**, 7 Mercer Walk, London WC2H 9FA (tel 020 7836 1321 www.stanfords.co.uk)
> - **The Map Shop**, 15 High Street, Upton-upon-Severn, WR8 0HJ (www.themapshop.co.uk)

Kümmerly & Frey also has a limited series of 1:120,000 sheets which provide a useful overview of regions such as Graubünden, Valais (Wallis) and the Bernese Oberland, and a separate sheet (*Wanderland*) at 1:301,000 showing all the main long-distance walking routes in Switzerland, with a comprehensive index on the reverse.

Guidebooks for walkers and trekkers
The majority of English-language guides to the Alps for walkers and trekkers are published by Cicerone (www.cicerone.co.uk), with the following list covering the Swiss Alps. Those produced by the Swiss Alpine Club are in either French or German.

Cicerone guides
100 Hut Walks in the Alps by Kev Reynolds (Cicerone, 3rd edition 2018)

Swiss Alpine Pass Route – Via Alpina 1 by Kev Reynolds (Cicerone, 3rd edition 2017)

Central Switzerland: a Walker's Guide by Kev Reynolds (Cicerone, 1993)

Chamonix to Zermatt: the Walker's Haute Route by Kev Reynolds (Cicerone, 6th edition 2019)

The Bernese Oberland by Kev Reynolds (Cicerone, 4th edition 2015)

Tour of the Jungfrau Region by Kev Reynolds (Cicerone, 3rd edition 2018)

Tour of the Matterhorn by Hilary Sharp (Cicerone, 2009)

Tour of Monte Rosa by Hilary Sharp (Cicerone, 2nd edition, 2015)

Trekking in the Alps by Kev Reynolds (Cicerone, 2011)

Walks in the Engadine by Kev Reynolds (Cicerone, 3rd edition 2019)

Walking in the Alps by Kev Reynolds (Cicerone, 2nd edition 2005)

Walking in Ticino by Kev Reynolds (Cicerone, 1992)

Walking in the Valais by Kev Reynolds (Cicerone, 4th edition 2014)

Other guides
Alpinwandern Graubünden (SAC)

Alpinwandern Rund um die Berner Alpen (SAC)

Alpinwandern Schweiz, Von Hütte zu Hütte (SAC)
Alpinwandern Tessin (SAC)
Alpinwandern Wallis (SAC)
Alpinwandern Zentralschweiz –Glarus –Alpstein (SAC)
Randonnées alpines, D'une cabane du CAS à l'autre (SAC)
Randonnées en montagne, Chablais–Valais francophone (SAC)
The Bernina Trek by Geoffrey Pocock (www.leisure-and-business.co.uk 2009)
The Walker's Haute Route by Alexander Stewart (Trailblazer, 2008)
Trekking and Climbing in the Western Alps by Hilary Sharp (New Holland, 2002)
Walking in Switzerland by Clem Lindenmayer (Lonely Planet, 2nd edition 2001)
Walking in the Alps by Helen Fairbairn et al. (Lonely Planet, 2004)
Wanderfitzig, Talein, talaus durchs Göschenertal (SAC)

Climbing guides
The following rock climbing guides have been published by the SAC, in German only.
Engelhornführer
Kletterführer Alpstein
Kletterführer Berner Voralpen
Kletterführer Bockmattli, Brügglerkette, Amden
Kletterführer Churfirsten–Alvierkette–Fläscherkette
Kletterführer Rätikon
Kletterführer Zentralschweizerische Voralpen

Editions Equinoxe publish sport climbing guides (mostly topos), and the Münich-based Bergverlag Rother (www.rother.de) has produced a useful pocket guide (in German) to the Swiss *via ferratas/klettersteigen*, while Eugen Hüsler's book gives details of all the *via ferratas* in both Switzerland and France.

Hüslers Klettersteigführer: Westalpen by Eugen H Hüsler (Bruckmann, 2001)
Klettersteig Schweiz by Iris Kürschner (Rother, 2004)
Schweiz Extrem: die Schönsten Sportkletteren by Jürg von Känel (Egger, Frutigen, 1989/Editions Equinoxe)
Schweiz Plaisir Ost by Jürg von Känel (Editions Equinoxe)
Schweiz Plaisir West by Jürg von Känel (Editions Equinoxe)

Mountaineering guides
The Alpine Club in London (www.alpine-club.org.uk) has an excellent four-volume series of mountaineering guides to the Swiss Alps, and a single guide to all the alpine 4000m peaks. Bâton Wicks also has a popular guide to the 4000m peaks translated from German. The West Col guide to Central Switzerland is long out of date, but is the only one in the English language to cover the Dammastock/Urner Alps district. The same publisher has a more up-to-date guide for the Silvretta Alps.

Bernese Oberland by Les Swindin (AC, 2003)
Bernina and Bregaglia by Lindsay Griffin (AC, 1995)
Central Switzerland by Jeremy Talbot (West Col, 1969)

Silvretta Alps by Jeff Williams (West Col, 1995)
The 4000m Peaks of the Alps by Martin Moran (AC, 2007)
The Alpine 4000m Peaks by the Classic Routes by Richard Goedeke (Bâton Wicks, 2nd edition 2003)
Valais Alps East by Les Swindin and Peter Fleming (AC, 1999)
Valais Alps West by Lindsay Griffin (AC, 1998)

The Swiss Alps are covered in near-comprehensive fashion by a series of German-language guides published by the SAC as follows.

Berner Alpen 1, Sanetsch bis Gemmi
Berner Alpen 2, Gemmi bis Petersgrat
Berner Alpen 3, Bietschhorn, Breithorn, Aletschhorngruppen
Berner Alpen 4, Tschingelhorn bis Finsteraarhorn
Berner Alpen 5, Von Grindelwald zur Grimsel
Berner Voralpen, Von Gstaad bis Meiringen
Hochtouren Berner Alpen, Vom Sanetschpass zur Grimsel
Bündner Alpen 1, Tamina und Plessurgebirge
Bündner Alpen 2, Vom Lukmanier zum Domleschg
Bündner Alpen 3, Avers (San Bernardino bis Septimer)
Bündner Alpen 4, Südliche Bergeller Berge und Monte Disgrazia
Bündner Alpen 5, Bernina-Gruppe und Valposchiavo
Bündner Alpen 6, Vom Septimer zum Flüela
Bündner Alpen 7, Rätikon
Bündner Alpen 8, Silvretta und Samnaun
Bündner Alpen 9, Engiadina Bassa – Val Mustair
Bündner Alpen 10, Mittleres Engadin und Puschlav
Säntis–Churfirsten, Von Appenzell zum Walensee
Glarner Alpen
Gotthard, Von der Furka zum Lukmanier
Zentralschweizerische Voralpen, Schwyzer Voralpen, Unterwaldner Voralpen, Pilatus–Schrattenflue–Kette
Tessiner Alpen 1, Vom Gridone zum Sankt Gotthard
Tessiner Alpen 2, Von der Cristallina zum Sassariente
Tessiner Alpen 3, Von der Piora zum Pizzo di Claro
Misoxer Alpen 4, Vom Zapporthorn zum Passo San Jorio
Tessiner Voralpen 5, Vom Passo San Jorio zum Generoso
Urner Alpen Ost 1
Urner Alpen 2, Göscheneralp – Furka – Grimsel
Urner Alpen 3, Vom Susten zum Urirotstock
Walliser Alpen 1, Vom Trient zum Grossen St Bernhard
Walliser Alpen 2, Vom Grossen St Bernhard zum Col Collon
Walliser Alpen 3, Vom Col Collon zum Theodulpass

Walliser Alpen 4, Vom Theodulpass zum Monte Rosa
Walliser Alpen 5, Vom Strahlhorn zum Simplon
Hochtouren im Wallis, Vom Trient zum Nufenenpass

The following large-format hardback describes easy routes to 50 summits of 3000m peaks in the Swiss Alps. Too big to carry on the hill, it nevertheless gives good background information for those with a reasonable command of German.

Freie Sicht aufs Gipfelmeer by Marco Volken and Remo Kundert (Salvioni Edizioni, Bellinzona 2003)

Ski touring/mountaineering and snowshoeing guides
Cicerone (in English) and the SAC (in French and German) have good coverage of the most popular regions.

Alpine Ski Mountaineering Vol 1: Western Alps by Bill O'Connor (Cicerone, 2002)
Alpine Ski Mountaineering Vol 2: Central & Eastern Alps by Bill O'Connor (Cicerone, 2003)
Alpine Skitouren 5, Glarus–St Gallen–Appenzell (SAC)
Alpine Skitouren Zentralschweiz – Tessin (SAC)
Die schönsten Skitouren der Schweiz (SAC)
Graubünden Nord, Vom Prättigau bis zur Surselva: Schneeschuhtouren (SAC)
Les plus belles randonnées à ski de Suisse (SAC)
Ski alpin Bas-Valais, Du Lac Léman jusqu'à la Dent-Blanche (SAC)
Ski alpin 3, Alpes valaisannes (SAC)
Skitouren Berner Alpen Ost, Lötschenpass bis Grimsel (SAC)
Skitouren Berner Alpen West, Waadtländer und Freiburger Alpen, Le Moléson bis Balmhorn (SAC)
Skitouren Graubünden (SAC)
Skitouren Oberwallis, Vom Bishorn zum Gross Muttenhorn (SAC)
Snowshoeing: Mont Blanc & the Western Alps by Hilary Sharp (Cicerone, 2002)
Tessin Misox: schneeschuhtouren (SAC)
Tessin/MisoxCalanca, Vom Val Bedretto zum Monte Generoso (SAC)
The Haute Route by Peter Cliff (Cordee)

BOOK SUPPLIERS

For details of all **Cicerone** publications, and to order online go to www.cicerone.co.uk

Alpine Club, Bâton Wicks, Rother and **West Col** guides are all available from Cordee www.cordee.co.uk

Swiss Alpine Club publications may be ordered online at www.sac-verlag.ch

HEALTH CONSIDERATIONS

At the time of writing no **immunisations** are required to enter Switzerland, unless you've recently been in an area of yellow fever or cholera infection, in which case an International Health Certificate will be needed. It's also sensible to be up to date with tetanus vaccination.

In view of the increase in the viral infection known as **tick-borne encephalitis** (TBE), walkers ought to consider protection. TBE is a debilitating and potentially life-threatening disease, spread by the bite of the *Ixodes* tick that lies in wait on the

Health Considerations

A rocky section of trail leading from the Gasterntal to the Lötschenpass above Kandersteg (Chapter 5:5)

underside of bushes and grasses in large areas of Europe, including Switzerland. Risk is seasonal, from March to September, and anyone taking part in outdoor activities below the snowline in summer (camping included) may be vulnerable. The risk of tick bites can be reduced by using an effective insect repellent, and by covering areas of exposed skin with suitable clothing, and a TBE vaccine is now available in UK travel clinics and some GP surgeries. For more information go to www.masta.org/tickalert.

If you take regular **medication**, make sure you have an adequate supply to last throughout your visit, and make a note of the generic name of the medication (not the brand name) which will make it easier to get a replacement should you inadvertently run out.

Water is safe to drink from most of the numerous fountains seen throughout the country, unless there's a notice stating otherwise: *Kein Trinkwasser* and *eau non potable* mean the water is unsafe to drink. Stream water should be treated with caution, as polluting animals may be grazing above the source. To ensure stream water is safe to drink, either boil thoroughly or use a special filter.

In winter as in summer, it's easy to get **sunburnt** or suffer from **heat stroke** in the mountains – especially at altitude – so protect yourself with a brimmed hat, a liberal coating of sunscreen and lip salve. At the other end of the spectrum, **hypothermia** can affect anyone in summer or winter when their body loses heat faster than it can produce it, and the core temperature falls to dangerous levels. This is most likely to happen in wet and windy conditions, and when suffering from exhaustion. Try to avoid getting soaked by wearing good waterproofs and layers of warm clothing, including gloves and hat. If you or your partner show early signs of hypothermia get out of the wind and into some form of shelter (tent, bivvy bag or large polythene bag), replace any wet clothing with dry, eat some high-energy food and drink hot sugary liquids. Do not drink alcohol, or rub the patient to restore circulation, and avoid further exertion.

The Dammastock group in central Switzerland (Chapter 6:1)

Health insurance

All medical treatment in Switzerland must be paid for, but note that the European health insurance card is also valid, which entitles the holder to reciprocal arrangements for the reimbursement of some costs of medical treatment (check limitations which are printed on forms available at UK post offices). However, the EHIC is no substitute for proper health insurance, so walkers, skiers and climbers should make sure they have adequate cover appropriate for their chosen activity; it should include personal accident, sickness and mountain rescue. The British Mountaineering Council (BMC) provides a comprehensive insurance service for its members, with policies covering travel, trekking, rock climbing, mountaineering and winter sports (www.thebmc.co.uk). Note also that the UK branch of the Austrian Alpine Club provides insurance cover to members for basic rescue, medical emergencies and repatriation (www.aacuk.co.uk).

THE MOUNTAINS

The Alps in winter – a pristine world of great beauty

Daubed with snow and ice and interspersed with lakes and lush green valleys, the Alps spread across the southern and central regions of Switzerland to give the country its dominant physical presence. Below the mountains to the north lies the more populated and industrial Mittelland, beyond which the relatively low limestone range of the Jura folds into France.

Despite being created some 90–100 million years ago when Africa collided with the Eurasian tectonic plate, pushing the land into waves of rock that eventually took shape as the mountains we see today, the Alps are still young in geological terms. Constantly reshaping, their youthful nature is characterised by jagged peaks and sharp ridges sculpted by ice and water. As they rise, the mountains are being worn down. Frost shatters immense blocks. Glaciers gouge chunks of rock and spew them out as moraine debris, and year upon year their torrents bring down tens of thousands of tons of mountain in the shape of silt and mud to nourish the fertile lowland fields.

Global warming increases that process of mountain destruction, not just by the melting of snowfields and glaciers, but the permafrost too. In many places the rock is so fragmented that it is only glued together by ice. When that melts, the mountains, or large portions of them, fall down. In April 1991 a large section of the Langenflueberg collapsed into the Mattertal near Randa, demolishing the railway, blocking the river and cutting the upper valley off for several days. In the July 2003 heatwave massive rockfalls marooned 70 climbers above 3400m on the Matterhorn's Hörnli ridge. A little under two years later 500,000 cubic metres of moraine collapsed onto the Lower Grindelwald glacier below the Fiescherwand, taking a restaurant with it. The following year an estimated 1.5 million cubic metres of rock broke away from the Eiger's southeast flank; shortly after an impressive 50,000 cubic metre flake of rock detached itself from the east flank of the same mountain and stood precariously in the glacier gorge above Grindelwald.

31

In common with all alpine glaciers, the Oberer Grindelwaldgletscher is shrinking fast

As this book goes to print the Swiss Alps are changing shape, and it is inevitable that some of the descriptions – not only of peaks, glaciers and snowfields, but routes to their summits – will have become outdated; such is the speed of change.

Climate change and global warming may be 21st-century buzzwords, but from about one million years ago the Alps have experienced a cycle of extended cold periods (ice ages), rapidly followed by climatically warmer intervals; each cycle lasting about 2000 years. Until these ice ages began, it is thought that the mountains consisted of bare rock peaks divided by narrow V-shaped river valleys, but then came the glaciers which covered all but the highest summits and ridges of the Central Alps, filling the valleys and stretching out into the lowlands. Reaching its peak about 25,000 years ago, the last great ice age smothered much of modern Switzerland, widening and deepening the alpine valleys, chiselling and sharpening peaks and smoothing rock walls. It was then that the Rhône glacier stretched 150km from its source near the Furkapass to the Lake of Geneva.

When the last great ice age drew to an end, glaciers slowly retreated, revealing characteristic U-shaped valleys, and great banks of terminal moraine formed dams that turned rivers of meltwater into the lakes for which Switzerland is also known. When the glacier that had filled the Surselva valley on the east side of the Oberalp Pass withdrew, a vast section of mountain collapsed into the valley below where Flims now stands, blocking the river for a length of something like 15km. When the pressure of water finally broke through the blockage, a wall of water swept downvalley causing much devastation.

In the warm period of 2000–4000 years ago, much less ice covered the Alps than there is today. Relics found near the 3301m summit of the Theodulpass show that it was snow-free in Roman times, and the tongues of 1st-century glaciers were then at least 300m higher than they are now. Throughout the Middle Ages, a number of passes that are covered by glaciers today were free from snow and ice and were in regular use.

But glaciers began to advance again from the 15th century onwards, reaching their greatest extent around 1850 during what has been referred to as a mini ice age. Visiting Grindelwald in 1723 Horace Mann reported that an exorcist had been

MOUNTAIN ACTIVITIES

GLACIER RETREAT: CONSEQUENCES FOR MOUNTAINEERING

Recent hot summers have seen the collapse of snow bridges adding to problems where access routes cross glaciers. In some years classic mixed faces have not been in condition (the White Spider section on the Eiger's *Nordwand* disappeared in the summer of 2003), and where glaciers are in retreat they often leave behind hazardous slopes of steep and unstable rock. Shrinking icefields have had a significant effect on numerous routes, especially where the climber transfers from glacier to newly polished rockface. Here, as on the approach to several huts, metal ladders may have been bolted to the rock to secure progress, while melting permafrost not only leads to increased danger from stonefall, but also threatens the stability of installations such as pylons carrying cable cars.

Glacier retreat and the increased possibility of rockfall can change the character of a route in significant ways. Climbers are therefore advised to check current conditions with great care before undertaking any alpine expedition.

employed to halt the advance of the glaciers that were threatening to engulf the village, while a century later James David Forbes described an advancing glacier invading fields of corn, and of seeing peasants gathering ripe cherries 'with one foot standing on the ice'.

The present glacial retreat began in the mid-19th century, and according to the Glacier Monitoring Service of the Swiss Academy for Natural Sciences, between 1850 and 2000 some 249 Swiss glaciers disappeared completely. Many more are in danger of disappearing within the next two or three decades, as satellite measurements recorded over the 15-year period from 1985 to 2000 show a 20 per cent loss of the glaciated surface of the Swiss Alps. Apart from the environmental consequences, glacier shrinkage can have a serious impact on mountain activities.

MOUNTAIN ACTIVITIES

Walking/trekking

Every region included in this guide holds almost unlimited scope for walkers of all ages, abilities and ambitions, and in the majority of cases superb multi-day routes exist that link huts, mountain inns and villages. Literally tens of thousands of kilometres of footpaths have been created throughout the Swiss Alps; some of these are ancient trading

Footpaths in the mountains are signed with customary Swiss efficiency. Unambiguous waymarks help walkers keep to their route

33

routes; others, hundreds of years old, were worn by farmers, chamois hunters and crystal collectors. Some have been made specifically to reach mountain huts, while yet more have been devised and constructed by local tourist authorities for the simple enjoyment of their visitors. The majority of trails are waymarked, signed and well maintained, with bridges constructed over large streams and rivers, and rope or metal handrails provided to give psychological support where a section of trail is narrow or exposed.

The easiest paths (*wanderweg*) are waymarked with yellow paint flashes. White-red-white striped waymarks are used on more challenging mountain trails (*bergweg*), while blue-and-white waymarks indicate a so-called alpine route (*alpenweg*). These alpine routes often involve cairned areas where no proper path exists; there could also be some scrambling involved, with *via ferrata/klettersteig* style sections of ladder, lengths of fixed rope/cable, or iron rungs drilled into the rock to enable users to surmount difficult crags. Agility and a good head for heights are essential.

Signposts are found at most trail junctions. Apart from a few major resort areas such as Zermatt, they conform to a national standard and provide information with typical Swiss efficiency. Coloured yellow these signs bear the names of major landmark destinations, such as a pass, lake, hut or village, or sometimes a name that appears on no map but which refers to a specific footpath junction. Estimated times to reach these places are given in hours and minutes, while some of the signposts include a plate giving the name and altitude of the immediate locality. In the early stages of a holiday, times may seem difficult to achieve, but most hill walkers soon find them less of a challenge.

In summer, gentle **valley walks suitable for families** with small children follow trails and tracks through meadows, alongside rivers and around lakes. Funicular railways, gondola lifts and cable cars provide opportunities to gain height and far-reaching views without effort, and in a number of cases enable modest walkers to enjoy easy trails to vantage points that would otherwise be beyond their ambition. Alp hamlets and the occasional

Bolted to the rockface, metal ladders like this one on the Pas de Chèvres, enable trekkers to scale otherwise impassable slabs

Stream crossing en route to the Vereinapass in the Rätikon Alps

farm restaurant make obvious goals. Neither prior experience (beyond common sense) nor specialised equipment will normally be required. But waterproofs, warm clothing and refreshments should be carried, and inexperienced walkers should never stray from a marked footpath. Local tourist offices often provide useful leaflets suggesting suitable walks.

Keen **hillwalkers** have a wonderland to explore, for countless footpaths seduce to mountain huts, passes, viewpoints and modest summits, every one of which will almost certainly reward with an unforgettable experience. For the newcomer to the Alps, however, ambition needs to be tempered with caution. On a first visit the sheer size and scale of the mountains can either excite or intimidate, and it may be difficult to appreciate just how long it will take to walk from A to B when the map's contours are so tightly drawn. Don't overstretch yourself on the first few outings. Keep ambition in check until routes have been found that match your capabilities, and make sure you enjoy the steep uphills as much as the level sections and downhill trails. Always carry a map and compass or GPS – and know how to use them. Stick to marked trails and

> **WEBSITES FOR THE INDEPENDENT WALKER AND TREKKER**
>
> www.wandersite.ch and www.wanderland.ch both give plenty of information and advice as well as outline routes for the walker in Switzerland.

avoid taking shortcuts that will lead to soil erosion, and where a route crosses terrain where no footpath as such is evident, keep alert for waymarks (paint flashes) and/or cairns that show the way.

Trekking, or walking a multi-day route, is for many the ultimate way to experience the mountains. In essence trekking consists of a series of linear day walks with each successive night spent in a different location. In some mountain regions trekkers need to be self-reliant and carry tent, cooking stove and food. But in Switzerland such backpacking is unnecessary, for there's a wonderful string of mountain huts, inns, dormitories and hotels almost everywhere below the snowline, enabling the outdoor enthusiast to make a whole host of journeys carrying little more than the basic essentials in a fairly small rucksack. Travelling light frees the spirit to roam the high places with maximum enjoyment and minimum sweat. This book outlines a number of hut-to-hut treks; some have dedicated guidebooks (listed where the route is described), while many more could be devised by careful study of the appropriate maps.

Equipment for the walker and trekker

Experienced hillwalkers will no doubt have their preferences, but the following list of clothing and equipment gives suggestions for newcomers to the Alps. Some items will obviously not be needed if outings are to be confined to low valley walks.

- lightweight walking boots with good grip – essential for dealing with rough terrain, scree and steep slopes
- wind- and waterproof jacket and overtrousers
- warm clothing such as fleece jacket, hat and gloves – even in summer
- brimmed hat, sunglasses, suncream and lip salve
- trekking poles – useful for crossing streams and rocky ground, and help reduce strain on leg joints
- rucksack with waterproof cover and liner
- closed cell sitmat to be used as an insulated seat on damp ground or rocks
- map and compass and/or GPS
- first aid kit
- sleeping bag liner (for use in mountain huts)

Climbing/mountaineering

The Swiss Alps have some of the finest, most historic and challenging of all the world's mountains, among which even a modest ascent can reward with memorable adventures played out in a fabulous setting. The 4000m peaks may jostle at the top of an ambitious climber's tick-list, yet numerous 'lesser peaks' would be worth the attention of anyone with a sense of adventure. This book suggests where some of these adventures may be won.

There are essential differences, of course, between climbing in Britain and climbing in the Alps; altitude for a start. Britain's highest summit (Ben Nevis) is 1344m, while most alpine climbs are on peaks of 3000m and more. While a day's mountaineering in Britain can net several summits, many alpine climbs are spread over two days – the first spent on the approach to a hut, with the second

The East Summit of Piz Palü (Chapter 4:4)

The icy heart of a glacier – to avoid close acquaintance rope up and stay alert!

day devoted to the climb itself, followed by descent to the valley.

The sheer scale and variety of alpine scenery is another major difference, and in Switzerland alone a climber could spend a lifetime of active holidays in one area after another without repeating a single route. But in the Alps climbing is a more serious business than in non-alpine areas, with objective dangers that should never be ignored. Rockfall, for example, can occur on almost any route, seracs can topple without prior warning, and even the most innocent-looking glacier may have hidden crevasses.

To climb safely in the Alps involves a number of skills, including a combination of rope management, route-finding ability, appreciation of snow and ice conditions, crevasse identification and an understanding of crevasse rescue, as well as fitness and good acclimatisation.

Knowledge of alpine mountains and mountaineering only comes with experience, but is essential to enable the climber to select a route that is in good condition, to recognise potentially hazardous snow and ice conditions, to detect the presence of crevasses, and predict changing weather patterns. Experience tells the climber what time to set out, when it is safest to deal with difficult or dangerous sections of the route, when and where the greatest threat of avalanche lies, or where rock is likely to be free from a glaze of ice.

Navigational skills are essential for safety and success in the mountains. Correct route-finding on both rock and glacier will save time and energy and limit a climbing party's exposure to danger. Close scrutiny of the appropriate maps and guidebook (where one exists) will be extremely useful. But with glacial recession and rockfall changing the mountains from one season to the next, quizzing other climbers who have recently done the route will often be the most beneficial approach. When on rock finding the correct way can be helped by signs of previous climbers, but beware of following other parties unless you're sure that they are on the same route you wish to climb. If the moves are much harder (or easier) than the grade your chosen route warrants, there's a good chance you're off-route.

As well as rock, snow and ice climbing skills, rope management should be practised in advance on climbs at home until they're second nature. But the alpine environment has demands beyond those of Britain's mountains, for safe movement on glaciers, for example, involves its own technique. While 'dry' glaciers (bare of snow) are usually safe to cross because crevasses are clearly visible, on snow-covered ('wet') glaciers where crevasses are hidden, parties should cross roped together 15m apart. Three on a rope is the minimum for safety on a glacier (four for preference), but even then it's not easy for two people to haul one unfortunate victim from a crevasse. Crevasse rescue is a skill that all would-be alpinists should practise.

Being fit on arrival in the Alps enables a party to move quickly and safely over a variety of terrain, and combined with good acclimatisation and stamina will allow them to complete long and arduous routes without fatigue impairing their judgement. Speed and efficiency equal safety.

ALPINE INSTRUCTION FOR BEGINNERS

Basic skills can be learned to an extent from various instruction manuals and DVDs, but mountaineering courses have a more immediate practical impact. Among those based in the Alps, the International School of Mountaineering (ISM) run alpine courses from their operations centre in Leysin (www.alpin-ism.com). Alpine instruction is also given by qualified British Mountain Guides (www.bmg.org.uk), and a number of commercial organisations run courses and mountaineering holidays in the Alps. Study advertisements in the outdoor press for details. For an entertaining primer, John Barry's *Alpine Climbing* (Crowood Press, 1995) is highly recommended.

Clothing and equipment for climbing/mountaineering

The list below is neither comprehensive nor prescriptive, but offered as a general guide for an alpine summer. If technical climbing is not on the agenda, a number of these items will not be required.

- A comfortable, well-adjusted rucksack (40–50 litres) with compression straps, and a waterproof liner.
- Clothing should be lightweight wherever possible. Layers allow flexibility with the varying

With their snow cover gone, 'dry' glaciers like this are safer to cross as crevasses should be clearly visible

temperatures encountered during an alpine climb; a thermal vest as a base layer is preferred. Trousers of a stretch material are ideal. Overtrousers should have long zips so they can be pulled on and off over crampons.
- Two pairs of gloves will be needed; an inner pair with leather palms allow good grip for technical climbing, while lined mittens provide protection in cold conditions.
- A fleece hat, brimmed sunhat and climbing helmet are all essential.
- Comfortable leather boots for most climbs in summer, but plastic boots in winter, in extra cold conditions, and for the very highest summits. Crampons must be compatible with your boots (plus point covers or a thick bag for safety in travel).
- Full length gaiters help keep legs and feet dry when ploughing through snow.
- A climbing sit-harness; ice axe (minimum 50cm) with curved pick, and an ice hammer.
- A single 9–10mm rope (minimum length 40m) is fine for glaciers and non-technical climbs. For advanced routes two 9mm ropes allow

MOUNTAIN ACTIVITIES

faces by way of metal rungs, ladders or footplates safeguarded by a continuous length of fixed cable. Some sections of the climbing community object to them for cluttering the mountain environment, but there's no denying their adventurous appeal, for those with no vertigo problems are able to tackle vertical and in some cases overhanging rock to reach vantage points and summits otherwise denied them. Cheating? Maybe. Exhilarating? Most definitely.

Safety equipment such as helmet, sit-harness, karabiners, rope and slings are essential, and their correct use should be rehearsed before setting off on any major *klettersteig* route. For these are frequently demanding, almost gymnastic undertakings that require a good level of mountain experience. Although non-climbers can successfully tackle some of the lower-grade routes, the ability to rock climb to at least grade III will be necessary on the longer and more challenging routes. A high level of fitness and stamina are also prerequisites.

The existence of many *klettersteig* routes are highlighted in this book, but the following German-language guide to 55 protected routes in Switzerland is recommended: *Klettersteig Schweiz* by Iris Kürschner (Rother, Munich 2004).

longer abseils on descent. Each member of a climbing party should carry spare cord or tape to back up any suspect abseil point; a belay plate, descender and two prusiks – and know how to use them.

- On many climbs essential bolts and pegs are often in place (treat all *in situ* gear with caution), but runners, slings and karabiners will be needed, and depending on the route, ice screws, friends, quick-draws and a full set of wired nuts may be required.
- Sunglasses with side protection, and a high-factor suncream and lip salve are absolutely essential, as is a first aid kit.
- Water bottle – beware of dehydration and drink copiously where possible.
- Head torch plus spare batteries and bulbs.

Klettersteig/via ferrata routes

Roughly translated as an 'iron way' or 'climbing path', *klettersteigen* (German) or *vie ferrate* (Italian) first appeared in Austria as early as 1869, developed as part of the armed struggle in the Dolomites during the First World War, and increased in popularity among climbers during the 1930s. In recent years a large number of these protected routes have been established right across the Swiss Alps, enabling activists to scale otherwise inaccessible rock

USEFUL WEBSITES

www.summitpost.org gives details of selected mountains and sample routes
www.viaferrata.org provides information on *via ferrata/klettersteig* routes in Switzerland, Italy, France and Spain

Ski touring/ski mountaineering

In winter there's an arctic, pristine beauty to the Alps that many find as appealing as summer's fine textures and colours. The crisp cold air, clear skies and glistening snows invite activity. Wearing snowshoes the walker can explore a winter wonderland that would be inaccessible equipped only with boots, and those who are fit and experienced are able to snowshoe their way even to modest alpine summits. For a guide to some of the best winter routes, see Hilary Sharp's *Snowshoeing: Mont Blanc & the Western Alps* (Cicerone, 2002).

While by far the majority of winter sports enthusiasts go for downhill skiing, with major resorts being Davos, Grindelwald, Klösters,

39

The Pers glacier basin below Piz Palü in the Bernina Alps (Chapter 4:4)

Mürren, Saas Fee, St Moritz, Verbier, Wengen and Zermatt, Switzerland also boasts some of the most important areas for ski mountaineering, and hosts some of the most compelling of tours. The classic Haute Route (Mont Blanc to the Matterhorn) is an obvious example, but there are numerous others, of shorter duration perhaps, but no less rewarding, that can be enjoyed in the Pennine and Bernese Alps, in the Engadine and Central Swiss Alps, in the Albula Alps and Silvretta.

Ski touring (or ski mountaineering) is one of the most demanding of mountain pursuits, and for those who have experienced it, it's certainly one of the most enjoyable, whose appeal lies as much in satisfactions found when exploring a snow-covered world far from crowded slopes as in the silent beauty of the high Alps. It's an activity that is growing in popularity as more and more accomplished skiers learn to appreciate the joys of off-piste adventure, and among mountaineers who wish to experience the Alps in winter as well as summer. As Bill O'Connor says: 'the Alps are, more or less, snowbound from November to June, and those unable to ski are virtually excluded from their heart for all but three months of the summer Alpine season.'

Those whose experience of the Alps has been largely restricted to the summer need to learn additional skills beyond those of skiing and mountaineering in order to tour safely. Knowing how to assess the stability of snow, avalanche awareness and what to do to survive one are perhaps the most important. This is not the book to teach those skills, but it's worth noting that 80% of avalanche victims are responsible for starting the avalanche they are caught in, and only four out of ten survive.

Bill O'Connor's inspirational two-volume guide *Alpine Ski Mountaineering* (Cicerone, 2002, 2003) is both rhapsodic in tone and down-to-earth with instruction; with a host of tours beautifully illustrated and described, it is highly recommended to anyone drawn to the sport.

Equipment for ski touring/ski mountaineering
Apart from warm but lightweight clothing, the primary needs of the ski mountaineer focus on the hardware without which touring becomes impossible. A more comprehensive list is included in Bill O'Connor's guides (see above).
- Comfortable ski mountaineering boots with good quality footbeds.

ALPINE CLUB DETAILS

Founded in 1857 the **Alpine Club** is the world's oldest mountaineering club and the leading UK organisation for climbers active in the Alps and greater ranges. Benefits of membership include access to the AC Library which houses over 25,000 books on mountain-related subjects, monthly evening lectures, free copy of the *Alpine Journal*; each year, an annual alpine meet and reduced rates in huts. Visit www.alpine-club.org.uk.

The **Swiss Alpine Club** (Schweizer Alpen-Club, Club Alpin Suisse, Club Alpino Svizzero, or Club Alpin Svizzer) dates from 1863, has over a hundred individual sections, many of which organise mountain tours, rock climbing and winter activities. The SAC produces a members' magazine, *Die Alpen*, publishes guidebooks for walkers, climbers and ski mountaineers, and through its member sections owns and maintains a great number of huts. See www.swiss-sport.ch/sac-cas, www.sac-cas.ch and www.alpenonline.ch.

The **Association of British Members of the Swiss Alpine Club** (ABMSAC) is an active UK-based club with a strong interest in alpine mountaineering. The Club organises a diverse range of meets to the European Alps and beyond. For information go to www.abmsac.org.uk.

- Wide, short, all-terrain skis with a touring binding.
- Climbing skins for uphill work.
- Harscheisen – removable ski crampons.
- Ski poles with powder baskets.
- Shovel – an essential piece of equipment.
- Transceiver and spare batteries.
- Avalanche probe.
- Ice axe, and crampons to fit ski boots.
- Climber's sit-harness.
- Two 30m ropes (for a touring party) plus prusiks for each member.
- Ski goggles, high-factor suncream and lip salve.

SAFETY DOS AND DON'TS

The following list of precautionary measures is valid for most mountain activities without reducing adventure in any meaningful way.

- Ensure you are physically and mentally prepared for the challenge of your chosen route.
- Plan your day with care; study the route details and time required to complete it. Don't overestimate either your own physical ability or that of your companions, but make a generous allowance for delays, imperfect conditions and bad weather.

A rescue helicopter in action in the Bernese Alps

- Carry liquid refreshment, emergency rations and a first aid kit.
- Check the weather forecast before setting out.
- Watch for signs of deteriorating weather, and don't be too proud to turn back should it be safer to do so than continue in the face of an oncoming storm.
- Don't venture onto exposed ridges if a storm is imminent. In the event of being caught by one avoid prominent rocks, metallic objects or isolated features, and refrain from taking shelter in caves, beneath overhanging rocks or in gullies.
- Should you be involved in an accident, stay calm, move yourself and, if feasible, the injured person (with care not to aggravate the injury) away from any imminent danger, and apply immediate first aid. Keep the victim warm by providing emergency shelter and adding any spare clothing available, and alert the rescue services – see below.

MOUNTAIN RESCUE

All mountain activities involve a degree of risk, and participants should be aware of the fact and accept responsibility for their own actions. Since accidents occur in the Alps every year and in every season, it is important to know the procedure for calling out the rescue services. Remember, the cost of an emergency rescue and subsequent medical treatment can be extremely expensive. Be properly insured – see the section in Practicalities above. (It's advisable to leave a copy of your insurance details with a responsible person at home, and to carry with you photocopies of important documents, such as passport information pages and insurance certificate, as well as an emergency home contact address and telephone number.)

Notification of an accident

Should you witness, or be involved in, an accident in the Swiss Alps, raise the alarm by calling the local police who organise mountain rescue; the number is 117. If you do not have a mobile phone, or cannot get a signal, remember that telephones are located in most mountain huts, including bivouac huts. Hut guardians will normally help co-ordinate the rescue call-out.

When reporting an accident the following information will need to be given:

- your name
- location and telephone number
- name of victim
- nature of injury
- exact location
- weather conditions at accident site
- any obstacles in the accident area (eg cables) which could hamper helicopter evacuation.

Established in 1952 the Swiss air rescue service REGA provides emergency medical assistance throughout Switzerland from its operations centre in Zürich. Its red-and-white helicopters carry a medic and paramedic, and the call-out number is 1414. A non-profit foundation, REGA relies on donations and patronage for its funding. *Do not request helicopter assistance for non-serious accidents.*

The following signals are used to communicate with a helicopter:

Help needed: raise both arms above head to form a 'V'

Help not required: raise one arm above head, extend other arm downwards

International Mountain Distress Signal
(*to be used in an emergency only*)
Six blasts on a whistle (and flashes with a torch at night) spaced evenly for one minute, followed by a minute's pause. In the event of no whistle being available, wave a brightly coloured item of clothing six times a minute, then wait a minute. Repeat until located by a rescuer.

The response is three signals per minute, followed by a pause of one minute.

RESCUE EMERGENCY CARE

First aid training courses designed especially for outdoor pursuits are available throughout the UK and Ireland. Go to www.recfirstaid.net. Cicerone publishes a very useful pocket-sized first aid handbook: *First Aid and Wilderness Medicine* by Drs Jim Duff and Peter Gormly.

Left *The extravagant spotted gentian* Right *Trumpet gentian (Photos: Linda Reynolds)*

PLANT AND ANIMAL LIFE

Plants and animals are vital to the alpine environment, and whether the visitor is intent on walking, trekking or climbing, an awareness of the rich variety of flora and fauna will help create a multi-dimensional experience. Plantlife is incredibly varied, thanks to the wide climatic differences that allow palm trees to flourish below the Lepontines of Ticino, while the glacier crowfoot has been found blooming near the summit of the Finsteraarhorn at over 4200m.

Alpine flora
While the range of mountain plants is enormous, they are grouped by habitat, soil and climate, rather than scattered in a haphazard manner, and are roughly divided between those that are lime-loving and those that exist only among non-calcareous formations. Habitats range from lush meadow to damp marsh and acid bog, from deciduous woodland and coniferous forest to virtually soil-less scree, moraine bank, high rock face and wind-scoured ridge. With such a diverse range of habitats, it's little wonder that Switzerland has around 620 species of flowering plant, and no matter how small some may be, no matter how remote and inhospitable their lodging place, each one is an integral part of the mountain world.

As the snow recedes in early spring, the lower valleys reveal such perennial favourites as soldanellas, gentians, primulas and anemones that flower, seed and then become dwarfed by the grass and coarse foliage of the burgeoning meadows. And when they're all-but forgotten, more of the same appear higher up the hillside as a later spring season arrives in late May and June to chase the departing snows from the true 'alps' – the summer pasturelands with their groups of chalets and hay-barns. In June and early July a profusion of mountain flowers adorn these pastures in a vibrant tapestry, until grazing cattle or the farmer's scythe have cleared them. In mid-July and August alpines are evident on glacial moraines, among screes, in narrow crevices and open rock faces; tiny cushions of flowering plants, some appearing little more than a stain on a rock, others that display a cluster of rosette-like leaves from which a stem of brilliant colour protrudes. Every one is a gem.

The **soldanella** referred to above is a tiny violet-blue tassle-headed snowbell (*Soldanella alpina*) that often appears to burn its way through melting patches of snow. Drifts of **crocus** appear at the same time, the white or purple *Crocus albiflorus* and *C. vernus*, the rose-red **primula** (*Primula hirsuta*), and the **spring anemone** (*Pulsatilla vernalis*) that also flowers as the snow melts.

The earliest of the gentians, the brilliant blue **spring gentian** (*Gentiana verna*) appears from March until August, and is followed at various altitudes and in different habitats by the extravagant **trumpet gentians** (*G. clusii* and *G. kochiana*), the blue-lilac field gentian (*Gentianella campestris*), the tall blue, multi-flowered **willow gentian** (*G. asclepiadea*) that appears in both wooded areas and damp meadows, and the tallest of them all, the **great yellow gentian** (*G. lutea*) that grows to more than 1m in height and flowers between June and August.

Growing among stony meadows and rock debris, the **large flowered leopardsbane** (*Doronicum grandiflorum*) is a 6–50cm tall member of the daisy family with custard yellow head, very similar in appearance to *Arnica montana* which appears in meadows and open woods.

Along the edge of woodland straggles of powder-blue **alpine clematis** (*Clematis alpina*) twist tendril-like around tree trunks and low branches, the flowers at their best in late June or July. But it is the **alpenrose**, or dwarf rhododendron (*Rhododendron ferrugineum*), that makes its presence known both nearby and from a distance, with its mass of pink-to-scarlet flowers spreading across the hillsides (preferring acid soils, but equally at home among limestone), from open woods to the edge of screes.

No alpine flower is more fragrant than the **daphne**, whose delicate perfume is often detected before the actual plant is seen. The bright pink, low-growing *Daphne cneorum* and taller, woody-stemmed *D. mezereum* are both lime-loving plants, while the straggly *D. striata* is also found among crystalline rocks.

If one mountain flower could be said to represent the Alps it would have to be the **edelweiss** (*Leontopodium alpinum*), its woolly grey-white bracts creating a distinctive star-shaped head on a slender stem. Growing in clusters, and favouring limestone and schist, it can be found in rocky places up to 3400m, but is equally at home on meadows as low as 1700m.

Much more showy than the edelweiss, the **moss campion** (*Silene acaulis*) forms a dense cushion of minute leaves out of which a mass of pink to bright red flowers appear. The white **Swiss rock jasmine** (*Androsace helvetica*) also produces a tight cushion which may grow to 15cm across. It grows on limestone, on rocky ridges and screes up to 3500m and comes into flower between May and August, while *A. alpina*, the **alpine rock jasmine** has a mat of white flowers blending to a bluey-pink flush. This is found among granite rocks and screes and has been discovered at a little over 4000m.

Thriving among dry moraines, damp streamsides, screes and rocky places, the lovely white **glacier crowfoot** (*Ranunculus glacialis*) holds the record for Europe's highest growing plant, while the azure blue **King of the Alps** (*Eritrichium nanum*) survives up to 3600m on acid rocks. This beautiful little plant forms a low, dense cushion of flower heads reminiscent of the dwarf forget-me-not, and is treasured by all who find it.

ILLUSTRATED GUIDES TO ALPINE FLORA

Two long-established and richly illustrated guides to mountain flowers that would aid identification are:
- *Mountain Flowers in Colour* by Anthony Huxley, with illustrations by Daphne Barry and Mary Grierson (Blandford Press, 1967)
- *The Alpine Flowers of Britain and Europe* by Christopher Grey-Wilson with colour illustrations by Marjorie Blamey (Collins, 1979)

Top Sporting large knobbly horns, a male ibex crops the short grass of an alp

Bottom The ubiquitous marmot, at home in almost every alpine valley

A small herd of chamois caught grazing at Busenalp (Photo: Linda Reynolds)

Alpine fauna

Of all alpine mammals the most endearing is the ubiquitous **marmot** that is seen in practically every district of the Alps, often enjoying the warm sunshine. A sociable furry rodent, the marmot lives in colonies among a range of habitats below the permanent snowline, with burrows excavated in pastures, among rock debris and even alongside busy trails. Growing to the size of a large hare, and weighing as much as 10kg, the marmot spends five or six months of the year in winter hibernation, emerging lean and scruffy in springtime, but soon growing healthy on the summer grasses. The famous shrill whistling sound, given as a warning of danger, is emitted from the back of its throat by an alert adult sitting up on its haunches. Prey to fox and eagle, by September the marmot has accumulated large reserves of fat and begins to prepare its 'nest' for the coming winter with a bed of dried grasses; then comes October and it settles into deep hibernation once more.

Chamois are members of the antelope family, characteristically shy of human contact and symbolic of the alpine regions. With short sickle-shaped horns, a white lower jaw and a dark reddish-brown coat in summer bearing a black stripe along the spine, the chamois is fleet-footed and agile. An incomparable sense of smell and acute hearing make them difficult to approach, but when surprised they make a sharp wheezing snort of a warning. During the winter the chamois spends most of the time in forests; the weakest members of a herd often perish, while others are killed by avalanche. As the snows recede, they return to higher altitudes; in May and June moulting takes place, with tufts of hair snagging on rocks and high shrubs, and during the summer months they prefer cool north-facing slopes and snowfields to warm sunny areas.

Much stockier than the chamois, the **ibex** has adapted perfectly to its hostile environment and can scale the steepest of cliffs with apparent ease. The adult male sports large, knobbly, scimitar-shaped horns and a short stub of beard, while the female could almost be mistaken for a goat with its smaller, less impressive horns and a grey or coffee-coloured coat. Males spend most of the year well away from the females, which inhabit lower regions, and they only come together for the brief mating season.

By contrast the shiny black **alpine salamander** is a curious newt-like amphibious creature that has adapted to the alpine environment by searching out the most humid areas and remaining concealed during dry weather, but emerging – often in large numbers – during or immediately after heavy showers of rain. It is more often seen in the Oberland than in the drier ranges of the Pennine or Lepontine Alps.

The dainty **roe deer** inhabits mostly low wooded areas and has a surprisingly raucous bark out of all proportion to its graceful appearance. The **red deer** stag, on the other hand, has a bellow to match its stately size, and during the autumn rut the forests and open glades echo to the sound. Both red and roe deer have highly developed senses of hearing, sight and smell, and spend most of the daylight hours hidden among the trees, emerging at daybreak and in the evening to graze meadows.

Red squirrels can often be seen scampering among larch, fir and pinewoods, their almost black coat and tufted ears being recognisable features. Conifer woods are also home to the **nutcracker** whose alarm cry of 'kre kre kre' makes it a rival to the jay as the policeman of the woods. It has a large head, strong beak, tawny speckled breast and a distinctive swooping flight, and is noted for breaking open pine cones in order to free the fatty seeds which it hides to feed on in winter.

The **alpine chough** is one of the commonest birds likely to be met in the Swiss Alps. The unmistakable yellow beak and coral-red feet mark it out from other members of the crow family, and they will often appear to scavenge leftovers of picnic food, perch on rocky summits and gather near mountain huts.

Practically all these creatures, and many more, can be seen in their natural habitats in the Swiss National Park in the Lower Engadine (see 4:5).

ENVIRONMENTAL ETHICS

Mountains are the ultimate symbols of wild nature, and mountaineering in its many forms both recognises and celebrates that wildness. But the growth of tourism and the sheer volume of walkers, climbers and skiers who flock to the Alps in summer and winter alike threaten to reduce and destroy the very wildness that is its primary attraction. Mountains are not eternal and unchanging; they're fragile,

The unchanging way of life of an Alpine farmer

with ecosystems endangered by pollution, climate change and overuse. We who love the Alps are a major part of the problem.

The ugly rash of ski tows and cable lifts that transport tens of thousands of downhill skiers in winter remain throughout the summer as unwelcome intrusions on snow-free slopes that often bear the scars of bulldozed pistes. On the other hand, snowshoeing, cross-country skiing and ski touring/ski mountaineering have no reliance on such mechanical aids, and make little or no impact on the environment.

Summer mountaineering is supported by a network of huts, by cable cars and funiculars that enable climbers, trekkers and walkers to gain height without physical effort; thus saving themselves both time and energy. Thousands of kilometres of trails wind across the hillsides, marked by splashes of paint or led by cairns; bolts and fixed anchors are applied to chalk-daubed crags; stairways of rungs, ladders and footplates scale rock faces in a rash of enthusiasm for *via ferrata* thrills; rescue helicopters and those that supply huts disturb the silence of the skies. All these are part of the infrastructure we've come to accept and rely on, yet they are alien to the appeal of wild nature.

While we may imagine that the Golden Age of Mountaineering was also a golden age of untarnished nature, it would be totally unrealistic to believe that the Alps could ever return to the conditions experienced by a handful of 19th-century pioneers who had the mountains virtually to

ENVIRONMENTAL ETHICS

INFORMATION AT A GLANCE

Communications When making a telephone call *to* Switzerland from the UK, the international dialling code is 0041. To call the UK *from* Switzerland use 0044. Cashless call boxes are operated by a phone card (Taxcard) on sale at post offices, newsagents and railway stations. Many call boxes also accept payment by credit card.

Currency The Swiss Franc (CHF); 100 centimes/rappen = CHF1. The Euro (€) is accepted as a means of payment in establishments near a border, but change will be given in Swiss francs. Major credit cards can be used in most hotels, mountain inns and some huts. ATM (cash machines) are located in the majority of towns and tourist resorts.

Emergency telephone number 117 for police/mountain rescue.

Formalities Visas are not required by holders of a valid UK passport or by other EU nationals. Visitors from other countries should enquire at their local Swiss embassy.

Health precautions There are no endemic contagious diseases in Switzerland, and at the time of writing no vaccinations are required for visitors entering the country, unless arriving from an area where cholera or yellow fever are prevalent, in which case an International Health Certificate will be needed. Consideration should be given to protection from tick-borne encephalitis (TBE) which is carried by the *Ixodes* tick. Risk is seasonal (March to September) and anyone engaged in outdoor activities could be vulnerable. Inoculation is available from travel clinics – seek advice from your GP. Any medical treatment in Switzerland must be paid for; make sure you have adequate health insurance.

Languages spoken French, German (*Schwyzerdütsch*), Italian and Romansch, but English is widely understood in many popular areas.

Mountain huts More than 350 huts (manned, unmanned and bivouac shelters) are located throughout the Swiss Alps, most of which belong to the SAC. Reductions in overnight fees are given to members of European Alpine Clubs, and to holders of a reciprocal rights card available to members of the British Mountaineering Council (www.thebmc.co.uk).

National mountaineering organisation Schweizer Alpen-Club, Monbijoustrasse 61, Postfach, CH-3000 Bern 61, Switzerland www.swiss-sport.ch/sac-cas.

Tourist information Switzerland Tourism, 30 Bedford Street, London WC2E 9ED www.MySwitzerland.com.

---

themselves. Yet those of us who cannot resist their lure can do several things to minimise our personal impact on them, no matter how small and insignificant they may seem. Multiplied many thousands of times, they can make a difference.

- Leave no litter and take your rubbish back to the valley for proper disposal.
- Recycle plastic bottles, glass and aluminium drinks cans (recycling bins are found in many Swiss resorts).
- Resist scree running; stick to footpaths and avoid taking shortcuts which can lead to soil erosion.
- If there is no alternative but to defecate in the open, do so well away from paths and places where others might take shelter, and at least 30m from streams and lakes. Dig a hole, bury faeces and cover, and burn used toilet paper, taking care not to set fire to vegetation.
- Do not pick wild flowers (many are protected, but even those that are not should be left for others to enjoy), and avoid disturbing wildlife.
- Wild camping is officially forbidden in Switzerland, but permission is often granted by farmers to those who request it. To minimise the impact, pitch your tent for one night only, light no fires and leave the site as pristine as you found it.

CHAPTER 1: CHABLAIS ALPS

The Dents du Midi group, together with frontier mountains south of Lac Léman and to the west of the Rhône valley, in Canton Valais.

CHABLAIS ALPS: CHAPTER SUMMARY

Location

In Canton Valais, south of Lac Léman (the Lake of Geneva) and west of the Rhône valley. The district's southern boundary is drawn by the Emosson lakes on the French border, and by the Vallée du Trient which drains to the Rhône above Martigny.

★ Highlights

🚶 Walks
- Tour des Dents Blanches (1:2)
- Tour des Dents du Midi (1:2)
- Tour du Ruan (1:5)
- Tour de la Vallée du Trient (1:5)

🧗 Climbs
- Via Ferrata de Tière (1:2)
- Assorted routes on the Dents du Midi (1:2)
- Traverse of the Sallière-Ruan Group (1:3)
- NE Face of the Tour Sallière (1:5)

⛰ Summits for all
- Haute Cime des Dents du Midi (1:2)
- Le Luisin (1:5)

Contents

1:1 Val de Morgins 53
Walks from the Val de Morgins 54

1:2 Val d'Illiez 54
The Barme Alpage 56
Tour des Dents Blanches (box) 58
Dents du Midi 59
Abbé Clément: First Man on Top (box) 61
Tour des Dents du Midi (box) 61

1:3 Vallon de Susanfe 64

1:4 Rhône Valley Approaches 66

1:5 Vallée du Trient 67
The Salanfe Basin 69
Tour du Ruan (box) 71
Lacs d'Emosson 73
The Vieux Emosson Dinosaurs (box) 75
The Upper Vallée du Trient 75
The Bisse du Trient (box) 76
Tour de la Vallée du Trient (box) 78

Access, Bases, Maps and Guides 80

◀ *Lac d'Antème lies at the foot of the NW Face of the Dents du Midi, with a small, privately owned refuge nearby*

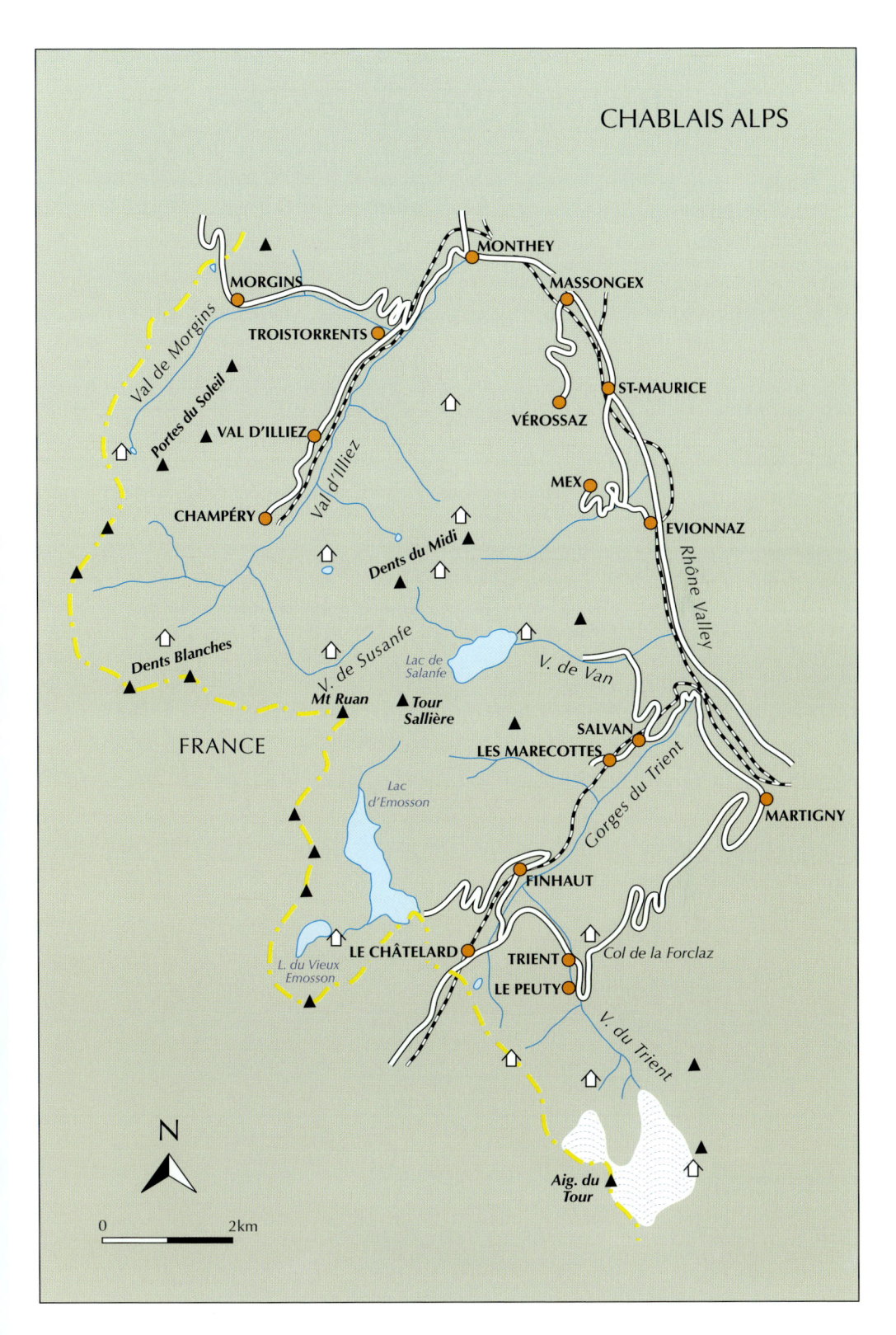

CHABLAIS ALPS

CHABLAIS ALPS: INTRODUCTION

The glaciers are small, only a few summits pass the 10,000ft mark, but the valleys are full of beauty.

R L G Irving, *The Alps*

As the plane circles to land at Geneva airport, the multi-pinnacled Dents du Midi appear at the far end of Lac Léman as alluring as the snowy Mont Blanc range beyond. These same peaks form a truly impressive backdrop to the castle of Chillon when viewed from the train running alongside the lake near Montreux, and are easily identifiable from several points at the western end of the Pennine Alps. Along with their neighbours in the Chablais region of Canton Valais, these are the most westerly mountains in Switzerland; a compact limestone group rising from green foothills to make a worthy introduction to the Swiss Alps.

Officially the Chablais region extends from St Gingolph, the little border town on the southern shore of Lac Léman, to St-Maurice north of Martigny in the Rhône valley, and includes all the mountains up to the French border. Of these, the Dents du Midi do not carry that border for they stand as an isolated block moated by valleys on three sides, unlike the Dents Blanches – the head-wall of the Val d'Illiez – which make an attractive neighbour and a natural frontier spreading eastward to the handsome Mont Ruan. There the border turns abruptly to the south to enclose on the Swiss side the two Emosson lakes, from whose slopes tremendous views are granted of the Mont Blanc range to the south.

South of the smaller of these lakes, the border twists northeast, then southeast at the barrage of the larger Lac d'Emosson above Le Châtelard in the Trient valley, which effectively separates the Chablais Alps from outliers of the Mont Blanc massif. Here, however, we extend the region

The small green lake at the Pas de Morgins

slightly to include all the Vallée du Trient, so that anything east of its bounding ridge can effectively be considered with the Pennine Alps in Chapter 2.

Straddling the Franco-Swiss border, a popular section of the Chablais region spreading out from Morgins is referred to in promotional literature as the Portes du Soleil, after a col on the ridge above Champéry, where a dozen resorts on both sides of the political divide are linked to exploit the skiing potential of the area and to promote both walking and mountain biking there.

But the whole region offers plenty of mountain walking opportunities, especially multi-day tours, some of which stray across the international frontier. Climbers are also well catered for, although there's very little in the way of snow and ice except in winter. Rock routes abound in the lower-to-medium grades, and there are some exciting ridges to traverse. The main centres are Morgins in the valley of the same name, Champéry and Val d'Illiez in the valley from which the latter village takes its name, and Finhaut high above the Gorges du Trient.

1:1 VAL DE MORGINS

Val de Morgins is pre-alpine; a broad, partly wooded pastoral valley whose upper reaches are linked to the Portes du Soleil ski playground. A short distance north of the valley's only resort lies a small lake at the 1369m Pas de Morgins on the frontier, from where a road descends to Abondance in France.

Ignoring the French side of the border, the normal route of approach is from the small industrial town of Monthey in the Rhône valley, from where a sinuous road writhes its way southwestward through the lower Val d'Illiez, at first between vineyards, then among chestnut and walnut trees to a junction on the outskirts of Troistorrents. The left fork is the one to take for Champéry (see 1:2), while the Morgins branch climbs a series of hairpins with retrospective views of the Dents du Midi and the Dent de Morcles on the far side of the Rhône's valley.

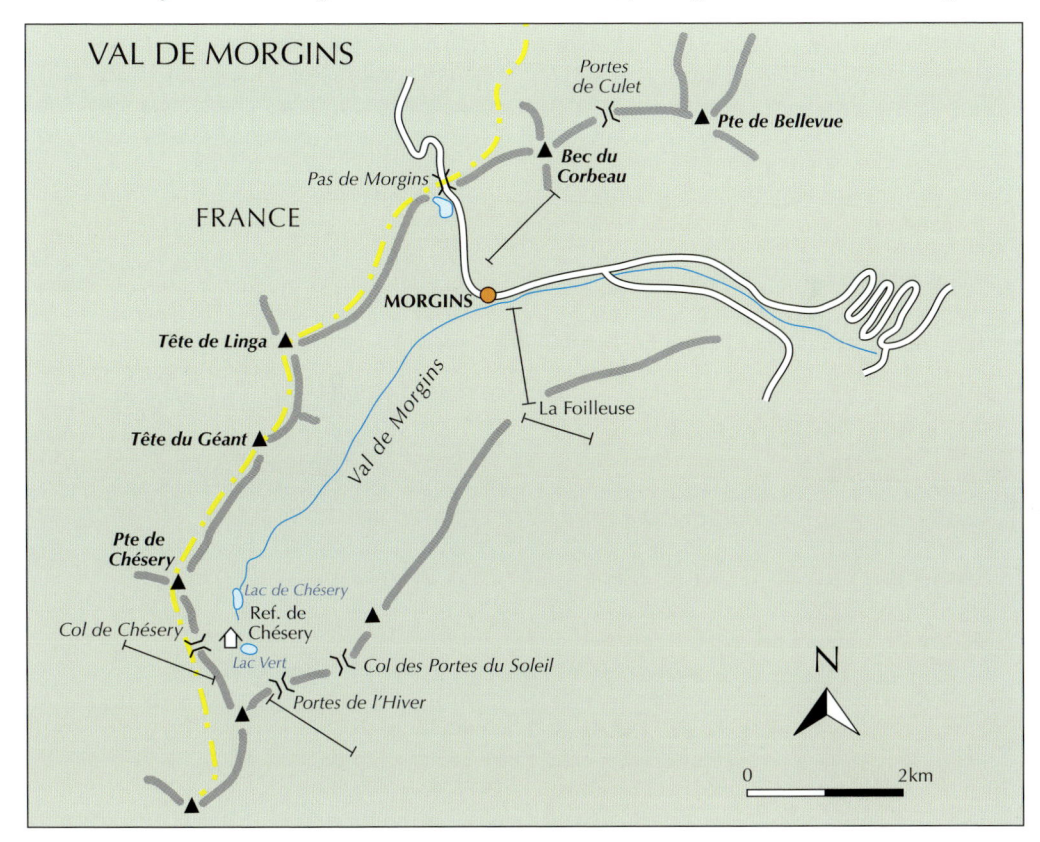

Having gained Val de Morgins the road then runs easily along the north bank of the Vièze de Morgins stream among alpine meadows and pinewoods, passing a minor road branching left (a pleasant cross-country route to Val d'Illiez) to gain the resort of **Morgins** at 1305m.

Spread across the meadows, the dark timber chalets, shops, campsite and two hotels (the Beau-Site and La Reine des Alpes) of this modest resort suggest a base for holidays of an undemanding nature. There are two chairlifts and two low-level skilifts, a climbing wall and some 800km of marked paths. In winter the extensive, but comparatively low ski area of Portes du Soleil that spreads across the border, gives access to 650km of pistes with 207 lifts (www.portesdusoleil.com), while cross-country skiing and snowshoe routes are also available, and at least 12km of footpaths are kept open. The Office du Tourisme (www.morgins.ch) located on Place du Carillon near the Foilleuse chairlift opposite the village church, produces a wealth of useful brochures and leaflets, although many of these refer to the French side of the border, and there's a handy footpath map available at a scale of 1:33,333: Carte des Sentiers à Pied et à Cheval.

Walks from the Val de Morgins

- Of the numerous walks in the valley, perhaps the easiest is that which takes just 20mins to reach the small green lake at the **Pas de Morgins**, where options for extending the outing in various directions become obvious. One of these options climbs to the **Bec du Corbeau** viewpoint; another makes for the **Portes de Culet**, then climbs the ridge to the east of the pass to gain the famed 2042m **Pointe de Bellevue** which gives such a splendid view of the Dents du Midi.

- Another recommended route follows the Vièze de Morgins upstream southwest of Morgins, wandering below the cliffs of the **Tête de Linga** and **Tête du Géant** to the head of the valley, and then climbs to the little Lac de Chésery at 1891m. **Lac Vert**, a second tarn nearby, lies just 20m below **Col de Chésery**, a walker's pass on the border with France at 1992m. Between the lake and the col, about 2½hrs from Morgins, stands the privately owned **Refuge de Chésery** (www.lacvert.ch) which offers refreshments, has 35 dormitory places and is often patronised by trekkers walking from Lac Léman to Chamonix along the GR5. Southeast of here the 2157m col of **Portes de l'Hiver** (also known as the Porte du Lac Vert) is well worth the extra 40–50mins of effort to reach, for it rewards with a truly breathtaking panorama. Yet again the Dents du Midi form an eye-catching part of that panorama.

- For more spectacular views of the Dents du Midi, however, the ridge that runs from **La Foilleuse** at 1814m to the 1950m **Col des Portes du Soleil**, takes a lot of beating. The ridge may be gained by footpath or chairlift from Morgins, and less than 2hrs of easy walking is needed to get from one end to the other. Views from here are not only of the Dents du Midi, but of Mont Ruan and the wall of the Dents Blanches to the south which is also impressive, as is the skyline of the Mont Blanc range beyond and above intervening ridges. And it would be perfectly feasible for a keen walker to continue as far as the Portes de l'Hiver (see the previous paragraph) and descend to Morgins by reversing the route suggested above.

- ★ The major walking challenge of the district, however, is the multi-day **Tour des Portes du Soleil** which, as its name suggests, makes a circuit of the region, much of it in neighbouring France. It's a longish tour demanding a total of about 44hrs of walking time on an assortment of trails, tracks and minor roads. Sadly there's a considerable amount of downhill ski terrain to contend with, with the inevitable tows and lifts that clutter the landscape, but the route also enjoys some splendid semi-wild sections with glorious vistas. Accommodation is available in the form of *gîtes*, refuges and hotels, but such places are not evenly spaced, so some stages are much longer and more demanding than others. The route is highlighted on the *carte des sentiers* mentioned above, which also gives approximate timings and contact numbers for information. Being a circuit, the Tour could, of course be started almost anywhere, but since this sub-chapter deals with Val de Morgins, the suggestion is to begin in Morgins itself to make a counter-clockwise tour.

1:2 VAL D'ILLIEZ

With the Dents Blanches at its head, the rolling heights of the Portes du Soleil to the west, and the Dents du Midi forming its eastern wall, Val d'Illiez is by far and away the most important valley from

1:2 Val d'Illiez

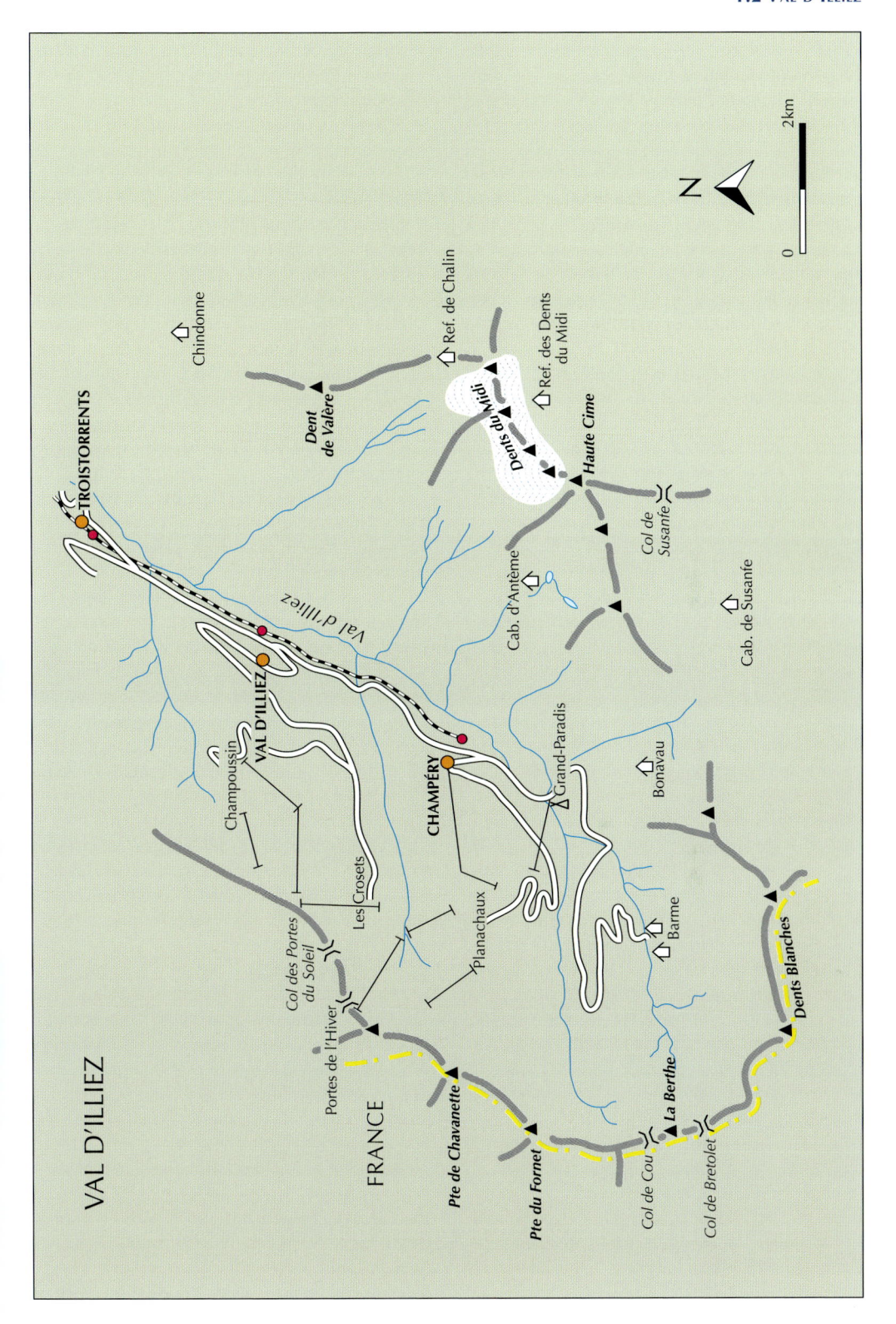

which to explore the highest and most dramatic section of the Chablais Alps. Since Troistorrents has only limited accommodation, Champéry and Val d'Illiez are the major resort villages, with direct access by railway from Aigle and Monthey.

By road the initial approach is identical to that for Val de Morgins (1:1), but on reaching the junction on the outskirts of **Troistorrents**, about 4km above Monthey, we branch left and skirt the tall, grey stone church, passing the post office, a bank and a handful of shops. Within the village accommodation is limited to five beds at the Chambres d'Hôtes Helvetia.

A short distance beyond Troistorrents a minor road cuts back to the right to climb in long loops up the hillside on an alternative route to Morgins, while the Champéry road continues above the Vièze to **Val d'Illiez** (948m), once the valley's main village. Larger than Troistorrents, Val d'Illiez has some old traditional chalets with projecting gables; there's a tourist office by the railway station (www.valdilliez.ch), and a choice of accommodation at Hotel Communal which has 31 beds, and the slightly smaller Hotel du Repos with 27 beds. There are also just four b&b rooms (a total of seven beds) available at the Chambres d'Hôtes en Play.

About 4km further along the road lies **Champéry** (913m), a pleasantly situated and modestly attractive summer and winter resort which, as if to underline the fact that it makes a good centre for mountain activities, has its own Compagnie des Guides, known as Montagne Experience (tel 024 479 14 30). The Office du Tourisme (www.champery.ch) is located near the railway station on the valley road which bypasses the crowded village centre where most of the shops, banks, restaurants and hotels are situated. There are around a dozen hotels, ranging from ungraded pensions and *chambres d'hôtes* to a handful of 3-star establishments – contact the tourist office for details. At the roadhead another 2km upvalley Camping du Grand-Paradis is a wooded site, open all-year with good facilities, and with the Auberge du Grand-Paradis nearby (www.grandparadis.ch). Almost opposite the tourist office stands the valley station of the Planachaux cable car, or Téléphérique Croix de Culet, which serves the Portes du Soleil ski area (www.telechampery.com), while upvalley near the campsite, a winter-only chairlift, the Télésiège du Grand-Paradis, feeds the same area.

With its ease of access and unrestricted views, the broad **Portes du Soleil** ridge is understandably popular year-round. There are paths, tracks and pistes, restaurant facilities and no shortage of accommodation. At **Champoussin** above Val d'Illiez, the 3-star Hotel Royal Alpage Club has 131 beds (www.royalalpageclub.com), while the less ostentatious Auberge Chez Gaby has 33 beds in 11 rooms (www.chezgaby.ch). Directly above Champéry, **Les Crosets** has the 3-star Hotel Télécabine (www.hotel-telecabine.com), and the 54-bed Hotel des Portes du Soleil (www.hotel-portes-du-soleil.com). Each of these makes the most of a magnificent panoramic view across the valley, while outline suggestions for walks on the ridge, from which even more extensive views are had, were given under the Val de Morgins sub-chapter (1:1).

But the Portes du Soleil region does not hold a monopoly either on views or on opportunities for mountain activity. On the eastern side of the valley opposite Champéry, a *via ferrata* route has been devised that picks a way up cliffs above the Tière, a tributary of the Vièze which drains the Lacs d'Antème on the slopes of the Dents du Midi. The ☆ Ⓑ **Via Ferrata de Tière** begins near the Sous Sex bridge at 913m, and crossing the river in three places, it meanders back and forth across the exposed 75° rock face, rising 125m over a course some 460m long. There is no charge for tackling this *via ferrata*, but the use of correct safety methods and equipment is compulsory. Specialist equipment can be hired from sport's shops in Champéry, or from the tourist office in Val d'Illiez. A short artificial climbing wall has also been created on one of the railway supports near the Champéry tourist office.

☆ **The Barme alpage**
At the head of the valley, about 11km from Champéry, but reached by track and footpath from Grand-Paradis, an open basin of pastureland lies at the foot of the Dents Blanches at an altitude of almost 1500m. This is the **Barme** alpage, also known as Barmaz, an utterly charming plateau almost completely enclosed by mountains and sliced with streams. Two rustic mountain inns provide accommodation and refreshments: Cantine de Barmaz, which has 50 places in dorms and bedrooms (tel 024 479 11 63); and Cantine des Dents Blanches which is open from the end of May to the beginning of October with 40 dorm places (www.

Backed by a line of crags, the Barme alpage lies about 11km from Champéry

barmaz.com). Nearby, on the edge of woodland overlooking the pastures, a small number of b&b places are available between June and September at Chalet Bicolet (tel 024 471 14 25).

It's possible to drive to the Barme alpage by way of a minor road that extends from Grand-Paradis, but a direct walking route will only take a little over 1½hrs by way of a good track used by the Tour des Portes du Soleil mentioned in 1:1, and is a much better option. There's also a scenic high route leading from **Planachaux** (cable car from Champéry) which joins the GR5 to curve below the frontier ridge on the way to Col de Cou in 2½hrs; and a more devious but highly recommended route from Grand-Paradis which begins by heading southeast to the privately owned **Bonavau refuge** (Cantine de Bonavau), then westward across a narrow saddle of about 1800m by the Signal de Bonavau, before descending to Barme in roughly 2½hrs.

But whichever route is taken to get there, a few days based at the alpage will not be regretted. By day there's plenty to see and do, while a night spent there has its own very special atmosphere.

The main block of the Dents Blanches, which rises some 1200m above the Barme pastures, has obvious appeal for climbers, but there's also a line of crags with routes up to 60m high; there are several paths for short walks and longer circuits that involve crossing cols, among them **Col de Cou** (Col de Coux: 1920m) and the slightly higher neighbouring **Col de Bretolet** that are noted as being on the route each autumn of large flocks of migrating songbirds heading south across the Alps to winter in Africa or the Mediterranean basin.

Close behind Cantine des Dents Blanches, the line of crags mentioned above is some 80m long and topped with trees, providing a choice of climbs varying in height from 30m to 60m, and ranging in grade from 3+ to 7b. The **Rocher de Barme** makes a useful training ground, and comes into its own when the higher mountains are out of condition.

Col de Cou across which a route leads down to Morzine, is less than 1½hrs from Barme. As has been noted, GR5 crosses this frontier pass, as do walkers tackling the Tour des Portes du Soleil. But for those staying at Barme, a recommended circular walk heads south from the col to ascend in 15mins to the 1989m summit of **La Berthe**, a fine vantage point, then continues along

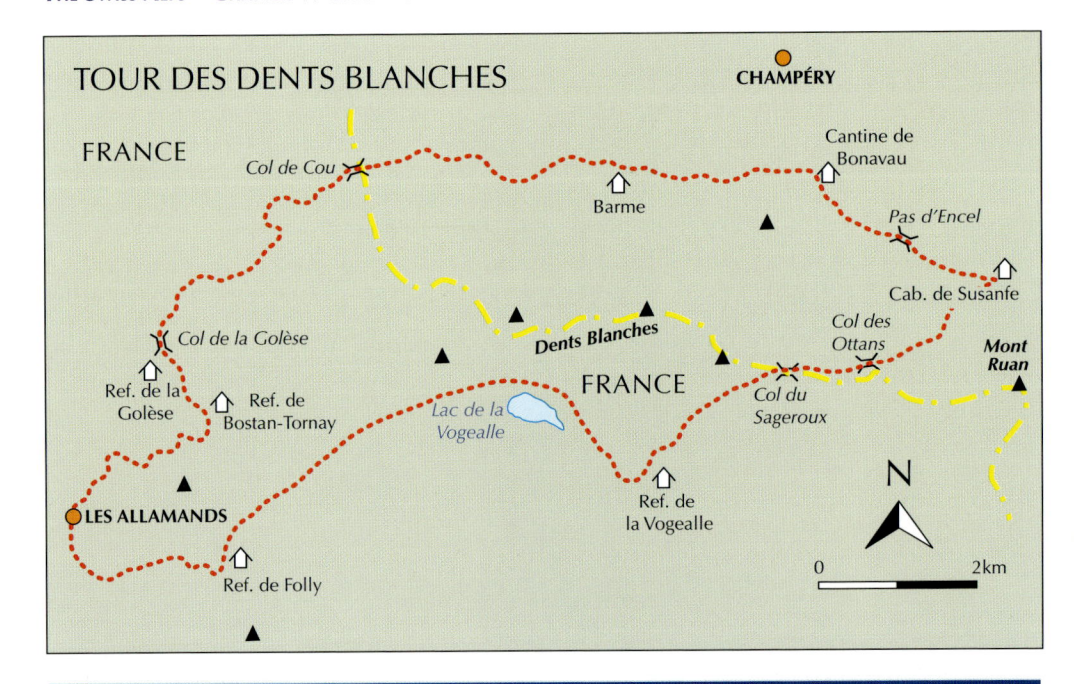

TOUR DES DENTS BLANCHES

Around the block of the Dents Blanches a three–four day trek has been created, most of which takes place on the French side of the mountains, and the suggestion here is to make a counter-clockwise tour, beginning at the Barme pastureland. (For information visit www.tour-dentsblanches.com).

Day 1: From one of the mountain inns at **Barme**, go up to the **Col de Cou** and follow GR5 waymarks on the French side below the Terres Maudites cliffs. Continue round to the **Col and Refuge de la Golèse** then, leaving GR5, branch away up to the **Refuge de Bostan-Tornay** which stands at 1763m below the Dents d'Oddaz, to conclude a short day's trek of about 4hrs. The refuge has 100 places and is manned from mid-June until the end of September (www.refugedebostan.com).

Day 2: The second stage is much longer than the first, during which you lose more than 800m of height by descending to **Les Allamands** and then curving round Le Crêt, followed by a long climb to **Refuge de Folly**, and an even longer ascent to Combe de Puaires just south of Pointe de la Golette at 2300m, about 7½hrs after setting out. A 300m descent brings the trekker to **Lac de la Vogealle** in 40mins, with another 20mins needed to reach **Refuge de la Vogealle** at 1901m. This hut has 40 places, and is manned from mid-June to mid-September (tel 033 450 89 77 59).

Day 3: Returning to Swiss territory by way of the 2395m **Col du Sageroux** 1½hrs after leaving the Vogealle refuge (beware of stonefall during and after heavy rain), the route of the TDB remains high along the frontier ridge west of Mont Ruan, then uses **Col des Ottans** (2496m) to descend into the stony Susanfe basin below the Dents du Midi. Reaching **Cabane de Susanfe** 4hrs after departing the Refuge de la Vogealle, it might be tempting to book a bedspace for the night, as there's still another 2½hrs or so of trekking left (including the crossing of a minor pass) before reaching Barme. But if you're not short of time and have plenty of energy, continue downvalley to descend the steep and exposed **Pas d'Encel** above a ravine, sharing for a while the Tour des Dents du Midi, then break away from that route by a stream, and head across a steep hillside to the privately owned **Cantine de Bonavau**. Above this a short but steepish climb brings you onto a narrow grass saddle on a spur overlooking the Barme pastures, with a steady descent of the west slope to conclude the trek.

the frontier ridge to Col de Bretolet, where you then cut back across the east flank of the mountain to rejoin the path between Col de Cou and the Barme pastures.

South of Col de Bretolet, the 2406m Tête de Bossetan more or less marks the western end of the **Dents Blanches** wall, which should not be confused with the better-known 4356m Dent Blanche in the Pennine Alps (see 2:6). While a short spur continues roughly westward, carrying the spectacular cliffs of Les Terres Maudites, the frontier ridge turns to the east, then kinks southeast across Col de Bossetan (2289m) before rising for almost 400m to the Pointe de la Golette which effectively marks a junction of ridges. To the southwest the crest of Les Dents d'Oddaz projects well into France, but the Dents Blanches ridge stretches a little north of east over a succession of minor summits and cols. Its precipitous north wall, whose highest point is the Dent de Barme (2759m), usually holds onto pockets of snow throughout much of the summer. According to an early Baedeker guide, its ascent from the Barme alpage was (in wonderfully restrained 19th-century prose) a 6hr climb 'without danger for proficients'.

☆ **Dents du Midi**

Not surprisingly it is the block of the Dents du Midi that attracts most of the attention of visitors to the Val d'Illiez. Seen from almost everywhere in the valley this abrupt wall, with its clean strata lines picked out by snow from autumn through to early summer, culminates in a row of seven prominent peaks – the famed *dents* or teeth. Aligned roughly northeast to southwest, these seven *dents* are: Cime de l'Est, La Forteresse, Cathédrale, Eperon, Dent Jaune, Les Doigts, and the highest of them all, the Haute Cime at 3257m.

Although not particularly high by comparison with summits in the nearby Mont Blanc or Pennine ranges, the Dents du Midi give every impression of being big mountains, and while there are only three small glaciers, and the rock is said to vary from good to mediocre and even bad, the range offers some fine expeditions. Generally speaking, the easiest routes are to be found on the west and south sides; the more difficult ascents being made on the north and east flanks. Most of the climbing takes place in the snow-free months of July to early October, but the Haute Cime is also climbed in winter on ski.

Signal de Soi gives a clear view of the Northwest Face of the Dents du Midi

THE SWISS ALPS – CHAPTER 1: CHABLAIS ALPS

There are huts on both the north and south sides from which to make a base. On the north there's the unmanned, eight-place **Refuge de Chalin** (2595m) which is owned by the SAC (www.cas-chaussy.ch), and the nicely situated, privately owned **Cabane d'Antème** (2037m) which has 35 places and is manned from July to mid-October (www.vs-wallis.ch/wallis/huetten/enteme). On the south side of the massif the **Cabane de Susanfe** (2102m) is SAC owned, with 72 places and a warden in residence from mid-June until early October (www.susanfe.ch); while high on the southeast flank close to the Plan Névé glacier, the SAC's **Refuge des Dents du Midi** (2884m) has just 20 places and self-catering facilities (info: tel 024 466 15 30), while overlooking the dammed Lac de Salanfe, the **Auberge de Salanfe** (1942m) is owned by the Commune d'Evionnaz. With 120 places, the auberge is manned from June to the end of September (www.salanfe.ch).

Since very little information about the Dents du Midi appears in English, a brief summary of routes on the main *dents* is offered here. But for a full rundown, see the SAC guide *Chaîne franco-suisse* (in French).

- 🔵 **Cime de l'Est** (3177m) is arguably the most impressive of all the peaks, but standing at the northeastern end of the chain (thus being the farthest from Val d'Illiez) it is seen at its best from the Rhône valley side where its triangular NE (St Maurice) Face tapers to a sharp point some 2800m above the valley. First climbed in October 1943 by André Roch, with P Bonnant and R Aubert, this remains one of the peak's classic routes, graded TD. The *voie normale* (PD+) is by the West Ridge, while a direct ascent of the Arête de Valère (North Ridge) foiled a number of parties before Chris Bonington, John Harlin and Rusty Baillie achieved its first full ascent in August 1965, a route now reckoned to be TD+ and accessible by a short approach from the unmanned Chalin refuge.

- 🔵 **La Forteresse** (3164m) is a double summited tower situated above the Col de la Cime de l'Est, first climbed in 1870 by one of the district's greatest advocates, Emile Javelle, with J Oberhauser. Their route, by the East Ridge (F), is today's *voie normale*, while more challenging climbs are to be had on the NW Couloir (AD) and the Soi Ridge/NW Face (AD+).

- 🔵 **La Cathédrale** (3160m) is the twin of La Forteresse, from which it is separated by a gap containing the Aiguillete Délez, named after the guide who made the first ascent in 1890. The popular Cathédrale-Forteresse traverse is graded AD, as is the SE Face, but the Délez Couloir goes at PD+. Rising from the Fenêtre de Soi, which separates the Cathédrale from L'Eperon, the SW Ridge rewards with one of the classic climbs of the Dents du Midi chain, an exposed 150m route first climbed in 1928 and now graded D, IV.

- 🔵 **L'Eperon** (3144m) rises above the secondary summit of the Petit Eperon by way of a series of rock steps which appear saw-like from the Val d'Illiez. The easiest route is by way of the SW Ridge above the Col de l'Eperon; the NE Ridge provides a traverse of the two summits at AD, while the NW Face is said to attract attention in winter.

- 🔵 **Dent Jaune** (3186m) is the elegant yellow thumb-like projection standing proud above the deep gap of the Col de la Dent Jaune, on the other side of which rise the Doigts de Champéry and de Salanfe. Originally there were two summits here, but one of these collapsed in the 19th century. The *voie normale* begins at the deep col mentioned above, cuts diagonally across the SE Face to join the NE Ridge, then follows this to the summit. Known as the Vire aux Genevois it was first climbed in 1894 by Georg and Malsch, and is now graded AD.

- 🔵 **Doigts de Champéry and de Salanfe** (3210m, 3205m) are grouped together with a secondary point known as the Pouce. Stonefall is a major concern here, especially in the Couloirs des Doigts, du Pouce and Dent Jaune. The NNE Face of the Doigt de Champéry offers the most challenging of the routes; a long and serious TD- climb pioneered by Lugon and Ramel in August 1937.

- ⊗ ☆ **Haute Cime du Dents du Midi** (3257m), despite being the highest of the group, its summit is easily reached by little more than a steep 2–2½hr walk from Col de Susanfe – 'very fatiguing, but without danger to the sure-footed,' is how Baedeker described the route from the col. First climbed (solo) in 1788 by local Val d'Illiez priest, J M Clément, the panorama from the summit is simply stunning, so much so that

ABBÉ CLÉMENT: FIRST MAN ON TOP

Abbé Jean-Maurice Clément, who it is thought made the first ascent of the Haute Cime du Dents du Midi at the age of 54, was a cultivated man with a library of a thousand volumes on natural history and medicine. Desperately unhappy with the parish to which he had been sent in 1780, he was on bad terms with his parishioners with whom he had frequent quarrels, and felt severely restricted by the limitations imposed by his valley. Perhaps this was why he climbed Haute Cime alone. According to a letter published in the *Journal de Lausanne*, he climbed what he termed 'two central peaks' on 22 August 1788. Although his description of the climb does not make it easy to identify his 'two central peaks', it has long been assumed that the Haute Cime was one of them. 'The weather was fairly fine,' he wrote, but despite the quality of the view from the summit, he was apparently not sufficiently inspired to describe it. 'The time I spent on the top was too short to enable me to give a useful and interesting account of the things which struck me. It would require a second climb, which I shall never make unless with a companion.' After that he abandoned any desire to climb elsewhere.

it has often been said that all climbers should visit it at least once in their lives. All the major peaks of the northern Alps are visible; in 1901 Baedeker said of it: 'The view of Mont Blanc and the Alps of the Valais and Bern is imposing; the background to the S is formed by the Alps of Dauphiné and Piedmont; the Lake of Geneva is visible from Villeneuve to Vevey.'

- Whilst routes to individual summits have their obvious attraction, one of the classic outings of the group is the **Traverse of the Dents du Midi** (D, IV). Starting from a base at the Auberge de Salanfe, this magnificent expedition is reckoned to require around 15hrs in all, under good conditions. First achieved in a southwest–northeast direction in 1893 by one-time President of the Alpine Club, J P Farrar, with the guides Pierre-Louis Délez and Daniel Maquignaz, the traverse is said to be considerably easier when tackled from east to west (AD, III+). Though normally attempted in summer, it was first completed solo in winter in 1974, but the route still demands to be taken seriously, for the ridge is over 3km long and prior knowledge of individual sections would be a great benefit to anyone considering tackling what is, after all, one of the finest outings of its grade in the Alps.

TOUR DES DENTS DU MIDI

The Tour des Dents du Midi (TDM) makes a rewarding trek. Although its full length is only about 42km, the terrain is such that most trekkers take three–four days to complete it. The scenic quality is high, with waterfalls cascading from steep slab walls; there are lakes and pools, and flowery pastures in which it's possible to study chamois and marmot. Accommodation is in *gîtes* and both privately owned and SAC huts, and there's a choice of at least three starting points: i) Champéry in Val d'Illiez, ii) La Doey above Vérossaz on the Rhône valley side of the mountains, reached by postbus from St-Maurice, or iii) Mex which stands above Evionnaz. In this brief summary we begin at Champéry, and tackle the route in a counter-clockwise direction (for information see www.dentsdumidi.ch).

Day 1: Wander upvalley from **Champéry** to the **Cantine de Bonavau** at 1550m. Shortly after, cross a stream to join the main path of the TDM which now climbs against steep slabs supporting the Dents de Bonavau (fixed cables and chains), then up the side of a ravine into the rocky groove of **Pas d'Encel**. Above this lies the small but wildly attractive Susanfe valley, and the SAC-owned **Cabane de Susanfe** (see above) standing at 2102m, about 3½–4hrs from Champéry.

Day 2: Aiming for the head of the valley among limestone ribs and rocks, this stage then rises over mounds of shale and grit before zigzagging up to the 2494m **Col de Susanfe** after 1hr. Lying between the Tour Sallière and the 3257m Haute Cime, the col provides an opportunity (given time and favourable conditions) to make the 2–2½hr ascent of the latter peak – allow 1½hrs back to the col. From the

THE SWISS ALPS – CHAPTER 1: CHABLAIS ALPS

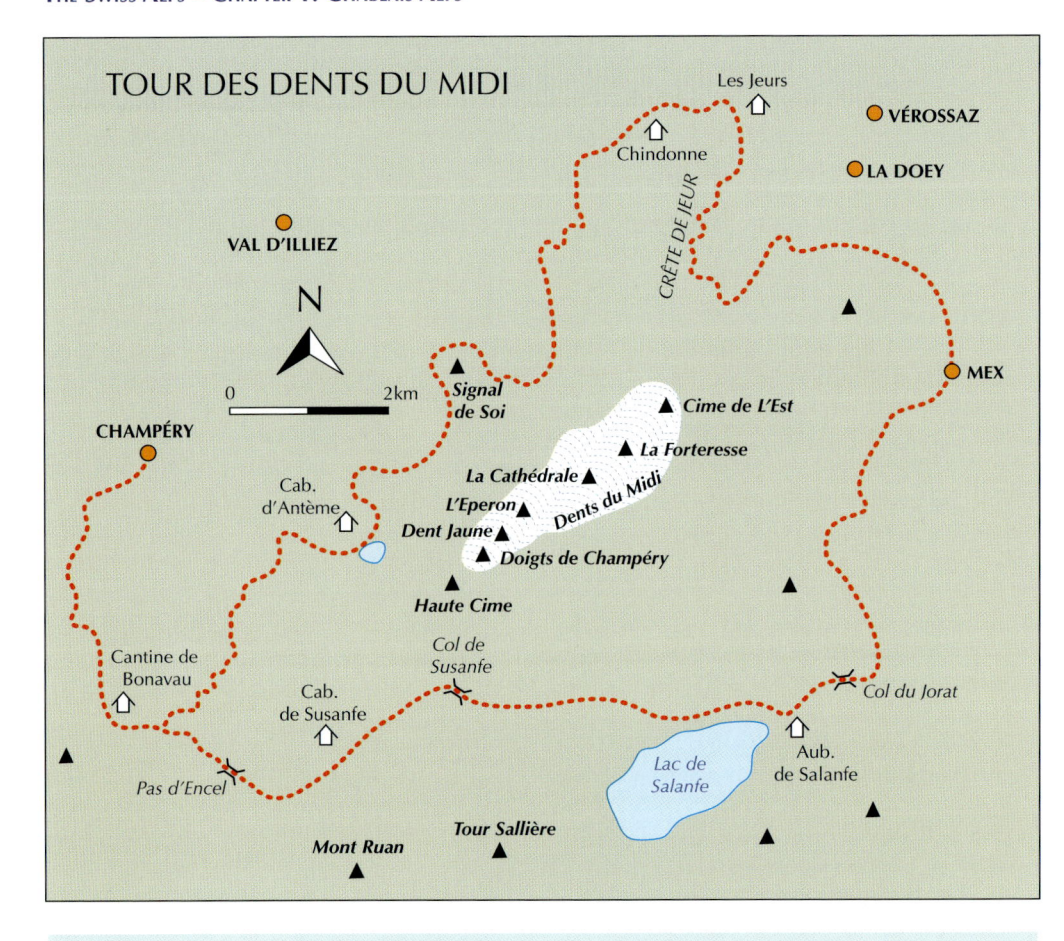

col either plunge directly down a steep slope of snow and scree, or follow a vague path down to a rock barrier and along an exposed ledge to join the direct route in a marshy meadowland a short distance from **Lac de Salanfe**, at the northeast end of which stands the **Auberge de Salanfe** (see above). This is reached in just 2½hrs from Cabane de Susanfe, or 6hrs including the ascent of the Haute Cime. If the latter has been climbed, then an overnight will be required here, otherwise it would be worth continuing as far as Mex (see below).

Day 3: The continuing route immediately heads for **Col du Jorat** (2210m) on a spur of the Dent du Salantin, reached in just 45mins from the auberge. From the col you look north down a steep slope, with the Rhône valley seen in the distance. A good path descends across screes and over high pastures, soon gaining views of the Cime de l'Est above to the left, and a little under 3hrs from Salanfe, arrives in **Mex**, a small huddle of a village at 1118m. Accommodation and refreshments are available at the comfortable Auberge de l'Armailli (www.armailli.ch) which has 18 dormitory places. A mostly woodland walk carries the route beyond Mex and into a combe north of the Cime de l'Est, followed by the ascent of a steep grass slope to the Crêt de Jeur (1555m) and on to the *gîte* of **Alpage de Chindonne** at 1604m (79 places in dorms and rooms, open June to end October; tel 024 471 33 96), about 7hrs from Salanfe.

Day 4: This final stage takes the route on a long traverse below the NW Face of the Dents du Midi, with some of the finest views of the whole tour, but with several high points to cross, this is also the most demanding day of all. Passing below hanging glaciers, it cuts into combes and crosses several

Reached from Champéry, the Cantine de Bonavau stands just off the Tour des Dents du Midi ▶

1:2 Val d'Illiez

THE SWISS ALPS – CHAPTER 1: CHABLAIS ALPS

glacial torrents, and about 3½hrs after leaving Chindonne, arrives at the little privately owned **Cabane d'Antème** (see above), set just below the Antème lake in a cirque at the foot of the Haute Cime. After crossing the lake's outflow, the TDM begins a long descent that passes the chalets of Métécoui, and 30mins later comes to a stunning viewpoint from which to study a long-drop waterfall cascading from a ravine below the Susanfe glen. Later, cross the stream below this waterfall at the lowest point of the whole tour, and in another 10mins desert the TDM proper to return to Champéry by way of the **Cantine de Bonavau**, at the end of a 6–7hr stage.

1:3 VALLON DE SUSANFE

Trapped between the western end of the Dents du Midi and the Dents Blanches–Mont Ruan–Tour Sallière wall, the Susanfe basin is a romantically wild mountain sanctuary rimmed with shrinking glaciers whose waters funnel through the Pas d'Encel ravine as the first major tributary of La Vièze, the river that drains the Val d'Illiez. As such it is really part of the Illiez valley system, but it seems so remote from that valley, and so distinctly different, that it deserves to be treated here as a separate entity.

There is no access by road, and apart from the Pas d'Encel route at 1798m, all other cols of entry are well above 2300m and likely to be confused with snow and/or ice until at best early July. Naming from west to east, these are the steep 2395m Col du Sageroux on the frontier ridge between Mont Sageroux and the Tête de Ottans; Col des Ottans at 2496m which forms a link with the former col; the glacial Col de la Tour Sallière (2834m) which offers a way down to Lac d'Emosson; and, easiest of all, the 2494m Col de Susanfe which gives access to the Salanfe basin and is used by trekkers on the Tour des Dents du Midi.

Within the valley, just an hour's walk away from Col de Susanfe, stands the **Cabane de Susanfe** in a landscape of rock-and-grass hillocks at 2102m (for details see the Dents du Midi section in 1:2).

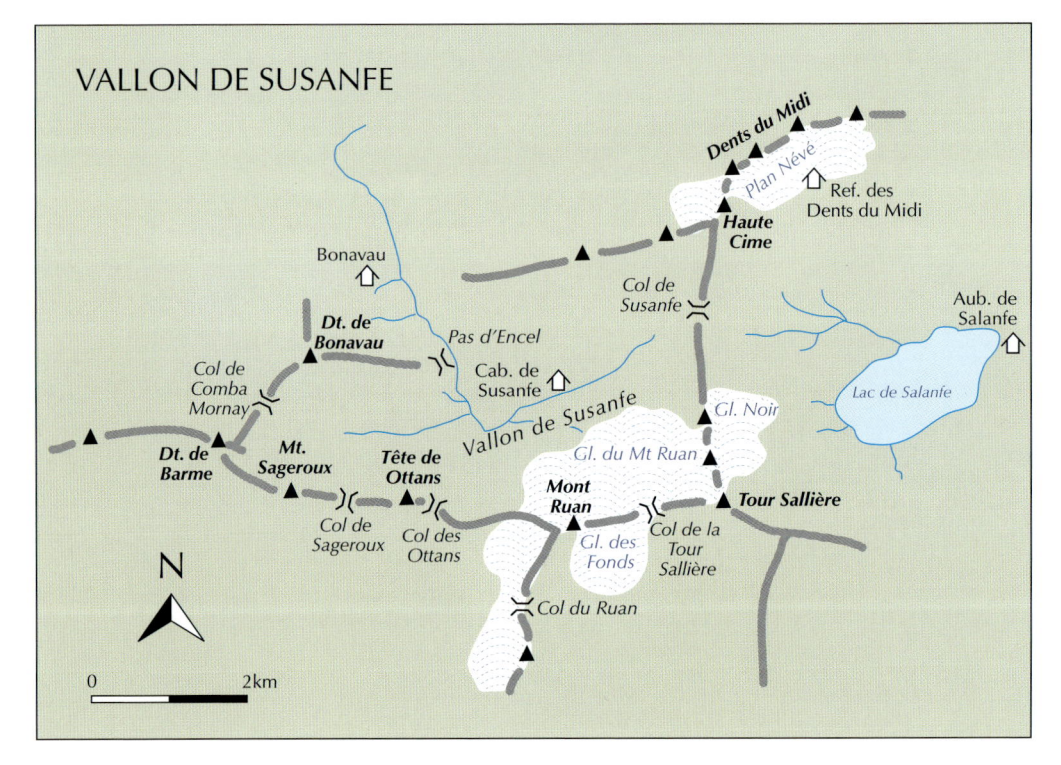

64

Located between Mont Ruan and the Dents du Midi, Cabane de Susanfe makes a useful base

This well-sited hut is useful as a base for a wealth of expeditions, not least a range of climbs on Mont Ruan which rises to the south, and on the Tour Sallière which forms the glen's massive southeast cornerstone.

Although by no means the highest peak in the district, the handsome 3057m **Mont Ruan** is a mountain with two tops, first climbed in 1875 (from the southeast) by G Béraneck, and well worth the attention of activists based here for a few days. The North Face is claimed to be around 1500m high; a rock wall broken by a steep ice shelf at about two-thirds height. However, routes on this face, graded D–TD, are said to be dangerous, for the quality of the rock is poor. But it is the ridges that give the best climbing from the Susanfe basin; the first of these being the West Ridge above Col des Ottans (2hrs from Cabane de Susanfe) which gives a PD traverse over the 2845m Petit Ruan; a route climbed in 1885 by Champéry guides. The East Ridge (AD, III) is a recommended minor classic beginning at the Col de la Tour Sallière (reached in a little under 3hrs from the Susanfe Hut), which offers mixed climbing in a fine situation. The final ridge leading to the summit is a narrow knife-edge of sometimes corniced snow or ice, while the summit itself gives a much-lauded panorama.

Tour Sallière (3219m) is an impressive rock pyramid at the head of the valley, with two secondary summits on its North Ridge, by which it is linked across the saddle of Col du Susanfe with the Haute Cime du Dents du Midi. These secondary summits are **L'Eglise** (3077m) and the higher **Le Dôme** at 3138m, both of which are usually traversed on the way to climb the Tour Sallière itself. The first of these is reached by a route graded D (IV-) in 4–6hrs from the col, then follows along the broad connecting ridge for 30mins to Le Dôme. In order to continue to the Tour involves a PD descent to the 3035m depression of the Col du Dôme, followed by a fairly direct and uncomplicated ascent of the main ridge (PD, II) in another 1–1½hrs. First climbed in 1858, the Tour Sallière has three faces; the NE (Grand Revers) which provides some very fine climbs from the Salanfe basin (see 1:5), the NW Face overlooking the Susanfe refuge and which has a steep, and at times a mostly snow, route with a total ascent of more than 1100m from the hut (PD); and the South Face whose ascent affords the easiest, albeit a rather monotonous, way

The Swiss Alps – Chapter 1: Chablais Alps

to the summit. If this latter route is to be attempted from the Susanfe glen, it will be necessary first to cross the glaciated Col de la Tour Sallière which is a much more demanding climb.

But the finest outing for climbers based at the Susanfe Hut is undoubtedly the ⑤ ☆ **Traverse of the Sallière-Ruan Group**, a long expedition requiring something like 15hrs of sustained effort. This ambitious route was first achieved in 1908 by R Perret, E Défago and S Grenon. By following the ridge crest throughout, it is graded D with pitches of III and IV.

1:4 RHÔNE VALLEY APPROACHES

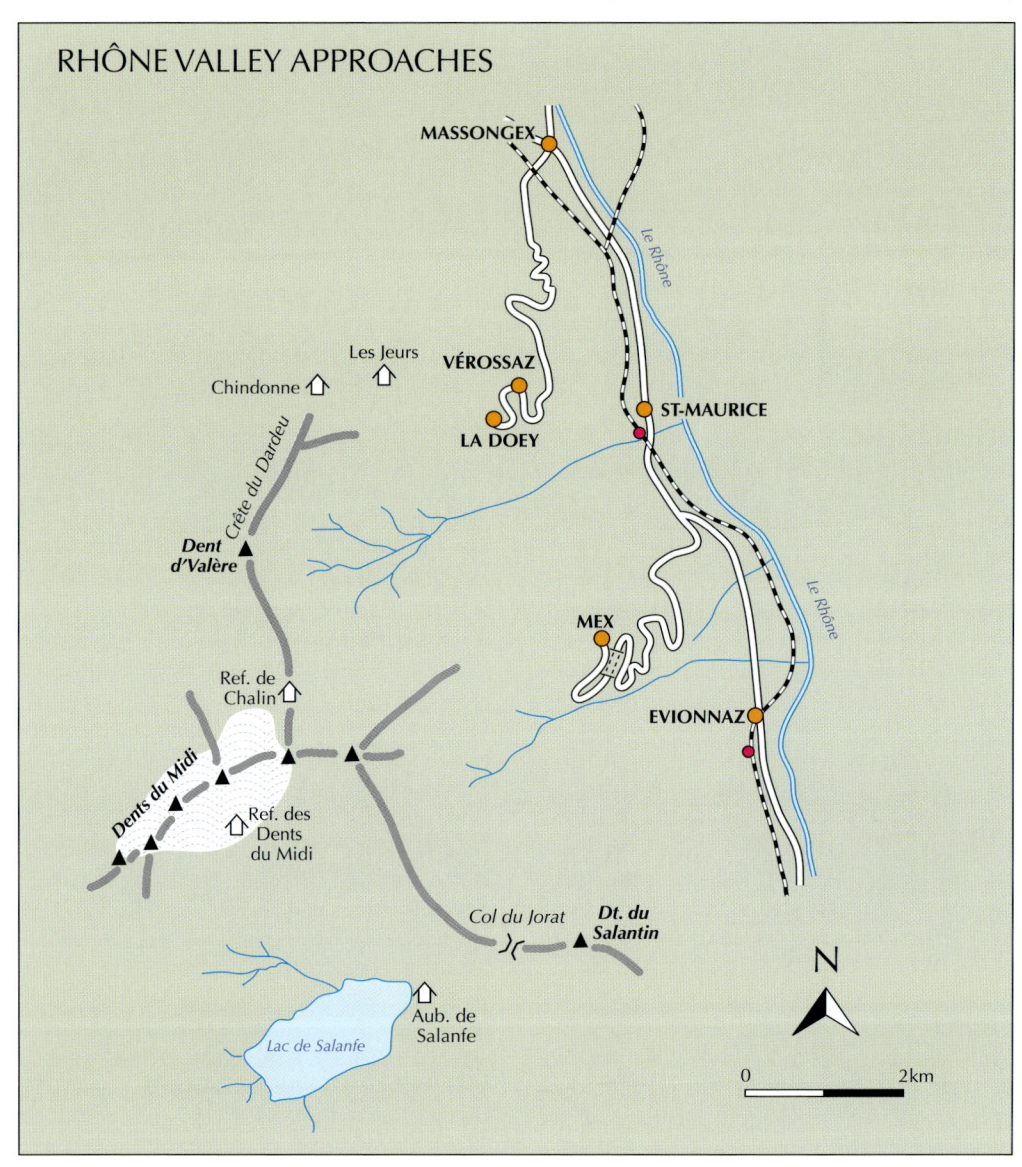

South of Lac Léman the broad, flat-bottomed valley of the Rhône makes an effective divide between the Chablais region and the Bernese Alps, and serves as a major artery of communication, carrying large volumes of traffic by both road and rail. Add to that a number of comparatively small industrial units and power lines, and the valley begins to lose any real aesthetic appeal. And yet, as we have seen on the journey from Monthey to Morgins and Val d'Illiez, it does not take long to be among vineyards and walnut and chestnut trees, with backward views across the valley to the Dent de Morcles and other peaklets and rocky outliers of the Alps of Canton Vaud.

And so it is when you approach the mountains from **St-Maurice**. Nestling in the valley at the foot of the Cime de l'Est, this is an old town which grew around a monastery of 515AD, and takes its name from the warrior-saint said to have been martyred nearby. A small, no-nonsense workaday town, it has its attractive corners and plenty of history, but for users of this guide its main importance is as a point of access to the east side of the Dents du Midi. The town has several hotels, a campsite, restaurants, shops and a bank, and a railway station on the main Geneva–Martigny–Brig line, although when coming from Geneva it's usually necessary to change at Lausanne to find a train that stops here. The tourist office (www.st-maurice.ch) is about 100m from the railway station, while from the post office opposite the station the local postbus begins its infrequent journey to either Vérossaz (La Doey) or Mex, both of which are on or near the route of the Tour des Dents du Midi (see 1:2).

Vérossaz is spread across an open hillside above and to the west of St-Maurice at 864m, but the road to it actually leaves the Rhône valley at Massongex, rather than St-Maurice from where the postbus sets out. The bus continues above the hamlet as far as **La Doey**, where a signpost directs walkers to the route of the Tour des Dents du Midi along a narrow metalled road heading into woodland. The TDM proper is reached where it enters a grassy combe containing the Fahy alpage, backed by waterfalls cascading ... Les Trois Merles and the Cime de l'Est, then swings round to cross the viewpoint of Les Jeurs and continues northward before an alternative path cuts away to the southwest. This strikes up the steep slopes of the **Dent de Valère** and along the **Crête du Dardeu** to gain the **Refuge de Chalin** (5hrs from Vérossaz). This small unmanned hut on the 2595m Tête de Chalin has just eight places, but serves as an overnight base for climbs on the Cime de l'Est and others of the Dents du Midi that rise immediately behind it (see 1:2). The hut enjoys a spectacular, airy situation, with distant views of the Pennine Alps being especially memorable (www.cas-chaussy.ch).

About 4km south of Vérossaz as the crow flies, but a mite longer via the waymarked TDM trail, the charming crowded village of **Mex** is reached by a short but tortuous road directly from St-Maurice. Located 700m above the Rhône, with woodland both above and below, a cutting dug by the St Barthélemy stream to the south, and the Cime de l'Est soaring above the village to the southwest, Mex has considerable merit as a staging post and short-term base, from some of whose upper houses a fine view can be had of the Grand Combin in the southeast. Overnight accommodation may be found here at the local café-restaurant, Auberge de l'Armailli (see 1:2).

A path descends from the village to **Evionnaz** in the valley south of St-Maurice, but by following the TDM southwestward, the **Salanfe basin** with its large dammed lake, busy auberge and views of the south flank of the Dents du Midi, may be gained by a walk of around 3½–4hrs. However, by a combination of road and mule-path, that same basin is approached by a somewhat more circuitous route that climbs above the deep cleft of the Trient gorge near Salvan.

1:5 VALLÉE DU TRIENT

The Trient valley proper begins on the outer edge of the Mont Blanc range in the snowfields of the Plateau du Trient, rimmed by the Aiguille du Tour, Aiguilles Dorées and Pointe d'Orny. From the northern edge of the plateau the fast-receding Trient glacier cascades steeply downhill to a funnel of moraines, pinewoods and pastures that spill out by the hamlet of **Le Peuty** which neighbours the small village of **Trient**, a village that's well-known to trekkers as an overnight halt on both the Tour du Mont Blanc and the Chamonix to Zermatt Walker's Haute Route.

The main road link between Martigny and Chamonix crosses Col de la Forclaz above Trient, and skirts the village on its way down the narrowing valley before turning southwest round a spur on the way to the French border at Le Châtelard. Before reaching that border, however, another road cuts sharply back to the right and climbs to Finhaut, built on a terrace high above the head of the Trient gorge. Meanwhile, the Trient river, boosted by the Eau Noire (which begins at the Col des Montets in France), burrows its way into a deep shaft heading northeast towards the Rhône's valley. Walking routes stretch the length of the ever-deepening gorge, but keep to its upper

Trient, a small village visited by hundreds of trekkers every summer

reaches. That which goes from Finhaut to Vernayaz on the sunny left bank has the pick of the views, while another on the right bank, beginning at the mouth of the Vallée du Trient and ending in the Rhône valley below Gueuroz, links a series of remote hamlets: Litro, Planajeur, La Crêta, La Tailla and Gueuroz itself.

While there are paths and farm tracks on both flanks, and the narrow-gauge Martigny to Chamonix railway (which carries the Mont Blanc Express) has managed to forge a route via stretches of tunnel along the north side of the gorge, the terrain is presumably too abrupt to encourage a road to be built all the way along the gorge walls – on either bank. There's a road at the upper end, as we have seen on the way to Finhaut, and there's another at the lower end that serves Salvan and Les Marecottes, but there's nothing in between. So in order to find access to the Salanfe basin below the Dents du Midi, other than by the walker's cols already mentioned, it is necessary to turn out of the Rhône valley along a minor road found on the northwest outskirts of Martigny at La Bâtiaz.

At first running parallel with the original valley road, it soon angles across the steep hillside of Mont d'Ottan, goes through a tunnel and emerges to cross the Pont du Gueuroz which spans the dramatic Gorges du Trient, here just a few paces wide with the river surging 180m below the bridge. Across this the road climbs on to the small resorts of **Salvan** and **Les Marecottes**, both of which have been built on natural shelves high above the gorge facing south and east. Salvan is the larger of the two, but hotel and b&b accommodation is available in both, while from Les Marecottes a cable car rises to Le Creusaz at 1777m for a panoramic view that includes the Mont Blanc range to the south. (Tourist information for both Salvan and Les Marecottes can be obtained from www.salvan.ch).

A narrow side road winds above Salvan heading north past the chalets of Les Granges on the way to the Lac de Salanfe. It is a narrow road too, mostly single-track with passing bays cut into the steeply wooded hillside, and with a couple of tunnels blasted through the rock, from the last of which you come out at the entrance to the Vallon de Van. This is a tight wedge of a valley; a valley of pasture and woodland with the tiny hamlet of **Van d' Haut** (1371m) its only habitation reached by shuttle minibus service from Salvan and Les Marecottes in the high summer season. A short distance beyond the hamlet the road comes to a halt at Camping Van d'Haut, from where a mule-path strikes ahead to make the final 500m ascent to the **Lac de Salanfe** reservoir, reached by a walk of about 1½hrs from the roadhead.

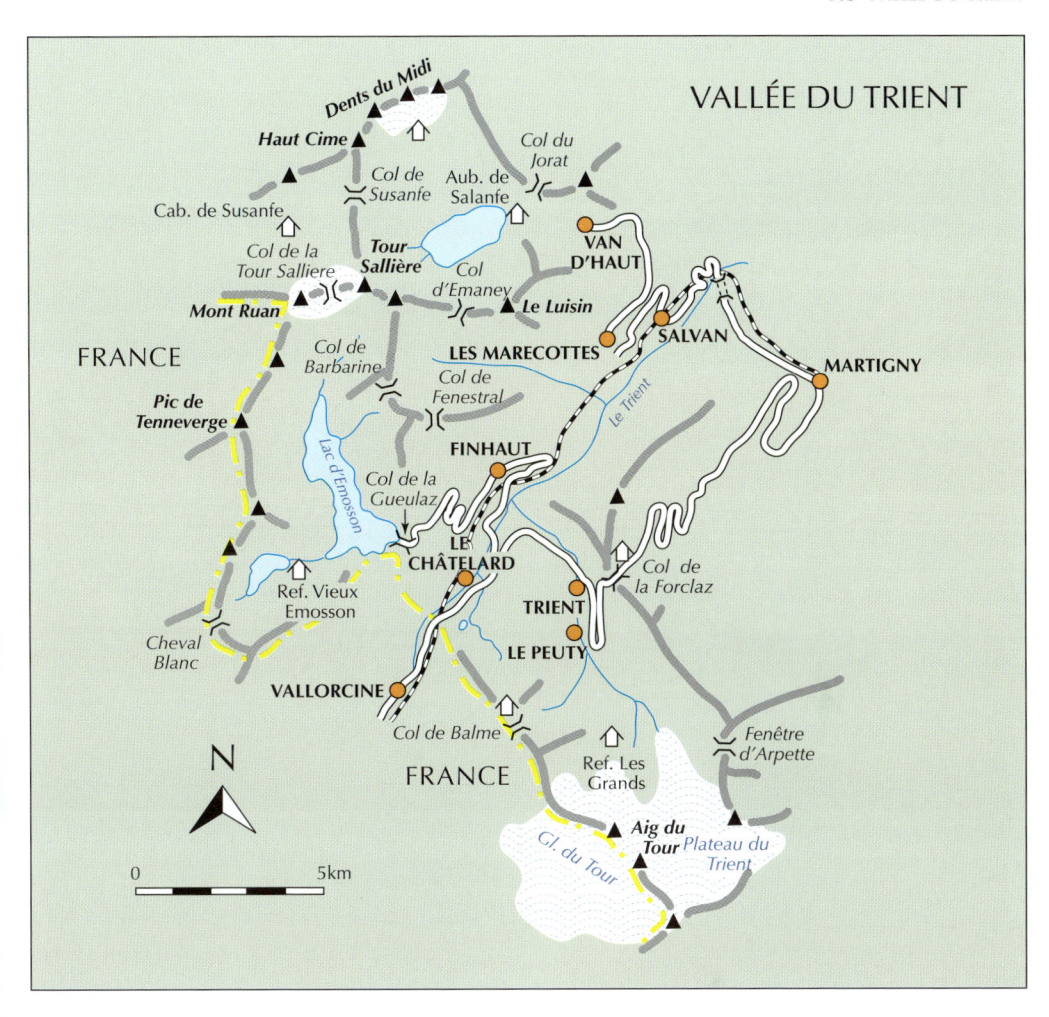

☆ The Salanfe Basin

'Whether you come to climb or not,' said R L G Irving, 'you should see the Salanfe basin from which [the Dents du Midi] rise; its praises were sung long ago by Emile Javelle and he has not exaggerated its charm' (*The Alps*).

With the ever-busy **Auberge de Salanfe** (see 1:2) standing at the northeastern corner of the reservoir at 1942m, the Tour Sallière apparently blocking the western end of the lake, and the SE Face of the Dents du Midi rising to its north, this is a truly dramatic and understandably popular location. No wonder the English-language interim guide to the district described it as 'a sort of "seaside" resort for the Rhône valley townships below'. With clouds hanging in the basin it can seem a haunted place, but on clear days of sunshine it has a unique and exquisite kind of beauty.

For a brief one-off visit a stroll along the south shore of the lake will provide perspective and memorable views (clouds permitting, that is), but the north side gives more variety, especially if you head through the marshy meadows and go partway towards the Col de Susanfe. And then there's an undemanding 45min walk northeast of the auberge that leads to **Col du Jorat** on a broad path used by the TDM (described in 1:2); the col being especially rewarding for those who are unfamiliar with the east side of the Dents du Midi range.

The SAC-owned Cabane de Susanfe stands in the wild little Susanfe valley

More challenging routes for the walker include the climb to **Col de Susanfe** and ascent of the **Haute Cime** (see 1:2); the crossing of the same col (in 2–2¼hrs) to gain access to the Vallon and **Cabane de Susanfe** (40mins from the col) on a path that continues to Champèry; while some 530m or so above and to the south of the lake at the head of a hanging valley, the 2462m **Col d'Emaney** (1½hrs from the auberge) offers walkers an opportunity to make the uncomplicated ascent of ⊗ ☆ **Le Luisin** (2786m) up the ridge to the left in another hour to gain some tremendous views.

By crossing the Col d'Emaney to its south side, however, you gain a choice of routes, the easiest being a descent along the left bank of the Vallon d'Emaney to Les Marecottes or Finhaut. A second option links with the highly scenic **Col de Barberine** (2481m) beyond which lies the Lac d'Emosson; while a third crosses the 2451m **Col de Fenestral** above Finhaut. This last is part of the Tour du Ruan, of which more below.

Those longer suggestions, of course, take walkers out of the Salanfe basin, while climbers might be persuaded to have a base at the Auberge de Salanfe and enjoy a few routes nearby. Alternatively, for those whose interest is in tackling climbs on the SE Face of the Dents du Midi, the unmanned 20-place **Refuge des Dents du Midi** is situated just below the almost level Plan Névé glacier at 2884m, and may be reached in about 3–3½hrs from the lake. From this hut both the South Face and WSW Ridge of the Cime de l'Est are obvious attractions; the first offering an exposed PD route with some delicate pitches of III; while the WSW Ridge via the Col de la Cime de l'Est provides the easiest route to the summit (F with pitches of II).

The massive triangular ⊕ ☆ **NE (Grand Revers) Face of the 3219m Tour Sallière** dominates the western end of Lac de Salanfe and holds a choice of routes for activists happy to be seduced away from the Dents du Midi. The 1280m Diagonal Route graded PD+ is one; the NE Buttress, or *Itinéraire*

1:5 Vallée du Trient

des Trois Français, is another which goes at AD (III). However, the Arête d'Emaney which rises from the Col d'Emaney ESE of the Tour Sallière and was first climbed direct in 1902, was long recognised as providing one of the best climbs of the district (IV with one pitch of V), although the Délez Chimney, which contains the main difficulty, can be avoided by an exposed variation.

TOUR DU RUAN

Though not so well known as the Tour des Dents du Midi described in 1:2, the clockwise Tour du Ruan is another multi-day trek worth the consideration of walkers wishing to understand better the topography of this corner of the Alps. Roughly half the route is spent across the French border, and views are memorable on every stage. (For information see www.toururuan.com) The route is also described by Hilary Sharp in *Trekking in the Alps*.

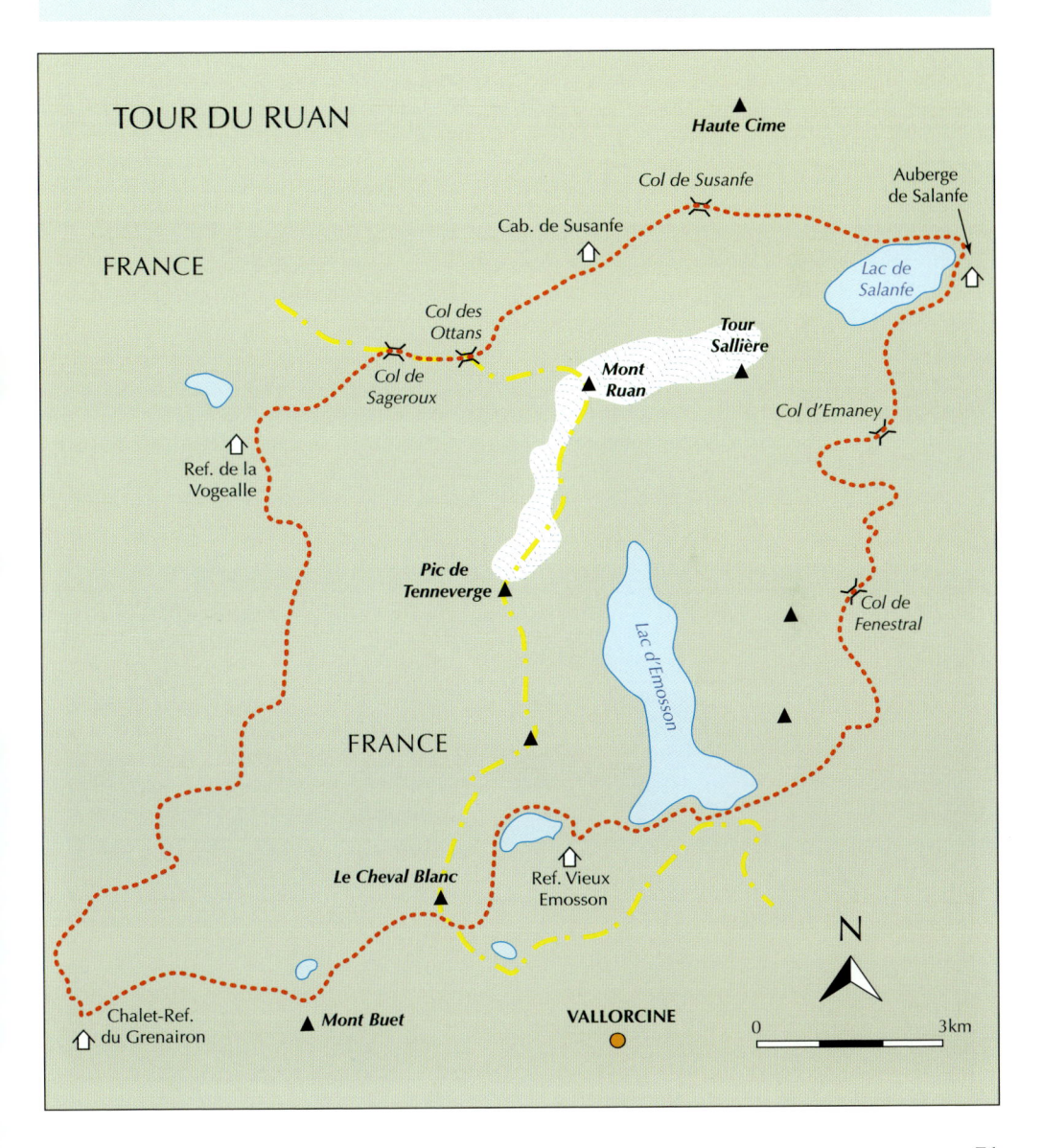

Day 1: Leaving **Auberge de Salanfe** go round the south side of the Salanfe lake and climb the narrow hanging valley leading to **Col d'Emaney**, from where the tip of the Matterhorn can be seen far to the east. Descend into the head of the little valley below the Pointes d'Aboillon, wander down the glen to the Emaney chalets, then break away on an alternative path which crosses the stream and climbs to the **Col de Fenestral** at 2451m. With the Mont Blanc range in view, go down to the Finestral alpage, then contour round to **Lac d'Emosson** and cross the massive dam wall (more great views of Mont Blanc). Either continue along a service road, or take a signed path through the Gorge du Vieux towards the southern end of **Lac du Vieux Emosson**. The timber-built **Refuge Vieux Emosson** (2200m) stands below the dam that closes the eastern end of the lake, and is gained about 7½–8hrs after setting out.

Day 2: A short walk above the refuge leads to the Vieux Emosson lake where you make an arc round its north shore, pass the dinosaur prints (see box) and cross the bounding ridge (with chain safeguards) into France at the cone-shaped **Cheval Blanc** (2831m). Should you have the energy, and the weather is good, an option here is to make the ascent of **Mont Buet** at 3096m. Descending into the Combe de Buet the Tour visits the little Lac du Plan du Buet, and continues among limestone towers before descending to the **Chalet-Refuge du Grenairon** which provides accommodation above the Giffre valley at 1974m, about 5½hrs from the Vieux Emosson refuge.

Day 3: Much of this day is spent working towards the head of the Giffre valley blocked by the Dents Blanche–Mont Ruan wall, and with the huge Tenneverge ridge which carries the Franco-Swiss border, soaring 1900m above to the right. A 1000m descent takes you down to the valley, at first on limestone, then through meadows lavish with flowers in early summer. Crossing the valley in its upper reaches near the Chalets du Boret, the way then climbs a little over 500m to gain the CAF-owned **Refuge de la Vogealle** at 1901m.

Day 4: The final stage of the Tour du Ruan returns to Switzerland at the 2395m **Col de Sageroux**, about 1½hrs above the hut, then cuts along the ridge heading east over the Tête des Ottans to **Col des Ottans**, which is 100m higher than Sageroux, and from where you descend steeply (caution required) into the Vallon de Susanfe. From **Cabane de Susanfe** head upvalley, cross **Col de Susanfe** and make the descent into the Salanfe basin to complete the circuit at **Auberge de Salanfe** at the end of a 6½hr day.

Mont Ruan and the Tour Sallière, seen from the Pas d'Encel

1:5 Vallée du Trient

Clouds hang low over Lac d'Emosson

Lacs d'Emosson

In common with the St Bernard Express (see Chapter 2) the Mont Blanc Express which begins in Martigny must be one of Europe's slowest 'express' trains. Grinding slowly along the left bank of the Gorges du Trient it has a station at **Finhaut**, an unpretentious resort whose buildings appear to cascade down the steep hillside. The tourist office is located at the railway station (www.finhaut.ch) at the lower end of the village which has a modest number of shops, a bank, a small choice of hotel and pension accommodation, and a 14-place *dortoir*, Les Alpes. A few kilometres further upvalley **Le Châtelard** marks the border with France, and it is here that rail passengers bound for Chamonix need to change trains. Le Châtelard has two hotels and a funicular, said to be the world's steepest with a gradient of 87%, linking with a narrow-gauge tourist train and a 'mini funicular' to provide access with Lac d'Emosson (www.emosson-trains.ch). The same reservoir's dam can also be reached in summer by road from Finhaut, and by a public bus service from Martigny.

The route to Finhaut and Col de la Gueulaz above the Emosson dam breaks away from the main Martigny to Chamonix road a short distance outside Le Châtelard. It makes for a scenically exciting drive, for as you sweep up the hillside a view opens through the upper Vallée du Trient to its glacier, then as you pass above Finhaut a retrospective view to the northeast reveals the Bernese Alps beyond the Rhône valley, and finally and most remarkably, Mont Blanc and the Aiguilles dominate the southern horizon with a vision of snow, ice and jagged granite ramparts.

Col de la Gueulaz (1965m) marks the roadhead with plenty of parking space, a bus stop, tourist information kiosk, a restaurant, public toilets, a small chapel and views overlooking the Lac d'Emosson. By walking up the steep path above the chapel for 10–15mins, the modest summit of Six Jeur unfolds a truly impressive panorama, and is recommended.

From the dam Lac d'Emosson is seen stretching north for about 4.5km towards the head of the Barberine valley where Mont Ruan and the Tour

Sallière close it off with an arc of rock and ice. Despite the intrusion of the massive dam wall, it is an enticing, wild-looking district with several worthwhile outings for both walkers and climbers, but it's difficult to resist speculating how lovely the valley must have been before the first dam was built here in 1926. Until then the Barberine valley was noted for its alpine pastures and small farms; it was visited by a few climbers, botanists and perhaps chamois hunters, and it was near the head of the valley on its west side that Jacques Balmat, who had made the first ascent of Mont Blanc with Dr Paccard, lost his life in 1834 when prospecting for gold.

The smaller Vieux Emosson lake which lies in a combe further to the west was dammed in 1950, then in 1975 the Barberine dam was superseded by a massive 150m high barrage created as part of a joint Franco-Swiss hydro scheme. This effectively drowned that part of the valley which had survived the initial flooding, including a number of chalets and an inn. Yet despite its effect on the valley, in truth the dam wall is not only a fine piece of civil engineering, but it makes an extraordinary vantage point, having an uninterrupted outlook to Mont Blanc in one direction, and to the Tour Sallière and the lake in the other. But it is also noteworthy for another reason – a line of holds has been fitted to make this one of the most impressive artificial climbing walls in the Alps.

On the east side of the lake a track extends towards the head of the valley, with a path cutting away from it two-thirds of the way along. This path climbs northeastward to the broad **Col de Barberine** (2481m) which lies at the southern end of the Pointes d'Abboillon, and is a wonderful viewpoint. In order to create a full day's circular walk, it would be possible to descend from the col into the Vallon d'Emaney, and wander down that valley as far as the Emaney chalets at 1855m, then return to Col de Gueulaz and Lac d'Emosson by way of **Col de Fenestral** (2451m).

The 2834m **Col de la Tour Sallière** is a different proposition. Located on the valley's headwall ridge west of the Tour Sallière, it is reached by way of the Glacier des Fonds, the upper reaches of which are sometimes threatened by stonefall. Once gained, the descent on the north side leads to Cabane de Susanfe in the Vallon de Susanfe (see 1:3) by way of the steep Glacier du Mont Ruan.

While the east side of the valley is contained, as we have seen, by the ridge of the Pointes d'Abboillon, the west side of Lac d'Emosson is largely overlooked by **Pic de Tenneverge**, a symmetrical 2985m pyramid of Jurassic limestone first climbed via its south flank in October 1863, nine years after his famous ascent of the Wetterhorn, by Sir Alfred Wills and C Gurlie starting from the Col de Tenneverge; a route today graded PD. Having been attracted to the Giffre valley on the French side of the mountain after climbing Mont Buet in 1857, Wills built a large chalet there, which he named The Eagle's Nest. From there he made at least two new ascents of Pic de Tenneverge; the first by the south flank, and the second a year later via the ENE Ridge after making a traverse of the entire Prazon glacier from the Col du Sageroux.

The majority of walkers who come here, however, make their way to **Lac du Vieux Emosson** with the aim of seeking out the dinosaur footprints discovered above the lake at an altitude of about 2400m in 1976. With a small refuge standing just below it, this lake is on the route of the Tour du Ruan, outlined in the box above, and is bounded by cliffs and screes to create a much more wild scene than that of its larger neighbour. After crossing the Emosson dam a narrow service road cuts roughly westward along the south side of the reservoir and actually goes all the way to Lac du Vieux Emosson via a couple of tunnels. If followed all the way, this walk would be achieved in about 1hr 20mins from Col de la Gueulaz; although it's possible to avoid the last third of roadway by taking an unmarked path through the steep little Gorge du Vieux which leads directly to the **Refuge Vieux Emosson** (2200m), a low, single-storey timber built hut (www.cabaneduvieux.ch) overlooking the Emosson lake to the east. Topos of local climbs are available at this hut.

A better option is to break away from the road at the second path junction where a sign directs a cairned and sparsely waymarked route to the dinosaur tracks in 2hrs. This path avoids the road altogether, and cuts through the peaceful Gorge de Veudale (much longer than the Gorge du Vieux) and is the one to take unless, that is, your plan is to go only as far as the refuge at Vieux Emosson, in which case the better plan is to remain with the road. The cairned footpath route leads to the southern end of Lac du Vieux Emosson, about 45mins beyond the refuge, and continues to the site of the now famous dinosaur footprints.

THE VIEUX EMOSSON DINOSAURS

Discovered above the southern end of the Lac du Vieux Emosson by a French geologist in 1976, a group of fossilized tracks has been identified as those belonging to dinosaurs that lived around 240–65 million years ago. The rock slab in which the surprisingly small footprints are embedded, was once part of a sandy beach frequented by the herbivorous creatures. Laid down in shallow water during the Triassic period (about 230 million years ago), the sand and sediments were compressed and hardened as earth movements led to the disappearance of the ocean with the collision of continental tectonic plates. As the African plate shunted against its Eurasian neighbour, so the Alps were born, and rocks that had been formed below sea-level were thrust up and outward to reveal evidence of creatures that roamed long before the mountains came into existence.

The dinosaur footprints are only a few centimetres long, and as the site is the most important yet found in Europe, it is protected by chains to prevent visitors from clambering over it. Further information is available at the tourist office in Finhaut (www.finhaut.ch), and at the Vieux Emosson refuge.

Carrying the Franco-Swiss border, the combe containing the Vieux Emosson lake and the dinosaur prints is formed by a rocky crest, much of which falls on its west flank into the Giffre valley, and which runs from Point de la Finive in the north across the Tête du Grenairon and Le Cheval Blanc to the Pointe de la Terrasse above the little Val de Tré les Eaux in the south. Within that crest will be found several crossing points, among them Col du Grenairon (2685m), Col du Vieux (2569m), Col des Corbeaux (2603m) and the 2645m Col de la Terrasse, which lies northeast of Pointe de la Terrasse. But it's also possible to cross the ridge over Le Cheval Blanc, as is the choice of the Tour du Ruan. However, not all these crossings are straightforward, and concentration may be required to find the way – especially in misty conditions.

An interesting return to Col de la Gueulaz and the Lac d'Emosson could be made by crossing Col de la Terrasse, descending on the French slope to the Chalets de Loria above Vallorcine, then making a long contour north across the steep hillside on a path which leads directly to the Emosson dam. An easier alternative is to follow the clear path round the north shore of Lac du Vieux Emosson, pass through a short tunnel at its eastern end and descend to the road at Refuge Vieux Emosson. The metalled service road which dates back to the building of the dam nearby, can now be followed down to Lac d'Emosson, or you could take the path which drops below the hut, goes through the Gorge du Vieux and brings you onto the road at a hairpin bend above the lake's western end.

The Upper Vallée du Trient

To conclude our survey of what we loosely term the Chablais Alps, we stray south of the Gorges du Trient to the very edge of the Mont Blanc massif where the upper reaches of the Vallée du Trient are neatly contained by clearly defined ridges; rocky and uncompromising in the southeast (the highest point being the 3540m Aiguille du Tour), but steeply wooded where they spill down towards the gorge at their northernmost limit. The French border traces the most westerly of these ridges, but only as far as Col de Balme. Here the ridge kinks northward from its former northwest alignment, but the frontier line ignores this slight change of direction and cuts straight down the slope to the Eau Noire stream and the Barberine chalets, before climbing the opposite slope to Lac d'Emosson.

Col de Balme is the only obvious crossing point in this westerly ridge. A broad grass saddle at 2204m, it is a justly famous vantage point with a direct view of the Aiguilles Verte, Drus, Charmoz and Blaitière, the graceful snow dome of Mont Blanc with the Chamonix valley below, and the Aiguilles Rouges forming its right-hand wall. Baedeker called it 'a superb view', while alpine connoisseur R L G Irving summed it up with the words: 'if that view does not thrill you you are better away from the Alps.' It's a view known to thousands of skiers who throng there in winter, and to the countless trekkers who make the crossing each year whilst tackling either the Tour du Mont Blanc or the Walker's Haute Route from Chamonix to Zermatt. On the pass itself stands the solid, gloomy, and privately owned **Refuge du Col**

The Trient glacier retreating into the upper reaches of the valley

de Balme, which is manned in summer and has 26 dormitory places (tel 04 50 54 02 33).

Reached by a good path in little over an hour from the col, another refuge stands on the Swiss flank below the Glacier des Grands at 2113m. **Refuge Les Grands** has 15 places but no permanent guardian; self-catering facilities are adequate but visitors need to provide their own food (for reservations tel 026 660 65 04). There are no views of Mont Blanc from here, for the hut has its back to the mountains and instead faces the valley's east wall across the deep trench scoured long ago by the receding Trient glacier. Of a summer's evening the sun's glow lingers on the Pointe d'Orny and the rocky needles that spread from it, and the only sounds to be heard are those of running streams and the occasional rattle of a stone falling through a distant gully.

Despite foreshortening, a wildly romantic scene is crammed with rocks, shrub-carpeted hillsides and glacial remnants immediately above the hut, which occupies the site of a one-time alp. From it a path descends steeply into the valley where a footbridge offers a goodly choice of walker's routes. You could cross that bridge to a little *buvette* (the Chalet du Glacier) in view of the Glacier du Trient, then climb first alongside, then above the glacier to reach the rocky gateway of the Fenêtre d'Arpette (2665m) which gives access to Val d'Arpette and Champex described in the Pennine Alps chapter (2:1); or you could turn left by the *buvette* along a near-level footpath that accompanies the Bisse du Trient across a wooded slope to Col de la Forclaz (see box). Or you could do neither of these things, and instead of crossing the footbridge simply turn left and wander downvalley between pastures to Le Peuty and Trient.

On the east side of the valley the Fenêtre d'Arpette is of course a crossing for mountain walkers, while the 1526m Col de la Forclaz carries the road from Martigny after labouring through vineyards and up a series of hairpins out of the Rhône

1:5 Vallée du Trient

THE BISSE DU TRIENT

Flowing from the foot of the Trient glacier to Col de la Forclaz, the Bisse du Trient is just one of more than 200 similar channels created throughout Canton Valais in order to carry glacial water sometimes a considerable distance to irrigate cultivated farmland, often in the Rhône valley. The oldest are believed to have been made in the 12th and 13th centuries; some channels being hewn from bare rock, others using hollowed tree trunks to bridge sections impossible to excavate; many were made by prisoners used as forced labour. Footpaths were invariably created alongside each *bisse* to facilitate its maintenance, but the track alongside the Bisse du Trient had rails laid on it in the 19th century to carry ice blocks from the glacier to the hotel at the col.

valley. Beside the road on the col stands the **Hotel du Col de la Forclaz** (35 beds, 40 dorm places plus camping; www.coldelaforclaz.ch) almost opposite the TMB path that goes to Champex via the Bovine alp.

Having gained the col from the northeast, the road now slants down into the Vallée du Trient and bypasses both Le Peuty and neighbouring Trient on its way to Le Châtelard and the French border. For those who plan to stay overnight in the valley, however, simple *gîte* accommodation is available at the **Refuge du Peuty** (40 dorm places, open June to mid-Sept; tel 027 722 09 38), while in Trient itself the **Relais du Mont Blanc** has 80 places (open all year; tel 027 722 46 23), with another 21 dormitory places to be found at the **Gîte La Gardienne**, which is also open all year (www.largardienne.ch). (For further information go to www.trient.ch)

Although there are a few local valley walks, in summer Trient is mostly used as an overnight halt

In summer Trient is a major overnight halt for countless trekkers

THE SWISS ALPS – CHAPTER 1: CHABLAIS ALPS

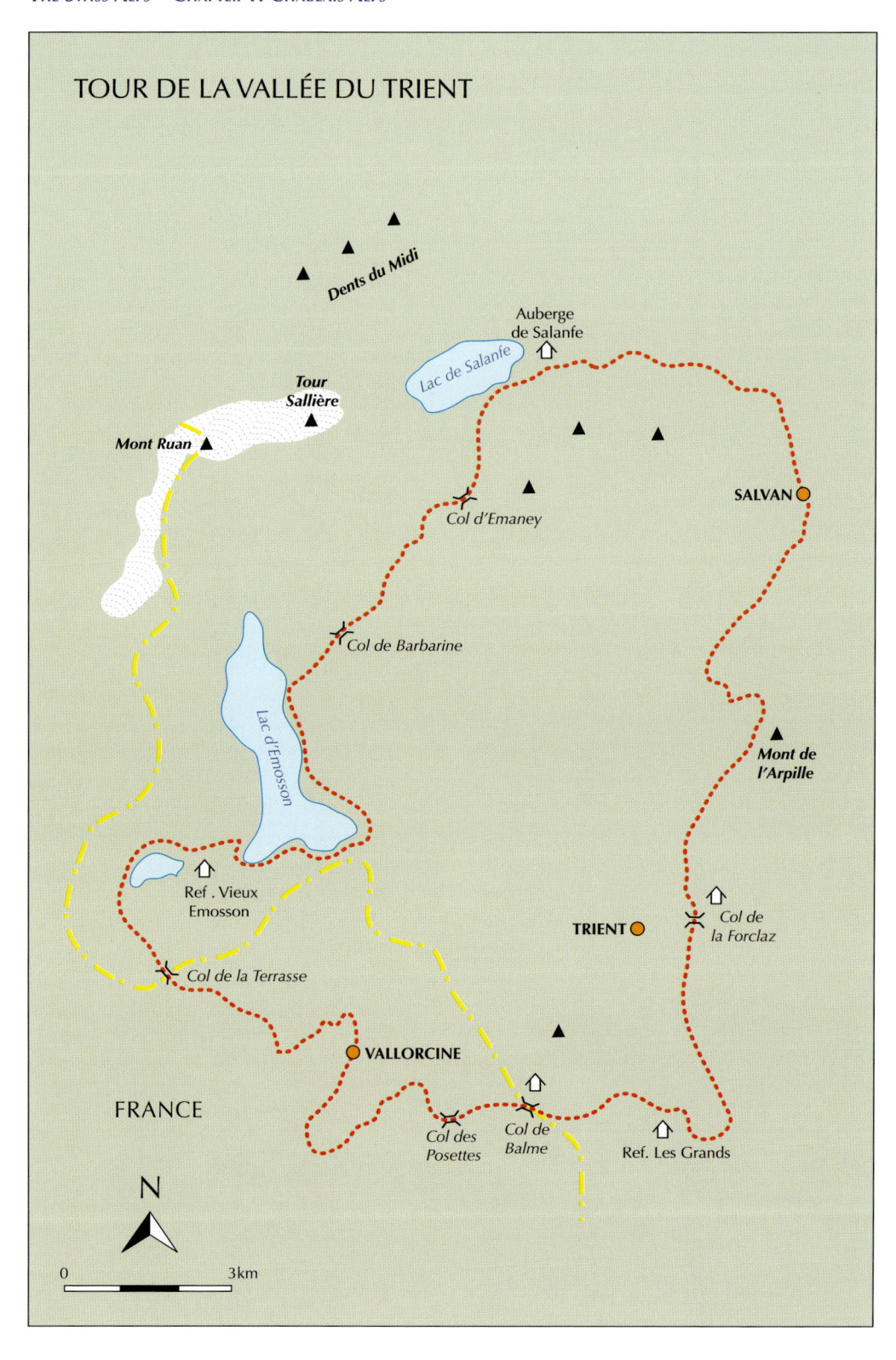

TOUR DE LA VALLÉE DU TRIENT

by trekkers passing through. There are no climbs easily accessible from the valley, for the main peaks of interest are approached from huts such as the **Cabane du Trient** under Pointe d'Orny at an altitude of 3170m, and the shortest route to that takes 5½–6hrs from the village. But in winter the upper Vallée du Trient can be explored on snowshoes and cross-country skis, while low-key ski tours are promoted on the Croix de Fer above Col de Balme, the Pointe Ronde massif southeast of the Col de la Forclaz and, of course, on the Plateau du Trient and Aiguille du Tour. The classic Haute Route ski tour avoids the Vallée du Trient by descending from Cabane du Trient into the Val d'Arpette by way of either the Fenêtre du Chamois or Col des Encandies, but in summer trekkers following the Walker's Haute Route pass through the Walker's Haute Route pass through the valley by a choice of routes, as do those tackling the ever-popular Tour du Mont Blanc. In addition, a third multi-day trek comes this way, intent on making a complete tour of the valley. This is the Tour de la Vallée du Trient.

TOUR DE LA VALLÉE DU TRIENT

This is a very fine walking tour which crosses no fewer than six cols and picks out virtually all the scenic highlights of the district. Since some of the cols hang onto their snow cover until quite late, it should not be tackled before about mid-July, by which time conditions ought to be fairly settled. The route is normally walked in a counter-clockwise direction.

Day 1: Begin at **Col de la Forclaz** where a path strikes uphill heading north to make the ascent of **Mont de l'Arpille** (2085m), over whose summit the way then descends to the Arpille alp, then much more steeply down to the Gorge du Trient which is crossed more than 1400m below Mont de l'Arpille. A steep climb out of the gorge leads to **Salvan** at the end of a 6–6½hr day.

Day 2: Although this is a much shorter stage (3hrs), it's uphill all the way. Leaving Salvan along the narrow road that works its way to the Vallon de Van, it concludes by taking the old mule-path from the campsite at the roadhead. This goes steeply uphill to the Salanfe basin in full view of the Dents du Midi where the night is spent at the **Auberge de Salanfe**.

Day 3: This third stage is similar to the first day's trek on the Tour du Ruan, in that it begins at Salanfe and finishes at the Vieux Emosson refuge. However, after crossing **Col d'Emaney**, our route descends into the head of the Vallon d'Emaney, then goes for the more direct **Col de Barberine** instead of Col de Fenestral, and descends to **Lac d'Emosson** with the Mont Blanc massif in view for much of the way. After crossing the dam at its southern end, the way then follows the narrow service road up to **Refuge Vieux Emosson** (5½–6hrs).

Day 4: Skirting the shore of Lac du Vieux Emosson, the continuing Tour de la Vallée du Trient is a 4hr stage that visits the site of the dinosaur footprints. It then crosses the 2645m **Col de la Terrasse** and descends past the Chalets de Loria to **Vallorcine**, the first village on the French side of the border.

Day 5: Leaving Vallorcine for the final stage of the trek, begin by following the cog railway upvalley towards Col des Montets, then break out of the valley with a 600m climb to the grass saddle of **Col des Posettes** with its big view of the Aiguilles du Chardonnet and Argentière, Verte and Drus, and of Mont Blanc itself. The way then loops round to **Col de Balme** to re-enter Swiss territory, but instead of plunging straight down into the Vallée du Trient, it adopts the path that remains high before cutting round the Remointse spur to **Refuge Les Grands**. From here you descend to the valley below the Trient glacier, cross the glacial torrent and finish the trek by a gentle stroll alongside the Bisse du Trient that leads directly to **Col de la Forclaz** (a 5½–6hr stage).

ACCESS, BASES, MAPS AND GUIDES

Access

Val de Morgins By minor road west of Monthey in the Rhône valley. By train from Aigle or Monthey to Troistorrents, then bus to Morgins.

Val d'Illiez As for Val de Morgins, but branch left at Troistorrents. By train from Aigle or Monthey to Champéry.

Vallon de Susanfe On foot from Champéry or the Salanfe basin.

Rhône Valley By train from Geneva to Monthey or St-Maurice via Lausanne. The postbus runs a service from St-Maurice to Mex and Vérrosaz.

Vallée du Trient By train (Mont Blanc Express) from Martigny through the Trient gorges to Finhaut and Le Châtelard on the French border. By bus from Martigny to Col de la Forclaz, Trient and Le Châtelard.

Valley Bases

Val de Morgins Morgins
Val d'Illiez Troistorrents, Val d'Illiez, Champéry
Vallon de Susanfe Cabane de Susanfe
Rhône Valley St-Maurice, Mex
Vallée du Trient Salvan, Les Marecottes, Finhaut, Trient, Col de la Forclaz

Information

Chablais Tourisme SA, Case postale 1429, CH-1870 Monthey 2 (Tel 024 471 12 12 info@chablais.info www.chablais.info)

Huts

Several huts, both staffed and unmanned, are situated in the main areas described, as mentioned in the text. Most of these belong to the SAC, although some are privately owned. In addition, a few mountain inns with low-priced dormitory accommodation may be found in secluded locations.

Maps

For planning purposes Kümmerly + Frey publish a useful Wanderkarte at 1:60,000: Grand-St-Bernard, Dents du Midi–Les Diablerets

The Swiss National Survey (Cartes Nationales de la Suisse) cover the same area at 1:50,000 with sheets 272 St-Maurice and 282 Martigny and at 1:25,000 with sheets 1284 Monthey, 1304 Val d'Illiez, 1324 Barberine, 1325 Sembrancher and 1344 Col de Balme

Walking and/or Trekking Guides

Randonnées en montagne – Chablais et Valais francophone by Philippe Metzker (SAC)

Trekking in the Alps by Kev Reynolds (Cicerone, 2011)

Trekking & Climbing in the Western Alps by Hilary Sharp (New Holland, 2002)

Snowshoeing: Mont Blanc & the Western Alps by Hilary Sharp (Cicerone, 2002)

Climbing Guides

Dents du Midi (West Col, 1967 – long out of print)

Chaîne franco-suisse (SAC, 2003)

Guide du Valais: Du Trient au Nufenen

Klettersteig Schweiz by Iris Kürschner (Bergverlag Rother, Munich, 2004)

See Also

Freie Sicht aufs Gipfelmeer by Marco Volken and Remo Kundert (Salvioni Edizioni, Bellinzona, 2003)

Walking in the Alps by Kev Reynolds (Cicerone, 2nd edition 2005)

CHAPTER 2: PENNINE ALPS

Also known as the Valais Alps. All mountains south of the Rhône valley, spreading eastward from the Mont Blanc massif to the Simplon Pass.

PENNINE ALPS: CHAPTER SUMMARY

Location
Although the range of the Pennine Alps is usually described as extending from the Col du Grand St Bernard to the Simplon Pass, for the purposes of this book we take its western limit to be the Petit Col Ferret on the Swiss-Italian border on the very edge of the Mont Blanc massif. The Rhône valley forms its northern limit, the alpine watershed which carries the frontier with Italy marks its southern extent.

☆ Highlights

🟢 Walks
- Walker's Haute Route (2:1)
- Tour des Combins (2:2)
- Tour du Val de Bagnes (2:3)
- Sentier des Chamois (2:3)
- Tour du Val d'Anniviers (2:8)
- Numerous routes from Zinal (2:8)
- Grächen–Saas Fee Höhenweg (2:10)
- Europaweg (2:10)
- Numerous routes from Zermatt (2:10)
- Tour of the Matterhorn (2:10)
- Gspon Höhenweg (2:11)
- Tour of Monte Rosa (2:11)

Climbs
- Assorted routes on the Grand Combin (2:3)
- Mont Blanc de Cheilon (2:5)
- Pigne d'Arolla (2:6)
- Various routes on the Dent Blanche (2:6)
- Ober Gabelhorn, Zinalrothorn & Weisshorn above Zinal (2:8)
- Weisshorn, East Ridge (2:10)
- Numerous climbs above Zermatt (2:10)
- Weissmies via the SSE Ridge (2:11)

Summits for all
- Grand Tavé (2:3)
- Bella Tola (2:8)
- Schwarzhorn (2:9)
- Mettelhorn (2:10)

Contents

2:1 Val Ferret 86
The Walker's Haute Route (box) 89
Walks and Climbs from Champex 90
Cabane du Trient 92
Orsières to La Fouly 92
Cabane de Saleina 93
La Fouly 93
Mont Dolent (box) 95
The Upper Val Ferret 95

2:2 Val d'Entremont 96
Tour des Combins (box) 98
The Upper Val d'Entremont 102
Col du Grand St Bernard: A Place in History (box) .. 102

2:3 Val de Bagnes 103
Tour du Val de Bagnes (box) 105
Cabane du Mont Fort 106
Le Châble to Fionnay 108
Combin Massif 109
The Upper Val de Bagnes 111
The Classic Haute Route (box) 113

2:4 Val de Nendaz 115

2:5 Val d'Hérémence 116

2:6 Val d'Hérens 120
Tour du Val d'Hérens (box) 124
Val d'Arolla 125
Ferpècle and the Dent Blanche 129
Dent Blanche: 'The grandest mountain in the Alps' (box) 130
La Sage and Ways East 131

2:7 Val de Moiry 132
Walks in Val de Moiry 135

2:8 Val d'Anniviers 137
Tour du Val d'Anniviers (box) 139
Val de Zinal 141

◀ *The Matterhorn and tranquil Stellisee*

Walks from Zinal 142
Climbs from Zinal. 143
Moving On. 145

2:9 Turtmanntal 146

2:10 Mattertal 149
Walks and Climbs from Grächen 152
St Niklaus to Täsch 153
The Weisshorn: 'An almost faultless mountain' (box) 153
Climbs from the Täsch Hut 155
Zermatt. 156
The Zermatt Basin. 157
Walks from Zermatt 158
Tour of the Matterhorn (box). 160
Climbs from Zermatt. 162
Ulrich Inderbinden: The Old Man of the Matterhorn
 (box). 166

Zermatt for Skiers 167
The Adlerpass. 167

2:11 Saastal 168
Climbs from Saas Grund. 170
Saas Fee 172
Johann-Joseph Imseng: Priest, Guide and
 Hotelier (box). 174
Walks and Climbs from Saas Fee 174
Tour of Monte Rosa (box) 176
The Upper Saastal. 176

2:12 Simplon Pass 179

Access, Bases, Maps and Guides 181

THE SWISS ALPS – CHAPTER 2: PENNINE ALPS

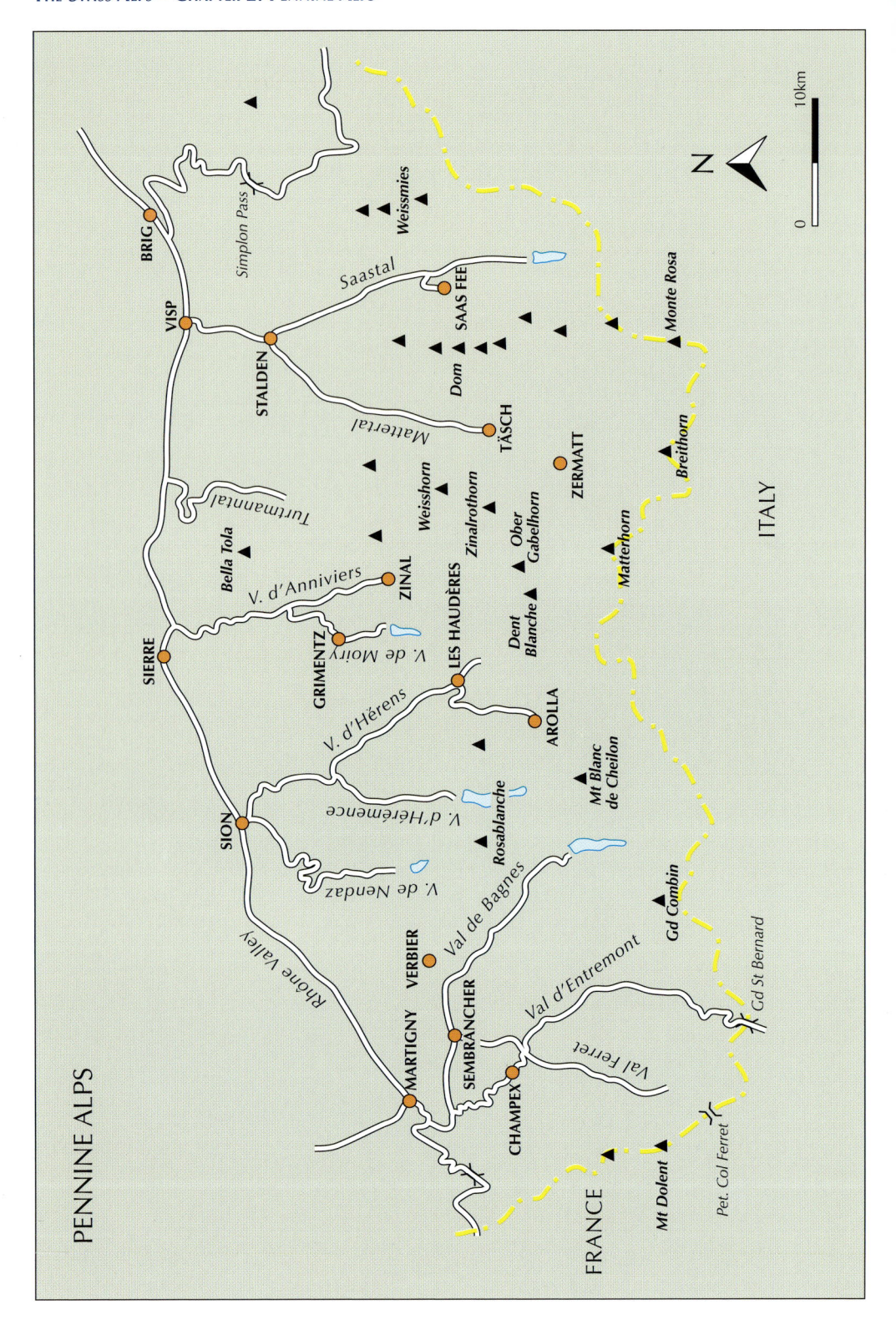

Col de Riedmatten, link between the Dix Hut and Arolla (Chapter 2.5) ▶

PENNINE ALPS: INTRODUCTION

Today the Pennines are the mecca of the classic-style mountaineer ... Such routes have lost none of their aura and belong to any list of the Alps' top climbs.

John Cleare, *Collins Guide to Mountains & Mountaineering*

This tremendous range of snow- and ice-clad mountains holds the largest concentration of 4000m peaks west of the Caucasus, among them Matterhorn, Weisshorn, Zinalrothorn, Monte Rosa, Ober Gabelhorn, Dent Blanche, Grand Combin and Dom – the highest mountain entirely in Switzerland. With some of the best-placed centres for mountaineering in all the Alps, there's also unlimited potential for walking holidays of all standards, immense scope for top-quality ski tours, and scenery to rival that of anywhere in Europe. Yet despite the popularity of the district, and the iconic status of so many of its peaks, it is still possible to walk and climb there in surprising isolation, even in the height of summer.

A succession of valleys and their tributaries drain northward into the Rhône. The headwall of many of these valleys is crowned with snowfields and glaciers, but in some cases the high mountains thrust forward away from the watershed crest along projecting ridge systems that effectively extend the snow cover further north. Beyond the snow and ice, these ridges are crossed by numerous cols of varying degrees of difficulty that attract the walker and trekker. And while mountaineering attention is naturally focused on the higher summits, more modest ascents are possible on numerous 'lesser' peaks which, standing as they often do apart from the more dramatic mountains, reward with some of the finest views of all.

Though it will no doubt be the mountains, either individually or as a group, that are the main attraction, many of their valleys are no less appealing. The majority are entered from the Rhône through a gorge that opens to bands of forest and sloping pasture or hay meadow. Alp hamlets, with their ancient barns, chalets and granaries (*mazots*) with stone slab roofs and almost black timbers perched on staddle stones, stand among the meadows, advertising an architectural heritage unique to Canton Valais. Closely grouped villages huddle above a river or spread in a line facing the sun, with the ubiquitous white-painted chapel standing to one side. Then come the resorts; not only Zermatt, Saas Fee and Verbier with their international reputations to protect and promote, but others that are much smaller and less overtly commercial, such as Arolla, Les Haudères and Zinal, to take just three examples.

Access to virtually every valley is straightforward and reliable, and there's plentiful accommodation of all standards in the resorts, while remote mountain inns and huts are numerous, making the Pennine Alps one of Switzerland's busiest and most dramatically attractive regions.

2:1 VAL FERRET

With the untamed tributary of Val d'Arpette above Champex, Val Ferret is the most westerly of all Pennine valleys. Distinctly pastoral, it boasts a string of unremarkable hamlets, and very little in the way of tourist infrastructure outside of Champex and La Fouly. Walled to the west by outliers of the Mont Blanc range, the east flank is snow- and ice-free in summer and at no point reaches 3000m, while the headwall is breached by the two Cols Ferret (Petit and Grand) and by the Fenêtre de Ferret. Walkers tackling the Tour du Mont Blanc (TMB) usually enter the valley from Italy via the Grand Col Ferret, while the narrow Fenêtre de Ferret a little west of the Col du Grand St Bernard is much less frequented, although it has been known for many centuries and is said to have been favoured by smugglers.

Road and rail access is from **Martigny** in the Rhône valley. At first heading roughly southwest out of town, the road (and railway) then curves to the east along the valley of the Drance to **Les Valettes**, where a minor alternative route breaks away to the south to climb through the wooded Gorges du Durnand on the way to Champex. The main road, however, continues alongside the Drance, and above the point where it crosses to the north side of the river, the 100m rock wall of ❺ **Les Trappistes** offers a choice of well-equipped sport climbs up to grade VI+. Meanwhile the road continues to **Sembrancher** (717m), a medieval village with a Baroque church standing opposite the entrance to the Val de Bagnes (see 2:3) about 12km from Martigny. It is here that the Ferret road turns south up the Val d'Entremont (2:2), then forks just before reaching **Orsières**, terminus of the branch line railway from Martigny. The right-hand option passes through the village and continues to the hamlet of **Som-La-Proz**, about 2.5km beyond Orsières, where the road forks once more. The main Val Ferret route goes ahead, but the right branch (served by bus from Orsières) heads northwest with a sweeping multi-hairpinned climb to reach **Champex**, or Champex-Lac as it's also known.

Cupped by mountains and built along two sides of a small lake at 1466m, this is an attractive little resort with year-round appeal and views of the Combin massif. Apart from its admittedly rather limited walking opportunities, in summer there's boating and fishing in the lake, while cross-country and downhill skiing are practised in winter and a few routes are worth tackling on snowshoes. Champex was once known as a base

2:1 VAL FERRET

VAL FERRET

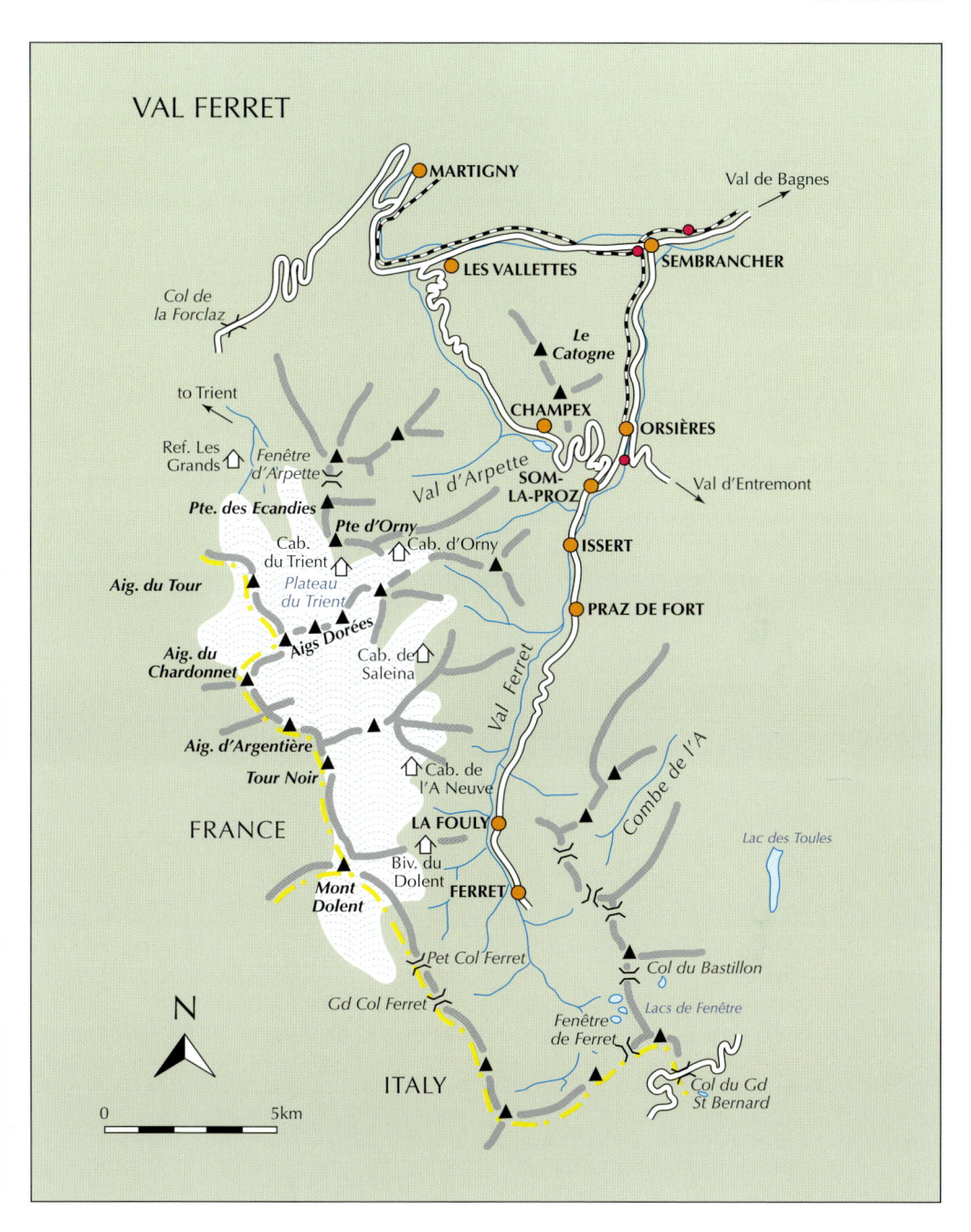

for making the ascent of several peaks on the edge of the Mont Blanc massif, most notably the Aiguilles du Tour, Chardonnet and Argentière – all unseen from the village – but it is the proximity of such huts as the Cabanes d'Orny and Trient that puts Champex-based climbers in touch with these mountains today.

Champex has an Office du Tourisme (www.verbier-st-bernard.ch) which is located along the main street on the northeast side of the lake. The village has only a few shops, but there's a post office, a handful of restaurants, a renowned alpine garden with an impressive collection of plants (open daily May to September), a chairlift to La

Champex, one-time mountaineering centre

Breya at 2194m, and a terraced campsite open throughout the year situated at the upper end of the village. A small selection of hotels range from 1 to 3-star, and dormitory accommodation is available at the Pension En Plein Air (www.pensionenplein-air.ch), and at the Au Club Alpin (www.auclubalpin.ch). Less than an hour's walk west of the village, just inside Val d'Arpette, the Relais d'Arpette has standard hotel bedrooms, 80 dormitory places, and space for camping at the rear of the hotel (www.arpette.ch). Being on the route of both the TMB and the Chamonix to Zermatt Walker's Haute Route, Champex is busy with rucksack-laden trekkers throughout the summer months, and in the spring ski-touring season Haute Route skiers arrive here from Cabane du Trient to await transport to Bourg-St-Pierre or Verbier for the next stage of their journey to Zermatt.

Above and to the west of the village, **Val d'Arpette** is very different from the immediate surroundings of Champex. This is a wild valley, wooded but with open meadows in its lower reaches, rougher in its middle section and rugged and untamed towards its head where it's confused by boulder tips and patches of grit and old snow. Though only one of the walling mountains reaches 3200m, the valley seems dwarfed by abrupt slopes. The south flank is swept by a vast ramp of scree, while the headwall is topped by a bristling ridge containing the spiked summits of Pointe d'Orny and Pointe des Ecandies; this latter summit pushes forward a spur that effectively divides the western end of the valley in two. Used by both the TMB and Walker's Haute Route (see box) the 2665m Fenêtre d'Arpette cuts through the ridge just north of Pointe des Ecandies, but the more challenging Col des Ecandies (2796m) below the Petite Pointe d'Orny is adopted by skiers on the classic Haute Route when departing the Trient refuge.

🚩 ⭐ WALKER'S HAUTE ROUTE

Making a two-week journey from Chamonix to Zermatt across the grain of the Pennine Alps, the Walker's Haute Route counts among the finest treks in Europe. The 180km route crosses 11 passes and gains in excess of 12,000m in height, so it's a reasonably tough undertaking.

Accommodation includes valley hotels, *dortoirs* and mountain huts – for full details see *Chamonix to Zermatt, the Walker's Haute Route* published by Cicerone.

Day 1: Assuming arrival in **Chamonix** on Day 1, this short first stage (2–2½hrs) remains in the valley and usually ends at Argentière.

Day 2: Three options exist here: the normal route crosses **Col de Balme** (2204m) and descends to **Trient**, the first village in Switzerland (see 1:5) for a 5–5½hr day, but an alternative from Col de Balme takes the trekker round to the unmanned **Refuge les Grands** (4½hrs), or continues from there to Col de la Forclaz where there's hotel and dormitory accommodation (6½–7hrs).

Day 3: Another stage with an alternative route, the choice is of either crossing the **Fenêtre d'Arpette**, or taking the less demanding trail past **Alp Bovine**. Much will depend on weather conditions; if good, the Fenêtre is the favoured option. Both routes lead to **Champex**.

Day 4: From Champex to **Le Châble** in Val de Bagnes is an easy trek of 3½–4hrs through a gentle landscape punctuated with small villages.

Day 5: By direct contrast with Day 4, this is a demanding trek with more than 1600m of height to gain in order to reach **Cabane du Mont Fort** after 6–6½hrs. But memorable views from the hut make the effort worthwhile.

Day 6: Once again two options are offered for the trek to Cabane de Prafleuri. From the Mont Fort Hut the main route goes along the balcony trail of the Sentier des Chamois with stunning views of the Combin massif, before turning to Col de Louvie; while the alternative takes a more direct route to Col de Louvie by way of the rocky Col de la Chaux. From **Col de Louvie** the way descends below the Grand Désert glacier, before making a long approach to Col de Prafleuri, followed by descent into a bleak basin in which stands **Cabane de Prafleuri** (6–6½hrs by the main route, 5½hrs via Col de la Chaux).

Day 7: A delightful 6½hr walk leads to Arolla via **Col des Roux** and either Col de Riedmatten or Pas de Chèvres, with an option of visiting **Cabane des Dix** below the North Face of Mont Blanc de Cheilon. This is one of the finest stages of the Haute Route, with a choice of accommodation to be had in **Arolla**.

Day 8: A gentle valley stroll takes the Walker's Haute Route down to Les Haudères, followed by a short uphill stretch leading to **La Sage** – a relaxing 4hr stage.

Day 9: Above La Sage either **Col de Torrent** or the rougher **Col du Tsaté** lead to the Val de Moiry (see 2:7). For accommodation **Cabane de Moiry** is highly recommended (5–5½hrs), otherwise you could stay in a *dortoir* above the Barrage de Moiry (5hrs), or descend to a choice of hotels in **Grimentz** in 6½–7hrs.

Day 10: The main Walker's Haute Route descends from Cabane de Moiry, then contours across a hillside above Lac de Moiry before climbing to Col de Sorebois and plunging steeply down to **Zinal** near the head of the wonderful Val d'Anniviers (5–5½hrs). If starting from the Barrage de Moiry, Zinal is reached in 4–4½hrs.

Day 11: Turning away from the big mountains, this stage either makes a 3½–4hr trek to **Hotel Weisshorn** (or continues for a further hour to Cabane Bella Tola) in readiness for crossing the Meidpass into the Turtmanntal next day, or it avoids the hotel and hut completely by crossing the lovely Forcletta on a direct route into the Turtmanntal (5½–6hrs), to overnight in the tiny village of **Gruben**.

Day 12: The final crossing of the Haute Route is the 2894m **Augstbordpass** which gives access to the Mattertal. Once over this the trail descends (with beautiful views throughout) for more than 1700m to

St Niklaus (7½hrs) by way of the charming little hamlet of Jungen (5½hrs), which has a limited amount of dormitory accommodation (but check first).

Day 13: It's possible to have a 5½hr valley walk of 18km to reach Zermatt, but the preferred option ascends the east flank of the valley to **Gasenried** (4hrs) where a night is spent before tackling the Europaweg.

Day 14: Created in 1996, the 31km Europaweg from Grächen to Zermatt is unstable in many places and there may be significant diversions, but it makes an exhilarating two-day trek high above the Mattertal with great views for much of the way. This first stage ends at the comfortable **Europa Hut** about 5½–6hrs from Gasenried.

Day 15: The final stage of the Walker's Haute Route completes the Europaweg by continuing beyond Täschalp and the hamlet of Tufteren to visit Findeln, with its spectacular Matterhorn view, before descending to **Zermatt** at the end of a 6½–7hr day.

Walks and climbs from Champex

Apart from a gentle stroll of an hour around the lake, most routes worth tackling from Champex are fairly long or strenuous, or both. The one exception is the approach to Cabane d'Orny using the La Breya chairlift to gain an initial 700m of height.

- ⊗ North of Champex, in effect backing the resort, a long mountain spine culminates in the summit crown of **Le Catogne** (2598m). The ascent, which begins at the lower end of the village, is not difficult, but has 1100m of height to gain. A major reward for making the ascent is the extent of the summit view, which is especially fine towards the Dents du Midi.
- ◐ A day's walk (4½–5hrs) leading to **Col de la Forclaz** via the Bovine alp is known to thousands of trekkers, as it forms a stage of the TMB. First visiting the chalets of Champex d'en Haut and Champex d'en Bas, it makes a lengthy slanting traverse of forest and pasture, with occasional views of the Dents du Midi, as well as the Alpes Vaudoises across the Rhône valley, and a backward view to the Grand Combin. Although not as strenuous as the alternative TMB stage via the Fenêtre d'Arpette (see below), this Bovine route is demanding enough. At the end of the day accommodation is available at Hotel du Col de la Forclaz (see 1:5 for details). To vary the return to Champex, consider making a round-trip by reversing the Fenêtre d'Arpette route (about 6½hrs from Forclaz to Champex).
- ◐ The crossing of the 2665m **Fenêtre d'Arpette** in the Val d'Arpette headwall should only be attempted under settled conditions and after any troublesome snow has cleared from the upper slopes. In a 'normal' summer, this is likely to be around early July, although snow patches often remain throughout the summer. Gained in about 3½–4hrs from Champex, the *fenêtre* is very much a window onto a different world, for the west side of the pass is dominated by the Trient glacier spilling from the Plateau du Trient, while a distant view includes the dammed lake of Emosson, with the Tour Sallière and Mont Ruan beyond it (see 1:5). TMB walkers crossing the pass descend to either Trient or Col de la Forclaz (see above) in another 2–2½hrs by a steep but straightforward route.
- ⊗ The ascent of **Pointe des Ecandies** (2873m) south of the Fenêtre d'Arpette may be made without major difficulties in about 1hr from the pass.
- ◐ In winter **Col des Ecandies** makes a worthwhile ascent on snowshoes – but only when conditions are stable, as the walling slopes of Val d'Arpette are prone to avalanche after snowfall (see *Snowshoeing: Mont Blanc & the Western Alps*).
- ⊕ The traverse of the **Ecandies ridge**, from Col des Ecandies to Pointe des Ecandies, or on to the Fenêtre d'Arpette (D, with two moves of V), is a classic route recommended by Rébuffet in his well-known *Mont Blanc Massif – 100 Finest Routes*.
- ◐ By using the La Breya chairlift from just above Champex, the approach to **Cabane d'Orny** (2826m) can be achieved in 2–2½hrs by an obvious path along the rocky upper slopes of the Combe d'Orny. Owned by the Diablerets section of the SAC, the hut has places for 86,

2:1 Val Ferret

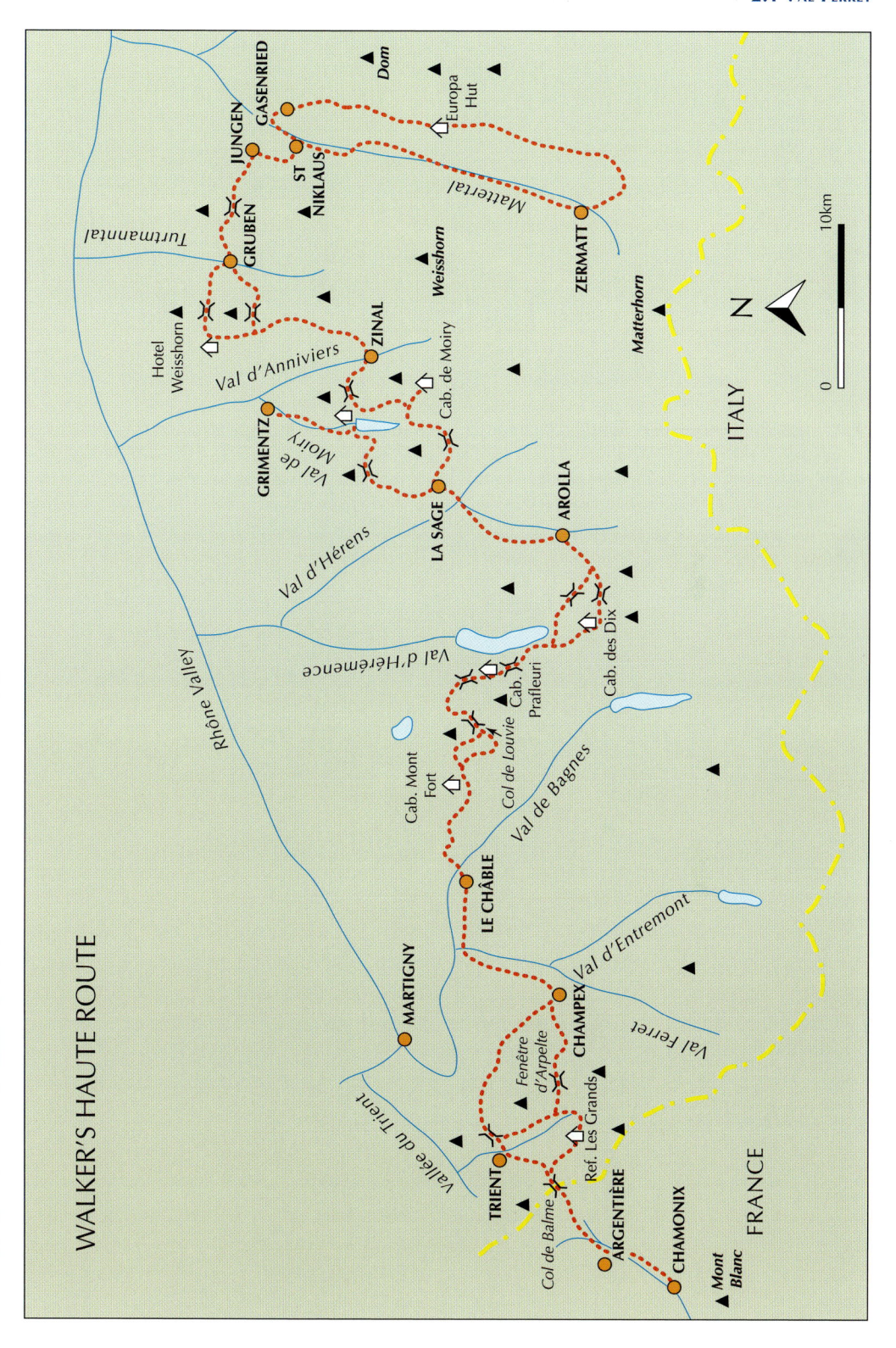

WALKER'S HAUTE ROUTE

with a resident guardian from early June to mid-September (www.cabanedorny.ch). From there **Cabane du Trient** is reached in 1hr, and 🚶 **Pointe d'Orny** (3269m) can be climbed by the NE Couloir (PD+) in about 3hrs.

Cabane du Trient

Cabane du Trient is a large and popular hut tucked below Pointe d'Orny on the edge of the Plateau du Trient at 3170m. With places for 130 and owned, like Cabane d'Orny, by the Diablerets section of the SAC, it is manned during the spring ski-touring season (mid-March to mid-May) and from mid-June to mid-September (www.sac-diablerets.ch). Of the climbs and tours to be made from a base here, the ascent of the 🚶 **Aiguille du Tour** is among the most obvious since it's the highest hereabouts, is located just across the glacial plateau, and is eminently suitable for first-season alpinists. The Aiguille has two distinct summits separated by a deep cleft, the 3544m north summit being higher than its southern counterpart by just 2m. The SE Flank of the north summit offers a pleasant F+ scramble, while similar-graded routes on the south summit are by way of the East Flank and the South Ridge. Both summits command tremendous views of the Mont Blanc range, as well as the Pennine and distant Bernese Alps, while across the Plateau du Trient, and blocking its southern end, the 🚶 **Aiguilles Dorées**, seen in profile, form a 1300m long wall of granite with around 14 tops, on some of which fairly short climbs at a modest standard are available. At a different level, however, the classic east–west traverse of the chain (AD+) was first achieved in the 1890s. As for the **Plateau du Trient** itself, though not unique, it's a very special site immortalised by Emile Javelle in his *Souvenirs d'un Alpiniste* with the following description: 'It is a perfect, ideal and quiet basin, scarcely tilted, and unfolding in vast and imperceptible undulations its immense surface … It is as if this dazzling plateau … was the high point of the Alps.'

Orsières to La Fouly

The lower Val Ferret is forested along the foot of its east and west slopes, but with open pasture and a succession of hamlets either strung along the road, or located a short distance from it. The TMB

Praz de Fort, one of the largest of the Val Ferret villages

passes through, linking some of these hamlets and enjoying pleasant if unremarkable landscapes, for despite the proximity of big mountains, the trail adopted by the TMB sees little of them, and it's only when crossing the mouth of the Saleina glen, or on arrival at La Fouly, that more than a hint is received of the true nature of its neighbourhood peaks.

The Saleina valley, or Vallon d'Arpette de Saleina to give its full name, opens a little south of **Praz de Fort** (1151m), one of the largest of Ferret villages, which boasts a grocery as well as a post office. Two huts of interest to climbers intent on one or more summits at this outpost of the Mont Blanc range can be reached from the village; these are the Cabane de Saleina and Cabane d'Orny. A metalled service road projects a short way towards the huts, with a car park at around 1250m. The road actually continues beyond this, but anyone planning to be away for a day or two should make use of the parking spaces available. From the end of the road a path remains on the true left bank of the Reuse de Saleina, then forks. The route to **Cabane d'Orny** (details above) works up the steep mountainside with a series of zigzags under the crest of the Pointes des Chevrettes, before joining the path from La Breya near a small tarn about 130m below the hut (4½–5hrs from Praz de Fort).

Cabane de Saleina

Cabane de Saleina, or Saleinaz as it's also known, is located above the right bank of the Saleina glacier at 2691m, with the glacial cirque rimmed by – among others – the Aiguilles d'Argentière and du Chardonnet, the Grande Fourche and Aiguilles Dorées. North of the hut the Petit Clocher du Portalet is an impressive shaft of smooth granite.

The hut approach begins at the same car park used by the Orny Hut route, although an alternative start could be made along a track on the south side of the Saleina stream. Where the Orny path forks to make the zigzag climb under the Pointes des Chevrettes, the Saleina route (waymarked blue and white for an 'alpine route') continues upvalley a short way before crossing the stream to join the south bank route, then climbs the terminal moraine of the Saleina glacier with the aid of fixed cables. It then follows the moraine crest to pass below the Clochers des Planereuses, and crosses a wide couloir to gain the hut.

Belonging to the Neuchâteloise section of the SAC, the modern Saleina cabane has dormitory places for 48 and is manned for a short period between late March and mid-April, and from late June to mid-September (www.cas-neuchatel.ch). Above it short, modest routes suitable for first-season alpinists, can be found on the easily accessible ● **Grande Pointe des Planereuses** and the ● **Grande Clocher des Planereuses**, although the little 2699m tower of the ● **Petite Clocher des Planereuses** holds more difficult climbs, especially via the SW Pillar. Near the head of the glacier, the 3619m ● **Grande Fourche** can be climbed by a PD route via its South Ridge in about 3½hrs from the hut. Of a very different proposition, the ● **Aiguille d'Argentière** (3902m) on the frontier ridge to the southwest has numerous quality routes of varying degrees of difficulty, mostly begun from the Argentière refuge on the French side of the mountains. However, the East Face which overlooks the Saleina glacier, attracts climbers based at Cabane de Saleina, the East Face Direct (AD) being one fairly popular route.

Further north along the frontier ridge, between the Aiguille d'Argentière and Grande Fourche, the beautiful ● **Aiguille du Chardonnet** (3824m) heads the Saleina cirque almost due west of the Saleina Hut. A very popular mountain with climbers based at the Albert Premier refuge, the narrow and exposed Forbes Arête, or East Ridge, is one of the classics of the region, often tackled from the Saleina Hut from which it is gained by first climbing a snow couloir at the head of the glacier to reach the Fenêtre Supérieure du Tour.

La Fouly

Continuing deeper into Val Ferret beyond Praz de Fort, more meadows, groups of chalets and hay-barns underline the pastoral nature of the valley. Shortly before reaching La Fouly, the hamlet of L'Amône has significance for climbers; not for the proximity of any great peak, but for the 400m white limestone crag known as the ● **Amône Slab** that gives delicate climbing of TD+ with individual moves up to VI-. Note however, that a storm can transform the slab in moments, so stay clear if the weather is threatening.

Standing astride the road at 1592m **La Fouly** is the undisputed mountaineering centre of the valley. Hardly a resort, this small village has a large campsite at the entrance to the l'A Neuve cirque crowned by the Tour Noir. La Fouly has a Bureau des Guides et Accompagnateurs, a ski school,

Mont Dolent, on whose summit the borders of Switzerland, France and Italy unite

some 15km of marked pistes for cross-country skiing, 160km of waymarked paths, several shops and restaurants, and an Office du Tourisme (www.verbier-st-bernard.ch) in the main street. For accommodation there are three hotels that also have dormitories: the Grand-Hotel du Val Ferret (www.ghvf.ch), Hotel Edelweiss, and Hotel des Glaciers, while Camping des Glaciers sprawls just below the village.

Built on the north side of l'A Neuve cirque, in a spectacular position under the crest of the Pointes des Essettes at 2735m, and with a direct view of Mont Dolent's steep North Face, **Cabane de l'A Neuve** is another SAC hut owned by the Diablerets section. With just 28 places it has a guardian from mid-March to mid-May, and from the middle of June to the end of September (www.aneuve.ch). The approach route, which takes about 3½hrs from La Fouly and is signed from near the campsite, is a challenging one, aided in places by fixed chains or cables and with a glacial torrent for company part of the way.

Above the hut the rock peaks of the 🚶 **Grand** and **Petit Darray** (3514m; 3508m) offer interesting, albeit modestly graded routes, while a traverse from one to the other entails about 400m of scrambling. Nearby the 🚶 **Grande Lui** is another of those easy snow peaks that makes an excellent first-season introduction to alpinism. At the southern end of the glacial cirque, the glorious North Face of 🚶 **Mont Dolent** is a very different proposition. With an air of remoteness, the 550m of this ice-plastered wall gives a fine TD outing, but with real danger from falling ice. Its *voie normale*, on the other hand is an uncomplicated PD ascent by way of the SE Ridge, as discovered by Whymper's party in 1864. For climbs on the East Ridge (AD), a small orange-coloured bivouac hut, **Bivouac du Dolent** (sometimes referred to as Cabane de la Maye), has been placed on the left bank moraine of the Dolent glacier at 2667m, and is gained by an approach of about 3hrs from La Fouly. Prospective users should take their own food and stove.

MONT DOLENT

Acting as the southeast cornerstone of the Mont Blanc range, the 3820m summit of Mont Dolent is significant for being the point where the borders of Switzerland, France and Italy meet. An attractive mountain with four irregular faces, it was first approached from the Italian side on 9 July 1864 by Edward Whymper and Adams-Reilly with their guides Michel Croz and Michel Payot, and Henri Charlet as porter. It was a straightforward climb from the Petit Col Ferret using the SE Ridge as the most obvious route; 'a miniature ascent' according to Whymper. As for the summit, 'it was the loveliest little cone of snow that was ever piled up on a mountain-top ... But there was nothing little about the *view* from the Mont Dolent' – as many have commented since. 'A superb view,' said Rébuffet, 'very extensive, over a whole series of different landscapes, from the wild to the pastoral.' Adams-Reilly was emphatic: 'Situated at a junction of three mountain ridges, it rises in a positive steeple far above anything in its immediate neighbourhood; and certain gaps in the surrounding ridges ... extend the view in almost every direction... The view is as extensive, and far more lovely than that from Mont Blanc itself.'

The Upper Val Ferret

Outside La Fouly the road curves southeastward, drawing away from the main wall of peaks and in so doing gains a better prospect of them. The path used by the TMB (albeit more often walked in the opposite direction) crosses the river and gives an option of climbing to the Petit Col Ferret, while the more popular Grand Col Ferret route keeps company with the Drance de Ferret as far as Ferret. Before reaching this final village (in reality little more than a hamlet), a short diversion leads to the Gîte de la Léchère which is open from June to the end of September, has 35 dorm places, self-catering facilities and meals provision (tel 027 783 30 64).

Ferret (1705m) clusters at what was formerly the roadhead, and now marks the terminus of the postbus route from Orsières. Standing near the tiny chapel with fine mountain views, Hotel

The tiny chapel at Ferret

THE SWISS ALPS – CHAPTER 2: PENNINE ALPS

High above Val Ferret the Lacs de Fenêtre lie in a charming plateau with views to the Grandes Jorasses, Mont Dolent and Tour Noir

Col de Fenêtre is open from June until the end of September, and provides the only accommodation, with 17 beds and 18 dormitory places (www.hotelcoldefenetre.theyellowpages.ch).

Upstream beyond Ferret the road passes through light woodland, then emerges to open pastures loud with the clatter of cowbells. Ahead the valley seems to be enclosed by rolling green hills, while a backward glance shows a dramatic cluster of peaks and glaciers. The official roadhead lies below the dairy farm of Les Ars dessous, where the original TMB route (now relegated to variant status) descends to the river, crosses a bridge and follows a farm track as the initial stage of the climb to the **Grand Col Ferret** (2½hrs) and the Italian side of Mont Blanc.

Meanwhile, on the other (east) side of the valley, a track winds up the hillside above the farm, and later becomes a footpath which leads onto an utterly charming plateau graced by the **Lacs de Fenêtre** at a little under 2500m. Reached in 2–2½hrs from Ferret, the first of these lakes presents a matchless foreground to a view of the Grandes Jorasses, Mont Dolent and the Tour Noir. To the south the frontier ridge is enticing for a different reason. In that ridge the 2698m **Fenêtre de Ferret** not only gives a sighting of Mont Blanc's Italian flank, but of the Gran Paradiso range to the south; it also suggests a way over the mountains into Italy where the Grand St Bernard road can be seen descending to the plains.

Northeast of the Lacs de Fenêtre, the 2757m **Col du Bastillon** takes walkers over a ridge descending from the Monts Telliers, where it's then possible to traverse the upper slopes of the Combe de Drône to Col de Chevaux and the **Col du Grand St Bernard**. Yet another option for walkers is to strike north from the lakes, passing below the Monts Telliers and rising to a saddle, over which a way descends through the long funnel of the **Combe de l'A** to gain the village of Liddes in Val d'Entremont.

2:2 VAL D'ENTREMONT

With the Col du Grand St Bernard at its head, Val d'Entremont has seen a steady procession of travellers since the earliest times. It was known to the Celts and the Romans; emperors and armies marched through the valley, as did countless pilgrims on their way to Rome. In the 11th century a

2:2 Val d'Entremont

VAL D'ENTREMONT

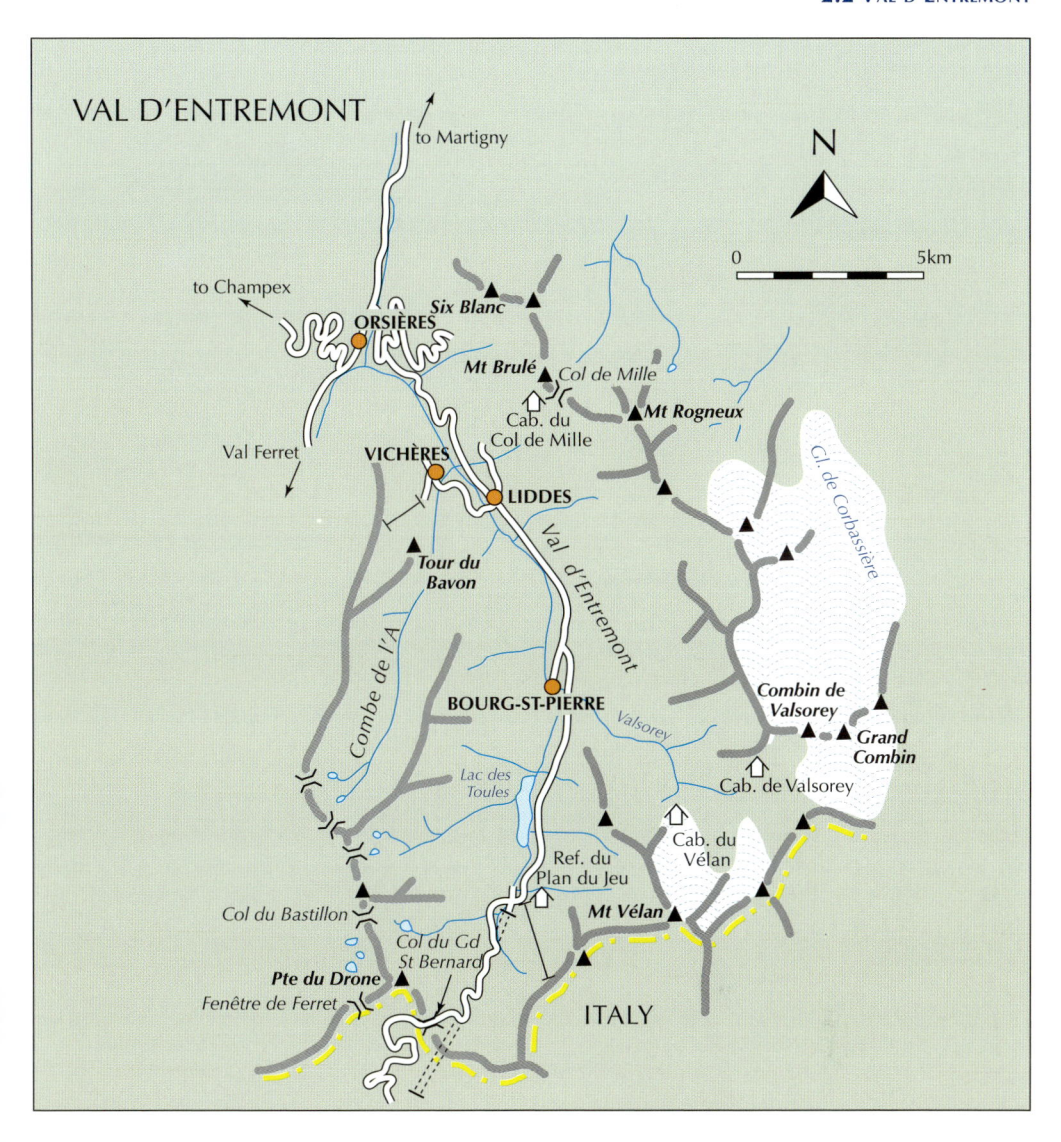

[Map of Val d'Entremont showing: to Martigny, to Champex, Orsières, Six Blanc, Mt Brulé, Col de Mille, Cab. du Col de Mille, Mt Rogneux, Val Ferret, Vichères, Liddes, Tour du Bavon, Combe de l'A, Gl. de Corbassière, Val d'Entremont, Bourg-St-Pierre, Valsorey, Combin de Valsorey, Grand Combin, Lac des Toules, Cab. de Valsorey, Cab. du Vélan, Ref. du Plan du Jeu, Col du Bastillon, Col du Gd St Bernard, Mt Vélan, Pte du Drone, Fenêtre de Ferret, ITALY]

hospice was founded on the pass, and on gaining it in the winter of 1178, the English monk John de Bremble uttered the heartfelt prayer: 'Lord restore me to my brethren that I may tell them that they shall not come to this place of torment.'

Scenically Val d'Entremont is unremarkable, for it lacks the grandeur of the majority of Pennine valleys. True, it has the Combin massif and Mont Vélan to wall its upper reaches, but these are not as prominently displayed as one might expect, other than in brief select places, and there's little to capture the imagination except perhaps by escaping the valley bed in order to gain a more elevated vantage point. The best of these will be found on the west flank, on the modest 2476m **Tour de Bavon** or the **Bec Rond** (2563m) above Vichères in the mouth of the Combe de l'A, for example.

A major highway cuts through the valley, bypassing its few villages and, since 1964, tunnelling beneath the actual pass to emerge on the Italian side of the mountains, leaving the old road to snake its way up to the Col du Grand St Bernard with its historic hospice, photogenic dogs and somewhat tacky souvenir stands.

It is at **Orsières** (901m), or rather just north of it, that the St Bernard road breaks away from the approach to Val Ferret. This little town, where the train from Martigny terminates, has most of the

Green hillsides lead to Orsières

necessities for stocking up with supplies for the hills, with supermarkets, a pharmacy, several banks and an ATM or two, a post office, restaurants and three hotels: Hotel des Alpes, Hotel Terminus, and Hotel Union which also has 100 dorm places. For tourist information go to www.verbier-st-bernard.ch.

TOUR DES COMBINS

Although the Grand Combin does not impress itself upon Val d'Entremont as it does on Val de Bagnes, it's a major massif with several high summits, big snowfields and glaciers. As its name suggests, the six-day Tour des Combins makes a circuit of the massif to give the experienced mountain walker some truly spectacular views and reasonably tough days. The trek leads through tracts of wild country and crosses several passes, but it also visits attractive small villages on the Italian flank. (For further information see: www.tourdescombins.ch)

Day 1: Leaving **Bourg-St-Pierre** the route heads north to the chapel of Notre Dame de Lorette where a path rises through forest on the east flank of the valley, leading to the alp of Creux du Mâ. It then sweeps up to the lower Boveire alp at 2230m and continues on a long contour with Mont Blanc's outlying peaks on show to the west. In a little over 4hrs from Bourg you reach the grassy **Col de Mille** and the timber-built **Cabane du Col de Mille** at 2472m. Views include the Grand and Petit Combin, Mont Vélan, Grandes Jorasses and Mont Dolent.

Day 2: Crossing Col de Mille above the hut, this 5–5½hrs stage descends into a grassy combe, then works a way round the hillside above Val de Bagnes to gain the privately owned **Cabane Brunet**, from where two options take the continuing route to the Panossière Hut. The most direct climbs steeply to cross **Col des Avouillons** (2647m) onto the Corbassière glacier, while the alternative descends into a tight little valley, then mounts a vegetated spur and eventually reaches the east bank lateral moraine

2:2 Val d'Entremont

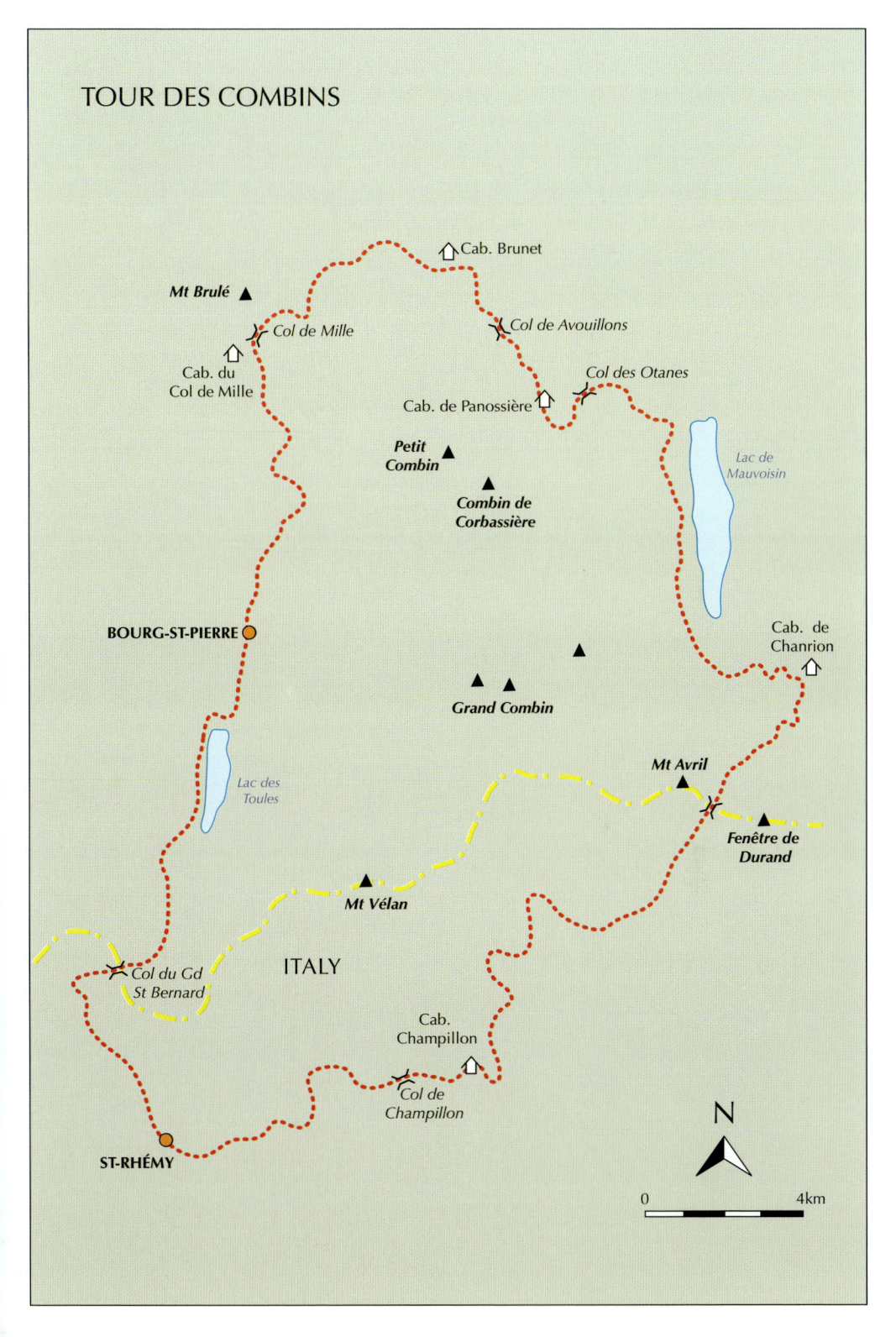

TOUR DES COMBINS

of the glacier on which the **Cabane de Panossière** (Cabane François-Xavier Bagnoud) is set at 2645m. The alpenglow on the Grand Combin is truly spectacular from here.

Day 3: This begins by climbing to **Col des Otanes**, at 2846m the highest point on the tour, followed by a steep descent towards Mauvoisin. After crossing the Pazagnou stream, veer away from the valley-bound route and cross the spur of Pierre d'Vire, then make an undulating traverse of the upper west flank of Val de Bagnes, near the head of which stands the 2462m **Cabane de Chanrion**. Ending with a seemingly relentless uphill drag, this is gained about 7hrs from the Panossière Hut.

Day 4: Taking the tour round the southern side of the Combin massif, all but the first 2½hrs of this stage are spent in Italy, where waymarks are painted yellow with the initials 'TDC'. The easy 2797m **Fenêtre de Durand** on the frontier reveals a complex and varied panorama, and from it the way slants down to the vast pastureland cirque of Conca di By. A *bisse* is followed for some way beyond the cirque, curving south through verdant pastures. From the Néan alpage a trail then begins to climb northwestward to reach the next overnight shelter at 2380m. **Cabane Champillon** was inaugurated in June 2005, and is gained at the end of a 7–7½hr stage from the Chanrion Hut.

Day 5: An hour's trek leads to **Col de Champillon** (2708m), which gives views of Mont Blanc in one direction, the Combin massif in the other. On the way down into the Vallée de Menouve the Grand St Bernard road intrudes into the landscape, yet the trail retains interest all the way, with one or two tiny hamlets and villages to pass through. **St-Rhémy** offers limited but comfortable hotel accommodation for the night at 1619m (6hrs from Cabane Champillon).

Day 6: Above the village the old road, now little more than a track, is followed all the way to the **Col du Grand St Bernard** at 2469m. Arrival can bring a shock to the system as the pass is invariably crowded with traffic and tourists, but it takes only a few moments to escape along a path that initially descends into Val d'Entremont along the right-hand side of the road, then crosses to the left through alp pastures and alongside the dammed **Lac des Toules**, before entering Bourg-St-Pierre about 5½hrs after leaving St-Rhémy.

From a ridge north of Mont Brulé, high above Val d'Entremont, walkers enjoy views to outliers of the Mont Blanc range

The main road loops up the hillside above Orsières, then strikes southeastward to ease into the valley proper, and after about 8km runs along the outskirts of **Liddes** (1346m). After Orsières this is the first village of any size on the way to the Grand St Bernard, with two small groceries, and a tourist office beside the road. The valley is broad and pastoral here; the eastern side being terraced, the lower hillsides wooded. Above the village to the north rises **Mont Brulé** (2572m), a walker's summit with commanding views of the Mont Blanc range, as well as the Bernese Alps and the Dents du Midi. A path ascends the east flank of the valley out of Liddes, making for Col de Mille and the small, timber-built **Cabane du Col de Mille** (2472m) in about 3½hrs. From there Mont Brulé is but a short and easy walk away. Being used by trekkers on the Tour des Combins and the Tour des Val de Bagnes, as well as walkers enjoying a few local routes, the hut can be very busy – especially at weekends. It has just 36 dorm places, is owned by the Liddes commune by whom it was built in 1996, and is staffed from mid-June to the end of September (tel 079 221 15 16).

Six kilometres beyond, and almost 300m higher than Liddes, **Bourg-St-Pierre** (1632m) is the largest village in the valley proper; an old place crowded just below the main road. This is about as close as you get to a mountaineering centre in Val d'Entremont, although it's little more than a place from which to set out for one or other of the huts that serve the Combin and Vélan massifs, or to retreat to in order to dry out when the weather turns foul. It's also used as one of the main starting points for the multi-day Tour des Combins. There's a long-established alpine garden here, a small supermarket, a few hotels, including the Auberge les Charmettes which has dorm accommodation, and a campsite, Camping du Grand St Bernard. For tourist information go to www.verbier-stbernard.ch.

Above Bourg to the southeast the **Valsorey** tributary drains the west flank of the Combin massif and the north side of Mont Vélan, and is the way through which to approach the Cabanes du Vélan and de Valsorey. Leaving Bourg-St-Pierre an underpass sneaks beneath the main road and leads onto a minor road which cuts for a short way into this small tributary valley. After about 45mins you reach the Cordonna chalets at 1834m, and continue above the stream for another hour or so to a fork. The right branch is the one to take for Cabane du Vélan (see below), but by keeping ahead you shortly reach the Chalet d'Amont (2197m) about 2hrs from Bourg-St-Pierre. The view of Mont Vélan is impressive from here. Now the path goes up to the Six Rodzes rock barrier, ascends a gully aided by fixed chains and sections of ladder, then swings round to the east, heading for pastures and a long spur to reach the **Cabane de Valsorey** at 3030m, about 4–4½hrs after setting out. Owned by the Chaux-de-Fonds section of the SAC, this stone-built hut, with its direct view of Mont Vélan, is used by Haute Route skiers as well as by climbers. It has 60 places and is staffed in the ski-touring season (mid-March to May) and from July until mid-September (www.valsorey.ch).

The ascent of **Combin de Valsorey**, the 4184m West summit of the Combin massif, is an obvious attraction. This is climbed either by the West Ridge (AD) via Col du Meitin, or by the SW Face (PD+) via the tremendous viewpoint of the Plateau du Couloir – the latter traversed by ski-mountaineers on the 'classic' Haute Route (there are alternative stages), of which it forms a key passage on the way to the Chanrion Hut via Col du Sonadon. The highest of the Combin summits, the 4314m **Combin de Grafeneire** (Grand Combin), is also climbed from the Valsorey Hut via Col du Meitin and the NW Face, or by first taking in Combin de Valsorey, then descending to a saddle at 4132m from where the NW Face route (see 2:3) is joined for the final ascent to the summit.

Southwest of the Valsorey hut **Cabane du Vélan** (2642m) serves climbers tackling the 3731m Mont Vélan, one of the earliest snow mountains to be climbed. The initial route of approach to the hut is identical with that to Cabane de Valsorey, but when the path forks just below the Chalet d'Amont, you branch right, cross a footbridge over the Valsorey torrent and climb south in a series of zigzags to gain the hut, which is situated below the Tseudet glacier with magnificent views of the Grand Combin in one direction, and the Mont Blanc massif in the other (3hrs from Bourg-St-Pierre). Property of the Genevoise section of the SAC, this modern-looking hut has 60 places and a resident warden usually from mid-March to the end of September, although the hut may not be permanently staffed in June (www.velan.ch).

To the southwest rises the 3202m Petit Vélan, but at the head of the glacier to the south the main block of **Mont Vélan** carries the frontier with a dome of snow and a complex of ridges at the culminating point of a great spur thrust out from the Grand Combin. As with so many Swiss mountains its glaciers are shrinking fast, as its moraine troughs testify, and it's very different from the Mont Vélan known to the pioneers. But in late winter and springtime, when the snow cover is consolidated, it attracts ski-mountaineers, for whom it affords a fine ascent by way of the Col de la Gouille and Valsorey glacier. Perhaps the finest summer route from the Vélan Hut is the NNW Ridge (the Tseudet Arête AD/AD+), first climbed in 1897 by a large party that included Tom Longstaff, one of the greatest of the early Himalayan explorers. From the Aiguille du Vélan the route goes along the linking snow crest to the Dôme du Vélan and the main summit (7–7½hrs) overlooking the vast cirque of the Conca di By on the Italian flank, while the Grand Combin nearby, Mont Blanc to the west, and the Paradiso massif to the southwest are highlights in a memorable panorama. Hubert Walker called it 'a panorama of equal magnificence with any in the Alps' (*Walking in the Alps*).

The Upper Val d'Entremont

Skirting the Lac de Toules reservoir above Bourg-St-Pierre the main road is protected by a long section of avalanche galleries and a tunnel. At the southern end the old road emerges to a moorland-like upper valley, while the main road enters the 6km long Tunnel du Grand St Bernard (open all-year, toll charged). The upper valley is clothed with rough slopes of grass, alpenrose, heather and scrub, but there's skiing on the north-facing slopes of the east flank at the so-called Super-St-Bernard resort, served by the Menouve *télécabine* whose valley station stands beside the road on emerging from the avalanche protection galleries at Bourg-St-Bernard. A 20min walk from here leads to the **Refuge du Plan du Jeu**, which has 26 dormitory places (tel 027 787 12 35).

Impassable to traffic in winter, the final approach to the pass goes along the fearsome-sounding, avalanche-prone Combe des Morts before arriving at the **Col du Grand St Bernard** and the frontier with Italy. For users of this guide its place in history is possibly more interesting than

---

COL DU GRAND ST BERNARD: A PLACE IN HISTORY

Reckoned to have been in use since the Bronze Age, the Col du Grand St Bernard is the oldest and best-known of the alpine pass routes. Tradition has it that Hannibal crossed with his elephants in 217BC, and in 57BC Julius Caesar marched with his army across the windblown gap in the mountains to attack Martigny. The emperor Augustus built a road across the pass, and there set up a temple to Jupiter, which was sacked with the fall of Rome.

Its earliest name was Mon Jovis, after the Roman temple, and between the 8th and 15th centuries it was regularly crossed by Rome-bound pilgrims, clerics and medieval emperors. But the pass was (and still is) prone to sudden storms and many travellers perished whilst attempting to cross, so in 1070 Bernard of Menthon, the archdeacon of Aosta, masterminded the construction of a hospice on the summit overlooking a small lake. This became a welcome haven for travellers, with the canons and lay brothers quartered there providing free shelter and food to all who requested it. These same custodians of the pass also rescued countless snowbound travellers, although the first mention of the famous St Bernard dogs was not made until 1708. (Today helicopters and sophisticated search equipment have more or less made the dogs redundant for rescue purposes, although a number have been retained by the hospice.)

During the late 18th century whole armies crossed the pass, the most famous being that of Napoleon who, between 14 and 20 May 1800 led 40,000 troops into Italy to defeat the Austrians at Marengo. Accounts of that crossing describe the future emperor's descent as a form of glissade: 'suffering himself, according to the custom of the country, to glide down upon the snow.' But as a result of the difficulties encountered in manhandling heavy pieces of artillery up to and across the pass, within three months of his victory at Marengo, Napoleon ordered the road across the Simplon from Brig to Domodossola to be made passable for artillery, and this was completed five years later.

As for Bernard of Menthon, he was beatified shortly after his death around 1080, and in 1923 Pope Pius XI confirmed him as the patron saint of the Alps. His statue now gazes out over a wild landscape near the Italian customs post.

its present (see box), for although the views can be enticing, and there are various walks and climbs to be tackled from the pass, including the ascent of the 2949m ⓑ **Pointe du Drone** with its sections of *via ferrata*, there are many more rewarding and atmospheric locations in the Pennine Alps to use as a base. However, for those who fancy a night here, accommodation can be had at the hospice itself in standard beds or dormitories (www.gsbernard.ch), and the museum is worth a visit.

2:3 VAL DE BAGNES

From its headwall backing pastures and old moraines south of the Mauvoisin reservoir, to the confluence of the Drance de Bagnes with that of the Entremont at Sembrancher, Val de Bagnes carves a deep swathe through the mountains east of Val d'Entremont. For the most part it's a narrow valley, steep-walled on its east flank, less so (except near its head) on the west where a few hamlets are

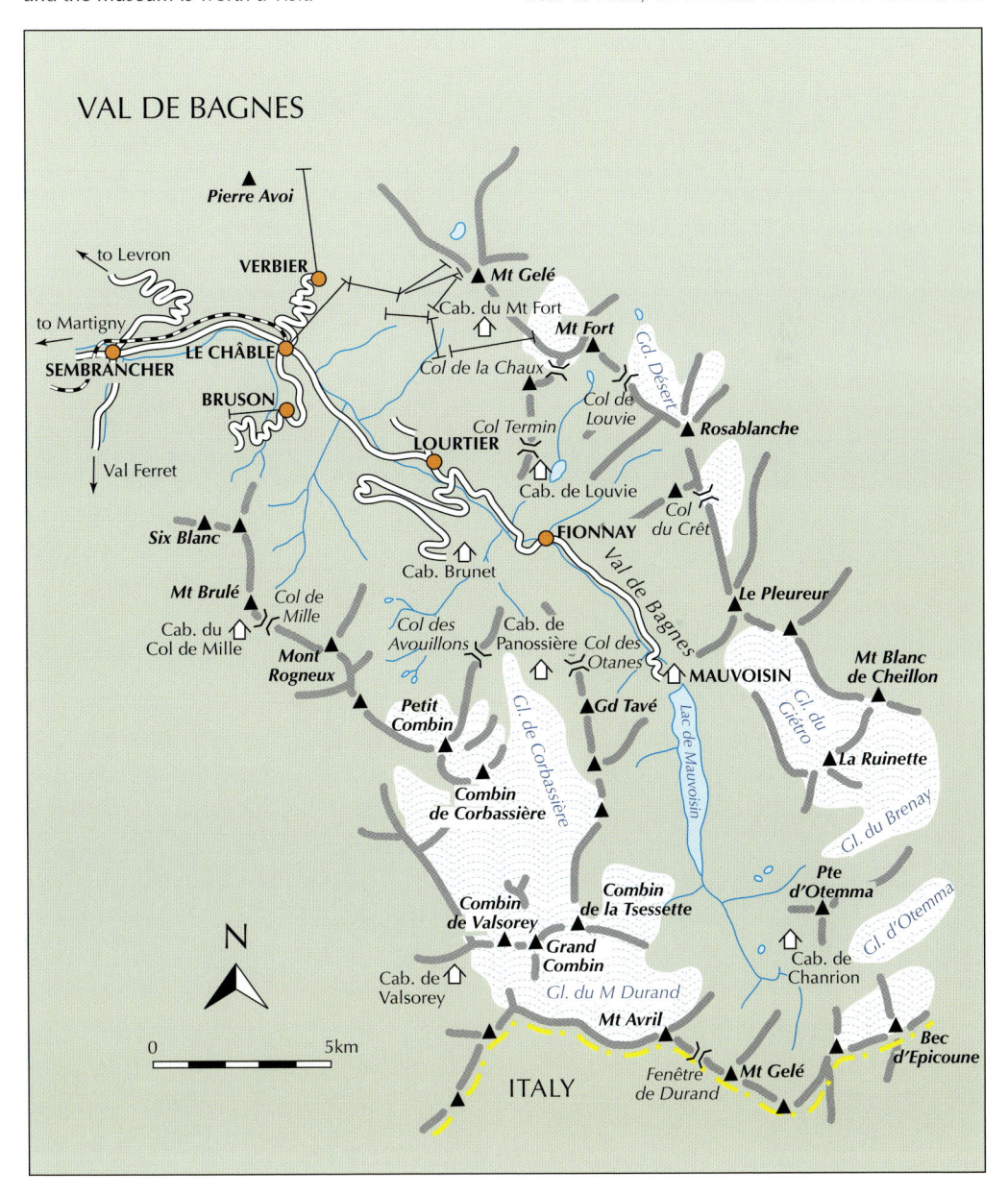

103

THE SWISS ALPS – CHAPTER 2: PENNINE ALPS

set among meadows and fringes of woodland. A string of small villages and hamlets line the valley bed, and with an area of 295 square kilometres the Bagnes commune claims to be the most extensive in all Switzerland.

Mountaineering interest is concentrated on the great Combin massif, but lesser summits grouped near the valley head have value too, and the Brenay and Otemma glaciers provide routes of access to peaks further east. Skiers working their way towards Zermatt on the Haute Route cross the Combin massif to use Cabane de Chanrion as an overnight stop before heading for the Vignettes Hut, while crowds of downhill skiers flock each winter to the slopes of Verbier. As for mountain walkers, there's enough to keep enthusiasts happy for many

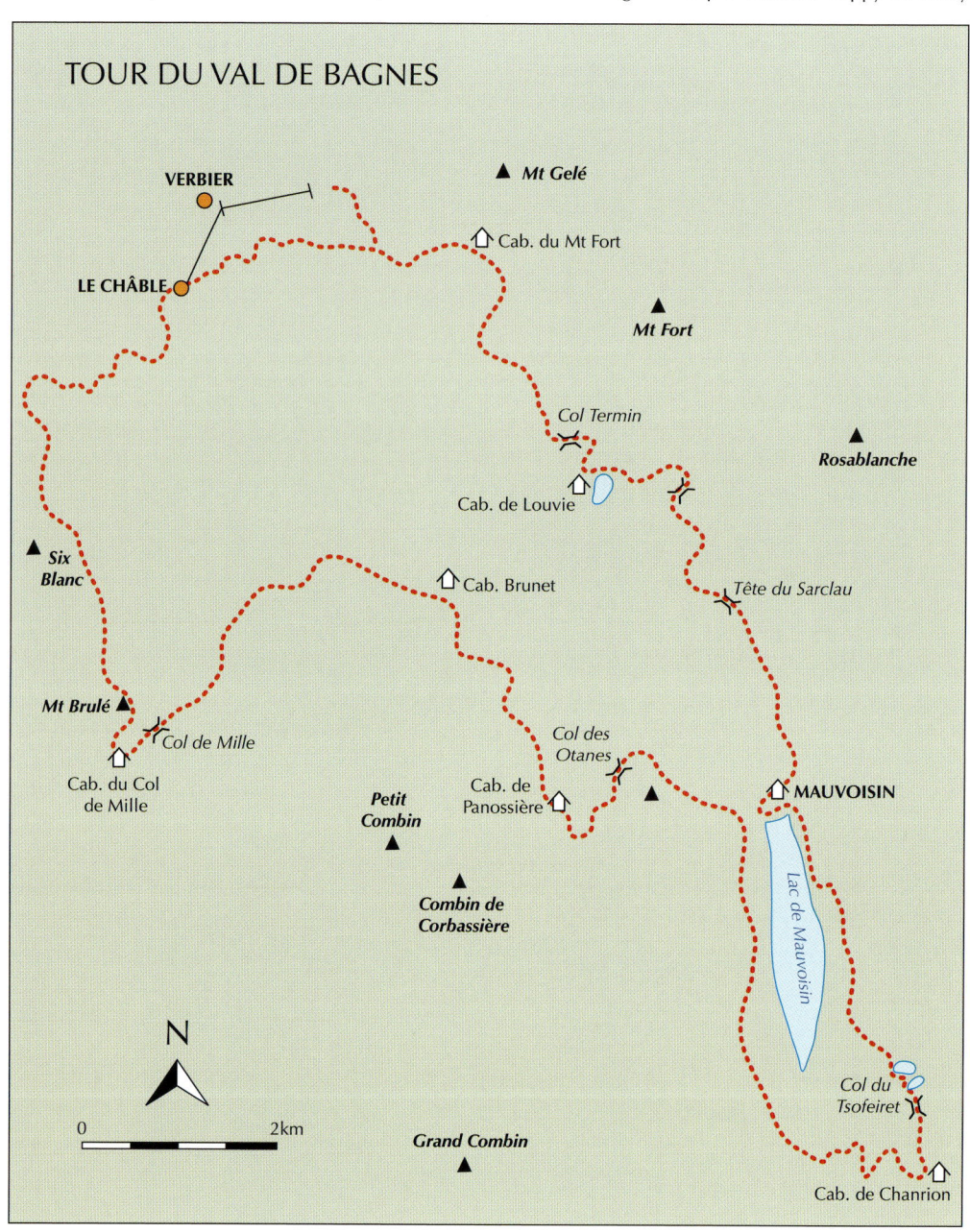

TOUR DU VAL DE BAGNES

a long day, although some of the routes can be brutally steep.

The branch line served by the St Bernard Express runs from Martigny to Le Châble via **Sembrancher**. An unpretentious stone-walled village, Sembrancher (717m) has limited pension accommodation, a campsite, foodstores and a restaurant. A little over 5km to the east, and surrounded on three sides by meadows, **Le Châble** (821m) is the main village of the valley. This too, is very modest in size, with some old buildings forming a square on the left bank of the Drance, while neighbouring Villette across the river has more modern development. Taken together there are just three hotels, several apartments, a post office, a handful of shops and restaurants and an Office du Tourisme located at the valley station of the cableway to Verbier (www.verbier.ch). The railway terminates here, but the postbus serves the rest of the valley as far as Mauvoisin, and also carries passengers up the northern hairpins to Verbier. A side road breaks away from Le Châble and winds through meadows to **Bruson**, above which small groups of commuter homes and holiday chalets enjoy a sunny aspect. Higher still, a few ski tows exploit the slopes of Six Blanc, from which the Dents du Midi can be clearly seen to the northwest.

The Walker's Haute Route comes through Le Châble, as does the Tour du Val de Bagnes, a fairly demanding six–seven day trek which adopts some dramatic trails that seek out a number of incomparable vantage points.

TOUR DU VAL DE BAGNES

With the option of a start by cableway, and with six huts and a hotel from which to choose accommodation, the TVB enables walkers to select their own itinerary. The first stage, for example, could be spent mounting the steep 1600m of hillside above Le Châble to reach Cabane du Mont Fort. But an alternative would be to ride the gondola to Verbier, thus avoiding the main climb, then take another to Les Ruinettes, and walk past the Mont Fort Hut to spend the first night at Cabane de Louvie. At a later stage of the Tour, there's the option of having a short day's walk from the Panossière Hut to Cabane Brunet, or of continuing to Cabane du Col de Mille. Much will depend on weather conditions, time available, and the fitness of the individual walker.

Day 1: From **Le Châble** cross the river to nearby Villette and take a series of linking footpaths up the steep slope to Les Verneys, and on to the suntrap of Clambin, where there's a restaurant. Above this the way continues to climb over open slopes, until a *bisse* is joined which leads round the hillside, and from which a final uphill drag brings you to **Cabane du Mont Fort** (2457m), about 6–6½hrs from Le Châble.

Day 2: A short but scenically spectacular day's walk takes the TVB along the exposed path of the Sentier des Chamois, with the Grand Combin fully displayed across the valley. **Col Termin** then directs the route northeastward above the Louvie combe, with a path descending to Lac de Louvie and (3hrs from Mont Fort) the cosy **Cabane de Louvie** (2250m) built in 1997 by the Bagnes commune.

Day 3: This is a demanding stage; not long (4½–5hrs) but reasonably tough and with exposed sections of trail that demand caution. It begins by climbing steeply to cross a ridge spur at about 2490m, the east side of which is exposed and precipitous. Descending into a hanging valley, the way then climbs again to cross the **Tête du Sarclau**, followed by a long descending traverse path that eventually reaches the valley bed at **Mauvoisin**, where a small hotel sits in the shadow of the massive concrete barrage wall.

Day 4: From Mauvoisin to Cabane de Chanrion near the head of the valley is a 3½hr delight. A road tunnel leads onto the dam wall, and on the eastern side of Lac de Mauvoisin a track gives 30mins or so of easy walking before you break away on a zigzag path rising into pastureland where ibex, marmot and chamois may all be seen. Passing between the Lacs de Tsofeiret the TVB mounts a grassy spur to **Col de Tsofeiret**; grass on one side, a steep rocky descent with fixed chains and timber steps on the other. (Some stonefall danger.) The trail continues across a wilderness of moraine to reach the SAC's **Cabane de Chanrion** at 2462m.

Day 5: Reversing Day 3 of the Tour des Combins (2:2), this 7½–8hr stage returns along the west flank of the valley on an undulating trail passing small tarns, pools and shepherds' huts, via rocky sections and long open pastures with views through the Val de Bagnes. A steep 700m climb to **Col des Otanes** (2880m) is rewarded by a sudden spectacular panorama that includes most of the Combin massif and its glaciers. A 200m descent then leads to the well-appointed **Cabane de Panossière** on the right bank moraine of the Corbassière glacier.

Day 6: After descending below the glacier, the TVB then wanders across a hillside carpeted with alpenroses, cuts into a cleft-like valley and climbs steeply to reach the privately owned **Cabane Brunet** (2103m) after about 2½hrs. Another 3hrs will be needed to complete this stage, which is mostly pastoral and with views of the Dents du Midi in the distance. Gaining **Col de Mille** in the valley's west wall, a few paces on the other side reveals the little **Cabane du Col de Mille** at 2472m.

Day 7: Less than 30mins after leaving the hut you stand on the modest summit of **Mont Brulé** from which the Mont Blanc massif is displayed in all its grandeur. That view remains as you wander along the ridge towards **Six Blanc**. Turning through a grassy col the Dents du Midi then take the place of Mont Blanc, before you descend through woodland and meadow to the Moay chalets where there's a restaurant, and continue downhill to **Le Châble** to complete the Tour du Val de Bagnes, 4½–5hrs from Col de Mille.

Almost 700m above Le Châble, with which it is connected by 9km of steeply winding road, **Verbier** (1526m) is one of the country's major ski resorts which grew from a tiny village in the 1950s to a sprawling complex of apartment blocks, hotels, shops and modern housing. The ski boom of the 1960s made Verbier fashionable as a place in which to spend the winter careering downhill, and today it attracts something like a million visitors a year. Short on charm, and with the slopes above it strung about with cableways, chairlifts and tows detracting from its aesthetic heritage, the lure of white gold has been used, no doubt, to justify the eyesores. It is said that rooms in apartments and private chalets outnumber hotel beds by a factor of ten to one. The tourist office on Place Centrale is worth a visit if you arrive on spec, but for more information go to www.verbier.ch.

Being the premier resort of the so-called Four Valleys ski area (www.4vallees.ch), Verbier is linked with Savoleyres above Isérables, and Nendaz in the next valley over the mountains (2:4), with cableways swinging up to Mont Gelé (3023m) and the glaciers of Mont Fort (3328m); and with the huge 'Le Jumbo' cable car transporting up to 150 people at a time via Col des Gentianes. But while skiing takes pride of place in and around Verbier, the resort also caters for other adventure sports. The mountain guides office is situated at the Maison du Sport, with climbing, high-level mountain walking and canyoning included in their prospectus (www.maisondusport.com), while the Ecole d'Alpinisme La Fantastique also runs mountaineering courses (www.lafantastique.com).

Before leaving Verbier it is worth mentioning the 2473m rock tower of ❸ **Pierre Avoi** which stands northwest of the resort overlooking the Rhône valley. Usually approached by taking the Savoleyres cableway followed by an easy walk, this limestone turret is not only accessible to tourists via steps, chains and ladders, but along with the neighbouring Clochetons de la Pierre Avoi, forms a rock climber's playground. The many equipped routes are marked on topos available from the Verbier guides' office.

Cabane du Mont Fort
To the east of the resort **Cabane du Mont Fort** is perched on a bluff at 2457m under the Monts de Sion. Property of the Jaman section of the SAC, the hut was refurbished in 2002, and its 66 places are now divided between conventional dormitories and 2, 4 and 6-bedded rooms (www.cabanemontfort.ch). Staffed in winter (December to mid-May) and from late June to mid-September, it's reached by a 3hr walk from Verbier, or 1¼hrs from the Ruinettes gondola. Although there are cableways nearby, the outlook from the hut is magical, with the Mont Blanc range concentrating one's attention.

- The Mont Fort Hut is well-used by walkers in summer, for there are several rewarding routes to follow, including the ascent of ⊗ **Mont Gelé** (3023m), for example. Having been assaulted by the ski industry, the mountain has lost any sense of isolation, but the cableway which rises to within a few metres of the summit does not operate in summer, and the uncomplicated 2hr walk and scramble from the hut via Col du Mont Gelé is made worthwhile for the extent and variety of the views. These include the Mont Blanc range, the Combin massif, and the western end of the Bernese Alps.
- The 3336m snowpeak of ⊗ **Rosablanche** rising some way southeast of the hut, but unseen from there, is another temptation for first-season alpinists, for whom the 4hr ascent via Col de Momin and the Grand Désert glacier is only graded F. Rosablanche is also climbed from the St Laurent (2:4) and Prafleuri (2:5) huts, the latter giving a much shorter climb of just 2½hrs.
- ◐ ☆ For the general mountain walker the number one route to take from Cabane du Mont Fort is without question the sensational **Sentier des Chamois**, which follows a belvedere course southeastward along the mountainside some 1600m above the valley bed. Narrow, exposed and safeguarded in places by fixed cable or chains, this is not a path to take in adverse conditions. But in summer when snow and ice have cleared and the weather's fine, the Sentier gives a memorable excursion. A sighting of ibex and chamois is almost guaranteed, and the direct prospect of the Grand Combin is unbeatable. Col Termin at the southern end of the Sentier gives a choice of continuing routes. One descends to **Lac de Louvie**, while another swings northeast towards **Col de Louvie** – this latter option being taken by trekkers on the Walker's Haute Route. Before reaching Col de Louvie, however, another trail cuts up to the left on a scrambly ascent to **Col de la Chaux** (2940m), over which a descent (confused among rocks and boulders) could be made back to the Mont Fort Hut.
- ◐ A descent path from **Col Termin** enters a little hanging valley at whose southern end lies Lac de Louvie. As you approach the tarn, careful to avoid boggy patches advertised with cushions of cotton grass, the Combin massif once again draws your attention. At the far end of the lake, and standing a few metres above it on a 2207m bluff, **Cabane de Louvie**

View from the terrace at Cabane du Mont Fort

was built by the Bourgeoisie de Bagnes. This light, modern hut has 54 dorm places and is manned only in the high summer season from July to mid-September (tel 027 778 17 40) – there's no winter access. Two onward routes are worth mention: the first is a direct 2hr descent to Fionnay; an extremely steep zigzag path with occasional fixed chains for safety. The other takes the path of the Tour du Val de Bagnes (see box) on a demanding and exposed up and down route, before slanting down to Mauvoisin (4½–5hrs).

Le Châble to Fionnay

'The lower part of the Val de Bagnes,' said R L G Irving in *The Alps*, 'is full of smiling villages. All the way up to Lourtier the valley bed is wide enough to allow plenty of room for road and stream and cultivation.'

Beyond Le Châble the main road bypasses Montagnier on the opposite bank of the river, but goes through Versegères and Champsec where it then crosses to the north side of the Drance de Bagnes and enters **Lourtier** (1072m). Having a supermarket, this is a useful place for stocking with supplies for the mountains. Overnight accommodation is possible here at La Vallée, which has 33 beds and 88 dormitory places (www.vallee.ch).

On the edge of the village a secondary road breaks away, recrossing the river to make a long winding ascent of the southern hillside, on the way topping a promontory known as La Ly to reach **Cabane Brunet** (Cabane Marcel Brunet: 2103m), which has a small pool lying before it. Owned, like the Cabane de Louvie, by the Bourgeoisie de Bagnes, this is understandably popular with day visitors for whom lunch with a view of the distant Dents du Midi makes the drive worthwhile. But it is also well used by ski-mountaineers in springtime, and by walkers tackling both the Tour des Combins and Tour du Val de Bagnes. Permanently staffed from July to September, and partially open from mid-December to the end of May, it has 65 dormitory places (tel 027 778 18 10) and a homely restaurant-dining room.

A little over 12km from Le Châble the main road enters the hamlet of **Fionnay** (1490m) trapped below soaring mountain walls. (For tourist information tel 027 776 16 82). This one-time mountaineering centre has a small shop, a post office and the 2-star Hotel du Grand Combin which has 48 dorm places as well as standard rooms (www.fionnay.ch). From Fionnay paths climb steeply on the northern side of the valley to Cabane de Louvie and the ruins of Le Dâ (above which Col de Severeu suggests a way over the mountains to Val des Dix); another makes the ascent eastwards to the Louvie–Mauvoisin high trail which it meets at Ecurie du Crêt; and yet another strikes south up the mountainside on the way to the Panossière Hut. Only a walk along the valley bed can be made without too much effort.

The valley's north (right) flank having been dealt with from Cabane du Mont Fort, we will look at the south side, and in particular the route to Cabane de Panossière, for this is the way chosen by climbers bound for the Grand Combin. This 4hr walk begins by crossing the Drance de Bagnes at Fionnay on a footbridge, then climbs steeply above a small lake to pass some ruins after about 1½hrs. The well-trodden path then swings to the south into the valley scooped out by the retreating Corbassière glacier, and comes to Plan Goli, a beautiful area of grass, flowers and streams in an ablation trough backed by old moraines. Now the way twists up to a tiny pool and continues along the moraine crest to reach **Cabane de Panossière** (Cabane F-X

2:3 VAL DE BAGNES

Bagnoud: 2645m). A splendid hut, built in 1996 to replace a former refuge destroyed by avalanche, its setting is magnificent with a direct view along the icy highway of the Corbassière glacier to the North Face of the Grand Combin, while directly opposite rise the Petit Combin and Combin de Corbassière. Although the former hut was owned by the SAC, the present building belongs to the Association François-Xavier Bagnoud of Sion. Of modern design, it has dormitory places for 103 and a resident guardian in April and May, and from July to September (www.cabane-fxb-panossiere.ch).

Climbers and ski-mountaineers will naturally focus their attention on assorted routes on the Combin massif (see below), but walkers have several options to consider when it comes to leaving the hut. The easiest of these simply reverses the approach route from Fionnay described above. Another, adopted by the Tour du Val de Bagnes (see box) descends into Plan Goli, then crosses the glacial torrent to a continuing path that works its way round the mountainside to **Cabane Brunet** in

Cabane de Panossière, base for climbs in the Combin massif

2½hrs. A third option also makes its way to Cabane Brunet, but instead of descending to Plan Goli, it crosses the lower reaches of the Corbassière glacier, then tackles **Col des Avouillons** for a more direct approach. And a fourth option entails crossing the 2846m **Col des Otanes** east of the Panossière Hut, followed by a steep descent into Val de Bagnes at Mauvoisin. Reached in just 40mins or so from the hut, the col makes a wonderful vantage point from which to study the Combin massif – a view of big mountains, sweeping glaciers and ice-bound cirques. Given sufficient time, it would be feasible to make an ascent of the 3158m ☆ **Grand Tavé** from Col des Otanes in about 45mins. This walker's peak rises south of the col, where a rock scramble (F) takes you onto the easy scree-cluttered North Ridge which rises to the summit for even more extensive views, especially of the great ice cliffs that make up the northern face of the Grand Combin.

☆ Combin Massif

Seen at its best from either Cabane de Panossière (for a close view), or the Sentier des Chamois (for a wider perspective), the Grand Combin is a major massif; high, majestic and complex, with an extensive glacier system, huge walls of rock on the south side, and on the north giant serac barriers, ice terraces and three distinct 4000m summits, namely: Combin de Grafeneire (4314m), Combin de Valsorey (4184m), and Combin de la Tsessette (4141m). Another 4000m top, the 4243m Aiguille du Croissant, was once considered the massif's highest point, but is in fact a secondary point on Combin de Grafeneire's snow dome, while other neighbouring mountains such as Combin de Corbassière and the Petit Combin, though not reaching the magical 4000m spot height, also make worthwhile goals.

It was three Val de Bagnes men, Benjamin and Maurice Felley, with Jouvence Bruchez, who in July 1857 discovered the route taken until recent years by most parties heading for the **Grand Combin** (Combin de Grafeneire), although they stopped short of the actual summit by assuming the Aiguille du Croissant to be the top. The real summit was gained two years later by Charles St-Clair Deville, Daniel, Emmanuel and Gaspard Balleys, and Basile Dorsaz. Approached from the north, the pioneers' route ascended glacier terraces to a long icy ramp, since named the Corridor which led to the Combin

109

The regal Combin massif and the long Corbassière glacier

de Tsesseret, but this ramp is threatened by collapsing seracs and over the years a number of parties came to grief while tackling the Corridor section. Nowadays the recommended route (AD-) avoids this by taking the rock crest that separates the NW Face from that of the Northeast, to reach a small bank of seracs which must be worked through in order to gain the summit dome. It's a long route from the Panossière Hut (8hrs+), with almost 1670m of height to gain, so climbers need to be fit and keep alert to any change in the weather.

- **Combin de Valsorey** is the West summit, and the massif's second highest. A broad snow ridge links it with Combin de Grafeneire, and it is usually tackled from the nearer Cabane de Valsorey (2:2), but since the NW Face route is gained from the Corbassière glacier, approach from Cabane de Panossière is equally valid.

- **Combin de la Tsessette** stands northeast of the main summit of the Grand Combin. From it a ridge pushes north then northeast to contain on its west side the glacial Corbassière valley, while the east flank of this ridge holds the little Tsessette glacier, which hangs above the southern end of the Mauvoisin lake. Rising from the Tsessette glacier, the impressive SE Face is climbed by three or four routes, each of which, being hampered by poor rock, requires good cold conditions to give some stability. These routes would best be tackled from a bivouac high above Lac de Mauvoisin, but the Panossière Hut is a practical base for climbers approaching via a course that diverts from the standard Grand Combin climb on a ridge-walk from Col du Croissant.

- At 3715m **Combin de Corbassière** makes an obvious goal across the glacier southwest of the Panossière Hut, from which several routes are feasible. The South Ridge is the shortest and most frequented (3½–4hrs; PD-); the NW Face gives an AD climb of about 5hrs; while the NE Face, clearly seen from the hut, has three couloirs prone to stonefall danger (PD).

- **Petit Combin** (3672m) lies just to the northwest of Combin de Corbassière and is often combined with a traverse of the latter peak. However, when conditions are favourable, an ascent by way of the Follets glacier and SE Face offers the most direct route (4hrs) from the Cabane de Panossière, while routes on the NW Face and NW Ridge are usually tackled from a base at Cabane Brunet.

2:3 Val de Bagnes

The Upper Val de Bagnes

Leaving Fionnay on the final stretch to the Mauvoisin barrage roadhead, the valley opens a little on the approach to Bonatchiesse (1565m), a small hamlet with a café and a large campsite, Camping Forêt des Mélèzes. Beyond this lie small patches of open meadowland, then where the road swings right to cross the river before the final hairpin ascent to Mauvoisin, a 50m limestone crag known as the ◉ **Madzeria Slab** provides a series of one-pitch climbs up to VI-.

Le Pleureur and Lac de Mauvoisin in the upper Val de Bagnes

Cabane de Chanrion

At the 1840m roadhead there's a small chapel and a hotel. Open June to September, **Hotel de Mauvoisin** has 20 beds and 30 dorm places (www.mauvoisin.ch). Behind it towers the massive 250m high dam wall holding back the Mauvoisin reservoir which forms part of the elaborate Grande Dixence hydro-electricity scheme. In 1818, almost a century and a half before the dam was built, a mass of ice broke away from one of the nearby glaciers and blocked the Mauvoisin gorge, causing a natural lake to form behind it. When the ice-and rock-barrier broke, a wall of water swept downvalley, killing 34 people and wreaking havoc as far as Sembrancher and Martigny, where the remains of trees and houses finally settled.

The road actually continues a short distance beyond the hotel to the barrage, and through tunnels emerges in the upper reaches of the valley on the west side of Lac de Mauvoisin, where a track (banned to private vehicles) continues almost as far as Cabane de Chanrion. On the east side of the barrage another track goes through more tunnels before heading south high above the water level. This is the preferred route by which to approach the Chanrion Hut, for about 30mins beyond the barrage a waymarked path strikes up the hillside, and crossing pastures eventually leads to the **Lacs de Tsofeiret**. Across the valley the abrupt wall of Combin de la Tsessette's East Face makes an impressive show. About 70m above the largest of the three lakes, Col de Tsofeiret is very much a col of two sides; on the north it's a grass slope, but the south side is precipitous rock down which steep zigzags lead to a chain-assisted stretch, then wood-braced steps before tucking against crags and descending to a moraine wilderness deposited by the Glacier du Brenay. About 40mins from the col you arrive at the **Cabane de Chanrion** (2462m), set in a basin of grass bluffs, pool-filled hollows, and mountains hung about with small glaciers, 3½hrs from the Mauvoisin roadhead (www.chanrion.ch).

When Whymper passed the night of 5 July 1865 at what he referred to as the chalets of Chanrion he was not impressed: 'a foul spot, which should be avoided' was his opinion. Cabane de Chanrion is very different. Owned by the Genevoise section of the SAC, it has 85 dormitory places and is permanently staffed from mid-March to the middle of May, and from mid-June to mid-September.

Using this as a base, a number of possibilities arise. For walkers a visit to the 2797m ⚬ **Fenêtre de Durand** on the frontier ridge southwest of the hut is an obvious attraction. There's nothing difficult about it, for a decent path mounts the flower-carpeted left bank lateral moraine of a small glacier in just 2½hrs, and views in all directions are very fine – the Gran Paradiso range especially catching your attention on the Italian side. The pass makes a natural crossing point between Val de Bagnes and Val d'Ollomont, and is used by trekkers tackling the Tour des Combins (see 2:2). Above the pass to the west rises a 'wonderful slag heap of shale' (Lindsay Griffin in the AC guide *Valais Alps West*). This description of ⚬ **Mont Avril** (3347m) may be apt, but the easy 1½hr ascent via an unmissable trail is worth the efforts of walkers, for the summit view on a good day is truly uplifting.

One of the most attractive peaks on show from the Chanrion Hut is the ⚬ **Bec d'Epicoune**, an elegant 3528m Ober Gabelhorn lookalike which stands on the frontier ridge southeast of the hut. Not surprisingly it's a popular goal for climbers, for whom the North Ridge is generally reckoned to offer the best route to the summit (PD; 5hrs). Looming over the hut to the east, the 3403m rock pyramid of the ⚬ **Pointe d'Otemma** is another popular target for climbers based here for a few days. It has three prominent ridges; the NE, South and West, each of which may be climbed by PD+ routes.

Then there's the 3875m ⚬ **La Ruinette**, another pyramid-shaped peak, this one located north of Pointe d'Otemma from which it is separated by the Brenay glacier. First climbed by Whymper with Christian Almer and Franz Biner on 6 July 1865, it is a tremendous vantage point, as Whymper was at pains to point out. 'As a standpoint it has not many superiors. You see mountains, and nothing but mountains. It is a solemn … view, but it is very grand. The great Combin, with its noble background of the whole range of Mont Blanc, never looks so big as it does from here. In the contrary direction, the Matterhorn overpowers all besides' (*Scrambles Amongst the Alps*). Whymper also stated (and there's no reason to contradict him) that 'There is not, I suppose, another mountain in the Alps of the same height that can be ascended so easily. You have only to go ahead: upon its southern side one can walk about almost anywhere.' Although his route of ascent is rarely followed these days, the *voie normale* by the Col de Lire Rose and the SW Ridge gives an enjoyable 5½hr PD- climb.

Ski-mountaineers working their way to Zermatt on the Haute Route have two options for progressing their journey from Chanrion to the Vignettes Hut above Arolla. The first is via the Brenay glacier and Pigne d'Arolla; the second and more direct route uses the long Otemma glacier and the plateau-like Col de Chermontane (3053m) at its head. This Otemma glacier route is also used in summer by climbers moving on to the Vignettes Hut; in good conditions it should be gained in 5–5½hrs. As Hubert Walker once said: 'All the stretch of country between the huts on the Col des Vignettes and Chanrion, including this glacier [the Otemma] and the parallel Glacier de Brenay, together with such fine peaks as Ruinette, la Serpentine and Mont Blanc de Seilon [Cheilon], makes up as fine and unfrequented a district as one could desire, providing ample scope for a splendid holiday' (*Walking in the Alps*).

THE CLASSIC HAUTE ROUTE

The Classic Haute Route ski tour between Mont Blanc and the Matterhorn has such a reputation that it attracts ski mountaineers from around the world, but as Bill O'Connor points out in Volume I of his *Alpine Ski Mountaineering*, which describes the route, its seriousness and difficulty are often underestimated, as a result many of those who set out on it, fail to complete the journey. The route has been refined several times since it was first achieved in January 1911, and today there are a number of variations from the main itinerary, and given decent conditions several summits could be claimed along the way. The outline given here is the main itinerary described in seven stages. For full details Bill O'Connor's guide (published by Cicerone in 2002) makes essential reading.

Day 1: From the village of **Argentière** upvalley from Chamonix, take the Grands Montets cableway to the top station and descend the steep and crevassed Argentière glacier from the 3233m Col des Grands Montets to **Refuge de Argentière** (2771m). This is a short and easy stage of about 2hrs.

The Swiss Alps – Chapter 2: Pennine Alps

THE CLASSIC HAUTE ROUTE

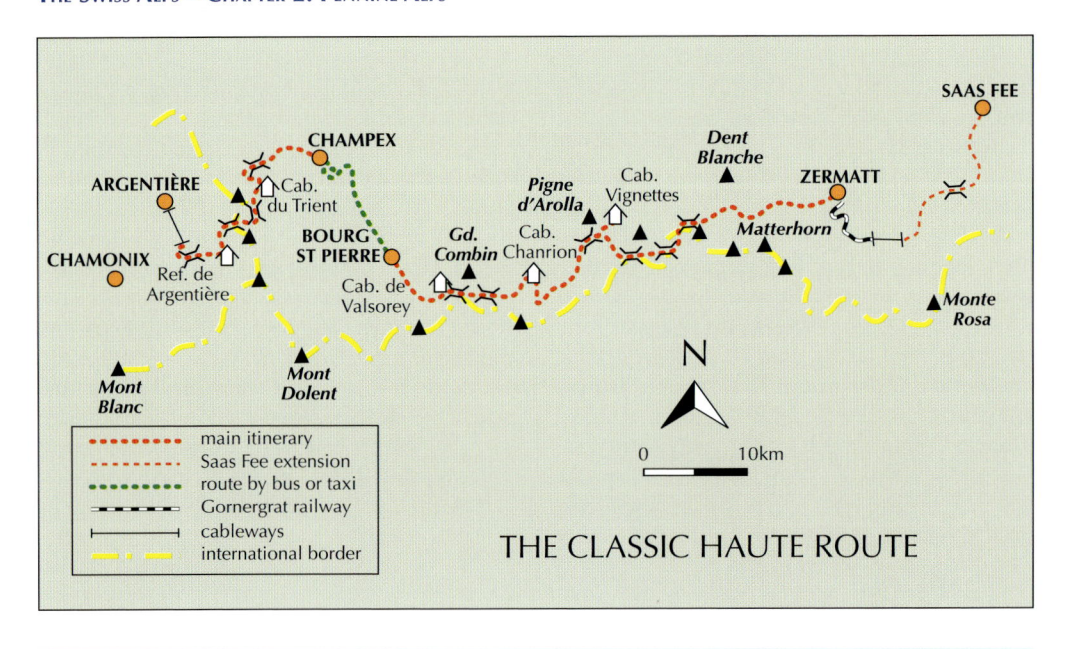

Legend:
- main itinerary
- Saas Fee extension
- route by bus or taxi
- Gornergrat railway
- cableways
- international border

Day 2: A challenging stage with a lot of height gain that involves steep climbing and an abseil or two. The impressive 3323m Col du Chardonnet is crossed to the Saleina glacier; then the Fenêtre de Saleina leads to the broad Plateau du Trient across which you make your way to the **Cabane du Trient** (3170m) at the end of a strenuous day.

Day 3: Although variations exist for the onward route from the Trient Hut, most ski tourers descend to the right of the Trient glacier's icefall, climb to the 2796m Col des Ecandies and descend (some avalanche danger) into the splendid Val d'Arpette and continue down to **Champex** (see 2:1). From there take either bus or taxi to Orsières and on to **Bourg-St-Pierre** in Val d'Entremont (2:2).

Day 4: A long and gruelling 5–6hr uphill slog leads to the **Cabane de Valsorey** at 3030m (2:2) in readiness for crossing the magnificent Combin massif next day.

Day 5: A serious stage demanding a high level of ski-mountaineering skills takes the Haute Route to the 3664m Plateau du Couloir, then down to Col du Sonadon across which descent of the Mont Durand glacier is made by one of two options. The route then works its way over moraine to make a crossing of the northeast ridge of Mont Avril, eventually gaining the CAS-owned **Cabane de Chanrion** (2462m) in the upper reaches of Val de Bagnes, about 6–8hrs after leaving the Valsorey Hut.

Day 6: The standard route to the Vignettes Hut above Arolla (see 2:6) pushes up the long and gently inclined Otemma glacier to gain the 3053m Col Chermontane. From there a short but steep climb leads to a traverse along the north side of a ridge to gain the **Cabane des Vignettes** (3160m) after about 4–5hrs. A longer (6–8hrs), more difficult, but potentially more interesting alternative goes by way of the Brenay glacier, Col du Brenay and Pigne d'Arolla Col, with an option of summiting the 3796m Pigne d'Arolla to enjoy one of the finest of all alpine panoramic views.

Day 7: A big day's effort marks this Haute Route finale that journeys among a whole series of dramatic mountains. Start by going up to the Col des Vignettes and on to the Col Chermontane (visited on Day 6) where you continue to Col de l'Evêque at 3392m. Col Collon is next, followed by partial descent of the Haute Glacier d'Arolla, before breaking away to Col du Mont Brulé on the Swiss/Italian border. The way continues on the Italian side to gain Col de Valpelline where there are opportunities to claim one or two summits, before skiing down interconnecting glaciers below the Matterhorn to reach **Zermatt** at the end of a long but memorable day's adventure.

Note: Some Haute Route skiers prefer to conclude their tour in **Saas Fee** by crossing the 3789m Adler Pass (see 2:10) from the Stockhorn cable car station above Gornergrat. This is another 'big day' among yet more magnificent scenery.

2:4 VAL DE NENDAZ

Known mostly to skiers, this short hanging valley between the Vals de Bagnes and Hérémence, is linked by cableway with the Verbier complex, and from its middle reaches footpaths lure walkers into a pastoral landscape that grows more wild and enticing the higher you go. The snow peak of Rosablanche effectively marks the head of the valley, with the Grand Désert glacier having left its moraine debris spilling down to the north; moraines that are slowly being invaded by alpine plants.

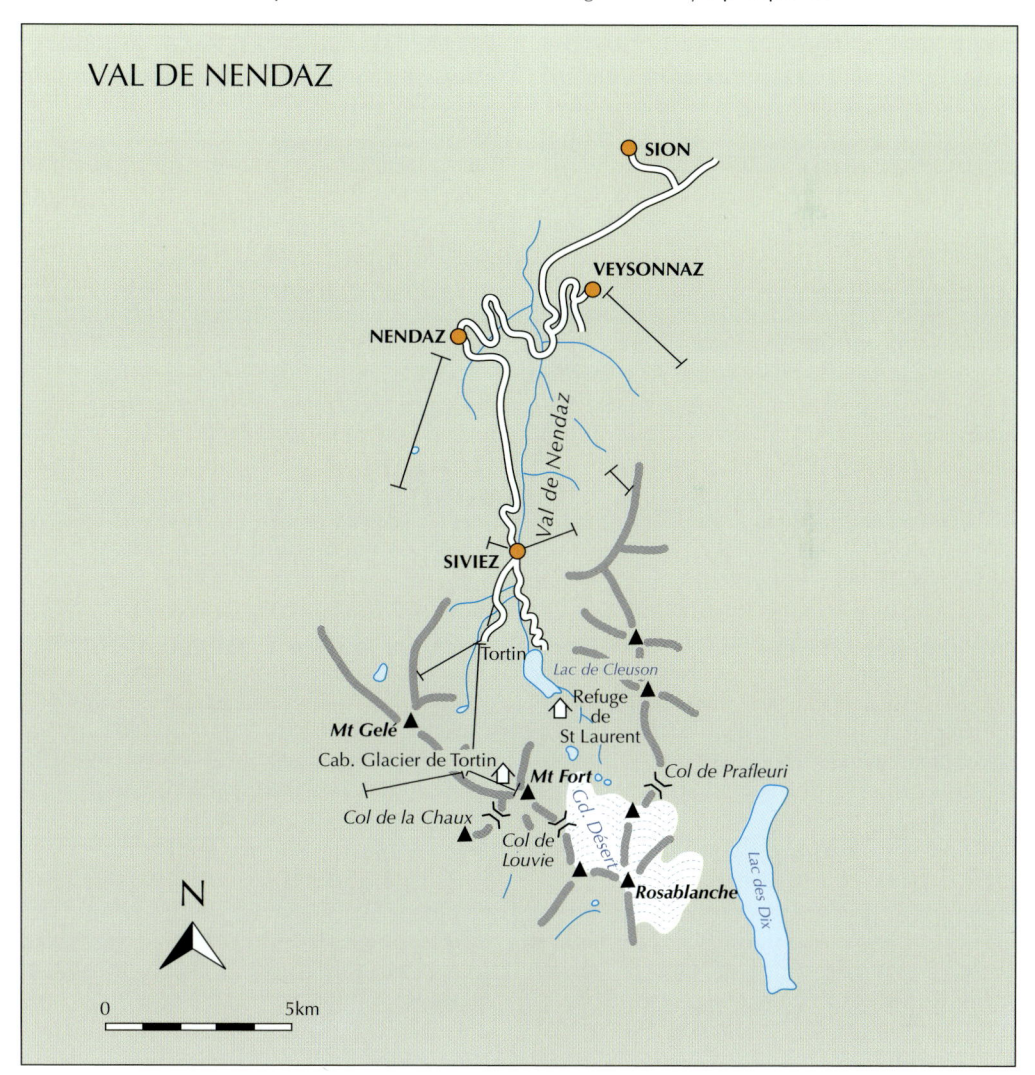

Val de Nendaz is approached from **Sion** in the Rhône valley by a road that climbs among orchards of peach and apricot to gain a terrace of shorn meadows and neat chalets. **Nendaz** (Haute Nendaz) overlooks the Rhône from this terrace, its hotels, pensions and *chambres d'hôtes* providing a modest amount of accommodation – for tourist information go to www.nendaz.ch. The road climbs higher, then projects south into the valley proper among tree-shrouded meadows, and when the woodland cover thins the valley opens out at the ski resort of **Siviez** (Super Nendaz; 1733m). This purpose-built development of apartment blocks and hotels is served by postbus from Sion, with a less frequent service continuing as far as Tortin.

Above Siviez the road forks. The right branch goes to **Tortin** at 2045m, from where cableways swing their passengers up to the Mont Gelé and Mont Fort ski slopes, to link up with the Verbier system. At around 3000m on the slopes of Mont Fort stands **Cabane Glacier de Tortin**. Owned by the Ski Club of Nendaz, it has 45 dorm places, and is staffed during the main winter and summer seasons (www.sonendaz.ch).

Beyond Siviez the continuing road (left branch) is not metalled, but it continues to the dammed Lac de Cleuson, from where a track goes along the lake's east shore as far as **Refuge de St Laurent** (2485m) – a walk of about 1hr from the dam. This privately owned hut is located south of Lac de Cleuson, and with places for 32 is staffed from July until the end of September (tel 027 288 50 05).

Although Val de Nendaz has limited appeal for climbers and walkers, the enterprising visitor would have no trouble discovering routes of interest. Modest walking opportunities will be found, for example alongside the Ancien Bisse de Chervé, which extends for almost 13km from Lac de Cleuson to Thyon at the entrance to Val d'Hérémence; or the Ancien Bisse du Milieu which links Haute Nendaz with the village of Veysonnaz on the opposite (right-hand) hillside entrance to Val de Nendaz. But the best and most interesting walks are to be had by pushing towards the head of the valley where, near the current tail-end of the Grand Désert glacier, a waymarked trail climbs to the west to cross **Col de Louvie**, then continues to Cabane du Mont Fort via Col de la Chaux; or from Col de Louvie to Cabane de Louvie (see 2:3) via a 650m descent with the Combin massif in view for much of the way. At the little lake below the Grand Désert glacier another waymarked route rises over rough stony ground heading southeast to **Col de Prafleuri** (2965m), from where a descent can be made to Cabane de Prafleuri (see 2:5).

Meanwhile the main mountain interest will be found on the ⓢ **Rosablanche** (3336m) where a straightforward ascent from the St Laurent Hut via the Grand Désert glacier – a popular route for skiers, as well as first-season alpinists – is only graded F, and will take about 3–3½hrs, while the NW Ridge offers a marginally more difficult route.

2:5 VAL D'HÉRÉMENCE

A little southeast of Sion the combined waters of the Vals d'Hérémence and Hérens spill through a gorge into the Rhône; the confluence of these two valley streams being close to the village of Euseigne. However, the road which serves these valleys from Sion divides in **Vex** (939m). The way to Val d'Hérens keeps ahead, while the right branch runs on to **Hérémence** (1237m), a village noted for its extravagantly modern church, built in 1971, which makes a stark contrast to the traditional timber buildings around it. (For tourist information tel 027 281 15 33.)

This upper road slides into Val d'Hérémence, the southwestern stem of the two valleys, with a linking road which cuts round the mountainside into neighbouring Val d'Hérens. Passing through **Pralong** (1608m), a pleasant base albeit rather far from the main areas of interest, there's the Hotel du Val des Dix (www.grande-dixence.com), a campsite and a few shops. The road then continues as far as **Le Chargeur** (2102m) below the massive Dixence barrage, some 16km from Vex. Here Hotel Grande Dixence has modestly priced rooms and dormitory accommodation (tel 027 281 13 22). A summer-only cable car swings visitors to the top of the barrage, thus saving about 30mins of walking up a steeply twisting path from the roadhead, while next to the car park a ⓢ **40m crag** has several short equipped routes up to grade V.

Measuring 287m, when built in the early 1960s the Grande Dixence barrage was the world's highest; it remains the tallest in Europe, and holds back the 6km long Lac des Dix which is fed by glaciers draped below Mont Blanc de Cheilon at the head of the valley, and several lesser ice sheets spilling from the west wall of what is known here as the Val

2:5 Val d'Hérémence

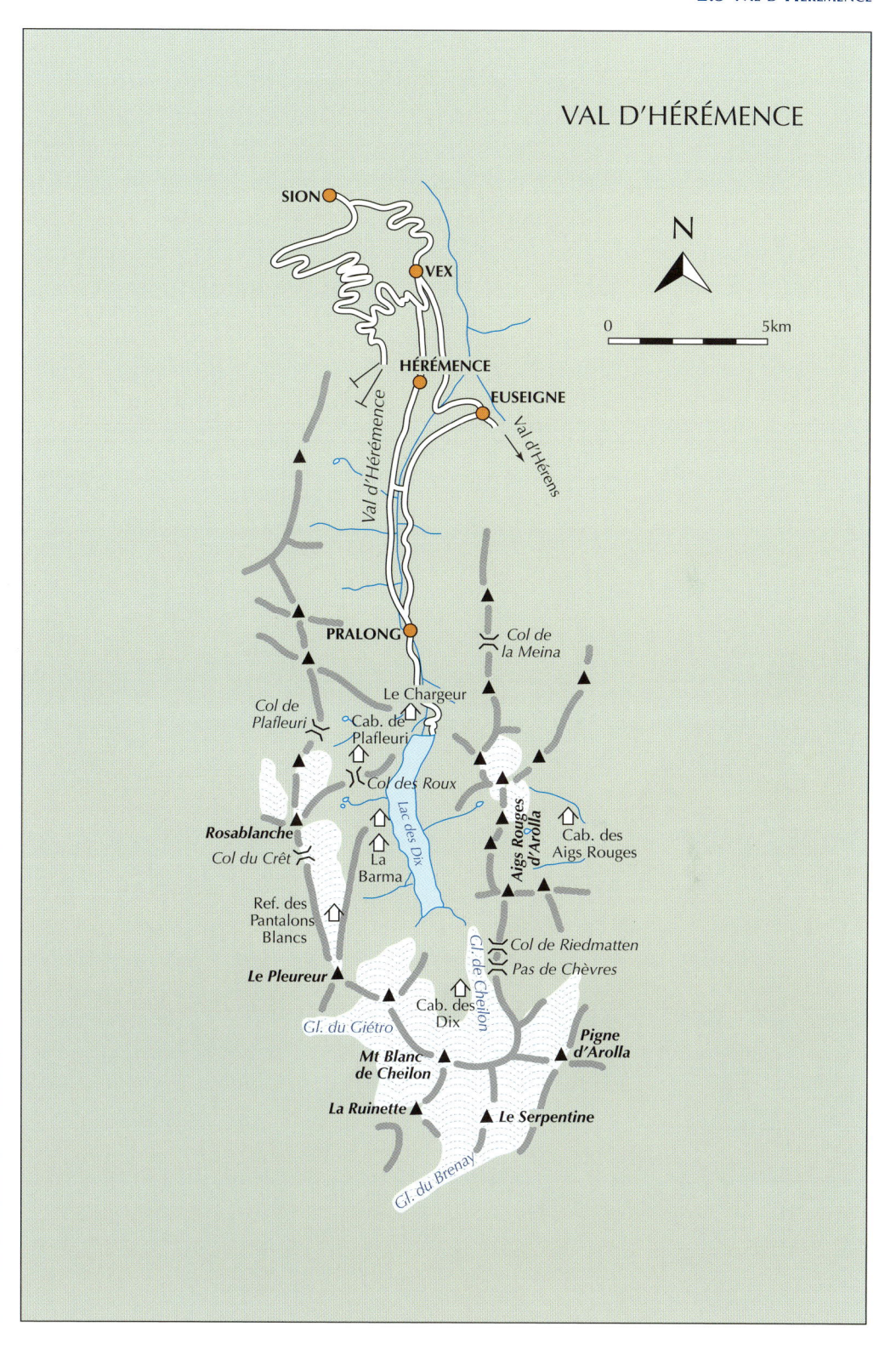

VAL D'HÉRÉMENCE

The Swiss Alps – Chapter 2: Pennine Alps

The track beside Lac des Dix that leads to the Dix hut and Mont Blanc de Cheilon

des Dix. A complex underground pumping system also brings glacial drainage via a series of tunnels from icefields as far distant as those around the Matterhorn.

To the west of Le Chargeur, the Combe de Prafleuri is a barren hanging valley that suffered the indignity of supplying crushed rock for concrete manufacture in the construction of the Dixence barrage. As a result it has the appearance of a gigantic quarry. Prafleuri – the 'plain of flowers' – is not what its name implies, although the herd of ibex that has adopted the combe seems not to mind. There is, however, a hut here, reached by a 4WD road from Le Chargeur. Conveniently set between two passes used by trekkers on the Chamonix to Zermatt Walker's Haute Route, **Cabane de Prafleuri** (2660m) is privately owned but open to all. It has places for 59 and is staffed in the spring ski-touring season (mid-March to the end of April) and from July until mid-September (tel 027 281 17 80).

At the head of the Combe de Prafleuri, **Rosablanche** sends down a small glacier, by which the shortest of the various ascent routes can be made. (Previous routes on this mountain are outlined in 2:3 and 2:4.) The Prafleuri glacier takes the climber onto a snow saddle between Rosablanche and the Petit Mont Calme, where you then climb southward to gain the mountain's NE Ridge just below the summit – about 2½–3hrs from the hut; grade F.

Above the Prafleuri Hut to the south, **Col des Roux** (2804m) is easily reached in just 20mins. From it you have a very fine view along the Val des Dix (the upper reaches of Val d'Hérémence) to the North Face of Mont Blanc de Cheilon. Below, Lac des Dix reaches deep within the valley, its eastern side walled by the Aiguilles Rouges d'Arolla, its western shore edged with pastures. A track cuts along the west shore from the Dixence barrage, and above it one or two alp buildings hint at the pastoral nature of the valley before the reservoir was created. The first of those alps is known as La Barma (2575m), where the farm has been converted to the **Refuge des Ecoulaies** by the Ski Club des Pyramides from Euseigne. It has 22 places, and a guardian is usually on duty during summer weekends (www.lespyramides.ch). A few paces beyond this one of the old dairy buildings has now become the **Refuge de la Gentiane la Barma**. Privately owned and manned only occasionally, it

◀ *The North Face of Mont Blanc de Cheilon seen across the deep 'V' of the Pas de Chèvres*

has cooking facilities and places for 30 (enquiries and/or reservations to Café de Amis, Hérémence tel 027 281 11 97).

These one-time farm buildings nestle below another combe, or rather, below the ridge of the Rochers du Bouc which helps contain that combe and the Glacier des Ecoulaies. Overlooking the head of the glacier above the Rochers du Bouc, stands the **Refuge-Igloo des Pantalons Blancs**, an unmanned bivouac hut at 3280m, reached by an interesting scramble along the Rochers du Bouc in about 3hrs from La Barma (4hrs from the Dixence barrage). It has places for about 17 and self-cooking facilities, and is used by climbers tackling the rock peak of **Le Parrain** (3210m) above the Col du Crêt, the flat-topped **La Sale** (3646m) which lies further south along the same ridge, and the 3704m **Le Pleureur** that can be gained by a traverse from La Sale in another 1½hrs.

At the southern end of Lac des Dix a path strikes uphill about 50m from the end of the track, wanders along a moraine rib beside the shrinking Cheilon glacier, and leads to a nub of rock on which stands the bustling **Cabane des Dix** (2928m), about 4–4½hrs from Le Chargeur. Owned by the Monte Rosa section, this 150-bed hut is one of the busiest of all those owned by the SAC (www.cabanedesdix.ch). Manned from mid-March to May, and from July until mid-September, it's very popular with day visitors from Arolla and, of course, with climbers in summer and ski tourers in the winter/spring season. About 1500m to the south rises the graceful Mont Blanc de Cheilon whose glacier forms a moat on the eastern side of the hut. Across that glacier, the dividing ridge beyond which lies Arolla, is crossed by two passes within a few metres of one another; the gritty **Col de Riedmatten** (2919m), and the 2855m **Pas de Chèvres**, which is surmounted by three near-vertical cal ladders. Before crossing to Arolla, however, it is necessary to look at the mountaineering potential here at the head of Val des Dix.

The most obvious attraction is ● ☆ **Mont Blanc de Cheilon** (3869m), whose perfectly formed North Face so dominates the view from the hut. In his autobiographical *Summits and Secrets*, Kurt Diemburger described it as 'a huge pyramid, mathematical in its regularity. Its steep North Face is, by one of nature's freaks, an exactly constructed equilateral triangle.' The summit is the culminating point of four ridges, a hub with radiating spokes; NW, NE, SE and SW, this last ridge extending with a kink to join up with La Ruinette, last visited from the Chanrion Hut at the head of Val de Bagnes (2:3). The SE Ridge descends with an easterly curve to the Col de la Serpentine, across which the classic traverse to Pigne d'Arolla is made, and from which the Cheilon glacier descends northwards, while on the south side the Glacier de la Serpentine falls away to the Brenay icefield. Until fairly recent times a major feature of the North Face was a distinctive ice couloir, but this has become another victim of global warming and it will be an unusual year when the couloir holds ice beyond the middle of July; indeed the whole face is generally snow-free after the avalanches of late spring/early summer have done their work.

The mountain was first climbed in 1865 by the guide Justin Fellay with J J Weilenmann, who is said to have climbed 320 mountains in 20 years. Their route was by the Col de Cheilon and the SW Ridge, the route now taken as the *voie normale* (PD; 3–4hrs), but the North Face had to wait until 1938, when it was climbed by Wolfgang Gorter and Ludwig Steinauer in a 30hr siege. The first British ascent of this face was not made until September 1971, when Dougal Haston and Bev Clark travelled over from the Leysin-based International School of Mountaineering where they were working at the time. Conditions have changed dramatically on this face in the decades since then, for winter or spring are now favoured when the rock is well plastered with ice (TD).

2:6 VAL D'HÉRENS

When the road from Sion forks in **Vex**, the Val d'Hérens stem continues along the fertile hillside some way above the river Borgne, then crosses the Dixence stream, makes a sharp left-hand bend and shortly after burrows beneath the Pyramides d'Euseigne; those curious moraine pillars protected from erosion by flat caps of rock. Turning the spur that separates the Vals d'Hérémence and Hérens, you then come to **Euseigne** village, nestling among walnut trees. A little south of this the road crosses the Borgne to its true right bank, and runs on for a few more kilometres to meet a side stream shortly before reaching Evolène. Here on the left of the road a ● **100m high crag** contains literally

2:6 VAL D'HÉRENS

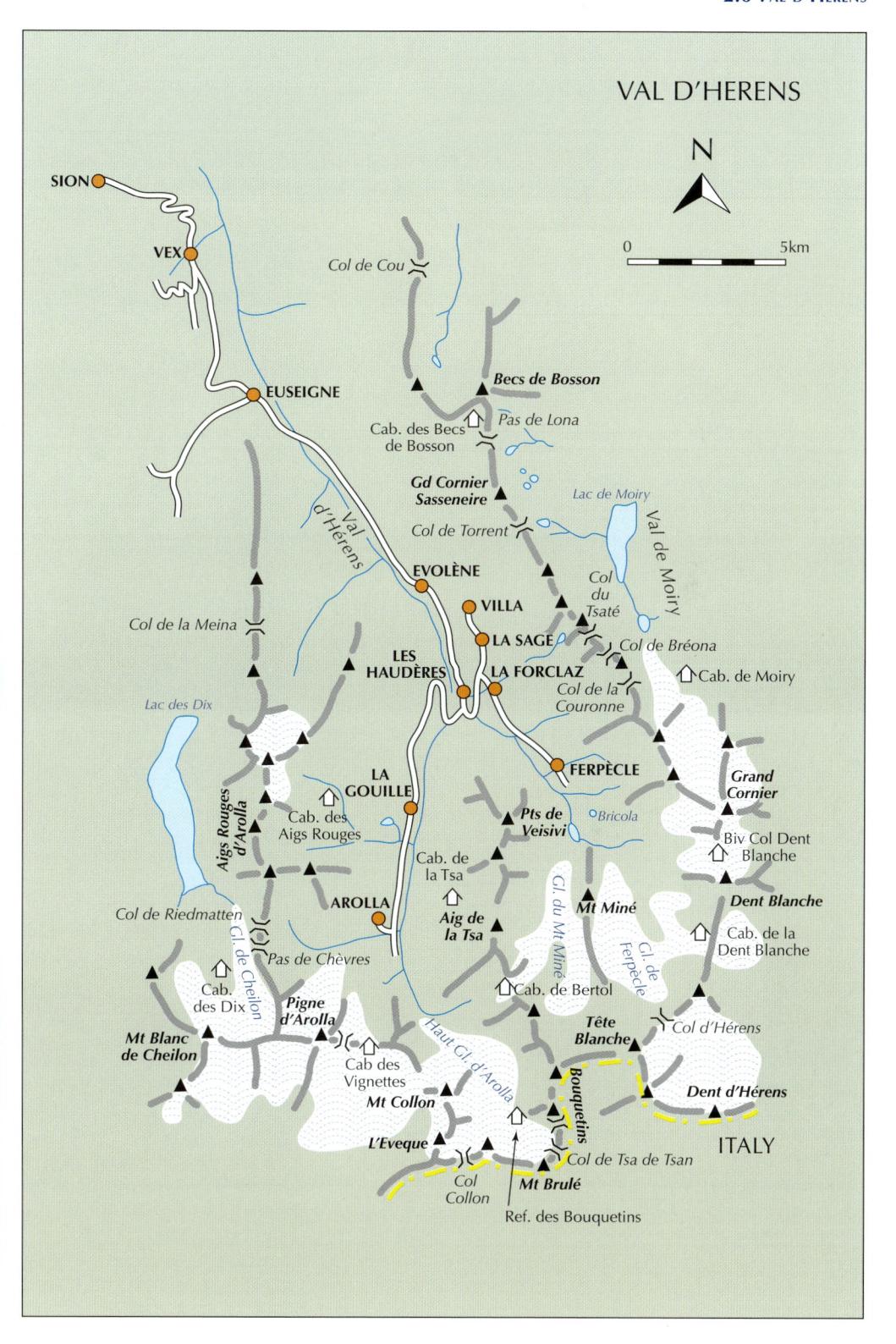

The curious Pyramides d'Euseigne at the junction of Vals d'Hérens and Hérémence

dozens of quality sport climbs on (as yet) unpolished gneiss. Well-equipped multi-pitch routes of anything from IV to VII+ on the five-pitch La Somital, will repay the attention of climbers before heading for the big hills above.

Evolène (1371m) is the main village of the valley, and one of the most attractive in Canton Valais. With its tall, dark-timbered, stone-based houses flanked either side of the narrow street among haybarns perched on staddle stones, Evolène is the quintessential Swiss picture postcard village. It has well-stocked foodstores, restaurants, a post office, banks and a tourist office (www.evolene-region.ch). There are three hotels, several *dortoirs* and a campsite with excellent facilities, open from May to the end of October. Across the river on the western hillside there's an extensive but fairly low-key system of ski lifts; above the road on its southern outskirts a short *via ferrata* has been created on the Ⓑ **Rocs de Villa**.

The valley here is pastoral, but a view upstream shows the great Dent Blanche and a swirl of glaciers, which should be sufficient to entice you to discover more. Across the river on the west bank, a riverside trail heads upstream to Les Haudères; another loops up the hillside, cuts into a hanging valley below the Pointe de Vouasson and crosses the 2702m Col de la Meina with a descent to Pralong in Val d'Hérémence (see 2:5); while a third option on the left flank of the valley rises to the alp hamlet of La Giette and works a way south to Arolla. There are, of course, other opportunities on the valley's east flank above Evolène, but one way to explore some of the best the valley has to offer, is to make the Tour du Val d'Hérens, another of those multi-day circuits created by the Association Valaisanne de la Randonnée Pédestre. Although it does not actually visit Evolène, it passes along the hillside above the village.

2:6 VAL D'HÉRENS

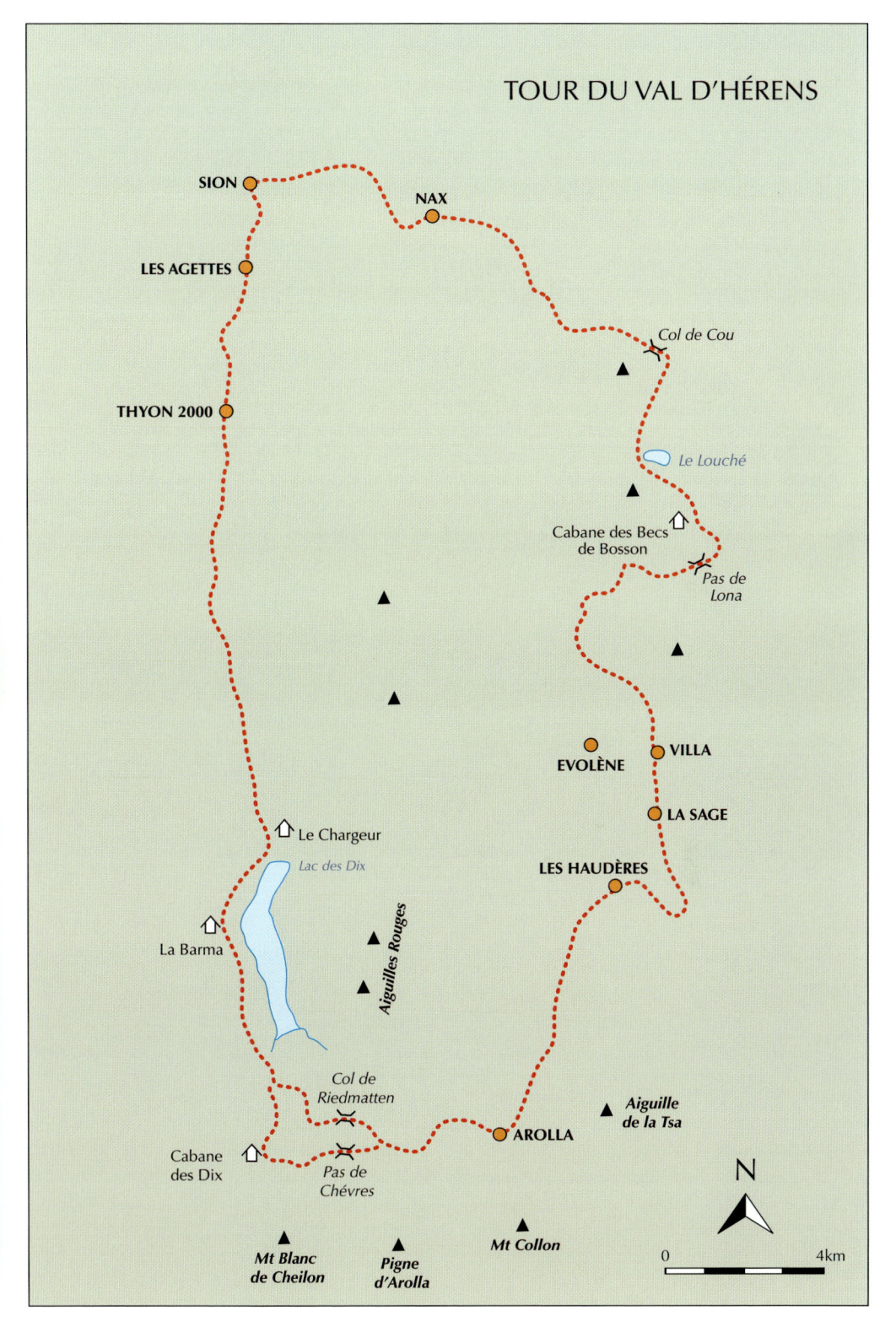

TOUR DU VAL D'HÉRENS

TOUR DU VAL D'HÉRENS

This six-day circuit also includes Val d'Hérémence and enjoys a whole range of scenic variations. Although it has some fairly strenuous sections, demands are on the whole reasonably modest, and it begins and ends in Sion, the capitol of Canton Valais, a town with a 2000 year history.

Day 1: From **Sion** cross the Rhône on a road bridge, then strike up the southern hillside on a path that leads to **Les Agettes** above Vex in 2hrs. Continue heading south, rising steadily to Mayens de Sion, Les Collons and up to **Thyon 2000**, an overall ascent from Sion of 1600m; a fairly tough 5hr stage as a starter.

Day 2: Progressing southward along the flank of Val d'Hérémence, the first hour is spent climbing to Les Gouilles d'Essertse at 2198m. You then descend a little before taking an undulating course to **Le Chargeur** (2102m) for hotel accommodation after 4–4½hrs, or continue to the **La Barma** alpage at 2575m where you can stay in either of the two buildings that have been converted to refuge accommodation – see 2:5 for details. But note that neither hut is permanently manned in summer, so food should be carried with you. (About 5½hrs)

Day 3: This is the first real high mountain stage, and a magnificent one at that. It follows the west bank of Lac des Dix to its southern end, then either traces the moraine path to **Cabane des Dix**, or crosses the stream issuing from the Cheilon glacier to find a path making for the **Col de Riedmatten** (2919m). Over this the continuing path descends to **Arolla**, while those walkers who chose the Cabane des Dix option will then cross the Cheilon glacier and climb the ladders to the 2855m **Pas de Chèvres**, where you join the Col de Riedmatten to Arolla path on the far side. Whichever option is taken, a memorable day is virtually guaranteed.

Day 4: From Arolla an easy stage slopes down through the upper Val d'Hérens to **Les Haudères**, then a short uphill section brings you to **La Sage** for hotel, or dormitory accommodation above the village restaurant (4hrs).

Day 5: After heading north along the hillside above Evolène, the Tour du Val d'Hérens then twists uphill on a long climb to gain the **Pas de Lona** (2787m) on the valley's walling ridge between the Sasseneire and Becs de Bosson. Having gained height it only takes 30mins to reach **Cabane des Becs de Bosson** at 2985m, at the end of a 6½hr stage.

Day 6: A 6hr day completes the trek, beginning by wandering along the east side of the ridge on a steady descent to a lake at 2567m, and continuing for about an hour on a gentle contour to **Col de Cou** at 2528m. Cutting through the col you then begin the long descent to the Rhône valley, passing through **Nax** on the way, and ending where the tour began, at the railway station in **Sion**.

The road continues southward, bypasses La Tour (1412m) and a little over 3km from Evolène, arrives at the lovely old village of **Les Haudères** (1436m) at the confluence of two glacier-fed rivers, the Borgne d'Arolla and Borgne de Ferpècle. Despite being rather low for a mountaineering base, the village has a lot going for it. The original village is crammed with typical Valaisian houses; near-black timbers and flowers at the windows; *mazots* squeezed between the houses, and a maze of narrow alleyways in which to get lost. More modern buildings are spread alongside the main road; there are currently six hotels and a *chambre d'hôte*; a campsite open throughout the year, Camping Molignon (www.camping-molignon.ch), a post office, a variety of shops and a tourist office (www.evolene-region.ch). Above the village, on the way to La Sage and Villa, two more ⓘ **sport climbing crags** are accessible, claiming routes of up to X-.

★ Val d'Arolla

Before looking at onward routes for the walker above Les Haudères, or at the climbing potential among big peaks that head the Ferpècle branch of the valley which forks here, we move into the Val d'Arolla stem of Val d'Hérens. For many in the past, as now, that valley leads to the promised land. 'Arolla', said R L G Irving in 1939, 'is the best place in the Alps to begin to climb them.' And four years before Irving, in her autobiographical

Climbing Days, Dorothy Pilley described the village thus: 'Perfectly situated amid pungent *arolles* [the Arolla pine] and at just the right altitude for general purposes, it offers an extraordinary number of interesting peaks.' More recently Lindsay Griffin agreed (in the AC guidebook *Valais Alps West*): 'Arolla is still one of the best bases anywhere from which to learn the rudiments of alpine climbing,' and the mountain and ski guide Bill O'Connor also gave it his enthusiastic thumbs-up before praising its ski-touring options: 'Arolla is a delightfully quiet village at the head of the Val d'Hérens, itself a splendid dead-end valley blocked by a magnificent barrier of mountains.' (*Alpine Ski Mountaineering: Vol 1*)

South of Les Haudères the road crosses the Borgne d'Arolla and swings in a loop to gain height before making the long slanting climb to Arolla itself. At the tiny hamlet of **La Gouille** (1844m) the friendly Pension du Lac Bleu right beside the road has 19 beds and 25 dormitory places (tel 027 283 11 66). Behind it a path climbs the wooded hillside to a group of chalets, and just above them, the well-known tarn of **Lac Bleu**, from which a path breaks away heading south along the hillside to Arolla, while another continues uphill, eventually reaching the Cabane des Aiguilles Rouges, of which more will be said later.

A short distance south of La Gouille huddles **Satarma** (1808m), a second hamlet with a side stream pouring from a wooded gully bringing snow-melt from the little glacial napkin draped beneath the Aiguilles Rouges. Here another path rises to Lac Bleu – a slightly shorter approach than that from La Gouille. Beyond this there's yet another crag worth noting near the road. **Pra Grassette** is a lengthy slab of gneiss facing east, and with a score or more equipped routes graded IV to VII+.

About 11km from Les Haudères you pass above Arolla's modest campsite situated in the valley bed on the other side of the river. Standing beside the road is Hotel-Restaurant Aiguille de la Tza with 64 *dortoir* places. A little further on, also beside the road, Le Sporting has 47 dormitory places. The

Les Haudères

road forks here, with a minor branch going ahead to a car park near a pumping station in full view of Mont Collon and the Arolla glacier; while the main road swings right in a hairpin for the final short climb to the compact village of **Arolla**, set among pinewoods at 2006m.

Small and unpretentious, but with the handsome iced gateau of Mont Collon as a backdrop and the stiletto point of the Aiguille de la Tsa prominent on the eastern ridge-line, Arolla offers the visiting walker, climber and ski-mountaineer a very different – some might say, welcome – experience from that which may be had in Chamonix, Zermatt or Grindelwald, say. By its somewhat limited infrastructure, night-life is virtually non-existent. So is shopping, beyond the necessities. You come to Arolla to fill your days with outdoor living, and sleep undisturbed when you hit the pillow at night.

A few shops are grouped near the village square. There are five hotels, and as well as Le Sporting and the Aiguille de la Tza already mentioned, four chalets with dormitory accommodation: the Edelweiss with 40 places, Les Ecureuils with 28 spaces, the 85 bed Centre Alpin, and Chalet de la Jeunesse with 60 places. Full details can be had from the Office du Tourisme (www.arolla.com).

As Irving had noted in his 1939 book *The Alps*, Arolla is one of the best of all centres for a first alpine season. The mountains that surround it have all the qualities one would specifically seek out; they *look* good, are clothed in snow and ice, are well-equipped with huts, and have routes of sufficient variety that their summits may be gained with satisfaction by both trainee and accomplished mountaineer. And, for a bonus, when you get to their top, most reward with simply breathtaking panoramas.

First, the huts. Nearest is the **Cabane de la Tsa** (2607m), a long, single-storey building on a rocky spur at the base of the Pointe des Genevois to the northeast of the village; reached by a steep path in 1½hrs. Owned by the Societé des Guides du Val d'Hérens, it has 50 places and is manned from the end of June to mid-September (tel 027 283 18 68). Since the backing wall of the Grandes Dents (consisting of Veisivi, Perroc, Genevois, Tsalion and the Aiguille de la Tsa) contains a wealth of rock routes, this is very much a climber's hut, although the approach path will give walkers decent exercise and a rather fine view when they arrive.

Plan Bertol below the Cabane de Bertol

Descending from Cabane de Bertol with the Haut Glacier d'Arolla as a background

Few huts anywhere have a more spectacular location than the **Cabane de Bertol**. Literally perched on a slender ridge above the Col de Bertol at 3311m, it is understandably popular, for it practically guarantees a memorable night's lodging. Built by the Neuchâteloise section of the SAC, it can accommodate 80 people and is staffed from mid-March to mid-May, and from mid-June until the end of September (www.bertol.ch). With glaciers on either side of the ridge (admittedly there's not much left now of the Bertol glacier), the final climb to the hut is via a series of exposed ladders – about 4½hrs from Arolla. Dorothy Pilley (in *Climbing Days*) repeats a famous story about a climber who fell into the bergschrund just below the cabane. His shouts alerted the guardian who emerged from the hut and looked everywhere – except in the bergschrund. Seeing no-one he went back inside, but the cries continued, and eventually the guardian became convinced that his hut was haunted. Fortunately a rope of climbers approached, heard the cries for help and fished the victim out, unhurt.

Standing on the right bank lateral moraine of the Haut Glacier d'Arolla at the foot of the Bouquetins ridge, **Refuge des Bouquetins** (2980m) has an impressive view of the ice cliffs of Mont Brulé on the frontier to the south, and of L'Evêque's rock walls seen across the glacier. Reached in 3½hrs from Arolla, the hut is located just off the skier's Haute Route (not the classic mountaineer's summer route which uses Col de Bertol) where it crosses between Col de l'Evêque and Col du Mont Brulé, while the Tour of the Matterhorn (see 2:10) uses Col Collon to the southwest in order to pass into Italy. With 28 dorm places, the refuge has only an emergency telephone, and no permanent guardian, although there's sometimes one in residence for a week or two during the main summer season (www.cas-valdejoux.ch).

Cabane des Vignettes (3160m) is perhaps the best known, and certainly one of the most frequented of the Arolla huts, and is another of those that enjoys a spectacular location (www.section-monte-rosa.ch). Airily positioned on a rock spur close to the Col des Vignettes, and gained in about 3½hrs from the village via the Pièce glacier, it is used for the ascent of Pigne d'Arolla, Mont Collon and L'Evêque, among others, as well as by

Haute Route skiers. Owned by the Monte Rosa section of the SAC, it has 125 dorm places and a resident guardian from mid-March until late May, and from July to mid-September.

Although **Cabane des Dix** has already been mentioned in the Val d'Hérémence sub-chapter (2:5), it is worth noting here as it is often visited by Arolla-based walkers on a long but rewarding there-and-back day hike, crossing the Pas de Chèvres ladders in one direction, and Col de Riedmatten on the return – or vice versa.

That only leaves **Cabane des Aiguilles Rouges**, which lies northwest of Arolla under the crest of the Aiguilles Rouges d'Arolla and its small glacier at 2810m. A comfortable hut with an easterly outlook to the Grandes Dents wall, and south to Mont Collon, the hut was built in 1948 by the Academic Alpine Club of Geneva, has 80 places and is fully staffed from mid-March to mid-April, and from late June to the end of September (tel 027 283 16 49). From Arolla an enjoyable 2½hr approach walk first visits the photogenic chalets of **Pra Gra**, then goes up into a wild region of boulder slopes and gravel beds before slanting roughly northward on a rocky contour. An alternative approach from Arolla via Lac Bleu is much steeper and takes about 3hrs.

So much for Arolla's huts, what of the peaks that make such an attractive arc around the village? If it's rock climbing or scrambling you're after, the Grandes Dents (Veisivi-Bertol) chain has plenty of attractions. The **Aiguille de la Tsa** is its most conspicuous feature, and when tackled from the Bertol Hut via the Mont Miné and Aiguille glaciers, gives a relatively short 80m PD+ climb on the East Face as its *voie normale*. However, the aiguille gives a much longer challenge when tackled from the west where the top of the pinnacle is some 700m above the remnant Tsa glacier, but both the SW and NW Face are subject to stonefall.

A little north of the Aiguille de la Tsa, the 3589m **Dent de Tsalion** has a West Ridge that gives a recommended climb of about 640m at AD (IV+), usually tackled from Cabane de la Tsa. Further north still, the highest point of the ridge is the 3677m **Pointe des Genevois** whose *voie normale* by the South Ridge (AD-) offers a scrambling experience with some big drops to add a certain frisson of adventure. And then there's the **traverse of the ridge** from Pointe des Genevois to the 3675m Dent de Perroc, the central summit of the Grandes Dents ridge; a fine outing graded AD+ (IV) taking about 1½hrs from summit to summit.

Moated on the west by the Haut Glacier d'Arolla and on the east by the Tsa de Tsan and Mont Miné glaciers, the 3838m **Bouquetins** crest should not be confused with the ridge which bears the same name stretching between the Grand Cornier and Pigne de la Lé above the Zinal valley (2:8). While the North, South and Central summits all have routes of varying degrees of interest, it is the long and committing **South to North Traverse** of the group, made famous by Joseph Georges with I A Richards in 1925, that is the major expedition here. Beginning at the Bouquetins Hut, the usual way is to gain the Col du Mont Brulé and work northwards over successive summits, gendarmes and couloirs, until finally reaching Cabane de Bertol after upwards of 12–13hrs of climbing. The overall grade is reckoned to be TD- but with moves of V- and V. Anyone attempting this epic traverse should consider travelling light and be very fit and competent, or be prepared to bivouac en route.

Mont Collon (3637m) is without question the most conspicuous of all Arolla's peaks, and is virtually its symbol, with the ice-crusted 1100m North Face seeming to block the head of the valley. It's very much an island peak, connected only by a rib on its south side to the elegant and higher fin of L'Evêque. Arthur Cust, who made the first ascent of Mont Collon's West Ridge, once famously said: 'Mont Collon is nothing but the braggart buttress of a ridge whose supreme point is L'Evêque.' That sentiment would be disputed by many today. On all other flanks glaciers effectively keep it aloof from its neighbours. The relatively short West Ridge carries the *voie normale* with an AD climb of 3½hrs from the Vignettes Hut, while the complex SE Face, with its choice of TD/ED routes, is tackled from a base at the Bouquetins refuge. The North Face is massive, and built upon buttresses it holds a number of different routes, the first climbed as early as 1890 by J Hopkinson, with A and J Maître. Their route was by the Left-Hand Spur, an 1100m climb now graded D/D+.

If Mont Collon is Arolla's symbol, the nearby (3796m) ★ **Pigne d'Arolla** is one of its most graceful, with a long plume-like snow crest reaching up to a summit which, though the easiest of the district's higher peaks, rewards with one of the most extensive panoramic views in all the Alps. Whether you can see the Mediterranean, as is claimed, or

The alp hamlet of Pra Gra, backed by Mont Collon

not, you should be able to make out most of the Pennine and Bernese Alps, as well as Mont Blanc, the Gran Paradiso and Grivola in the Graians. 'It is hard for me to imagine how any one can look up at the Pigne … and not long to share its outlook on the world,' said R L G Irving in *The Romance of Mountaineering*. The Pigne not only makes a must-climb summit for the aspirant alpinist, it is regularly visited by ski tourers on the Haute Route, can be climbed on snowshoes and, regrettably, is popular with heli-skiers who are dropped off on the summit to enjoy an exhilarating descent to the valley without undergoing the effort of getting to the top under their own steam. First climbed via the West Flank in 1865 by Horace Walker, A W Moore and Jakob Anderegg, the *voie normale* today is from the Vignettes Hut via the ESE Flank (F) in 2hrs, and is often continued with a traverse (AD) that takes in Mont Blanc de Cheilon and a descent to the Dix Hut (see 2:5).

The last of our mountain groups to be briefly visited from Arolla are those of the ⊕ **Aiguilles Rouges d'Arolla**. Forming part of the valley's extreme west wall, with Lac des Dix below them on the other side, the saw-tooth crest is more than 3km long from Col des Ignes to the Cols de Darbonneire. Although there are only three main summits, certain sections bristle with gendarmes; 'the pinnacles of the Aiguilles Rouges are legion,' said Dorothy Pilley who made an aborted traverse in 1921. It is the traverse of this ridge, however, that is the ultimate expedition here. It's a long and exacting outing (12hrs) with an overall grade of D, but with a few individual pitches of IV+ and V. However, northeast of this ridge ⊗ **Mont de l'Etoile** (3370m) provides an uncomplicated and easy ascent (F) of less than 2hrs from the Aiguilles Rouges Hut, as does its neighbour the 3490m ⊗ **Pointe de Vouasson** which rises northwest of the Darbonneire cols; both summits being superb vantage points.

Ferpècle and the Dent Blanche

The Ferpècle stem of Val d'Hérens which branches southeast above Les Haudères is considerably shorter than its Val d'Arolla counterpart, and is blocked in the south by a great sweep of glaciers headed by the Tête Blanche, Wandfluehorn and, towering above to the southeast like a massive cone, the splendid Dent Blanche – one of the truly great peaks of the Alps.

The road out of Les Haudères angles up the wooded hillside above the village heading north almost as far as La Sage, then in a tight hairpin doubles back to **La Forclaz** (1744m), built on a terrace catching the sun. Beyond this small village the road continues to **Ferpècle**, which has the Hotel Col d'Hérens, open mid-June to mid-October. From here a pleasant walk of about 1½hrs among meadows and pines leads to **Bricola** (2415m), a grassy alp belvedere overlooking the Ferpècle glacier below a cascade of seracs falling away from the Plateau de Hérens, which lies between Tête Blanche and Wandfluehorn. At the crest of this plateau lies the 3462m **Col d'Hérens**, one of the oldest glacier passes in the Pennine Alps, and a way for mountaineers and ski tourers to cross via the Stockji glacier to the Zmutt valley and Zermatt. Meanwhile, across the Ferpècle glacier rises the dark mass of Mont Miné, and beyond that the Grandes Dents wall. But above and behind the alp it is the Dent Blanche that makes its presence felt most effectively.

The Dent Blanche is a serious objective for the climber, and offers no ground for the walker, but two further outings above Bricola are worth a walker's attention. The first takes an hour or so to reach the moraine crest between the Manzettes and Ferpècle glaciers; the other goes up to a combe below the West Face of the Dent Blanche in a little less than an hour. Both are rewarding for their wild, high mountain points of view.

Two huts serve climbers on the Dent Blanche. On the north side of the mountain, close to the glacier pass after which it is named, the stone-built **Bivouac au Col de la Dent Blanche** (3540m), owned by the Jaman section of the SAC, has places for 15, an emergency telephone, but no guardian, and can be reached in 5–5½hrs from Ferpècle (www.cas-jaman.ch). The other is located on the south side of the peak on a 3507m rocky knoll at the base of a short spur, with the Plateau d'Hérens and Wandflue stretching away to the south. Also owned by the Jaman section of the SAC, **Cabane de la Dent Blanche** is reached in about 6hrs from Ferpècle; it has 55 places and is permanently manned from July to the middle of September (www.cas-jaman.ch).

The 4356m ☻ ☆ **Dent Blanche** is an obvious goal for the experienced alpinist. Not only is it one of the élite 4000ers, but it's a mountain with a history of its own (see box), a peak with four great ridges that endow it with graceful proportions and no shortage of challenges. The easiest and most popular route is by the South Ridge (the Wandfluegrat), chosen for the first ascent in 1862 and now graded AD with pitches of IV/IV- (4–6hrs from the Dent Blanche cabane). But the Dent Blanche is a big mountain with more rock than snow or ice to climb, and other features tackled from the Ferpècle side are the West Ridge (Ferpècle Arête; D+), on which Owen Glynne Jones was killed in 1899; the NW Face, NNW Ridge and the NNE Face (various routes graded TD/ED); all of which are serious and committing.

Other faces and ridges of the mountain are approached from either the Cabane Mountet at the head of Val d'Anniviers (2:8), or from the Schönbiel Hut at the confluence of the Schönbiel and Zmutt glaciers (2:10).

DENT BLANCHE: 'THE GRANDEST MOUNTAIN IN THE ALPS'

When he gazed north from the Dent d'Hérens in 1863, William Hall proclaimed the Dent Blanche to be 'without exception the grandest mountain in the Alps'.

Examining the mountain from Col Durand, Geoffrey Winthrop Young spoke of 'the ranked precipices of the Dent Blanche, assembling symmetrically against the sky into a single ice-tipped spearhead'. Whymper was more prosaic, saying little of its beauty, but remarking that it was 'a mountain of exceptional difficulty'.

On 12 July 1862 T S Kennedy made his first attempt to climb the Dent Blanche with Peter Taugwalder and his son as guides, but after the older Taugwalder almost fell and lost his nerve when they were high on the South Ridge, the attempt was abandoned. Kennedy returned six days later, this time with William Wigram and the guides J B Croz and Johann Krönig. In very cold and windy conditions they fought their way up the ridge, and at last reached the summit, where they noted the temperature to be -20°F. Making the third ascent in 1865 by the SW Flank, Whymper also experienced intense cold on the mountain, and his guides were lucky to escape with only slightly frostbitten fingers.

The ENE Ridge (the Viereselsgrat) separates the Durand and Grand Cornier glaciers, emerging from the ice of the former at around 3000m. Setting out from the Mountet Hut on 11 August 1882, J Stafford Anderson, George Baker and the guides Aloys Pollinger and Ulrich Almer took 12hrs to fight their way up 1300m of very difficult climbing to reach the summit at 3pm, whereupon Almer commented: '*Wir sind vier Esel*' (We are four asses) – hence the name by which the ridge is known today.

The same year (1882) the Ferpècle Arête (West Ridge) was *descended* by Aloys Pollinger and his party, but seven years later Pollinger returned to make its first ascent leading his client Walter Gröbli. This same ridge was the scene of a tragic accident that occurred on 28 August 1899, when Owen Glynne Jones (one of the finest rock climbers of his day), was attempting the route with F W Hill and their guides. One of the guides, Elias Furrer, slipped, knocking Jones and Clemenz Zurbriggen from their stance. As they fell Jean Vuigner, the third guide, was also dislodged, the combined weight breaking the rope between Vuigner and Hill. Jones and the guides all fell to their deaths, leaving Hill as the sole survivor on the mountain. With just a short remnant of rope and his ice axe, Hill continued to the summit, then began to descend the South Ridge, but was stopped by a snowstorm above the Grand Gendarme. After a forced bivouac, he was at last able to resume the descent at noon next day, got lost on the way down, but finally made it to Zermatt 48hrs after the accident had happened. His was an epic escape.

The NNW Ridge (often referred to as the North Ridge) is the shortest and hardest on the mountain, and is broken by a formidable rock barrier at mid-height. In 1926 it was descended – mostly by abseil – over two days by Zinal guides Marcel Savioz and Jean Genoud with their client, M Kropf. Two years later I A Richards and Dorothy Pilley made the first *ascent* of this ridge during their honeymoon, taking the brothers Joseph and Antoine Georges as their guides. It was a difficult and taxing climb recorded in some detail in *Climbing Days*: 'a detached pinnacle clinging to the edge of slabs … a crack which passed at its critical point out of sight into the unknown … An occasional pinch-hold was a luxury.' In one place Richards and his bride had to share 'a nook the size of a dinner-plate, with one handhold' between them. Antoine emerged over a bulge to see the couple clinging to the solitary hold, and exclaimed: '*Ah, les amourex!*' At the crux it took the party almost 3½hrs to climb just 60m, and they did not reach the summit until 5pm. This somewhat fierce and dangerous mixed route is now graded TD, with individual pitches of up to V+.

La Sage and ways east

Above Les Haudères on the east flank of Val d'Hérens, the road goes up to La Sage and continues only as far as Villa. **La Sage** (1667m) is a delightful little village of stone-roofed chalets and *mazots* set upon a slope of meadowland backed by steep pinewoods. Reached by postbus from Les Haudères, it has a café, foodstore and tourist office (www.evolene-region.ch). For accommodation there's Hotel de la Sage (www.hoteldelasage.com); Café-Restaurant L'Ecuriel, which has 40 dormitory places (tel 027 283 11 28); and *chambres d'hôtes* with 19 beds – apply for the latter at the small foodstore at the entrance to **Villa**.

On the walling ridge above these two small villages, several walker's passes rightly suggest entertaining ways over the mountains to Val de Moiry (2:7). The easiest and most popular of these is the ◐ **Col de Torrent** at 2916m. Gained by a steady 3–3½hr walk over rolling pastures above Villa, this is a scenic outing that is recommended whether or not your plan is to continue down into Val de Moiry, where Grimentz may be reached by a continuing trail in a further 3hrs or so from the col. The panorama from the col is tremendous. Retrospective views to the south and west reveal the Tête Blanche, Mont Miné, Grande Dent de Veisivi, Pigne d'Arolla, Mont Blanc de Cheilon, Grand Combin, Aiguilles Rouges d'Arolla, Rosablanche and, far off, Mont Blanc. Turning to the east Lac des Autannes sparkles in a green plateau a little over 200m below the col; beyond that the jade-green Lac de Moiry is caught

Tiny pool below Col du Tsaté

in the deep trough of Val de Moiry, and above and beyond the ridge that walls that valley, Weisshorn, Schalihorn and Pointe Sud de Moming can all be seen.

For an even more extensive panoramic view, the easy ascent of the ⊗ **Sasseneire** (3254m) which rises along the ridge northwest of Col de Torrent, can be made in a little under an hour. From the summit Dent Blanche, which is unseen from the col, dominates the southern view, while to the north it is said that the heights of the Jura are often visible beyond the Bernese Alps.

North of the Sasseneire, **Pas de Lona** (2787m) gives walkers a direct link between Evolène (Villa) and Grimentz, while a third crossing point, the 2868m **Col du Tsaté** lies above and to the east of La Sage, and is the choice of Walker's Haute Route trekkers heading for Cabane de Moiry (5–5½hrs from La Sage to the hut).

Col de Bréona (2915m) is located a short distance southeast of Col du Tsaté, but is much less popular than its neighbour, except as a means of gaining the summit of the 3159m **Couronne de Bréona** (PD+) in about 2hrs from the col. The SE Ridge of the Couronne drops down to the **Col de la Couronne**, a 2987m pass which a study of the map would suggest is the most direct crossing point between Val d'Hérens and Cabane de Moiry, but seriously loose rocks below the col make this route one to avoid.

2:7 VAL DE MOIRY

North of the Dent Blanche the summit of Grand Cornier forms the meeting point of three valleys: Hérens, Moiry and Anniviers. Its NW Ridge extends by way of an arthritic kink as far as Pointe de Bricola, while breaking away to the north of that ridge is the projection of the Bouquetins whose collective summits form the east rim of the Moiry glacier's *névé* plateau. To all intents and purposes this wedge of ice under the Grand Cornier may be seen as the head of Val de Moiry, the short southwestern tributary of Val d'Anniviers.

It's a valley of two parts. The lower reaches around Grimentz (about 23km from Sierre) consist of steep green slopes of forest and meadow, with the ski industry having laced the west flank above the village with cables and tows. But as you work

2:7 VAL DE MOIRY

VAL DE MOIRY

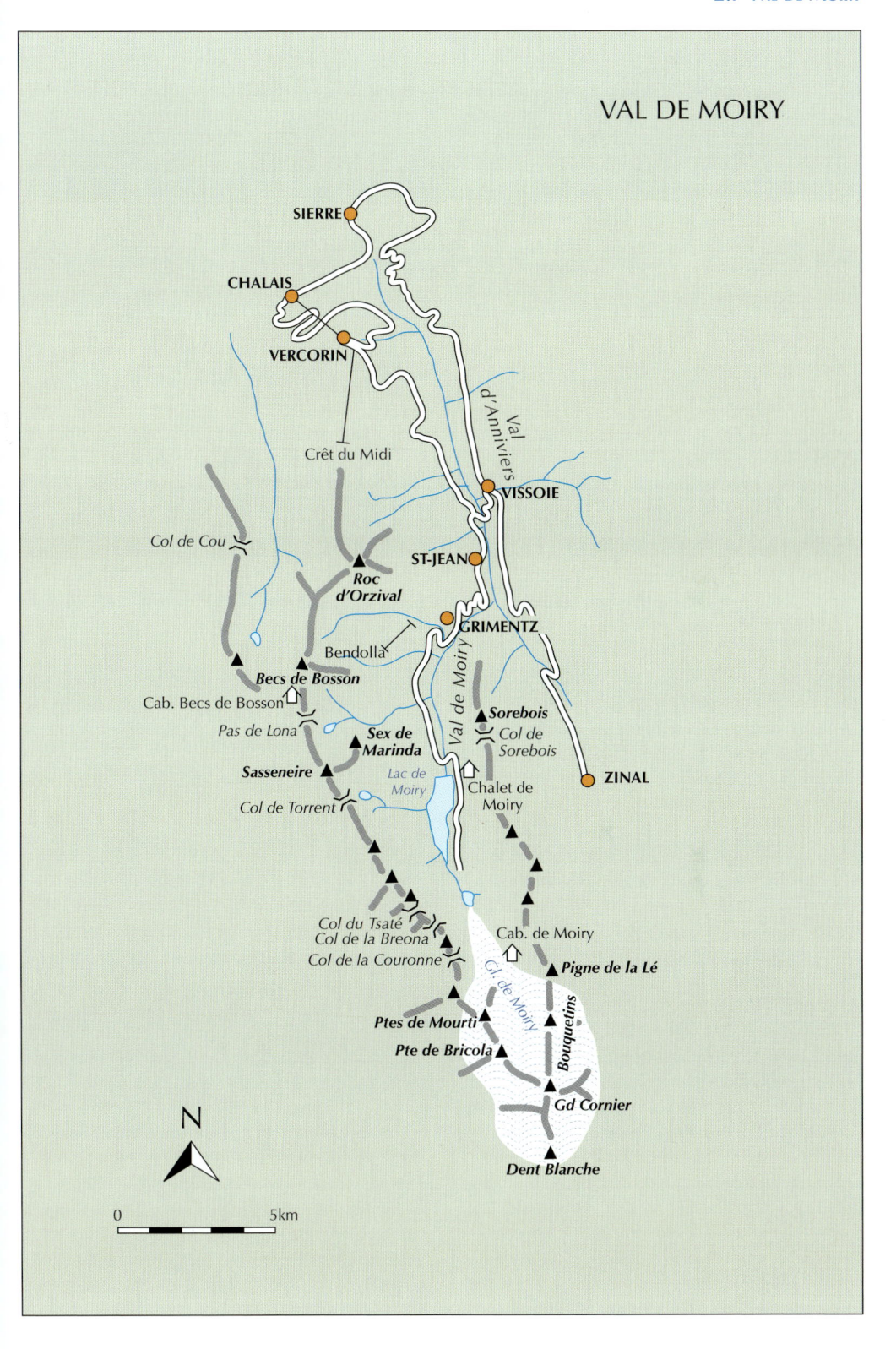

133

Walkers on the moraine wall below Cabane de Moiry

southward the valley narrows further, becomes even more steeply walled and is then blocked by the Moiry barrage. The road snakes up towards that barrage, goes through a tunnel and emerges on the edge of the dam in the upper part of the valley. Here the east wall rises abruptly, but the west side of the valley opens out to fold gently up and over pastures to a ridge that only becomes more rocky and challenging towards the south. And there, at the far end of the reservoir, stretches the Moiry glacier, a shrinking tongue of ice spilling from an icefall that deserves closer inspection. For that we need to visit Cabane de Moiry, a fine SAC hut set upon a rock promontory at 2825m.

A narrow path goes along the east bank moraine crest, drops into the ablation trough, then climbs a rocky slope, aided in places by chains and fixed cables, to emerge at the hut 1½–2hrs from the roadhead at the southern end of the lake. The recently enlarged **Cabane de Moiry** has 96 places, and is permanently staffed from the end of June to the end of September (www.cabane-moiry.ch). Having a direct view of the icefall, it overlooks the lower glacier that is receding at an alarming rate. In 1864 A W Moore came through the valley to attempt the Grand Cornier, and was greatly impressed by this glacier, which he described as 'a noble ice-stream, comparable to any other in the Alps'. He continued:

Between the Pigne de l'Allee on the east, and a spur running down from the highest peak of the Zatalana [the Pointe de Mourti] on the west, is a tremendous ice-fall of great height and very steep. The lower part of this extends completely from one side of the glacier to the other ... Below this great cascade of séracs, the ice is as compact and level as above it is steep and dislocated. Indeed, I never saw an ice-fall confined within such plainly defined limits, or terminate so abruptly.'

(The Alps in 1864)

Above the hut to the southeast the 3396m **Pigne de la Lé** (Moore's Pigne de l'Allee) is an excellent viewpoint easily reached by way of the Col du Pigne and the NNW Ridge (PD) in 1½–2hrs. South of that stretches the crusty **Bouquetins** ridge whose highest point is at 3627m. Again, of no great difficulty when tackled from the Moiry Hut, a traverse of the group of summits from north to south is graded PD. But difficulty of route need not be the only criterion by which to judge an outing, and the Bouquetins is a good example of this. During his 1864 visit, Moore failed in his attempt to climb the Grand Cornier, but what he had to say of the scene which he surveyed from the Bouquetins ridge is worth repeating:

> Our annoyance at missing the larger game was quickly forgotten in the contemplation of a view which for grandeur and interest is without parallel in my Alpine experience. I have seen many more extensive prospects, but extent is but a single and by no means the most important feature of a panorama, and I cannot call to mind having been on any other point ... from which I have had so perfect a view of so many elevated summits within a reasonable distance.

And he goes on to list practically every major summit of the Pennine Alps except those of Matterhorn and Dent d'Hérens, which were hidden behind the Dent Blanche. In support of his appreciation of the view his guide, Christian Almer also ranked it as 'the finest that even he had ever seen'.

Had he made it to the **Grand Cornier** (3961m), perhaps Moore would have been even more ecstatic with the panorama from this summit, which is another 300m higher than that of the Bouquetins. It was climbed only a year after Moore and Almer had turned back, but this time it was Whymper who claimed the first ascent with the same Christian Almer among his guides. Their route was via the East Ridge, starting from Zinal shortly after 2am and reaching the summit at 12.30pm – a route now usually begun from the Mountet Hut. However, the Moiry Hut is closer and offers a more convenient base, the normal ascent route from here tackling the NW Ridge (AD), with 3½hrs being a good time – about half that needed from Cabane du Mountet.

On the west side of the upper glacier **Pointe de Bricola** (3658m), the **Dent de Rosses** (3613m) and the twin peaks of the **Pointes de Mourti** (3529m; 3564m) are all worthwhile objectives from the Moiry Hut, offering routes in the PD/AD range.

Walks in Val de Moiry

Being accessible by postbus, and with parking places at either end of the reservoir, Lac de Moiry makes an obvious attraction. Paths cut along both flanks of the valley, visit small tarns, walker's cols, viewpoints and minor summits. Although Grimentz with its hotels is not far away, for those who would choose to make a base here for a day or two, simple *dortoir* accommodation is available just above the dam at the Chalet du Barrage (2350m) (www.moiryresto.ch). With room for 26 and basic self-catering facilities, it's open from June to October; meals are available at the café/restaurant at the dam, where enquiries should be addressed.

- Almost 600m above the barrage **Col de Sorebois** (2840m) is gained by an obvious zigzag path in little more than 1½hrs, to be greeted by a splendid panorama of high mountains dominated by the Weisshorn. Although this is the way taken by trekkers moving on to Zinal, to the left of the col the 2895m **Corne du Sorebois** is only 5mins walk away, and the view from there is even better.

- A 4–5hr walk publicised locally as the **Haut Tour du Lac** makes a circuit of Lac de Moiry, not along its shoreline, but by contouring across high pastures. It's a visual treat, not especially challenging, but worth giving a day to by any walker based in the district.

- **Lac des Autannes** is a beautiful mountain lake spread across a pastoral basin below Col de Torrent on the west flank of the valley at 2686m. Reached by an easy walk of 1½–2hrs, it would be feasible to continue up to **Col de Torrent** in another 40mins, and from there head up the right-hand ridge to the **Sasseneire**, an uncomplicated summit of 3254m previously mentioned in 2:6 and reached in less than an hour from the col.

- Another modest peak worth the attention of walkers is the 2906m **Sex de Marinda**, a rocky, round-topped summit overlooking Grimentz, and gained from Lac de Moiry by a path that crosses the col of Basset de Lona on the mountain's West Ridge. The walk could be continued from the col down through the Lona pastures (a lovely basin littered with tarns) and on to Grimentz itself.

- And then there's a 4hr walk from the Moiry dam which goes by way of the Basset de Lona, Lac de Lona and Pas de Lona to reach **Cabane des Becs de Bosson**, a privately owned hut at 2983m just below the summit of the mountain after which it is named. With room for 50, it is staffed from Christmas to mid-April, and from

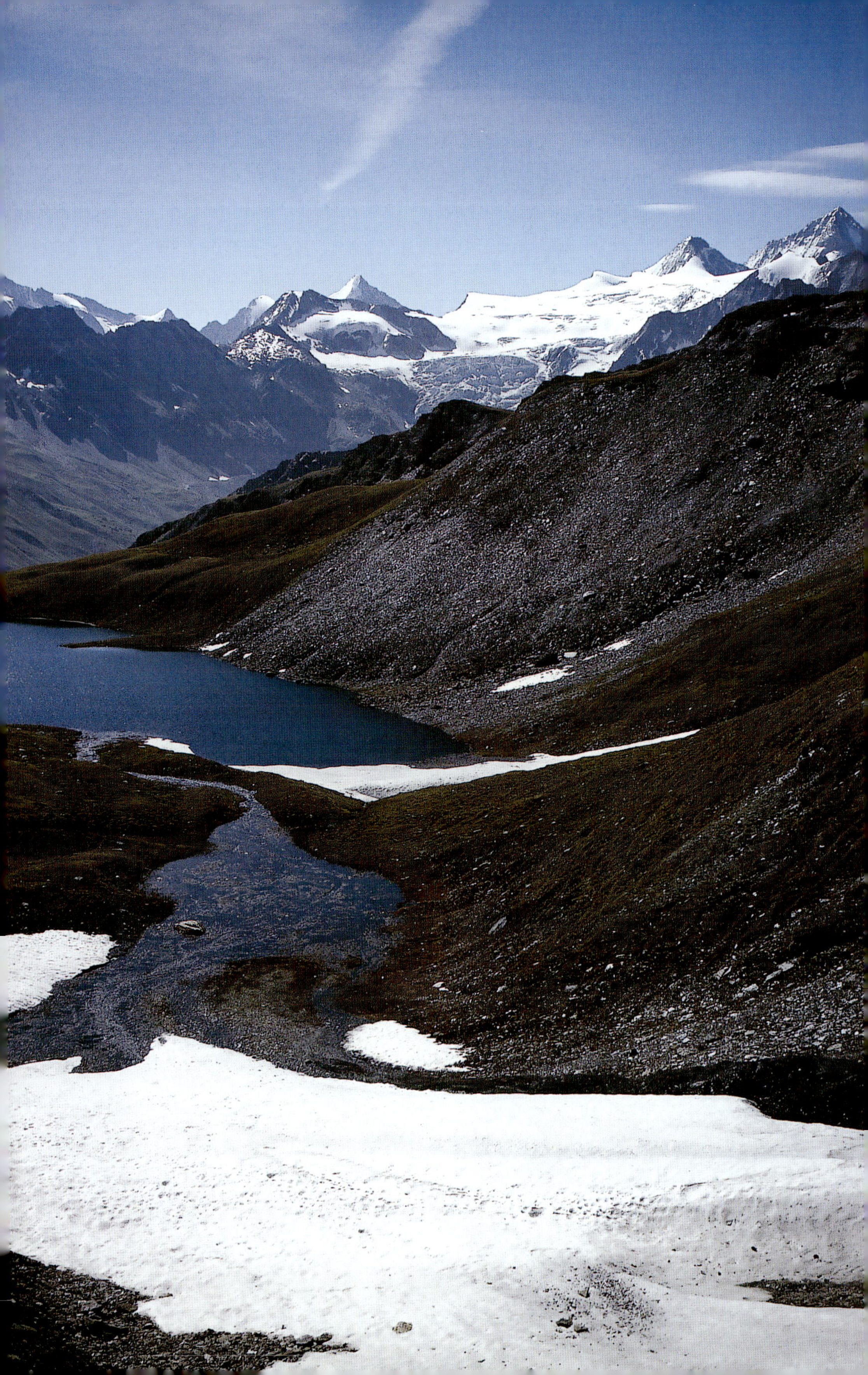

the end of June to the end of September – reservations essential (tel 027 281 39 40).
- Finally, a pleasant walk of about 1½–2hrs takes you downvalley to ⬤ **Grimentz**. The path begins at the western end of the dam, twists down a densely vegetated hillside, then crosses the road to a meadow and woodland trail. Meanwhile, an alternative and higher route contours along the western hillside among alpenrose and damp meadows rich in alpine flowers, and eventually leads to the **Bendolla** alp (2112m) where a gondola could be taken down to Grimentz. This trail is used by the Tour of the Val d'Anniviers (see 2:8).
- **Grimentz** (1572m) more or less guards the entrance to Val de Moiry. Once a simple village of dark-timbered chalets and *mazots*, it has expanded to attract skiers in winter, with gondolas that swing up to Bendolla for north and east-facing runs. In summer the village is noted for the troughs of flowers that appear to grace every window and balcony; it has six hotels, a number of apartments, *chambres d'hôtes*, all-year camping, and tourist information (www.grimentz.ch). From here, or rather just below the village, a forest path curves round the lower slopes of the Corne du Sorebois and into the Val d'Anniviers.

2:8 VAL D'ANNIVIERS

To the general tourist Val d'Anniviers remains largely unknown. It has no resort to match neighbouring Zermatt or Saas Fee, for example, and its mountains – though among the most dramatic in the Alps – are mountaineer's mountains, their names conjuring visions of splendour to the climber, but passing unremarked by those unschooled in alpine history. Yet the valley is, to put it quite simply, magnificent. Irving pointed out that it shares with Zermatt's valley 'the greatest row of climbers' peaks in the Alps'. In his *Walking in the Alps*, Hubert Walker wrote of it with unbridled enthusiasm: 'I would say that not only is Val d'Anniviers far and away the finest valley on the Swiss side of the Pennine Alps, but also the cirque at its head is much grander even than the head of the neighbouring valley of Zermatt.' Those who know the valley well will no doubt endorse that view.

◀ *Lac des Autannes and Val de Moiry*

Approached from Sierre, the rich visual heritage of Val d'Anniviers is concealed at first by a narrow gorge which forces the road to writhe in coils up its east flank, then having gained a toehold (so to speak) on the steep wall, it sneaks along a ledge in truly dramatic fashion, until at last the gradient eases and the valley begins to open out on the approach to **Vissoie** (1204m).

It is here that a side road, served by postbus, cuts up the eastern hillside in numerous hairpins to **St-Luc** (1655m) and **Chandolin** (1920m). The first of these small resorts spreads across the hillside facing south and west, with four hotels and a funicular serving Tignousa at 2180m where there's additional accommodation available, and nearby stands the F-X Bagnoud Observatory (tourist information www.saint-luc.ch). The second, Chandolin, has a few shops, post office, apartments and hotels, and a tourist office in the village square where the postbus terminates (www.chandolin.ch). With mechanical lifts linking the slopes above them, both St-Luc and Chandolin offer a modest amount of downhill and cross-country skiing with some 75km of pistes, but in summer the walking opportunities seem unlimited.

Above Chandolin, and reached by footpath from the village square in just 20mins, **Cabane d'Illhorn** (2145m) is a charming, atmospheric hut set on the edge of pinewoods. Now privately owned, it was originally an SAC refuge, and in it the panelled dormitories and dining room conjure visions of the past. With 32 places, hot showers and meals provision (tel 027 475 11 78), it makes a good base for a few days of a walking holiday, or from which to embark on a classic 5½–6hr panoramic walk to Zinal, or to begin the Tour du Val d'Anniviers (see box) which shares that classic trail on its first stage.

Northeast of the hut the conical ⬤ **Illhorn** (2716m) is the northernmost summit on the valley's walling ridge. Gained by an uncomplicated route via the 2544m Pas d'Illsee in 2hrs, its situation is such that the line of the Bernese Alps across the Rhône valley is seen in a single undisturbed glance; Les Diablerets, Wildhorn, Wildstrubel and Bietschhorn being prominent in that view.

Lying a little less than 200m below the Pas d'Illsee on its eastern side, the **Illsee** tarn makes an obvious destination for a walk, while the 2790m ⬤ **Schwarzhorn**, which overlooks that tarn from its position east of the Illhorn Hut, can be climbed by a marked route in 2½hrs. However, the most obvious summit temptation from Cabane d'Illhorn

The Swiss Alps – Chapter 2: Pennine Alps

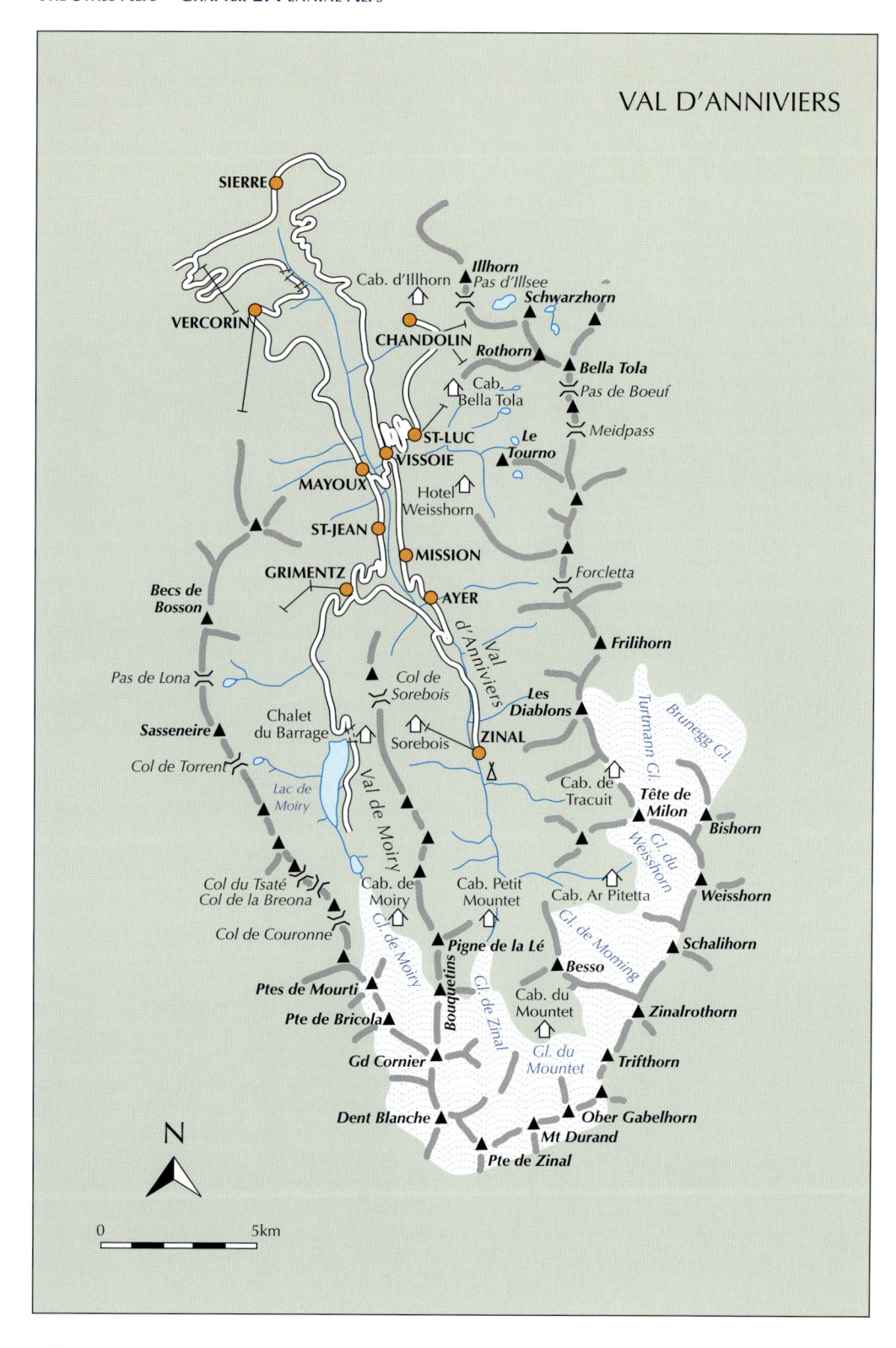

is that of the well-known 3025m ☆ **Bella Tola**, a vantage point much loved by the Victorians, which stands southeast of the hut. There's nothing difficult in the climb, for a good path leads all the way to the summit in 3½–4hrs. For such an easy ascent the 360° panorama from this modest mountain is one of the best and most extensive in Switzerland, with (it is claimed) some 250 peaks on show. Baedeker called it 'an admirable and favourite point of view … [which] embraces the whole of the Bernese and Valaisian Alps'.

The path of ascent comes onto a connecting ridge between Bella Tola and the 2998m **Rothorn**, so another summit may be collected in the same outing, while instead of returning to the Illhorn Hut, walkers planning to move on eastward, could descend Bella Tola's SE Ridge to the **Pas de Boeuf** (2897m) and from there drop into the Turtmanntal (see 2:9).

Directly below Bella Tola, and set among pastureland just 20mins from the Tignousa funicular, the cosy **Cabane Bella Tola** (2346m) has 92 places and is manned from mid-June until the end of September, and from mid-December until the middle of April (www.funiluc.ch). The view towards the head of the valley is very fine, there's good walking country easily accessible from it, and the mountain after which it is named can be climbed in just 2½hrs.

🚩 ☆ TOUR DU VAL D'ANNIVIERS

A three–four day trek, starting at Cabane d'Illhorn and ending at Vercorin on the west slope of the valley, makes a recommended shorter version of the locally publicised TVA which begins and ends in Sierre in the Rhône valley. Given sufficient time, the tour described below could be extended to include the ascent of Bella Tola, a visit to Cabane du Mountet at the head of the valley, and a diversion to Cabane de Moiry overlooking the Moiry icefall (see 2:7). However, the basic route as outlined makes a very fine trek in its own right. For further information contact the Association du Tour du Val d'Anniviers, Office du Tourisme de Sierre, Case postale 706, CH-3960 Sierre (www.anniviers.ch).

Day 1: Just above **Cabane d'Illhorn** (2145m) a farm track takes the TVA round the hillside to join a balcony route blazed with the letter 'Z' (for Zinal). Used by the annual Sierre–Zinal marathon, this is a very scenic route with growing views of the valley's headwall. In its early stages it follows the Chemin Planétaire which has large models of the planets beside the trail, and in 2½hrs passes **Hotel Weisshorn** at 2337m (www.weisshorn.ch). Beyond this large Victorian hotel views become increasingly impressive, and 5½–6hrs after setting out the trail brings you down to **Zinal** (1675m) at the roadhead. Unless your plan is to trek next day to Cabane du Mountet under the valley's headwall (4½hrs), an alternative to staying in Zinal would be to continue for another 1½hrs to spend the night in **Cabane du Petit Mountet** built on the Zinal glacier's moraine wall at 2142m. Across the valley the Weisshorn's great West Face is in direct view.

Day 2: Assuming the previous night was spent at the Petit Mountet Hut, this 5½hr stage of the TVA climbs the grass-covered west slope of the valley to gain the pastures of Alp La Lé, then contours northwestward, with a couple of exposed sections safeguarded with fixed cable or chains. Less than 3hrs from Petit Mountet you reach the **Sorebois** cable car station where there's a restaurant, after which the route crosses and recrosses ski pistes on the way up to **Col de Sorebois** (2840m) on the ridge separating the upper Val d'Anniviers from Val de Moiry. A short (40min) descent on the west flank leads to the **Chalet du Barrage** (2300m) set just above the Moiry barrage, where there's dormitory accommodation (reservations essential) – see 2:7 for details. An alternative option would be to take a path heading south just above the *dortoir*. Making a traverse of the steep east slope of Val de Moiry above the reservoir, at the far end it climbs to **Cabane de Moiry** (2825m) in another 2hrs or so.

Day 3: From the Chalet du Barrage cross to the west side of the dam, then after descending a short distance, follow a trail across slopes of alpenrose, juniper and bilberry, and in a little over 2hrs come to the gondola lift station of Bendolla where refreshments are available. A series of tracks and footpaths progress the route northward, passing farms and weaving through woodland before descending a long slope to the lovely old village of **Vercorin** (1322m: 5hrs), from which you can descend to Sierre by bus, or by cable car to Chalais.

THE SWISS ALPS – CHAPTER 2: PENNINE ALPS

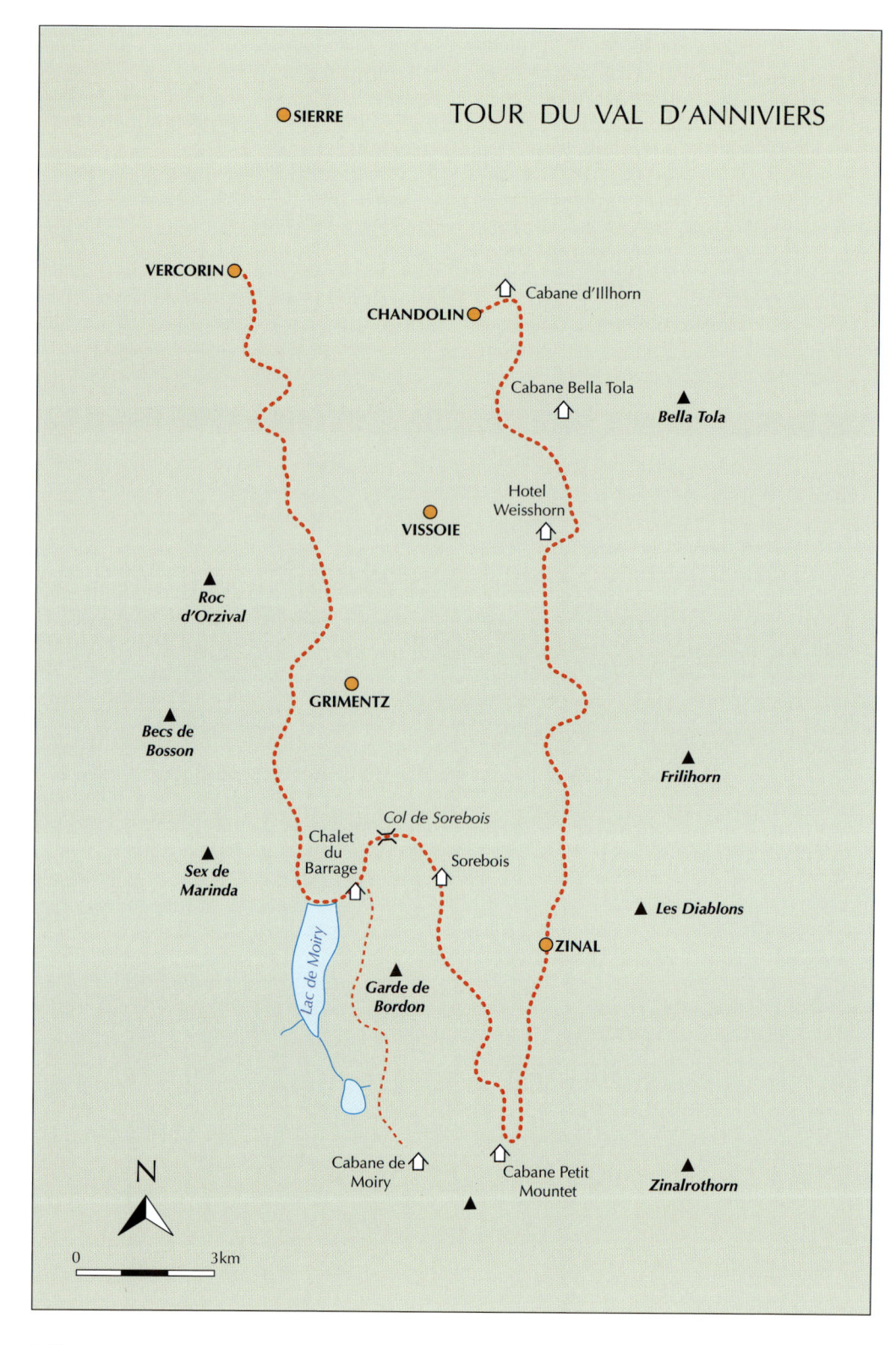

2:8 VAL D'ANNIVIERS

Heading south along the Tour du Val d'Anniviers, walkers are teased by the Zinalrothorn and rock peak of Besso

At Vissoie not only does a side road break away to climb to St-Luc and Chandolin, another descends to the Navisence river, then climbs the opposite bank to **Mayoux** (1205m) where it joins the west flank road which runs from Vercorin to Grimentz.

This road climbs out of the Rhône valley at Chalais, southwest of Sierre, in order to reach **Vercorin** (1322m), an attractive village of traditional houses set high above the Rhône but facing south. It has a couple of supermarkets, post office, bank, restaurants, a few hotels and pensions, and a tourist office (www.vercorin.ch). Rising above the village, a gondola lift takes visitors to the 2332m viewpoint of the Crêt du Midi from where footpaths suggest routes into the uninhabited little valley of the Rèche which lies to the west; or a ridgewalk heading south over the summit of La Brinta and on to the Roc d'Orzival above Grimentz.

Out of Vercorin the road continues southward along the left flank of the valley to Pinsec, Mayoux, St-Jean and Grimentz (see 2:7), and extends as we have seen as far as the southern end of Lac de Moiry. But as we have already looked at Val de Moiry; it's time to return to the main valley at Vissoie.

Val de Zinal

Leaving Vissoie the road has a fairly straight run, rising all the while to **Mission** (1312m) and **Ayer** (1419m) where you enter the upper valley, known here as Val de Zinal. Narrow and wooded at first, on reaching the final village just short of the roadhead, the valley opens again and every lover of fine scenery will realise they've arrived somewhere rather special. Big mountains gather round (Geoffrey Winthrop Young's 'perpetual semicircle of great Pennine peaks, rounding off the valley'); others remain concealed behind ridge spurs and buttresses, but you sense their presence and know they are within reach.

Zinal (1675m) is an unpretentious village and long-time mountaineering centre. Despite the addition of apartment blocks at the northern end, and ski slopes above to the west, it retains its basic character, and a stroll among the old dark-timbered chalets and *mazots* of the original village underline that fact. A few shops, post office and supermarket line the wide village square where the postbus terminates its journey from Sierre. Here will be found the small tourist office (www.zinal.ch) and next door the bureau des guides (www.anniviers-montagne.

141

ch). Zinal has a number of 1, 2 and 3-star hotels and pensions; dormitory accommodation is available at Auberge Alpina, and Auberge Les Liddes, and there's a campsite nearby on the southern edge of the village, Camping Les Rousses, open from June until the end of September. Dormitory accommodation is also available on the western hillside above the village at the Sorebois cableway station. Cabane de Sorebois has 35 places and is staffed from mid-December to mid-April, and from mid-June to the end of September.

🟢 ☆ Walks from Zinal

Zinal is, I repeat, a major mountaineering centre, but before we look at its mountains from a mountaineering perspective, it's worth getting to know them from the footpaths. As a base for a walking holiday Zinal comes close to Paradise; but you need to be mountain fit, for there are very few trails without their steep and challenging sections, and some of the best walks will be both long and demanding.

- One of the first to check out is located on the west flank of the valley, a high-level path which runs from the **Sorebois** cable car station southward to **Alp La Lé** and then back down to Zinal in about 4hrs or so. A steep forest path climbs to Sorebois, but as this 760m ascent can be made by cable car, you can save your energies for later. The way begins on a track, but soon gives way to a narrow and sometimes exposed path which has a rocky section to negotiate, and another which crosses an area of rockfall (both places safeguarded with fixed cables or chains) before mounting a grassy shoulder above Alp La Lé. Across the valley Les Diablons, Tête de Milon, Weisshorn, Schalihorn, Zinalrothorn, Besso, and a crowd of glaciers hanging like ice curtains over the cirque of Ar Pitetta – all these form but one section of an unforgettable panorama.

- In the walling ridge that contains Alp La Lé the 3141m Col du Pigne is a climber's pass linking Cabane de Moiry (2:7) with Val de Zinal. But below the col, perched on the left bank lateral moraine of the Zinal glacier, is the privately owned **Cabane du Petit Mountet** (2142m) (www.petitmountet.ch). The original hut was built in 1899, but this was destroyed by fire in June 2001. The present hut was built on the same site and opened in 2003. With a direct view of the Weisshorn to the east, and along the glacier to the glorious Ober Gabelhorn to the southeast, it has 40 places and is fully staffed from mid-June to mid-October (reservations essential). One of the easiest and most popular walks from Zinal visits the hut in less than 2hrs.

- Standing below Le Mammouth at the head of the valley overlooking the confluence of the Mountet and Zinal glaciers, **Cabane du Mountet** (2886m) is reached by an exhilarating walk of about 4–4½hrs from Zinal. A path climbs high above the east bank of the Zinal glacier across the flank of Besso (fixed cable aid in places), with Grand Cornier and Dent Blanche assuming Himalayan proportions on the opposite bank. On arrival at the hut the scene is truly awesome. Walker called the view 'one of the most glorious in all the Alps'. G D Abraham wrote of 'an almost unsurpassed prospect of stupendous peak, and glittering glacier'. The hut is the property of the Diablerets section of the SAC; it has 115 places and is staffed in April and May, and from late June to the end of September (www.cas-diablerets.ch). Climbers should note that the SE wall of 🔵 **Le Mammouth** above the hut offers a good selection of routes of 180–200m in length, at grades of up to V+.

- Another 'must-visit' hut is **Cabane d'Ar Pitetta** (or Arpitettaz; 2786m) which stands below the West Face of the Weisshorn in an ice-crowded cirque southeast of Zinal. The 4–4½hr approach walk via Alp d'Ar Pitetta (the 'little alp') makes a splendid outing, climbing first among shrubs and low-growing trees, then onto a bluff with the tiny Lac d'Ar Pitetta in the mouth of the cirque reflecting the shapes of Grand Cornier and Dent Blanche. In 1864 Whymper, Moore, Almer and Croz came here on their way to make a crossing of the Moming Pass, and spent a night at the Ar Pitetta alp in 'a hovel … roofed with rough slabs of slaty stone … surrounded by quagmires of ordure, and dirt of every description' (*Scrambles Amongst the Alps*). Deeper into the cirque and some 500m higher than the tarn, Cabane d'Ar Pitetta is a small, stone-built SAC hut awarded the Wilderness Prize in 1995 for its facilities, ecological standards and maintenance. With 32 places it is staffed from late June to the end of September (www.arpitettaz.ch).

Cabane d'Ar Pitetta

- A long ridge slanting round from Tête de Milon to the Pointe d'Ar Pitetta forms part of the north wall of the Ar Pitetta cirque. At the lower end of the ridge it makes a kink to the northwest to the wonderful viewpoint of the **Roc de la Vache** at 2581m. A very steep path rises over 900m from Zinal to gain the saddle of the Roc in about 2hrs, but the effort is rewarded by a stunning outlook to the head of the valley and a crowd of glistening snow- and ice-capped peaks. That view is rearranged and reordered as you descend to the Ar Pitetta alp, where other peaks and glaciers are revealed, among them 'that magnificent pair of giants the Weisshorn and Rothorn … seen in all their greatness' (Walker). A round trip from Zinal to the Roc, then down past the crumbling hut of Tsijière de la Vatse to the Ar Pitetta alp and back to Zinal, will take care of at least 5hrs, although with so much natural beauty on show the connoisseur will take much longer than that.
- **Cabane de Tracuit** (3256m) is yet another SAC hut that deserves to be visited by strong, fit walkers. Located on the ridge linking Diablon des Dames with the Tête de Milon, a little southeast of Col de Tracuit, it looks up to the Bishorn across the Turtmann glacier. It will take from 4–4½hrs to reach from Zinal on a steep and demanding path which climbs through the Combautanna pastures, then up and across the north flank of the cirque to gain the ridge close to the col. The hut has 110 places and is fully staffed from July to mid-September (www.cas-chaussy.ch).

☆ Climbs from Zinal

With so much on offer to the climber on both flanks of the valley and on its great headwall, it's difficult to know where to begin and where to stop. Perhaps the Grand Cornier is as good a place as any to start, and from there we will work counter-clockwise round the headwall, then northward along the east flank.

- Briefly studied from Val de Moiry (2:7), the 3961m **Grand Cornier** is a handsome mountain that suffers both by comparison with its better-known neighbour, Dent Blanche, and by failing (just) to reach the 4000m contour. It was first climbed in 1865 by Whymper with his guides Croz, Almer, and Biner by the

East Ridge, the route now taken as the *voie normale* (AD) from the Mountet Hut. Having studied the mountain in advance of his ascent, Whymper decided 'to have nothing to do with its northern side', and when you look up at it from the hut path which runs across the flanks of the Besso, it's easy to understand why, for the NE Face which extends into the Bouquetins ridge rises in a sudden upthrust from a much-broken cascade of ice that falls to the Zinal glacier in the valley bed. That face is swept by stonefall, while for the most part the Bouquetins glacier makes an unacceptably dangerous approach to it. Nevertheless, the face received its first ascent (by Devies and Lagarde) in 1932.

- The **Dent Blanche** (4356m) has already been described in 2:6, but one cannot ignore the historic Viereselsgrat (ENE Ridge), a climb now graded D that is usually approached from a base at the Mountet Hut; nor the great NNE Face which overlooks the upper reaches of the Zinal glacier. However, this face is usually approached from the bivouac hut on Col de la Dent Blanche, itself reached from the Mountet Hut by a PD+ route of 4hrs or so.

- Southeast of Dent Blanche, Winthrop Young's 'beautiful fan-shaped summit' of the 3789m **Pointe de Zinal** is dwarfed by its more illustrious neighbour, but it nonetheless gives a rewarding ice climb of about 500m on its North Face (D), while the *voie normale* tackles the short NE Ridge (PD) from Col Durand. The prominent South Ridge descends to the Schönbiel Hut from where the mountain is also often climbed (see 2:10).

- One of the most attractive of all alpine peaks, the **Ober Gabelhorn** (4063m) is the central feature in the Val de Zinal headwall, a beautifully proportioned mountain with four ridges culminating in a short, chisel-shaped summit. Despite three unsuccessful attempts to climb it in the summer of 1865, Lord Francis Douglas was beaten to its first ascent by just one day. The accolade went to A W Moore, Horace Walker and Jakob Anderegg, who forced a route up the East Face on 6 July 1865; next day Douglas and his guides Peter Taugwalder and Josef Vianin made their ascent via the NNW Ridge (the Coeurgrat). While relaxing on the summit, no doubt disappointed by missing the prize of first ascent, Douglas said 'the whole top fell with a crash thousands of feet below, and I with it'. Taugwalder was also avalanched from the summit, but the two were miraculously held on the rope by Vianin.

Dent Blanche and the Grande Cornier

A week later Lord Douglas was to lose his life in the Matterhorn tragedy, while Taugwalder survived once more. Today the normal route on the Ober Gabelhorn is by the ENE Ridge (AD), starting from the Rothorn Hut (2:10), but the Douglas/Taugwalder/Vianin route on the Coeurgrat is most often climbed from the Mountet Hut, a 5–6hr climb mostly on snow (AD), while the steep 450m of the North Face give a straightforward TD- climb also from the Mountet Hut.

- The **Zinalrothorn** (4221m) forms a distinctive pinnacle from which three ridges of consistently good rock provide the climber with classic routes. Leslie Stephen, who made the first ascent in 1864 with F C Grove and the guides Jakob and Melchior Anderegg, described the short North Ridge as a 'fin from a fish's back'. Crusted with gendarmes, this ridge makes a first-rate climb from the Mountet Hut (AD), although when he reached the summit along it, Stephen reckoned it had given him 'the nastiest piece of climbing I have ever accomplished'. The *voie normale* is by the SE Ridge, approached from the Rothorn Hut, but the SW Ridge (the Rothorngrat) gives an AD+ ascent with individual moves of IV and V, starting from the Mountet Hut, and is considered by some to be the finest of the mountain's classic routes.
- On the approach through the valley to Zinal the rock peak of **Besso** (3668m) appears to be a major summit, for it dominates the east flank of Val de Zinal. Until, that is, the full splendour of both the Ar Pitetta cirque and the valley's headwall are revealed. But Besso is still worth a climber's attention, especially by its very fine SW Ridge where an AD route (IV+) on decent rock takes around 4–5hrs from the Mountet Hut.
- Buttressed at its southwest corner by the Besso, the great glacier-hung Ar Pitetta cirque is dominated by the 4506m **Weisshorn**, beaten only by the Dom and the Monte Rosa massif in the hierarchy of Swiss mountains. 'This perfect pyramid, standing well away from the central chain, draws attention at once, whenever it appears,' wrote R L G Irving in *The Alps*. 'One face of the pyramid, which overlooks the Zinal valley, is an immense rock wall. To climb it near the centre without falling off or being knocked off requires skill, great endurance and bad shooting by the mountain.' As Irving indicated, this West Face is desperately loose (it was here that Munich climber Georg Winkler died in 1888), but it was by a long rock rib on this very face that in 1900 Geoffrey Winthrop Young made one of his four new routes on the mountain, now known as the Younggrat – an ascent of 1719m from the Ar Pitetta Hut; grade D-. Young compared this rib to 'a petrified giant snake, hung by the neck to the Tower [the Grand Gendarme] above, with its tail whipping out upon the glacier below' (*On High Hills*). Though several routes have been made on the West Face, practically all other climbs on the mountain begin either from the Weisshorn Hut (2:10), the bivouac hut on the Schalijoch or, in the case of the North Ridge, from the Tracuit Hut and over the summit of the Bishorn – a long route of 8–9hrs at a grade of AD+.
- While the 4153m **Bishorn** overlooks both the Turtmanntal (2:9) and Mattertal (2:10), and is unseen from Val de Zinal, the normal route to its summit via its NW Flank begins at the Tracuit Hut on the headwall of the Combautanna cirque above Zinal. This is the route by which it received its first ascent in 1884; an uncomplicated climb (grade F) which remains on the Turtmann glacier as far as a saddle between the mountain's twin summits. This same route also makes a popular ski ascent.

This catalogue of Zinal summits and suggested routes is by no means comprehensive, as a glance at the map would immediately reveal. Climbers wishing to examine all the possibilities are advised to study the two Alpine Club guidebooks, *Valais Alps East* and *Valais Alps West*, or the SAC guide *Alpes valaisannes 3* detailed at the end of this chapter. Winthrop Young's autobiographical *On High Hills* is also recommended reading for anyone coming to Val de Zinal with a tick-list of routes, for it serves as a reminder of what may be achieved by a strong, fit climber burning with ambition.

Moving on

The next valley east of Val de Zinal is the Turtmanntal (2:9) which stretches to the north from the tail end of the Turtmann glacier, its walling ridge more or less beginning at the Tête de Milon. Located at the head of the Combautanna cirque, Col de Tracuit gives access onto the Turtmann glacier, from where it would be possible to descend to the Turtmann Hut and thence into the valley below,

Ober Gabelhorn (4063m) above the Zinal glacier

but as there are many crevasses, this is reserved for roped parties.

The first crossing point for walkers is the 2874m **Forcletta** located east of Alpe Nava and gained in 3½–4hrs from Zinal. A narrow windblown saddle between horns of rock, a rich panorama of distant peaks can be seen from it. The pass is one of two chosen by trekkers on the Walker's Haute Route, and on the eastern side a long descent leads past the alp chalets of Chalte Berg to eventually reach Gruben. A short way below the pass you gaze across a sweep of craggy peaks and glaciers; 'I doubt whether there is a more spiky panorama to be seen in the Alps than this view across the Turtmanntal,' wrote Showell Styles in *Backpacking in the Alps and Pyrenees*.

Further north, and easily reached from either Hotel Weisshorn or Cabane Bella Tola in 2–2½hrs, the **Meidpass** (2790m) offers a direct crossing to Gruben. This pass lies just below the Corne du Boeuf in an upper basin of crag and scree, a narrow stony gap between upstanding rocks, but on arrival a view that encompasses the Brunegghorn, Bishorn and Weisshorn among others, is one to enjoy.

Looking back to the west, Grand Combin and Mont Blanc can be seen far off.

Between Corne du Boeuf and Bella Tola, the **Pas de Boeuf** (2897m) is another option, but this is less well marked than either Meidpass or the Forcletta, and takes you down first through the hanging valley of the Bortertälli which drains into the Turtmanntal some way below Gruben.

And finally, from Cabane d'Illhorn above Chandolin, a route crosses the 2544m **Pas d'Illsee**, skirts the north shore of the Illsee tarn and works its way to Oberems at the northern end of the Turtmanntal.

2:9 THE TURTMANNTAL

The most westerly of the German-speaking valleys of the Pennine Alps, this is one of the least known of all. Headed by Weisshorn, Bishorn and Brunegghorn, it's a comparatively short hanging valley with a romantically remote ambience. Winthrop Young referred to it as being wild and seldom visited when he was there in the 1890s;

2:9 THE TURTMANNTAL

TURTMANNTAL

[Map of the Turtmanntal region showing villages including Turtmann, Unterems, Oberems, Gruben; peaks including Illhorn, Schwarzhorn, Bella Tola, Le Tourno, Frilihorn, Les Diablons, Tête de Milon, Weisshorn, Bishorn, Brunegghorn, Barrhorn, Stellihorn, Ergischhorn, Signalhorn, Dreizehntenhorn, Augstbordhorn, Schwarzhorn; passes including Pas de Boeuf, Meidpass, Forcletta, Jungpass, Augstbordpass; huts including Turtmann Hut, Tracuit Hut, Topali Hut; and glaciers including Turtmann Gl., Brunegg Gl., Gl. du Weisshorn. Scale 0-5km.]

and 80 years later Showell Styles commented that it was the most charming valley he'd seen on his trek from Martigny to the Simplon Pass, and that Gruben, its highest village, was like something out of mountaineering's Golden Age. 'The Weisshorn at the head [of the valley] looks stupendous,' he wrote, 'and the Turtmann Glacier is a marvel, all icefalls.'

These suggestions from the past that the Turtmanntal is a wild and lonely alpine backwater remain largely true today. Refreshingly free from development, it's a gem of a valley and one in which the connoisseur will gain much from exploring. Leslie Stephen, who made the first ascent of the Zinalrothorn, came here in 1864 and having remarked upon its primitive seclusion, he then described the scene which greeted him from a pine glade:

Above us rose the Weisshorn in one of the most sublime aspects of that almost faultless mountain. The Turtmann glacier, broad and white with deep regular crevasses, formed a noble approach, like the staircase of some superb palace. Above this rose the huge mass of the mountain, firm and solid as though its architect had wished to eclipse the Pyramids. And higher still, its lofty crest, jagged and apparently swaying from side to side, seemed to be tossed into the blue atmosphere far above the reach of mortal man. Nowhere have I seen a more delicate combination of mountain massiveness with soaring and delicately carved pinnacles pushed to the verge of extravagance.

(The Playground of Europe)

The village of **Turtmann** lies in the Rhône valley midway between Sierre and Visp, and houses the valley's tourist office (www.turtmanntal.ch). From there a road climbs to **Unterems** (1003m) and **Oberems** (1348m), the latter having cableway connections with Turtmann, and an outlook over the Rhône from the west flank of the valley's initial gorge. From Oberems the road then pushes on into the wooded lower reaches of the Turtmanntal proper for another 11km to reach **Gruben** (1822m). Also known as Meiden, this small village of summer chalets set in meadowland fringed with trees, is limited in tourist facilities to a small grocery, post office and a single hotel, the Schwarzhorn, which has dormitory places as well as standard beds, and is open from June to October (tel 027 932 14 14). Just 5mins downvalley, Restaurant Waldesruh also has dormitory accommodation, and is open from mid-June to mid-September (tel 027 932 13 97).

The official roadhead lies beyond Gruben at Vorder Sänntum (1901m), some way below a small dammed lake passed on the way to the **Turtmann Hut**. This medium-sized stone-built refuge is located on a rock spur just north of the Brunegg and Turtmann glaciers at 2519m, and is approached by an easy walk from the roadhead. Owned by the Prévôtoise section of the SAC, it has 74 places and is fully manned from mid-March to mid-May, and from mid-June to the end of September (www.turtmannhuette.ch). For the visiting climber nearby crags have been equipped to offer a number of mostly one-pitch routes ranging from III to IX. The hut guardian can provide details.

Although the hut is naturally popular with day-visitors, climbers overnighting there are often bound for the 🧗 **Bishorn**, whose summit soars 1640m above it to the south. While the ordinary route involves negotiating 6km of the Turtmann glacier's crevasses, of more interest are the East Ridge (AD) via the Bisjoch, and the complex NE Face (TD), both of which deserve consideration.

The 3833m 🧗 **Brunegghorn**, and twin summits of the 🧗 **Barrhorn** (3610m; 3583m) are also accessible from the Turtmann Hut. The first is an elegant snow peak with three faces, three ridges and the long Brunegg glacier sweeping down its northwest flank to join the Turtmann glacier above the hut. The stony Barrhorn, on the other hand, rises directly above the hut but is less interesting to look at, although the higher summit (Üssers Barrhorn) can be reached by an uncomplicated ascent of a little over 3hrs, and the north to south traverse makes a pleasant F-grade outing of about 6hrs.

🚶 Walkers based in the valley for a few days can enjoy a good path that extends beyond the Turtmann Hut heading southeast below the Barrhorn, from where spectacular views may be had across gleaming icefields to the Weisshorn. Other vantage points that reward a few hours of exercise can be won by mounting the west flank of the valley into the wild little **Blüomatttälli** headed by the **Forcletta** (or Furggilti), one of the cols leading to Val d'Anniviers. From the alp of Chalte Berg in the mouth of this hanging valley, the upper Turtmanntal shows its true nature, while the continuing trail gives an even more savage outlook.

🚶 On the **Turtmanntal's east flank** a high trail contours along the hillside above the treeline linking tiny alps and again presenting memorable views of the big snow peaks at the head of the valley, before angling up to the Turtmann Hut.

🚶 A 1000m climb above Gruben leads to the **Augstbordpass**, the 2894m crossing taken by Walkers' Haute Route trekkers to reach St Niklaus in the Mattertal. Used since the Middle Ages as part of a trading route between the Rhône valley and Italy, the waymarked trail rises through the hanging valley of the Grüobtälli without any unduly steep sections until just below the actual pass, which is gained in about 3hrs. A wild view to the east across a basin of rock and scree leads the eye to the Fletschhorn and outliers of the Mischabel wall above the Saastal. While the continuing route to St Niklaus plunges into a rocky basin below, an hour's climb up the ridge north of the pass leads without difficulty onto the 3201m ⛰ ⭐ **Schwarzhorn**, a fabulous viewpoint considered by Baedeker to be even better than that of the Bella Tola (2:8). Walker agreed: 'It includes especially all the Oberland peaks from the Doldenhorn to the Finsteraarhorn, the St Gotthard and Ticino mountains, and the round is completed by Fletschhorn, Weissmies and Mischabel, Monte Rosa, Lyskamm, Weisshorn

2:10 THE MATTERTAL

Below the Augstbordpass a view across the Mattertal shows the Ried glacier with the creamy Dom on the right

and Dent Blanche – a wonderful array all from one point' (*Walking in the Alps*).

🟢 And there's also the **Jungpass** (2990m), a narrow gap in the ridge between Furggwanghorn and Rothorn which also leads from Gruben to St Niklaus, but is a much tougher crossing than that of the Augstbordpass. On the eastern side the way descends through the lonely Jungtal where one trail joins the Augstbordpass route just above Jungen, that glorious little alp hamlet that seems almost to hang from the precipitous hillside 800m above St Niklaus (see 2:10).

2:10 THE MATTERTAL

Thanks to the magnetic draw of the Matterhorn, the Mattertal is without question the busiest and best-known valley in the Pennine Alps, if not in all Switzerland. Access by both road and rail is through the lower Vispertal south of Visp in the Rhône valley, although a road tunnel now misses the northernmost 3km or so of the Vispertal's narrows. At Stalden (799m) the valley divides like a tuning fork; the southeast branch becoming the Saastal (2:11), the southwest being the Mattertal.

At first it's a gloomy defile and you need to be up on the mid-height slopes to gain an impression of the valley's true worth. One means of doing this is to take a side road snaking up the north flank just beyond Stalden. This leads to Törbel (1497m), a village with a sunny outlook built on several levels (www.toerbel.ch), where another road, served by bus from Stalden, continues up the hillside to reach Moosalp (2048m). From here the 9km long Moosalp–Jungen Höhenweg works along the steep slope heading southwest to join the historic path mentioned in 2:9 which links Gruben in the Turtmanntal with St Niklaus in the Mattertal.

Midway between Stalden and Törbel another road breaks to the south through a tunnel, before snaking along the hillside to reach Embd (1358m), an enchanting village of stone-roofed chalets built on an impossibly steep slope above Kalpetran, with which it is connected by cable car. Accommodation can be had at the Restaurant-Gasthaus Morgenrot, which has standard rooms and a 12-place dormitory. Footpaths explore the upper hillsides and link up with traverse routes, and just above the village yak trekking has become a local novelty. For information, contact Embd Tourismus (www.embd.ch).

THE SWISS ALPS – CHAPTER 2: PENNINE ALPS

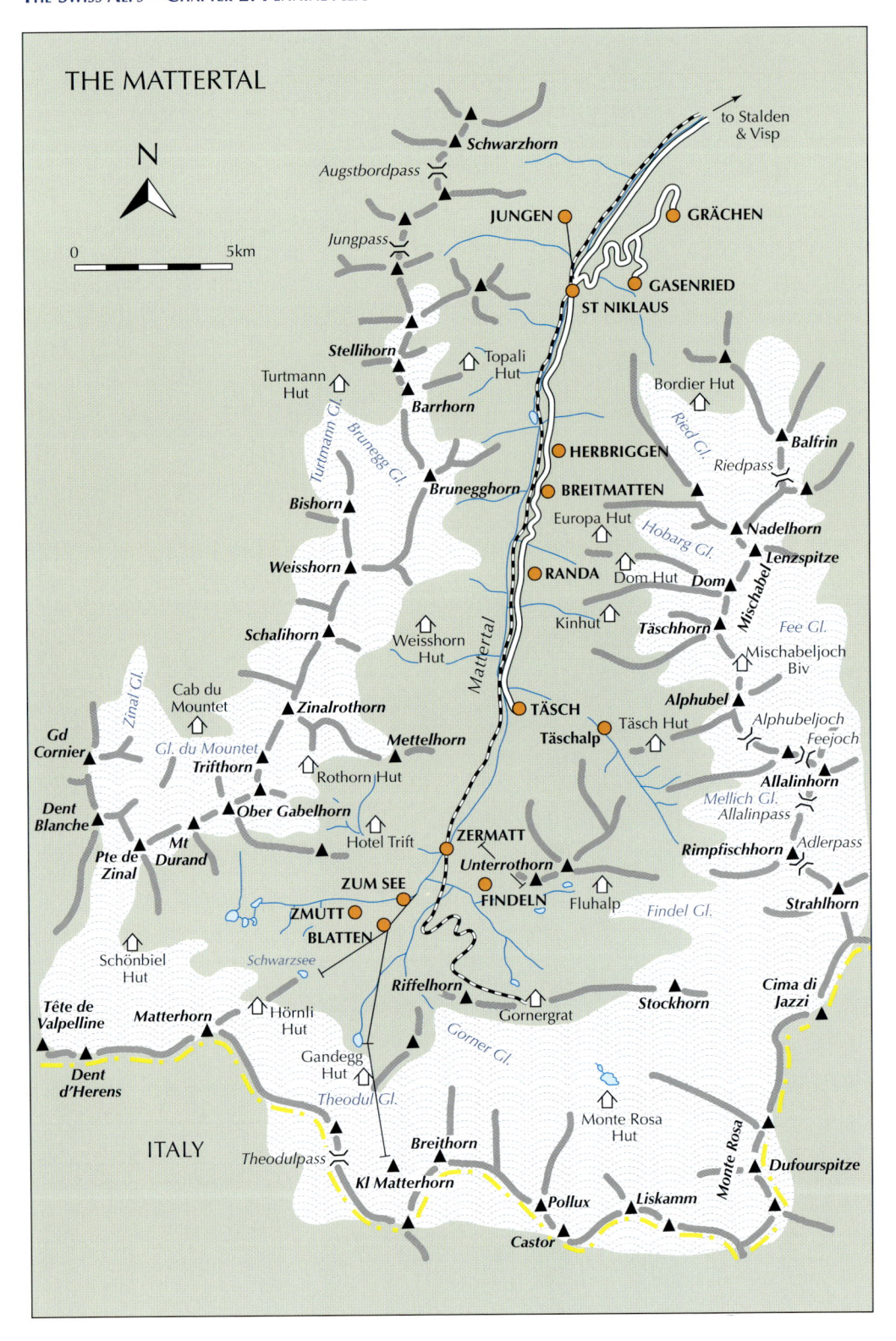

THE MATTERTAL

2:10 THE MATTERTAL

Jungen is perched on a steep slope high above St Niklaus

At **St Niklaus** (1127m) the Mattertal's defile begins to open out. An old workaday village, St Niklaus was the valley's one-time capital, and in mountaineering terms is remembered as the home of three great guiding families, the Knubels, Lochmatters and Pollingers – the local museum is partly dedicated to mountain guides (Bergführer & Heimatmuseum, open at set times in summer). Now bypassed by the main road, the village would make a reasonable base for a few days of a walking holiday. It has at least seven hotels and pensions, shops, restaurants, a post office and bank, and a tourist office near the railway station (www.st-niklaus.ch). Close by, a cableway links St Niklaus with **Jungen** (or Jungu; 1955m), a glorious alp hamlet perched precariously on a sloping meadow with an exquisite view along the valley to the great snowpeaks that carry the Swiss-Italian border at its head, and southeast to the Ried glacier extending below Nadelhorn, Lenzspitze and Dom. Limited dormitory accommodation may be available here; check at the Junger-Stübli restaurant (tel 027 956 21 01).

⊙ From Jungen one could walk to Moosalp along the signed *höhenweg* mentioned above, or follow a much more challenging route (some danger of stonefall) into the hanging Jungtal, then head south across a stony wilderness, at the head of which a steel ladder and fixed ropes safeguard the ascent of crags topped by the 3114m Wasulicke, on the ridge linking Wasuhorn and Festihorn. Over this a way continues below Stellihorn and Barrhorn to reach the **Topali Hut** (2674m), about 5½–6hrs from Jungen. Owned by the Genevoise section of the SAC, the hut has 44 places and is staffed from July until mid-September (www.topalihuette.zaniglas.ch). From there a continuing trail, exposed in several places, reaches Randa in 4–5hrs, but there's another trail cutting from it which makes a very steep descent through the Guggigraben ravine to Herbriggen.

On the eastern side of the valley above St Niklaus, **Grächen** (1618m) is a straggle of flower-decked chalets, hotels and apartments spread across a sunny terrace reached by bus. With a very fine view of the Weisshorn, and with no shortage of accommodation or other tourist facilities, plus a network of footpaths and two gondola lifts, Grächen makes a good base for a walking holiday. It's also a modest winter resort, whose helpful tourist

The box-like Topali Hut, high on the west flank of the Mattertal

THE SWISS ALPS – CHAPTER 2: PENNINE ALPS

office has plenty of leaflets, brochures and recommendations for all seasons (www.graechen.ch).

A short walk of an hour or so south of Grächen brings you to **Gasenried** (1659m), a much smaller and therefore much quieter village with accommodation, including *matratzenlager* (dormitory), at Hotel Alpenrösli (tel 027 956 20 16). This also makes a relaxing base for a few days' holiday, with access to lots of walking opportunities.

Walks and climbs from Grächen

- ◐ ☆ One of the finest walks from Grächen, and a true alpine classic, is the **Grächen–Saas Fee Höhenweg**, also known as the Balfrin Höhenweg. Opened in 1954, several existing paths were linked by newly created trails, which involved blasting tunnels through the rock and cutting ledges in cliffs, to create a walk of about 6½hrs from Hannigalp (reached by gondola lift from Grächen), to Saas Fee in the Saastal (see 2:11). It's a committing walk, and unsuitable for anyone who suffers vertigo, but an absolute 'must' for the sure-footed. A special ticket (*Kombi-Billet Höhenweg*) can be bought which covers the gondola lift and the return bus from Saas Fee.

- ◐ By using the gondola to gain height, the 3037m **Seetalhorn** above the village to the southeast is accessible by a climb of less than 200m from the upper gondola station, with steep paths of descent on three sides of the mountain from which great panoramic views can be enjoyed. One of these paths descends through the Seetal on the east side of the ridge to join the Grächen–Saas Fee Höhenweg to give a 5½hr walk to Saas Fee.

- ◐ ☆ On a par with the Grächen–Saas Fee Höhenweg, the 31km long **Europaweg** gives an

The Europaweg is threatened by rockfall in several places

epic two-day trek from Gasenried to Zermatt which teeters along the steep east flank of the Mattertal. With some short sections exposed to stonefall, and others where the path negotiates precipitous terrain (safeguarded with fixed chains, cables or ropes), the Europaweg also goes through several tunnels and requires constant maintenance. There may be significant diversions on the route. Roughly halfway along the route accommodation is available at the **Europa Hut** (2220m), and also at **Täschalp** 3–3½hrs further on. (See below for details).

- Approached via Gasenried, a 4–4½hr hike leads to the **Bordier Hut** (2886m) on the east bank of the Ried glacier. A path crosses below the glacier's snout to Alpja (2099m), then climbs the west bank lateral moraine to 2600m, follows cairns up the hillside a little higher, then crosses the glacier (usually 'dry' and with marker poles) to the hut. Owned by the Genevoise section of the SAC, it has places for 44 and is fully staffed from mid-June to mid-September (www.bordierhuette.ch). From it ascents are made of the Gross Bigerhorn, Balfrin, Ulrichshorn, Nadelhorn and other peaks at the northern end of the Mischabel massif.

- The 3626m **Gross Bigerhorn** rises directly east of the Bordier Hut and offers a scrambling PD ascent of about 2hrs via its WSW Ridge, or a more interesting AD climb along the gendarme-encrusted NNW Ridge.

- The 3796m **Balfrin** can also be climbed from the Bordier Hut by first crossing the Gross Bigerhorn, then ascending the NW Ridge (PD); making an ascent of about 3½–4hrs. The Victorian mountain traveller and art critic W M Conway climbed the Balfrin by this route in 1878.

- Almost directly opposite the Bordier Hut across the Ried glacier, the Galenjoch marks the lower, northern extent of the Nadelgrat, a long spine of rock extending from the 4327m **Nadelhorn** and punctuated by no fewer than three other 4000m tops: the **Stecknadelhorn** (4241m), **Hobärghorn** (4219m), and the 4035m **Dürrenhorn** (shown as Dirruhorn on the latest LS maps). Each of these summits may be climbed by a variety of routes from the Bordier Hut; see the Alpine Club guide *Valais Alps East* by Les Swindin and Peter Fleming, for details.

St Niklaus to Täsch

Between St Niklaus and Randa the road keeps to the east bank of the Mattervispa river, passing through the hamlets of Mattsand (1227m), **Herbriggen** (1262m) and **Breitmatten** (1280m). Linking footpaths and tracks enable walkers to avoid both road and railway for most of that distance, but although occasional views to the head of the valley act as a lure, the avenue of high mountains through which the valley carves a deep trench is almost always unseen. This is a great pity, for this section of the Mattertal is flanked by an astonishing collection of peaks that include Barrhorn, Brunegghorn, Bishorn and Weisshorn on the west, and Nadelhorn, Lenzspitze and Dom on the east. But as was mentioned above, two high routes enable sure-footed walkers to avoid the valley bed and thereby enjoy the dramatic scenery. The first of these is the Jungen–Topali Hut–Randa *höhenweg* along the west flank; the other being the Europaweg that extends from Gasenried to Zermatt on the east flank.

In April 1991 a massive rockfall blocked the valley between Breitmatten and Randa when a vast section of the Langenflueberg collapsed, demolishing the railway, damming the river and cutting off the upper Mattertal for several days. Hundreds of large boulders still litter the valley meadows today, unnervingly close to chalets and haybarns.

Randa (1409m) retains the atmosphere of an alpine village and offers a low-key alternative to Zermatt as a valley base. It has limited shops or tourist facilities, but accommodation is to be had at the Hotel Dom (www.hotel-dom.ch). There's a *touristenlager* (dormitory) at the Alpenblick (www.haus-alpenblick.ch), and a popular campsite on the south side of the village with good facilities – Camping Atermenzen (www.camping-randa.ch). This is probably the best campsite in the valley, and 'Freddy' taxis operate a reliable summer service between it and Zermatt. Randa also has a post office, railway station and tourist office (www.randa.ch).

Southwest of Randa the **Weisshorn Hut** stands high above the Schalikin gorge on the south flank of the Wisse Schijen at 2932m. Gained by a steep walk of about 4½hrs, this small hut has just 30 places, and is owned by the Basel section of the SAC, with a guardian in residence from mid-July until mid-September (www.sac-basel.ch). As its

THE WEISSHORN: 'AN ALMOST FAULTLESS MOUNTAIN'

Whymper called it 'the peerless Weisshorn', and 'the noblest in Switzerland'. Leslie Stephen proclaimed it to be 'an almost faultless mountain'. Irving described it as a 'perfect pyramid'.

One of the great 4000m peaks of the Alps, the Weisshorn is also one of the most sought-after, with its three neatly defined ridges from which fall three stupendous faces. Geoffrey Winthrop Young climbed it eight times by six different routes, four of them new, and in the account of his impressive alpine career, *On High Hills*, he depicted each of the faces in typically eloquent fashion. The complex West Face he described as being of 'furrowed rock, prognathous', and concealing its height; the SE Face as 'a triangular shield, [which] races to the sky in upright lines of exquisite lightness'; while the NE Face above the Bis glacier he likened to a 'storm-cone of snow, in line faultlessly composed, self-contained, and content to hold our eye within its assertion of complete mountain form'.

Today the normal route traces the long and tiring East Ridge from a base at the Weisshorn Hut, and is the one by which the mountain was first climbed in August 1861 by the Irish scientist and one-time Vice President of the Alpine Club, Professor John Tyndall. Together with his guides Bennen and Wenger, Tyndall set out from Randa and found a way to a ledge at the foot of the East Ridge, where a bivouac was arranged beneath an overhanging rock. The rest of the afternoon was spent on reconnaissance, during which Tyndall and Bennen came to a point where 'the whole colossal pyramid stood facing us. When I first looked at it my hope sank, but both of us gathered our confidence from a more lengthened gaze [until] Bennen decided on the route.'

At 3.30am the next morning they began their ascent in clear moonlight, only roping up after two hours as the ridge narrowed, 'and the precipices on each side [became] more sheer'. One troublesome section was crested by pure white snow which Tyndall feared would not hold their weight. But Bennen tested the snow, then started across. Tyndall followed like 'a boy walking along a horizontal pole, with toes turned outwards'.

After six hours on the ridge the summit seemed no nearer, and Bennen, the lead guide, began to despair. But a halt was called for food and a sip of champagne, which sharpened his determination; '*Herr! Wir müssen ihn haben.*' (Sir, we must make it!) A final rock pitch was scaled, followed by another knife-edged crest of snow which led to the point where the three ridges meet on the summit. Tyndall was ecstatic. 'I had never witnessed a scene which affected me like this,' he confessed. In an age when scientific enquiry still played a part in mountain exploration, the great scientist gave up any attempt to record his observations. 'There was something incongruous, if not profane, in allowing the scientific faculty to interfere where silent worship was the reasonable service.' A red handkerchief was tied to the handle of Bennen's ice axe to act as a victory flag and proof of their success, then the trio began their descent, arriving back in Randa the same evening, almost 20 hours after leaving their bivouac.

---

name implies, the hut is used as a base by climbers with ambitions for several routes on the magical ❸ ☆ **Weisshorn**, including the East Ridge (AD), NE Face (TD), and NE Buttress (TD).

On the east side of the Mattertal above Randa, no fewer than three huts are accessible by very steep paths: the Europa Hut, built in a single summer as a service to trekkers on the Europaweg; the Dom Hut standing nearly 700m above the Europa; and the newest of them all, the privately owned Kinhut located southeast of Randa.

The timber-built **Europa Hut** (2220m) is almost exclusively used by trekkers walking the Europaweg between Gasenried and Zermatt, or those following the Tour of the Matterhorn in the opposite direction. The property of the Randa *gemeinde*, it has 42 places, is fully staffed from late June to the end of September (www.europaweg.ch), and can be reached in 2–2½hrs by a direct path from Randa.

About 5mins from the Europa Hut, the approach to the **Dom Hut** crosses the Europaweg at 2149m, and continues up to the Festiflüe, a rocky barrier initially avoided by turning to the south to locate a way through via steps, ledges and fixed cables. Standing at 2940m on the Festi glacier's north bank lateral moraine, the hut is reached about 2–2½hrs from the Europa Hut, or 4½–5hrs from Randa. With a stunning view across the valley to the Weisshorn, it forms a natural base for climbs on the Dom and other peaks of the Mischabel group. Owned by the Uto section of the SAC, the hut has 75 places, and is fully staffed from July to the end of September (www.domhuette.ch).

Since the ✪ **Dom** (4545m) is the highest mountain wholly in Switzerland (as opposed to the highest *summit*, the accolade for which goes to the 4634m Dufourspitze in the Monte Rosa massif on the Swiss/Italian frontier), the ascent is usually high on the wish-list of alpinists. Standing amid a long line of pointed summits, it does not show its prominence from every view, but the glacial ramps which sweep down its west and northwest flanks make it an obvious ski-mountaineer's peak. Indeed, it was first climbed on ski as long ago as 1917 by Arnold Lunn and Josef Knubel, who managed to remain on their skis all the way up the Hohbärg glacier to the very summit. The *voie normale* is also a long PD-grade glacier plod *sans* ski via the Festi glacier, while the first ascent of the mountain was made in 1858 via the more interesting NW Ridge, the Festigrat (PD+), by the Revd John Llewellyn-Davies and three guides from Zermatt, Johann Zumtaugwald, Johann Krönig and Hieronymus Brantschen.

Nestling below the Dom's Western Arête at 2582m, the **Kinhut** was opened in 2001. Reached in about 3½hrs from Randa by a path that climbs from the Europaweg through the Wildikin combe, this privately owned hut can also be used for climbs on the Dom, as well as Täschhorn and Kinhorn. It has 30 dormitory places and is staffed from mid-July to mid-September (tel 027 967 86 18). Out of this staffed period the hut is kept locked.

At the Mattertal roadhead **Täsch** (1450m) is dominated by massive car and coach parks, and what must surely be one of Switzerland's busiest railway stations, dedicated to the efficient transfer of as many tourists as possible, out of the village and away to Zermatt. The vast majority of these visitors have little idea that a short distance from the station lies the old village, barely touched by the tourist invasion just across the valley.

So far as the tourist is concerned, Täsch has six 3-star hotels, a large number of apartments for rent, and a campsite on the west bank of the Mattervispa. There are a few shops in the main street, a bank, post office and tourist office (www.taesch.ch). The rather more attractive old village stands in a huddle on the east side of the valley with the Täschbach channelled along its southern edge. This drains an unspoilt hanging valley, the Täschalpen, which lies beneath four 4000m peaks – Täschhorn, Alphubel, Allalinhorn and Rimpfischhorn.

To reach Täschalp from the Mattertal involves either taking a taxi up a hairpin road, or a 2½hr walk up a very steep footpath above the old village. **Täschalp** (Ottavan on the LS map) consists of

The Täsch Hut, traditional base for climbs on several 4000ers

a scattering of chalets, cowsheds, a tiny chapel and a dairy farm, but dormitory accommodation may be had at Restaurant Täschalp-Ottavan, also known as the **Europaweg Hut** (www.europaweghuette.ch). This is open from June to mid-October with 40 places. About 1–1½hrs, and almost 500m above the buildings, the **Täsch Hut** (2701m) has 60 dormitory places, is manned from late June to the end of September (www.taeschhuette.ch), and is used by climbers as a base for attempts on several neighbouring peaks.

Climbs from the Täsch Hut

- The **Täschhorn** (4490m) is an obvious attraction. With three ridges and three great faces, it's the most difficult and impressive of the Mischabel peaks. The SW Face is said to be as serious as the North Face of the Matterhorn, but the rock is dangerously loose. The SW Ridge (Teufelsgrat) is almost 2km long, while the normal route from the Täsch Hut uses the SE Ridge, the upper part of which is usually reached via the Weingarten glacier and SW Rib (AD, III).

- From the west the 4206m **Alphubel** shows itself to be a rock peak, while above Saas Fee it assumes the stance of a classic snow and ice mountain with a long, mostly level summit ridge. The first ascent was made in 1860 by Leslie Stephen, Thomas Hinchliff and their guides, Melchior Anderegg and Peter Perren, by way of the Alphubeljoch and SE Ridge, and it is the SE Ridge which today is one of the *voies normales*, graded PD. The West Ridge, or Rotgrat (AD+), is also tackled from the Täsch Hut, as is the West Rib (D: IV, IV+).

- Southeast of the Alphubel, the **Allalinhorn** (4027m) is the obvious snow dome on the skyline above Saas Fee, and is usually climbed from the Britannia Hut, or the so-called Metro-Alpin which deposits visitors onto the snow at 3456m. The Täsch Hut approach is therefore much quieter and more aesthetically pleasing. From here the WNW Ridge gives a PD ascent of 4½–5hrs, while the SW Ridge is also a PD climb, but taking around 6hrs from the hut.

- The **Rimpfischhorn** (4199m) stands isolated from both its nearest neighbours, the Allalinhorn and Strahlhorn, and is flanked on all sides by glaciers, the Mellich and Längflue glaciers draining directly into the Täschalpen valley. A 6–7hr climb from the Täsch Hut gives a PD/PD+ route on the WSW Ridge, or via the NW Face by a D grade route pioneered in 1923 by Emile Blanchet and the guide Heinrich Imseng.

About 5km south of Täsch the railway terminates at the entrance to Zermatt, where the expectations of the vast majority of visitors, active or not, are focused

Zermatt, mountaineering capital of Switzerland

on the Matterhorn, the symbol not only of this most enigmatic of resorts, but of all Switzerland. For the few who choose to walk up through the woods from Täsch, its gracefully kinked and unmistakable upper section comes into view about 40mins before reaching the town. It's a vision that seldom disappoints.

Zermatt

If Chamonix is the greatest mountaineering centre in the Alps, then Zermatt runs it a close second. But apart from mountaineering, the two also share a common bond of ruthless exploitation by bulldozer, cable car and mountain railway to maximize the year-round tourist potential, with the number of skiers in winter rivalling and even outnumbering those of summer visitors. Zermatt's mountain basin has become a 365-day commodity.

In summer, trails that climb out of the town are all signed, timed and waymarked; climber's routes on some of the more difficult peaks have been fixed with bolts, ropes and chains; and peak-ticking visitors with a fat bank balance are helicoptered up to a variety of snow passes from which convenient 4000m summits may be reached by a minimum of effort, thus enabling a guide's well-heeled client to be transported safely back to his hotel in time for dinner.

When Whymper was here the Matterhorn still had 'a *cordon* drawn round it, up to which one might go, but no farther'. Today Zermatt is the epitome of Leslie Stephen's Playground of Europe. And yet, despite it all, even in the height of summer it remains possible to find solitude amidst impeccable scenery, and one can still climb routes on the most popular of peaks without the fear of being bombarded by rocks dislodged by other parties above, and experience again the mystique that made the pioneers gasp in awe. Zermatt may be bursting at the seams, its slopes tunnelled through and laced with cableways, but all is not yet lost.

Zermatt (1620m) still claims to be car-free, yet electric taxis and buses bully the crowds more often than the horse-drawn carriages that greet arrivals at the station. Old Valaisian houses line the main street south of the church, and a few jealously guard their small vegetable plots against the ceaseless development that has brought capital city *chic* to upmarket shops and one hotel after another crowding for a view of the Matterhorn, the one mountain everyone is anxious to see. The town (for it can no longer be classed a village) has every modern facility for the visitor, with a vast array of hotels and apartments, a youth hostel, a basic campsite near the railway station, supermarkets, banks, post office, restaurants, bars, internet cafés, shops selling climbing equipment, books, guides and maps, and an interesting alpine museum. In the main street there's a mountain guides' office (www.zermatt.ch/alpincenter), and a few paces from the railway station, a well-stocked tourist office (www.zermatt.ch), with free hotel booking facilities.

The Zermatt Basin

One would be forgiven for thinking that the Matterhorn was the only mountain above Zermatt. In fact it is just one of a great collection of 4000m peaks rimming the basin at the head of the Mattertal. Working clockwise round that basin we begin with the Rimpfischhorn (already mentioned as a climb from the Täsch Hut), then to the Strahlhorn and south from there to the frontier with Italy and the shared summits of the Monte Rosa massif (Jägerhorn, Nordend, Dufourspitze, Signalkuppe and Parrotspitze), followed by Liskamm, the 'twins' Castor and Pollux, then the massive Breithorn leading the frontier ridge round to the Theodulpass and on to the Matterhorn. Next comes the Dent d'Hérens and the Tête de Valpelline, followed by the modest Tête Blanche where the rim then strikes northeast away from the frontier, and north to the Dent Blanche. Now the basin wall works roughly eastward to include Pointe de Zinal, Mont Durand, Ober Gabelhorn and Unter Gabelhorn. But another ridge pushes north or northeast from Ober Gabelhorn across the Wellenkuppe and Trifthorn up to the Zinalrothorn and beyond. And although one might be tempted to include Schalihorn and Weisshorn in this fabulous collection, in truth they belong to the Mattertal's west wall above Täsch and Randa.

Glaciers sweep from the majority of those peaks, the largest of which is the famed Gornergletscher draining westward below Monte Rosa, overlooked by the ever-popular **Gornergrat** (3090m) reached by rack-railway from Zermatt, whose hotel (Gornergrat Kulm www.zermatt.ch/gornergrat.kulm) affords spectacular sunrise views. A two-stage cable car continues from there via the Hohtälli to the Stockhorn perched above the ice at 3407m.

Other cableways exploit the upper reaches of Zermatt's basin. One goes to the Schwarzsee at the foot of the Matterhorn, another ascends via Trockener Steg to the **Klein Matterhorn** at 3883m between the Theodulpass and Breithorn, while an underground funicular from Zermatt, the so-called Sunnegga Alpen Metro, emerges at 2285m, where a cable car then swings visitors to Blauherd (2571m) and on to the flat rocky summit of the 3103m Rothorn (Unterrothorn on the map). But while these mechanical aids grant access for all to sites otherwise the preserve of determined walkers, they at least help reduce pedestrian traffic on the actual footpaths – of which there's an almost matchless network.

☼ ☆ Walks from Zermatt

There's no shortage of well-maintained paths here, and anyone with a map and imagination could happily spend weeks wandering from lake to lake, or hut to hut with routes punctuated by viewpoints that challenge superlatives. The following is merely a sample, for to include every possibility would demand a book of its own. As with the list of peaks on the basin rim, walks mentioned here follow a clockwise trend.

- By riding the Alpen Metro to Sunnegga you quickly gain a trail that descends to the tiny Leisee, then follow a route to the **Stellisee** for an almost perfectly framed view of the Matterhorn (arguably more satisfactory than the better-known view from the Riffelsee). From here you continue over rough grass slopes to the big timber-faced **Berghütte Fluhalp** at 2616m (beds and dormitory places; tel 027 967 25 97); a base for climbers tackling the Rimpfischhorn. Nearby a path goes along a moraine crest overlooking the Findelgletscher, then descends to **Grindjisee** to join a track leading to the **Grünsee**, from where a return can be made to Zermatt via exquisite **Findeln** and Winkelmatten to complete a 5hr tour.

- From Rotenboden station just below the Gornergrat, the **Monte Rosa Hut** may be reached in 2½hrs by crossing the Gornergletscher. It's not a difficult walk, and the way is usually marked with poles, but the glacier is crevassed, so normal safety precautions should be taken. It first visits the **Riffelsee**, then takes a path slanting down the south side of the Gornergrat ridge to gain access to the glacier. From there to the hut takes at least 1½hrs, and on arrival a very fine view is to be had along the glacial highway to the Matterhorn. The very modern Monte Rosa Hut has 120 places, is manned in late March, April and May, and from July

Easily reached from Sunnegga, the Stellisee provides a perfect foreground to views of the Matterhorn

to mid-September (www.section-monte-rosa. ch). After returning to the Riffelsee it's worth continuing all the way down to Zermatt via **Gagenhaupt** and **Riffelberg**, making an overall hike of about 7hrs.

- Used by the majority of climbers tackling the Matterhorn's normal route via the Hörnli Ridge, the **Hörnli Hut** (3260m) makes an interesting destination for a walk, for the views that gradually expand as you ascend towards it, reveal more of the Zermatt basin than from almost any other route. If the Schwarzsee cable car is taken, the ascent to the hut should need no more than about 2hrs – but add another 2½–3hrs if you walk all the way from Zermatt. The path is signed and obvious; there's a ladder, a steel platform over an exposed section, and fixed ropes higher up, but the way is mostly straightforward. Together with the adjacent Berghotel Matterhorn, the Hörnli Hut has 170 places and is staffed from July to the end of September (www.hoernlihuette.ch). From the terrace you gaze eastward along a line of 4000m peaks to Monte Rosa.

- From the **Schwarzsee** a rewarding return to Zermatt takes a path through the Zmutt valley below the Matterhorn's North Face, visiting on the way Stafelalp, Kalbermatten and Zmutt. Allow about 3hrs to reach Zermatt, plus stops.

- A visit to the **Schönbiel Hut**, perched upon the Zmutt glacier's lateral moraine opposite the Dent d'Hérens at 2694m, affords one of the finest of all walks from Zermatt. There are two routes. The first and most direct heads upvalley on a busy trail to **Zmutt** at the entrance to the Zmutt valley. The continuing path keeps to the north flank of the valley and, beyond the Arben tributary, follows the moraine crest to the hut, which is gained about 4hrs from Zermatt. With 80 dormitory places, it is fully staffed from Easter until mid-May and from the end of June to mid-September (tel 027 967 13 54).

- The second route to the Schönbiel Hut is longer, more demanding, but a real classic. It begins by climbing through the Trift gorge to the west of Zermatt. At the head of the gorge stands the Victorian **Hotel du Trift** (2337m; 30 places in beds and dormitories, tel 079 408 70 20). Cross the Triftbach here and rise southward to gain the tremendous balcony meadows of **Höhbalmen** (2665m) where an immense view can be had of the Zermatt basin, with the Matterhorn's Hörnli Ridge and North

The Schwarzsee lies at the foot of the Matterhorn

Face directly ahead. Across the meadows the way veers west and continues high above the Zmutt valley before descending through the Arben glen, then following the moraine wall up to the hut to give a 6hr walk, with another 3hrs needed for the most direct return to Zermatt.

- 🌟 The ascent of the 3406m **Mettelhorn** is included in this selection of walks since the summit may be reached without any technical skills, and for many years was seen as a classic training peak on which to get fit before tackling something more serious. Standing as it does at the eastern end of a mountain crest reaching from the Zinalrothorn, it serves as an ideal vantage point from which to survey many of Zermatt's great peaks. The way rises through the Trift gorge, continues beyond **Hotel du Trift** into a glacial basin, then breaks to the right to ascend steep grass slopes of the Triftkumme. At the head of the combe a narrow saddle is crossed below the Platthorn. Beyond this cross a slope of *firn* to gain the Mettelhorn's summit; an ascent of 1786m and 5–6hrs from Zermatt.

TOUR OF THE MATTERHORN

Making a 10–11 day circuit of the most famous mountain in Europe, the ToM covers 145km, crosses six passes (two of which are glacier passes), strays into Italy and wins a whole series of spectacular views. As all of the route on the Swiss side, from Zermatt to Arolla, reverses the Walker's Haute Route described in 2:1, in the high summer months of July and August accommodation may be at a premium, so make a point of booking ahead (the recommended guidebook includes telephone numbers). Outlined below the route follows the seven stages as set out in the *Tour of the Matterhorn* guidebook by Hilary Sharp, but is divided here into convenient day treks.

Days 1 & 2: Beginning in **Zermatt** the first day's trek traces the Europaweg high on the east side of the Mattertal, as far as the **Europa Hut**, and next day continues as far as **St Niklaus**, below **Gasenried**.

Day 3: This tough, 8hr stage has a long 1700m climb to the **Augstbordpass**, followed by descent to **Gruben** in the Turtmanntal, but at least 2hrs of this time could be saved by taking a cable car from St Niklaus to Jungen.

Day 4: Leaving German-speaking Switzerland behind, the ToM uses the 2790m **Meidpass** to reach Val d'Anniviers. Descending at first to **Hotel Weisshorn**, the route then takes a spectacular high-level trail with exciting views all the way to **Zinal** – another 8hr stage, but less demanding than on Day 3.

Day 5: The guidebook describes an 11hr stage between Zinal and Les Haudères, but for practical purposes this should be divided into a two-day trek, unless you are prepared to take the cable car from Zinal to Sorebois, that is, and perhaps a bus from Villa to Les Haudères. So on Day 5 climb steeply out of Zinal on a long haul up to the **Col de Sorebois** – a 1600m ascent – then make a short, easy descent to a *dortoir* above the **Barrage de Moiry**.

Day 6: A very pleasant ascent over pastureland, passing Lac des Autannes, leads to **Col de Torrent** (2919m). This is followed by another long stretch of pastureland down to **Villa** and **La Sage** on the east flank of Val d'Hérens. A short and easy walk downhill then brings you to **Les Haudères** in the bed of the valley.

Day 7: This is a short walk which ends at **Arolla**. The only demanding section being a steep climb from La Gouille to Lac Bleu, followed by an undulating trail through woodland. Some trekkers, however, take a rest day and ride the bus from Les Haudères.

Day 8: On this lengthy stage, the first glacier crossing of the tour is experienced – crampons and ice axe essential, and when the glacier is snow-covered the party should be roped for safety. From Arolla make your way onto the Haut Glacier d'Arolla below Mont Collon, and follow this to the 3087m **Col Collon** on the Swiss-Italian border. On the Italian side the descent leads to **Prarayer** at the end of a demanding 9hr day.

2:10 THE MATTERTAL

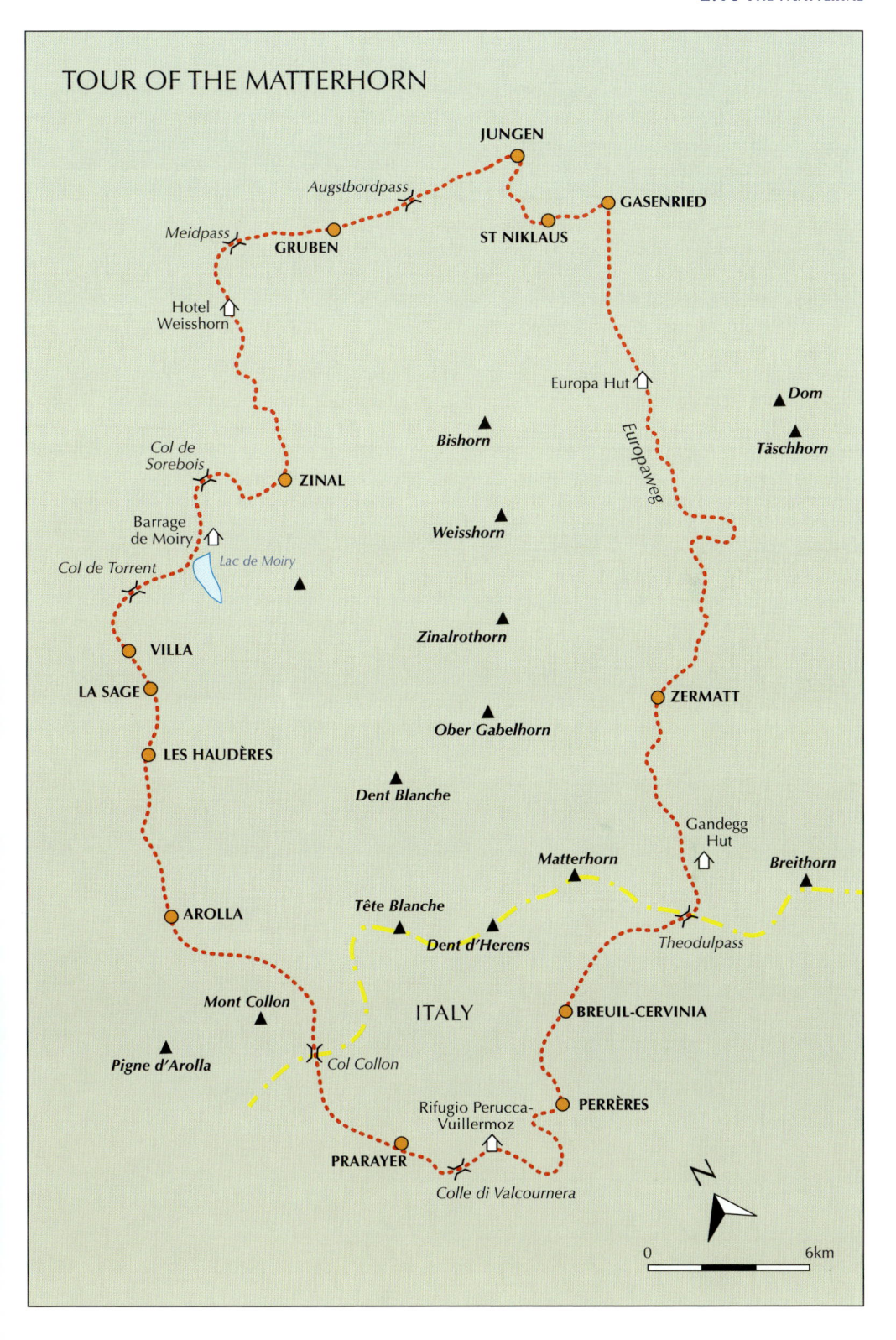

TOUR OF THE MATTERHORN

Day 9: This stage begins with a tough 1000m ascent to the **Colle di Valcournera** (3056m), but on arrival the panoramic view makes all the effort seem worthwhile. There follows a very short descent into a charming landscape, where **Rifugio Perucca-Vuillermoz** is too tempting to ignore.

Day 10: The descent continues to Breuil-Cervinia on the south side of the Matterhorn. But it's not all downhill, for after reaching **Perrères**, you're faced with a steady uphill drag through the valley to **Breuil-Cervinia**, Italy's answer to Zermatt.

Day 11: Cervinia lies at 2006m, and the **Theodulpass** is 3301m, so the first part of the day can be quite gruelling, unless, that is, you choose to take a cable car to Plan Maison to save a little over 1½hrs of walking. Once at the pass a tremendous view opens up, with the Matterhorn (of course) dominating. Descend via the Oberer Theodulgletscher to the **Gandegg Hut**, and either take the cable car from Trockener Steg, or walk down to **Zermatt**.

Climbs from Zermatt

Many summits on the Zermatt rim that played an important role in the history of mountaineering retain their appeal today. These are mostly snow- and ice-mountains with some bare rock ridges. Where rock is exposed on faces, it is more often than not frighteningly loose and, unless held in place by a glaze of winter ice, perhaps best left alone. In recent summers the danger and frequency of rockfall has increased, as illustrated by a notorious incident in 2003, when the Matterhorn shed a massive amount of rock from its East and North Faces, and from the Hörnli Ridge, above which 70 stranded climbers had to be airlifted off. Bearing this in mind, climbers should take note of the effect climatic conditions may have on their chosen route.

Classical alpinism comes into its own on these mountains, for their size and make-up calls for good rope technique and the ability to move quickly over mixed terrain. Fitness, acclimatisation, and the ability to 'read' snow conditions are prerequisites for safe climbing here, yet countless alpine novices serve their apprenticeship on these very mountains. If in doubt about current

Monte Rosa and the Gornergletscher

Monte Rosa and the glacier-hung headwall of the Zermatt basin, seen from the Hörnli Hut

conditions, enquire at the local guides' bureau or tourist office, or ask hut guardians who will have up-to-date local knowledge.

A good number of huts and *berghotels* reduce the length of approach to select routes, as do various mechanical lifts. In the following selection, only the normal routes are outlined, but for a broader range of climbs consult the appropriate Alpine Club guidebooks: *Valais Alps East* and *Valais Alps West*.

- For training purposes, or for the pleasure of rock climbing pure and simple, two neighbouring crags below the 2927m **Riffelhorn** are easily accessible from the Gornergrat railway: the **Gornerflüe** and **Gagenhaupt**. Both give a variety of routes ranging in difficulty from IV to VIII, with those of the Gornerflüe being the longest. The Riffelhorn itself gives a number of climbs on its south-facing wall, its couloirs and along the East Ridge.
- Though often climbed from both the Britannia Hut above Saas Fee, and from the Täsch Hut (see above), the 4199m **Rimpfischhorn** is considered above all to be a Zermatt mountain, and was first climbed from the Fluhalp by Leslie Stephen, Robert Liveing and their guides in 1859 via the WSW Ridge (Rimpfischwänge).

Now graded PD+ the ascent by this route takes about 5hrs from Berghütte Fluhalp.
- The **Strahlhorn** (4190m) neighbours the Rimpfischhorn across the Adler Pass and, like its neighbour, was first climbed (by the three Smyth brothers, with Franz Andenmatten and Ulrich Lauener) from the Fluhalp. Popular on both foot and ski, this first ascent route is a glacier expedition that reaches the Adler Pass, then ascends by the right-hand snow crest leading to the summit ridge. Any difficulties are likely to be found on the section linking the Findel and Adler glaciers (PD).
- The **Monte Rosa Group** is a major attraction. Boasting ten 4000m tops, it's possible to traverse them all in a two-day expedition, overnighting in the CAI's Margherita Hut on the summit of the 4556m **Signalkuppe**. For Zermatt climbers bound for the highest summit, the 4634m **Dufourspitze**, the Monte Rosa Hut, standing beside the Gornergletscher, makes a rather distant base (6–7hrs). From there the ascent by its normal route (PD) involves a height gain of more than 1800m, and is reckoned to be a somewhat tedious snow plod. Perhaps its most famous ascent was by John Tyndall who, despite a number of crevasses

The Matterhorn, with the Hörnli Ridge facing

needing circumspection, climbed the mountain alone in 1858, lightly clad and sustained by a ham sandwich and flask of tea.
- **Liskamm** (4527m) is a double-summited peak with an impressive 5km ridge tracing the Italian border. The North Face is 3km wide and at its highest, rises some 1100m above the Grenzgletscher. According to Oscar Meyer, 'the beauty of the mountain is celestial, as no other in the Zermatt area'. The east summit is the higher point by as much as 50m, and the normal route traces that of the first ascent party along its East Ridge; grade AD. Either the Monte Rosa Hut, or CAI's Gniffeti Hut are used as a base for this climb.
- Dwarfed by both Liskamm and Breithorn, the 'twins' **Castor** (4226m) and **Pollux** (4091m) are predominantly snow mountains whose northern approaches are confused by heavily crevassed glaciers, so they are more frequently climbed via the Italian flank, although the 4km long North Ridge of Pollux gives a 5–6hr AD climb from the Monte Rosa Hut.
- The 4164m **Breithorn** is very much the 'broad mountain' its name implies, and its SSW Flank has the distinction of giving the easiest ascent route of any alpine 4000er (F) – although it becomes a very serious proposition when the mist descends. By use of the Klein Matterhorn cableway the snow saddle of the Breithorn Plateau is reached in just 10mins (or 2½hrs from the Gandegg Hut). The route then goes to the Breithorn Pass where you head up a steep slope to the mountain's SW Ridge, and on to the summit (1–2hrs). Meanwhile the North and NNW Faces of the main summit offer routes of a very different order.
- The **Matterhorn** (4477m) is an elegant pyramid only when seen from afar, for close acquaintance reveals it to be a disintegrating tower of rubble. Well, it does have some redeeming features, and its history and charisma continue to attract like no other mountain. But its most popular route via the Hörnli Ridge (the route of Whymper's first ascent in 1865) is both very long and loose, and much more serious than might be expected by many climbers of average ability who are attracted to it. The 1200m route is graded AD and, in good conditions involves rock climbing of no more than II+, but congestion on the fixed rope sections can add an hour or more to the overall time suggested for the climb on a busy day. In addition, the scarcity of decent

natural belays, and the need for parties to move together on a short rope for the majority of the ascent and descent – and the way the mountain attracts storms – combine to make this a route for the alpine novice to consider only with care. With its three other ridges and four faces, the Matterhorn, of course, has many other challenges for the serious alpinist to aim for. Most of the face routes are infrequently climbed, and the classic NW (Zmutt) Ridge – long considered to be one of the finest mixed routes in the Alps – was controversially equipped with fixed aids by the Zermatt guides in 1999. Despite these it remains a serious undertaking.

- The Matterhorn's western neighbour is the **Dent d'Hérens** (4171m), whose ice-sheathed North Face, rising 1300m from the chaos of the Tiefmatten glacier, looks so impressive from the Schönbiel Hut, and was described by Geoffrey Winthrop Young as 'a lacquer of dark slab and hanging glacier, forcing the eye perpetually outward to the order of its outline' (*On High Hills*). That outline is most clearly expressed by the 2.2km long East Ridge which connects the mountain with the Matterhorn. Although a beautiful crest with plenty of exposure, the rock is said to be appalling, and its ascent is therefore not recommended. Until recently the *voie normale* was by the SW Flank, but with reduced snow cover this has become very loose and dangerous. The West Ridge (AD-) has now become the most popular route, using the CAI's Aosta Hut at the foot of the Tête de Valpelline as a base. Accessed from the Tiefmattenjoch, the West Ridge is therefore a possibility from the Schönbiel Hut, although the approach is long, and the climb to the *joch* threatened by stonefall. Meanwhile the North Face Direct, which became a classic following its first ascent in 1925 (by Welzenbach and Allwein), relies on good conditions to minimise the objective dangers that have increased in recent years.

- The 3799m **Tête de Valpelline** makes a wonderful vantage point for views of the Matterhorn, and is often climbed from the nearby Col de Valpelline by ski-mountaineers nearing completion of the Haute Route. Parties heading west from the Schönbiel Hut, whose journey takes them across the heavily crevassed col, might consider the 45min diversion worth taking.

Ober Gabelhorn, Zinalrothorn and Weisshorn, viewed from the Matterhorn's Hörnli Ridge

- Rising at the head of the Schönbiel glacier, the massive **Dent Blanche** (4356m) has been discussed at some length in 2:6. Traditionally the normal route via the South Ridge was tackled from the Schönbiel Hut, but this lengthy approach via the Wandflue has fallen out of favour, and the mountain is climbed nowadays from the Cabane de la Dent Blanche (see 2:6).
- North of the Schönbiel Hut, the 3789m **Pointe de Zinal** sends down its rocky South Ridge as a division between the Schönbiel and Hohwäng glaciers, and makes a rewarding climb (AD: III/III+) of between 5 and 6hrs. This route was pioneered in 1891 by Norman-Neruda and his favourite guide, Christian Klucker. The normal route, however, is via the NE Ridge (PD), which is gained from the Schönbiel Hut in about 4½hrs by way of the Hohwäng glacier and Col Durand.
- The **Ober Gabelhorn** (4063m) is best seen from the north where its chisel-headed summit peers down the length of Val de Zinal (see 2:8). The *voie normale* is via the ENE Ridge from the Rothorn Hut, but its abrupt South Face, rising from a narrow band of ice above the Arbengandegge which spills out to the Zmutt valley, and being almost entirely good quality rock, gives a very respectable 600m climb (D: IV/IV+) – preferably from the 15-place Arben bivouac hut at 3224m. Another recommended route from the Arben bivouac is the WSW Ridge, otherwise known as the Arbengrat. Longer than the South Face and graded AD: III+ it was first climbed in 1874.
- One of the most dramatic-looking and satisfying rock peaks of the Zermatt basin is the 4221m **Zinalrothorn**, approached from Zermatt through the Trift gorge. Reached by a very steep trail, and perched almost 1600m above the town, the **Rothorn Hut** is the base for climbs on all but the North Ridge. Owned by the Oberaargau Section of the SAC, it has 68 places and is staffed from July to the end of September (www.sac-oberaargau.ch). From it the intricate *voie normale* tackles the SE Ridge (AD: III-), avoiding its upper section, known as the Kanzelgrat, by climbing a snow couloir on the South Face up to the Gabel Notch on the SW Ridge, above which a pinnacle forces the route onto the Biner Slab and a slanting crack. Once back on the ridge, an exposed traverse of a small gendarme then leads to the Kanzel rock tower. This is turned by a ledge above the East Face, and then on to the actual summit with its extensive panoramic view. On the first ascent of this route in 1872, the successful party of Clinton Dent and George Passingham, with the guides Ferdinand Imseng, Franz Andenmatten and Alexander Burgener, were descending the Biner Slab when a dislodged boulder slid between the climbers, was deflected by Andenmatten and bounced over the head of the unroped Imseng.

ULRICH INDERBINDEN: THE OLD MAN OF THE MATTERHORN

In the summer of 2004 Zermatt lost its oldest guide, a simple man whose fame had spread far beyond the valley in which he'd been born and from which he rarely strayed. For 70 years Ulrich Inderbinden guided clients up the local mountains, and only retired from his calling when he was 95, a year after he'd given up skiing.

Inderbinden was born in Zermatt during the exceptionally cold winter of 1900. His parents were poor farmers who, with their nine children, spent the summer months moving between the hamlets of Zmutt and Blatten where they grazed their four cows. From the age of four, Ulrich helped tend the cattle, but by the time he'd reached 20, he had decided on a career as a guide. Yet after qualifying he found it difficult to find work, and it was not until July 1925 that he made his first climb as a professional, taking a client up the Matterhorn. It was a climb he was to make some 370 times.

The early years were hard, as he combined guiding work with helping on his parents' farm, and out of season earned money by clearing snow or labouring for local builders. He became a first-class ski guide, leading clients up 4000m peaks like the Breithorn, and guiding parties on the Haute Route from Mont Blanc to the Matterhorn, yet it was not until after the Second World War that he began to earn a comfortable living from the mountains. Though never one to seek out new routes, he established a reputation as a steady and reliable guide with an impeccable sense of direction in bad weather.

Quoted in his biography, *Ulrich Inderbinden: As Old as the Century*, he claimed that he lived life as he climbed mountains – 'at a pace that is slow and deliberate but also purposeful and regular'. That pace was not as slow as one might expect, for when he climbed the Matterhorn in 1990 for the last time, he reached the summit only four hours after leaving the Hörnli Hut – he was then just short of his 90th birthday, and already an institution. Two years earlier a client had complained that he'd gone too fast on the ascent of the Dufourspitze. 'My dear sir,' he replied, 'if you want to climb more slowly, you must engage an older guide.' He was 87 at the time.

Ulrich Inderbinden attributed his good health and longevity to a positive attitude, and a love of nature and his profession. 'As a child I learnt to be satisfied with little,' he said, 'to make no demands on life and always to work.' The old man of the Matterhorn died in June 2004 at the age of 103, and was buried in the shadow of the mountain on which he had spent so much of his working life.

Zermatt for Skiers

While summer skiing is a possibility for fanatics on the Theodulgletscher, in winter three major sectors served by their own lift systems concentrate all the downhill activity. Top of these is the Schwarzsee–Theodulgletscher region, with the Trockener Steg/Testa Grigia complex giving access not only to the extensive north-facing slopes, but to the Italian side of the border served from Breuil-Cervinia. The Gornergrat–Stockhorn and Sunnegga–Blauherd–Rothorn systems also have a number of runs at most levels of ability, with some good long downhills that descend all the way to Zermatt.

Of course, there's plenty of scope for snowshoe expeditions, and the ascent of such major peaks as the Breithorn from the Klein Matterhorn (see Hilary Sharp's *Snowshoeing* guide).

But perhaps best of all late winter snow expeditions is a week-long tour that links a number of huts and a few lofty summits in a ski-mountaineering journey from Zermatt to Saas Fee. Fitness, and a high level of competence of both skiing and mountaineering is essential, but the rewards are considerable. Bill O'Connor describes such a tour in *Alpine Ski Mountaineering, Vol I*.

The Adlerpass

A series of glacier passes link the upper Mattertal with the Saastal: the Alphubeljoch, Feejoch and Allalinpass (all above Täschalp), the Adlerpass above Fluhalp, and the Schwarzberg Weisstor virtually on the Swiss-Italian frontier. Of these the Allalin and Adler are the best known, with the 3789m **Adlerpass** presenting one of those unforgettable high mountain views by which the geography of the landscape is revealed. Frequently crossed during the ski touring season, but less so in the summer, those arriving at the pass, which lies between Rimpfischhorn and Strahlhorn, first gaze across the upper Saastal to the Weissmies and Portjengrat, then look back to what Alfred Wills (in *Wanderings Among the High Alps*) called a 'scene of surpassing beauty'. Looking into the great glacial basin which falls from the Monte Rosa massif, Wills described what he saw:

> From where we stood to Monte Rosa, and again, from Monte Rosa to the Matterhorn, is one vast amphitheatre of precipitous summits, connected by long lines of glacier, such as I have never seen before or since. Opposite to us was the amazing peak of the Matterhorn, an object which never failed to fill me with astonishment and awe ... A line from the Rimpfischhorn ... to the Matterhorn, would have made the diameter of a semi-circle which was marked by the several peaks of the Strahlhorn, the Cima di Jazzi, Monte Rosa, the Lyskamm – the finest precipice I have ever seen – the twin peaks of the Zwillinge ... the dark frowning crags of the Breithorn, and the Klein Matterhorn [while] over and beyond [the Theodulpass], we saw many of the Piedmontese Alps.

Having noted the view, and tearing ourselves away – metaphorically turning our backs on Zermatt's great basin – it's time to explore the neighbouring Saastal.

2:11 THE SAASTAL

In many respects matching the Mattertal's dramatic mountain scenery, the Saastal is the last of the major valleys of the Pennine Alps, beginning just outside **Stalden** where the Saaservispa spills out of its gorge to join the Mattervispa. On the east bank of the valley, directly opposite but 200m higher than Stalden, the chalets of **Staldenried** cluster on different levels, and are linked with Stalden by cable car. An upper section of cableway continues as far as **Gspon** (1895m), a traffic-free hamlet scattered across sloping meadows with views north across the Rhône valley to the Bietschhorn, and south up the Saastal to the Balfrin. For tourist information contact the Staldenried/Gspon Verkehrsverein or visit www.staldenried.ch.

While the main road into the Saastal follows the left bank of the river, a magical high path ripples along the right flank of the valley between 2000m and 2400m all the way from Gspon to the Kreuzboden lift on the slopes of the Lagginhorn, above Saas Grund. This ◉ ☆ **Gspon Höhenweg** is one of the great walks of the Valais region: 13km and about 5hrs long, with a steadily unfolding panorama of big snow and rock mountains to gaze on as the route makes its way southward. From Kreuzboden there's also an opportunity to extend the walk further by continuing for another 10km (4–4½hrs) on the **Höhenweg Almagelleralp**, which eventually leads down through the Almergellertal into the Saastal proper. The main Gspon Höhenweg is very much the east slope equivalent of the Grächen–Saas Fee Höhenweg (or Balfrin Höhenweg) on the west slope of the valley mentioned in 2:10.

There is no railway in the Saastal, but a frequent postbus service from Visp feeds each of the villages, with some buses going as far as the roadhead at the Mattmark dam in summer. The lower Saastal has one or two tiny hamlets below the road, but before the valley begins to open, **Eisten** (1089m) is the first actual village you reach, although admittedly that is a very small one. About 6km further on lies **Saas Balen** (1483m) below and between the Lammenhorn on a spur from the Balfrin, and the Fletschhorn (tourist information: www.saas-balen.ch). The village is a modest one, but it has some attractive houses, two churches (one with a noted circular nave dating from 1812) and a fine waterfall behind it; it is linked by footpath with Saas Grund, and also has a trail that climbs the eastern hillside to summer alps and the *höhenweg* from Gspon. A route continues above

The alp hamlet of Trift above Saas Grund

2:11 THE SAASTAL

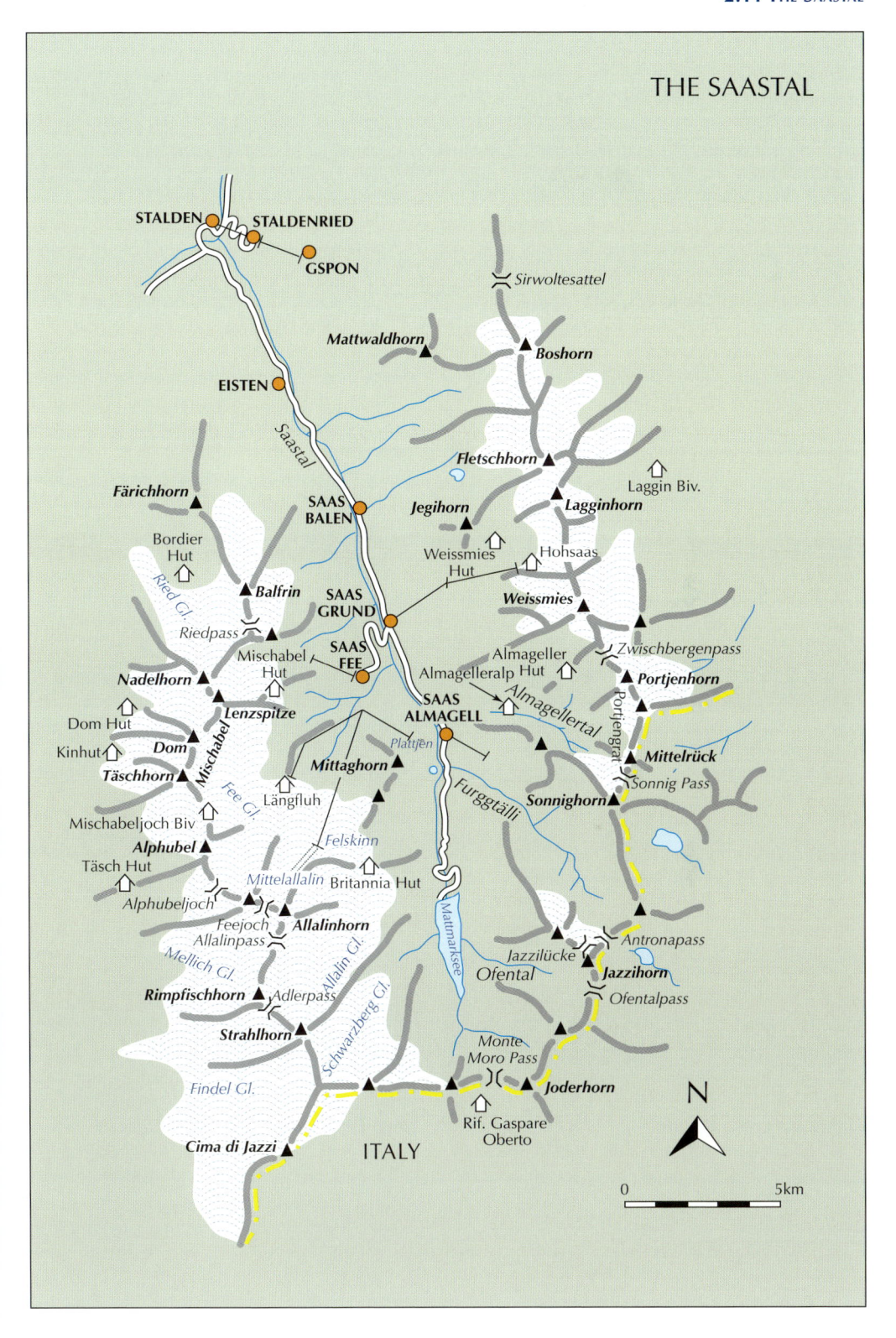

THE SAASTAL

the highest of the alps into the glacial basin under the West Face of the Fletschhorn, while another crosses the 3022m Simelipass on the way to the Simplon Pass. Yet another route makes the uncomplicated ascent of the ◉ **Mattwaldhorn** (3245m) just 45mins above the Simelipass – a minor summit but an excellent vantage point with views of the Bernese Alps to the north, Monte Leone to the east and the Mischabel peaks to the west.

The valley opens out on the approach to its main village, **Saas Grund** (1559m). Despite being overshadowed by the year-round popularity of Fee, which lies on a natural terrace some 250m above to the southwest, Grund has much to offer, with at least 16 hotels up to 3-star standard, plenty of holiday chalets and apartments, and no fewer than five campsites. There's a range of shops and restaurants, a bank, a post office and a climbing school (Bergsportschule Weissmies, www.weissmies.ch). The helpful tourist office is found in the main street (www.saastal.ch), and there are cableways to Kreuzboden and on to Hohsaas. Both provide easy access to the **Weissmies Hut** (2726m), the main base for climbs on this eastern side of the valley. There are two huts in effect, both belonging to the Olten Section of the SAC, with a total of 135 places, staffed from June to the end of September (www.sac-saas.ch/hutten.html). The **Bergrestaurant Hohsaas** (Hohsaashaus; 3100m) by the upper lift station, also has dormitory accommodation and a fine outlook. It's open during the ski season, and from June to late September (www.marnet.ch/over-the-top).

Being centrally placed, Saas Grund makes a good base for a walking or climbing holiday. The climbing potential of the valley's west wall is tapped into from Saas Fee, and this in turn is easily reached by postbus, while the east flank cableway makes the Fletschhorn–Lagginhorn–Weissmies chain an obvious target. Walkers, on the other hand, have a wealth of trails within reach, especially when the postbus is brought into use.

Climbs from Saas Grund

This brief summary of climbs from Saas Grund concentrates on that fine group of mountains on the east side of the valley immediately above the village, dominated by the Weissmies.
- At 4023m the ◉ **Weissmies** is (only just) the easternmost 4000er in the Pennine Alps. But is it still a 4000er? Summit readings in 2004 suggested that global warming had taken its toll, with the snow and ice melting to such an extent that its altitude had dropped to 3999m. Whatever the statistics say, it remains an impressive, handsome mountain that attracts plenty of attention. While there are three main ridges and three principal faces, most of that attention is focused on the NW Flank and the SSE Ridge; the first is served by the Weissmies huts and Hohsaas, the latter by the Almageller Hut (see below for details). Until the late 1980s there were at least six routes on the NW Face, but below the serac barrier of the upper Trift glacier, the mountain has now shed its summer snow cover. In its place a slabby rock wall is threatened by the overhanging seracs. The standard route (PD), which is more popular than the SSE Ridge route through ease of accessibility, uses the NW Flank to gain the broad snow crest of the upper SW Ridge, gaining the summit in about 3½hrs from Hohsaas. (For the SSE Ridge route, see The Upper Saastal sub-section below.)
- The ◉ **Lagginhorn** (4010m) is the central peak of the Fletschhorn–Weissmies chain, but unlike its slightly loftier neighbour to the south, is a rock peak with very little snow remaining on its flanks in summer. The summit ridge runs north–south, with two subsidiary ridges projecting roughly westward, the more southerly of these being above the Weissmies huts, from which the majority of climbs are made. The West Ridge was taken during the Lagginhorn's first ascent in 1856 by a party led by J J Imseng, the Saastal priest (see box), and is the normal route chosen today. Graded PD, the climb from the hut is some 1300m in length, taking around 4–5hrs under good conditions. The SSW Ridge (sometimes referred to as the SW Rib) offers an ascent at the slightly higher grade of AD with a down-climbing section of III.
- At 3993m the ◉ **Fletschhorn** has the lowest summit but is by far the most complex of the three-peak chain above Saas Grund. From the west, Saastal, side the mountain's upper reaches are defended by a barricade of spurs and glaciers; the Rothorngrat and Jegigrat being the main arêtes which support the summit ridge. Its most impressive feature, however, is the North Face with the Rossbodegletscher spilling in a curve towards the Simplon road. From the

The Weissmies, most easterly of the Pennine 4000ers ▶

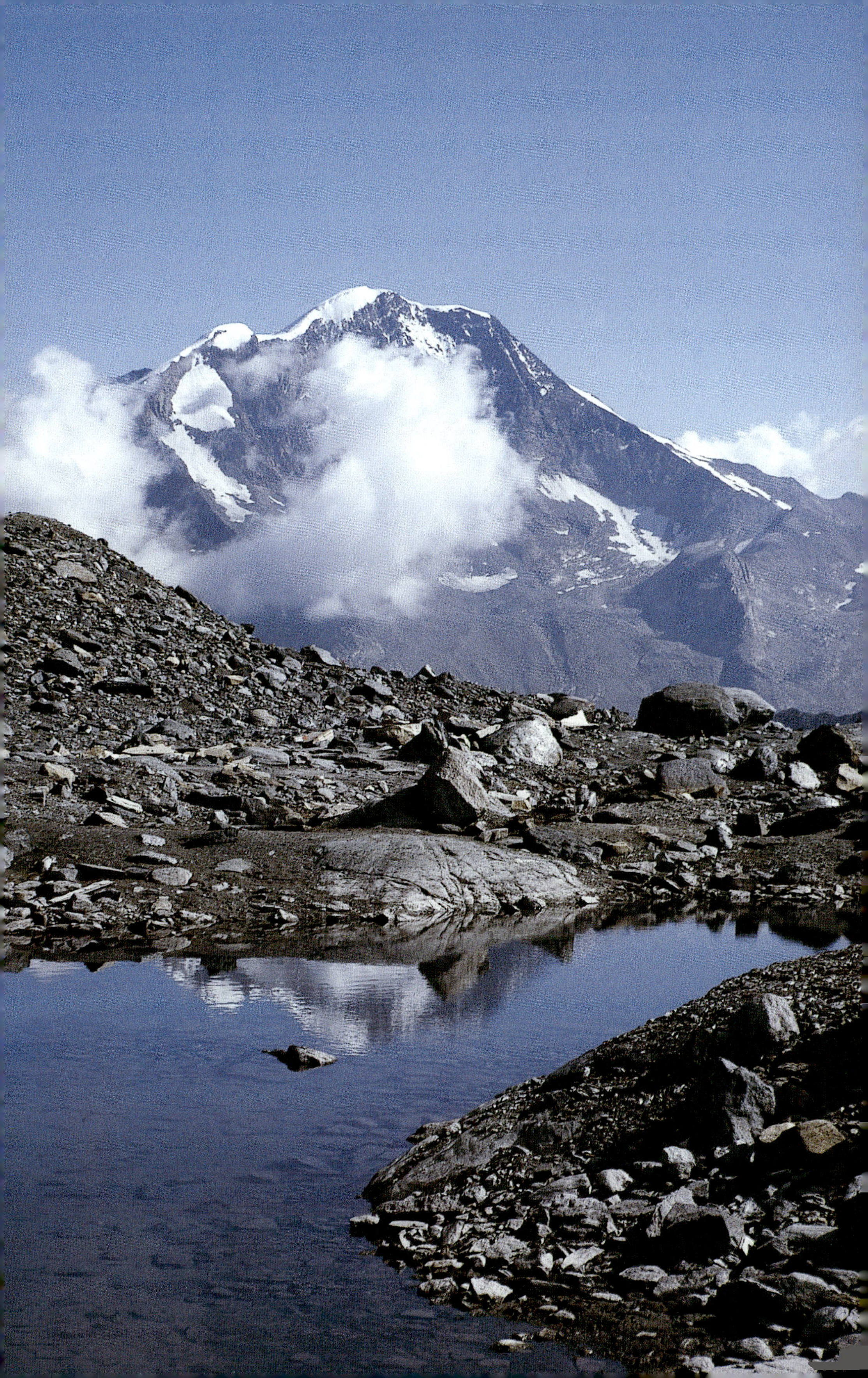

Simplon Pass itself, the Fletschhorn assumes a stature greater than its actual height, while the East Face above Simplon-Dorf is almost entirely rock, broken by a long central ridge spur. The normal route from the Weissmies Hut is a meandering one of some 1300m by way of the West Flank and NW Ridge. Graded PD, allow 4–5hrs.

- The ⊗ **Jegihorn** at 3206m rises above the Weissmies huts at the lower end of the Jegigrat, offering splendid views and a very pleasant scramble of about 1½hrs. There's a path and/or waymarks virtually all the way. There's also a *via ferrata* (*klettersteig*) leading up to the ⓑ **Jegilücke** (3098m), before turning southwest along the Jegigrat to the summit, making this the highest *via ferrata* in the Western Alps (see www.klettersteig.ch).

Saas Fee

The valley road forks in Grund. While the main road continues to Saas Almagell and the Mattmark dam, the other branches right, crosses the river and swings up the wooded hillside in two long loops to emerge onto an open terrace looking into a vast natural amphitheatre gleaming with a curtain of ice. The road ends here, at the entrance to **Saas Fee** (1809m).

Saas Fee has become one of the top mountain resorts of Switzerland, thanks to its unbeatable location at the foot of a string of 4000m peaks, with year-round skiing on the Feegletscher and plenty of mechanical uplift to tease visitors to outstanding viewpoints. The traffic-free village has all modern facilities, including hotels of all standards and lots of chalets and apartments for rent. There's no shortage of shops, restaurants, a bank and bars. There's a post office, a large and efficient tourist office (www.saas-fee.ch), and a mountain guides' office (Bergführerbüro, www.mountain-life.ch). From its origins as a tiny alp hamlet, Fee is expanding across the meadows and steadily filling the amphitheatre floor as the glaciers retreat above it. Its outlook is impressive.

From the village the view south is framed on the left by the steep rock wall of the Mittaghorn, which forms the eastern limit of the Feegletscher. Above the summer-streaming glacial rocks, the ice of this glacier is being drawn ever higher like a blind at a window (a large portion collapsed in September 2009), but at its head the graceful

Saas Fee

The Britannia Hut

snow domes of Allalinhorn and Alphubel, hung with billowing white pelmets, stand either side of the Alphubeljoch. The Alphubel is a cornerstone, from which the west wall of the amphitheatre extends northward along a collection of lofty summits known as the Mischabelhörner, comprising Täschhorn, Dom, Lenzspitze and Nadelhorn. Each of these peaks, plus Allalinhorn and Alphubel, belongs to that noble group of alpine 4000ers.

Three manned huts and a simple bivouac hut provide high altitude bases from which to set out on a variety of climbs, while several mountain restaurants are patronised by walkers and general tourists alike.

With glaciers on either side, the **Britannia Hut** (3030m) stands on a cleft between the Klein Allalin and a ridge of the Hinter Allalin. It's a large hut (134 places) belonging to the Genevoise Section of the SAC, but was partly funded by British members of the Swiss Alpine Club (BMSAC), hence its name. Fully staffed from March to the end of May, and from July to the end of September (www.britannia.ch), when conditions allow it may be reached in 40–45mins from the Felskinn cableway, or by a very fine 2hr walk on a high level path from the Plattjen gondola.

Standing almost at the top of the Längflue rock rib which divides the Feegletscher, the privately owned **Berghütte Längfluh** (2870m) has 120 places, meals provision, is open in the ski season, and from July to the end of September (tel 027 957 21 32). Directly accessible by cableway, it is also reached by a steep path from Saas Fee in about 3hrs.

Built some 1500m above and to the west of Saas Fee, the **Mischabel Hut** (3329m) belongs to the Academic Alpine Club of Zürich. Actually there are two huts built one above the other, with 120 places in total and a full complement of staff from July to the end of September (www.ssf.ch). The 4hr approach path from Saas Fee is unremittingly steep, and has sections of fixed cable but wonderful airy views.

The **Mischabeljoch Bivouac Hut** (3847m) is built on a stilted platform close to the foot of the Alphubel's North Ridge. Unguarded, it has 24 places, cooking facilities and an emergency telephone, and is reached in 4hrs from the Mittelallalin, or from the Täsch Hut.

JOHANN-JOSEPH IMSENG: PRIEST, GUIDE AND HOTELIER

In the village square at Saas Fee there stands a statue of a 19th-century priest decked out in traditional cassock and flat, broad-brimmed hat, his hands resting not on a bible or lectern, but on an ice axe. Johann-Joseph Imseng (1806–1869) was born in Saas Grund the son of a peasant farmer, and spent his childhood tending sheep and goats on the Saastal hillsides. He must have been gifted with intelligence as well as curiosity, for when Alfred Wills met him in 1852, he described him as being 'a good Latin scholar, and [he] can talk Latin with an ease and fluency that would shame many a professed scholar'. He also commented on Imseng's knowledge of rocks, alpine flowers, and the history and topography of the Saastal.

Imseng became the priest of Saas Fee, and in 1836 set out to attract visitors to the valley by opening an *auberge*. A few years later he was running two hotels in Saas Grund and a small inn at the Mattmark lake. Though they were rather grubby places, Imseng was an agreeable and congenial host, beloved and respected by all who came into contact with him. Among his many roles, he became the adviser to practically all visiting climbers; he guided parties across the glacier passes that led to Zermatt, climbed the Nadelhorn, Allalinhorn, Fletschhorn and Balfrin, and attempted the Dom with E S Kennedy. Many of those whom he led commented on his picturesque figure. They described his greasy old cassock ('patched in places innumerable'), and told how he tied it up when an ascent became difficult, betraying a pair of torn breeches beneath. They also remarked on his tremendous vitality, the stamina that left many a client in awe.

When the priest guided Wills and his party across the 3564m Allalinpass in 1852, thereby making the first direct crossing from Saas Grund to Täsch, they set out at 2.30 in the morning. Imseng carried 'a tremendous alpenstock, eight or nine feet long ... and a pair of shoes, all soles and nails, and wore a white low-crowned hat with the top knocked in'. Fresh snow lay on the Allalin glacier, which made the going pretty laborious, and they did not reach the pass until 12.55. The descent to the Mattertal was equally difficult, but when the party finally reached Täsch at 5.15pm, almost 15 hours after leaving Saas Grund, Imseng said farewell to his charges, and continued downvalley to St Niklaus. On arrival he 'sat and slept, with his head on the table, for two hours', before heading off again for Stalden, then marched through the night up the Saastal in order to celebrate mass in Saas Fee at five the following morning.

In 1869, at the age of 63, the priest's body was discovered in the Mattmark lake. It was assumed that he'd had a stroke, fallen from the path and drowned. But not everyone was convinced. Tradition has it that Imseng caught a local guide in the act of poaching. The two men quarrelled, the priest was killed and his body thrown into the lake. Whatever the truth, it was a sad end to the man who did more than anyone to put the Saastal onto the map.

Walks and climbs from Saas Fee

- The 2hr approach to the ◐ **Britannia Hut** from the Plattjen top station is a must, provided, that is, you don't suffer from vertigo, for a good section of the path is exposed with a long view directly onto the rooftops of Saas Almagell. A brief ascent of a glacial remnant takes you to the hut, and (when possible) it's worth ending the walk by following a marked path along the Chessjen glacier to the Felskinn cableway for descent back to Saas Fee. With glacial recession, the route to Felskinn is becoming less popular.
- Another walk using the **Plattjen** gondola lift to gain height, follows what is known as the ◐ **Gemsweg** (chamois path). This makes a 3–3½hr undulating traverse of the headwall of Fee's basin keeping below the glaciers, and cuts right round to the west flank at Hannig, where another gondola takes you back down to the village.
- The multi-day ◐ ☆ **Tour of Monte Rosa** visits Saas Fee, and is well worth considering by experienced mountain walkers. An outline of this route is given below in a boxed section.
- The 3143m ◉ **Mittaghorn** has been secured with a *via ferrata* on its NW Ridge to give a 3hr ascent from the Morenia middle station of the **Felskinn** lift. The *via ferrata* can also be reached

The big Mischabel wall above Saas Fee supports a number of 4000m summits

- by a path cutting away from the Gemsweg mentioned above.
- The snow dome of the 🯂 **Allalinhorn** (4027m) is the easiest of the Saastal's 4000m summits, thanks to the construction of the Metro-Alpin underground funicular leading to the **Mittelallalin**, the effect of which has been to seriously degrade the high mountain environment with piste-making vehicles and other invasive paraphernalia. From the top station at 3454m, the ascent (F) is less than 2hrs via the Feejoch and NW Ridge. But by the Hohlaubgrat (ENE Ridge), the true alpine ambience may be experienced on a climb of more than 1000m starting from the Britannia Hut; grade AD, 4–5hrs.
- Seen to the south of the Allalinhorn across the Allalinpass, the 🯂 **Rimpfischhorn** (4199m) is an imposing mountain topped by a rocky spire. Climbed either from the Täsch Hut, Fluhalp or the Britannia Hut, the usual route from the latter via the WSW Ridge involves a long approach over the Allalin and Mellich glaciers (linked by the Allalinpass), then via the Rimpfischsattel. The summit is gained about 6hrs from the hut (PD+). The North Ridge offers a more direct and exacting route (AD) for climbers based at the Britannia Hut.

- The 🯂 **Strahlhorn** (4190m) is also on the list of Britannia Hut-based climbers, for whom the peak is seen to good effect across the Allalin glacier. A direct route via the Adlerpass and WNW Flank (PD) is equally popular on ski (4–5hrs).
- Seen directly from Saas Fee, the 4206m 🯂 **Alphubel** is a snow mountain pure and simple, but its west flank is buttressed by rock walls emerging from the Weingarten glacier. Climbers based in Saas Fee usually tackle it following an overnight at Berghütte Längfluh, by either the SE Ridge, or the East Flank – both routes graded PD and involving a long glacier approach. If begun from the Mittelallalin, reached by cableway and Metro-Alpin, the approach is shorter, but has the disadvantage of a lack of accommodation, so the only chance of an early start is to bivouac.
- One of the most impressive 4000m peaks in the Pennine Alps, the 🯂 **Täschhorn** (4490m) is usually climbed from the Mattertal. Above Saas Fee the East Face is part of the formidable Mischabel wall, but objective dangers effectively deter the amount of attention its other flanks and ridges receive. The bivouac hut on the Mischabeljoch gives direct access to the classic SE Ridge, and to reach it from the Fee side usually involves a convoluted 4hr route

from the Mittelallalin. The Täschhorn's SE Ridge is then climbed in 5hrs to the summit (AD, III), while a traverse along the NNE Ridge to the Domjoch, followed by the ascent of the Dom, is considered to be one of the finest of its kind in the Alps.

- Despite its proximity to Fee, from where it is seen as the highest part of the Mischabel wall, the ⓘ **Dom** (4545m) is rarely climbed from this side, except as part of a traverse from the Täschhorn (see above).

- The 4294m ⓘ **Lenzspitze** carries the Mischabel wall to its northern limit, while at the same time being the most southerly point of the Nadelgrat. Its NE Face is draped with the Hohbalm glacier, and it is via this face that the mountain received its first ascent in 1870 by Clinton Dent, his guide, Alexander Burgener, and a porter, Franz Burgener. The *voie normale* for Fee-based climbers is the ENE Ridge above the Mischabel Hut. Graded AD, this is one of the hardest of 'normal routes', with its crux being the ascent of the Grand Gendarme (II+) about 2hrs from the hut. The NNE Face (Dreieselwand) has become a popular test piece, and is said to be similar to the Ober Gabelhorn's North Face.

- Close neighbour of the Lenzspitze, the ⓘ **Nadelhorn** (4327m) is the highest of the Nadelgrat's summits, and is climbed from the Mischabel Hut by its NE Ridge (PD), or the SE Ridge (AD) by which it is linked with the Lenzspitze.

The Upper Saastal

The final and most southerly settlement in the Saastal is **Saas Almagell** (1673m), a modest-sized village about 4km beyond Grund. Although it has

---

🚶 ⭐ TOUR OF MONTE ROSA

Making a circuit of the Monte Rosa massif, the TMR is a spectacular 9–11 day trek to match that of the Tour of the Matterhorn (2:10), with which it shares at least three stages. Being a circular tour it could be walked in either direction, but is outlined here as a counter-clockwise route beginning in Saas Fee. See the highly recommended English-language guidebook *Tour of Monte Rosa* by Hilary Sharp (Cicerone, 2007), for a full description, including accommodation details.

Day 1: From the start the trek tackles one of the classic long walks of the Pennine Alps, the **Balfrin Höhenweg** (also known as the Saas Fee–Grächen Höhenweg) which follows a truly dramatic trail from **Saas Fee** to **Grächen** in the Mattertal.

Day 2: This leads the TMR southwards along the famed **Europaweg** high above the Mattertal, but note that sections of this trail are threatened by stonefall. The day ends with an overnight at the **Europa Hut**.

Day 3: Completing the Europaweg, on this stage the trek arrives in **Zermatt** at the foot of the Matterhorn.

Day 4: The glacial **Theodulpass** has to be crossed into Italy, and the TMR trekker can either take two days to walk all the way, staying perhaps in the **Gandegg Hut** on the first night, or take the easy way with cable cars to the Schwarzsee or Klein Matterhorn, and cross the pass to **St Jacques** above Champoluc in Valle d'Ayas in one hard day.

Day 5: Once St Jacques has been reached, the next stage takes the trek eastwards on the south side of Monte Rosa, crossing the mountains to reach **Gressoney-la-Trinité** in Valle di Gressoney.

Day 6: From Valle di Gressoney to Valle della Sesia the route makes its way to **Alagna**, the lowest village on the tour at 1190m.

Day 7: A long day's walk progresses the TMR northward now to **Macugnaga** at the foot of Monte Rosa in readiness for a return to Switzerland.

Day 8: With almost 1700m to gain in order to reach the Monte Moro Pass, this is a tough day's walk, but an overnight is spent just below the pass at **Rifugio Gaspare Oberto** at 2796m.

Day 9: The circuit is completed after crossing the **Monte Moro Pass** and descending into the Saastal, taking the paved Kapellenweg at the end of the day from Saas Grund up to **Saas Fee**.

2:11 The Saastal

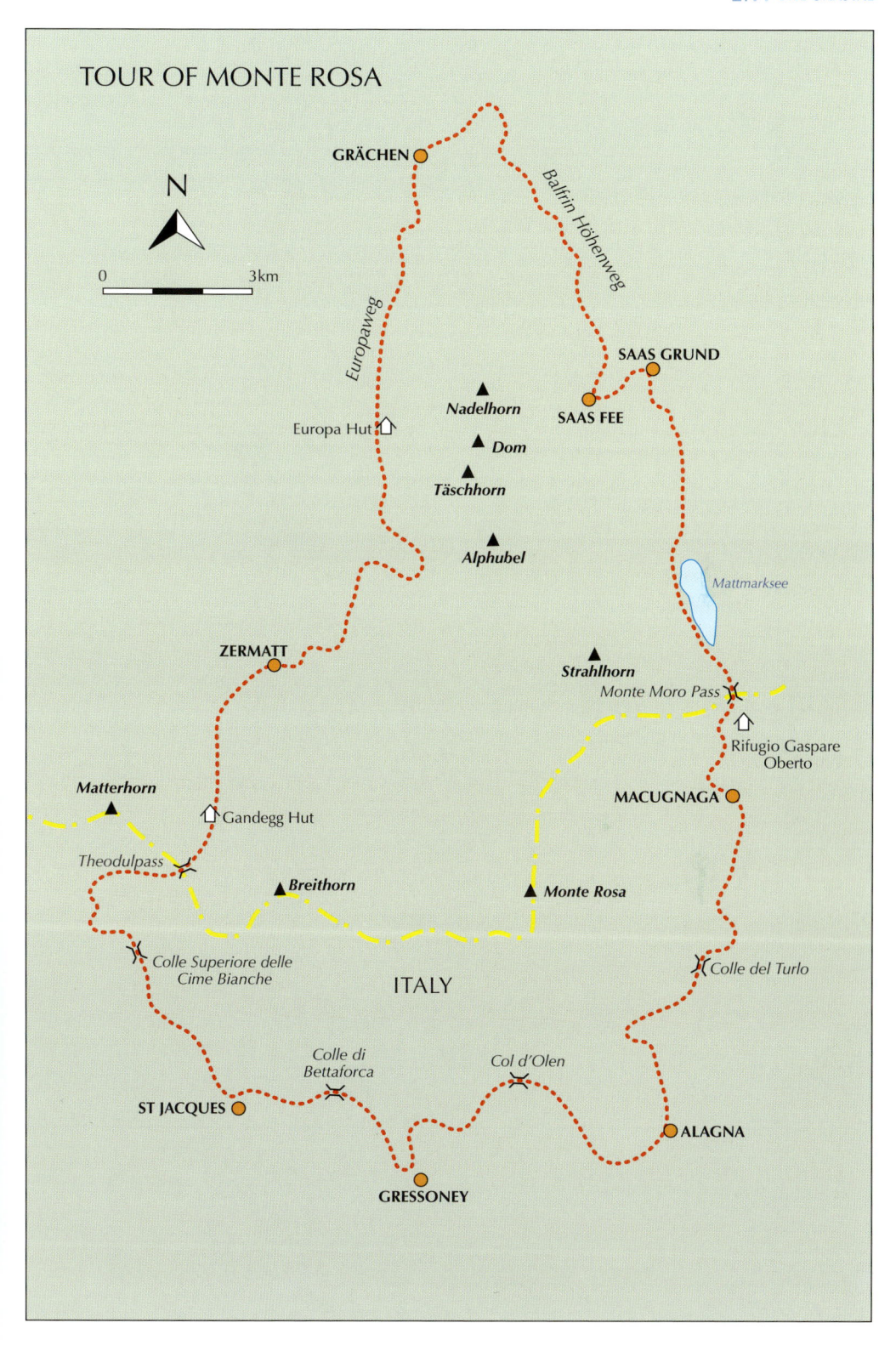

TOUR OF MONTE ROSA

limited shopping facilities, there are at least 14 hotels and pensions, a number of holiday chalets and apartments, restaurants, a post office and a tourist office (www.saastal.ch). From the southern end of the village a chairlift connects with the hamlet of Furggstalden near the mouth of the Furggtälli, a lonely glen at the head of which the Antronapass leads to the Valle d'Antrona in Italy. Meanwhile, at the northern end of Saas Almagell, the Almagellerbach flows from the Almergellertal in which lies the romantic **Berghotel Almagelleralp**, set deep within the glen about 500m above the village, with neither road nor cableway access, but having both standard beds and dormitory places and inspiring views across the Saastal to the Mischabel wall (tel [mobile] 078 644 57 97). High above the inn on the south side of the Dri Horlini in the Wysstal spur, about 3½–4hrs from Saas Almagell, the **Almageller Hut** (2894m) is owned by the Niesen Section of the SAC. With 120 places, it is manned from July to the end of September (www.almagellerhuette.ch).

The road continues south of Almagell for a further 6km, but then ends at a restaurant by the dam holding back the **Mattmarksee** reservoir. Fed by glaciers and streams draining the valley's headwall, the lake was originally formed when the upper valley was blocked by moraines of the protruding Allalin glacier. A hotel stood on the Mattmark alp, but this was submerged when the lake grew and spread further south. As the glacier started to recede, work on the dam began. However, in August 1965 an estimated three million cubic metres of ice broke away and fell onto the construction site, killing 88 workmen.

A service road cuts along the west bank of the lake for a short distance, and after going through a tunnel a track continues further south. A broad path also traces the east bank and, the two routes coming together, leads to the Tälliboden pastures, after which the way steepens on the ascent to the 2868m ⬤ **Monte Moro Pass** on the frontier with Italy (5½hrs from Mattmark). Before the mid-day clouds build up, this is a great vantage point with the huge East Face of Monte Rosa on show, while to the north the Saastal appears as a long trench at the foot of glaciers that sweep below the valley's west wall. On the south side of the pass and a few metres below it, lies the privately owned 40-place **Rifugio Gaspare Oberto**, and an old trail continues the long and steep descent to Macugnaga, while a cableway makes the same journey with less effort.

The Monte Moro is an historic pass that has been in use since at least the 13th century, for it is said that as early as 1250 Italian migrants came this way in order to settle in the Saastal, while a little over a decade later German-speaking Valaisians crossed in the opposite direction. The first mention of a route over the pass is in a treaty of 1403 concerning its maintenance, and in the 16th century it was regularly used by pilgrims on the way to Varallo.

Berghotel Almagelleralp, a peaceful setting with inspiring views

Just 35mins from the gilded Madonna on the Monte Moro Pass, an uncomplicated ascent of the 3035m ⬣ **Joderhorn** leads to the point where the frontier ridge kinks sharply to the northeast. The route along the broad, boulder-cluttered ridge is easy enough in good visibility, but could be problematic in mist. Views are far-reaching and make the diversion from the pass worthwhile. The East Face, which falls on the Italian flank, is a very different proposition, with a variety of respectable routes of around 200m on good quality rock.

Southeast of the Mattmark lake lies the shallow **Ofental**, a peaceful little glen flanked to north and south by ridge spurs extending towards the Saastal from frontier summits. At its head the ◓ **Ofentalpass** (2837m) carries a route down into the Valle d'Antrona, while an alternative trail breaks away before the pass is reached, crosses the rocky and briefly exposed **Jazzilücke** (3081m) and, straying across the Italian slope, cuts north round the **Jazzihorn** to the wild and uncompromising landscape of the **Antronapass** at the head of the **Furggtälli**. From there you can either descend into Italy, or veer left and wander down through the Furggtälli to Saas Almagell to complete a tough but rewarding 7–8hr trek.

The head of the **Almagellertal** is rimmed by a lofty ridge running roughly northward from the Sonnighorn to the Weissmies. The southern half of this ridge borders Italy, but north of Pizzo d'Andolla both sides fall into Swiss territory. The impressive ⬣ **Portjengrat** carries a large section of this ridge across the divide, acting as a vast bracket of quality rock whose traverse is a popular local classic (AD+) of about 10hrs.

At the head of the Rotblatt glacier between Sonnighorn and Mittelrück in the southern section of the frontier ridge, the 3147m ◓ ⬣ **Sonnig Pass** offers a challenging route into the Italian Valle d'Loranco, with long metal ladders fixed to the very steep crags on the east flank – part of the so-called Via Ferrata del Lago.

At the northern end of the Portjengrat the ◓ **Zwischbergenpass** (3268m) gives access to the Zwischbergental and the Simplon road. A waymarked route leads to it in a little over an hour from the Almageller Hut. Since the east side of the pass consists of a steep rock wall, the point of crossing is about 25m higher than, and a little north-east of, the lowest section of ridge. On the eastern side a trail initially cuts along the north flank of the Zwischbergental, just avoiding a tiny glacial remnant, and continues all the way down-valley to Gondo (855m), the last Swiss village on the Italian border at the foot of the Simplon Pass. The Simplon road may actually be reached at a higher point than Gondo by breaking out of the Zwischbergental at the Zwischbergen hamlet, and following a minor roadway that joins the Simplon route at Gabi.

The Zwischbergenpass is also the starting point of the main (SSE Ridge) route on the ⬣ ☆ **Weissmies** for climbers based at the Almageller Hut. With a PD grade, the route keeps to the east side of the ridge for much of the way, before treading a fine snow crest rising gently from the foresummit to the main top – 4½–5hrs from the Almageller Hut. The descent is often made via the Trift glacier to the Weissmies huts or the Hohsaas cableway. (For the normal route from the Weissmies Hut, see the section on Climbs from Saas Grund.)

2:12 THE SIMPLON PASS

Linking Brig in the Rhône valley with Domodossola in the Italian Valle d'Ossola, the Simplon Pass (2005m) not only marks the eastern limit of the Pennine Alps, but is also the official end of the Western Alps. To the east of the broad green plateau rise the Lepontines, and the Central Alps.

The pass itself does not lie on the international frontier. For that it is necessary to descend another 20km or so below the snowy Fletschhorn, Lagginhorn and Weissmies to **Gondo**, a tiny village hemmed in by the granite walls of a gorge, and home of the Swiss customs post.

On the northern, Rhône valley side the road leading to the pass is an exciting one, for the engineers have excelled themselves with a series of short tunnels, galleries, and the beautiful 678m long Ganter Bridge which, supported by two great concrete piers, spans the deep Gantertal. On the approach to the bridge the 3194m Bortelhorn is the first of the Lepontine Alps to be seen, and shortly after crossing, the road comes to the small village of **Berisal** (1524m) and swings round to the west then southwest below the Wasenhorn. Climbing steadily to **Rothwald** (1745m), the road then turns to the south with the protection of avalanche galleries and two more short tunnels before the pass is reached.

THE SWISS ALPS – CHAPTER 2: PENNINE ALPS

THE SIMPLON PASS

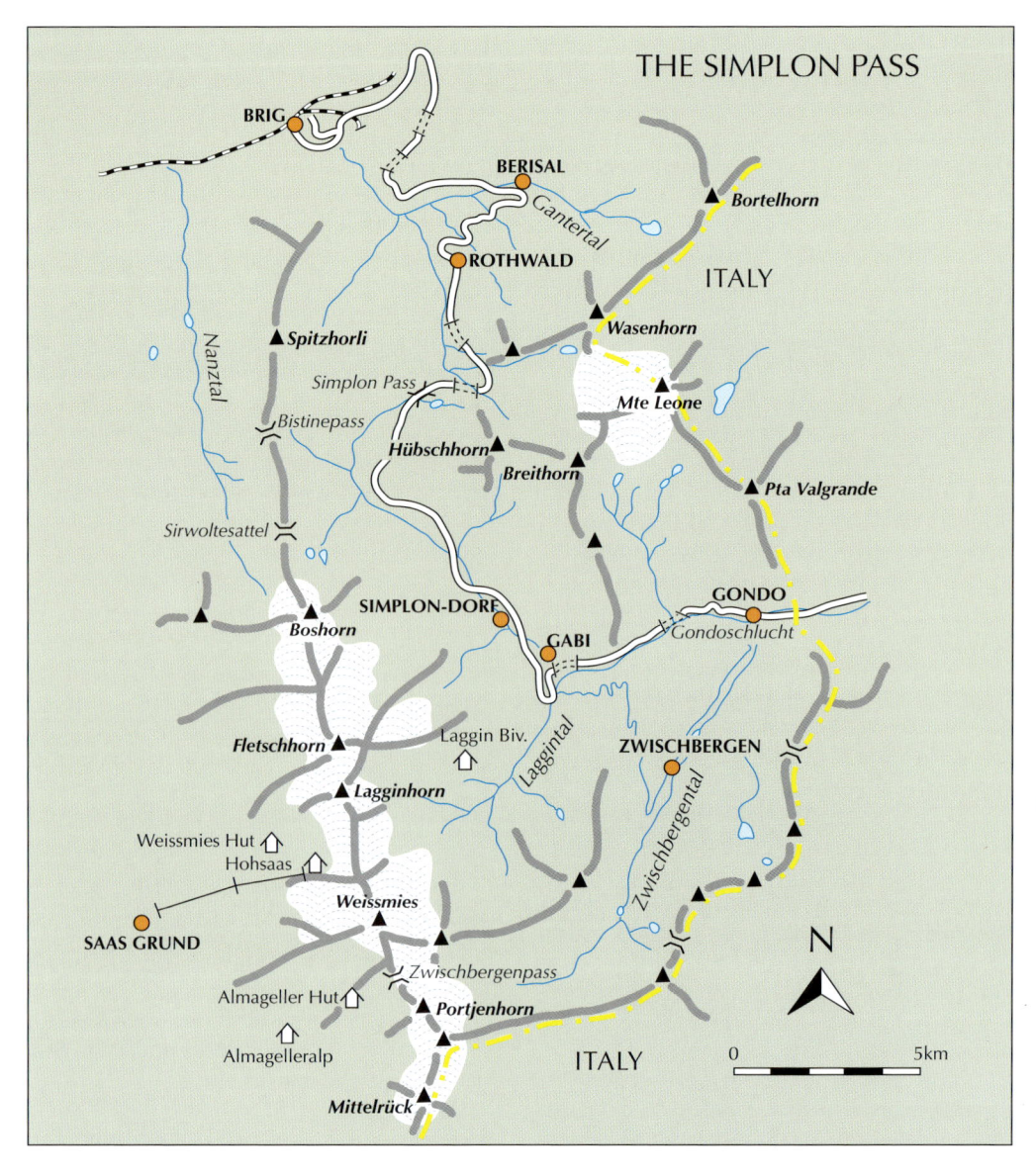

Though neither as dramatic nor impressive as a number of other major crossings, the **Simplon Pass** is a long, gently tilted pastureland, from which a very fine retrospective view shows the Aletschhorn as the dominant feature in the craggy line of the Bernese Alps, while to the south it is the North Face of the Fletschhorn that captures your attention. Nearer to hand Monte Leone is the highest of the Lepontines, and with its two small glaciers makes a worthy neighbour of the Pennine Alps. A number of buildings stand alongside the road, including the Hotel Bellevue-Kulm, and the old hospice which has been occupied since 1825 by monks from the Grand St Bernard Hospice. But the Simplon has thankfully been spared much of the tackiness that adorns many alpine road passes, and footpaths seduce across the meadows. Whilst leaving those on the eastern side to the Lepontines chapter, it is worth noting that one signed trail accompanies the road along its western side, then plunges down to the cobbled village of **Simplon-Dorf** (1472m) in 2½hrs. From there a continuation could be made to Gondo via Zwischbergen and the lower Zwischbergental. This is part of a longer two-day hike which follows the 35km long mule-track of the 🟢 **Stockalper Weg** between Brig and Gondo.

From Simplon-Dorf, the **Laggin Bivouac Hut** (2428m) on the eastern slope of the Lagginhorn, may be reached by a walk of 3½hrs. The hut is unmanned, but with 10 places, cooking facilities and an emergency telephone, it makes a useful base for climbing the 🟢 **Lagginhorn's East Rib**, and the SE Ridge (Hosaasgrat) of the 🟢 **Fletschhorn**, a long AD route first climbed in 1876.

ACCESS, BASES, MAPS AND GUIDES

Access

Val Ferret From Martigny to Ferret via Sembrancher and Orsières. By railway from Martigny to Orsières. A side road climbs from Som-La-Proz to Champex.

Val d'Entremont By road from Martigny via Orsières. Daily buses (summer only) to the Col du Grand St Bernard from Martigny, but more frequently from Orsières.

Val de Bagnes From Martigny via Sembrancher. By railway from Martigny to Le Châble, from where the postbus continues as far as Mauvoisin.

Val de Nendaz By road (postbus) from Sion to Nendaz, Super Nendaz and Tortin.

Val d'Hérémence From Sion to Le Chargeur by road (postbus).

Val d'Hérens By road (postbus) from Sion to Les Haudères and Arolla, with a side road climbing to Ferpècle, La Sage and Villa.

Val de Moiry From Sierre to Grimentz via Vissoie; the road extends (in summer only) to the southern end of Lac de Moiry and is served by postbus.

Val d'Anniviers Sierre to Zinal by road (served by postbus), with a side road climbing from Vissoie to St-Luc and Chandolin (postbus from Vissoie).

Turtmanntal By road from Turtmann to Gruben, or cableway from Turtmann to Oberems, and bus from there to Gruben.

Mattertal By road from Visp to Täsch, with side roads to Torbel and Grächen above St Niklaus, and from Täsch to Täschalp. No motor vehicles, other than those owned by locals, are allowed between Täsch and Zermatt. Use the Brig–Visp–Zermatt railway for this final leg.

Saastal By road from Visp via Stalden, with postbus to all Saastal villages.

Simplon Pass From Brig take the E62 road. A daily postbus service crosses the pass to Domodossola.

Valley Bases

Val Ferret Champex, La Fouly

Val d'Entremont Orsières, Bourg-St-Pierre

Val de Bagnes Le Châble, Verbier, Fionnay

Val de Nendaz Nendaz, Siviez

Val d'Hérémence Pralong

Val d'Hérens Evolène, Les Haudères, Arolla

Val de Moiry Grimentz

Val d'Anniviers Zinal

Turtmanntal Gruben

Mattertal Grächen, St Niklaus, Randa, Täsch, Zermatt

Saastal Saas Grund, Saas Fee, Saas Almagell

Simplon Pass Simplon-Dorf

Information

Valais Tourism, Rue Pré-Fleuri 6, CH-1951 Sion (tel 027 327 35 70 www.valaistourism.ch)

Huts

Numerous huts and bivouac shelters, both SAC and privately owned, as well as remote mountain inns or *gîtes*, are located in all the main areas described. The vast majority of these are staffed during the high summer season. Details are given in the text.

Maps

Kümmerly + Frey produce a 1:120,000 sheet (Wallis) of the whole Pennine Alps range which is useful for planning purposes

Cartes Nationales de la Suisse publish two composite maps that cover most of the range at 1:50,000 – numbers 5003 Mont Blanc–Grand

Combin and 5006 Matterhorn–Mischabel, while six standard sheets at the same scale are required to cover all the Swiss side of the Pennine Alps – 282 Martigny, 292 Courmayeur, 283 Arolla, 273 Montana, 274 Visp, and 284 Mischabel

Walking and/or Trekking Guides

Walking in the Valais by Kev Reynolds (Cicerone, 4th edition 2014)

Walking in Switzerland by Clem Lindenmayer (Lonely Planet, 2nd edition 2001)

Chamonix to Zermatt: the Walker's Haute Route by Kev Reynolds (Cicerone, 6th edition 2019)

Tour of the Matterhorn by Hilary Sharp (Cicerone, 2006)

Tour of Monte Rosa by Hilary Sharp (Cicerone, 2007)

Trekking in the Alps by Kev Reynolds (Cicerone, 2011)

Trekking & Climbing in the Western Alps by Hilary Sharp (New Holland, 2002)

Snowshoeing: Mont Blanc & the Western Alps by Hilary Sharp (Cicerone, 2002)

Climbing Guides

Mont Blanc Massif Volume II by Lindsay Griffin (AC, 1991)

Valais Alps West by Lindsay Griffin (AC, 1998)

Valais Alps East by Les Swindin and Peter Fleming (AC, 1999)

The Alpine 4000m Peaks by the Classic Routes by Richard Goedeke (Bâton Wicks, 2nd edition 2003)

The 4000m Peaks of the Alps by Martin Moran (Alpine Club, 2007)

Guide du Valais – du Trient du Nufenen by Hermann Biner (SAC)

Alpes valaisannes 1 – Trient–Gd-St-Bernard by Maurice Brandt (SAC)

Alpes valaisannes 2 – Gd-St-Bernard–Col Collon by Maurice Brandt (SAC)

Alpes valaisannes 3 – Col Collon–Theodulpass by Maurice Brandt (SAC)

Alpes valaisannes 4 – Theodulpass–Monte Moro by Maurice Brandt (SAC)

Alpes valaisannes 5 – Monte Moro–Simplon by Maurice Brandt (SAC)

Hochtouren im Wallis/Guide du Valais by Hermann Biner (SAC)

Escalades en Bas-Valais by François Roduit (Atelier Imprimex)

Escalades en Valais by Eric Blanc and Dominique Lugon (Atelier Imprimex)

Escalades en Valais Central by Daniel Blanc, Dominique Lugon and Patricia Procellana (Atelier Imprimex)

Kletterführer Oberwallis by Beat Ruppen (topo diagram guide to crags in Turtmanntal, Mattertal, Saastal and the Simplon Pass area)

Schweiz Extrem by Jürg von Känel (Editions Equinoxe)

Schweiz Plaisir West by Jürg von Känel (Editions Equinoxe)

Les Plus Belles Courses dans les Alpes Valaisannes by Michel Vaucher (Denoël, 1979 – also published in German as *Walliser Alpen, Die 100 schönsten Touren*)

Skitouring/Mountaineering

The Haute Route by Peter Cliff (Cordee)

Alpine Ski Mountaineering: Vol I: The Western Alps by Bill O'Connor (Cicerone, 2002)

See Also

The High Mountains of the Alps by Helmut Dumler and Willi P Burkhardt (Diadem, 1994)

Walking in the Alps by Kev Reynolds (Cicerone, 2nd edition 2005)

Walking in the Alps by J Hubert Walker (Oliver & Boyd, 1951)

Freie Sicht aufs Gipfelmeer by Marco Volken and Remo Kundert (Salvioni Edizioni, 2003) describes modest routes to 3000m summits in several regions of the Swiss Alps.

Klettersteige Schweiz by Iris Kürschner (Rother, 2004) describes 55 *via ferrata* (Klettersteig) routes throughout the Swiss Alps.

CHAPTER 3: LEPONTINE AND ADULA ALPS

The Alps of Ticino, spreading northeast of the Simplon to the Splügen Pass, but south of the Rhône and Vorderrhein valleys.

LEPONTINE AND ADULA ALPS: CHAPTER SUMMARY

Location
South and east of the Oberland at the hub of the alpine chain, the Lepontine Alps straddle the Swiss-Italian border from Monte Leone overlooking the Simplon Pass, as far as Passo di San Giacomo at the head of Val Formazza. But east of the San Giacomo a block of mountains spills southward in a complex group contained within Canton Ticino (Tessin), where they are sometimes referred to as the Ticino Alps. The Lepontines continue east to, and just beyond, the Lukmanier Pass where the Adula Alps begin. These spread south and eastward beyond Valle di Blenio to fill the gap which ends at the Splügen Pass.

☆ Highlights

☁ Walks
- Griesspass (3:3)
- Passo di Cristallina (3:3)
- Tour of Val Piora (3:4)
- Passo di Redorta (3:5)
- Tour of Valle di Blenio (3:7)
- Sentiero Alpino Calanca (3:8)
- Plaun la Greina (3:9)

⊙ Climbs
- Monte Leone (3:1)
- Ofenhorn (3:2)
- Pizzo Campo Tencia (3:4)
- Basòdino (3:6)
- Rheinwaldhorn (3:7 and 3:9)

⊗ Summits for all
- Wasenhorn (3:1)
- Cristallina (3:3)
- Piz Terri (3:7 and 3:9)
- Pizzo Tambo (3:9)

Contents

3:1 Simplon Pass East 189

3:2 Binntal 191

3:3 Val Bedretto 194
Capanna Corno-Gries 196

◂ *Pizzo del Prévat and the SAT-owned Capanna Leit*

Capanna Piansecco 197
The Cristallina Massif 199

3:4 Valle Leventina 200
Val Piora Nature Reserve 200
Valle Leventina's South Flank 203

3:5 Val Verzasca 205
Lavertezzo's Valleys 207
Val d'Osura 207
Upper Val Verzasca 209

3:6 Valle Maggia and Its Tributaries 211
Valles di Campo and Bosco 211
Val Bavona 212
Val Bavona North 214
Val Lavizzara 215
Val di Prato 215
Val di Peccia 216
Fusio and The Upper Valley 216

3:7 Valle di Blenio 217
Val Malvaglia 219
The Rheinwaldhorn (box) 220
Malvaglia to Olivone 220
Valle Santa Maria 221
Valle Camadra 221
Tour of Valle di Blenio (box) 223

3:8 Vals Calanca and Mesolcina 224
Val Calanca 224
Valle Mesolcina 227

3:9 The Northern Valleys 229
Rheinwald 229
Surselva 231
Ruin' Aulta (box) 232
Valsertal 232
Val Lumnezia 234
Val Sumvitg 234
Plaun la Greina (box) 235
Val Medel 235
The Oberalp Pass 236

Access, Bases, Maps and Guides 237

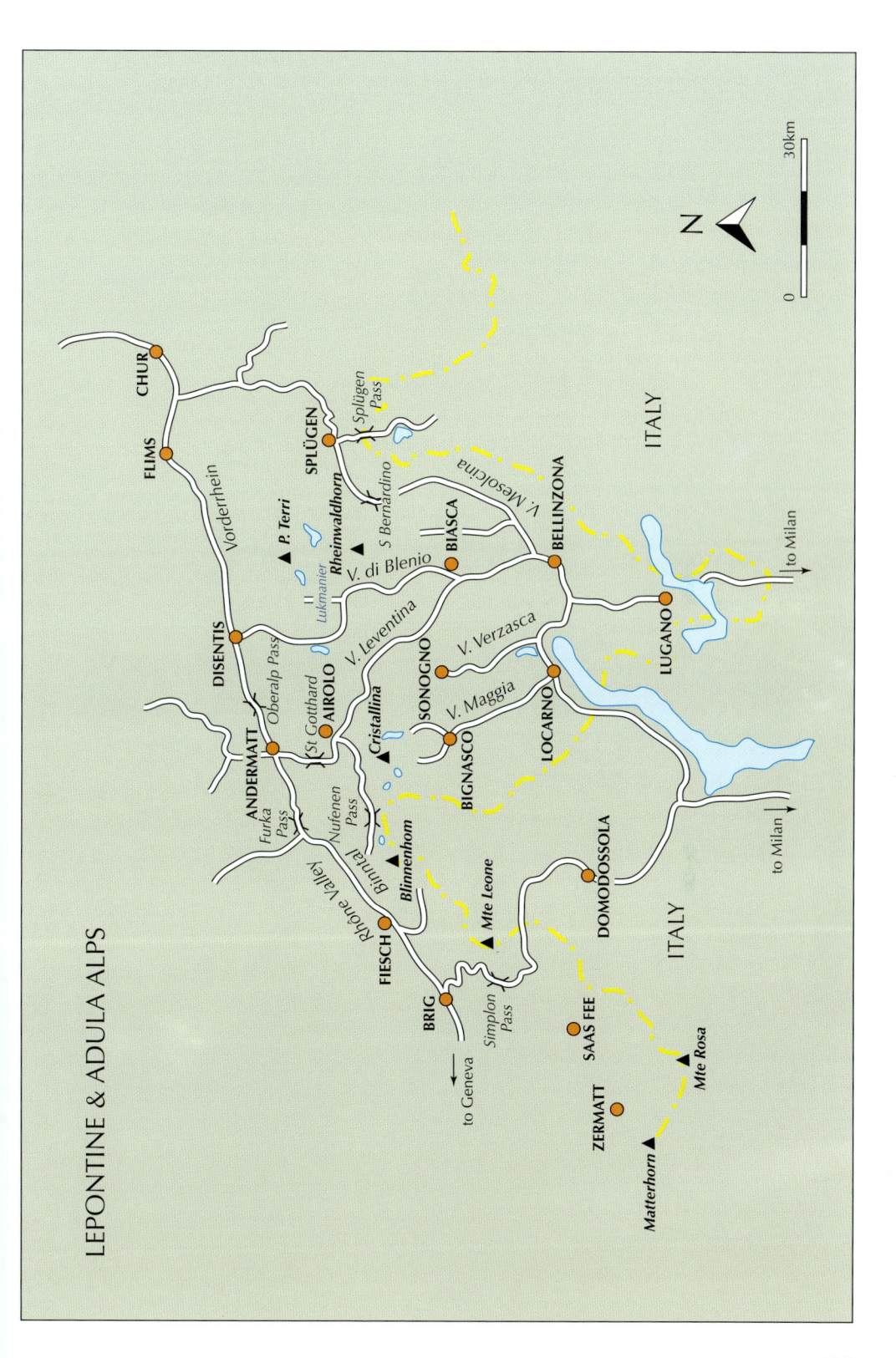

LEPONTINE & ADULA ALPS

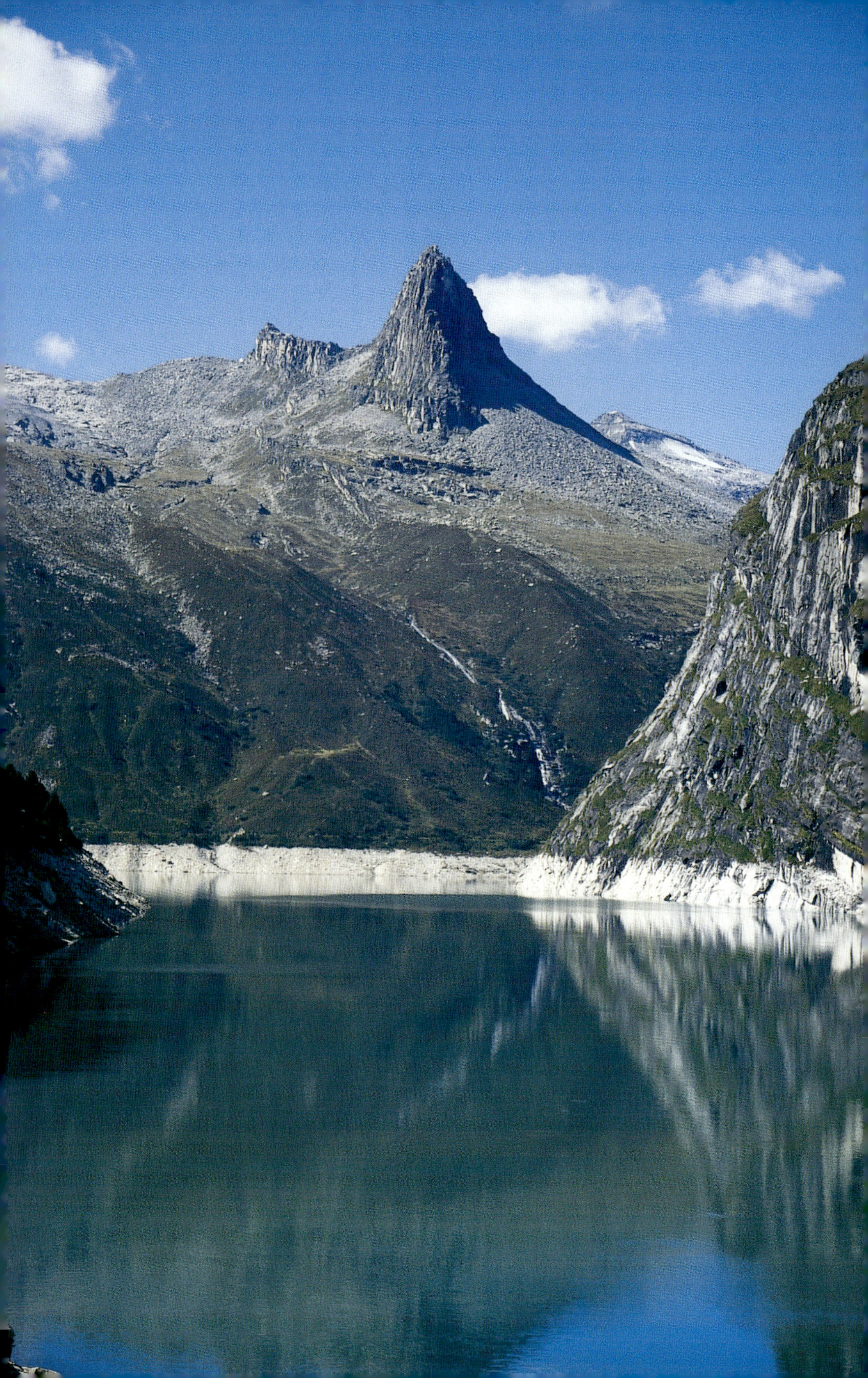

LEPONTINE AND ADULA ALPS: INTRODUCTION

The characteristics of this Alpine Group ... are warmth, sunshine and light – a noble combination of atmospheric qualities.

J Hubert Walker, *Walking in the Alps*

By direct contrast with the neighbouring Pennine and Bernese Alps, the Lepontine and Adula groups are, to English-speaking activists, among the least known and most scarcely documented of all Swiss mountains which, for some of us, adds considerably to their appeal.

Spreading in a well-defined arc to form the alpine watershed, they rise on their northern side from the upper Rhône and Vorderrhein valleys, but fall steeply to the south in a complex system of ridge, spur and valley to the lakes of Maggiore, Lugano and Como. Between the Simplon and Splügen four other road passes breach this watershed: the Nufenen, St Gotthard, Lukmanier and San Bernardino, but beyond their highways lies a surprisingly remote country. The inner valleys have roads and villages, of course, but there's little in the way of tourist infrastructure, and during the last 100 years or so the mountains of Ticino have experienced serious depopulation. But some of the crumbling chalets of long-gone farmers are now being restored as holiday homes for city dwellers in search of solitude.

All the Ticino region is Italian-speaking. In fact it was part of Italy until the early 16th century, and sharing many of the features of Lombardy – not just language, but climate, architecture and culture – the district clearly reflects its origins. As Walker pointed out, warmth, light and sunshine are its main characteristics. The inner valleys remain largely undisturbed, the villages unspoilt, and it's perfectly feasible to wander for days at a

Val d'Osura

◀ *The Zervreilahorn stands like a finger above the Zervreilasee* time without seeing more than a handful of other visitors.

It's true that the hydro engineers have tamed some of the high mountain lakes, but in the decades since they left, nature has worked its magic and partly camouflaged the workings. In only a few districts concrete dams may be found that insult the wild places, and with no skiable terrain to challenge the popularity of neighbouring groups, both the Lepontines and Adula Alps have been largely spared the bulldozing of pistes, creation of lift systems and other developments associated with winter resorts. As Hubert Walker put it: 'For the lover of pure mountain beauty, whose mind is unmoved by the popular appeal of places just because they are popular, but whose aim is rather to find other places where he may enjoy mountain landscape of the most exquisite loveliness in comparative solitude, this is the district' (*Walking in the Alps*).

There are no famous names among these mountains, no major expeditions to be made, no routes of notoriety. Good rock climbing is in short supply, and there's little to tempt those who dream of either big walls or mixed routes with ice or snow that lasts much beyond winter. Although excellent granite does exist, there's some rather unpleasant scrambling to be had on schist and slate unless you have an eye for route-finding. In the original Conway and Coolidge guide of 1892, it was said that these mountains were 'not suited for the purposes of the gymnastic climber and do not offer the comforts demanded by the centrist, but … they are admirable for the wanderer'.

This last comment has been echoed by others. Freshfield was one, but here's Walker again, his claim perhaps rather overstated in his understandable enthusiasm for the region: 'There is no single district of the whole alpine chain better suited to a continuous walking-tour from valley to valley, from glen to glen, and there is scarcely a mountain in it whose summit cannot be reached by a rough uphill walk.'

R L G Irving, as always, put it in context. 'Though of inferior height to the great peaks west of the Simplon,' he wrote, 'and of little interest to ambitious climbers, this comparatively unfrequented part of the main range offers great attractions to those who like to get away from tourists and are content with mountains built on a smaller and less formidable scale than the giants of Zermatt' (*The Alps*).

The topography is confusing, access often lengthy. There's no major crestline, such as that which defines the Pennine and Bernese Alps, but a straggle of interconnecting ridges linked by comparatively low saddles that have been crossed since at least the Middle Ages. The highest summits are concentrated in the most northerly quarters on or near the outer edges. The heartland is disconnected, for isolated groups of mountains thrust away from the watershed to divide valleys that radiate and multiply above and beyond the great lakes. In turn these valleys are subdivided by projecting spurs, so a multitude of side glens create a variety of routes for the discerning wanderer.

To give a rough sense of the district's geography, the Lepontines begin at the Simplon Pass and spread northeast above the Italian enclave of Val d'Ossola and its tributaries the Vals Devero, Antigorio and Formazza. So far as Swiss territory is concerned, this is a narrow line of mountains accessed first from the Simplon Pass, then by the very lovely Binntal, whose head is crowned by the Ofenhorn and threaded by the Italian border. The line of mountains continues north of the Ofenhorn where the Blinnenhorn tips its glacier towards the Griessee above the Nufenen Pass, whereupon the arc curves eastward either side of Val Bedretto which drains down to Airolo at the foot of the St Gotthard.

Near the head of Val Bedretto the Passo di San Giacomo redirects the Italian border southward, and all the mountains east of this pass and south of Val Bedretto are Swiss mountains belonging to Ticino – Basòdino, Cristallina and Campo Tencia being the best known – with valleys cutting south as tributaries of Valle Maggia.

Below the St Gotthard Pass Airolo links Bedretto with the much-abused Valle Leventina, the main arterial valley hereabouts, whose major transalpine highway, railway and power lines run southeastward to Biasca, Bellinzona and on to the Italian lakes. This valley effectively divides the Ticino mountains into two blocks, with the watershed ridge continuing its eastward trend as far as the Lukmanier Pass, and mostly gentle mountains easing in an extensive line south of east, then roughly southward down to Biasca, with Valle di Blenio and its tributaries marking its eastern limit. From here to the Splügen the geography becomes confused, and the mountains challenge any attempt to group them into easy categories.

3:1 SIMPLON PASS EAST

Fortunately, the Lukmanier Pass carries less traffic than the St Gotthard, and the Valles Santa Maria and di Blenio are therefore much more attractive to visit than Leventina. East of the Lukmanier the watershed ridge makes a brief northward kink round the head of Valle Camadra, but at Piz Tgietschen it concludes its eastbound course, for a long crest of mountains now runs in a north–south line via Piz Terri and the Rheinwaldhorn to carry the Adula Alps between Valle di Blenio and Valle Mesolcina, the latter headed by the San Bernadino Pass a little west of the Splügen.

At the eastern end of the Pennine Alps the alpine watershed makes a northward turn by the Monte Moro Pass at the head of the Saastal (2:11), continues north along the Weissmies–Lagginhorn–Fletschhorn crest, and only resumes its eastward trend near the Tochuhorn above the Simplon. As was noted in 2:12, the Simplon not only carries the watershed, but effectively marks the divide between the Pennine and Lepontine Alps.

Reached by postbus from Brig, the Bellevue-Kulm Hotel (tel 027 979 13 31) stands on the

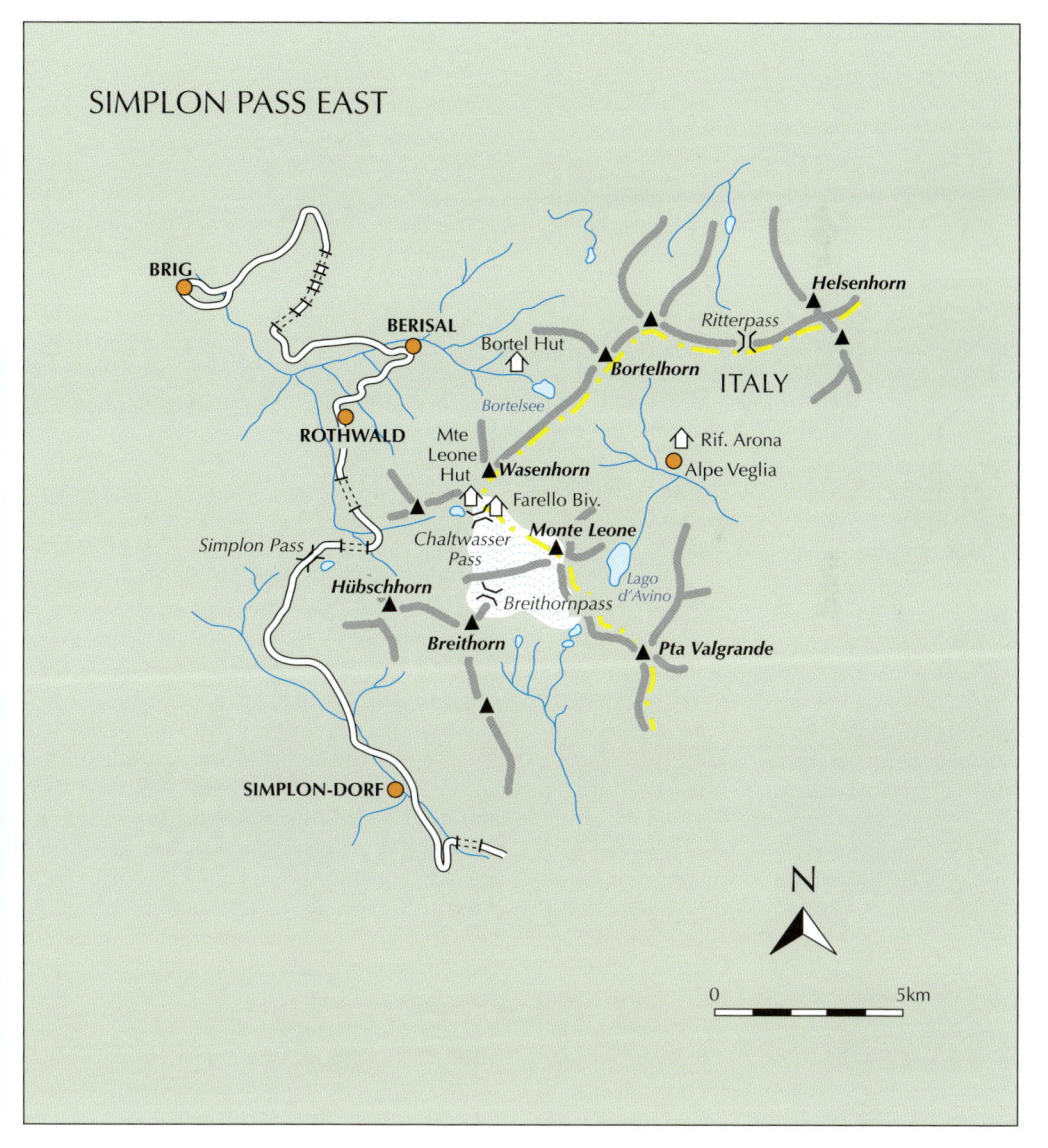

189

Monte Leone, easily reached from the Simplon Pass

highest point of the pass, the massive pink-walled Simplon Hospice a little further to the north. With 132 places, and open throughout the year, this historic building which dates back to Napoleonic times and is now run by Augustinian monks, makes a useful base for a variety of walks and climbs (tel 027 979 13 22).

From the plateau-like saddle the glacier-draped Fletschhorn seen to the south is the most dominant mountain feature, while the Aletschhorn captures your attention across the Rhône valley. Though much closer on the eastern side of the Simplon, Monte Leone, highest of all Lepontine summits, is only on show from a few select places. Above the pass the Hübschhorn is the first of the Lepontine Alps, its higher neighbour the Breithorn (yet another to bear this name) stands just to the east of that, with a ridge linking it with Monte Leone.

The **Hübschhorn** is a double-summited peak whose western top measures 3187m, while the main, east summit (3192m) is reached along an unstable connecting ridge, and is marked with a cross. The steep NW Face looks down on the pass, but the mountain also has some decent rock on its north and east flanks, while scree and boulder slopes fall from the southwest and south. Routes of II, III and IV exist on the various rock faces, with a grade IV route on the NW Ridge, while the normal route tackles the WSW Ridge. Like most of its neighbours, the Hübschhorn makes an outstanding viewpoint, with the Bernese Alps to the north and Pennine Alps stretching off to the southwest.

Few Lepontine mountains carry glaciers, but the 3553m **Monte Leone** has the Chaltwasser (or Kaltwasser) glacier on its west flank, and the tiny Homatten on the southwest side below the **Breithornpass**, which forms a link with the Alpjer glacier on its south flank. The north side tilts remnants of the Aurona and Leone glaciers towards Alpe Veglia in the Italian Valle Cairasca, while the east side of the mountain is ice-free. Divided by a prominent spur, this East Face consists of steep rock walls that soar above **Lago d'Avino**. The normal route on the Swiss flank is a basic snow and ice climb usually approached from the Simplon Pass, by which the summit may be reached in about 6hrs – a ski ascent is also possible from March to June. It uses the Homatten glacier to gain the Breithornpass, then heading east traverses the crevassed Alpjer glacier to the southern ridge (Stickelgrat). The easy but friable rocks of this ridge enable the summit cross to be reached without difficulty. From here the panoramic view is considered to be one of the finest of the alpine chain, with the whole of the Bernese Alps laid out for inspection, a cluster of major Pennine summits on show – Mischabelhörner and Weisshorn among them – as well as the mountains of Ticino swelling to the east.

Reached in 2½hrs from the Simplon Hospice, the ◐ **Monte Leone Hut**, as its name implies, is also used as a base for ascents of Monte Leone, but even for walkers with no interest in climbing, the hut approach is well worth making. The route begins at the hospice where a signed track gives way to a footpath rising over pastures, and after about 20mins is joined at a large pylon by an alternative path coming from the Bellevue-Kulm Hotel. Shortly after, a *bisse* (irrigation channel) is followed, with Monte Leone now in view directly ahead, the crevassed Chaltwasser glacier spread across its west flank. Beyond the *bisse* the way labours up a slope below the glacial moraine and continues to a tarn below the **Chaltwasser Pass** (Bocchetta di Aurona). On the east side of the pass a descent of less than 2hrs leads to the beautifully situated Alpe Veglia, where the Italian Alpine Club has a hut. (There's also the **Farello bivouac hut** on the Italian side of the pass.)

Owned by the Sommartel section of the SAC, the small, single-storey Monte Leone Hut stands almost 80m above the Chaltwasser Pass at 2848m. With places for 34 it is usually manned from June to the end of August, and sometimes in September (www.cas-sommertel.ch). It can also be reached by a path from Rothwald on the road from Brig in 3½hrs. The prominent 3246m pyramid of the ◈ ☆ **Wasenhorn** rises immediately above the hut. Also known as Punta Terrarossa, it was first climbed by James David Forbes in 1844. Its ruddy schistose rock is said to be of poor quality, but the normal route from the hut involves no more than a steep and exposed scramble of a little over an hour.

Northeast of the Wasenhorn, the 3194m ⦿ **Bortelhorn** is the next summit of note. Standing astride the frontier, its southeast flank plunges almost 1400m to the chalets of Alpe Veglia, while its west side looks down on the Brig road. From **Berisal** on that road, a walk of less than 2hrs leads to the Simplon Ski Club's **Bortel Hut** (2113m), which makes a near-perfect base for the ascent of the Bortelhorn. Staffed from mid-June to the end of September, it has 40 dormitory places (www.bortelhuette.ch). From the hut a path continues up to a little tarn at 2450m, while another makes for the foot of the Bortelhorn's SW Ridge, which can then be followed to the summit.

3:2 THE BINNTAL

Northeast of the Simplon Pass this gem of a valley is hidden away between the frontier ridge and a secondary spur which effectively conceals it from the upper Rhône valley. Narrow, pastoral, and with wooded flanks, it's sparsely populated and protected as a nature reserve.

The Binntal is accessible by postbus from **Fiesch**, about 18km above Brig. Crossing the Rhône, it takes a narrow side road through meadows to **Ernen**, an utterly charming village of almost black timber-on-stone chalets, where the way forks. The 10km branch that leads to Binn cuts along steep hillsides covered with larch, pine, rowan and birch, and passes through tiny **Ausserbinn**, which has accommodation at Gasthaus Jägerheim (www.jaegerheim.ch). Beyond this hamlet the road goes through a tunnel above a ravine before emerging at a confluence of valleys and another fork. To the south lies the Lengtal (Längthal), to the east, the Binntal.

The **Lengtal** road ends at the small collection of chalets, church and tall free-standing cross of **Heiligkreuz** (1450m) at the foot of a spur projecting northwest from the frontier ridge, and crowned by the Helsenhorn. This spur effectively divides the upper Lengtal from the Kriegalptal, at the head of which the ◐ **Kriegalppass** (2508m) takes walkers into the Italian **Valle Devero** – a route of 7–8hrs. The upper section of the Lengtal proper is a stone-strewn hanging valley known as the Kummental (Chummibort), and at its head the 2764m ◐ **Ritterpass** breaches the frontier ridge west of the Helsenhorn to give access to **Alpe Veglia** below Monte Leone (see 3:1) in a long day's effort of about 9hrs.

First climbed in 1863, the ⦿ **Helsenhorn** (3272m) is the main mountaineering interest in the Lengtal. The normal route, which is only graded F, follows a path towards the Ritterpass, but then breaks away to climb the little Helsen glacier towards the SE Ridge, along which a final scramble leads to the summit.

A walk of about an hour links Heiligkreuz with **Binn** (1400m), in the Binntal proper. The postbus from Fiesch terminates on the edge of this attractive

THE BINNTAL

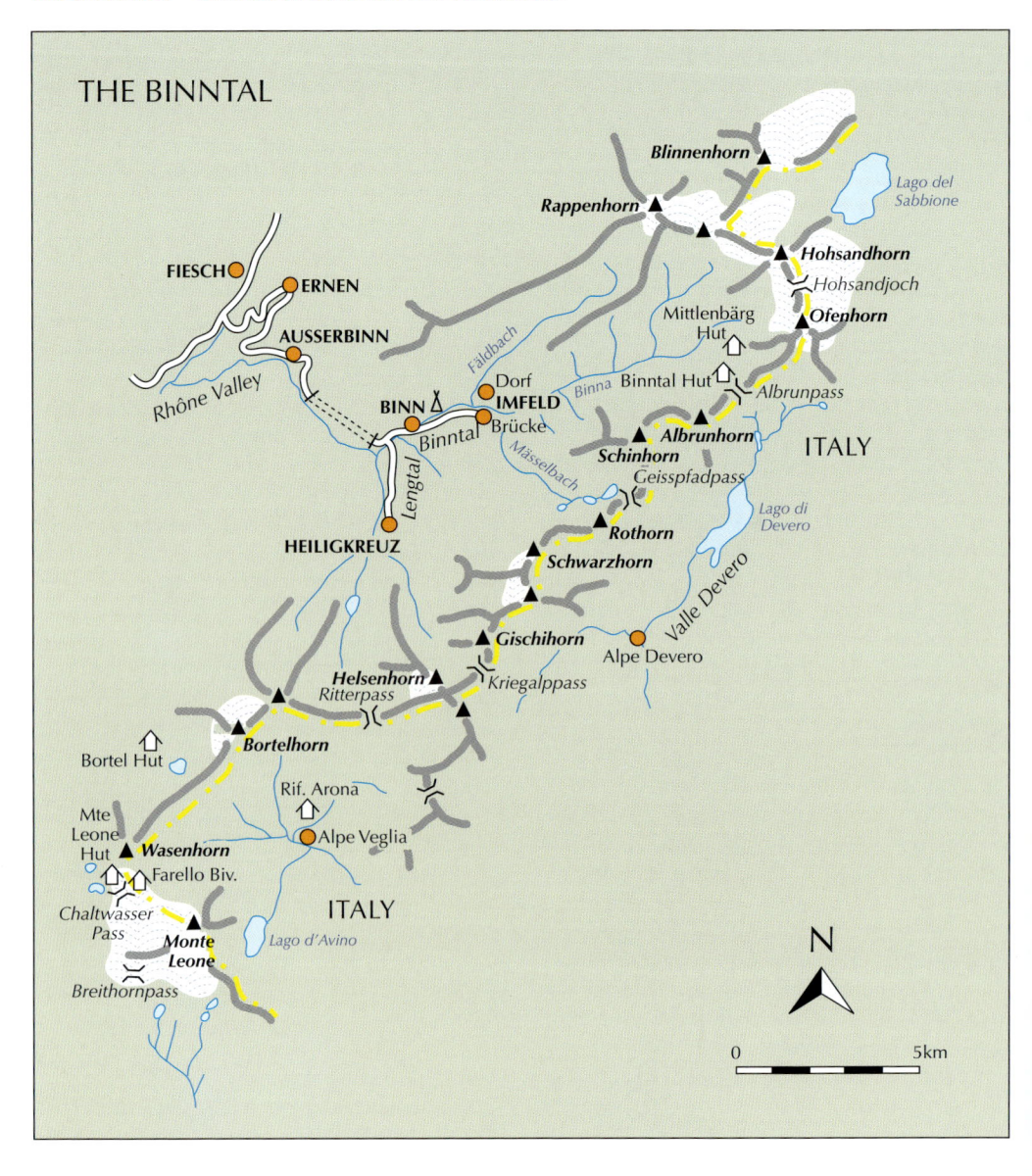

village of typical Valaisian buildings; a near-perfect huddle of timber-and-stone houses and barns, and an ancient hump-backed bridge spanning the Binna stream. The village has a bank, a post office, restaurant, supermarket and very helpful staff at the tourist office (www.binn.ch), while accommodation is available at Pension Albrun, and the more upmarket Hotel Ofenhorn (www.ofenhorn.ch). A campsite is situated 2km upstream at the hamlet of Giesse on the way to Imfeld.

Known for its rare minerals and crystals, the Binntal has a year-round population of little more than 150. There are a number of fine walks of different lengths, and the lure of the Ofenhorn for climbers. Hubert Walker enthused about the valley and its prospects: 'The chief delight that Binn has to offer,' he wrote in *Walking in the Alps*, 'is the variety of walking rounds and passes across the frontier-ridge to an equally beautiful and unfrequented part of Italy, and back. Tosa Falls is one objective, reached either by the beautiful Hohsand glacier and the Blindenhorn, or by the Albrun Pass and Bocchetta del Gallo … Devero is another Italian village, reached over the Geisspfad Pass and a path which winds as steeply as any anywhere underneath jagged peaks and towering crags on the Italian side. And a third line across the range leads through Heiligkreuz and over the Ritter Pass down to Veglia Alp, walled in by yet another colossal rocky amphitheatre.'

Easily reached from Binn by a walk of 50mins lies **Imfeld** (Feld or Fäld on some maps), a village of two parts. Imfeld Brücke is located in the valley bed by the river where private vehicles must be left, while Imfeld Dorf stands on the hillside on the north side of the Binna at 1547m.

There's a gathering of streams on the outskirts of the village. To the northeast the Fäldbach drains a hanging valley headed by the Rappenhorn (also known as the Mittaghorn), whose upper reaches cling to a small glacial remnant. To the south, the Mässelbach spills down from the watershed ridge, while the Binna itself collects a number of streams under the valley's headwall and carries them down through the main valley.

By following up into the Mässelbach's valley a choice of routes can be made. One leads to the little Mässersee tarn at 2137m. A continuation of this trail climbs another 300m to two further lakes nestling beneath the frontier ridge, the Geisspfadsee and smaller Züesee, while the ○ **Geisspfadpass** can be crossed in about 3–3½hrs from Imfeld. From there a 3hr descent leads to **Alpe Devero**.

The best opportunities for walkers and climbers, however, push on towards the Binntal's headwall, where Ofenhorn and Hohsandhorn are the dominant peaks. The frontier ridge rises to the Ofenhorn from the comparatively low ○ **Albrunpass** (2409m), known to have been crossed by Swiss troops as early as 1425. Popular in summer, the east side overlooks the head of Valle Devero, and descent into what has aptly been described as a land of waterfalls takes the walker down to **Lago di Devero**, Alpe Devero and the roadhead at Goglio in 4hrs from the pass. Just 30mins below the pass on the Swiss flank, the **Binntal Hut** (2265m) has 50 dormitory places and is manned from the end of June to the end of September (www.cas-delemont.ch). Owned by the Delémont section of the SAC, it's reached by a 3hr walk from Imfeld. From the hut a number of fairly modest ascents may be made, including Ofenhorn, Blinnenhorn, Albrunhorn, Schinhorn and Hohsandhorn.

The 3235m Ofenhorn and the Sabbione glacier

Another hut, privately owned but open to all, stands a little north of, and 100m or so higher than, the Binntal Hut, and is often used by climbers tackling various routes on the Ofenhorn. The **Mittlenbärg Hut** (2393m) can sleep 24, is permanently manned from June to the end of October, and staffed when booked during the rest of the year except November (www.mittlenberg.ch). In addition to climbs on the Ofenhorn, Hohsandhorn, Rappenhorn and Blinnenhorn, a crossing of the Hohsandjoch (between Hohsandhorn and Ofenhorn) gives an opportunity for those with glacier experience to undertake tours into Italy.

First climbed in 1864, the ● ☆ **Ofenhorn** (3235m) captures most attention, being prominently placed at the northeastern end of the valley, with the small Tälli glacier draped below the ridge by which it is connected to the Hohsandhorn. Quite possibly the most frequently climbed of all Lepontine mountains, it has two summits, four main ridges (West, NW, South and SW) and two glaciers – the Tälli already mentioned, and the larger and more impressive Hohsand glacier plastered on the Italian flank where it pushes down towards Lago del Sabbione. The South Ridge (F), reached via the narrow gap of the Eggerscharte, provides the most popular ascent of about 3hrs from the Binntal Hut. The SW Ridge gives moderate rock climbing (PD-, II) on reasonably sound gneiss, and is the route by which W A B Coolidge and Christian Almer climbed the mountain in 1888. The same team made at least three other ascents of this peak, including the West Couloir (PD+) in 1893, and the near-classic North Ridge (PD+) in 1891. Two days before their ascent of the North Ridge, Coolidge and Almer crossed the 3044m Mittlenbergpass west of the Hohsandhorn, to climb the SW Ridge of the Blinnenhorn (see 3:3).

3:3 VAL BEDRETTO

The Blinnenhorn (formerly Blindenhorn) is an appealing mountain, made especially so by rising above the long Gries glacier that flows northeastward to the Griessee not far from the Nufenen Pass (Passo della Novena). The right-hand wall of its glacial trough carries the watershed ridge, but on the eastern side of the Griesspass which overlooks the Griessee, the watershed departs from the frontier, veering north across the walker's saddle of Passo del Corno, crossing the Nufenenstock and the road pass below it, and on up to Piz Gallina. Here the watershed suddenly breaks to the east to form the north wall of Val Bedretto, while the south wall of this, the first of Ticino's valleys, carries the Swiss-Italian frontier only as far as Passo di San Giacomo before that frontier swings south to enclose the Italian Val Formazza, long noted for the beauty of the Tosa Falls.

Val Bedretto begins, then, at the 2478m **Nufenen Pass**, the road link between Obergoms (the upper Rhône valley) and Ticino, that was only opened to traffic in 1969. Not as bleak as many alpine passes, it has a fine view of the snow-free crest of peaks that carries the south flank of Val Bedretto, as well as the Bernese Alps to the west, and the Blinnenhorn and Gries glacier to the southwest. To the keen mountain walker and the climber of modest ability, the Nufenen provides opportunities to get to grips with some rewarding landscapes before descending into Val Bedretto proper.

The Blinnenhorn and Gries glacier are the most obvious local attractions, and the easiest way to reach them is via a path on the south side of the pass, which soon descends to the second hairpin bend on the west flank (bus stop and small parking area). Here a contractor's road cuts along the hillside to the barrage at the **Griessee**. Across the lake the glacier gives the appearance of a highway of ice, seen at its visual best when carpeted with fresh snow.

First climbed in 1866, the 3374m ● **Blinnenhorn** is the highest summit between Monte Leone and the Rheinwaldhorn. From the Griessee two routes are possible, one on either side of the glacial trough, and both graded F. Not surprisingly, the glacier invites ski ascents in late winter, and the summit has a much-lauded view – especially across the Rhône to the Bernese Alps.

To the south and east of the Griessee two walker's passes enable circuits or cross-border expeditions to be made. On the Swiss-Italian border the 2479m ● ☆ **Griesspass** is an old 'wine pass' used as a trade route between Domodossola and Central Switzerland. Reached by footpath from the Nufenen road in less than 1½hrs, the pass itself is a stony, desolate place, but a short descent on the Italian side brings improvement, where a small bivouac hut overlooks Lago di Morasco, some 650m below, and a hint of the deep Val Formazza beyond in which the Tosa Falls may be gained in

3:3 Val Bedretto

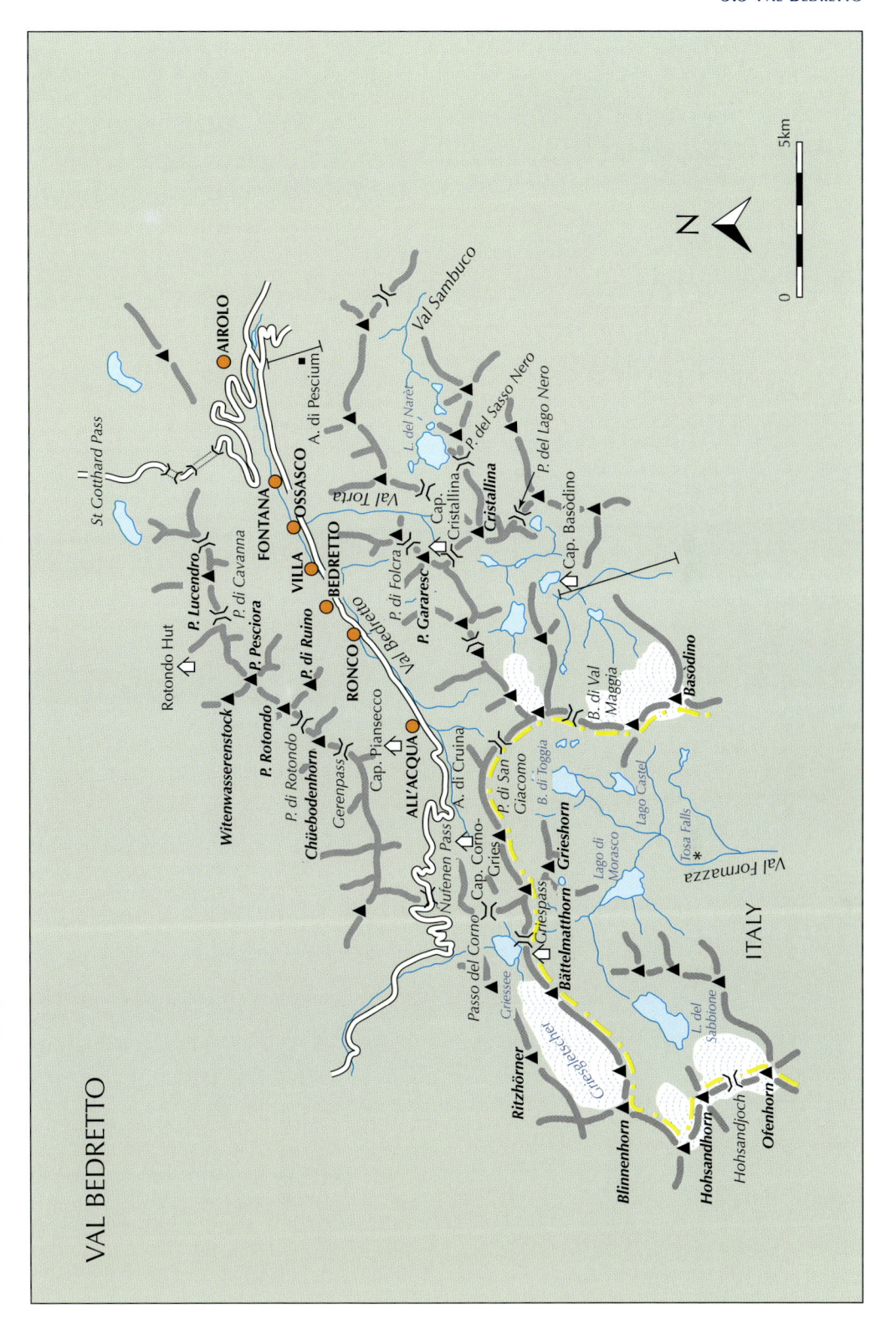

Val Bedretto

another 3hrs. Nearer to hand the curious ribbed face of the Bättelmatthorn guards the entrance to the Sabbione glen with its lake and glacier topped by the Ofenhorn (see 3:2).

The 3044m **Bättelmatthorn** enjoys a privileged situation, standing northeast of the Blinnenhorn above the Gries glacier, with a grandstand view of Valle di Morasco and the mountains of Ticino, and the highest peaks of the Bernese Alps. An uncomplicated ascent via its NE Ridge from the Griespass should take less than 2hrs.

The **Passo del Corno** (2485m) on the east side of the Griessee leads into Val Corno, the first tributary of Val Bedretto. Like its neighbour to the south, this is an easy pass to gain from the Nufenen, and it has a narrow strip of a tarn lying just below in the Val Corno trough through which a well-used path descends in less than 30mins to the Corno-Gries Hut.

Capanna Corno-Gries

Owned by the Bellinzona section of the SAC, **Capanna Corno-Gries** (2338m) overlooks the upper reaches of Val Bedretto. It has 80 places and is fully staffed from July to the end of September, and from February to the end of April when booked in advance (www.capanneti.ch). A winter room is otherwise available, with wood-burning stove and solar-powered lighting.

Several onward route options are possible from this hut. One contours across the hillside heading east towards the San Giacomo chapel, then up to the 2313m **Passo di San Giacomo** (in less than 2hrs) and on into Val Toggia and Val Formazza in Italy. It's also possible to reach **Capanna Basòdino** (see 3:6) via this pass for there's a connecting route across the Bocchetta di Val Maggia into the granitelands spreading between the Basòdino peak and the hut itself.

Another route flanks the right-hand side of Val Bedretto before descending to **All'Acqua**, while yet another path continues below the hut for about an hour to reach **Alpe di Cruina** on a hairpin bend on the Nufenen road (bus stop).

A pleasant **circular walk** of 4½–5hrs can be made by taking the path up through Val Corno to **Passo del Corno**, then heading north towards the Nufenen Pass. Do not go as far as the pass, however, but from the hairpin bend below it follow a path climbing eastward to cross high ground just south of the pass, then continue down this trail to **Alpe di Cruina** where you then cut back up to the hut.

In winter the hut is used by ski-touring parties, for whom ascents of the following peaks are often made: **Grieshorn** (2969m – 2hrs), **Blinnenhorn** (3374m – 5hrs), and **Ritzhörner** (3023m – 3½hrs).

☆ **Val Bedretto** is sparsely populated, and being tucked away between high ridges that deflect its flow from west to east, Tuscany's influence is barely felt. A string of tiny villages and summer-only settlements scattered among the pastures, it has a history of avalanche devastation stretching back to the 18th century when Ossasco was overwhelmed and 13 villagers lost their lives. The highest of its villages, and that a very small one, is **All'Acqua** at 1614m. A peaceful hamlet, it's linked with other Bedretto settlements by a string of footpaths known as the Strada bassa, and offers accommodation at the Ristorante All'Acqua, which is open from February to October. Downvalley a short distance from All'Acqua, a higher trail than the Strada bassa visits a series of alps and pastures on the right flank of the valley. This path of the alps, the Strada degli alpi Bedretto, goes as far as Pesciüm above Airolo.

Capanna Piansecco

On the north side of the valley and just an hour's walk from All'Acqua, **Capanna Piansecco** (1982m) makes a useful base for various ascents and both walking and ski tours. Built among larchwoods by the Bellinzona e Valli section of the SAC, it's a modern building with 50 places, is fully staffed from June until mid-October, and at weekends from February to March when booked in advance (www.capanneti.ch).

Above it the 3070m ⊗ **Chüebodenhorn** stands on the watershed ridge between the Gerenpass and Passo di Rotondo. An uncomplicated 3½hr ascent from the hut climbs through the mountain's southern combe to reach the **Gerenpass** (2691m). This gives onto the head of the Chüeboden glacier which lies in a *firn* basin on the mountain's southwest flank, almost 400m below the summit. Winter ascents of this peak are also made on ski.

It's closest neighbour, and the highest along Val Bedretto's watershed ridge, is ⊗ **Pizzo Rotondo** at 3192m. First climbed in 1869, the normal route by the SW Couloir is only graded F, although early Baedeker guides described it as being difficult and 'for experts only'. As with the Chüebodenhorn, Pizzo Rotondo also attracts ski mountaineers, for whom the 1200m ascent from Capanna Piansecco takes about 3½–4hrs. Baedeker thought the summit view 'very grand and picturesque'.

Rotondo's SE Ridge leads to a 2964m secondary peak, ⊗ **Poncione di Ruino**, with a granite tower projecting a little further down which has some commendable grade IV/V rock climbs of about 150m, while the next summit along the main ridge is the 3122m **Pizzo Pesciora**, just south of the Witenwasserenstock. Pesciora is yet another goal for ski-mountaineers, albeit one that should not be underestimated, with a 5hr route which crosses Passo di Rotondo and turns the north side of Pizzo Rotondo to gain the Geren glacier, then via the SW Ridge to the summit.

Although Pizzo Rotondo is the highest on the ridge, it is the **Witenwasserenstock** (3082m) that claims the distinction of not only being the meeting point of three cantons (Ticino, Valais and Uri), but as being the source of three major rivers – the Rhône, the Rhine and the Ticino (a tributary of the Po) which flow, respectively, into the Mediterranean, the North Sea and the Adriatic. Coolidge and Almer were drawn to it in 1892, and made its first ascent. The usual base for climbs here is the **Rotondo Hut** which lies below the northern side of the ridge at the foot of the Witenwasseren glacier at 2570m. The hut is approached from the Furka Pass in 4½–5hrs, from Realp in 3–3½hrs, or in 1hr from a motorable road climbing above Realp. Property of the Lägern section of the SAC, the hut is popular with ski tourers as well as walkers and climbers in summer. Manned from late December to mid-May, and from July to mid-October, it has 92 dormitory places (www.jo-sac.ch/rotondo). From here the normal route (F+) only takes about 2hrs, climbing first to a saddle between the Hüenerstock and a secondary summit of the Witenwasserenstock, then gains that lesser summit at 3025m, to follow the East Ridge to the top. From the south, Val Bedretto, side of the mountain, a much longer climb is necessary – 5hrs being the normal time taken from Bedretto village.

Between All'Acqua and Bedretto, **Ronco** (1487m) sits astride the old valley road. Another tiny group of buildings (there are no large villages in Val Bedretto), it has limited accommodation at the 2-star Stella Alpina, open throughout the year with 20 beds (www.stellaalpina.ch). A short distance downstream, and lying at the foot of the Witenwasserenstock on

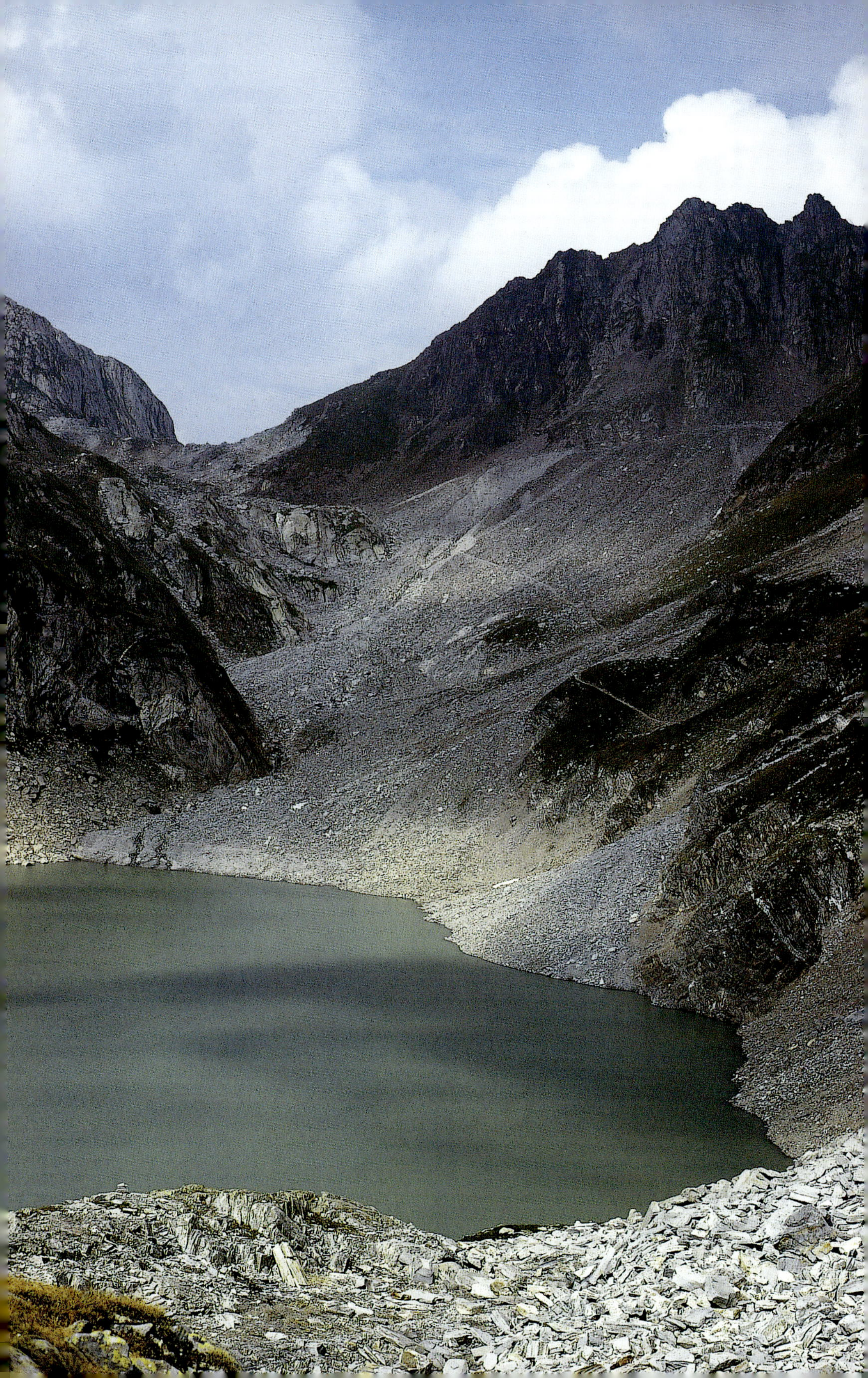

the left bank of the Ticino river, **Bedretto** (1402m) also has limited accommodation with just 12 beds at the Pizzo Rotondo, open from April until December (tel 091 869 21 61).

Continuing downvalley, the old road passes through **Villa**, where a trail climbs steeply up the northern slope to cross **Passo di Cavanna** (2613m), an old route linking Val Bedretto with Realp. The main road is rejoined below Villa, shortly before reaching **Ossasco** (1313m) on the right bank. Although it has no accommodation, Ossasco has a restaurant, and behind it to the south wooded narrows conceal the charming Val Torta, Val Bedretto's gateway to the Cristallina massif whose only downside is the existence of high-tension power lines whose pylons insult the otherwise wild nature of the region.

The Cristallina Massif

An impressive district of rock peaks, screes, shrinking glaciers and dammed lakes, the Cristallina massif drains into no less than five valleys – Bedretto to the north, Sambuco to the east, Peccia in the southeast, Bavona in the south and Formazza in Italy on the western side. Vals Sambuco, di Peccia and Bavona are all tributaries of Valle Maggia, and will be visited later in this chapter, but suffice to say that their headwaters are linked by a series of stony cols that provide excellent opportunities for walkers to make circuits or crossings of the region.

When approaching the massif through **Val Torta** from Ossasco there are various options to consider. Those in search of summits will be attracted to Cristallina, the peak that lends its name to the surrounding area and offers a pleasant scramble – or perhaps the impressive double-summited Pizzo Gararesc north of Passo di Cristallina. Walkers intent on passes have three to consider: Passo del Narèt, Cristallina and di Folcra, while the modern **Capanna Cristallina** (2575m), standing close to the Cristallina pass, makes a worthwhile objective in itself, and is reached in 4hrs from Ossasco. As the former hut which stood at the base of the mountain was destroyed by avalanche, when its replacement was planned a better site was chosen, and hopefully this one is free from avalanche danger. In recognition of the district's popularity, the hut has 120 places and excellent facilities. Sometimes manned in winter (mid-December to mid-April), it is fully staffed from late June until early October (www.capannacristallina.ch).

Not to be confused with Piz Cristallina (3128m) which stands northeast of the Lukmanier Pass, the usual route of ascent for ☁ ☆ **Cristallina** (2912m) from its namesake hut gives an easy scramble (F) of just 1½hrs. The NE Ridge offers another route which was often favoured by climbers staying in the old hut, and by combining these two a popular traverse of the peak can be achieved. Once again the summit vista is both extensive and revealing of a large part of the Ticino Alps. As for ◉ **Pizzo Gararesc**, this has two peaks; the north summit known as the Campanile (2729m) holds several moderate rock climbs, while its southern counterpart is the main peak at 2751m. Below the Campanile, **Passo (or Bassa) di Folcra** gives access to Val Cassinello which drains into the Ticino river near Bedretto village.

Probably the most popular route for walkers is the crossing of the 2568m ☁ ☆ **Passo di Cristallina** as part of a major traverse of the district linking Vals Bedretto and Bavona, and which is highly recommended. The pass overlooks Lago Sfündau lying on the south side in a drab, scree-walled well, across which a trail cuts high above the lake's east bank and eventually leads to **Capanna Basòdino** (see 3:6), about 2hrs from the Cristallina Hut. From there a well-made path descends steeply to the glorious Val Bavona, described in more detail in 3:6.

That traverse route is justifiably popular, but a long and full day's ☁ **circular walk** of about 7–8hrs based on Capanna Cristallina, which crosses no less than four passes, is every bit as rewarding. To achieve this, descend into the head of Val Torta, then veer right on a path which makes for the 2438m **Passo del Narèt**, across which you take a minor path down to the dammed **Lago del Narèt**. Skirt its southwest shore to reach a much smaller tarn, before climbing a short distance to a grass saddle a little west of **Passo del Sasso Nero** (2420m). Here you enter a rocky landscape aiming southwest, then later drop into, and climb steeply out of, a depression to gain a boulder tip in Val del Coro, a wild little valley below Cristallina just north of **Passo del Lago Nero** (2563m). Over this pass views of the snowy Basòdino (3:6) are magnificent as you traverse high above Lago Nero on a path occasionally safeguarded with fixed cables. Descending towards the lake's southwest corner, a path then crosses steep grass slopes angling northwest. When it forks take the right branch (the

◀ *Lago Sfündau lies between the Cristallina and Basòdino huts* alternative trail leads to a road above Lago Bianco) to reach the scree-draped basin in which Lago Sfündau is the final lake on the circuit. Above this come to **Passo di Cristallina** and the hut where the walk began.

3:4 VALLE LEVENTINA

At first glance Valle Leventina, the central and most important valley of the Ticino Alps, fails to impress. At its upper, northwestern end where it joins Val Bedretto, both road and rail traffic spew into the valley from the Gotthard tunnels, and below Airolo the motorway and railway continue downvalley, following a line of high tension cables to destroy any semblance of harmony.

But the glacier-carved trough of Leventina is more than a major artery for transport; it's a fertile valley inhabited by attractive villages, and above both banks hanging valleys or tarn-sparkling plateaux invite walkers along their paths. There are walker's cols, and a few summits to entice climbers, and several huts give the opportunity to spend a night or two well away from the constant noise of Leventina's heavy traffic. From 2012, when the Gotthard Base Tunnel is due to open, the valley should be spared much of this traffic, for the main terminus will be at Bodio near the confluence with Valle di Blenio. Perhaps then it will have a partial restoration of the peace that is its due, though the visual scars will no doubt remain.

Airolo (1142m) is the gateway to Leventina and is its main valley base, the old town centre standing some way above the railway station. It's a quiet, unremarkable town with most facilities, including the valley's main tourist office on the Via San Gottardo (www.leventinaturismo.ch). Accommodation is plentiful, with eight, mostly small to medium-sized hotels, and a couple of apartments.

High above Airolo and reached by little more than a walk of about 3½hrs from the historic St Gotthard Pass (Passo del San Gottardo; 2108m), **Pizzo Centrale** (2999m) has the reputation of an outstanding viewpoint. Below its south flank Lago della Sella dominates the little **Val Torta** (not to be confused with the valley of the same name above Ossasco in Val Bedretto), and at its head the 2776m **Giübin** is another easy summit to reach by a path that traces the SW Ridge from **Passo Posmeda** (2569m) in less than 3hrs from the St Gotthard. On the west side of Giübin, **Passo Sella** directs a long walk down to Andermatt in the Central Swiss Alps, while east of the summit yet another pass, the **Unteralp**, leads into Val Canaria which drains down to the Ticino river outside Airolo.

Val Canaria is a beautiful little valley with tiny hamlets, isolated farms and neatly shaved meadows, with paths leading into it from **Valle** and **Madrano**, which guard its entrance. The valley's upper reaches are very different from the lower section. Some 1100m above its opening, the Pian Bornengo gathers several streams under the headwall topped by Piz Alv, while almost 300m above the Pian, the easy pass of **Bocchetta di Cadlimo** looks onto a wildly attractive alpine scene. The minor subsidiary ridge on which this pass lies, actually carries the watershed in a brief southerly kink before it resumes its eastward trend along the south wall of Val Cadlimo as far as the Lukmanier Pass (3:7).

Overlooking the valley after which it is named, **Bocchetta di Cadlimo** also gives access to one of the highest mountain huts in the Ticino Alps, **Capanna Cadlimo** at 2570m. Owned by the Uto section of the SAC, it has a total of 80 places, and is fully staffed from July to the end of September (www.cadlimo.ch).

Val Cadlimo slopes away to the east below the hut among old moraines and tiny lakes and pools, its stream slipping down to the Lukmanier Pass by which it makes its way north to the Rhine. While the south wall forms the alpine watershed, the north wall of the valley carries the canton boundary, and on its ridge the conical **Piz Blas** (3019m) gives a 2hr ascent (F) from Capanna Cadlimo by its south flank.

From the hut one path follows the stream downvalley, another heads south to Lago Scuro, then rises to cross the watershed at the Bassa del Lago Scuro which enables walkers to descend into the charming plateau of **Val Piora**.

The Val Piora Nature Reserve

The lawn-like meadows and dreamy blue lakes of Val Piora make this one of the best-loved districts of mountain Ticino. It's a nature reserve rimmed with woods of larch and pine, with more than 500 species of flowering plants, gentle rolling pastures and modest summits and ridges that effectively cradle a broad plateau above and between the Valles

3:4 Valle Leventina

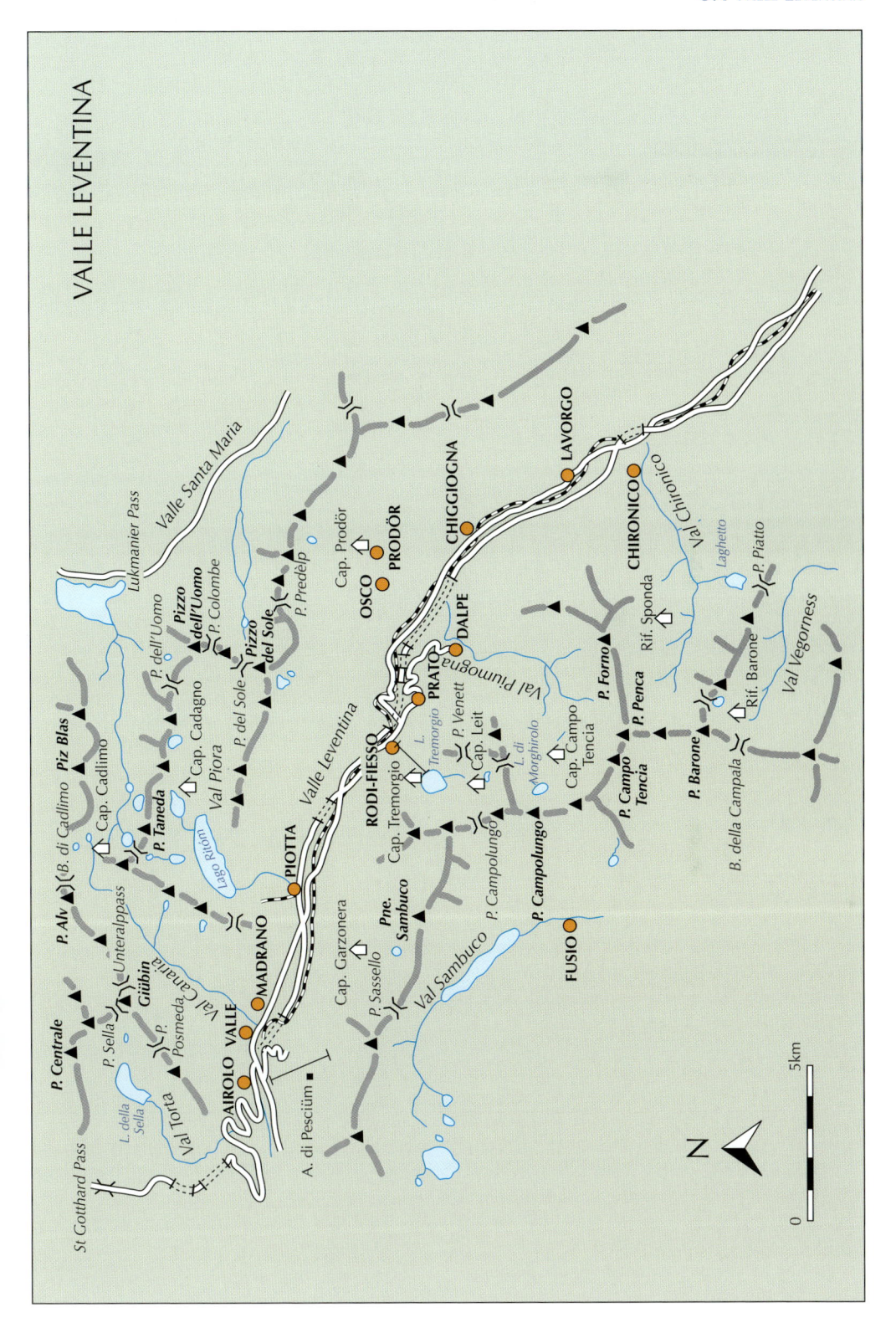

The Val Piora nature reserve

Leventina and Santa Maria. Idyllically set in the middle of this plateau at a junction of trails near Lago Cadagno at 1987m, **Capanna Cadagno** has room for 60 in its dormitories, is staffed in March and April, and from June to the end of October (www.capanna-cadagno.ch). Owned by the SAT (Sociéta Alpinistica Ticinese), it's used by cross-country skiers, ski tourers and snowshoe enthusiasts in late winter, as well as by walkers and day visitors during the summer months.

From Valle Leventina the nature reserve is most easily reached via the Funicolare Piotta-Ritóm, said to be Europe's steepest mountain railway, whose valley station is located at **Piotta** (1005m) about 6km east of Airolo and reached by postbus (www.ritom.ch). The village has accommodation at the Ristorante Vais (tel 091 868 15 31), and Motel Gottardo Sud (www.gottardo-sud.ch). The upper station is at 1793m, and from it a 20min walk leads to the dammed **Lago Ritóm** on the southern edge of the plateau, where hotel accommodation may be had at the Albergo Ristorante Lago Ritóm. It has 34 beds and is open from May to October (tel 091 868 14 24).

Having arrived at the lake a variety of tours, day walks, pass crossings and modest climbs can be made. By far the best **circular walking tour** is that which works a way north from roughly halfway along the lakeside, then on a track that leads to the shallow Lago di Tom at 2021m. Above this continue climbing to reach two small tarns below the Bassa del Lago Scuro (c2480m) mentioned above. Lago Scuro lies just beyond, but before going to that lake it might be worth clambering over rocks on the right of the pass to gain the summit of **Piz Taneda** (2667m) for a very fine outlook across the Val Piora plateau. Should it be your plan to make this a two-day tour, then Capanna Cadlimo will be your immediate goal. If not, then veer right at the northern end of Lago Scuro and descend into Val Cadlimo. When the path forks, branch right to climb back up to the southern ridge where, virtually on the crest, lie the tiny Miniera tarns east of the domed Piz Corandoni at 2525m. On the south side of the ridge the way cuts round the upper wall of the combe in which Lago di Dentro is seen, then slopes down into Val Piora to Capanna Cadagno and the Lagos Cadagno and Ritóm to complete the circuit in about 6hrs.

A longer variation of that tour (7½hrs) misses the Miniera and di Dentro tarns by walking the

3:4 VALLE LEVENTINA

length of Val Cadlimo, and returning to Val Piora by way of Val Termine and the broad saddle of ◯ **Passo dell'Uomo**, while yet more tours can be made by linking some of the easy passes that give access to neighbouring valleys. At the eastern end of the plateau, for example, ◯ **Passo Colombe** and **Passo del Sole** lie either side of the handsome cockscomb of Pizzo Colombe. Both take routes over the rim into Valle Santa Maria below the Lukmanier Pass, but could be combined to make an interesting day's circuit. On the east side of Passo del Sole another path breaks away to cross ◯ **Passo Predèlp**, with a descent on the south side to **Osco**, an old village on the north flank of Valle Leventina (5hrs from Capanna Cadagno), from where a postbus can be taken down to Faido in the valley bed. An alternative would be to follow a minor road heading east from the hamlet of Predèlp along the steep flank as far as **Prodör** where, 30mins above the village, **Capanna Prodör** is set among pinewoods at 1757m. Owned by the UTOE (Unione Ticinese Operai Escursionisti), it has 49 places but no permanent guardian. When unmanned the key is collected from Ristorante Pensione Carì; but for reservations tel 091 866 18 33.

As for summits that surround Val Piora, many of these can be reached without difficulty; a number being on a tick-list for ski tourers in springtime. Two of these help contain the valley to the east of Capanna Cadagno. Above Passo Colombe, the 2663m ◯ **Pizzo dell'Uomo** makes an outstanding vantage point, with the Rheinwaldhorn clearly seen across Valle di Blenio to the southeast. South of Pizzo dell'Uomo, and on the far side of Pizzo Colombe, ◯ **Pizzo del Sole** (2773m) is also easily climbed from the Cadagno Hut, but has the added advantage of two lakes lying immediately beneath it on the Leventina side, and an uninterrupted view of the Cristallina massif to the west, as well as a direct view of Pizzo Campo Tencia on the south side of Valle Leventina.

Valle Leventina's South Flank

The south side of Valle Leventina is easily accessed by the Sasso della Boggia cable car, which begins just below Airolo, and whose middle station, **Pesciüm** (1745m) has a splay of trails spreading

Lago Cadagno and Val Piora

from it. One of these leads to the 2334m **Passo Sassello** for a long 7hr trek across the mountains to Fusio in Val Lavizzara (see 3:6); another goes to the unmanned **Capanna Garzonera** at 1973m in about 2½hrs. Built on a terrace of larch and spruce trees below Poncione Sambuco (2581m), the hut has 20 places, cooking facilities and solar-powered lighting, and is owned by the Ritóm section of the SAT (for information tel 091 869 15 33). From a base here several summits may be reached on ski in winter, among them **Pizzo di Sassello** (2480m) and the 2710m **Madone**, both peaks taking about 3hrs. **Poncione Sambuco** is an obvious goal for climbers in summer.

A third trail from Pesciüm visits a string of hamlets and small alps before reaching **Lago Tremorgio** (1830m) after 4–4½hrs. Almost entirely surrounded by steep slopes, this charming lake forms part of a pumped hydro scheme by the Azienda Elettrica Ticinese, which owns the chalet-style **Capanna Tremorgio** found by the upper station of the cable car rising from **Rodi-Fiesso** (940m), about 12km downstream from Airolo. With 42 places, the hut is manned from June to September (tel 091 867 12 52), and several fine outings are possible from it.

Directly above the lake to the south, Pizzo Campolungo (2714m) forms the northwest buttress of a profound cirque enclosing the wooded Val Piumogna, topped by **Pizzo Campo Tencia**, one of the most important peaks in this part of the Lepontines. On the north slope of Campolungo and reached by a good path in 1½hrs from Lago Tremorgio, **Capanna Leit** is yet another hut that would make a good base for a few days of exploration. Owned by the SAT it stands in wild, rocky country overlooking a small tarn at 2260m, and has 64 places but is only temporarily staffed from June to mid-October (www.capanneti.ch) (on other occasions there are 10 beds available, and self-catering facilities). To the west of the hut, the neat spire of **Pizzo del Prévat** (2558m) suggests it could reward the attention of rock climbers, as does **Pizzo Campolungo** itself, while below to the north of Pizzo del Prévat, the 2318m **Passo Campolungo** enables walkers to cross the mountains to Fusio (see 3:6) in 4hrs.

Northeast of Capanna Leit, **Passo Venett** (2138m) crosses a long spur projecting from Pizzo Campolungo's east summit, and is the easiest way for walkers to reach **Dalpe**, the uppermost village on the large green terrace at the mouth of **Val**

Passo Venett (2138m)

Piumogna above Valle Leventina. Dalpe is served by bus, and has a single hotel, the Delle Alpi, with 19 beds, open all year except October (tel 091 867 14 24).

Dalpe is the closest village on the north side of Pizzo Campo Tencia, and is where most walkers and climbers begin their approach to the hut which serves the mountain. It's a 3hr walk through Val Piumogna and via Alpe di Croslina, with another 150m or so to climb above the alp huts before reaching the SAC-owned **Capanna Campo Tencia** at 2140m, below and due north of the main summit of the peak after which it is named. It has 80 places, and is fully staffed from mid-June to mid-October (www.campotencia.ch). It's also linked in 2hrs with Capanna Leit by way of the 2481m **Passo di Leit** (Passo Lei di Cima) on a shoulder of Campolungo.

For walkers an unmissable highlight of a visit to the Campo Tencia hut, is an extension up the northwest slope to ● **Lago di Morghirolo** which lies at the very head of the valley, a little over 100m above the hut under the crags of Pizzo Campolungo. From this truly delightful site, a view east shows the glacier-crowned Rheinwaldhorn in the Adula Alps. But naturally the main interest for climbers is the ascent of ● ☆ **Pizzo Campo Tencia** (3072m), the normal route being more or less that which was pioneered by D W Freshfield and the Chamonix guide François Dévouassoud in 1873. It begins by heading south of the hut to where a glacial stream comes down from a rock barrier under what's left of the Croslina glacier, marked on the map as point 2271m. From here you climb rock and loose scree and follow a trail towards the mountain's NW Ridge which is gained at the Bocchetta di Croslina (2867m), about 2hrs from the hut. The summit is reached along this ridge in another hour.

This is what Walker had to say about it: 'Campo Tencia is a superb view-point, and the rough scrambling along the ridge from peak to peak over good sound granite, is wholly delightful' (*Walking in the Alps*). Baedeker also commented on the view, but said the ascent was 'trying'. In the West Col guide (*Mittel Switzerland*), the author Michael Anderson called it 'one of the notable viewpoints of the region' and said its three main points 'have been likened to a miniature Grindelwald Wetterhörner'. The mountain is also climbed in winter, partially by ski, while its frozen waterfalls bring another dimension to the climber's world here in the heart of Ticino.

Campo Tencia's summit ridge angles southeast to a secondary peak, Pizzo Penca at 3038m, then forks. One ridge strikes southward, the other veers a little north of east across Poncione del Laghetto to Pizzo Forno (2907m). These two ridges form part of the headwall of Val Chironico, a wooded glen similar to that of Piumogna, with the village of **Chironico** (787m) huddled below its entrance. Reached by a sinuous minor road that leaves Val Leventina at Nivo, the village has one hotel, the Pizzo Forno, which has 11 beds and is open from March until December (tel 091 865 16 26).

The road pushes deep within **Val Chironico**, with a path climbing steeply from it to reach the alp hamlet of Cala high on the left bank at 1467m. The trail continues heading west, and beyond Alpe Sponda comes to **Rifugio Sponda**, set on a wide and sunny terrace at 1997m directly below Pizzo Forno. Property of the SAT, the three-storey hut is only manned at weekends between mid-May and mid-October, has 56 places and cooking facilities (www.satchiasso.ch). Of the ascents made from here, **Pizzo Forno** (in 3hrs), **Pizzo Penca** (in 4hrs), and the 2864m **Pizzo Barone** (3hrs) are also tackled on ski in winter.

In addition to accessible summits, Rifugio Sponda offers an overnight stay for walkers planning to cross ● **Passo Barone** (2582m) into Val Vegorness in which lies the lovely village of Sonogno (see 3:5). On the south side of the pass, and 400m below it, **Rifugio Barone** is another unmanned hut with 32 places and self-catering facilities located on the Alpe Barone at 2172m (3:5). Between the pass and the hut, Lago Barone is trapped among steep mountain walls.

A larger tarn, the **Laghetto**, or Lago di Chironico, lies in a deep scoop on the south flank of Val Chironico at 1763m and is reached by a path that continues above it to gain the **Passo di Piatto**, a 2108m dip in the ridge between Pizzo dei Laghetti and Cima Bianca, which offers another way over the mountains into **Val Vegorness**, the northernmost tributary of Val Verzasca.

3:5 VAL VERZASCA

The Ticino river, which rises near the Nufenen Pass at the head of Val Bedretto and flows through Valle Leventina, finally discharges into Lago Maggiore near **Locarno**. Only a matter of metres from its entry

THE SWISS ALPS – CHAPTER 3: LEPONTINE AND ADULA ALPS

VAL VERZASCA

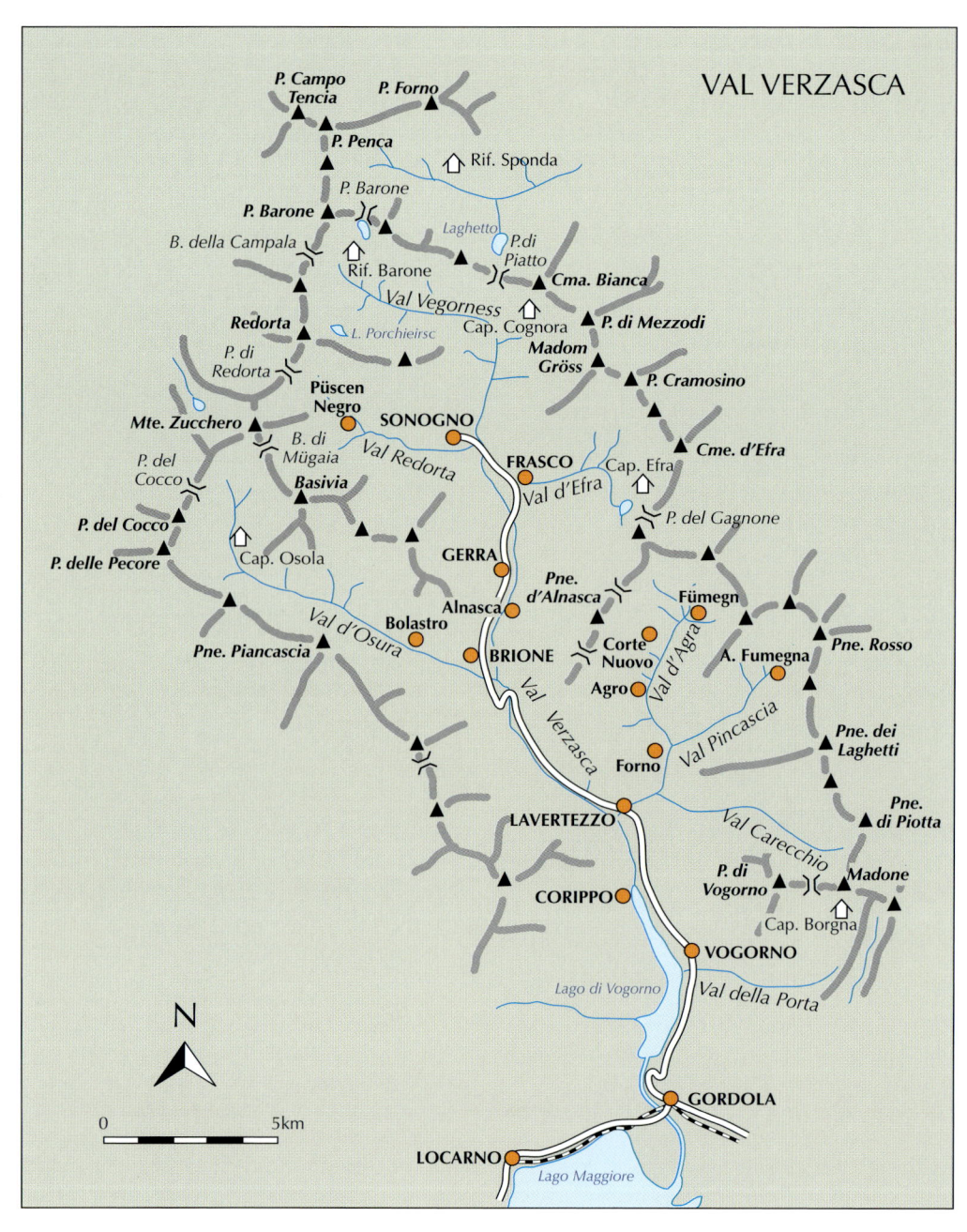

into the lake, another river spills its bounty from the mountains. It's one of the loveliest of all Lepontine streams. Clear as crystal in its higher channels, it glides into green pools banked by polished granite slabs, and dashes through shady defiles as it scores a way through Val Verzasca, a comparatively short but deep and narrow valley that pushes into the Alps of Ticino between the Valles Leventina and Maggia.

There's little in the way of tourist infrastructure in Val Verzasca. No resorts, few hotels, no campsites. But there's a handful of charming villages and barely inhabited side valleys, and sufficient trails to keep the wanderer happy for many a long day.

Access is via **Gordola** at the eastern end of Lago Maggiore, where vine terraces force the road on a snaking hairpin course before reaching the reservoir of Lago di Vogorno at the valley entrance. Here a series of brief tunnels leads the road along the east bank to **Vogorno** (three small hotels with a total of 37 beds), beyond which the way continues for another four kilometres to **Lavertezzo** (536m). Apart from Sonogno, Lavertezzo is the nearest any Verzasca village comes to being a resort, thanks to its picturesque medieval bridge with two stone arches spanning the river. The beauty of the scene is famed throughout Switzerland, with the inevitable result that during the summer traffic blocks the narrow streets as crowds gather on and below the bridge. But peace and solitude may still be found, and those prepared to take to the hills will not be disappointed. As a base for exploring the trio of side valleys behind the village, Lavertezzo has just two hotels, the Osteria Vittoria and Ristorante Posse. For tourist information contact the Ufficio Turistico in Tenero (tel 091 745 16 61).

Lavertezzo's Valleys

Lavertezzo sits at a confluence of streams, for one drains out of the mountains immediately behind the village to join the main Verzasca river just below the bridge. The tributary stream gathers the waters from three short side valleys – Vals Carecchio, Pincascia and Agro, each of which has an old trail (in places a partially paved mule trail) enticing into it. There's plenty of woodland and the walling mountains are all of modest stature, for not one reaches 2600m. But each of these valleys has plenty of charm and would reward a few hours of exploration, while several passes suggest ways of making longer journeys across the mountains, or circuits that would eventually bring you back to Lavertezzo.

Take **Val Carecchio** first. The most southerly of the three, it flows east to west from a cirque topped by Poncione dei Laghetti, Poncione di Piotta, Madone, and Pizzo di Vogorno. Despite some of these names being familiar from travelling along Valle Leventina's south flank, they're very different mountains that simply share a common title. A few huddled groups of stone huts gather on the bank of Carecchio's stream, and the trail squeezes from one to the other between the trees along the steep north flank of the valley, then forks near its head. One path climbs abruptly north up the lower slopes of Cima Pianca, then angles below a band of cliffs before cutting through a cleft to reach the one-time alp of Eus at 1603m on the southern rim of Val Pincascia.

The continuing trail curves round the lower headwall of Val Carecchio to gain the ◓ **Bocchetta di Rognoi** (2219m) on the ridge linking Pizzo di Vogorno and Madone. On the south side of this pass Val della Porta drains out to Vogorno, but high up on its headwall at 1912m, the unmanned, 25 place **Capanna Borgna** makes a useful overnight stay (www.verzasca.com), and is reached by path from the Bocchetta. Another path descends from the pass directly to the Rienza alp, then cuts west along the flank of the valley to Vogorno.

Val Pincascia is the central of the three valleys above and behind Lavertezzo, and is reached by either a narrow road or old mule trail as far as Cugnera, then a continuing path that remains high above the river on steep, heavily wooded slopes as far as the large hamlet of **Forno** at the junction of Vals Pincascia and Agra. Here you descend to the river, cross on a hump-backed bridge and take the right-hand path into Val Pincascia. Once again the way climbs high above the Pincascia stream and pushes upvalley where the tree cover is less extensive and Poncione Rosso (2505m) guards its upper reaches. Right at the head of the valley **Alpe Fumegna** makes a good turning point at 1810m, some 4hrs from Lavertezzo.

The third of these tributaries is the charming ◓ **Val d'Agra** which, with its traditional stone-built huts and alp hamlets, its beautiful natural pools and cascades, counts among the nicest of Val Verzasca's feeder glens. **Agro** is its largest hamlet, at 1173m, reached in 2–2½hrs from Lavertezzo, and it is here that the trail divides. One continues alongside the stream to the few hutments of **Fümegn**, some 300m higher than Agro at 1494m, while another angles up the hillside above Agro to **Corte Nuovo** (1873m). Yet another option is to take the signed trail from Agro to Alpe Cremenzé, then cross the ridge directly above it at a 2143m saddle north of Poncione d'Alnasca, and descend to **Alnasca** in Val Verzasca above Brione.

Val d'Osura

At **Brione** (756m), 6km upstream from Lavertezzo, the valley bifurcates, with the main stem curving slightly east of north, and the Val d'Osura tributary inviting to the northwest. Brione is the main village of Val Verzasca, yet it is still only a small place with a shop, post office and limited accommodation (eight beds) at Ristorante Ai Piee, which is open from March to October.

A clear Lepontine stream flows through Val d'Osura

Walker called Val d'Osura 'a particularly beautiful glen', and that it surely is. Pastoral in its lower reaches, with groups of broad-leaved trees and small hay meadows, it grows more rugged in the Sambuco cirque that closes its head under Monte Zucchero. The stream which flows through the valley is one of the finest in the district, rushing over little cascades and through smooth runnels, with deep translucent pools that invite the passing walker or climber to delay ambition and bathe. How Baedeker, a hundred years ago, could dismiss the path through Val d'Osura as 'uninteresting' defeats me.

A narrow lane delves into the valley for 3km or so from Brione, to serve the hamlet of Bolastro, then a track continues a little farther beyond the buildings of Daghei. Thereafter footpaths either break out of the valley to climb to higher alps, or push on upstream, eventually curving to the north under the wall of mountains that divides it from Valle Maggia and its tributaries. Here the trail climbs among wild raspberry canes, alpenroses and rowan trees to gain an upper level of grassland with the Sambuco cirque closing around it. This is Alpe d'Osura on which the small, stone-built **Capanna Osola** stands at 1418m (2½hrs from Brione). Unmanned, and with 18 places, the hut has cooking facilities, solar-powered lighting and a water supply outside (information: www.verzasca.ch or www.capanneti.ch).

Above the hut on the west walling ridge, **Passo del Cocco** (2142m) suggests a way to cross the mountains to Val Cocco, one of the feeder glens for Val Lavizzara (3:6), but the main continuing route here climbs steeply up the west slope, then contours round to Alpe Sambuco in another 1½hrs. This alp lies directly below **Monte Zucchero** (2735m), on whose South Ridge the **Bocchetta di Mügaia** is a 2518m pass leading to Sonogno (a 10hr round from Brione), upvalley from Brione. A straightforward ascent of Monte Zucchero can be made in 30mins from the pass, to be rewarded with an excellent view over the surrounding country.

Upper Val Verzasca

The next village beyond Brione up the main stem of Val Verzasca is **Gerra** (808m), another small group of buildings with overnight accommodation (24 beds) at Ristorante Froda, open year-round except in February. A short distance beyond this the road crosses to the east bank of the river and comes to **Frasco** (885m), a scattered community at the mouth of Val d'Efra.

Val d'Efra is short, narrow, steep-walled and loud with the rushing of waterfalls, but it opens to a wild and rugged little valley with a tarn lying almost 1000m above Frasco, two passes in its headwall, and an unmanned hut some 200m above the tarn on the way to ⬤ **Passo del Gagnone**, which leads to Val d'Ambra and the lower reaches of Val Leventina. Gained in 3½–4hrs from Frasco, **Capanna Efra** (2039m) belongs to the Società Escursionistica Verzaschese of Vogorno, has 24 places, cooking facilities and is open from June to October (www.verzasca.com). Even without being tempted to overnight at the hut, or cross either of the passes, it would be worth the effort to reach little Lago d'Efra in its rock-girt basin, by a walk of 3–3½hrs from Frasco.

About 7km north of Brione **Sonogno** (918m) stands at the end of the public road at the entrance to Val Redorta, with the rocky walls of Madom Gröss rising abruptly to the northeast. An understandably popular destination for day visitors, the village has become a small-scale tourist centre, with its attractive stucco or stone-walled houses hung about with flowers. There's a folk museum, a shop selling local crafts, food stores, a restaurant and post office, but only one hotel, the Ristorante Alpino with 15 beds, open all year (tel 091 746 11 63).

Striking west of the village **Val Redorta** is the glen through which the route crossing Bocchetta di Mügaia from Val d'Osura came down to Sonogno. It's a shorter tributary than Val Vegorness, the upper Verzasca stem that projects northeast of the village, but it enables the walker to make a crossing to Prato in Val Lavizzara by way of the 2181m ⬤ ☆ **Passo (or Forcarella) di Redorta** in 7hrs. This is one of those crossings that has been known and appreciated by mountain wanderers for more than 100 years, for on both sides of the pass beautiful valleys are traversed. As far as the little hamlet of **Püscen Negro** (1½hrs) the route from Sonogno is the same as that for the Bocchetta di Mügaia, but thereafter the Prato trail takes a different route and climbs to Alpe di Redorta on the way to the pass.

Another long route crossing the mountains to Prato uses the higher **Bocchetta della Campala** (2323m) in the Val Vegorness headwall south of Pizzo Barone, but it's a much longer route than the Redorta option.

Out of Sonogno the paved road soon becomes a rough track, then a footpath through the **Val Vegorness** stem. For the first hour beyond Sonogno the landscape is distinctly pastoral and dotted with small alp hamlets, but once the valley makes its westward curve at Cabioi (1079m), it takes on a more alpine stature. At Cabioi a path swings up the north flank of the valley, making for ⬤ **Passo di Piatto** (2108m) west of the Cima Bianca. Less than an hour from the pass a one-time herder's hut has been converted to the **Capanna Cognora** at 1938m, reached in about 3½hrs from Sonogno. With 20 places, the hut is unmanned, but delightfully situated (www.verzasca.com). From here the way to the pass follows a good track, but in one or two places short sections of ladder or fixed cable have been provided for security. Over the pass the way descends to Alpe dei Laghetto and its tarn, known as Lago di Chironico, already visited in 3:4.

Continuing deeper into Val Vegorness beyond Cabioi, the walling slabs gleam with waterfalls, and as you progress, climbing to a higher level near the building of Corte di Fondo, the valley floor is littered with rocks and boulders. Pizzo Barone dominates the bounding cirque wall, and the path climbs towards it, but on topping a rocky shelf near another alp hut at 1950m, the trail divides. One strikes off for the **Bocchetta della Campala** (the crossing that leads to Prato), with another breaking away from that to visit the little **Lago dei Porchieirsc** on the south wall of the valley at 2190m.

Meanwhile the main path tacks up the steep north slope to **Rifugio Barone**, 4hrs from Sonogno. This is another unmanned hut owned by the Vogorno-based Società Escursionistica Verzaschese. With 32 places, it has self-catering facilities and a very fine outlook (for information go to www.verzasca.com). About 40mins above the hut, the kidney-shaped Lago Barone lies in a rugged cirque at 2391m, with the **Passo Barone** leading to Val Chironico (3:4) another 200m above that.

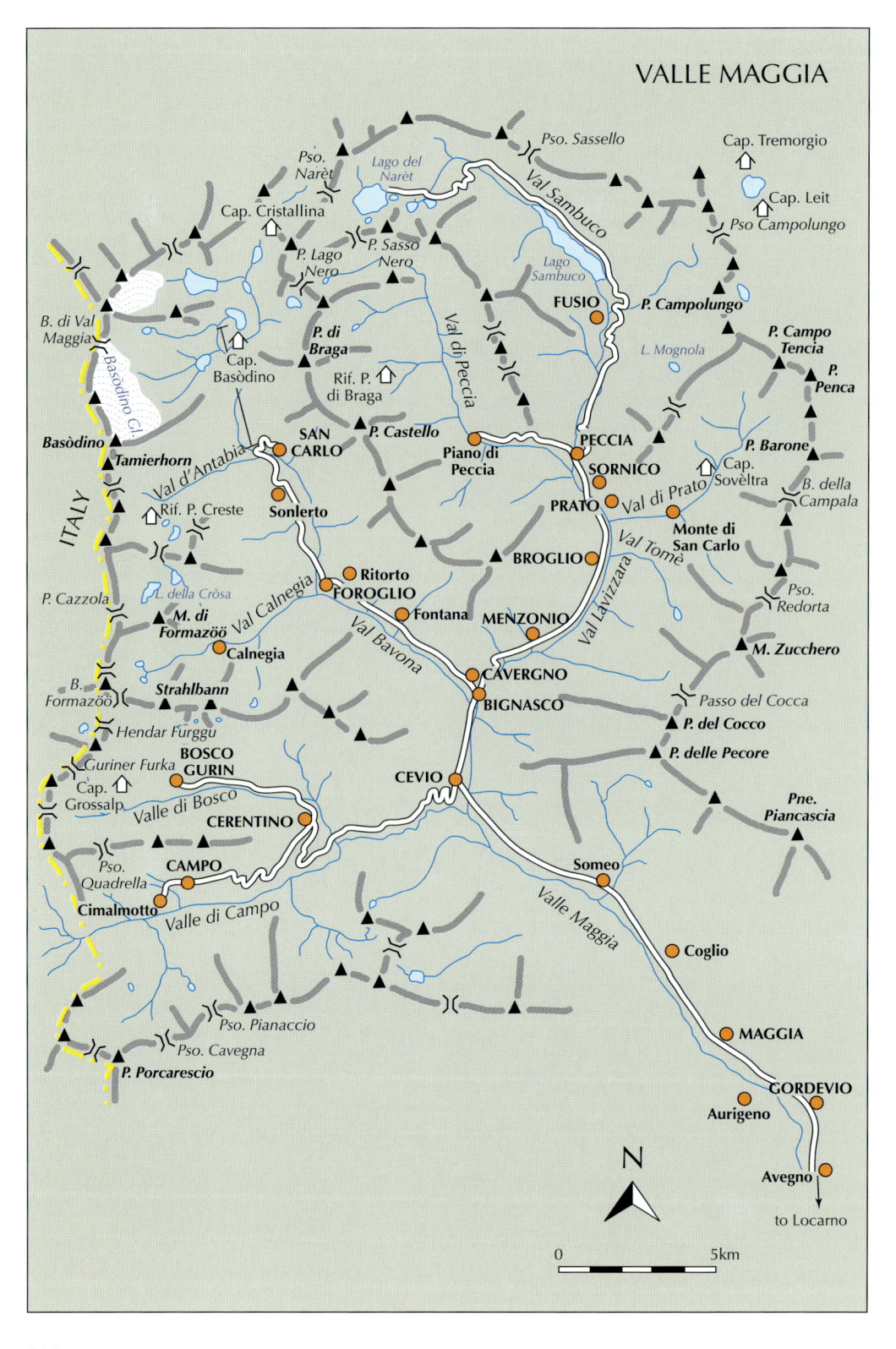

The Swiss Alps – Chapter 3: Lepontine and Adula Alps

VALLE MAGGIA

3:6 VALLE MAGGIA AND ITS TRIBUTARIES

With its many tributaries, Valle Maggia is the largest of the valleys draining the Lepontine Alps north of Lago Maggiore. Slicing into the mountains above Locarno and Ascona west of Val Verzasca, it begins modestly enough, but as you journey deeper into it, from Cevio on the landscape begins to impress. D W Freshfield drew attention to the walls of the valley which 'close in and bend, and huge knobs of ruddy-grey rock thrust themselves forward' (*Italian Alps*). Baedeker wrote of its 'bold rock-scenery, rich vegetation, pretty villages, and fine waterfalls' (*Switzerland*), while Walker, writing of Val Verzasca and the three upper arms of Valle Maggia which begin under the Cristallina massif (Vals Bavona, di Peccia and Lavizzara), claimed that they contain 'such delights of nature's loveliness as few other places possess' (*Walking in the Alps*).

The lower valley has something of the Riviera about it. Broad and flat-bottomed, with barely a perceptible rise for several kilometres, it's not exactly alpine, despite being flanked by mountains streaked with waterfalls. But characteristic villages such as Gordevio, Aurigeno, Maggia, Coglio and Someo all have hotels and, a rarity for Lepontine valleys, campsites at Avegno and Gordevio. Buses serve just about every village that has a paved road to it, while the valley's tourist information office is sited in **Maggia** (www.vallemaggia.ch), roughly midway between Locarno and Cevio.

Cevio (418m) is located at the entrance to Valle di Campo which has an off-shoot into Valle di Bosco. But before exploring these, it's worth noting that Cevio makes a reasonable base, for it has four small hotels, restaurants, shops, a bank, post office and a weekly market.

Valles di Campo and Bosco

The road into Valle di Campo climbs a series of tight hairpins among houses built on vine terraces, then through chestnut woods and the villages of Linescio and Collinasco to **Cerentino** where it forks. The right branch enters Valle di Bosco, the left continues as Valle di Campo.

Valle di Campo is unusual in that the Italian border cuts right across it less than 5km upstream of **Campo**, the main village which sprawls along the north flank of the valley at 1318m. The headwall runs from Corona di Groppo to Pizzo del Forno, on the far side of which lies Valle Antigorio. That headwall does not carry the border but stands well within Italian territory, even though Valle di Campo is only accessible from Italy by walker's passes. Apart from Campo, several other villages and alp hamlets grace the meadows of this lovely, if undramatic, little glen, and there are small hotels in Cerentino, Campo and Cimalmotto.

This is all walking country, with alps to visit, viewpoints to enjoy, and passes to cross. Above **Cimalmotto** on the south side of the valley, for example, two passes – **Passo della Cavegna** and the 2183m **Passo Pianaccio** – carry paths over the mountains to Vergeletto where you can catch a bus through Valle Onsernone to Locarno. Perhaps a better option, however, is found north of Cimalmotto where a 4½hr crossing of 🟢 **Passo Quadrella** (2137m) takes the walker to Bosco Gurin in the neighbouring Valle di Bosco.

Valle di Bosco is shorter than its neighbour, and at 1503m its only true village, **Bosco Gurin**, is the highest in Ticino. Settled in the 13th century by German-speaking Walsers from the upper Rhône valley, the inhabitants today still speak a form of *Schwyzerdütsch*, rather than Italian. There's hotel accommodation at the Edelweiss, and the 3-star Walser, and dormitory beds at the Ostello Giovani Bosco. At Grossalp, formerly a hamlet of semi-deserted stone huts under the headwall, a new ski complex is linked via a tunnel with Valle Antigorio in Italy. The timber-built, UTOE-owned **Capanna Grossalp** (1907m) overlooks the valley. Manned from June to September, it has 36 places (tel 091 754 16 80) and is reached in about 1hr from Bosco Gurin.

On a high and stony terrace about 900m above Bosco Gurin, three tiny tarns lie under the Strahlbann–Piz d'Orsalia ridge to give an energetic 5hr circular walk, while even more demanding trails cross the **Guriner Furka** (Passo di Bosco; 2323m) and the 2419m **Hendar Furggu** on the frontier ridge, or the **Bocchetta Formazöö** (2670m) east of the Wandfluhhorn near the head of Val Calnegia.

Valle Maggia narrows above Cevio on the approach to **Bignasco** (443m), which Walker, in his enthusiasm for the Lepontines, considered to be the gateway to a wonderland. Walker's understandable love for the district echoed that of Freshfield who, 70 years earlier, described the scene:

As we draw near the first scattered houses of Bignasco, the mountains suddenly break open, and reveal a vision of the most exquisite and harmonious beauty, one of those masterpieces of nature which defy the efforts of the subtlest word-painters ... At the gate of Val Bavona a white village glistens from amidst its vineyards. Sheer above it two bold granite walls rise out of the verdure, and form the entrance to a long avenue of great mountain shapes ... Each upper cliff flows down into a slope of chestnut-muffled boulders in a curve, the classical beauty of which is repeated by the vine-tendrils at its feet. In the distance the snows of the Basòdino seen through the sunny haze gleam, like a golden halo, on the far-off head of the mountain.

Bignasco commands a fork in the valley, where the main stem of the Maggia, known here as Val Broglio but higher up as Val Lavizzara, descends from the northeast to be joined by Val Bavona coming from the northwest. Both stems drain the Cristallina mountains, but while the first is dominated by Pizzo Campo Tencia, the latter is crowned – as we have seen – by the Basòdino. With nearby **Cavergno**, Bignasco smiles in the benediction of both, and with much to explore on their doorstep, the two villages make a natural base for walker and climber. Between them there are four hotels or *pensiones*, the Ostello, Posta, Pensione Stella, and the 3-star Ristorante Turisti; a few shops, a bank and a post office.

Val Bavona

The loveliest and most interesting of Valle Maggia's feeder glens, Val Bavona may well lay claim to being the finest of all among the Lepontine Alps. Once again let Walker summarise its appeal: 'The valley is a deep and narrow trench, the mountain walls crowd in closely and rise up in tier upon tier of granite, with chestnuts clothing their lower slopes. All the way up the scenery has character, and is grand and striking in the extreme' (*Walking in the Alps*). It would be impossible to disagree with that.

Working upvalley among small meadows and a clear running stream, among chestnut and walnut trees and hamlets of local stone that are the very

The tiny huddle of buildings of Sonlerto in the lower Val Bavona

3:6 Valle Maggia and its Tributaries

essence of vernacular architecture, one is struck by a sense of order. Not the order imposed by a dominant authority, but a natural orderliness – the harmony of which Freshfield hinted. The soaring granite slabs, waterfalls and the lure of a distant summit, set against a lowly woodland glade in which a group of weather-stained haybarns or granaries have lizards scrabbling across their walls. Boulders patched with lichens stand among the meadows where they landed, who knows how many centuries ago? Though randomly set, they have their place. They simply *belong*.

Linking footpaths cross and recross the Bavona stream, meandering from one hamlet to the next: Mondada, Fontana, Sabbione and Ritorto, their white-walled chapels decorated with frescoes, each crammed huddle of buildings as much a part of the landscape as the mountains that wall them.

Then you come to **Foroglio** (684m) on the right bank of the river among stands of chestnut, linden and beech trees. So closely set are its houses that the slab-stone roofs almost overlap, and only the narrowest of pathways manage to squeeze through. Behind the village a bold spout of a waterfall erupts from the lip of a hanging valley. This is ◯ **Val Calnegia**, and it's worth giving a day to an exploration of its abandoned or semi-deserted hamlets, visiting the tarns that lie high up on the slopes of Madone di Formazöö, or crossing one or other of the passes in its headwall.

The woodland path from Foroglio emerges above the waterfall in the mouth of the glen not far from the buildings of Puntid where you cross the stream on an attractive hump-backed bridge. The valley is dotted with silver birch, and the path pushes ahead along the south side of the stream among straggles of wild raspberry canes and rosebay willowherb. The semi-deserted buildings of Gerra are seen on the opposite bank tucked against a slab of rock, then 1½hrs from Foroglio you come to the uppermost hamlet, **Calnegia**, at 1108m. Forgotten and deserted, its old stone buildings are crumbling amid rampant vegetation. Shortly after working your way through, the path begins to climb abrupt slopes of the headwall under Madone di Formazöö. At 1703m another lost group of alp buildings is met on a grassy shelf. This is Gradisc, and 400m above it lie the two beautiful tarns of **Laghi della Cròsa** in an impressively wild location where it's possible to see chamois or ibex.

The wild Val Calnegia, a tributary of Val Bavona

Some 300m above these tarns a gap in the ridge west of Pizzo Solögna takes a route into **Val d'Antabia** where the two buildings that comprise **Rifugio Piano delle Creste** (2108m) are usually manned at weekends between June and October. Owned by the Società Alpinistica Valmaggese (SAV), the huts sit among pastures about 3½hrs from San Carlo, have a total of 36 places and cooking facilities (tel 091 755 14 14).

Other crossings at the head of Val Calnegia include **Passo Cazzola** (2411m) on the frontier ridge, with a descent into Val Formazza, and the 2670m **Bocchetta Formazöö** on the valley's south-flanking ridge east of the Wandfluhhorn, with a descent to Bosco Gurin in Valle di Bosco.

Val Bavona North

North of Foroglio more small hamlets shelter beneath the valley's rock walls: Rosed (Roseto), Fontanelada, Faed and best of all, **Sonlerto** at 808m on a twist in the road, with a show of flowers bright against sun-warmed stone. And beyond that, not far from Val d'Antabia's drainage stream, the roadhead village of **San Carlo** (938m) with its 16th-century church and cableway to Robièi in the Cristallina massif. Reached by public transport from Locarno (change at Bignasco), San Carlo has limited accommodation at Ristorante Basòdino, open from June to October.

One other hamlet lies beyond San Carlo. Campo's few buildings are passed by the trail that climbs out of the valley to reach **Capanna Basòdino** (1856m) on the southern edge of the Cristallina massif, about 3hrs from San Carlo, or 10mins from the Robièi cable car station. One of the few huts in Ticino to be owned by the SAC, it has 60 places, is permanently manned from early June to early October, and often at weekends during the rest of the year (www.cas-locarno.ch).

The cableway from San Carlo was originally built to aid construction of the Robièi hydro scheme, and near the dammed Lago di Robièi, the obtrusive six-storey Hotel Robièi offers alternative accommodation to that of the Basòdino hut, and is similarly open from early June to October.

This southern side of the Cristallina massif bears evidence of the hydro engineer in the form of service roads and dams, for most (if not all) of the lakes have been harnessed for electricity. And yet in many places one looks over a surprisingly

Capanna Basòdino

rugged landscape, and the scenery is magnificent, with the great peak of Basòdino forming the district's southwest cornerstone.

First climbed by a party of Italian guides in 1863, ❸ ☆ **Basòdino** (3272m) is one of the most inspiring of Ticino's summits and an obvious attraction to mountaineers of modest ability. With its broad but shrinking glacier lying like a napkin under its summit crest, the mountain carries the Italian frontier along its main ridge, but it also has a long secondary ridge pushing eastward, whose southern walls fall with impressive abruptness into Val d'Antabia. Whilst it's also climbed via the Italian flank (F), and from the Piano delle Creste Hut via the Tamierhorn and the South Ridge (PD), the standard route from Capanna Basòdino (F) is a classic expedition of about 4½hrs by way of the Basòdino glacier. It begins by wandering round to the Robièi cable car station, just beyond which a good path climbs southwest to the Randinasca alp at 2156m. The path forks here. One continues another 500m to the ◯ **Bocchetta di Valle Maggia**, across which descent is made to Val Toggia and either the Tosa Falls or Passo di San Giacomo for the Corno-Gries Hut (see 3:3). The other trail is the Basòdino ascent path which crosses a stream and angles up and over a series of rock bands to gain an old moraine slope. This leads to the glacier which is crossed towards the summit cone, the final section being via a minor saddle on the East Ridge. The summit view is extensive, with the main peaks of the Pennine and Bernese Alps of especial interest.

Val Lavizzara

This northeast stem of Valle Maggia which extends beyond Bignasco, is longer than the Bavona branch, and although it does not have the immediate appeal of Bavona, lacks nothing in either beauty or interest. For the first few kilometres it's known locally as Val Broglio, while the upper reaches beyond Fusio go by the name of Val Sambuco. It also has the added charm of tributaries like those of di Prato and di Peccia.

The valley's bus service goes as far as Fusio, but a series of paths and mule-tracks also head upvalley from village to village. Unlike those of Val Bavona, these are real villages, albeit mostly small ones, with year-round inhabitants, and very few have either accommodation or even a shop. Val Broglio rises steadily between steep wooded slopes, the mountains closing in around Brontallo and Menzonio, between which Val Cocco cuts back into the east flank mountains. Both Brontallo and Menzonio stand above the road – **Menzonio** (731m) has a single hotel, the Osteria Camesi – while **Broglio** (703m) lies in the bed of the valley about 6km from Bignasco.

Across the Maggia river opposite Broglio a track hugs the bank and a short distance upstream meets a path which climbs into **Val Tomè**, a small tributary rising under the steep West Face of Monte Zucchero. In the stony cirque near the head of that valley, about 2½hrs from Broglio, Lago di Tomè can be found at 1692m, with a few larches and low-growing shrubs attempting to colonise the screes.

Val di Prato

Handsome, stone-built **Prato** (742m), and its neighbouring village **Sornico**, are reached a little under 3km from Broglio. With accommodation at Ristorante Lavizzara or the Casa Antica, either village would make a useful base for a night or two, for there's easy access into nearby ◯ **Val di Prato**, a valley that deserves to be on the list of all keen walkers exploring the upper reaches of Valle Maggia. About 45mins from Prato a dirt track rising through the chestnut woods of this side glen brings you to the hamlet of Monte di San Carlo (Monte di Predee on the map), situated at a junction of valleys at 1001m. Walker reckoned it to be one of the loveliest alps he knew. 'The alp occupies an angle between two tremendous waterfalls,' he wrote, 'and from its green lawns whichever way you look you see glittering cascades backed by forests of chestnut and ringed by graceful peaks.'

Of the two valleys converging at Monte di San Carlo, the south branch is Val di Pertüs, through which a route climbs to **Passo di Redorta**, the 2181m pass which gives access to Sonogno at the Val Verzasca roadhead (see 3:5). Val di Prato itself veers northeast, and beyond sloping meadows a footpath brings you to a gorge spouting another waterfall. In typical Ticinese fashion, a staircase has been hewn out of the rock to carry an old mule-trail up to a few more alps where the valley opens a little beneath the southern face of Pizzo Campo Tencia. There are more cascades, and in the bed of the stream deep seductive pools; the hillsides are tufted with trees, alpenrose and low carpets of juniper and bilberry, and on the west side of the stream a small mountain hut, **Capanna Sovèltra** (1534m) is reached about 2½hrs from Prato. Property of the SAV, it has 25 places and is occasionally manned from June to October (www.sav-valmaggia.ch). Using this as a base, the ascent of 🔴 **Pizzo Campo Tencia** can be achieved in 4–5hrs (see also 3:4). 'The steep grass of the upper alp,' said Walker, 'will be the only difficulty.'

Val di Peccia

A very short distance upvalley beyond Prato, **Peccia** (840m) guards the entrance to yet another tributary valley, this one draining from the west. Smaller than Prato, the village offers accommodation at Ristorante Medici, and is served by bus from Locarno, as are all the villages along Val Lavizzara. The valley it looks into is Val di Peccia, which digs into the southeastern corner of the Cristallina massif. Shorter than Val Bavona which it parallels, Val di Peccia shows clear evidence of pastoral decline, with abandoned farms and deserted alp buildings on its slopes, and some of the old pathways overgrown and hard to find.

Despite all that, it's a very pleasant valley with just a few small villages or hamlets: Veia, Cortignelli, San Carlo (not to be confused with San Carlo in Val Bavona), and **Piano di Peccia** (1034m) where the paved road – and the bus service – ends. From it a track continues to a quarry near Ghieiba from which high-quality marble is extracted.

High on the west flank at 2003m stands the little **Rifugio Poncione di Braga** on the slopes of the peak after which it is named. Gained by a waymarked path from Piano di Peccia in 2½–3hrs, the hut belongs to the UTOE, has 22 places and is occasionally manned between mid-June and mid-October (for information see www.capanneti.ch). Locals who use this hut often make the ascent of either the 2864m 🔴 **Poncione di Braga**, or 🔴 **Pizzo Castello** (2808m), both of which reward with stunning views of Basòdino to the west across the depths of Val Bavona.

On the same flank as the *rifugio*, one or two rough alps and goatherds' huts are linked by paths of varying degrees of clarity, but perhaps the most obvious excursion for walkers in Val di Peccia is the crossing of either **Passo del Lago Nero** or the nearby **Passo del Sasso Nero** (2420m) at its head, for these both lead into the Cristallina massif (see 3:3). From either of these passes, on the edge of a wonderland of lakes and granite peaks, one has a choice of continuing to Capanna Basòdino and Val Bavona, to Capanna Cristallina and Val Bedretto, or descending via Lago del Narèt into Val Sambuco and the head of Val Lavizzara. Any of these options, or another being a circuit of the Cristallina massif, would provide the fit mountain walker with a day or two of adventure in a memorable set of landscapes.

Fusio and the Upper Valley

The final village of Val Lavizzara consists of mostly tall, solid-looking, pastel-coloured houses with tiny balconies standing above the west bank of the river at 1289m. **Fusio** has accommodation at the Osteria Dazio Antica, Albergo Pineta, and the Ostello Communale. It also has a shop or two and a post office, is the terminus of the bus route from Bignasco, and has a car park about 100m beyond the bridge leading into the village. Above it to the north a huge dam holds back the waters of Lago del Sambuco, with Val Sambuco stretching beyond that to the eastern edge of the Cristallina mountains.

The valley walls are steep on both sides, and Fusio is suitably dwarfed by them, so apart from valley-bed trails, it's inevitable that effort will be required to tackle the best walks on offer. The east flank has the prime choice, and almost 800m above Fusio on a little shelf of grass and rock below L'Uomo, the sparkling tarn of 🟢 **Lago di Mognola** makes an excellent destination for a walk. The path climbs through forest, rising to a pasture with cascades streaming behind the alp of Corte Mognola, almost 200m below the lake. From the lake a high trail contours northward with Lago Sambuco seen far below and the Cristallina mountains ranged at the head of the valley. Then a steep path plunges back down to Fusio to complete an energetic 4½hr circuit.

Northeast of Fusio a full-day's trek crosses 🟢 **Passo Campolungo**, the 2318m pass on the far side of which stand Capanna Leit and Capanna Tremorgio on the south flank of Val Leventina described in 3:4. This is a classic crossing, taking 6½hrs of persistent walking from Fusio to Rodi-Fiesso, and is highly recommended.

A second route that crosses the mountains to Val Leventina aims further north with Airolo as its ultimate destination. The trail for this tacks up the hillside just beyond the uppermost end of **Lago Sambuco**, and crosses the 2334m 🟢 **Passo**

Fusio, a pastel-coloured village in Val Lavizzara

Sassello with a 900m descent on the Leventina side leading to Nante in a little over 6hrs, followed by another hour's walk down to Airolo.

Long walks are a feature of these upper reaches of Val Lavizzara, for yet another pass crossing can be made which leads to Ossasco in Val Bedretto (3:3) by way of 🟢 **Passo del Narèt** and Val Torta in 6–6½hrs. For the first 3½hrs the route pushes through Val Sambuco on the way to **Lago del Narèt**, and it is here that an alternative long walk becomes possible, with an 8hr loop trip ending in **Peccia**. This route cuts round the south bank of the lake, crosses **Passo del Sasso Nero**, then descends into and through Val di Peccia.

3:7 VALLE DI BLENIO

With the Lepontines forming its west flank and the Adula Alps the east, Valle di Blenio is headed by the 1914m Lukmanier Pass (Passo del Lucomagno), while at its southern extreme the Brenno river flows into the Ticino at Biasca at 301m. In truth the Lukmanier heads only the western stem of the upper valley, known here as Valle Santa Maria, which joins the northern branch at Olivone, giving the valley the shape of a crooked letter Y. Directly above Olivone the Brenno rises at Passo della Greina at the head of Valle Camadra, virtually at the point where the Lepontine Alps give way to the Adula Group on the borders of Ticino and Graubünden.

Although the Lukmanier has been used since at least Roman times, it carries far less motor traffic than that of the St Gotthard Pass, and as there's no railway in Valle di Blenio, except at Biasca at its southern entrance, and no *autostrada* either, the tranquillity lost in neighbouring Valle Leventina may be gathered here.

There are few similarities with the Leventina, for while that valley is narrow, deep and rocky, Valle di Blenio is an open sun-trap, with vines straggling on granite terraces along with figs, mulberries, walnuts and chestnuts. Known locally as the Valle del Sole ('the valley of the sun'), it seems to be flooded with a soft warm light that fills each feeder glen, meadow and mountain alike.

Biasca is a small industrial town overlooked by the 2329m Pizzo Magn and a Romanesque 13th-century church at the confluence of the Ticino

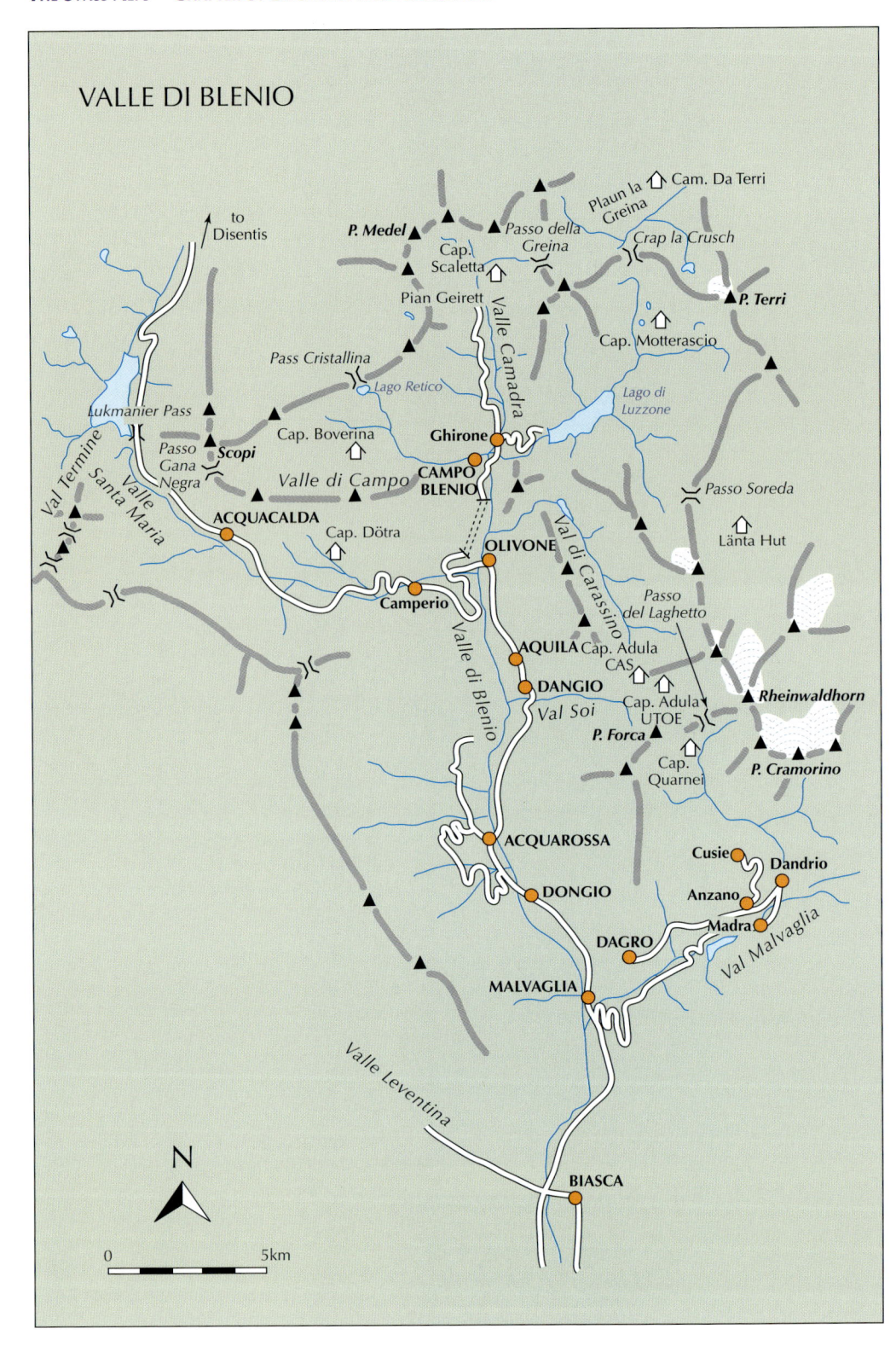

The Swiss Alps – Chapter 3: Lepontine and Adula Alps

VALLE DI BLENIO

Val Malvaglia leads to the Rheinwaldhorn

and Brenno rivers. Though of modest size, it is still the valley's largest township, with six hotels, holiday apartments, shops, restaurants, a post office, banks and a tourist office on the Via Lucomagno (tel 091 862 33 27). It is also the hub of the valley's public transport system, with buses run by the Autolinee Bleniesi company (www.autolinee.ch) feeding practically all the villages further north.

A little over 6km upstream the main road bypasses **Malvaglia** (366m), where a narrow lane breaks northeast to climb in dramatic fashion into Val Malvaglia at whose head stands the Rheinwaldhorn. Malvaglia is an old village with two small hotels, the Notari and Ristorante della Posta, both of which are open throughout the year.

Val Malvaglia

The road into Val Malvaglia is steep and dramatic. It rises out of the village by innumerable hairpins twisting among vine terraces before plunging into chestnut woods, then through a narrow unlit tunnel above a ravine. A covered bridge, replacing the romantic old arched original, spans the ravine to reach the hamlet of Pontei. The road ignores this, however, and continues along the south bank to pass a row of stone-built cottages before coming to a massive dam holding back a lake. The road twists above this, now on the north bank, for an easy glide into the inner valley. Across the reservoir rock walls soar above the water.

This inner section of the valley is a mixture of woodland and pasture. Just before reaching the hamlet of **Madra** (1086m) the little Val Madra presses into the east wall of mountains before being blocked by an abrupt cirque, on whose far side lies Val Calanca (see 3:8).

The road continues to **Dandrio** (1220m) in a magical setting – refreshments at the Ristoro Alpino – then crosses the Orino to angle up the steep west slope of the valley in an amazing feat of engineering. At **Anzano** (1354m) this narrow road forks. One branch maintains direction along the hillside to **Dagro** (1367m) which has gondola access from Valle di Blenio a little north of Malvaglia (accommodation at Ostello Dagro). The other makes a sharp right-hand turn and climbs still higher to the alp chalets of **Cusie** (1666m), 18km from Malvaglia, where the road becomes a track. Northward, the Rheinwaldhorn may be identified among a confusion of ridges.

THE RHEINWALDHORN

With Canton Graubünden to north and east, the 3402m Rheinwaldhorn is the highest peak in Canton Ticino and the crowning glory of the Adula Alps (its Italian name is l'Adula). Though offering a comparatively easy ascent by any of its normal routes, it is nonetheless a complex mountain with five ridges and three glaciers, two of which drain into the Rhine and thence to the North Sea; the other feeds the Brenno, then by way of the Ticino and Po to spill eventually into the Adriatic. The shortest but steepest approach is from Dangio via Val Soi below the West Face. On this side of the mountain there are two huts, both named Capanna Adula; one belonging to the SAC, the other to the UTOE, and both usually reached by way of Val di Carassino. The north side is climbed from the Länta Hut near the head of the Valsertal, the east from a base at the Zapport Hut near the source of the Hinterrhein, and the south side from Capanna Quarnei in Val Malvaglia.

First climbed from the east in 1789 by Father Placidus à Spescha, there were traditionally three technically easy standard routes, although in recent hot summers glacier shrinkage may have increased difficulties and the danger of rockfall. The mountain also offers a popular ski ascent (best from the north) in late spring. (See the SAC guidebook *Alpi Ticinesi Vol III/Tessiner Alpen 3* by Giuseppe Brenna.)

Wander along the track towards that mountain, and in a little under 1½hrs you will come to **Capanna Quarnei** at 2107m. This modern hut with 58 places, makes a useful base for climbs on the ★ **Rheinwaldhorn** (see box), **Pizzo Forca** (2582m) and the 3130m **Pizzo Cramorino** among others. Built by the Società Alpinistica Bassa Blenio (SABB) of Malvaglia, the hut is permanently manned from June to September, and at weekends in May and October when booked in advance (www.quarnei.ch). From there a 4hr crossing of Passo del Laghetto leads to **Capanna Adula** (see below), while the 2938m Passo dei Cadabi takes a route over the Rheinwaldhorn's SE Ridge onto the Paradies glacier and down to the **Zapport Hut**, normally reached from Hinterrhein (see 3:9).

Malvaglia to Olivone

The west flank of Valle di Blenio has its fair share of trails linking alp hamlets, but the main mountain interest is to be found on the east side. On the journey north to gain access to these mountains beyond Malvaglia, accommodation can be found at **Dongio** (478m), where on the Via Cantonale the Della Piazza has 12 beds and is open throughout the year. **Acquarossa** (526m), the next village, has three hotels: Ristorante Valsole (www.valsole.ch), the Rubino, and the Stazione. A short distance north of the village on the east bank of the river about 13km from Biasca, there's a very pleasant 2-star campsite, Camping Acquarossa, open all year and with a 22 place dormitory.

At **Dangio** (801m), 5km upvalley beyond Acquarossa, a very narrow road squirms up the steep hillside at the entrance to the little **Val Soi**. Wandering through this glen, the way climbs steep zigzags above the buildings of Soi to gain the SAC-owned **Capanna Adula** (2012m) in 3hrs. Perched on a small grassy shelf overlooking the valley, the hut has 34 places and is manned from mid-June to mid-October (www.capanneti.ch). A continuing trail leads in a further hour to the other Capanna Adula, which stands at 2393m with far-reaching views and is owned by the Bellinzona section of the UTOE. Larger than its SAC namesake, it has 58 places and is manned from mid-June to the end of September (www.utoe.ch). Both huts are popular with walkers, as well as with climbers tackling the Rheinwaldhorn, and are linked across the Passo del Laghetto with Capanna Quarnei in Val Malvaglia.

Stretching below Passo Termine, and roughly north of the lower Adula Hut, **Val di Carassino** suggests a pleasant walk down to Olivone. It's a gentle but narrow valley dotted with old stone buildings and with a farm road running for most of its length. At its northern end there's a small reservoir, beyond which you turn left and descend to **Olivone** which lies at 889m.

It is at Olivone that the main road through Valle di Blenio makes a sharp bend to the left to begin the climb into Valle Santa Maria, while another keeps ahead to a gorge through which the Camadra stem of the valley is reached. As for Olivone itself, it houses the valley's tourist office (www.blenio-turismo.ch), has a post office, small supermarket and four hotels: the upmarket Olivone e Posta with 45 beds, Albergo Arcobaleno (www.albergo-arcobaleno.ch) with 59 beds, the San Martino which has 35 beds, and the smaller 18-bedded Osteria Centrale. With these accommodation possibilities the village makes a useful base for walks and climbs in the upper northern stem of the valley, but before heading through its guarding ravine, we will first explore the Santa Maria valley which leads to the Lukmanier Pass.

Valle Santa Maria

At **Acquacalda** (1758m), another 8km up the road towards the Lukmanier, Hotel Acquacalda offers 40 beds (open March to November) and also has a simple campsite at the rear (www.uomonatura.ch). From here a choice of paths take walkers to various destinations, including Passo Colombe in the west, and Campo in the east.

Between Aquacalda and the Lukmanier Pass, **Valle Santa Maria** is particularly fine walking country; a verdant swathe of pastureland broken here and there with stands of trees, small meandering streams and marshy sections betrayed by cotton grass. On either side peaks of modest stature stand back to be admired; there is no crowding in these upper reaches, and the only habitation is seasonal, where cheese-makers spend the summer months in low, stone-built farms. A summer-only tourist office is located in a car park on the east side of the road on the way to the pass.

The **Lukmanier Pass** (Passo del Lucomagno) is an undramatic saddle at 1914m, across which there lies a lake. The boundary between Cantons Ticino and Graubünden crosses 50m from the Hospezi Santa Maria which has standard hotel beds, 24 dormitory places and a large restaurant (www.lukmanierpass.ch). On the north side of the pass a good road runs down to Disentis (see 3:9) in Surselva, and the Lukmanier may be reached by bus from either direction.

There's plenty of good walking to be had. West of the hotel a farm road skirts the lake and brings you to the mouth of ◯ **Val Termine** through which a stony track leads to Passo dell'Uomo (1hr 20mins from the Lukmanier) and on to Capanna Cadagno in Val Piora in a little over 2hrs (see 3:4).

A short way towards Passo dell'Uomo another path veers off to work through ◯ **Val Cadlimo** to Capanna Cadlimo in 3hrs 20mins from the Lukmanier (see 3:4). By combining these routes a very fine circular walk, or a longer multi-day tour, could be created.

On the east side of the pass another recommended walk follows a path across attractive green slopes to the 2430m ◯ **Passo di Gana Negra**, and down past Alpe di Boverina and Valle di Campo to Campo Blenio upvalley from Olivone (see below) in 4hrs. Also on the east side of the Lukmania, the 3190m summit of ◯ **Scopi** is said to be a superb viewpoint, easily gained in 3–3½hrs by a footpath rising above the avalanche gallery protecting the lakeside road. The canton boundary runs across the summit.

Valle Camadra

As has been noted, Valle di Blenio has two upper stems, both drained by streams known as the Brenno, which come together at Olivone. Having already visited the western, Valle Santa Maria, branch, we will now look at the northern stem known as Valle Camadra, which flows from Piz Medel and Passo della Greina. At the upper end of Olivone a minor road breaks away from the Lukmanier route, swings up the hillside above the village, enters a 1.5km long tunnel, and emerges in a gorge. Where this opens, **Campo Blenio** huddles in the valley bed with Valle di Campo rising to the west. Overnight accommodation can be found at the Ristorante Genziana.

While the valley road curves round Campo on its way to Ghirone, it's worth straying into **Valle di Campo** where two walker's routes cross the intervening mountains to reach Valle Santa Maria, while a third visits **Lago Retico** in a rock-girt basin at 2372m, and crosses Pass Cristallina, less than 30m above the lake on the watershed crest. The UTOE's **Capanna Boverina** makes a good base for exploring here. Standing among pastures at 1870m about 2–2½hrs from the village, it has 50 places, and is staffed from June until the end of October (www.utoe.ch).

On the outskirts of Campo the road crosses to the east bank of the Brenno, and shortly arrives at **Ghirone** where it forks. The right branch loops up the hillside to reach a large dam holding back Lago di Luzzone at 1603m, where there's a restaurant and plenty of parking spaces. The 165m

The artificial Lago di Luzzone

high ⊗ **Luzzone barrage** has been equipped with 650 bolt-on holds, thus creating an exposed five-pitch artificial climbing wall with a F6a grade (fee charged).

At the far end of the reservoir rises Piz Terri, at whose foot **Capanna Motterascio** may be reached by a hike of a little under 3hrs from the dam. This SAC-owned hut has 70 places and a resident guardian from mid-June until mid-October (www.capannamotterascio.ch), and from it the ascent of ⊗ ☆ **Piz Terri** (3149m) can be made in 2½–3hrs via the West Ridge (PD). First climbed in 1802 by Placidus à Spescha (see 6:3), Piz Terri is a cornerstone of the Lepontine and Adula Alps. Its south and west flanks are bare rock, but a small glacier hangs on its northwest flank above a glacial lake which lies on the alternative route of ascent often taken from the 100-place **Camona da Terri** (see 3:9).

Beyond Ghirone and the last scattered hamlets, a road (with seasonal bus service) extends as far as Pian Geirett at 2048m under the Valle Camadra headwall, whose principal summit is that of 3210m ⊗ **Piz Medel**, the ascent of which is usually made from the tent-shaped Scaletta Hut, built on the east side of the valley between Pian Geirett and the Greina Pass. **Capanna Scaletta** belongs to the SAT, has 52 dormitory places and a guardian in residence from June until the end of October (www.capanneti.ch/scaletta). Above the hut to the east, the 2357m **Passo della Greina** not only marks the alpine watershed, but it also carries the Ticino–Graubünden cantonal border and is a linguistic boundary, with Italian being spoken in the south and west, and Romansch in the north and east. An easy trail across the pass takes the walker into the nature reserve of **Plaun la Greina** which holds great significance for many Swiss (see 3:9).

3:7 VALLE DI BLENIO

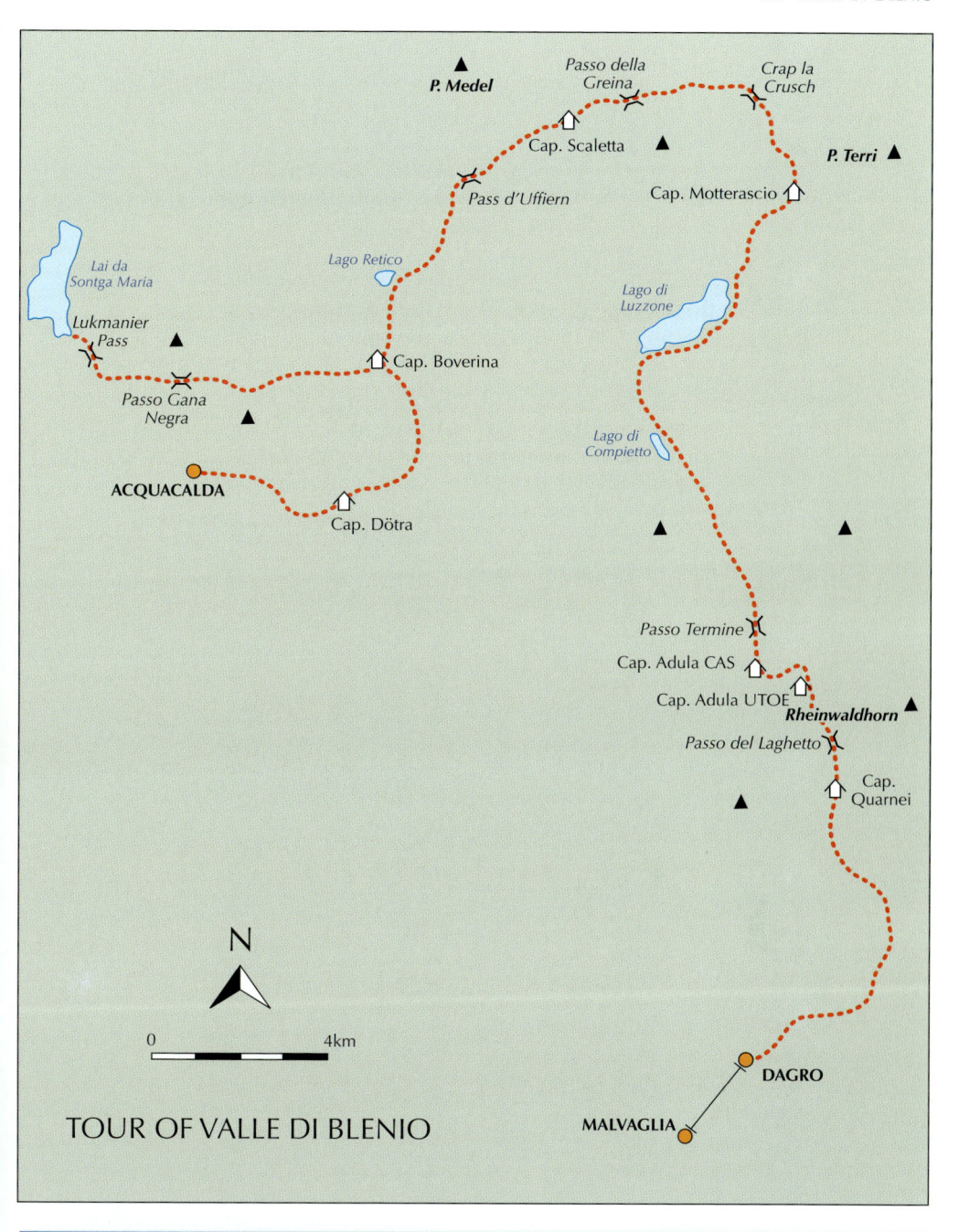

⛺ ⭐ TOUR OF VALLE DI BLENIO

Before leaving Valle di Blenio it's worth looking at a multi-day tour of this eastern district of the Lepontine Alps. Beginning in the south at Malvaglia, it works north then west to finish either in Valle Santa Maria at Acquacalda or the Lukmanier Pass. Accommodation is provided by a variety of mountain huts.

223

Day 1: From **Malvaglia**, north of Biasca in the lower Valle di Blenio, take the gondola to **Dagro**, then walk from there along the upper flank of Val Malvaglia, and spend the first night in **Capanna Quarnei**, nestling at 2107m below the Rheinwaldhorn.

Day 2: This stage of the tour crosses spurs and ridges of the Rheinwaldhorn on the way to **Capanna Adula**, the highest of these crossings being made at the 2646m **Passo del Laghetto**. As noted elsewhere, there are two Adula huts; the higher of the two, at 2393m, is owned by the UTOE, while the SAC's Capanna Adula is considerably lower at 2012m. The first gives the better views, while the second effectively reduces the amount of time needed for the following stage.

Day 3: Crossing **Passo Termine** the route now sweeps through the length of Val di Carassino, but at the northern end of this narrow valley, instead of swinging left to descend to Olivone, the way continues heading roughly north, comes to **Lago di Luzzone** and follows its southern shore to Alpe Garzott and on to **Capanna Motterascio** below Piz Terri – a 5–5½hr trek.

Day 4: North of Capanna Motterascio the tour crosses briefly into Graubünden at the **Crap la Crusch**, beyond which lies the Plaun la Greina nature reserve. Turning west through this you cross **Passo della Greina** and descend to **Capanna Scaletta** for an easy 3hr stage.

Day 5: On what is likely to prove the most demanding stage of the tour, it's quite possible that ibex will be seen at some point along the way – this section is known as Il Sentiero degli Stambecchi (the Steinbockweg, or Ibex trail). As befitting an 'alpine route' (blue-white markers), good visibility is essential when crossing wild and rocky areas where no actual path has been made. Should the weather be poor, or much snow lying, it would be wise to choose an easy valley route alternative. However, for the main route, the day begins by descending below Piz Medel, then rising to cross the 2628m Pass d'Uffiern – again on the cantonal border – before heading south and southwest along the rocky Sasso Lanzone ridge, then dropping to **Lago Retico** on the way to **Capanna Boverina**.

Day 6: This final stage will either cross the easy **Passo di Gana Negra** at the head of Valle di Campo and finish at the **Lukmanier Pass**, or head south from the Boverina Hut to Passo Cantonill, then follow a trail southwest and west via **Capanna Dötra** to **Acquacalda** in Valle Santa Maria.

3:8 VALS CALANCA AND MESOLCINA

South of the alpine watershed, these two valleys, which belong to the Adula Alps, represent an Italian-speaking enclave of Canton Graubünden; Calanca is a deep and narrow trench of a valley which ends in a headwall dominated by the 3132m Zapporthorn, while Mesolcina is broader, more open, and with one of the nicest of all road passes at its head, the San Bernardino, creating a link with east and central Switzerland.

Val Calanca

Val Calanca is the major tributary of Mesolcina which it enters near Rovaredo. Flanked by abrupt, cliff-like walls, the turbulent Calancasca is fed by several waterfalls. Alongside the river a string of picturesque stone-built hamlets suggest a reluctance to submit to the valley's final abandonment, while others, reached by veritable stairways of flagstone, occupy terraces several hundred metres above the river.

At the lower, Mesolcina, end of the valley, the access road passes beneath vine terraces, then winds up to a tunnel before crossing a bridge to the east bank of the Calancasca. Woods cover the hillsides, and between Molina and Buseno there's a small dammed lake. Beyond Buseno the road returns to the west bank and remains there all the way to Rossa. With Arvigo seen apparently hanging above the road, the route passes a large granite quarry. At **Selma** a cableway swings up the western hillside to Landarenca, after which little meadows open across the valley bed. **Bodio** has a tiny, decorated chapel; then comes **Cauco** on the opposite side of the river. The road keeps to the west bank, and steep rock walls once again squeeze the valley on the way to **Santa Domenica**, from where a steep ascent of the western hillside takes a route across the mountains via Pass Giumela to Biasca

3:8 Vals Calanca and Mesolcina

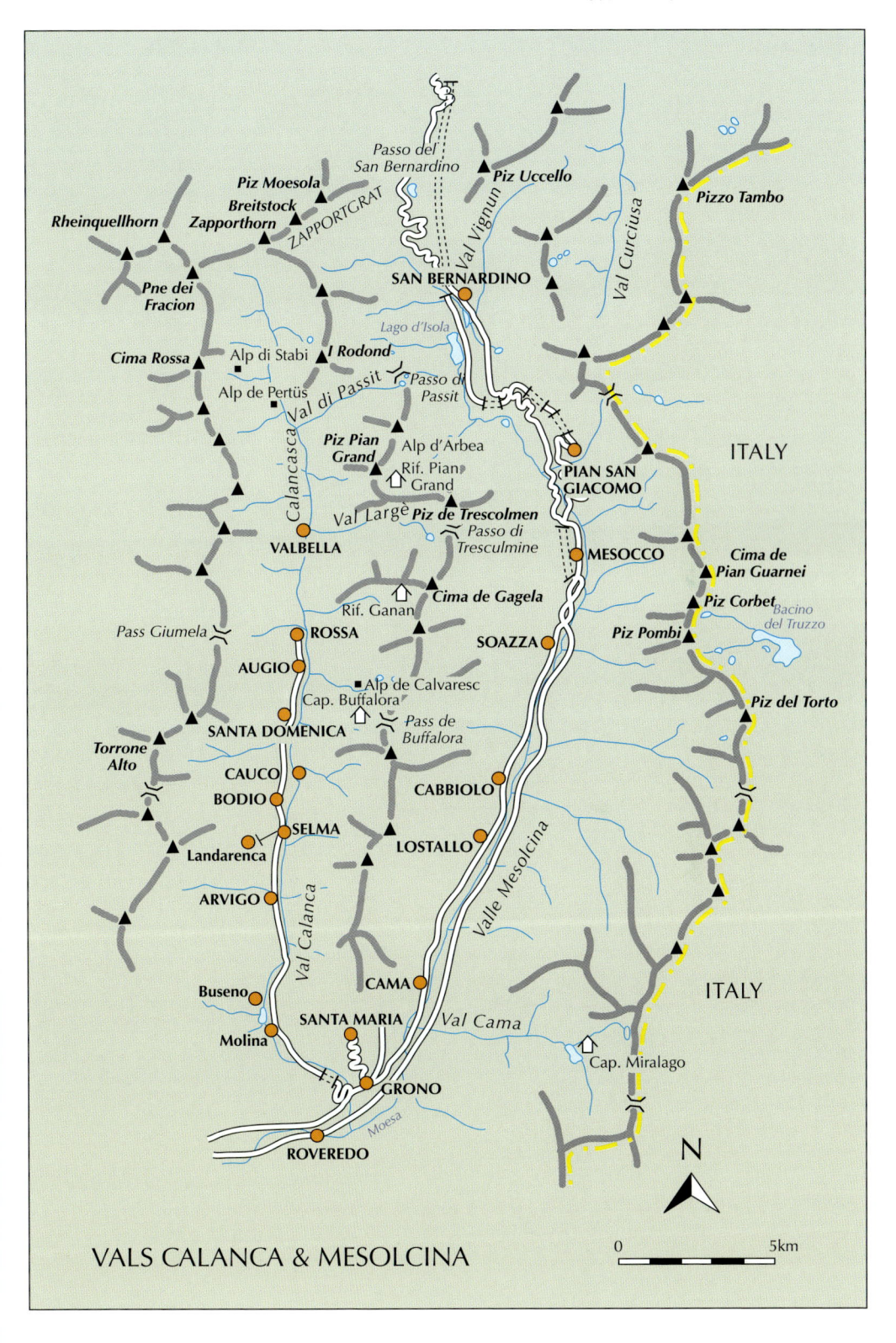

VALS CALANCA & MESOLCINA

The decorated chapel in Bodio, Val Calanca

in Valle di Blenio (see 3:7). **Augio** is next; a village with an attractive heart, it's noted for the Ristorante El Cascata, and slender waterfalls which cascade down the eastern cliffs.

Rossa (1069m) stands at the roadhead, and with accommodation at Ristorante Valbella and Ristorante Alpina (the latter of which looks as though it's seen better days), the village is the obvious base for an exploration of the valley. From here a trail climbs southeastward for almost 800m to Alp de Calvaresc (in 2–2½hrs), then trends south, still climbing, to where the timber-clad **Capanna Buffalora** is located at 2078m, about 3hrs from Rossa. Property of the Associazone Sentieri Alpini Calanca, the hut can sleep 24 in its dormitories, and is manned between June and mid-October (www.sentiero-calanca.ch). Above it the 2261m Pass de Buffalora can be reached in just 40mins, with a long sweeping descent on the east side of the dividing ridge leading to Soazzo in Valle Mesolcina.

About 3km upstream beyond Rossa, **Valbella** is the highest of Calanca's hamlets, its buildings strung in a line where the Calancasca is joined from the east by a stream spilling from Val Largè, at whose head the 2161m **Passo di Tresculmine** invites another uncomplicated crossing of the mountains to Valle Mesolcina (5hrs to Mesocco). An alternative trail breaks away from the route to this pass, cuts round the west flank of Piz del Largè and contours across the steep cirque walls that tower over Rossa, to reach the simple unmanned **Rifugio Ganan** below the Cima de Gagela, about 4½hrs from Valbella – there is no direct route from Rossa, which lies 1300m below. The *rifugio* stands at an altitude of 2375m, it has just eight places, basic cooking facilities, and is owned by the same organisation that built Capanna Buffalora.

A track-then-path pushes on beyond Valbella, still on the west bank of the river, before veering northeast into Val di Passit, the last of the tributary valleys of Val Calanca. Through this upper glen a trail seduces up to and over **Passo di Passit** (2082m) with its two small tarns, then down to the resort village of San Bernardino, gained about 6½hrs from Rossa.

The head of Val Calanca beyond **Alp de Pertüs**, with the 'grand mountain basin' (Baedeker) of Alp di Stabi cupped below the savage south-facing crags of the Zapporthorn, is not so easy to reach. This is rugged terrain, flanked by uncompromisingly steep mountain walls, and is rarely visited.

3:8 Vals Calanca and Mesolcina

Valle Mesolcina

Formerly known as Val Mesocco, the Mesolcina is broad and flat in its lower reaches, with vines, pomegranates, mulberries, fields of maize, and fig trees revealing a distinctly southern influence, while mountains rising on either side appear surprisingly high; those forming the eastern wall carry the Italian border, and beyond Roveredo and the entrance to Val Calanca the hillsides are heavily wooded, except where big rock slabs defeat vegetation. There are no towns, only villages with handsome churches, a few ruins and groups of mottled stone barns that stand hunched in meadows, some having been converted into holiday homes and weekend retreats. For much of the valley's length, the old road which links the villages runs west of the *autostrada* to unfold Mesolcina's history and culture.

The landscape becomes more interesting as you journey north. A few kilometres beyond Roveredo, **Val Cama** is a seemingly insignificant tributary which cuts into the eastern mountains. Under its headwall lies a small lake, where the privately owned 34-place **Capanna Miralago** provides a tranquil overnight lodging, some 2½–3hrs on foot from Cama (staffed mid-June to September: tel 091 827 17 42).

Between Cabbiola and Soazza figs and vines run out, but a 150m high waterfall attracts attention on the left of the road. Some way above it **Pass de Buffalora** provides a route across the bounding ridge into Val Calanca, as briefly described above. **Soazza** stands above the road, with a fine view of the ruined Castello di Misox commanding a bluff in mid-valley, just before you reach **Mesocco**, a village of cobbled streets and thick-walled houses. On the east side of the valley here, Piz Corbet tops the 3000m mark, where the Swiss-Italian border teeters along a splendid crest linking such summits as Piz del Torto, Piz Pombi and Cima de Pian Guarnei, on whose Italian flank (above Valle San Giacomo) the lake of Bacino del Truzzo is trapped in an extraordinary truncated cirque valley.

The Mesolcina road climbs towards the San Bernardino Pass, with attractive mountains to right and left soaring above high pastures dotted with barns and houses. A 400m rise brings the road to **Pian San Giacomo**, from where a footpath labours up the western hillside to **Alp d'Arbea**, eventually to gain the two basic bivouac huts that comprise **Rifugio Pian Grand**, about 4hrs from Pian San Giacomo. Owned by the Associazione Sentieri Alpini Calanca, the *rifugio* is unmanned, but there

Lago Moesola at the Passo del San Bernardino

are cooking facilities, an emergency telephone and sleeping spaces for 14 (www.sentiero-calanca.ch).

Northwest of Pian San Giacomo the valley opens out with fir woods and pastures, while impressive angular slab walls soar above to the left. On either side now the mountains take on a more serious tone. These mountains, rock peaks of the so-called ❂ **Alpi Mesolcinisi**, have been explored and devoured by local activists from both sides of the border. Though not high by alpine standards, there's much to reward a visit from climbers, especially on those peaks that run between the San Bernardino and Splügen passes, where classics from such names as Bramani and Vitali have been won on rock faces of excellent gneiss. (Consult the CAI guide *Mesolcina–Spluga* by Allesandro Gogna and Angelo Recalcati.)

There's also much to appeal to walkers, for the upper valley, before you actually reach the pass, is a plateau with lakes and streams, stands of Arolla pine and fir woods, meadows full of flowers and footpaths. **San Bernardino** (1608m), about 6km short of the pass, is the one real resort of Valle Mesolcina catering for both winter and summer visitors. Built on the site of a mineral spring which, during the late 19th century, became popular with Italian invalids, the modest-sized village has just four hotels, but several holiday apartments, plenty of restaurants and bars, shops, two banks, a post office and centrally placed tourist information (www.sanbernardino.ch).

The east-facing slopes of the 2829m **I Rodond**, and those below Pass di Omenit, have a limited number of ski lifts serving mostly red and blue runs, but in common with many winter resorts, both cross-country skiing (*langlauf*) and winter walking are also catered for. Yet it is in the summer that this largely unsung alpine outpost comes into its own, with a number of opportunities for mountain walkers. Linked with the road pass several choice routes could be taken, either as one-way walks with the possibility of return by bus, or as longer, circular outings. The ◐ **Strada alta** is just one of the recommended routes, giving a 7hr hike from the hospice on the pass to Pian San Giacomo. An exploration of **Val Vignun**, northeast of the village, is another option, with a trail that pushes into **Val Curciusa**, with the possibility for strong

Piz Uccello guards the San Bernardino Pass

walkers of descending all the way to Nufenen in the Rheinwald (see 3:9).

For those who might be looking for a short hut-to-hut tour, there's a fine (45km) three-day trek promoted locally as the ⬤ ☆ **Sentiero Alpino Calanca**, which begins in San Bernardino and makes an easy first day's hike to **Refugio Pian Grand**. The second stage crosses the walling mountains to end at **Capanna Buffalora** overlooking Val Calanca, and the third and final day takes the route as far as the village of **Santa Maria** which stands above the point where Val Calanca opens into Valle Mesolcina. The village has a postbus service with Bellinzona via Grono.

Out of San Bernardino the old road twists up among dwarf pine, while the *autostrada* tunnels through the mountains to avoid the pass altogether, emerging near Hinterrhein in the Rheinwald. The **Passo del San Bernardino** (2065m) is another alpine watershed, a broad and appealing scoop with a tiny lake set midway between Piz Moesola and Piz Uccello. Known to the Romans, this is one of the most pleasing and least bleak of all the major road passes across the Alps, with long views to be won from neighbouring slopes, and a route or two worth tackling on those western peaks that line the ridge leading to the Zapporthorn. The ⬤ **Zapportgrat** is a splendid long ridge which, apart from its eastern extremity, remains above the 3000m mark, linking the Rheinquellhorn, Zapporthorn, Breitstock and Piz Moesola (or Marscholhorn), its glaciated north side, on which there's some outstanding climbs to be made, plunging into the head of the Hinterrhein's valley (see 3:9).

3:9 THE NORTHERN VALLEYS

Of course, the Lepontine and Adula Alps do not end at the watershed, but drain on their northern side through a series of valleys that feed into either the Hinterrhein or Vorderrhein in the canton of Graubünden. The shortest of these are tributaries of the Hinterrhein, lying directly below the Adula Alps, but as this flows beyond Splügen and on to its confluence with the Vorderrhein a few kilometres southwest of Chur, so the river is flanked by the Albula Alps, described in Chapter 4. Before straying to that new chapter, however, it's worth making a brief survey of the valleys which lie between the Splügen and Oberalp passes.

Rheinwald

The short but sinuous descent from the San Bernardino to the village of Hinterrhein in the Rheinwald valley reveals a more open landscape, and on the final run-down into the valley bed the Zapportgletscher presents an attractive scene off to the left, where the Rheinwaldhorn stands proud at its head, with the nearer Rheinquellhorn also making its presence felt. The first recorded ascent of this latter peak was made in 1834, when a human skeleton, a dagger and the remains of clothing were found on the summit.

That upper section of the Rheinwald valley is flat-bedded and contained between long ridges of 3000m peaks: Hohberghorn, Lorenzhorn and Chilchalphorn on the north, Rheinquellhorn, Zapporthorn and Breitstock on the south. The Swiss military use it for training purposes, so access is sometimes restricted (for information tel 081 660 11 11 or 081 725 11 95). Below the Hohberghorn, about 4hrs walk from Hinterrhein village, the **Zapport Hut** stands at 2276m, not far from the source of the Hinterrhein river which comes from the Paradies glacier. The hut is owned by the Chur-based Rätia section of the SAC; it has 30 places and is usually manned at weekends or when booked in advance (www.zapport.ch). From it, climbs are made on the Güferhorn, Rheinwaldhorn, Vogelberg, Rheinquellhorn and the Zapporthorn, while a crossing of the Vogeljoch or neighbouring Passo dei Cadabi (both of which are over 2900m), leads to Capanna Quarnei in Val Malvaglia (3:7).

At the foot of the San Bernardino pass, **Hinterrhein** (1620m) enjoys an almost uninterrupted view of the snowy Adula Alps. Here the architecture is very different from that of the south side of the pass, and clearly shows the Romansch influence. An attractive village with a handsome square, the houses are solid-looking, with thick stone walls and deeply set windows, and there's a small amount of accommodation for those inclined to stay awhile. **Nufenen** is another 4km downvalley on the way to Thusis and is almost directly opposite **Val Curciusa**, which squeezes into the mountains between Einshorn and the rocky Guggernüll, the two guardian peaks that serve as gateposts. A 5hr trek through the length of that valley takes the mountain walker across a 2420m pass and down to San Bernardino village, while midway along the east wall of Val Curciusa stands the shapely, isolated **Pizzo Tambo**, at 3279m clearly the most significant

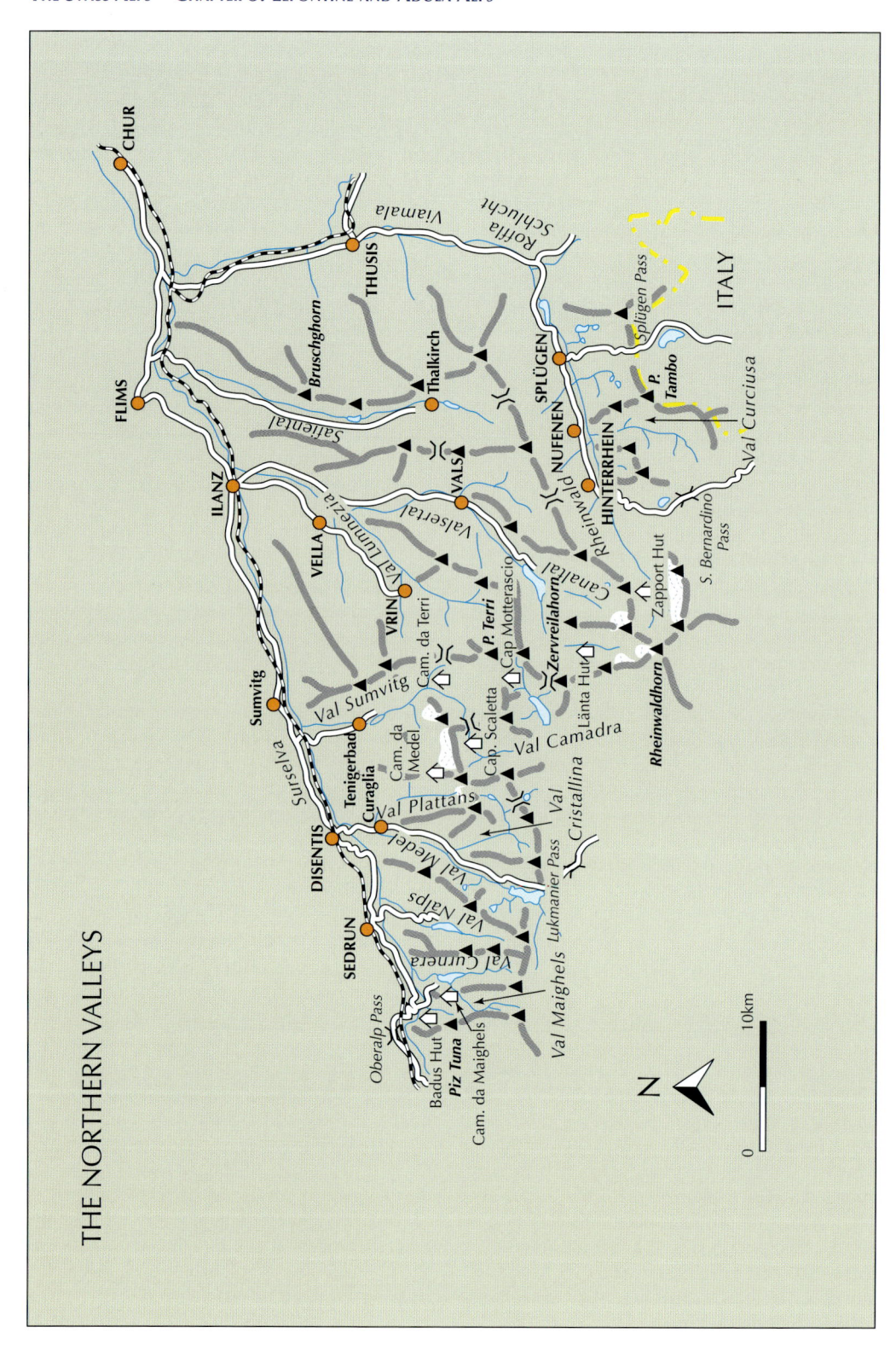

THE SWISS ALPS – CHAPTER 3: LEPONTINE AND ADULA ALPS

THE NORTHERN VALLEYS

The Rheinwald valley near Nufenen

summit at this end of the Adula Alps. (See below for notes on an ascent from the Splügen Pass.)

Still on the north bank of the Hinterrhein, Medels stands as a cluster of buildings on a slope above the road which then makes a straight run between hay meadows to **Splügen** (1457m), the 'capital' of the Rheinwald. With a campsite nearby, the village also has five hotels, restaurants, shops, a bank and post office, and a useful tourist office (www.splugen.ch or www.viamalaferien.ch). To the south lies the **Splügen Pass** at the head of a short, bleak valley, the original road to it having been constructed by the Austrian government from 1819 to 1821. The Italian border is met at the pass, and on the south side Valle San Giacomo drains down to Lake Como. The locally promoted 65km long ⬤ **Via Splüga** crosses the pass on a four-day hike which follows the traditional trade route from Thusis to Chiavenna.

It is from the pass that a recommended ascent is made of ⬤ ☆ **Pizzo Tambo**. Graded no higher than F, the normal route first makes its way towards the summit of the 2857m Lattenhorn, but passes just below the top and remains on the south side of Tambo's East Ridge, mainly on scree and occasional snow patches in summer. This ridge steepens considerably towards the summit, but there are no technical difficulties, and the top should be gained about 3½–4hrs from the pass.

Flanked by the Surettahorn on the east, and Piz Tamborello on a spur extending from Pizzo Tambo and the Lattenhorn, the Splügen Pass effectively marks the eastern end of the Adula Alps, so as all the remaining mountains and valleys on the south side of the Rheinwald belong to the Albula Alps, we will quickly journey downvalley, passing the dammed Sufner See and descending into the gloomy defile of the Roffla Schlucht where the river makes its northward bend on its way to join the Vorderrhein below Tamins, some 34km from Splügen.

Surselva

The distance by road to the Oberalp Pass from the Vorderrhein's confluence with the Hinterrhein is about 75km. Known by the Romansch name of Surselva ('above the forests'), this valley separates the Glarner Alps to the north from the Lepontines

RUIN' AULTA

The 400m deep gorge of Ruin' Aulta owes its origin to Europe's largest landslide, which occurred around 14,000 years ago when a huge block of mountain, estimated at 15 billion cubic metres of rock and earth, collapsed into the Surselva valley from a point thought to be where Flims stands today. A 15km stretch of the river was effectively dammed by this epic fall, causing a lake to form, whose weight eventually broke through the natural dam, wreaking havoc downstream. Over time the Vorderrhein scored a channel through the limestone debris; erosion by wind, frost and water has since helped create a remarkable landscape which consists of chalky caves, fingers, columns and strange pillars of white rock. The Chur to Disentis railway passes through the gorge, and a recommended 3½hr walk descends into it from Trin, with a way out by train which can be taken at the Valendas-Sagogn station at its western end.

and Adula Alps to the south, and for centuries has been an enclave of the Romansch language. A 100km walking route, the ◯ **Senda Sursilvana**, travels from Chur to the Oberalp Pass, visiting some of the nicest tributary valleys and picking out cultural highlights. The famed Glacier Express passes through the valley, with only minimal tunnelling at the pass, while the ubiquitous postbus service connects just about every village and side valley that has a road. And it is in these southern side valleys that flow from the Lepontines that our main interest lies – although not exclusively so, for a short distance west of its joining the Hinterrhein, the Vorderrhein is channelled through an impressive gorge, known in German as the Vorderrheinschlucht, but to local Romansch speakers as the Ruin'Aulta, and this is worth exploring.

The Oberalp road climbs above the gorge, goes through a 2km long tunnel near Trin, and soon after enters **Flims**, a busy, year-round resort in a sunny location backed by a row of crags. The resort has all services, including campsites, two climbing schools – Alpine Action Unlimited (www.alpineaction.ch) and Mountain Fantasy (www.mountain-fantasy.ch) – and a tourist office (www.alpenarena.ch) in both sections of the village, Flims-Dorf and Flims-Waldhaus. Cableways reach up the south-facing slopes, while across the wooded valley enticing views reveal little-known side glens cutting into a range of modestly proportioned mountains.

The first of these is the **Safiental**, with Versam sitting above a gorge at its entrance (www.safiental.ch). A few scattered hamlets lie deep within the valley, most of which are accessible by postbus from the Versam-Safien railway station, and a little over 1km beyond **Thalkirch**, the highest of these hamlets, accommodation can be found at the Berggasthaus Turrahaus, about 23km from the valley entrance. Overlooking the valley at this point is its loftiest peak, the 3056m **Bruschghorn**, which offers a rewarding ski ascent from the east in winter. But from the Turrahaus a walker's route slants up the western hillside to cross the 2412m ◯ **Tomülpass** to reach Vals in the Valsertal (see below), while another continues upvalley on an historic mule-trail which crosses the 2486m saddle of ◯ **Safienberg**, then descends southeastward to Splügen in the Rheinwald valley, a walk of about 5hrs.

The Valsertal

Out of Flims the Oberalp road passes through Laax and then slopes down to **Ilanz** on the south bank of the river. Once an important town, Ilanz is now of interest in the context of this book only on account of its position at the mouth of **Val Lumnezia**, a beautiful valley of open meadows, cherry trees and a string of neat villages. From here two minor roads enter the valley, both served by postbus. One remains on the west bank of the Glogn and 21km later arrives at the village of Vrin. The other soon crosses the river and rises steadily to reach Uors, where it then curves into the narrow, wooded **Valsertal**, named for the Walser people from Canton Valais who migrated here in the 13th century.

After passing through two small gorges, the road eventually arrives in **Vals** (1252m), some 20km from Ilanz. As well as a bottling plant for Valser water, the village has a modern spa building with hotel attached, modest downhill ski facilities and a tourist office (www.vals.ch). There are walker's passes to the east (the Tomülpass leads to the Safiental) and to the south, where the Valserberg carries a route over the mountains to Hinterrhein in the Rheinwald

3:9 THE NORTHERN VALLEYS

At the head of the Valsertal the Zervreilahorn has a distinctive shape

valley. But greater potential for walkers and climbers is to be found by continuing along the road for another 8km where, rising through forest and a single-track tunnel, you reach Gasthaus Zervreila near the Zervreilasee dam. This is as far as the postbus goes from Ilanz, although it's possible to take private vehicles to a parking area below a small chapel above the lake. From the dam wall, the solitary rock peak of the **Zervreilahorn** (2898m) dominates the view southwest at the far end of the reservoir, whose creation flooded the hamlet of Zervreila in which there was formerly an inn used by climbers before the Länta Hut was built.

Standing behind, but nudging slightly to the east of the Zervreilahorn, the 3383m glacier-hung **Güferhorn** has been celebrated as the most interesting of all Adula peaks. First climbed in 1806 by Placidus à Spescha, its south flank plunges into the head of the Rheinwald, while the East Ridge forms part of the dividing wall that separates that valley from the Valsertal which, at the southern end of the reservoir, splits into two stems, the Länta and the Canaltal. A walk of a little under 3hrs from the dam leads to the **Länta Hut** which, as its name suggests, is located within the narrow, steep-walled Länta valley at 2090m. Owned by the Boden section of the SAC, the hut has 33 places, is fully staffed from mid-June until mid-October (www.laenta.ch), and is the base from which the normal route on the Güferhorn is climbed via the 2979m Läntalücke and West Ridge (PD).

Proceeding further into the valley beyond the hut, the **Rheinwaldhorn** (3402m) towers overhead as the culminating point of tapering ridges. The normal route from the Länta Hut also uses the Läntalücke that links the mountain with the Güferhorn, in order to gain the NE Ridge, but due to glacier shrinkage the traditional route to this pass has changed (the current route is clearly marked). From the pass the ascent is made directly up the ridge (grade F).

For those not here to climb, high in the valley's western wall above the Länta Hut, but approached by a trail from the Lampertsch Alp, the 2759m **Passo de Soreda** provides a challenging way for mountain walkers to reach Lago di Luzzone and Capanna Motterascio in the upper reaches of Valle di Blenio (see 3:7).

233

On the other side of the Zervreilahorn, and curving left at the far end of the Zervreilasee, a good path seduces into the **Canaltal**, and in 1½hrs leads to the Canalalp, described in an early Baedeker guide as being 'grandly situated at the foot of the Kanal and Güfer Glaciers and dominated by the Güferhorn and Lentahorn'. Both of these glaciers have receded a long way since those words were written, but the scene is still a rewarding one, for it is here that the Adula Alps are seen at their best.

Val Lumnezia

With a reputation for being one of the most beautiful of all Graubünden valleys, Val Lumnezia is rather different from the Valsertal stem, for it is more open and much less wooded than its counterpart, its villages glow with sunlight and enjoy mostly unrestricted views of mountains at the head of the valley. This high region of hay meadows is blocked in the southwest by a cirque rimmed by Piz Terri, Piz Scharboda and the domed Frunthorn at the western end of the Adula group, but the 3121m Piz Aul, which effectively divides Lumnezia from the Valsertal, commands much of the valley. All the villages stand well above the river, and the road which links them is a joy to travel, especially in springtime when the cherry trees are in full blossom. **Vella** is perhaps the most important for the visitor, for it hosts the valley's tourist office (www. vallumnezia.ch) and has at least four hotels. Vattiz has the only campsite, while **Vrin** has an extraordinary Baroque church, some attractive dark-stained timber buildings with stone slab roofs, and lovely views of Piz Terri. Hotel Piz Terri is the only place to stay, but it has dormitory accommodation as well as standard hotel rooms.

The road continues for another 4km beyond Vrin, passing through Cons and Sogn Giusep, before ending at the hamlet of Puzzatsch. From there a trail entices up to Alp Diesrut, then aims for Pass Diesrut, at 2428m the lowest point on the Adula ridge at the head of the valley. On the west side of the pass lies Val Sumvitg, with Camona da Terri nestling at 2170m close to the nature reserve of Plaun la Greina, about 4½hrs from Vrin (see below for hut details).

Val Sumvitg

Returning to Ilanz, the main road through the Surselva valley keeps to the north bank of the Vorderrhein for a few more kilometres before briefly crossing to the south bank, then returning to the north side to enter Trun. But on reaching **Sumvitg**, midway between Trun and Disentis, it is worth diverting across the river to follow a minor road into the wild and sparsely inhabited Val Sumvitg. About 7km into the valley stands the hamlet of **Tenigerbad** at 1305m. A small dammed lake lies a little further upvalley, and the road ends not long after. But a track-then-trail pushes on towards the south, with the tributary of Val Lavaz cutting off to the west below an icy crest carrying Piz Valdraus, Gaglianera, Piz Vial and Piz da Stiarls, each one still clutching glacial remnants. The trail through Val Sumvitg becomes steeper beyond the Lavaz junction as the towering peaks squeeze the upper rock-girt valley. Yet there's a breach in what would otherwise appear to be the headwall, with Piz Miezdi to the right and Piz Tgietschen on the left, the latter peak forming a cornerstone of the Lepontine and Adula Alps. The breach in this headwall, through which the trail passes at 2102m, is known as the Crest la Greina, on the south side of which stands the **Camona da Terri** (2170m) at a junction of trails (4–4½hrs from Tenigerbad).

Property of the SAC, the Terri Hut has 110 dormitory places, and is fully staffed from July until the end of October, and when booked in the winter months of January to April (www.terrihuette.ch). More easily reached from Campo Blenio (3:7), the hut is not only a perfect base to explore the Plaun la Greina (see box) which stretches to the south and southwest, but is popular with climbers tackling Piz Terri and other summits of the Medel group.

Previously outlined in 3:7, the isolated ☆ **Piz Terri** (3149m) is an iconic peak with a handsome profile, and an ascent from Camona da Terri gives an enjoyable day's exercise (4–5hrs to the summit). The standard route from the hut initially takes the path towards the Pass Diesrut (one fixed rope section), but after crossing a stream you leave that trail and turn right into the Plaun la Greina before breaking off to follow cairns into a small valley below Piz Terri's west flank, where there's a small glacial lake. Pass along the northeast side of the lake, then cross glacial debris to gain a 2720m col at the foot of the mountain's West Ridge and follow the ridge to the summit.

From the Terri Hut it only requires a short walk to reach the region known as the Plaun la Greina which spreads round in a curve below the watershed ridge and is guarded at its southeastern corner

PLAUN LA GREINA

The nature reserve of Plaun la Greina covers about ten square kilometres of protected grassland through which meandering streams and boggy moors are outlined with cotton grass. Flanked by craggy peaks, the whole area, which lies just below the alpine watershed of Passo della Greina, is rich in alpine flowers and wildlife. Now recognised as a 'landscape of national significance', in the 1980s it became the focus of a long drawn-out battle between conservationists and the electricity authority who planned to flood the Plaun la Greina as part of a major hydro-electricity scheme.

by Piz Terri. So idyllic is it that a full day (or more) could easily be given to a lazy exploration. But a recommended walk continues through the meadows, crosses the 2357m Passo della Greina, and descends to **Capanna Scaletta** in a little over 2hrs. The Scaletta Hut looks across to Piz Medel at the head of Val Camadra, and an easy walk down that valley leads to Campo Blenio, described in 3:7.

Val Medel

Continuing along the Vorderrhein's valley towards the Oberalp Pass, **Disentis** (Mustér in Romansch, 1130m) is the next place of note, with its most obvious feature being the large Benedictine monastery in which Placidus à Spescha, the 18th-century monk-mountaineer, served. From its terrace above the river, this modest health resort is the capital of the upper valley, with plenty of accommodation of all standards, and a campsite on the road to the Lukmanier Pass. The town has most facilities, and a tourist office (www.disentis-sedrun.ch) located near the railway station. To the south stretches Val Medel, at the head of which lies the Lukmanier Pass (3:7) and the most practical way of entry into Ticino.

After crossing the Vorderrhein, the Lukmanier road enters the Medelserschlucht, a narrow ravine loud with the noise of crashing waters, then, having passed through a series of tunnels, the way climbs to **Curaglia**, a small, huddled resort with a

Disentis, with its Benedictine monastery

few hotels, a bank, post office and tourist information (tel 081 947 54 00). On the eastern side of the village, **Val Plattans** reaches up into the Lepontine Alps, where the Medels glacier hangs between Piz Cristallina, Piz Ulliera and Piz Medel. A trail climbs through the valley to reach **Camona da Medel** in 3½hrs.

Also known as the Medelser Hut, Camona da Medel stands on the 2524m Fuorcla da Lavaz, which links Val Plattans with the Lavaz tributary of Val Sumvitg. Property of the Uto section of the SAC, the hut has 55 places and is fully staffed from February until Easter, and from mid-June until mid-October (www.medelserhuette.ch).

South of Curaglia, Val Medel is distinctly pastoral, with several tiny hamlets and farms hugging the east bank of the river, until the road curves briefly into the mouth of Val Cristallina by the chalets of Pardatsch (1559m). The wild **Val Cristallina** extends southeastward into the mountains for 4.5km until it breaks into two stems, Val Casatscha and Val Uffiern, both being hemmed in by 3000m peaks. It is from the second of these stems that a trail crosses Pass Cristallina (2398m), descends to Lago Retico, and continues past Capanna Boverino to Campo Blenio, described in 3:7. Anyone planning to travel through Val Cristallina, however, should note that this is another of those uninhabited valleys used by the military for exercises, and is sometimes closed to the public. A noticeboard at the entrance provides details, but for advance information tel 081 725 11 95.

Beyond Pardatsch the road swings round to San Gions, described by Baedeker in 1901 as a 'group of hovels with a hospice'. Most of the climb to the pass has been achieved at this point, with a final twist shortly before the dam is reached which holds back the waters of Lai da Songta Maria, whose southern end marks the summit of the **Lukmanier Pass** at 1914m, making this the lowest of Switzerland's transalpine road passes. Beyond it, Valle Santa Maria eases down into Valle di Blenio, that sunlit glen walled by mountains representing both the Lepontine and Adula Alps.

The Oberalp Pass

Between Disentis and the Oberalp Pass, **Sedrun** lies in the upper valley of the Vorderrhein, known as Val Tavetsch. Located 300m higher than Disentis, it's a modern resort with good facilities, including banks, at least 10 hotels, numerous holiday apartments and two campsites. Tourist information is on Via Alpsu,

The 2044m Oberalp Pass marks the border between Graubünden and Uri

south of the railway station (www.disentis-sedrun.ch). North of the village, at the head of Val Strem, the 3327m Oberalpstock is one of the major peaks of the Glarner Alps, while across the Vorderrhein to the south, **Val Nalps** is a long tapering valley in which hydro engineers have dammed the Lai da Nalps midway between its entrance and the Lepontine headwall. Clamped between summits of around 3000m, this is a lonely valley, but at its head the Nalps Pass (2750m) suggests a way over the mountains to Val Cadlimo (see 3:4).

Immediately west of Val Nalps, and running parallel with it, **Val Curnera** is guarded above Tschamut (the final village before the pass) by a forbidding and pathless ravine, but there is access via a service road which comes from a little below the Oberalp Pass, and ends at the barrage built across the northern end of the Lai da Curnera. Like Val Nalps, this is another uninhabited valley trapped between abrupt mountain walls, while **Val Maighels**, the last of these northern valleys of the Lepontine Alps before reaching the Oberalp Pass, also marks the western limit of Canton Graubünden. The 100-place **Camona da Maighels** is conveniently sited at 2314m less than 2hrs walk from the road pass. The hut is staffed throughout the year, except May-early June, and November–Christmas (www.maighelshuette.ch), and from it several walker's passes and circular tours may be enjoyed. Streams that drain into Val Maighels flow into the Lai da Curnera by way of the little interconnecting groove of Val Platta below the Maighels Hut, but just north of this lie the ponds, marshes and streams which give birth to the Vorderrhein and hence the Rhine itself.

The true source of the Rhine here is generally considered to be Lai da Tuma (Thomasee in German) which lies in a hollow at the foot of Piz Tuma, due south of the **Oberalp Pass**. At 2044m the pass forms the border between the cantons of Graubünden (Grisons) and Uri, and is often closed by snow from November to May. But protected by tunnels and galleries, the railway remains open throughout the year and when the road is blocked, cars are transported by rail between Sedrun and Andermatt. As well as its railway station, the pass is noted for its lake, the Oberalpsee, which is said to be teeming with trout, hence its popularity with anglers. Accommodation can be found at Hotel Rheinquelle and Gasthaus Piz Calmot, and several interesting walks can be achieved from a base here. One of the most popular is that which takes 2½–3hrs to reach Lai da Tuma after first visiting the SAC's **Badus Hut.** Nestling against a south-facing crag at 2503m, the hut has 22 dormitory places, is permanently open, and is manned between July and the end of September. Taking a different route back to the pass gives a pleasant circular walk of about 4–4½hrs.

ACCESS, BASES, MAPS AND GUIDES

Access

Simplon Pass East From Brig take the E62 road. A daily postbus service crosses the Simplon on its way to Domodossola.

Binntal By minor road south of Fiesch in the upper Rhône valley. The road passes through Ernen and Ausserbinn, and is served by postbus from Fiesch.

Val Bedretto Across the Nufenen or St Gotthard Passes, both served by postbus; or by train to Airolo on the trans-Gotthard railway.

Valle Leventina By train on the trans-Gotthard railway, or by postbus. The valley road is a major artery leading to the Italian lakes.

Val Verzasca By road from Tenero or Gordola near Locarno. The valley has a bus service as far as Sonogno. There's a railway station at Tenero on the Locarno line.

Valle Maggia Road access from Locarno, with bus services to all villages.

Valle di Blenio Rail access via Biasca, then bus services to practically all villages. The Lukmanier Pass is also reached by postbus from Disentis.

Val Calanca Road access via Roveredo in Valle Mesolcina, with infrequent postbus service as far as Rossa.

Valle Mesolcina The valley is accessible via the San Bernardino Express bus route (Chur to Bellinzona). A scenic road serves all the main villages and crosses the San Bernardino Pass, while a motorway tunnels beneath the pass and provides a speedy transit from one end of the valley to the other.

Rheinwald All villages in this valley are connected by postbus services from Chur.

Surselva Good rail services on the Chur–Oberalp–Andermatt line run throughout the valley, and there are postbus connections with side valleys and villages away from the railway.

Valley Bases
Simplon Pass Hotels at the pass
Binntal Binn
Val Bedretto All'Acqua, Ronco, Bedretto, Airolo
Valle Leventina Airolo
Val Verzasca Lavertezzo, Brione, Sonogno
Valle Maggia Cevio, Bosco Gurin, Bignasco, Prato, Fusio
Valle di Blenio Biasca, Acquarossa, Olivone
Val Calanca Rossa
Valle Mesolcina San Bernardino
Rheinwald Hinterrhein, Splügen
Surselva Flims, Vals (Valsertal), Vella and Vrin (Val Lumnezia), Disentis, Sedrun

Information
Ticino Turismo, Casella Postale 1441, Via Lugano 12, CH-6501 Bellinzona (www.ticino-tourism.ch)
Graubünden Ferien, Alexanderstrasse 24, CH-7001 Chur (www.graubuenden.ch)

Huts
There are more than 50 huts in the Lepontine and Adula Alps, by far the majority being owned by local Ticino-based alpine clubs such as the SAT, UTOE and FAT (Federazione Alpinistica Ticinese). The Swiss Alpine Club has only a dozen or so. Many Lepontine huts are unmanned, but have cooking facilities and, in a number of cases, solar-powered lighting.

Maps
For planning purposes, Kümmerly + Frey produce two useful sheets at 1:120,000: Tessin, which covers everything south of the alpine watershed, from the upper Binntal to the Splügen Pass; and Graubünden which includes all the northern valleys as far west as the Oberalp Pass. The same company also publish Wanderkarten at 1:60,000 – 26 Tessin Sopraceneri, 811 Surselva and 812 Hinterrheintäler

More detailed mapping is available from the Swiss National Survey (Landeskarte der Schweiz) with the following sheets at 1:50,000 – 274 Visp, 265 Nufenenpass, 256 Disentis, 257 Safiental, 266 Valle Leventina, 267 San Bernardino, 275 Valle Antigorio, 276 Val Verzasca, 277 Roveredo

Walking and/or Trekking Guides
Walking in Ticino by Kev Reynolds (Cicerone, 1992)

Walking in Switzerland by Clem Lindenmayer (Lonely Planet, 2nd edition 2001)

Alpinwandern Tessin by Marco Volken, Remo Kundert and Teresio Valsesia (SAC)

Climbing Guides
Mittel Switzerland by Michael Anderson (West Col, 1974 o/p)

Alpi Ticinesi Vol I – Gridone to S. Gotthard Pass (SAC)

Alpi Ticinesi Vol II – Cristallina to Sassariente (SAC)

Alpi Ticinesi Vol III – S. Gotthard Pass to Pizzo di Claro (SAC)

Alpi Mesolcinesi Vol IV – Zapporthorn to S. Jorio Pass (SAC)

Prealpi Ticinesi Vol V – S Jorio Pass to Monte Generoso (SAC)

Mesolcina–Splüga (CAI)

See Also
Walking in the Alps by Kev Reynolds (Cicerone, 2nd edition 2005)

Walking in the Alps by J Hubert Walker (Oliver & Boyd, 1951)

Italian Alps by D W Freshfield (Longmans, 1875; Blackwell, 1937)

Freie Sicht aufs Gipfelmeer by Marco Volken and Remo Kundert (Salvioni Edizioni, 2003)

CHAPTER 4: BERNINA, BREGAGLIA AND ALBULA ALPS

Southeast Switzerland, from the Splügen Pass to Val Poschiavo, and north to the Flüela and Ofen Passes, including the Swiss National Park.

BERNINA, BREGAGLIA AND ALBULA ALPS: CHAPTER SUMMARY

Location
Sometimes grouped together under the heading of the Rhaetian Alps, the mountains spread diagonally across southeastern Switzerland. The Albula group extends east of the Adula Alps as far as the Maloja Pass, then northeast along the left bank of the Inn to the Flüela. The Bernina and Bregaglia Alps begin south and east of Maloja to straddle the Swiss-Italian border, while the official northern boundary of the Bernina group reaches the Stelvio Pass above Val Müstair. In order to include all of the Swiss National Park, this chapter strays beyond Val Müstair and the Ofen Pass (its link with the Engadine) as far north as the S-charl valley.

★ Highlights

☁ Walks
- Pass da la Prasignola (4:1)
- The Forcellina: Juf to Maloja (4:1)
- Casaccia to Soglio via Pass da Cam (4:3)
- Sentiero Panoramico (4:3)
- Fuorcla Surlej to Pontresina or the Coaz Hut (4:4)
- Tour of the Bernina Alps (4:4)
- Tour of the Swiss National Park (4:5)

⦿ Climbs
- Piz Kesch (4:2)
- N Ridge, Piz Badile (4:3)
- NE Face, Piz Badile (4:3)
- La Fiamma (4:3)
- Biancograt, Piz Bernina (4:4)
- East–West Traverse, Piz Palü (4:4)

⦿ Summits for all
- Piz Gallagiun (4:1)
- Piz Lunghin (4:2)
- Piz Languard (4:4)

Contents

4:1 Val Madris and The Averstal 244
Pass Crossings from Juf 248

4:2 Engadine Valley: Left Bank 248
Walks and Climbs from the Ela and Jenatsch Huts . . 251
St Moritz to the Albula Pass 252
Piz Kesch (box) 253
Albula Alps: North to the Flüela Pass 254

4:3 Val Bregaglia 256
Bregaglia North 258
Val Bondasca 261
Piz Badile: Icon of the Bregaglia (box) 261
Val Albigna 264
Val Forno 267

4:4 The Bernina Alps 270
Val Fedoz 270
Val Fex 272
Val Roseg 273
Climbs from the Tschierva Hut 274
Climbs from the Coaz Hut 277
Val Morteratsch 278
Johann Wilhelm Coaz: First on the Bernina (box) . . . 278
Val Bernina 281
Val Poschiavo 282
A Tour of the Bernina Alps (box) 283

4:5 The Swiss National Park 285
Val Trupchun to Val S-charl 287

Access, Bases, Maps and Guides 289

◀ *Lägh da Cavloc at the entrance to Val Forno*

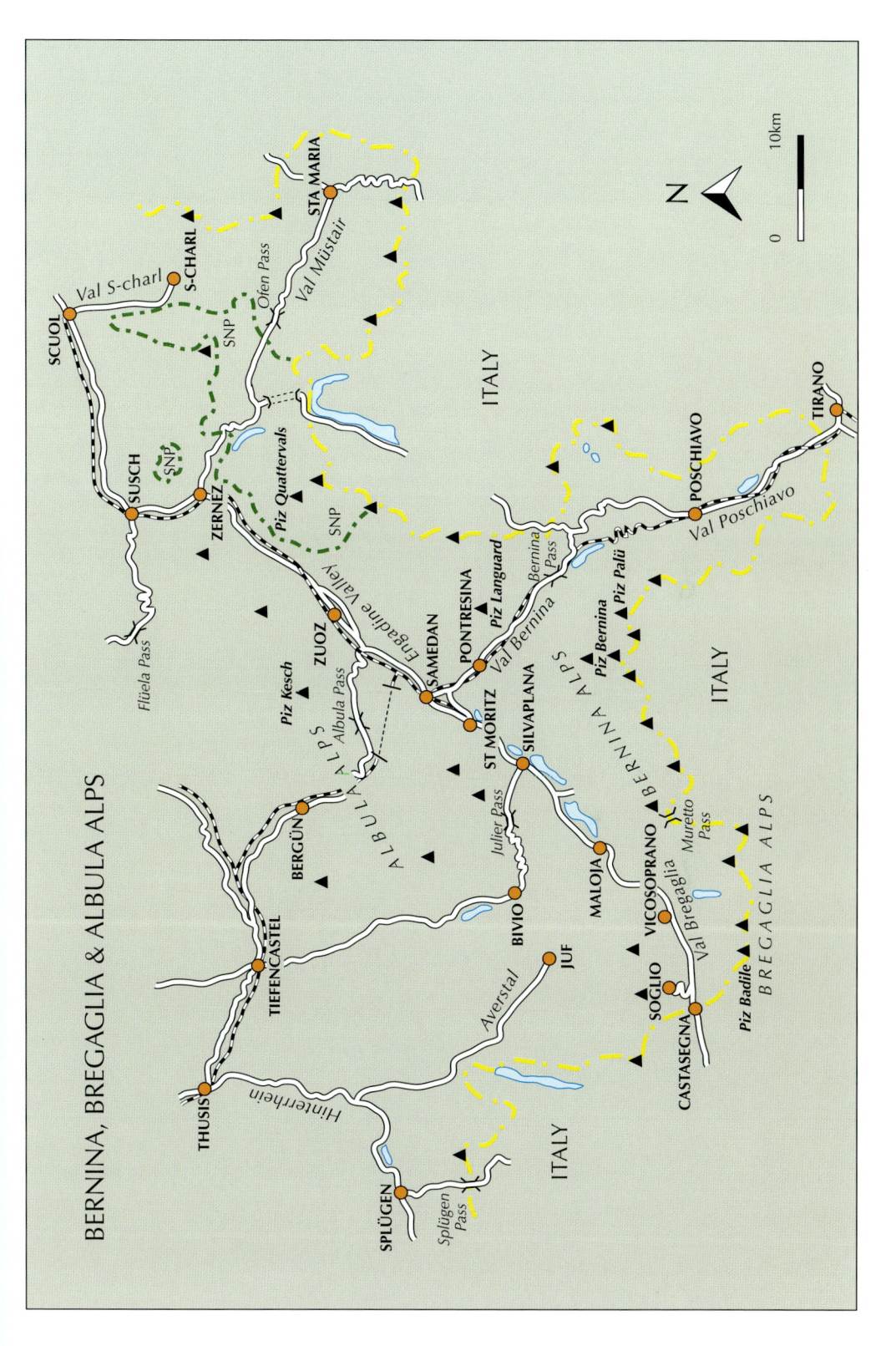

BERNINA, BREGAGLIA & ALBULA ALPS

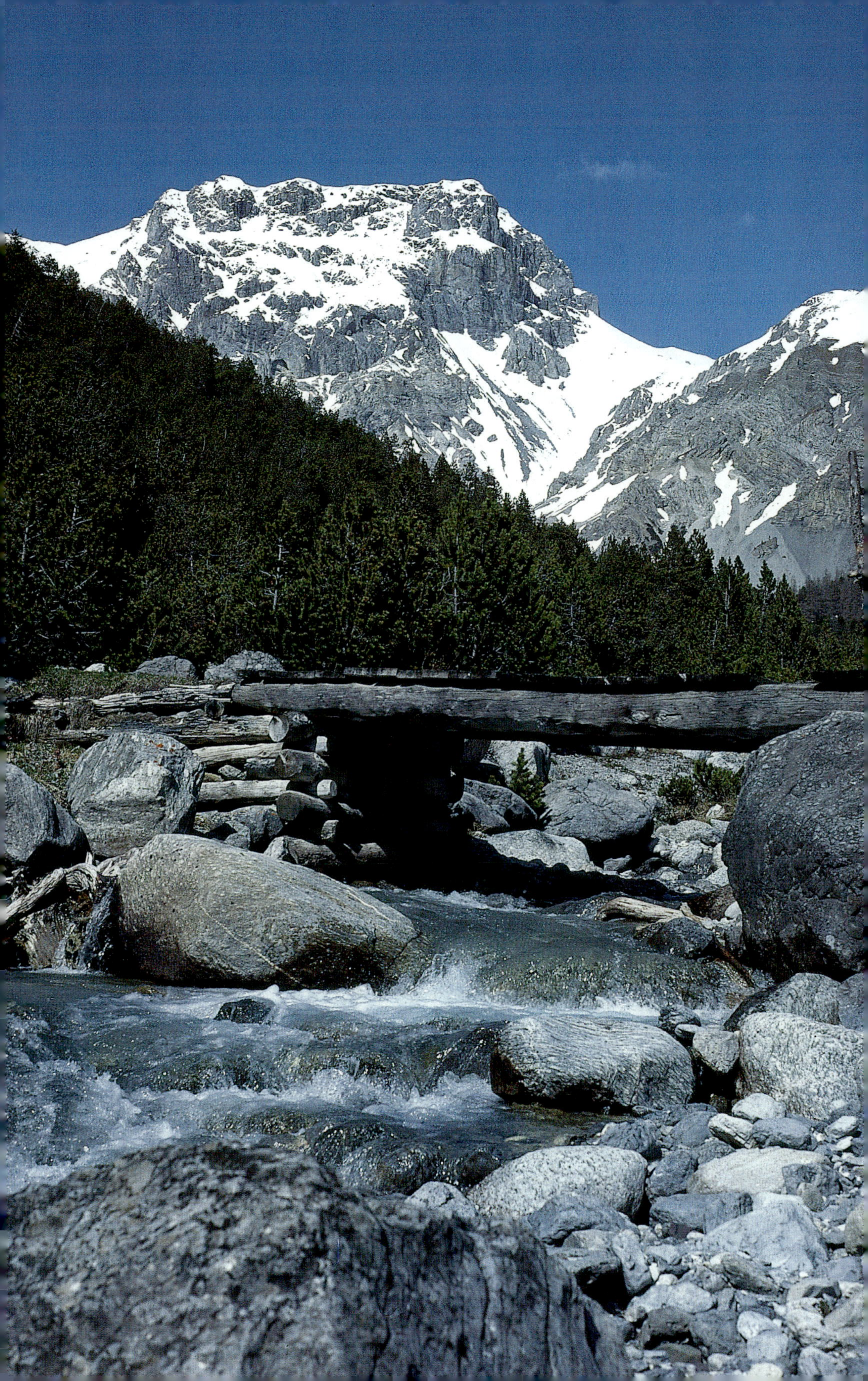

BERNINA, BREGAGLIA AND ALBULA ALPS: INTRODUCTION

The mighty forms of Piz Roseg, Monte di Scerscen, the Bernina, and the Morteratsch, and the glittering Tschierva Glacier below, with its multitudinous fissures and ice-falls, were a feast for hungry eyes.

Christian Klucker, *Adventures of an Alpine Guide*

These are districts full of contrasts. Divided by a number of ravine-like valleys, the Albula Alps are mostly snow-free in summer, and the few glaciers that remain tucked under the north-facing crags of Piz Kesch, Piz Vadret and Piz Grialetsch, are not likely to be there much longer. Yet the main block of the nearby Bernina Alps is a majestic group containing what its greatest guide, Christian Klucker, once described as an armour of ice, whose highest peak is the most easterly 4000m summit in the Alps, and whose neighbours still glisten with *névé*. Treading Piz Palü's delicate corniced crest, or climbing the famed Biancograt on Piz Bernina, one could imagine oneself in the Pennine or Bernese Alps. By contrast the Bregaglia is noted for its abrupt granite walls and bristling spires, in places reminiscent of Chamonix, while the deep luxuriant valley bears the Swiss hallmark of orderliness, yet in almost every other respect it's Italian, for architecture, language and even the light seems to belong to Lombardy.

In the Albula Alps lie some of Switzerland's most remote settlements, yet the Engadine which flows northeast of the Maloja Pass and claims to have sunshine on at least 300 days a year, contains one or two of the country's busiest resorts.

Alp Es-cha Dadaint above Madulain, with Piz Kesch behind

◀ *Piz Cristanas stands to the northeast of S-charl*

Here, Switzerland's only national park preserves and protects wild nature, innocent of the fact that only a few kilometres away, mountain slopes and the peaks above them have been strung about with cableways – hillsides sacrificed to the white gold of downhill skiing.

Mountaineering of a traditional kind can be found at the head of the Roseg and Morteratsch valleys, with snow and ice and fine ridges leading from one lofty summit to another. Hard rock routes abound on Bregaglia's slabs and walls; demanding cross-country treks are there to be discovered in the Albula back-country; hundreds of kilometres of well-marked trails greet walkers of all abilities throughout the district, and when snow falls the Engadine is transformed into a winter wonderland, acknowledged as one of the ultimate alpine playgrounds whose appeal is also recognised by the experienced ski-mountaineer, for away from the glitz and glamour of St Moritz there lie dozens of peaks, passes and valleys among which winter sport can be enjoyed without the crowds.

West of the Engadine the Albula district is broken into sizeable chunks outlined by three road routes: those that cross from Tiefencastel to Silvaplana via the Julier Pass; the Albula route (Filisur to La Punt), and the Flüela Pass which links Davos and Susch. East of the Engadine the Bernina Pass carries a road and railway line from St Moritz and Samedan to Poschiavo and then to Tirano just over the Italian frontier, while the Ofen Pass road gives a clear run from Zernez to Santa Maria at the foot of the Stelvio, and on to nearby Müstair. No roads penetrate the Swiss side of the Bregaglia Alps, but an old trade route enables walkers to cross the Muretto Pass which effectively separates the Bregaglia from the Bernina Alps.

4:1 VAL MADRIS AND THE AVERSTAL

From Splügen to Thusis the Hinterrhein threads its way through deep and gloomy gorges interspersed with open meadows. The first of these gorges, the Roffla Schlucht, lies below the barrage of the Sufer See, but before it breaks out of this defile, the Hinterrhein is strengthened by a mountain torrent which gathers the run-off from two sparsely inhabited valleys, namely Val Madris and the Averstal which, lower down, become the Val Ferrera. Along

The lonely Averstal

4:1 Val Madris and the Averstal

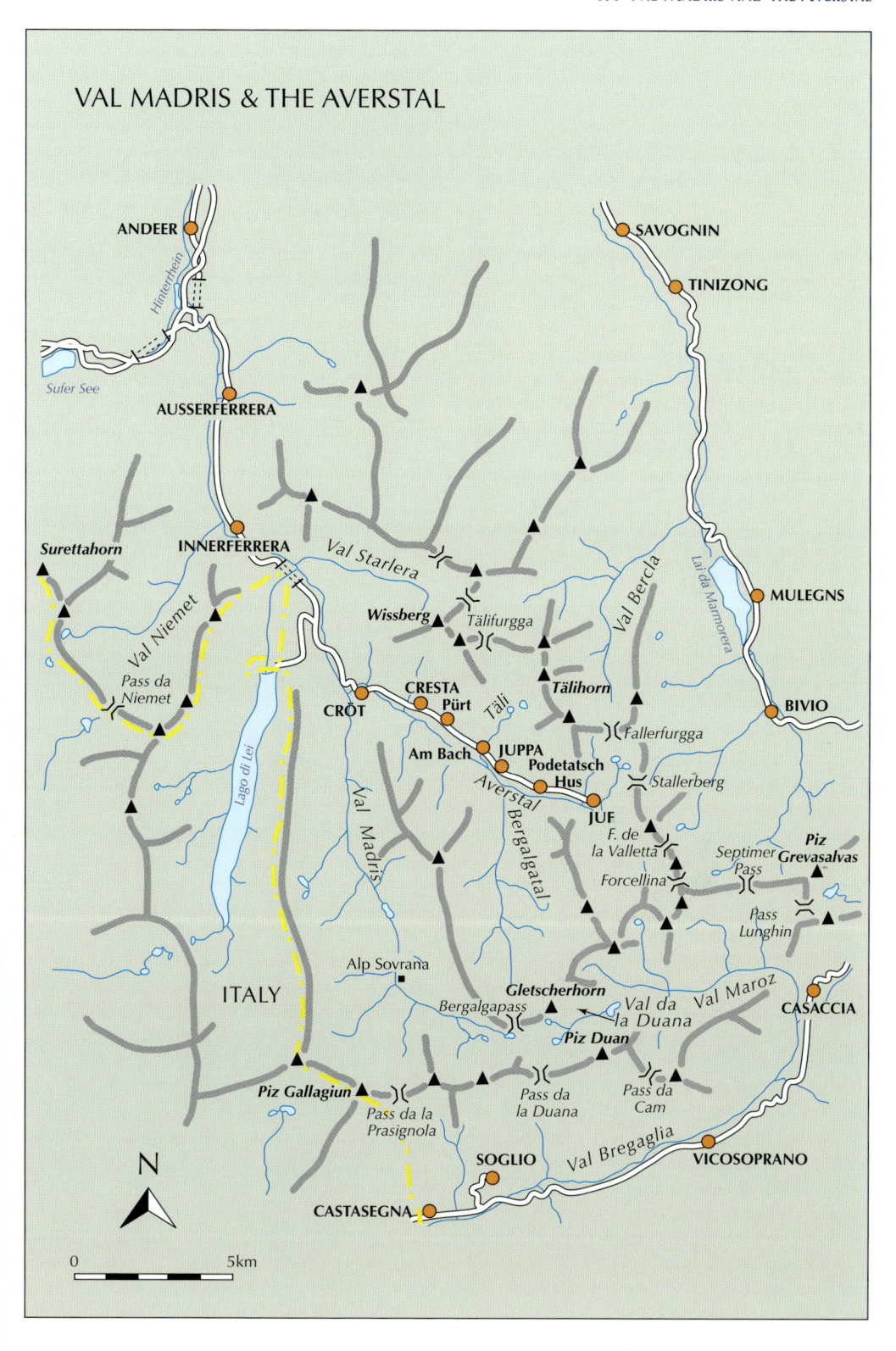

with their tributaries, these remote valleys emanate from Val Bregaglia's north wall, and count among the loneliest in all Switzerland.

Despite its remoteness the Averstal, the valley of the Averserrhein, is served by postbus from Thusis. The road climbs south through the wooded defile of Val Ferrera at its confluence with the Hinterrhein, and comes first to **Ausserferrera**, a small village in which Gasthaus Edelweiss advertises *touristenlager* (dormitory accommodation) as well as standard rooms. At the head of the gorge the valley expands a little, and passing a small dammed lake you arrive at **Innerferrera**, where Gasthaus Alpenrose (www.alpenrose-gr.ch) makes a suitable overnight base. Just below this hamlet **Val Niemet** can be seen cutting into the mountains to the southwest. At its head **Pass da Niemet** (2295m) carries a walker's route into the Italian enclave of Valle San Giacomo, but it is the Surettahorn northwest of the headwall that captures most attention.

Skirting around Innerferrera the road crosses the river, known here as the Ragn da Ferrera, and goes through two tunnels before emerging to a savage landscape of big rock walls, with pines and fir trees growing at impossible angles. With the Italian border encroaching almost to the road, the valley forks. To the south lies the Valle di Lei, Italian throughout, except for a tiny wedge of Switzerland providing access to a dam at the northern end of Lago di Lei. The Swiss-Italian border traces the walling right-hand ridge of this valley, on the east side of which lies Val Madris, most conveniently accessed from the hamlet of **Avers Cröt** (1715m) where there's a single *gasthaus* (the Walserstuba) with 12 beds.

Running due south of Cröt **Val Madris** (or Madrisch) is the second longest tributary of the Averstal, and by far its finest. At its head above **Alp Sovrana** (about 9km or 3–3½hrs from Cröt) the valley breaks into four stems, at least two of which have passes that lead across the mountains into Val Bregaglia. In his 1951 classic, *Walking in the Alps*, Hubert Walker was eager to promote Val Madris and the passes at its head, describing the walk upvalley as being 'remote and away from the frequented routes [and] altogether delightful'.

The second of the four upper stems is Val da la Prasignola which falls from the northeast flank of Piz Gallagiun, the 3107m peak on whose east ridge lies the rocky pass favoured by Walker. ☆ **Pass da la Prasignola** (2724m) is gained in 2hrs or so from Sovrana by a 'well constructed path with stone steps in the steeper parts'. On breaching it, a wonderful scene is revealed to the south across the depths of Val Bregaglia, whose villages lie more than 2100m below the vantage point. This is what Freshfield had to say about it in Italian Alps, first published in 1875:

> *Opposite, and separated from our stand-point … only by the deep but narrow trench of Val Bregaglia, a great mountain-mass glowed in the afternoon sunshine. Its base was wrapped in chestnut woods, its middle girt with a belt of pines, above spread a mantle of eternal snow. The sky-line was formed by a coronet of domes and massive pinnacles carved out of grey rocks, whose jagged yet stubborn forms revealed the presence of granite. Full in front the curving glaciers of Val Bondasca filled the space beneath the smooth cliff-faces …*

Only the curving glaciers of Val Bondasca fail to live up to that description today, but almost eight decades after Freshfield, Walker, inspired by the Victorian traveller's words, enjoyed the same outlook, then went on to recommend an hour's diversion from the pass to make the ascent of ☆ **Piz Gallagiun** by what he termed an easy scramble, for this, he vowed, would provide 'a worthy introduction to the promised land at whose threshold you now stand'.

Bregaglia is indeed a promised land, but to gain it demands a steep and knee-crunching descent to Castasegna or Bondo via Soglio. However, as Bregaglia and its feeder glens will be described in detail in 4:3, we will delay entry for now and return to the uppermost reaches of Val Madris where Val da Roda, its final stem, takes a route heading southeast to join a crossing of the Bergalgapass by some tiny ponds in a hollow below Piz dal Märc, about 5½hrs from Avers Cröt. From this point the 2694m **Pass da la Duana** can be reached and this, too, provides a route into Val Bregaglia by way of Soglio.

Back in the Averstal, after leaving Cröt the road climbs by a series of hairpins, then crosses a ravine to enter the upper valley with its string of hamlets set among slopes of shaven grass topped by rocky peaks of modest proportions. Some 200m above Cröt, **Avers Cresta** is an attractive village whose church stands alone beyond the houses. There is no accommodation for the visiting walker or climber,

4:1 VAL MADRIS AND THE AVERSTAL

Avers Cresta in the quiet backwater of the Averstal

but the village does boast a bank, and the valley's tourist information is based here (tel 081 667 11 67). An enticing trail strikes away from the road. At first it angles across the hillside heading east, then more energetically in steepening zigzags to enter a minor valley (**Täli**) which leads into a mountain sanctuary under the Tälihorn. Two small lakes lie within this sanctuary, while a crossing may be made of the **Tälifurgga** (2817m) on a shoulder of the Wissberg. Baedeker recommended an ascent of this peak, which he described as 'attractive', in 3hrs from Cresta. The walker's route over the Tälifurgga continues with options to eventually reach the Surses valley below Lai da Marmorera on the Julier Pass road, or via two further walker's passes heading west through Val Starlera to arrive back at Innerferrera.

Both **Avers Pürt** and **Am Bach** are tiny; the first has the six-bedded Pürterhof Gasthaus in an old stone and timber building, the second has some pretty houses. There are no more trees up here; just pastures and hay meadows and the ageless dwellings of farmers. Then the valley bifurcates at **Avers Juppa**. Set at 2004m, the village faces south into the Bergalgatal, at whose entrance there's a solitary drag lift with a restaurant nearby. This is ideal terrain for *langlauf* (cross-country) skiing in winter, and for long-distance walks in summer. Just beyond the village Hotel Bergalga serves as a convenient base for both activities. It has 32 beds and is open throughout the year except November (www.bergalga.ch).

A trail strikes south through the ○ **Bergalgatal** along the east bank of its river, and in a walk of a little over an hour from Juppa, it brings you to Alp Bergalga. In the closing years of the 19th century the valley was said to be 'enclosed by fine glaciers'. Well, not any more, and today you can continue all the way to the **Bergalgapass** at 2790m and not touch snow, let alone ice. Even the 3107m ○ **Gletscherhorn** which overlooks the pass is mostly snow-free in summer, and a complete misnomer that may be climbed by a straightforward route in 4hrs from Juppa. It will take 3–3½hrs to reach the Bergalgapass from that same hamlet, but arrival there gives little cause for celebration, for unlike the Gletscherhorn's summit, there are no expansive, breathtaking views to reward the effort of reaching it. Instead you need to descend into the pond-littered hollow which lies between Val da

Roda (on the west) and the head of Val da la Duana (to the east), and then go on to the **Pass da la Duana** to overlook the deep Val Bregaglia and appreciate the exciting serrated crest on its far side. But an alternative option would be to descend through **Val da la Duana** and continue into Val Maroz which lies beyond it, and there (if you have energy to match imagination – plus a bivvy bag and supplies for a day or two) trek on across a whole variety of passes that make this delightfully unsung country of sparsely inhabited pastures a mountain wanderer's wonderland.

One other suggestion, whilst in the region of the Bergalgapass, is to descend partway down Val da la Duana to the second lake, then break to the south to make the straightforward ascent of 🔺 **Piz Duan** (3130m) via the last vestige of the Duan glacier. According to the Alpine Club guide, the summit gives magnificent views of the ragged peaks of the main Bregaglia chain to the south.

Back in the Averstal the road eases out of Juppa and passes a group of old houses and barns (**Podestatsch Hus**) before ending at **Juf** (Avers Juf), about 25km after leaving the valley of the Hinterrhein. At 2126m it is said to be the highest permanently inhabited hamlet in Europe. Though perhaps the least attractive in the Averstal, the collection of rustic buildings, and the numerous piles of firewood stacked in readiness for winter isolation, help create the impression of a forgotten world, despite the fact that it is served by postbus. There's a small shop, and accommodation may be had (not May or November) at Pension Edelweiss where there are 30 beds (www.juf2126.ch).

Though modest in facilities, Juf's situation is everything. Remote and other-worldly, it bears little relation to the Switzerland often portrayed as a mix of tradition and sophistication. That is part of its charm. A sense of isolation creeps into the hamlet as shadows of evening fill the valley. On a lonely alp, such solitude is to be expected; in a village having a postbus link with the outside world, it is a rarity. On all sides 3000m summits look down on Juf. But it is not summits that are the lure; rather it is the sheer number and quality of pass crossings that make the hamlet and upper reaches of the Averstal so appealing.

Pass crossings from Juf

- 🟢 In the walling ridge to the north, between the Mazzaspitz and Piz Suparé, the 2838m **Fallerfurgga** (Fuorcla da Faller) offers a walker's route into Val Bercla and on to Mulegns in the Surses valley.

- 🟢 East of Juf the 2581m **Stallerberg** is the lowest of the neighbouring passes. Gained in little more than an hour, a view now opens of mountains that gather above the Julier road pass, while the continuing trail descends to Bivio below that pass in another 2hrs.

- 🟢 Next comes **Fuorcla de la Valletta**, a 2586m crossing below the peak of Uf da Flüe, whose descent path also leads to Bivio, but by way of the little tarn of Leg Columban (2hrs from Juf) and the Valletta da Beiva.

- 🟢 ★ The **Forcellina** (2672m) is the best-known of Juf's passes, for it combines with other crossings to make a classic route between the Averstal and the Engadine. Located southeast of Juf, the path of approach is the same as that for the Fuorcla de la Valletta, but just 20m below the Valletta this path splits and the Forcellina trail contours south for a while before swinging to the east for the final climb to the pass (1½hrs from Juf). More than 300m below the Forcellina lies the **Septimer Pass**, one of the oldest of alpine trade routes, and one that was known to the Romans. Gained in an hour from the Forcellina, the Septimer is a four-way crossing: north to Bivio using a section of Roman paving; south to Casaccia in Val Bregaglia; and east to Maloja (5½hrs from Juf) in the Engadine by way of Pass Lunghin (see 4:2).

4:2 ENGADINE VALLEY: LEFT BANK

The Upper Engadine is a broad, almost level valley that effectively divides the Albula group from the Bernina Alps. At its head Maloja lies at 1815m, and in the first 14km to St Moritz it loses only 40m of height. For much of that distance four river-linked lakes give the landscape much of its character. Larchwoods cluster along the right-hand Bernina flank, while the road runs along the left side of the valley, connecting Maloja with Sils Baselgia, Silvaplana, Champfer and St Moritz. At Silvaplana another road heads west for the Julier Pass, rather conveniently containing a block of mountains and valleys whose western limit may be taken as the ridge running from Maloja to the Septimer Pass, south of which lies the Bregaglia.

4:2 ENGADINE VALLEY: LEFT BANK

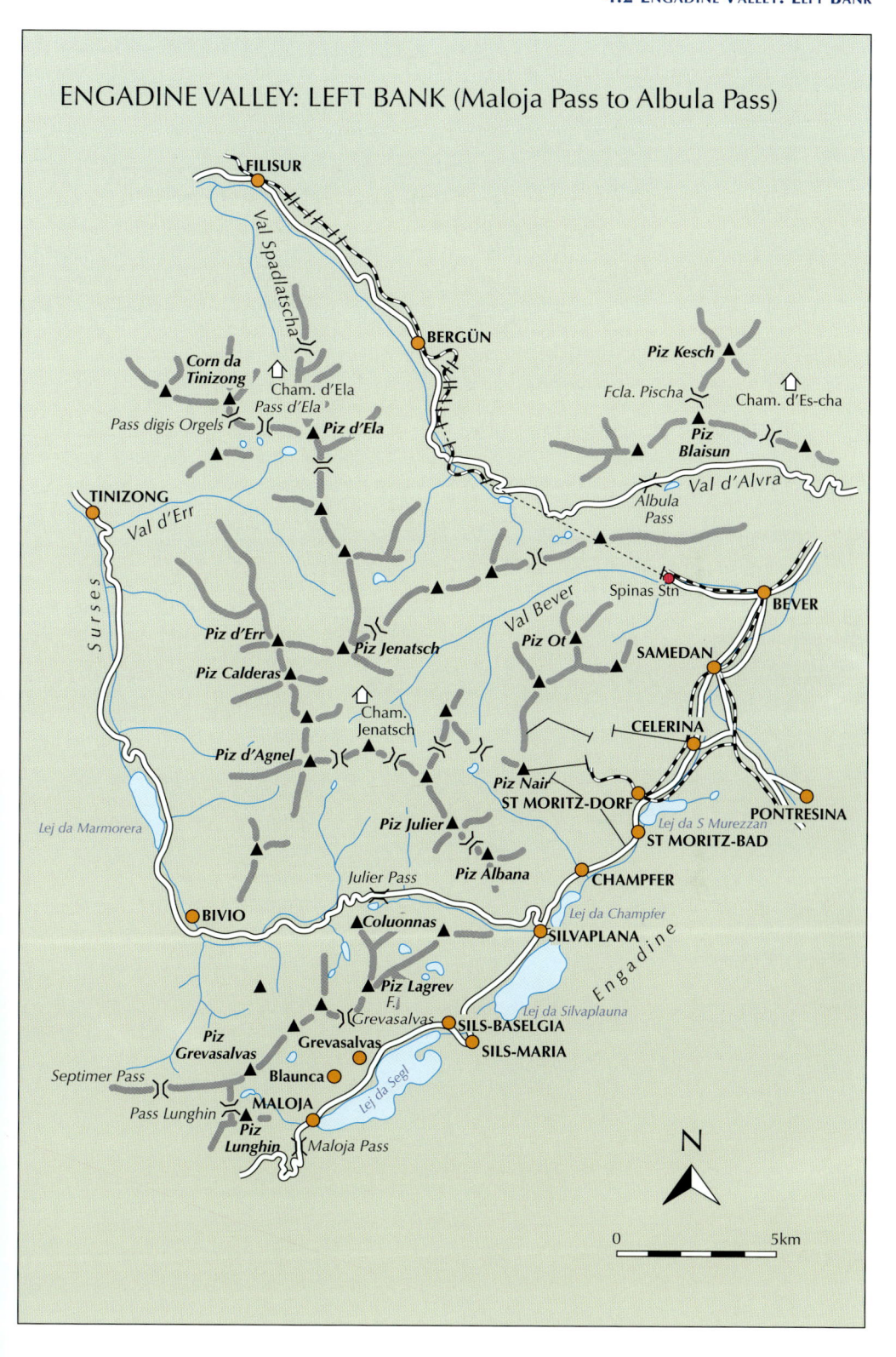

Despite its position at the southwestern limits of the Engadine, **Maloja** belongs politically to Val Bregaglia. It's not a large village, but it does have a few shops, several hotels, numerous holiday apartments, a youth hostel, a fairly low-key campsite at the southern end of the Lej da Segl, and tourist information (www.maloja.ch). With a number of modest ascents, no shortage of walks of varying length, and good prospects for *langlauf* ski tours in winter, it has much going for it, without the razzamatazz, say, of St Moritz or Pontresina. Among its many attractions, Maloja is at the start (or finish) of the ◯ **Via Engiadina**, a mid-level walking route which links the village with St Moritz by combining several trails above the valley's left bank. It's also the starting point of the annual Engadine Ski Marathon which takes place on the second Sunday in March, and covers a distance of 42km to S-chanf in the Lower Engadine with something like 13,000 competitors taking part (www.engadin-skimarathon.ch).

Directly above the village, and providing a grandstand view of both the Bregaglia and Engadine valleys, Piz Lunghin acts as a gatepost, its partner to the southeast being the armchair-shaped Piz de la Margna (4:4), whose bulk and unmistakable outline dominates much of the upper valley. Nestling in a basin of scree and rocks below Lunghin's north flank, Lägh dal Lunghin is recognised as the source of the River Inn. From the road a short distance outside Maloja, a path climbs up to this tarn, then curves southwest to reach ◯ **Pass Lunghin** at 2645m. This is a major alpine watershed, for on its east side the Inn eventually feeds into the Black Sea; on the west slope an insignificant stream (unseen from the pass) becomes the Maira which flows through the Bregaglia and on to the Mediterranean; while northwest of the pass a tributary of the Gelgia feeds into the Rhine, which makes its way to the North Sea.

From Pass Lunghin a marked trail breaks away to the south to wind without complication up to the 2780m summit of ⦿ ☆ **Piz Lunghin**, reached in about 3–3½hrs from Maloja. Easily gained, this summit makes an outstanding vantage point from which to study the district, with a veritable sea of peaks and valleys spread out in all directions.

As was noted in 4:1 above, the trail over Pass Lunghin connects with the ◯ **Septimer Pass** (2310m) whose crosstracks offer several choice hikes. One heads north along a path which leads

Lej da Segl – the Lake of Sils in the Upper Engadine

down to **Bivio** on the west side of the Julier Pass; from there it's possible to return to the Engadine by postbus to complete a good day's outing. Another route descends south of the Septimer Pass, reaching Casaccia in Val Bregaglia, from where you could again catch a postbus over the Maloja Pass to the Engadine.

The left bank of the Engadine between Maloja and Plaun da Lej conceals a pastoral terrace upon which two small groups of alp buildings are inhabited during the summer months. **Blaunca** and **Grevasalvas** are backed by a short but abrupt rocky wall, at the southern end of which the 2932m ✤ **Piz Grevasalvas** looks directly down on Lägh dal Lunghin. A scrambling ascent of this peak can be made from a path which rises above the Grevasalvas chalets, then via the tiny Lej Nair and the North Ridge. But a more challenging route (IV) is found on the SE Ridge, with the prospect of a rewarding traverse being made by descending the SW Ridge to Pass Lunghin.

North of the hamlet with which it shares a name, the **Fuorcla Grevasalvas** is a 2688m col with a walking route that crosses the mountains to the Julier Pass, while the highest peak south of that road pass, the 3164m ✤ **Piz Lagrev** offers a choice of climbs on its southeast and southwest ridges. In common with Piz Grevasalvas, Lagrev is composed of crystalline granite which gives enjoyable climbing, and the slabs of **Piz da las Coluonnas**, its near neighbour directly above the Julier Pass, also claims some interesting routes.

North of the Julier a second block of mountains may be further defined by the Albula Pass road which snakes a way between Filisur and the Engadine at La Punt. Sporadically explored by Victorian climbers in the second half of the 19th century, this splendid district contains a cluster of 3000m summits that give mostly short but entertaining routes on either granite or limestone, while the region is crossed by several connecting trails along which a choice of one- or two-day walking tours can be made. In winter ski tours and ascents are also possible, for the snow record is good, and the local season sometimes extends into May. Bill O'Connor's inspirational guide *Alpine Ski Mountaineering: Volume 2* describes a superb six-day ski tour of the Albula Alps between the Julier Pass and Val Sarsura near Zernez, and to make the most of the district, the SAC has provided hutted accommodation in two locations; one in the dolomitic Ela group, the other further south near the head of Val Bever.

Walks and climbs from the Ela and Jenatsch huts

The most northerly of these huts is **Chamona d'Ela** which stands at 2196m at the head of **Val Spadlatscha**, to the south of Filisur and roughly midway between Savognin and Bergün. With 34 places, it's only partly wardened in the high season of July to September, but it has self-catering facilities and an emergency telephone (www.sac-davos.ch). The other hut, **Chamanna Jenatsch** (2652m), is owned by the Bernina section of the SAC and is larger than its neighbour, with 60 dormitory places (www.chamannajenatsch.ch). Lying below the Jenatsch crest that extends from Piz d'Err near the source of the Beverin stream, it's usually manned at the New Year, then from mid-February until the end of April for ski-mountaineers, and from July until the end of September.

Southwest of the Ela Hut, the 3172m ✤ **Corn da Tinizong** is sometimes referred to as the Matterhorn of the Albula Alps. First climbed by its NE Face in 1866 by D W Freshfield and his party, the steep 470m South Face rises directly from the Pass digis Orgels, while the West Ridge falls towards Piz Migel (the latter also climbed by Freshfield a year after his Tinizong success). The Orgels Pass carries an approach route to the Ela Hut from Savognin and Tinizong, while southeast of that pass, the higher, 2724m **Pass d'Ela** is crossed by a well-made path that skirts the south side of the great dome of Piz d'Ela and, via Fuorcla da Tschitta, continues down to Preda below the Albula road pass.

At 3338m, ✤ **Piz d'Ela** is a sprawling peak which casts out a number of ridges, most of them pointing towards Bergün. The normal route (PD) from Chamona d'Ela tackles the West Ridge from a point near Pass d'Ela and takes 4–5hrs, with individual pitches of II+/III-. The summit panorama is said to be magnificent and far-reaching.

Among the many routes available to activists overnighting at Chamanna Jenatsch, the pyramid-shaped ✤ **Piz d'Agnel** (3205m) counts among the easiest. Rising south of the hut, the mountain's normal route (F) is by the broad NW Ridge, gained at the Fuorcla da Flix, while the longer East Ridge offers more of a challenge with moves of III. This ridge cannot be compared, however, with the 4km crest that stretches in a long line northeast of the hut, and passes over 🔵 **Piz Jenatsch** (3251m) before ending on the 3378m summit of 🔵 **Piz d'Err**. Although individual pitches are graded no higher than III, a full traverse of the ridge counts as a serious expedition.

South of Piz d'Err 🔵 **Piz Calderas** is the highest of the group at 3397m, and reckoned by many to be the finest, with an incomparable view from the summit. A traverse of the peak which also takes in Piz d'Err via the North Ridge is graded PD+ with moves of III-, but it is claimed that the sharp East Ridge has the best climbing of all (see the Alpine Club guidebook *Bernina and Bregaglia* for details).

St Moritz to the Albula Pass

Overlooking not only the Julier Pass, but rising above the Engadine resorts of St Moritz, Champfer and Silvaplana, ⚫ **Piz Julier** is a distinctive peak, and at 3380m, is one of the highest of the Albula Alps. The normal ascent route by the East Ridge (I/II) is a straightforward scramble with fixed ropes and chains; another goes by the South Ridge (II/III) – both starting from the Fuorcla Albana, a 2870m cleft in the ridge linking Julier with Piz Albana and reached as easily from Alp Julier below the road pass, as from Alp Suvretta and the Signal cableway above St Moritz. In common with several other semi-isolated peaks in the district, the summit panorama is extensive, and includes the Bernese and Pennine Alps, the Tödi group, nearby Bernina summits, and the distant Ortler and Ötztal mountains.

Self-aware and aloof just above its lake, **St Moritz** is the unquestioned tourist capital of the Upper Engadine, its reputation for opulence and glamour concentrated mostly on the winter season when the rich and famous, and those who wish to be seen among the rich and famous, glide furbound through the streets, indulge a fascination for the renowned Cresta Run, or practice their ski turns on the crowded slopes of Corviglia and Piz Nair, or on Corvatsch above Surlej on the Bernina flank of the valley. Despite its setting in a landscape of lakes, forests and mountains, and in spite of having all facilities, a wealth of hotels, a youth hostel in St Moritz Bad and tourist information in Dorf (www.stmoritz.ch), there is little here to detain the serious mountaineer or walker, although there's no shortage of marked trails and accessible summits for those who do choose it as a base. And of course, it is one of the great alpine ski resorts which enjoys a long winter season, thanks to the altitude of its more challenging runs.

St Moritz is a railway terminus; the end of the line for the spectacular Glacier Express which crawls (it is surely one of the world's slowest express trains) between Zermatt and the Engadine valley by way of the Oberalp Pass. (For information look to www.glacierexpress.ch) Other trains head away from St Moritz bound for Pontresina, the Bernina Pass and Val Poschiavo, which lies more than 800m below the level of the Engadine and gives every impression of belonging to a different country. Another line extends downstream from St Moritz to Scuol in the Lower Engadine, while its main railway link is with Chur, the cantonal capital.

The Inn's outflow from the Lej da San Murezzan drops through a mini-gorge behind St Moritz railway station, the first serious change in the valley's level since Maloja, for it descends 40m or so in a wooded step before spilling out around the edge of Celerina. Between Celerina and Samedan the Inn is swollen by the Flaz which drains Val Bernina, seen here stretching off to the southeast. At this point the Engadine is at its widest, but it soon contracts again between Samedan and **Bever**.

Val Bever stretches behind the village. For the first 3.5km as far as Spinas station, there's a minor road which briefly accompanies the Chur-bound railway line, but then the valley takes an anti-clockwise curve into more lonely country below the granite pyramid of ⚫ **Piz Ot** (3246m). The normal route of ascent here tackles this graceful peak from the east on a blue-white marked path known as the Piz Ot-weg, accessible either from Samedan, Marguns (cableway from Celerina), or by a trail striking south of Alp Spinas through the Valletta da Bever.

Four kilometres downstream beyond Bever, another narrow road breaks out of the Engadine at La Punt bound for the Albula Pass. Twisting above the village it then enters **Val d'Alvra**. Hidden from view by the valley's north walling ridge, the highest – and some would claim, the finest – peak of the Albula Alps may be approached by a path which leaves this road near Alp Nova, crosses the saddle of Fuorcla Gualdauna (gaining a splendid view of the Bernina Alps to the south), and contours below **Piz Kesch** to reach the Es-cha Hut in less than 2hrs. An alternative, albeit longer (2½–3hrs), approach to this hut comes from **Madulain**, a small, attractive Engadine village with a lovely onion-spired church,

Chamanna d'Es-cha with Piz Kesch above a huge moraine bank

two hotels, a campsite, and tourist information (www.madulain.ch).

Property of the Bernina section of the SAC, the traditional stone-built **Chamanna d'Es-cha** stands on an old moraine below the southeast flank of Piz Kesch at 2594m. With 60 dormitory places, it's staffed at Easter, and from late June until mid-October, making a good base for tackling several routes on Piz Kesch, and on a few neighbouring peaks (www.sac-bernina.ch).

Two cols enable activists to cross from one side of Piz Kesch to the other. The 3008m **Porta d'Es-cha** is situated at the foot of the Keschnadel's NE Ridge with which it is joined to Piz Val Müra. A marked path leads to this col, via scree slopes and with fixed cable or chains on the final section, while descent on the north side is made down the Porchabella glacier directly to the Kesch Hut. The other col lies well to the south of Piz Kesch, and just below Piz Blaisun. This **Fuorcla Pischa** (2871m) gives a straightforward crossing (1½hrs from the Es-cha Hut) and takes walkers down through the little Val Plazbi to Chants at a junction of valleys northeast of Bergün in another 2hrs. From Fuorcla Pischa, the ascent of **Piz Blaisun** (3200m) takes only 1hr, but is highly recommended. Standing alone to the south of Piz Kesch it commands a tremendous view of its neighbour's southern ramparts, as well as Piz Bernina in the opposite direction.

PIZ KESCH (3418M)

Seen from the southeast, the grey crags of Piz Kesch that appear to support a sharp pointed summit (it is in fact a secondary summit) are seamed with cracks and gullies in which the last vestige of winter's snow lingers into mid-summer. The two glaciers (Pischa and Es-cha) that helped shape this fine mountain have all but disappeared, leaving in their wake monstrous walls of moraine and scree. The north side is rather different, for the Vadret da Porchabella still presents a wide sheet of ice above the Kesch Hut (see below). From that glacier the rock face is shorter than its southern counterpart (about 150m) and the mountain's outline is less severe and therefore less challenging in appearance, with the summit presenting a domed aspect. First climbed in September 1846 by a four-man team led by the 24-year old Johann Coaz (see box in 4:4), Piz Kesch has attained the status of a minor classic among what may be termed the second division of alpine mountains, and it also makes a fine winter ascent, partly on ski. The PD- grade normal route is via the East Face, while the Keschnadel, the prominent aiguille standing southwest of the Porta d'Es-cha, rewards with some of the finest climbs of the whole Albula group.

Piz Kesch and the Porchabella glacier

Albula Alps: North to the Flüela Pass

A short distance downvalley beyond Madulain, **Zuoz** was once the home of the important Planta family, and for several centuries was considered the main village of the Upper Engadine. Today it retains a number of traditional 16th-century houses, mostly grouped in or around the Dorfplatz, and with its various hotels and holiday apartments, makes a low-key base from which to explore the nearby national park, whose boundary lies on the east side of the valley. For tourist information go to www.zuoz.ch.

The next tributary valley draining out of the Albula Alps is the charming ◐ **Val Susauna** whose stream, the Vallember, spills into the River Inn a little south of Cinuos-chel. A campsite is located just below the valley entrance, and refreshments are available at the small farming hamlet of **Susauna** which lies about an hour's walk from the Cinuos-chel/Brail railway station. The only other habitation within Val Susauna consists of farm buildings or simple cabins used by chamois hunters. The valley is partly wooded and rich in wildlife, with red and roe deer, chamois and, in the pastureland of Alp Funtauna (2–2½hrs from Susauna), which opens above a section of rocky narrows, there are colonies of marmots. For walkers with a love of solitude, the whole valley, with its upper tributaries, is immensely rewarding.

The sunny, open pastures of **Alp Funtauna** (2192m) gather several streams, for this is a crossroads, a confluence not only of mountain torrents,

4:2 ENGADINE VALLEY: LEFT BANK

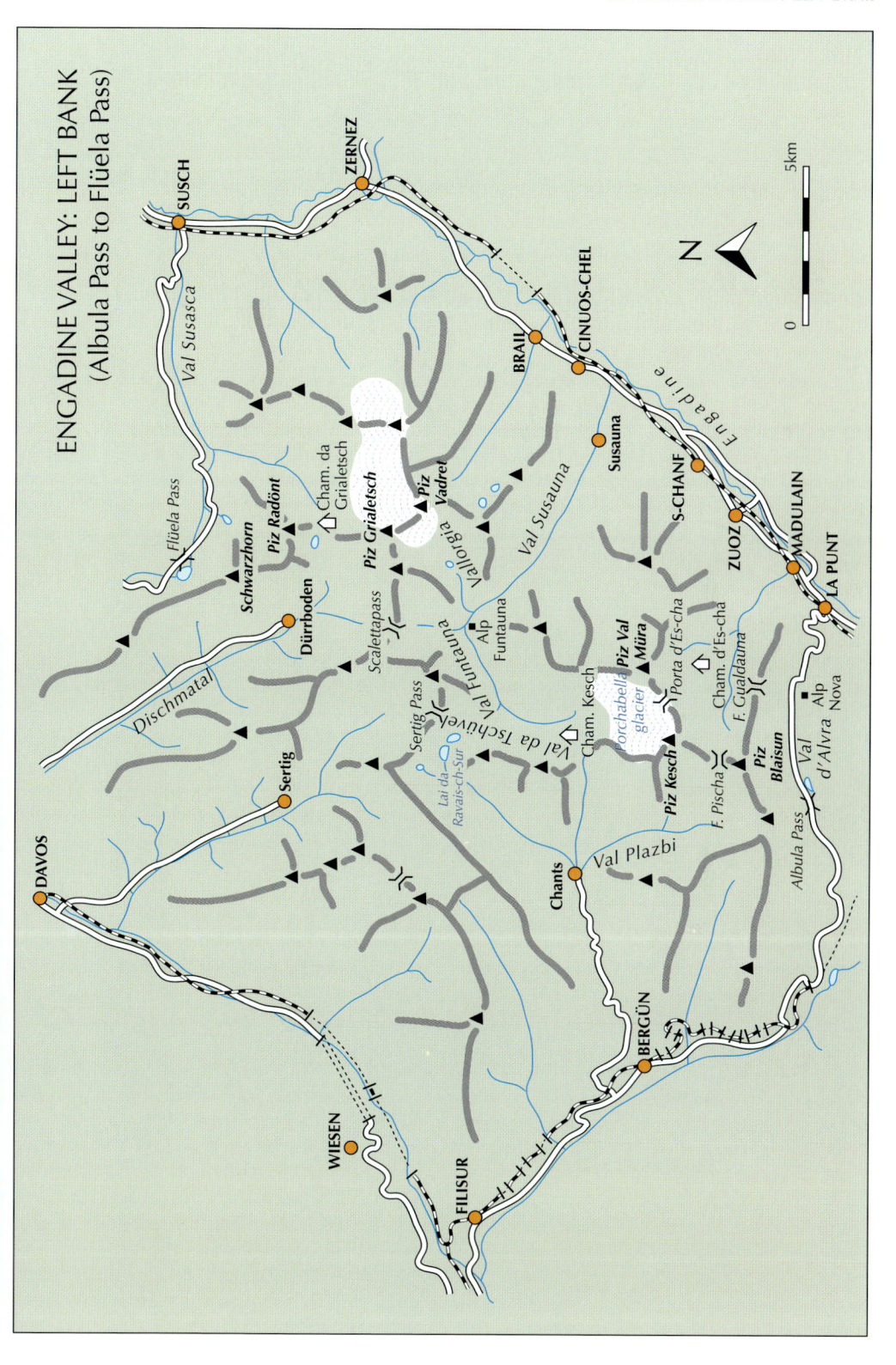

but of valleys: Val Funtauna to the southwest; and the Vallorgia to the east, hanging below Piz Vadret and Piz Grialetsch. Directly ahead to the north, another stream rushes down from the 2606m **Scalettapass** which invites walkers to make a cross-country hike over the mountains and down through the Dischmatal to **Davos**, while stretching off to the southwest a trail through Val Funtauna leads to a pair of lakes (the **Lai da Ravais-ch-Sur**) near the Sertig Pass, but another trail curves south out of Val Funtauna, and rising through Val dal Tschüvel, arrives at the remote but eye-catching Kesch Hut in 1½–2hrs from Alp Funtauna.

Chamanna digl Kesch (2632m) serves climbers tackling Piz Kesch from the north. It's a modern timber-and-glass-walled hut with obvious environmental credentials and, thanks to its design by Toni Spirig of Celerina, was awarded the Swiss Solar Energy Prize in 2001. Owned by the Davos section of the SAC, it has 92 places and is fully staffed over the Christmas/New Year period, in March and April, and from late June until mid-October (www.kesch.ch). Other approach routes come from Davos (4½hrs) via either the Scaletta or **Sertig** passes, or from Bergün (in 4½hrs) via **Chants**. The hut has a commanding position on the Fuorcla da Funtauna, from which it not only looks across the Porchabella glacier to the North Face of Piz Kesch, but also has a direct view to the west down through Val Tuors, below which lies Bergün, midway between Filisur and the Albula Pass.

Apart from Piz Kesch, the other climbing interest in this final block of the Albula Alps, is found above Alp Funtauna, or rather, between Alp Funtauna and the Flüela Pass where **Chamanna da Grialetsch** makes an obvious overnight base. Another SAC hut, this one has 60 places, is owned by the St Gallen section, and stands at 2542m at the head of Val Grialetsch southeast of the Flüela, with Piz Radönt to the north and Piz Grialetsch to the south. Fully staffed in March and April, and from July until mid-October (www.grialetsch.ch), the shortest route of approach is from Chant Sura on the Flüela road in 2hrs, but note that the pass is usually closed from December until the end of April. Other hut approaches are from Davos via **Dürrboden** and the Fuorcla da Griavaletsch, or from Alp Funtauna by way of the **Scalettapass**.

Climbs of interest can be found on the 3181m ● **Piz Grialetsch** (also sometimes tackled in winter from Alp Funtauna via the Vallorgia and the West Ridge); ● **Piz Vadret** (3229m) by the spiky NW Ridge (III+); and the 3065m ● **Piz Radönt** on which a west to east traverse is said to make a worthwhile outing first achieved in 1892. And finally, it's worth mentioning the 3146m ● **Schwarzhorn**, which overlooks the Flüela Pass from the south, and is pretty much an outlier of the Albula Alps. Thanks to its attractive pyramid shape, its convenient location and a path which leads right to the summit, this is climbed more often than any other in the district.

4:3 VAL BREGAGLIA

The distance between the Maloja Pass at the Engadine watershed and the Italian border at Castasegna is only 23km, but there's a difference in altitude of more than 1100m leading to an abrupt change in vegetation. But the difference between the Upper Engadine and Val Bregaglia is far more striking than simply an exchange of larchwood for chestnut, walnut and beech trees, for the Bregaglia (Bergell in German) induces another climate, another culture; it seems to belong almost to another age. A hint of its uniqueness was gained from the Pass da la Prasignola (4:1), and any mountain wanderer who took the hint and descended into the valley would have been won over by its appeal before arriving in Soglio – that utterly magical village described by painter Giovanni Segantini as being at 'the threshold of paradise'. Soglio, with its cluster of old houses and almost overlapping stone-laid roofs, is perched upon a natural terrace above the valley, facing south to the ragged granite fenceposts of the Sciora group whose appearance is sufficient to make a climber's fingers itch with longing.

The Scioras are not all, of course. In fact they are almost minor players, a chorus-line in a cast headed by Piz Badile, with Cengalo a worthy co-star. This is a vertical landscape, a climber's paradise with a well-founded reputation, although it is the Italian flank that often wins the plaudits these days; especially the slabs and cragging opportunities of Valle di Mello. That is not to dismiss the Swiss side. Indeed, despite regular ascents of the original Cassin Route, and numerous alternative lines having been created, the great NE Face of Piz Badile would capture attention in almost any mountain arena, and the valley it overlooks (Val Bondasca)

4:3 VAL BREGAGLIA

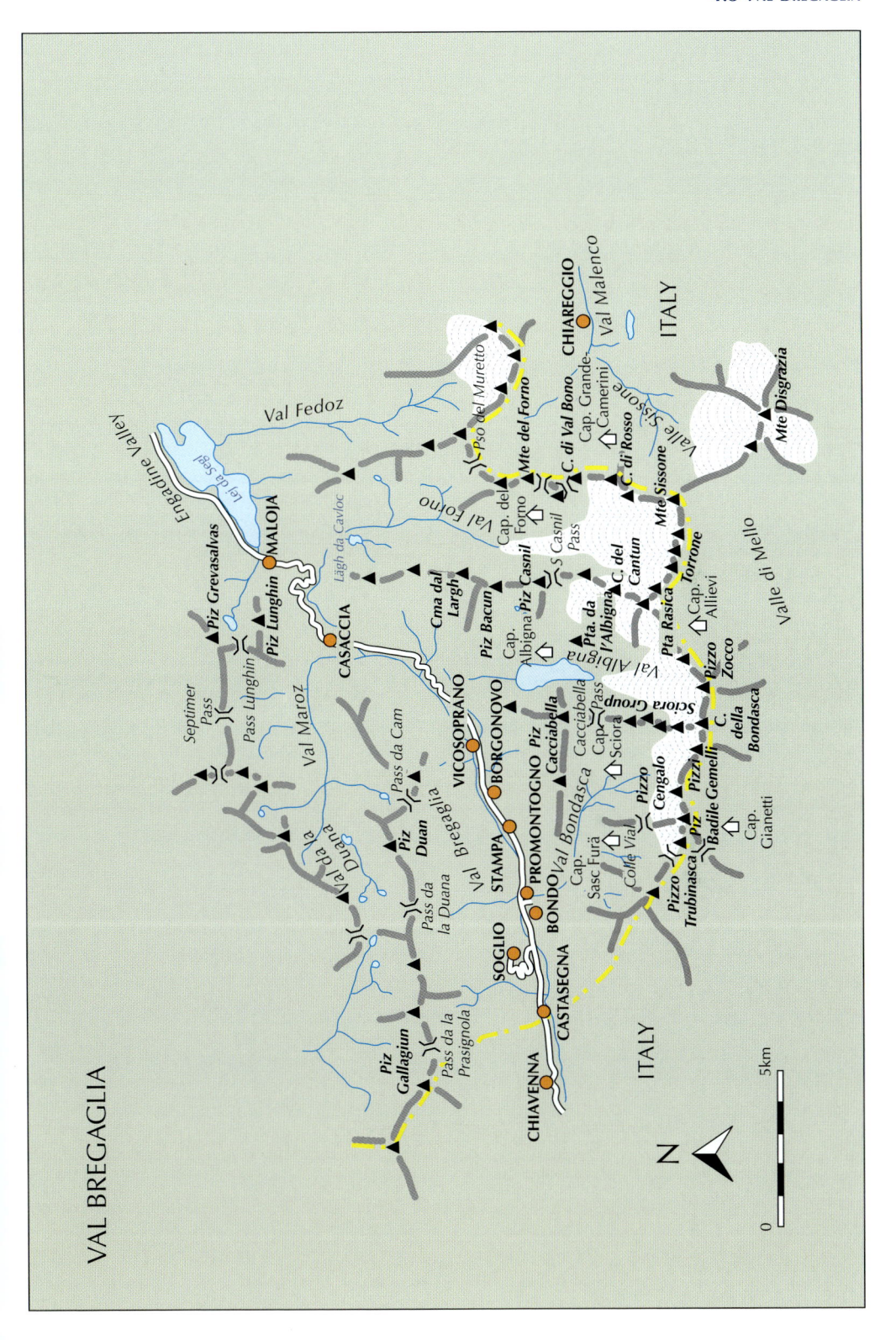

is one of the most wildly romantic of any in the Alps. In *Starlight and Storm*, Rébuffet summed it up in just 16 words: 'The Piz Badile is situated in the most enchanting cirque of mountains that one could imagine.' And none could argue with that.

Val Bregaglia *is* special. 'He must be very dull of soul indeed,' said Walker, 'who could not see without a catch of his breath the sudden upward surge of the Bondasca peaks of Badile and Cengalo, as he turns into that glen, or the cascading sheer descent of turret on turret of rock, falling from the perfect peak of Bacone, as seen from the Albigna glen' (*Walking in the Alps*).

Bondasca, Albigna and Val Forno all flow from the ragged peaks that carry Bregaglia's southern border, but before giving them due attention, both the north slope and the valley itself deserve more than a fleeting glance.

Bregaglia North

Descending from the Maloja Pass the road unravels before reaching **Casaccia**, a tiny village at 1458m behind which lies Val Maroz and the old trade route to the Septimer Pass. Despite its modest size overnight accommodation can be found at Hotel Stampa, which has dormitory places as well as standard bedrooms. Several long walks begin here. One follows the historic route over the **Septimer Pass** to Bivio on the Julier Pass road in 4½–5hrs. A more demanding 8hr route heads west through ◐ **Val Maroz**, continues into the higher Val da la Duana, then crosses Pass da la Duana to descend to Soglio. A third route (6½hrs) also climbs through Val Maroz, but then heads south just beyond the alp buildings of Maroz Dent to find a way into the little ◐ ☆ **Val da Cam**, out of which the trail goes through a minor pass to follow a rough belvedere course many hundreds of metres above the valley, going from one alp to another before joining the path from Pass da la Duana and descending steeply to Soglio. From Pass da Cam to Soglio views are (forgive the overworked cliché) simply breathtaking.

Then there's a fourth route to consider, the so-called ◐ ☆ **Sentiero Panoramico**, a 14km long (5hr) valley classic which begins in Casaccia and ends (yet again) in Soglio. Although its German name, Panoramahöhenweg, suggests a high trail, in truth it's a mid-level walk that weaves its way through mixed woods with several sudden vantage points that exploit views across the valley to the soaring peaks of Bondasca.

The postbus carries on down into **Val Bregaglia** below Casaccia, from where it ought to be possible to gaze up into the Albigna glen, were it not for a huge dam wall that blocks its entrance between Piz Casnil and Piz Cacciabella. Despite the dam's looming presence, the journey downvalley holds plenty of interest with spacious woodlands interspersed with open meadows in which stone barns and lichened boulders cast small islands of shade. A scattering of chalets can be seen from the road, but there's no further village until you come to **Vicosoprano**. Rightly considered Bregaglia's most important community, the village is bypassed by the main road, although the postbus manages to squeeze through the narrow streets between a number of old houses. Situated midway between Maloja and Castasegna at 1067m, it is arguably the best and most convenient valley base for both climbers and walkers. It has a few shops, a bank and a post office, three hotels (the Corona, Piz Cam and the Crotto Albigna), several apartments and a campsite a short distance northeast of the village. There's also an indoor climbing wall for use on those occasions when outdoor activity is rained off. Paths climb steeply out of the village, work their way up to and across the Panoramico trail, and continue to the Duana and Cam passes. These are old trails created by farmers and chamois hunters, and although strenuous, are also rewarding to follow.

Stampa straddles the old road below Piz Duan at 994m. A huddle of buildings, the village was the birthplace of painter Augusto Giacometti and his sculptor son Alberto, whose former home, the Ciäsa Granda, now houses the Bregaglia museum. Despite being much smaller than Vicosoprano, Stampa hosts the valley's tourist office (www. bergell.ch), and like its larger neighbour, contains three hotels: the Stampa (which also has dormitory accommodation), Val d'Arca, and the Walther, but apart from a post office it has few other facilities.

Another 3km brings the postbus to **Promontogno** (821m) and **Bondo** (823m), the two divided by the torrent which bursts out of **Val Bondasca**. These are lovely old Italianate villages clamped in the Bregaglia's narrows where the road to Soglio begins its climb, the rumble of rivers fed by snowmelt being all that disturbs nightfall. It is said that for three months each winter Bondo never sees the sun, but in summer its shade can be a godsend. A *boccia* court near the river is littered with

Soglio, one of the gems of Val Bregaglia

chestnut leaves; tiny curved balconies hang over the streets, and mountains are so close as to have their intricacies concealed. There's a small supermarket, a post office, two hotels (the Bregaglia and Hotel-Pension Sciora) and a campsite patronised by climbers.

The final village on the Swiss side of the border at 697m is **Castasegna**. With two small hotels, banks and a post office, it has less obvious charm than other Bregaglia villages, and mountain activists based in the valley often drive through it and continue across the border to restock with supplies from the supermarkets in Chiavenna, where there are also shops selling climbing equipment.

Castasegna lies directly below the Pass da la Prasignola, with which it is linked by a relentlessly steep path that strays first to **Soglio**. And before we turn to the south side of the valley, we too should stray to this wonderful village, for no visit to the Bregaglia would be complete without climbing the hillside (on foot or by the special short-wheelbase postbus that comes from Promontogno) to explore Soglio's cobbled alleys and absorb its special atmosphere.

Perched like an eyrie above chestnut woods at 1097m, Soglio is outstanding. One of the most picturesque of Swiss villages, its narrow alleys are crowded with close-set stone buildings dwarfed by the church with its Italian-style campanile, and overshadowed for elegance by the Palazzo Salis, built for the von Salis family in 1630, but now given new life as a hotel with a magnificent vaulted hall, four-poster beds, antique stoves and suits of armour. The village has four other hotels or pensions, a number of holiday apartments, restaurants, two grocery stores and a post office. And memorable views at almost every turn.

Views from the village, and from meadows on either side, are worthy of their reputation. But difficult though it may be to believe, they're even better from Alp Tombal, an hour's stiff climb above Soglio, or from Plän Vest which lies 270m and another hour above Tombal. From there the world falls at your feet. Val Bregaglia is a bottomless defile, and lazing in the grass it's impossible to direct your eyes away from a scene dominated by the bristling granite spires and smooth, steeply angled walls of Val Bondasca opposite. Rébuffet was right: it *is*

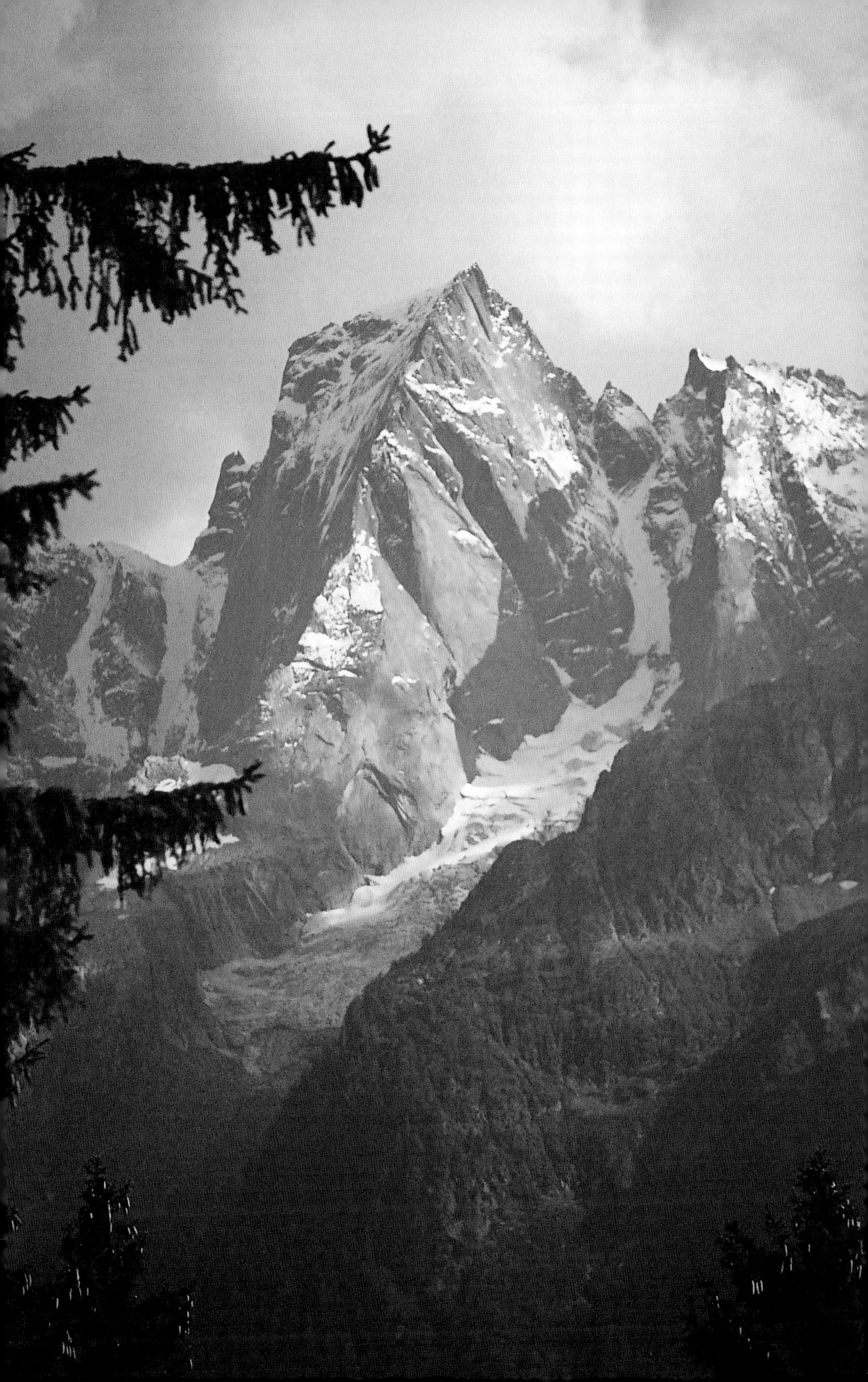

the most enchanting cirque of mountains that one could imagine.

Val Bondasca

Rising steeply from a riot of sub-tropical vegetation, where ferns grow as high as a man's shoulder, to a headwall of granite teeth, soaring slab walls and a necklace of screes and glacial moraine, Bondasca's reputation is assured. The 'flamelike' Scioras, Pizzi Gemelli, Cengalo and Badile are compelling features in Christian Klucker's famous 'land of granite' where several chapters of alpine history were written: the unhappy but productive partnership in the 1890s of Klucker and the Russian Anton von Rydzewski; the inspired leadership of Riccardo Cassin on the first tragic ascent of Piz Badile's NE Face over three days in 1937; Rébuffet's account (in *Starlight and Storm*) of the second ascent of the face 11 years later; and Hermann Buhl's astonishing 4½hr solo climb of the same route in 1951 – all these have given the valley a romantic appeal, and made it a magnet, not only for climbers of ambition, but for all who love wild and uncompromising landscapes. Land of granite indeed. In August 2017 a massive rock fall from Piz Cengalo forced the valley's closure for several seasons.

Behind Bondo and Promontogno the valley's entrance is guarded by a gorge, into which a dirt road forces a way (a local taxi can be taken as far as Laret, to save an hour's walking). When this road ends a path continues, then divides 10mins later. The left branch pushes on upvalley to reach the **Sciora Hut**, but the right fork crosses the Bondasca torrent by footbridge, then climbs steeply through mixed woods to reach the **Capanna Sasc Furä**, about 2hrs or so from the roadhead. This climber's hut, built on a rock rib directly below Badile's North Ridge at 1904m, is the property of the Promontogno-based Bregaglia section of the SAC. It's a comparatively small hut with a traditional appearance and cosy atmosphere, with 43 places and a warden on site from July to the middle of September. Out of season the winter room can sleep just five (www.sascfura.ch). Thanks to its position, it's used as a base for routes on Piz Badile and **Pizzo Trubinasca**, Badile's close neighbour to the west, whose austere North Face looms above the Vallun da Trubinasca, and also for the crossing of the Passo della Trubinasca into

---

PIZ BADILE: ICON OF THE BREGAGLIA

By no means the highest of Bregaglia's peaks Piz Badile, though only 3308m, has an unmistakable presence that impresses in a way that many higher mountains do not, and few could approach either its 800m NE Face, or its graceful North Ridge and remain unmoved. However, the first ascent of the mountain was made, not from Val Bondasca, but via its south flank which overlooks the old Italian spa of Bagni del Màsino. Now graded PD, the route taken in 1876 by the alpine historian W A B Coolidge, with the Dévouassoud brothers as his guides, follows a rather complex line above the Gianetti Hut. But of course, it is the north flank that demands most attention and the greatest respect. Here the elegant 🚶 ⭐ **North Ridge** (D-/IV+) gives superb climbing on slabby, compact granite, and was first attempted (solo and in socks) as a reconnaissance by Klucker in 1892, but was climbed successfully in 1923 by Alfred Zürcher with the guide Walter Risch. The ridge gives about 1000m of climbing, and rightfully belongs to the repertoire of alpine classics – as does the masterpiece of the 🚶 ⭐ **NE Face**. Listed by Rébuffet as one of the six great north faces of the Alps, Cassin's route (TD/V/AO) joined a succession of 'last great problems' that in due time inevitably came to be hailed a true classic reserved for the top players. Nowadays, with its reputation somewhat diminished by familiarity, it is one that countless alpinists aspire to, for the main difficulties are not high by modern standards and it's not at all unusual to find several parties at work on the face at any one time in the summer, and there are now in excess of a dozen other lines spread right across it. That being said, Piz Badile should never be underestimated, for it attracts sudden and fearsome storms, and rain or snowfall can transform the face within minutes – as experienced by the Cassin party in 1937.

On 14 July of that year, Riccardo Cassin and his two companions, Esposito and Ratti, started up the face as two other young Como climbers, Molteni and Valsecchi, tried an alternative route further to the right. Molteni had already made two attempts on the face, and was eager to succeed this time, but for

---

◀ *Piz Badile with its NE Face (left) and North Ridge facing*

days he and Valsecchi had been sleeping rough to avoid paying hut fees, and living on meagre rations to such an extent that their stamina suffered, so after sharing a bivouac with Cassin and his partners at the end of the first day, the two ropes joined forces. After a second day on the face, the five climbers bivouacked on a ledge at the foot of a light-coloured slab, and whilst they were there a storm broke over the mountain with rainwater streaming down the rocks. As they resumed the climb on the third day, conditions were appalling; the slabs were wet, greasy and difficult. Rain turned to hail, then to snow. Visibility deteriorated; the rocks were smeared with verglas, every tiny ledge was covered with snow, yet with tremendous skill and determination, at 4pm on the 16 July Cassin brought the unwieldy rope onto the summit in a blizzard.

But the epic was far from over, for as they began to descend the Italian side, the weather grew even wilder. In a weakened state the five men were battered by the fearful conditions, and Molteni sank to the ground with exhaustion. Cassin later wrote, 'I tried to support him when he no longer had the strength to continue, but in vain. Without so much as a moan he sank to the ground, never to rise again.' Now four, the storm-battered climbers struggled on, searching for the Gianetti Hut. Then Valsecchi, who had not been aware of his friend's death, suddenly realised that Molteni was no longer with them. When he learned the truth, he burst into tears, sank down, and also died. Failing to find the hut, Cassin, Esposito and Ratti, soaked through and frozen, were forced to endure a third bivouac. Fortunately for them, after so many hours of fury, the storm blew itself out overnight, and in the morning the survivors managed to reach the hut and tell their grim story.

Italy's Val Codera or, as is more often the case, by climbers returning to Val Bondasca from the Gianetti Hut, having summited Piz Badile and descended by its south flank.

East of Piz Badile, the massive Pizzo Cengalo rises directly above the **Capanna di Sciora**, another SAC hut with 42 dormitory places, and a guardian in residence from July until the end of September (www.sachoherrohn.ch). Set among moraine debris left by the shrinking Bondasca glacier, the hut is reached by a straightforward, albeit fairly steep, approach path in 2½hrs from the Laret roadhead, or in 3½hrs by an entertaining and, in places, slightly exposed route from the Sasc Furä Hut which crosses the ⬛ **Colle Vial** on the lower slopes of Badile's North Ridge. Thanks to its situation, the Sciora Hut is perfectly placed for tackling numerous climbs, not only on Cengalo, but on the slabs, pinnacles, ridges and arêtes of the Sciora group, and the celebrated 'Flat Iron' ridge of Pizzi Gemelli.

Take ⬛ **Pizzo Cengalo** for a start. At 3370m, it's the second highest of the Bregaglia peaks, and seen from certain angles, it dwarfs its more famous neighbour, although the huge North Face (the biggest in the Bregaglia Alps) cannot compare for architectural elegance with Badile's. Chamonix guide François Dévouassoud, who led Coolidge on the first ascent of Piz Badile, was also with Freshfield and Comyns Tucker in making the first ascent of Cengalo in 1866. Their route was via the West Ridge, which is usually approached from the Italian side, and it took another 31 years before the complex North Face was climbed. At the time, these mountains had a considerable covering of snow, and the first North Face ascensionists were forced to tunnel through a great cornice below the summit. The following day their entire route was swept by avalanche following the collapse of the summit ridge. This original 1300m route, put up in 1897 by Prince Scipio Borghese, with the Pontresina guides Martin Schocher and Christian Schnitzler, has retained a reputation as a serious undertaking, with a grade of TD (V/A3), but stonefall can be a serious problem.

The NW Pillar (sometimes referred to as the North Buttress) has little, if any, danger from stonefall. Another TD route, it leads onto the West Ridge some way below the summit, and gives about 900m of climbing. It was won by Fred Glaiser and Bertel Lehmann on 15 July 1937, the day after Riccardo Cassin had begun his epic route on Badile's NE Face. It was another 13 years before a second ascent was made, this time by Walter Bonatti and B Sala.

In the 1890s Christian Klucker found himself in the employ of Anton von Rydzewski, a Russian baron who lived in Dresden and who had taken up mountaineering late in life, yet had ambitions

The granite Sciora peaks at the head of Val Bondasca

beyond his natural capabilities. It was an unhappy partnership, as Klucker's autobiography testifies, but it resulted in a good many explorations, new pass crossings and first ascents, all in the Bregaglia Alps and mostly with a second guide, Mansueto Barbaria from Cortina. (Although not all were with Rydzewski, Klucker had a tally of 21 first ascents in this district alone.) **Pizzi Gemelli**, the twin-summited peak to the east of Cengalo, was one of those that fell to the Rydzewski/Klucker/Barbaria rope in June 1892. Noted for the distinctive 'Flat Iron' (Bügeleisen) on the NW Ridge, when climbed in 1935 this gave the first grade VI in the Central Alps. It is now considered TD-/V/AO (7–8hrs from the Sciora Hut) and, as was found by Alpine Club activists who enjoyed a 2005 summer meet in Val Bregaglia, it gives superb climbing 'on peerless granite in a magnificent mountain environment'.

As for the **Sciora group**, there are four main summits which form the eastern headwall of Val Bondasca, and therefore do not carry the Italian border. Naming from the south, the first of these is **Sciora Dadent**, the highest at 3275m (Klucker with Theodor Curtius and Richard Wiesner by the SW Flank in 1888: PD+), but by contrast to the rest of the group, it is of little interest to the rock climber.

Then comes **Ago di Sciora** (3205m), first climbed via the South Face in 1893 by Rydzewski, Klucker and Emile Rey (AD/IV-), and whose NW Ridge Direct, dating from 1969 is said to give excellent free climbing on sound granite (TD/V+). **Punta Pioda di Sciora** (3238m) is another Rydzewski/Klucker/ Barbaria success from 1891. Their route was by the South Face/East Ridge, while the great slabs of the NW Ridge that were first climbed in 1935 offer a local mountaineering classic graded D+/TD-. But it is the tremendous near-vertical 550m NW Face that was the focus of attention in August 1980, when Czechoslovak climbers Belica and Obuch put up a sustained and exposed ED2 route over two days.

North of Punta Pioda the fourth summit is the 3169m **Sciora Dafora** (also known as Sciora di Fuori), which once claimed the best ridge climb of the group on the Fuorikante, or NW Ridge. A good technical climb (TD/V+/A1/2) with lots of exposure, it has since been surpassed for interest by the 450m West Face Direct (TD+/V+/A2), put up by a three-man team over five days in 1970.

Backing the Sciora Hut, Val Bondasca's eastern headwall is most easily crossed at the southern **Cacciabella Pass** (2897m), the higher but more convenient of two passes on the ridge between Sciora Dafora and the south summit of Piz Cacciabella. An old chamois hunter's pass, it's waymarked on both sides, and takes trekkers and climbers from Capanna di Sciora to the Albigna Hut in 4½hrs.

Val Albigna
Descending through Val Bregaglia below Casaccia, the view south is dominated for a while by the looming presence of a dam which blocks the end of the Albigna reservoir high above the valley meadows. Before this dam was created the Cascata dell' Albigna, considered to be one of the finest waterfalls in the Alps, could be admired spraying through the ravine whose head has now been closed by that huge concrete wall. When it was proposed, Klucker ranted: 'To hear no more of the sound of the magnificent Albigna waterfall, because industry has devoured it? Come, liberator Death!' At Pranzaira, about 5km from Casaccia, there's a bus stop, car park and the valley station of a cableway that swings visitors some 900m up to the base of the dam in just 15 minutes. By making that effortless approach to Val Albigna and its hut, the visiting climber misses out on a truly delightful walk along a path which leads through what was once described as 'a glen of almost legendary wildness and beauty [that] ought to be trodden by the feet of all mountain pilgrims' (J Hubert Walker). If he has neither the energy nor the inclination to walk up to the Albigna glen (in 3–3½hrs), then the visitor ought at least to give himself the pleasure of descending by that path to Vicosoprano.

Val Albigna drains north from a 3000m headwall that makes a gentle arc between the Cima della Bondasca and Cima di Castello, from which the Albigna glacier spills its ice towards the reservoir. The valley is short, rugged, and flanked by comparatively little-known but inviting peaks, and it contrasts in many ways with its more romantic western neighbour.

Val Bondasca, for example, flows roughly east to west; Val Albigna drains northward. Bondasca is heavily vegetated in its lower regions; Albigna is a stony hanging valley that has no comparable lower regions and only sparse vegetation. To access either of the Bondasca huts requires a stiff walk, while the Albigna Hut is gained by a short, 40min stroll from a cable car. Bondasca has Badile, Cengalo and the Scioras to seduce the climber and lover of wild scenery; Albigna is less showy, but no less rewarding.

Capanna da l'Albigna

Conveniently set below the little Piz dal Pal on the east bank of the reservoir, and about 170m above the water, the 94 bed **Capanna da l'Albigna** is often very busy in summer, thanks to its ease of access and number of climbing opportunities near at hand. Owned by the Hoher Rohn section of the SAC it is fully staffed from mid-June until the end of September (www.sachoherrohn.ch), but it has 18 places in the permanently open winter room.

Some of the best and most accessible climbing opportunities will be found close to the dam, where **Spazzacaldeira** has some alarmingly exposed routes and sensational views from some of them onto miniscule Bregaglia rooftops. Forming the western gatepost at the entrance to Val Albigna, this 2487m peak, though of modest height, has become one of the most popular climbing venues in the district. A 10–15min walk from the cable car terminus leads to the foot of the NE Ridge where a 300m ascent (IV/IV+) is among the most frequented, while the *voie normale* tackles the south flank by a fairly well-defined path and a bit of scrambling (II-). The 300m SE Face has a rich variety of routes, mostly five to eight pitches long and graded V or VI, from which it's usually possible to rope down once completed. But the slender and highly photogenic rock spire of **La Fiamma**, which juts out north of the summit, gains the most publicity and is high on the list of visiting climbers who would dare to balance on its tip to impress the folks back home. Windfree conditions and a lack of imagination are essential for this.

Of similar appeal, but with longer climbs than those on Spazzacaldeira, the 2905m **Piz Frachiccio** lies south of Spazza, and its NE Face, which contains some routes with up to 12 pitches, can be reached within 30mins of leaving the cable car. Here the Kaspar Pillar (VII), first climbed in 1963, has become a much-respected classic.

The 2980m north summit of the twin-peaked **Piz Cacciabella** makes a splendid vantage point from which to survey virtually the whole of the Bregaglia Alps, and rising southwest of Piz Frachiccio (combined with which it makes an excellent traverse), it marks the point where the north walling ridge of Val Bondasca meets the west walling ridge of Val Albigna. Although it is more often climbed from the Sciora Hut by a somewhat tedious route, it's as easily won by climbing a snow couloir on the Albigna flank leading to the gap between the north and south peaks. Both peaks received their first recorded ascent in June 1897 by the ubiquitous Klucker, along with von Rydzewski and Mansueto Barbaria.

Between Piz Cacciabella and Cima della Bondasca, the ridge is defined by the Sciora group, whose attractions, which have been briefly enumerated above, are best appreciated from Val Bondasca. The southern end of this ridge forms the head of the Bondasca glacier on the west, and the Albigna glacier on the east, while the south flank plunges into Valle di Mello. Here, between Sciora Dadent and Cima della Bondasca, the broad snow saddle of the Colle dell'Albigna (3160m) gives a worthwhile ice climb in winter or spring when attacked from the Albigna glacier.

Rising steeply from the Albigna glacier, **Cima della Bondasca** (also known as Pizzo del Ferro Centrale) has two summits separated by a small saddle, then the frontier ridge runs east and north-east to close off the Albigna cirque at the Cima di Castello. In the middle of this ridge, **Pizzo di Zocco** (3174m) draws the attention of all who study the cirque, for it is one of the finest and most complex of Albigna summits, with an impressive glaciated wall which drops into the glacier between rocky buttresses. The normal route (PD+) from the Albigna Hut tackles the NW Flank and is another of those pioneered by von Rydzewski, Klucker and Barbaria in their first season together in the Bregaglia mountains. The Alpine Club guide claims this to be (under good conditions) one of the finest expeditions in the valley.

At 3388m **Cima di Castello** is the highest of the Bregaglia peaks in Switzerland (Monte Disgrazia being Italian), first climbed in 1866 by Alpine Club stalwarts Freshfield and Tuckett, with François Dévouassoud and A Flury. Its position at a junction of ridges makes it an ideal viewpoint, and the summit panorama is unequalled in this corner of the range. As its *voie normale* is not exactly demanding (no higher than PD-), and its vantage point reputation well known, it receives probably more ascents per season than any other 'high' mountain in the district. It also makes a popular ski ascent in the springtime.

The long ridge stretching north of Cima di Castello effectively separates the Albigna and Forno valleys. Several passes interrupt the line of 3000m peaks to give connecting routes between these two valleys and their huts. Between Cima di Castello and Cima dal Cantun, the most southerly

Lägh da Cavloc and the Muretto Pass

of these passes is the broad snow saddle of Passo dal Cantun (3265m). Too remote to be of practical use in going from one hut to the other (except as an expedition to gain experience), since there are more direct routes to consider, its main value is providing access to the peaks on either side. The attractive 🐻 **Cima dal Cantun** (3354m) is a good example of this, for a recommended route on the SW Flank (PD-) would make a fine outing for first-season alpinists, which first heads towards the Cantun Pass. It's also popular as a ski ascent in springtime, and is yet another von Rydzewski/Klucker/Barbaria route, as is the NE Ridge which is gained at the Furcela dal Scalin. Both of these routes were climbed within 10 days of each other in June 1892, and the team also added the first traverse of the peak after their NE Ridge ascent.

The NW Ridge of Cima dal Cantun sweeps down towards the Albigna lake and terminates on the 🐻 **Punta da l'Albigna**. Within a short stroll of the Albigna Hut, this eye-catching rock pyramid naturally attracts the attention of climbers based in the valley, and a good number of lines have been developed on it; one of the favourites being the 24-pitch Steiger Route (D+), although the best-known is the 1961 Mueli Route graded AD+ which has plenty of bolts *in situ*. Then there's the nearby 2843m 🐻 **Bio-Pillar** (1hr from the hut) which offers short-length, but high-quality rock climbing and glorious views. To quote Lindsay Griffin in the AC guide: 'For the rock athlete this is a big crag in a mountain setting – what more could one ask for?'

Back on the valley's walling ridge, the most popular crossing points are the two Casnil Passes that breach the crest east of the Albigna Hut. These are old routes, said to have been used for centuries by chamois hunters and traders, and they were quickly adopted by climbers as the most convenient means of moving between districts. The lower 2941m **South Casnil Pass** is preferred in order to avoid the steep and unstable couloir on the east side of the more northerly pass, but in recent hot summers the Forno slope has suffered from considerable stonefall, so caution is needed whichever pass is chosen. To the north rises **Piz Casnil** (3189m). Though not as impressive as its neighbour, Piz Bacun, it's understandably popular, and with fine summit views; the most frequented route (II) is from the North Casnil Pass via the South Ridge.

Continue north beyond Piz Casnil, and the 3244m summit of 🟢 **Piz Bacun** is the culminating point of four ridges. This 'magnificent granite pyramid' (Christian Klucker), with an exquisite panoramic view of the Forno glacier leading the eye to Monte Disgrazia, is probably climbed as often from the Forno side as from the Albigna Hut. Here Klucker's name is inextricably linked with that of Theodor Curtius, the man who, beginning in 1883, was most responsible for the exploration of the northern side of Bregaglia's frontier mountains. By direct contrast with his later employer von Rydzewski, Klucker and Curtius formed a harmonious partnership, and their friendship remained intact until the very end. Together they made the first ascent of Piz Bacun, not from Val Albigna, but from the Forno glacier via the NE Face and East Ridge (III-), and two years later, in August 1885, they returned to climb the North Ridge (III) – also from the Forno side. The SW Ridge, generally reckoned to be the best, is interrupted by several granite projections, and this had to wait until 1912 for its first ascent (by Bonacossa and Botsford). The South Ridge (IV) dates from 1921, while the splendid South Pillar has a reputation for some exciting routes and possibilities for further development.

Piz Bacun stands at about the halfway point along the ridge, but the northern half extends beyond Val Albigna's entrance to form the left-hand wall of the upper Val Bregaglia. Along it the **Cima dal Largh** (or Cima del Largo) is another that fell to the Curtius/Klucker partnership in 1887. There are, in fact, three spires to this peak which projects north of Piz Bacun, each being won by Klucker; the highest measuring 3188m. After this, there's only one more 3000m summit (Cima da Splüga) before the crest makes a gradual decline towards the entrance to Val Forno.

Val Forno

The longest and highest of the three tributary valleys that feed into the Swiss Val Bregaglia, Val Forno at first appears to be directed towards the Upper Engadine, but just as it opens a little south of Maloja, its river (the Orlegna) suddenly swings to the left and pours into the Bregaglia. This goes against its natural inclination, for Val Forno once was a tributary of the Engadine valley, whose headwaters, it is thought, were located further south, more or less where Vicosoprano now lies. But since Bregaglia's slope is much more aggressive than that of the Engadine's, and rainfall greater on the south side of the range than the north, the Maira, which is the main Bregaglia river and was then much more powerful than it is today, gradually bit back into the original watershed and eventually captured both Val Albigna and Val Forno from the Engadine.

At its entrance today Val Forno gives no impression of its true nature. Meadow and woodland give way to the beautiful tree-fringed 🟢 **Lägh da Cavloc** (otherwise known as the Cavolocciasee), easily gained by a pleasant 1hr walk from Maloja. There's a restaurant by the lake, and on a calm summer's day mountains are turned on their heads in the water; in September bilberries cluster ripe and black where shrubs form cushions over rocks around its shores. The low stone buildings of Alp Cavloc huddle just to the south, and beyond them, barely 20mins from the lake, the valley forks at Plan Canin. Val Forno proper curves to the right, but directly ahead a stream comes down from the short, narrow and steeply inclined Val Muretto, at the head of which the 2562m 🟢 **Passo del Muretto** carries an old historic trade route, in use since at least the 14th century, between the Upper Engadine and Italy's Valtellina.

The Muretto Pass is not only the border between Switzerland and Italy: it's also the demarcation point between the Bregaglia Alps to the south and west, and Bernina Alps to north and east. Although this is as far as we need go in our concentration on the Alps of Switzerland, whoever reaches this pass owes it to himself to descend a short distance on the Italian flank to gain a heart-stopping view of the majestic Monte Disgrazia, the highest, most handsome and gracefully proportioned of all Bregaglia mountains.

Returning to Plan Canin, just below a confluence of streams there's a path junction with a sign indicating the way into the main Val Forno, with 2½hrs being given as the time needed to reach the Forno Hut. As you make your way to the south, the valley is narrow and uncompromisingly rough underfoot, the path picking a way over a chaos of rocks, with a few spindly larches and low-growing shrubs being all that relieves the raw, untamed nature of the place. It has about it a Himalayan ruggedness. Huge granite slabs soar on either side, and as you draw near the snout of the Forno glacier, so the valley opens out and the view ahead draws one's attention through a long avenue of grey peaks daubed with patches of snow and ice; the

The Forno glacier

highway between those peaks being a broad and gently inclined river of ice closed off at its southern end by the Torrone peaks, across which lies Italy's Valle di Mello.

The steady withdrawal of the **Forno glacier** has been plotted for decades, with some alarming results. In the 115 years from 1887 to 2002, for example, the glacier shrank by more than 2.5km; the average annual rate of shrinkage being 22m, and there's no reason to assume that rate will lessen in the foreseeable future. For now the way to the hut crosses the glacier and is usually marked by poles, and as the ice is almost completely flat, crevasses should not be a major problem. The main danger comes from the unstable nature of the east bank moraine up which the path makes its final approach to the hut.

Owned by the Rorschach section of the SAC, from its 2574m eyrie **Capanna del Forno** enjoys a privileged balcony view of the glacier, the upper valley and most of the peaks that rim its enclosing cirque. An enlarged hut with 104 places, it is often used by the SAC as a base for climbing courses. It is fully staffed from late March until early May, and from the end of June until the end of September, and there's a winter room permanently open with 25 places (www.fornohuette.ch). Once again the name of Klucker crops up, for it was he who chose the site for the original hut, which was built here in 1889 and largely paid for by his great friend Theodor Curtius, before being taken over by the Rorschach section in 1920. Klucker arrived with a group of five on the evening of 15 August 1889, and was the first to spend a night there. For a while, he also acted as hut guardian.

Despite his close association with the hut, Klucker's most prestigious Bregaglia climbs were made elsewhere. Among the first ascents that he did make from here (with L Norman-Neruda), was that of the nearby **Monte Rosso** (3088m) which rises to the southeast, and whose summit may be gained in 4hrs by the Neruda/Klucker route via the NE Ridge (AD-). Klucker referred to his ascent as 'a stimulating, and at times rather exposed clamber'.

Northeast of the hut the 3214m **Monte del Forno** makes a less demanding ascent than that of Monte Rosso, but it's rewarding for first-season alpinists when there's still a decent snow cover in the early summer, and for ski mountaineers in winter and spring. The normal route is along the

South Ridge, which is gained at the Sella del Forno col. First climbed in 1876, it is not unduly difficult (PD- with individual moves of II/II+), but is subject to stonefall when the snow has melted. By traversing across the summit and continuing northeast, it's possible to reach the Passo del Muretto, thereby giving a choice of descent to either Maloja or Chiareggio. Most climbers and ski mountaineers aiming for Chiareggio, however, would use the 2768m **Sella del Forno**, for this lies almost due east of the Forno Hut and offers a much shorter and more direct route into Italy.

All along the east and south walling ridges of Val Forno, superb views are gained of Monte Disgrazia to the south or southeast, and often northeast too, to the high peaks of the Bernina massif. While most of the local summits were won in the second half of the 19th century, more technical climbs were established from the 1920s on, almost exclusively led by Italian climbers. Giusto Gervasutti was one. Along with Chabod and Corti he helped pioneer the East Ridge of ❸ **Cima di Val Bona** in 1933; a route today graded AD+ and probably tackled more often from the Grande-Camerini Hut which lies below it on the Italian flank.

Further south, a strange intrusion of limestone in this otherwise granite region has produced an interesting but brittle crest culminating in the 3301m ❸ **Cima di Vazzeda**, one of Klucker's routes undertaken when guiding von Rydzewski in 1892. Klucker commented that caution was required when climbing the NE Face from the bergschrund at its foot, on account of loose stones, and the current guide also warns that heavy stonefall puts the mountain's flanks out of bounds in summer, but the East Ridge (Corti/Foianini/Albertini in 1929) offers a long but safer route at AD (III+). It's interesting to note that having made the first ascent of this peak, Klucker then led his rope on a traverse of the ridge leading to the lovely Cima di Rosso in 2hrs. 'The clamber over this bizarre ridge' he wrote, 'was to me a *Wanderung* of great beauty.' They then returned to the Forno Hut, and later that evening went down to Promontogno. It must have been quite a day!

❸ **Cima di Rosso** is an obvious goal for climbers based at the Forno Hut. Not only is it one of the highest in the district at 3366m, it's certainly one of the most handsome of all Forno peaks, whose impressive North Face was pioneered by Walter Amstutz with Aldo Bonacossa in 1930, the latter being very active here in the inter-war years. First climbed via the SW Flank (PD-) by Coolidge with François and Henri Dévouassoud guiding, three days after they'd made the first ascent of Piz Badile (see Val Bondasca section above), the Cima has a wide variety of other climbs, is popular with ski-mountaineers in winter and spring, and enjoys exquisite summit views.

Having made the ascent of Cima di Rosso, climbers often include ❸ **Monte Sissone** in the same expedition. Rising to the south of the Cima across the broad snow saddle of the Passo Sissone, this easy 3330m snow peak was first climbed by Freshfield's party in 1864, and is located where the frontier ridge makes a sharp turn to the west to close off the Forno valley, while another ridge sweeps to the southeast across the head of both Valle di Mello and Valle Sissone. As this ridge connects directly with Monte Disgrazia, it will come as no surprise to discover that Monte Sissone has one of the finest of all views of its noble neighbour seen in profile, as it were, from a distance of just 4km. But the graceful form of Monte Disgrazia is not all (though that view alone would make the ascent worthwhile), for the full length of the Forno glacier stretches off to the north; the depths of Valle di Mello fall away to the southwest; and to the east Valle Sissone and Val Malenco direct one's gaze to the central block of the Bernina massif. It is easy, claims Walker, to descend from the summit into the head of Valle di Mello as an obvious traverse route for those aiming for San Martino and/or the Valle dei Bagni.

West of Monte Sissone the frontier ridge passes across the three ❸ **Torrone peaks**: Orientale (3333m), Centrale (3290m), and the highest of them all, the 3351m Torrone Occidentale. Serious routes will be found on each of these peaks, as well as on the conspicuous 40m granite finger of the Ago del Torrone (3233m) poking skyward between Orientale and Centrale. The beautiful pyramid-shaped **Torrone Orientale** is perhaps the most appealing, and is more easily accessible than its neighbours. First climbed on 29 July 1882 by R Paulcke and Alexander Rzewuski, with Klucker and J Eggengerger as guides, it was Klucker's earliest first ascent in the Bregaglia Alps. Their route, by the NE Flank, is a fairly long (5–6hrs) but recommended mixed expedition from the Forno Hut, which carries a grade of AD- (III/III+). Klucker also made the first ascent of Torrone Centrale in 1891, with von Rydzewski and Barbaria. The following year, the same party climbed another rock pyramid, the 3306m ⊙ **Punta Rasica** on the ridge between Torrone Centrale and the Cima di Castello, their route following the sharp SE Ridge (AD) above Colle Rasica.

The frontier ridge pushes north and northwest from Punta Rasica, but on gaining Cima di Castello it then makes a sharp southwesterly turn, while another ridge projects north, effectively dividing Val Forno from Val Albigna. As this dividing ridge has already been described in the Val Albigna section above, we've effectively completed this survey of the Bregaglia Alps.

4:4 THE BERNINA ALPS

The main block of the Bernina Alps, the picturesque and heavily glaciated range that is so reminiscent of the Western Alps, is contained between four main valleys: the high, lake-filled Engadine in the west, comparatively narrow Val Bernina to the north, the deep Val Poschiavo in the east, and Italy's Val Malenco to the south. Each of these four valleys is fed by tributaries of varying degrees of importance to the climber and walker. For a start the pastoral Vals Fedoz and Fex drain western outliers of the range before spilling out to the Engadine, but neither has direct access to huts or the main summits. Vals Roseg and Morteratsch are the most heavily glaciated, flow north into Val Bernina and have the most obvious appeal, while short and seemingly insignificant hanging valleys cut into the more remote eastern fringes above Val Poschiavo. As for the southern flank, two main valleys draw the snowmelt and run-off from the Scerscen and Fellaria glaciers, with a service road that leaves Val Malenco to climb up to a pair of dammed lakes below Piz Palü.

From Piz Palü in the east, to Piz Glüschaint in the west, there runs an almost unbroken crest of glittering snow and ice. Much of this crest is obscured from all but a select handful of vantage points on the south side of the range, but from the north, wave upon wave of graceful summits announce their presence to the approaching walker and climber. The symmetry of Piz Palü's triple buttresses; the long and almost horizontal sweep of Bellavista's ridge; the clearly defined snow arête of the undisputed 'monarch', Piz Bernina; Piz Roseg's slender spire; the graceful fin of Piz Glüschaint and the rolling snow domes of the neighbouring Sella group from which crumbling stairways of ice wait to collapse into the head of Val Roseg. All these, and more, help give the range an elevated status that is not simply altitude related.

Compact but majestic, the Bernina Alps reward with numerous traditional routes, each one in a setting of extraordinary beauty, while their feeder glens are no less appealing than the peaks that guard them.

Val Fedoz

About 3km from Maloja at the head of the Engadine, and roughly halfway along the southeastern shore of the lake of Sils (Lej da Segl), the few buildings of **Isola** occupy the edge of an alluvial meadowland created by deposits brought down from Val Fedoz. Behind the hamlet a waterfall thunders from a little gorge at the valley entrance, and a path tacks up the hillside to the north of this, before turning into the valley itself. Another way into Val Fedoz follows a track from the open meadow of Plan Brüsciabräga on the Maloja side of Isola, and the two routes are linked by a path at the chalets of Ca d'Starnam.

Overlooking Val Fedoz south of Ca d'Starnam, ⊗ **Piz de la Margna** is the most conspicuous of local mountains, its massive armchair shape dominating practically every Engadine view throughout the valley's upper reaches to such an extent that it has virtually become its unofficial emblem. Gracing countless postcards and calendars, the 3158m peak is by no means one of the highest hereabouts, yet its bulk – and its dominant position at the head of the valley – gives it more than an edge over many of its loftier neighbours, and the summit panorama is exceptional, embracing not only the great lake-filled trench below, but more especially the Bernina, Bregaglia and Albula Alps in all their rich diversity. By its normal route, la Margna is not a difficult mountain to climb (F) for a path strikes up the slope above and to the south of the chalets, leading to scree and sometimes snow, before you desert this and make for the NE Ridge, which is then followed directly to the summit. Most of the mountain's snow cover having disappeared by the middle of summer, the higher rocks – and even some of the exposed turf – may be in an unstable condition, in which case a degree of caution is advised.

4:4 The Bernina Alps

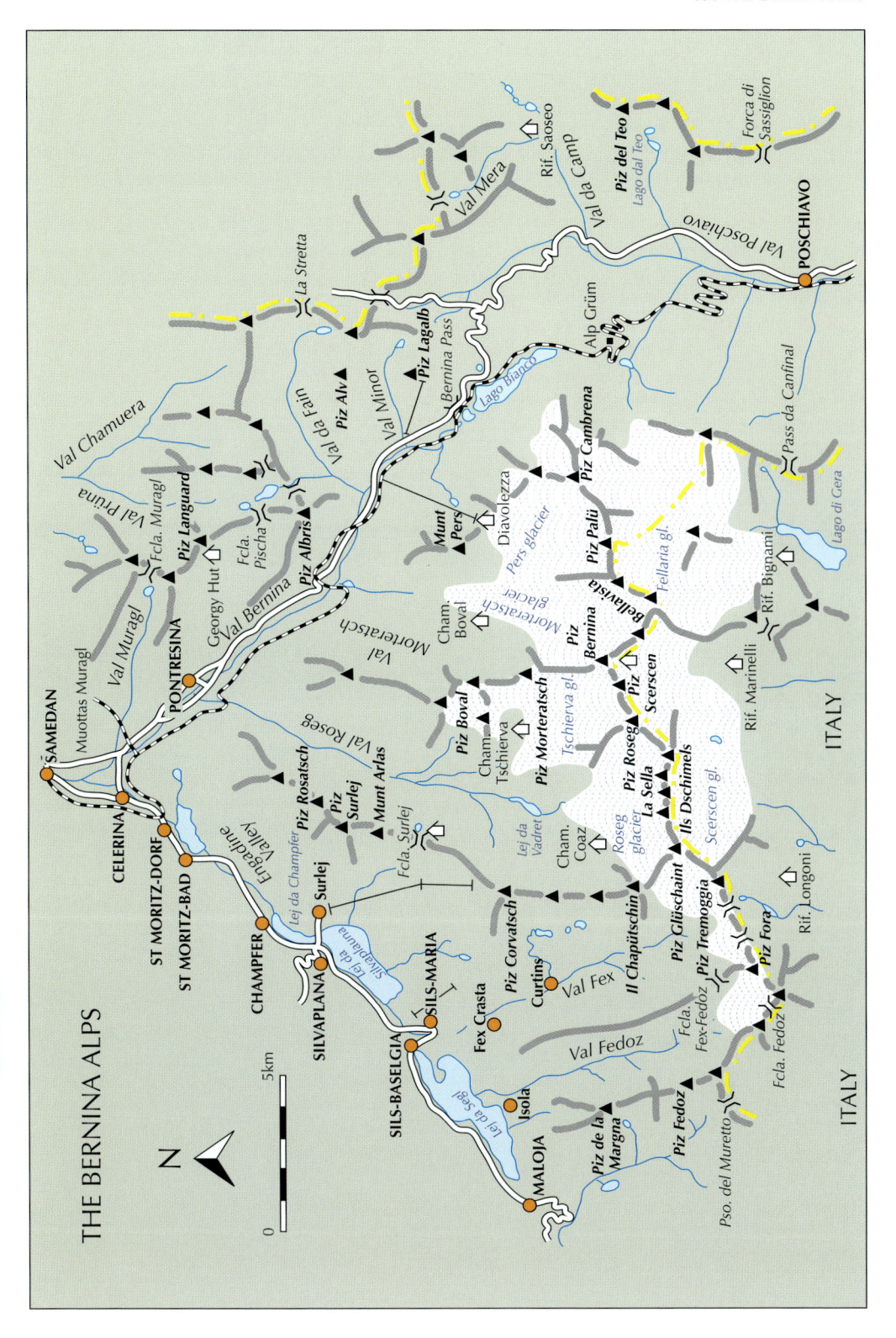

Val Fedoz is a rugged little glen, only occasionally inhabited in summer, and with a sense of remoteness that is all the more noticeable by comparison with the tourist-haunted Engadine valley from which it is entered. Its southern end is closed off by a narrow cirque whose ridge carries the Italian border from Piz Muretto across Monte dell'Oro and on to the attractive Piz Fora, under which the last remnants of the Fedoz glacier still linger. But north of Piz Muretto, which rises just above the Passo del Muretto (4:3), and on the ridge between that peak and Piz de la Margna, **Piz Fedoz** (3190m) gives an undemanding ascent with yet more rewarding views. Meanwhile, in a fairly central position on the frontier ridge southeast of Monte dell'Oro, the **Fuorcla da Fedoz** suggests a direct way across the mountains to the Disgrazia district, and was first crossed in 1866 by Freshfield, C C Tucker and François Dévouassoud. But this pass has since lost much of its appeal, in favour of cols in the headwall of neighbouring Val Fex.

Val Fex

There is a seductive tranquillity to Val Fex that was missing in Val Fedoz. Gentle and distinctively pastoral, in the early summer herds of cattle are brought from lowland Switzerland to graze the pastures of the Plaun Vadret (the 'Glacier Plain'). It was here that the young Christian Klucker was set to work as a cowherd at the age of six 'amongst the beautiful flowering pastures of the Fextal'. It was from here that he set off as a guide to explore the granitelands of Bregaglia and lead his clients in many other alpine districts; from where he embarked in 1901 to accompany Whymper on his expedition to the Canadian Rockies; and it is here, in the trim little churchyard of Fex Crasta, that Klucker now lies at peace.

With **Sils Maria** (www.sils.ch) nestling below its entrance, Val Fex may be gained by a path which cuts through its protective gorge, part of the way along a timber gallery to emerge among meadows just short of the chalets of Fex Platta. Beyond these lies **Fex Crasta** with its tiny church set beside the service road that comes from Sils. Near the church there's a small hotel, Hotel Sonne (www.hotel-sonne-fex.ch).

Above the road on the west side of the valley a path contours along the hillside, while another takes a much higher course along what is known as the Muott 'Ota, from where you gain a fine overview of Val Fex and the southern crags of Piz Corvatsch that rise on the far side.

Midway between Fex Crasta and the Plaun Vadret lies the hamlet of **Curtins**, with Hotel Fex nearby (www.hotelfex.ch). From here a ○ **recommended path** slants up the valley's right-hand hillside heading north. The path offers several options for the return: either returns to Sils Maria; turns the Marmorè spur to make a scenic contour along the lower slopes of Piz Corvatsch, with views over and along the Engadine lakes before dropping to Surlej opposite Silvaplana; or cuts back to the southeast, then climbs to the remote tarn of Lej Sgrischus at 2618m. These, and various other trails, are all worth exploring.

When the road runs out at Curtins, a footpath continues upvalley through patches of marsh and grassland to reach an old moraine at Muot-Selvas, where there's a small tarn and the upper pastures of Plaun Vadret seen stretching ahead. The nature of the valley changes here, for the walls on either side are more abrupt, rising to 3000m summits, steep cliffs fall from remnant glaciers, and between Piz Fora and the West Ridge of Piz Glüschaint, no less than three passes suggest ways to cross the frontier ridge to Val Malenco. The lowest of these is Fuorcla dal Chaputsch (2929m); then there's the easy Pass dal Tremoggia (3014m), and finally the rather complicated 3122m Fuorcla Fex-Scerscen at the head of the Tremoggia glacier. Two further crossings are found in the east wall of the valley between Il Chapütschin and the Italian border, but these take climbers, not into Italy, but to the Coaz Hut at the head of Val Roseg.

There's very little to attract climbers to Val Fex, although ✪ **Piz Tremoggia** (3441m) makes an excellent viewpoint and a pleasant training climb along its NE Ridge (F+/PD) via the Fuorcla Fex-Scerscen, or by way of the jagged SW Ridge from Pass dal Tremoggia (AD: III/IV), this latter route first climbed solo in 1879 by Klucker at the request of the cartographer, J M Ziegler. (Klucker also made a new route on Piz Tremoggia via the NW Face with Norman-Neruda in 1890.) ✪ **Piz Fora** is another option worth considering by a climber found straying into Val Fex. This 3363m snow pyramid, which stands on the dividing ridge between Vals Fedoz and Fex, may be climbed from the Fex side by the Chapütschgrat, the ENE Ridge which runs gently down to the Fuorcla dal Chapütsch, while a second route worth considering is via the NNW Ridge (F)

Lej da Vadret in Val Roseg

which separates the two valleys. On this ridge the 3143m saddle of Fuorcla Fex-Fedoz also provides an interesting crossing point between these valleys, but note there are small glaciers on either side.

Val Roseg

A 13km long wall of mountains runs roughly northeastward from Il Chapütschin above Val Fex before sweeping down to Val Bernina close to Pontresina. The highest point on this wall is the celebrated ski mountain of **Piz Corvatsch** (3451m) which has cable car access from Surlej on the right bank of the Inn. This Engadine flank has one or two other cableways strung upon it, but there are long stretches of mid-height trail that enjoy uncluttered views and make worthwhile outings for visiting walkers in summer. A few of these paths sneak into the barren scoop of Margun directly above Surlej. It's not an attractive area, but at its head lies the magnificent vantage point of the Fuorcla Surlej, an easy saddle and a classic crossing point that takes walkers and climbers from the Upper Engadine to the exquisite Val Roseg. Actually, it's not necessary to trudge all the way to the pass from either Surlej or St Moritz (although a very fine trail climbs from St Moritz-Bad to the little Lej dals Chöds (Hahnensee), before slanting into and up the Margun basin), for the middle station of the Corvatsch cable car is located on the Murtèl spur overlooking the stony basin, from which an easy walk of just 45mins leads to the saddle.

At 2755m **Fuorcla Surlej** is one of the great viewpoints of the Alps, for beyond a tiny tarn and a clutter of rocks the mountain drops away into Val Roseg, while directly across that valley Piz Morteratsch, Piz Bernina, Piz Scerscen and Piz Roseg present a classical pose above the cascading icefall of the Tschierva glacier. It's a view no mountain lover could tire of; a view to excite every mountaineer with imagination.

On the saddle stands the **Berghaus Fuorcla Surlej** where one could happily spend a night, enjoy the alpenglow staining Bernina's snows, and from there make the ascent of one or more of the neighbouring summits. Of these, **Piz Corvatsch** is by far the most popular with an easy climb (F) via Piz Murtel. The summit, of course, has a noteworthy panorama that takes in most of the main Bernina peaks, as well as Monte Disgrazia and the Bregaglia Alps, the Albula range to the west

273

and north, and the Engadine lakes 1600m below. On the other, northern, side of Fuorcla Surlej, an uncomplicated scramble over **Munt Arlas** leads in little more than 1½hrs to ◯ **Piz Surlej**, at 3188m the highest summit on the broad Rosatsch massif. (This massif has a long line of summits, at least four of which exceed 3000m, that may be climbed from St Moritz by strong walkers with a bit of scrambling experience; the initial path for these ascents is located behind the French Protestant Church in St Moritz-Bad.)

Five minutes below Fuorcla Surlej the path forks. The left branch descends directly to Hotel Roseggletscher (1hr from the pass) where a track leads down through the lower Val Roseg to ◯ ☆ **Pontresina** in a further 1½–2hrs. The right-hand path descends a little further below the junction, then cuts along the hillside and contours across the slopes and terraces of grass and rock of Alp Ota with its celebrated view of the Tschierva icefall, before reaching ◯ ☆ **Chamanna Coaz** (see Climbs from the Coaz Hut for details), about 2½hrs from Fuorcla Surlej. Both these paths are highly recommended, but especially the scenically spectacular Coaz Hut route. (By backtracking about 25mins from this hut, an alternative descent can be made to Lej da Vadret below the Roseg glacier, where a continuing trail goes all the way to Pontresina in 3½–4hrs.)

Enclosed by two parallel spurs that project northward from the gleaming frontier ridge, Val Roseg is without question one of the finest of those tributary glens that poke into the Bernina massif, with pleasures to be won by all who are drawn from its entrance below Pontresina to its headwall above the Roseg and Sella glaciers.

Facing directly into Val Roseg **Pontresina** (1809m) is, after St Moritz, the busiest Engadine resort, but one that is noted more for its climbing potential than for skiing. Sprawling along a terrace above the Bernina torrent (the Flaz), it's home to the well-known Schweizer Bergsteigerschule (www. bergsteiger-pontresina.ch), the largest mountaineering school in Switzerland. The town has a strong mountaineering tradition, with a large body of guides, so it's not surprising to find that several of its shops stock climbing equipment. Accommodation ranges from a youth hostel and modest pensions to upmarket hotels; there are two campsites nearby, plenty of restaurants, an indoor swimming pool, post office and banks, and the tourist office is located in the Rondo Convention Centre on Via Maistra (www.pontresina.com). Pontresina is served by the Rhaetian Railway with regular trains from Chur running through Val Bernina and across the Bernina Pass into Val Poschiavo. It also has a frequent bus link with the main Engadine valley resorts.

As for Val Roseg, there is no vehicular access for the public, but from the town's railway station horse-drawn carriages ferry visitors with no desire for exercise as far as Hotel Roseggletscher. But to ride is almost sacrilegious, and should be reserved for those who are infirm and simply cannot walk. Val Roseg needs to be entered on foot, for it rewards every step taken by those who are drawn along its footpaths in winter as in summer. The undemanding 2hr approach to ◯ **Hotel Roseggletscher**, at first through woods of larch and Arolla pine, then across small rock-littered meadows, is almost certainly the most popular outing for visitors to Pontresina, which is quite understandable, for there's so much to enjoy along the way. Shortly before reaching the hotel, an open glacial plain gives unrestricted views towards the head of the valley where the Sella group, with Piz Glüschaint and Il Chapütschin, dazzle with a spectacular series of icefalls.

As the building's name implies, the Roseg glacier once extended much closer to the hotel, but the glacier's tongue is now almost 5km further south. Nevertheless, Hotel Roseggletscher makes a romantic lodging for a night or two, and in addition to standard rooms, there's dormitory accommodation for at least 100 (www.roseggletscher.ch). But of more interest for those intent on scaling the peaks, the valley has two SAC huts, Tschierva and Coaz, the latter having already been briefly visited along the high trail from Fuorcla Surlej.

Climbs from the Tschierva Hut

The popular **Chamanna da Tschierva** is the choice of climbers with ambitions on Piz Morteratsch, Bernina, Scerscen and Roseg, and some of the district's finest ice climbs begin here, and high above the hut to the northeast, in the ridge between Piz Morteratsch and Piz Boval, the 3347m Fuorcla da Boval is a much-used crossing point for activists making a traverse to the Boval Hut in the Morteratsch valley. With a hideous, container-like square block of an extension, the Tschierva Hut, which belongs to the St Moritz-based Bernina section of the SAC, has 100 places and is fully staffed in April and early May, and from mid-June until mid-September (www.sac-bernina.ch). Situated at 2583m on the north bank of the Tschierva glacier immediately below Piz Morteratsch, the approach to it leads up through the glacier's ablation valley before rising onto the crest of the right-bank lateral moraine and gaining dramatic views across the Tschierva icefall to Piz Roseg. During the evening and early morning, it's not unusual to watch ibex and chamois from the terrace.

Several summits above the hut are climbed just as frequently (or perhaps even more so) from the Boval Hut on the east side of the ridge dividing the Roseg and Morteratsch valleys, **Piz Morteratsch** being one. This 3751m peak is probably climbed more often than any other in the Bernina range except, perhaps for Piz Palü, for it is one of the easiest of its height in the Alps. The normal route is a snow climb via the North Ridge (PD-), the route taken by the team of four who made the first ascent in 1858, and thanks to its position on the ridge due north of Piz Bernina, the summit panorama is unrivalled for extent, variety and dramatic beauty.

While the majority of routes on **Piz Bernina** (4049m) start either from the Boval Hut or the CAI's Marco e Rosa situated on the Italian flank near the Fuorcla Crast'Aguzza, the long and complex ice climb of the West Face (D+) naturally enough begins at Chamanna da Tschierva. First climbed by T Graham Brown in 1930, with A Graven, Joseph Knubel and A Zurcher, this route is marred by several objective dangers, and is best tackled in cold conditions when a glaze of ice reduces the chances of stonefall.

Although virtually all routes on Piz Bernina are worthy of consideration, it is the famed ☆ **Biancograt** (AD) that wins most of the plaudits, for it has become one of the most celebrated of all alpine ridge routes, and despite being pioneered more than 130 years ago, it remains the ultimate prize. Access to the North Ridge is gained at the Fuorcla Prievlusa (3430m), about 3–4hrs from the hut, after which the route goes up its rocky right-hand side for about 50m, before working onto the actual crest. From here the Biancograt rises as a beautifully defined and elegantly formed line of crystal snow tapering against the sky. On 12 August 1876 Henri Cordier, Thomas Middlemore and the guides Johan Jaun and Kaspar Maurer made the first ascent of this

Piz Bernina (left) and Piz Morteratsch

ridge as far as Piz Bianco (or Piz Alv, 3995m), where they discovered that they were separated from the true summit by a 25m deep gap, now known as the Berninascharte. Exactly two years later, German climber, scientist and politician Paul Güssfeldt, along with the Pontresina guides Hans Grass and Johan Cross, made the difficult descent into the gap, then completed the route to the summit proper. Today the ascent of the Biancograt takes 7–9hrs from the Tschierva Hut (5–6hrs down by the same route), but in 1950, Hermann Buhl climbed the whole route – to the summit and back – from the Boval Hut in just 6hrs to win a wager of 200 Swiss francs (see Buhl's *Nanga Parbat Pilgrimage*).

From Bernina's summit the southwest ridge carries the Italian border in an almost straight 3.5km line to Piz Sella, passing across the summits of Piz Scerscen and Piz Roseg, both of which are climbed by classic ice routes from the Tschierva Hut. The Eisnase, or NW Spur (AD+) of **Piz Scerscen** (3971m) is the first of these, put up in September 1877, a year before his Biancograt climb, by Güssfeldt with Caspar Capat and Hans Grass. Being especially attracted to the Bernina region, in 1879 Güssfeldt returned to Piz Scerscen to pioneer its SW Couloir (PD/PD+), and 10 years after this, he climbed the SW Ridge (PD+) for the first time.

Between Scerscen and Piz Roseg the 3522m **Porta da Roseg** is sometimes referred to as the Güssfeldtsattel since Güssfeldt was the first to climb it from the Roseg side (in 1872) with Hans Grass, Peter Jenni and Caspar Capat. On 12 September the guides cut steps up almost half the wall, and the next day all four completed the route in which another 450 steps had to be cut. In 1898 von Rydzewski, with Christian Klucker and Mansueto Barbaria, made the first traverse from the Italian side, and Klucker's account of their descent to the Tschierva glacier is one of the best in his autobiography. For some time after, the Porta da Roseg was one of the most coveted of ice climbs in the Bernina range, but it has since lost much of its appeal.

When studied from the northwest, the elegance of **Piz Roseg** is difficult to exaggerate; it is an imposing wall of rock and snow billows

Piz Bernina (left) and Piz Roseg, from Fuorcla Surlej

whose ridges sharpen to a gleaming ice pinnacle, acting as a counter-balance to Piz Bernina. Klucker, who was intimately acquainted with a good many spectacular mountains, referred to 'the proud structure of beautiful Piz Roseg' of whose NE Face he dreamed of making the first ascent. In Ludwig Norman-Neruda, he had the perfect companion for this, for he was one of the leading amateur climbers of the day who would (and could) go almost anywhere with Klucker. In July 1890 the two had already claimed the NE Face of Piz Bernina and a new route on the NW Face of Piz Scerscen when, at 6.30 on the morning of the 16th they stood at the bergschrund at the foot of Roseg's NE Face and contemplated the way above.

'Our route led up from this,' wrote Klucker, 'in a line directly below the snow-cap ... to a rockband on the wall which ran across the ice slope of the mountain about 350 feet above the bergschrund. On account of an ice coating, this band of rock gave us a good deal of trouble, though it is not high. Above it we made our way to the left, slightly ascending, till we came to a deep ice-gully about thirty-five feet wide.

'The crossing of this ice-filled gully or ravine, which plunges down at an angle of exactly 60° called for some hard step-cutting work. Each separate step had to be made big enough to allow easy room for both feet, and in addition hand-holds were cut in the ice.'

Thus began a 5½hr epic of step cutting, since they did not have the benefit of crampons. Later, Norman-Neruda claimed that each step called for about 70 strokes of the ice axe. But eventually 'the layer of snow grew thinner and thinner, and about 350 feet below the peak disappeared entirely. To avoid [more] weary step-cutting, we gave up the direct ascent to the peak and crossed over to the right towards the summit ridge, which we reached at the last gap above the saddle between both peaks, at 12.37. After a halt of twenty-five minutes we clambered up the last stretch to the highest peak, on which we set foot at 1.20' (*Adventures of an Alpine Guide*).

The Klucker/Norman-Neruda route is now graded D+, while the TD+/ED1 Directissima was pushed through in July 1958 by Austrians Kurt Diemberger and 'Charlie' Schonthaler, to make what is generally reckoned to be the hardest route on the face – and the most dangerous too. This Directissima was just one ascent in a Bernina blitzkrieg that summer when the duo also ticked off the North Face of Piz Palü, NE Face of Piz Bernina, and the NW Spur of Piz Scerscen.

Climbs from the Coaz Hut
Designed by Jakob Eschenmoser, the 16-sided, stone-walled **Chamanna Coaz** has a spectacular location at 2610m on the so-called 'Plattas' rock below the Val Roseg headwall, and backed by the turmoil of the Roseg glacier's icefall. Under this headwall the Roseg and Sella glaciers are among the most heavily crevassed in the Bernina Alps. Owned by the Chur-based Rätia section of the SAC, the hut is named after the well-known Johann Coaz who first climbed Piz Bernina in 1850 (see box). With 80 dormitory places (20 in the winter room), it is manned from March until mid-May and from mid-June until early October (www.coaz.ch), and is invariably busy. From a base here a number of expeditions are possible.

The first of these entails a short and direct plod up the glacier above the hut to climb the snow and rock pyramid of ❸ **Il Chapütschin** (3386m) – the 'Monk's Cowl' – by its North Ridge (F) in 2hrs. This is another Johann Coaz route dating from 1850, and from the summit it's quite possible to descend into Val Fex, should you have plans to move on.

In the centre of the headwall the 3594m ❸ **Piz Glüschaint** is an obvious attraction, the normal route being via the NE Face (PD), which has a tortuous approach up the multi-fissured Roseg glacier. The steep NW Face (AD+/D-) needs a decent cover of frozen snow to reduce the risk of stonefall, so is best tackled early in the season, while the superb North Ridge (AD+) is reputably the finest mixed route in the Sella group.

The twin rock peaks of ❸ **La Sella** (3584m; 3564m) are separated by a saddle from which both summits may be climbed. Another set of twin peaks, ❸ **Ils Dschimels** (3508m; 3479m) barely protrude above the ridge, and may be reached by simply following the frontier crest from La Sella.

The 3517m snow dome of ❸ **Piz Sella** marks the point on the Roseg headwall where the frontier breaks from the ridge to slant northeastward across the Fuorcla de la Sella to Piz Roseg. More frequently climbed from the Marinelli Hut, it can be climbed from the Coaz Hut by first crossing the heavily crevassed Roseg and Sella glaciers to reach the Fuorcla, where you then turn southwest to gain the summit.

And finally, a ⑤ **Traverse of the Sella Ridge** from Piz Sella to Il Chapütschin is without question one of the finest high level routes in the district (PD+). Allow 6–8hrs for the traverse, plus time to reach Piz Sella from the Coaz Hut; a big but rewarding day.

Val Morteratsch

Leaving Pontresina bound for Poschiavo and Tirano, trains cross the mouth of Val Roseg and make their sedate way along the left bank of Val Bernina, and after 6km stop briefly at Morteratsch Station. Next to the station the 2-star Hotel Morteratsch has both standard beds and dormitory accommodation (www.morteratsch.ch), while to the south stretches the once ice-filled trench of Val Morteratsch headed by a magnificent line of snowpeaks: Piz Bernina, Crast'Aguzza, Piz Argient, Piz Zupò, Bellavista and Piz Palü. Billowing waves of snow tumble as almost motionless glaciers spilling into the valley which, lower down, is bare of ice but on whose old moraines clusters of larch, pine and alpenrose add colour and shade. The Morteratsch glacier has been steadily shrinking for decades, and marker posts have been set along the valley bed to graphically illustrate the rate of its recession.

About 2hrs from Morteratsch Station, at the foot of Piz Boval and the ridge which divides the valley from Val Roseg, stands the Boval Hut, while across the Morteratsch and Pers glaciers Berghaus Diavolezza enjoys a privileged position on the saddle of the Diavolezza Pass between Munt Pers and Piz Trovat. Both huts are understandably popular with climbers and day visitors, and the two are linked by a glacier route via the Isla Persa, an island of rock surrounded by ice.

Hubert Walker was a bit sniffy about the **Chamanna da Boval**, or rather its immediate surroundings, which he likened to 'Hampstead Heath on a Bank Holiday, swarming with tourists who walk up for the day from Pontresina'. It is without question one of the busiest hereabouts, but the walk to it deserves to be enjoyed by all who truly appreciate wild and sumptuous mountain landscapes such as that in which it resides. The first Boval Hut was built in 1877, but was destroyed by an avalanche in 1906. The present building dates from 1913, stands at 2495m and belongs to the Bernina section of the SAC; it has 90 places (12 in the winter room), is fully staffed from late March until mid-May, and from mid-June until mid-October (www.sac-bernina.ch), and it occupies a site near that of a one-time herdsmen's chalet that was frequented by the early climbers. In 1861, E S Kennedy and the Revd J F Hardy came here to climb Piz Bernina with the brothers Peter and Fleury Jenni as their guides. The chalet was deserted when they arrived, but: 'The wind whistled through the crannies of the stone walls; the fir beams creaked in their uneasy beds; the wooden shingles rattled on the roof; the rain drops pattered on the earthen floor; and the log fire freshly kindled, filled the dwelling with pungent smoke.' After a while the two herdsmen arrived, 'followed by the goats and sheep', reported the Alpine Club stalwarts. 'These were closely followed by a she-ass and her foal. Hospitality could be stretched no further' (*Peaks, Passes and Glaciers*).

Perhaps this account is worth remembering when spending a night in a crowded Boval Hut *matratzenlager*.

JOHANN WILHELM COAZ: FIRST ON THE BERNINA

A commemorative plaque below the Boval Hut was unveiled in 1922 to mark the centenary of the birth of Johann Wilhelm Coaz, who made the first ascent of Piz Bernina on 13 September 1850 with local guides, the brothers Jon and Lorenz Ragut Tscharner. Born in Chur, the young Coaz was soon at home among the mountains of his native Graubünden and by the time he became private secretary to General Henri Dufour, the map maker, at the age of 28, he had already made at least 30 ascents in the Bernina and Albula ranges, including Piz Tschierva, Piz Corvatsch and Piz Kesch. The ascent of Piz Bernina was connected with his cartographic work, but from 1875 when he was appointed Federal Chief Inspector of Forests, Coaz was involved with conservation work and in devising avalanche safety measures. During his time in office, the Swiss National Park was founded in the Lower Engadine with strict laws to protect alpine flora and fauna. Johann Coaz was active into his nineties, and died in 1914 at the age of 96.

4:4 THE BERNINA ALPS

The famed triple buttresses of Piz Palü

Of the various climbs to be made from here, the easiest and nearest must surely be that of ❸ **Piz Boval** (3353m) whose broad East Ridge gives a pleasant PD route via Corn Boval. **Piz Morteratsch** has already been mentioned as an ascent from either the Tschierva or Boval Huts, with the Fuorcla da Boval being used as a convenient crossing point from one hut to the other.

But it is to ❸ **Piz Bernina** that all eyes and ambitions will inevitably turn, for in the words of Helmut Dumler, the mountain 'portrays a constant and unmistakable allure'. Some of that allure results from it being the most easterly of all the alpine 4000m peaks, but its purity of form and also its history add much to the stature of this Monarch of the Eastern Alps. First climbed on 13 September 1850 by Johann Coaz and the Tscharner brothers as his guides, their day began at 6am when they set out from the Berninahaus inn below the Morteratsch glacier. Their route then took them through the so-called 'Labyrinth' of the upper Morteratsch glacier to gain the East Ridge along which they worked their way to the summit. This was gained at 6pm, and the descent was made largely in darkness, ending some 20hrs after setting out.

Because of glacial recession, the original route is no longer feasible, so today's *voie normale* is via the SE Ridge, the Spallagrat (PD+), which is reckoned to be the safest and easiest way of ascent, despite considerable exposure. This was climbed in 1866 by Francis Fox Tuckett and Frederick Brown with their guides, Christian Almer and Franz Andermatten, while the NE Face features a major ice climb (D+) put up by Norman-Neruda and Christian Klucker in 1890. This latter route, however, is rarely climbed in summer nowadays, due to the extent of glacier retreat, while the famed Biancograt is mostly tackled from the Tschierva Hut (see above).

East of the Boval Hut, across the Morteratsch and Pers glaciers, **Berghaus Diavolezza** is the alternative base for climbers here, as well as being a honeypot for tourists in summer and skiers in winter. Usually approached by cable car from near the Bernina Suot railway station, this large, privately owned hotel and restaurant has a magnificent, classic view of the North Face of Piz Palü, and provides access to all the main summits at the eastern end of the massif. Although more expensive than SAC huts, Berghaus Diavolezza offers hut-style accommodation, on condition that users buy a meal in the restaurant. Open throughout the year, except mid-October until the end of November, it has around 200 places in bedrooms and *matratzenlager* (www.diavolezza.ch).

Walkers who come here for the day are recommended to follow a clear path heading northwest from the *berghaus* to the 3207m summit of **Munt Pers**, a tremendous viewpoint with a 360° panorama. On the other side of Diavolezza, **Piz Trovat** (3146m) is another option worth considering, reached in less than 1hr.

The most easterly of the Bernina peaks is the 3604m double-summited **Piz Cambrena** which stands south of Piz d'Arlas, and across which the mountain's North Ridge is gained for a PD+ ascent. This same ridge is also used on descent. Once known for its ice routes (especially the Eisnase or NNW Spur) activists need to consider spring visits these days in order to enjoy decent conditions on Piz Cambrena.

Naturally **Piz Palü** is a prime attraction for visitors to Diavolezza, for who could fail to be drawn to its sublime architectural lines, the triple buttresses and elegant crest? There are three summits: the East (3882m) stands entirely in Switzerland, but the Central peak (at 3905m it is also the highest) and the West summit (3823m) both straddle the frontier, and were first climbed in 1866 by K Digby, P Jenny and a porter. The East summit was climbed much earlier, in 1835, by Oswald Heer (who also climbed Piz Linard) with M and P Flury and the guides Colani and Madutz. Huge cornices are a feature of the summit ridge, and the normal route to the East Peak involves negotiating an icefall, weaving around monstrous crevasses and seeking out safe snow bridges. That being said, this route only goes at PD under 'normal' summer conditions. The **East–west Traverse** of the three peaks makes a tremendous expedition, and when combined with a continuation over the **Bellavista** to spend a night at the Marco e Rosa Hut by Fuorcla Crasta'Aguzza, a rewarding day may be anticipated.

The three buttresses, or pillars, of Piz Palü provide a range of TD climbs: the Central Peak's North Spur (the Bumillergrat) is arguably the most difficult; the North Spur of the East Peak is the easiest of the three (AD+), while the North Spur of the West Peak, which dates from 1899, is mostly a snow and ice route with some mixed ground.

Piz Palü's Central and highest peak

Val Bernina

From its confluence with the Engadine valley near Pontresina, to the broad, flat Bernina Pass at 2328m, Val Bernina forms a clear divide between the big snow and ice peaks on one side, and a group of less dramatic snow-free mountains on the other. Though lacking the obvious appeal of such summits as Palü, Bernina and Roseg, those on the right (northeast) flank of the valley make accessible grandstands from which to view them. The Bernina range has its traditional mountaineering routes, but here a bounty of walker's trails and easily gained summits may be enjoyed by activists with more modest ambition. Val Bernina has something for everyone. In winter downhill skiers are not only drawn to Diavolezza, they also flock to Piz Lagalb, to the slopes of Alp Languard and Muottas Muragl; *langlauf* (cross-country) enthusiasts explore valley-bed *pistes*, while ski mountaineers have a choice of tours to make among the highest of the Bernina peaks (see Bill O'Connor's *Alpine Ski Mountaineering: Volume 2*).

At the valley's entrance, but overlooking the Upper Engadine, **Muottas Muragl** is one of the great vantage points of the district. Served by a funicular dating from 1907, the upper station is sited adjacent to Berghotel Muottas Muragl, some 700m above the Samedan basin (www.muottasmuragl.ch). Immediately behind it a trail cuts into a shallow hanging valley, at the head of which lies Lej Muragl, a small tarn below the 2891m ● **Fuorcla Muragl**. The trail continues across this pass, descends on the far side into **Val Prüna**, then heads downvalley into Val Chamuera by which the Engadine can be rejoined at Chamues-ch and La Punt to give a 6hr trek. Another, shorter, option cuts up the northern hillside above Lej Muragl, crosses ● **Fuorcla Champagna** (2806m) and descends through the narrow and seemingly remote Val Champagna to reach Samedan in 3½–4hrs.

The view for which Muottas Muragl is primarily known is incomparable; a view that stretches across the string of Engadine lakes to Piz de la Margna and, rising out of the hinted Val Bregaglia, the summit wedge of Piz Badile. But to view the Bernina range, a recommended outing leads in 1½hrs to the Segantini Hut (Chamanna Segantini), named after the artist Giovanni Segantini (1858–99) who made numerous paintings of Engadine and Bregaglia landscapes, and died here at the age of 41. The hut (no accommodation) is perched at 2731m high above Pontresina on a ridge running between Piz Muragl and Munt de la Bes-cha (the Schafberg), and from it the creamy waves of Piz Palü, Bellavista and Piz Bernina concentrate all one's attention to the southeast. Paths continue beyond the Segantini Hut across the flanks of Piz Languard, while others give knee-crunchingly steep descents to Pontresina.

All these paths are worth following, for without exception they reward with a choice of splendid views. But the best-known of Pontresina's vantage points must surely be that of ● ☆ **Piz Languard**, the 3262m peak which towers above the resort. Known to generations of visitors, but unjustifiably dismissed by alpine snobs, Piz Languard must be one of the easiest of 3000m summits to reach on foot, for a path climbs all the way to the top in 3½–4hrs. Just 76m below the summit the privately owned **Georgy Hut** (also known as Berghaus Languard) provides accommodation with 20 dormitory places, and is manned from about mid-June until mid-October; reservations are essential (tel 081 833 65 65). From the hut the panoramic view across the depths of Val Bernina to all the high snow-laden peaks of the range is stupendous, and is what draws hundreds of walkers to it every summer, especially to watch sunset and sunrise paint the distant snowfields and glaciers with a palette of colours. However, Piz Languard's summit gives a much more extensive view than that from the Georgy Hut, and one deemed worthy of a pull-out panorama in the early Baedeker guides, with the author listing recognisable far-off peaks such as Monte Rosa, Adamello, the Tödi and the Zugspitze.

A herd of ibex roams the slopes of Piz Languard, while others may be seen around Piz Albris. On the ridge which links these two, the 2837m ● **Fuorcla Pischa** carries a route eastward to a group of tarns (Prüna and Pischa), crosses a second saddle, Fuorcla Tschüffer, then heads north through the remote Val Prünella which feeds into **Val Chamuera**. This, as we have already seen, spills out to the Engadine at Chamues-ch and La Punt to give the adventurous mountain walker a memorable day's wandering.

On the east side of Fuorcla Pischa another trail breaks away to the right and soon descends southward into **Val da Fain** below Piz Alv. At the head of this tributary of Val Bernina, a path crosses the frontier ridge at a saddle known as **La Stretta** (2476m), and drops down into the upper reaches of

Italy's Valle di Livigno. Meanwhile, the lower end of Val da Fain joins Val Bernina at the foot of the Diavolezza cableway, with Piz Lagalb (a popular and challenging ski mountain) nearby. **Val Minor**, a botanical paradise, partially moats **Piz Lagalb**, and a circular walk may be made around the mountain, passing Lej Minor at almost the highest point of the tour. Shortly after, another path branches to the south and leads directly to the **Bernina Pass**.

The 3km long **Lago Bianco** lies virtually on the pass, between the railway line and the slopes of Piz Cambrena. At over 2300m snow and ice lingers late here, long after the first hay crop of summer has been shorn from the meadows of the valley far below to the south. 'The Hospice on the pass must be difficult of access in some winters,' said R L G Irving in his 1939 volume, *The Alps*, and went on to recall how many years earlier he had taken a party there, when 'thunder, lightning, wind and snow gave us a boisterous welcome. Several windows were blown in and though the heads of the beds in which my sons were sleeping were at the greatest possible distance from where the window had been, the snow blew straight upon their faces.' It is a bleak pass, as many alpine passes are, but it provides an enticing glimpse of another land, a valley whose name, architecture and atmosphere belong (as surely as does that of Val Bregaglia) to Italy – Val Poschiavo, a low-lying enclave, a finger of Switzerland nestling some 1200m below the Bernina Pass, but poking into Italy's Valtellina district.

Val Poschiavo

The road and railway part company at Lago Bianco, for the road heads to the east before writhing down into ever-more green and welcoming country, soon passing across the mouth of the tributary glen of ◐ **Val da Camp**. This is worth a diversion, for Val da Camp is an enchanting valley with meadow and woodland and a string of lakes, tarns and pools in the upper section known as Val Viola. **Rifugio Saoseo** stands at 1986m about 1½hrs from Restaurant Sfazù on the Bernina road, and makes a welcoming base. Owned by the SAC, it has 80 places and is staffed from mid-February until early May, and from mid-June until mid-October (www.sac-bernina.ch). The trail that leads to it gives several options. One takes off into Val Mera behind the refuge and crosses Pass da Val Mera (and the

Val Poschiavo lies far below Piz Palü

Italian border) on its way to Livigno. Another continues northeast to visit the Val Viola lakes before making another border crossing and descending through the Italian Val Viola to reach Valdidentro and Bormio in the upper reaches of the Valtellina. Yet other paths make the most of Val da Camp's south flank, where Lago dal Teo lies cradled in an intimate little cirque under Piz dal Teo and the Cresta della Sperella, and gives a surprise view west to Piz Palü.

About 600m below the lake another trail links one alp to another high above the road, before dropping down to **Poschiavo**, a sunny, tranquil place despite being the main town of the valley, and with more than a hint of Italy in its flagstone piazzas. To suit its size, it has a modest amount of accommodation, several restaurants and shops, banks and a tourist office located near the 15th-century church of San Vittore (www.valposchiavo.ch).

Away from the road, the Bernina Railway (built 1906–10) spirals southward from the Bernina Pass in a series of extraordinary hairpin bends protected here and there by avalanche galleries. A path accompanies the railway as far as Poschiavo, and on the way to **Alp Grüm** the walker looks up at the Palü glacier, and down to the shimmering Lago di Poschiavo far below. West of Alp Grüm lies the little Lagh da Palü, and the path makes a welcome diversion to it, then resumes the descent to rejoin the railway in the flat meadowland of Alpe Cavagliola. From here another trail cuts away towards Alpe Varuna, crosses the Varuna torrent, and rises again across the western wall of Val Poschiavo, in and out of woodland before entering the tributary glen of Val d'Ursè. A steep hike up this glen leads to the 2628m **Pass da Canfinal** which marks the Swiss/Italian border. An Italian bivouac hut has been placed about 20m above the pass. Walkers making a tour of the Bernina range descend from here to the meadows of Alpe Gembrè, then skirt above the artificial Lago di Gera and head for the CAI's Rifugio Bignami located near the base of a ridge sweeping down from the Sasso Moro.

There are other walker's passes that cross the west walling ridge of Val Poschiavo, and these include the Pass d'Ur (1493m) a little south of Corno Campascio, and Pass da Cancian (2464m) a short distance further south again, both of these giving access to the Valle Poschiavina which spills down to Lago di Gera on the route of the Alta Via della Valmalenco.

On the eastern side of Val Poschiavo, 1500m above Poschiavo town, the 2542m **Forca di Sassiglion** carries a route over the mountains into the Italian Val Grosina which leads down into the Valtellina. Apart from these pass crossings all other trails either go from alp to alp along the flanking hillsides, or skirt valley meadows and the lovely

⭐ TOUR OF THE BERNINA ALPS

The following outline tour is not an officially recognised trek, but one that has been created by linking known trails into a multi-day circuit. Experienced trekkers could use this as a basic route with a number of possible variations. It starts and ends at Maloja at the head of the Engadine valley, and makes a clockwise tour of the central block of the Bernina Alps.

Day 1: Leaving **Maloja** wander along the southeast shore of the Lej da Segl to **Sils Maria**, then walk into Val Fex as far as **Curtins** where a trail climbs the eastern hillside, turns a spur at Marmorè, then follows a belvedere course high above the Engadine valley. This trail eventually turns into a stony hanging valley, passes the middle station of the Corvatsch cableway, and brings you to the pass of **Fuorcla Surlej** (2755m) whose Berghaus gazes across Val Roseg to Piz Bernina.

Day 2: Although a direct descent into Val Roseg is possible, the recommendation is to follow a very fine route to the **Coaz Hut** at the head of the valley, then descend to the post-glacial **Lej da Vadret** and wander north all the way through the valley to **Pontresina**, where there's a wide range of accommodation.

Day 3: An easy stage, this works along Val Bernina as far as the entrance to Val Morteratsch. You then take the moraine path above the Morteratsch glacier to the **Boval Hut** where a night is spent at 2495m with another view of Piz Bernina.

Day 4: Either cross the Morteratsch and Pers glaciers to the **Diavolezza**, and descend from there to the **Bernina Pass**; or return downvalley from the Boval Hut as far as **Morteratsch Station**, then head along

Val Bernina to the Bernina Pass to rejoin the main route. From the pass take a popular trail alongside the railway to **Alp Grüm** where there's hotel accommodation in a splendid setting.

Day 5: On this stage the tour descends a little, then rises across the west flank of Val Poschiavo before making an energetic ascent of the hillside to gain the 2628m **Pass da Canfinal** on the Swiss/Italian border. Now on the Italian flank the way descends towards the dammed **Lago di Gera**, then climbs to **Rifugio Bignami**, a CAI hut at 2382m.

Day 6: A short (3hr) stage carries the tour northwestward below the Fellaria and Scerscen glaciers, ending at the large **Rifugio Marinelli** at 2813m reached via the tiny Caspoggio glacier. This hut has places for about 250 in its dormitories, being extremely popular with climbers tackling various routes on the south side of the Bernina range. It's also used by walkers on the Alta Via della Valmalenco.

Day 7: This penultimate stage, which ends at the Longoni Hut, has two main options: a direct route via the 2381m **Forcella d'Entova**, or a more circuitous trail which first descends to **Alpe Musella** and visits Lago Palü before making a long rising traverse to **Rifugio Longoni**, another CAI hut with places for about 37.

Day 8: Monte Disgrazia is on show for most of the first half of this final stage of the trek, as the *Alta Via* is followed round to **Chiareggio**, the uppermost settlement in Val Malenco, after which you begin the climb along an old trade route to the **Passo del Muretto**. Back in Switzerland, the trail now descends to **Lägh da Cavloc** and **Maloja** to complete the tour.

Note: An alternative recommended seven-day linear tour has been devised as a hut-to-hut trek across the Bernina range, starting at Bever and ending at Poschiavo. The Bernina Trek is described and illustrated in a guide of the same name published in 2009 as an e-book by Geoffrey Pocock (see www.leisure-and-business.co.uk).

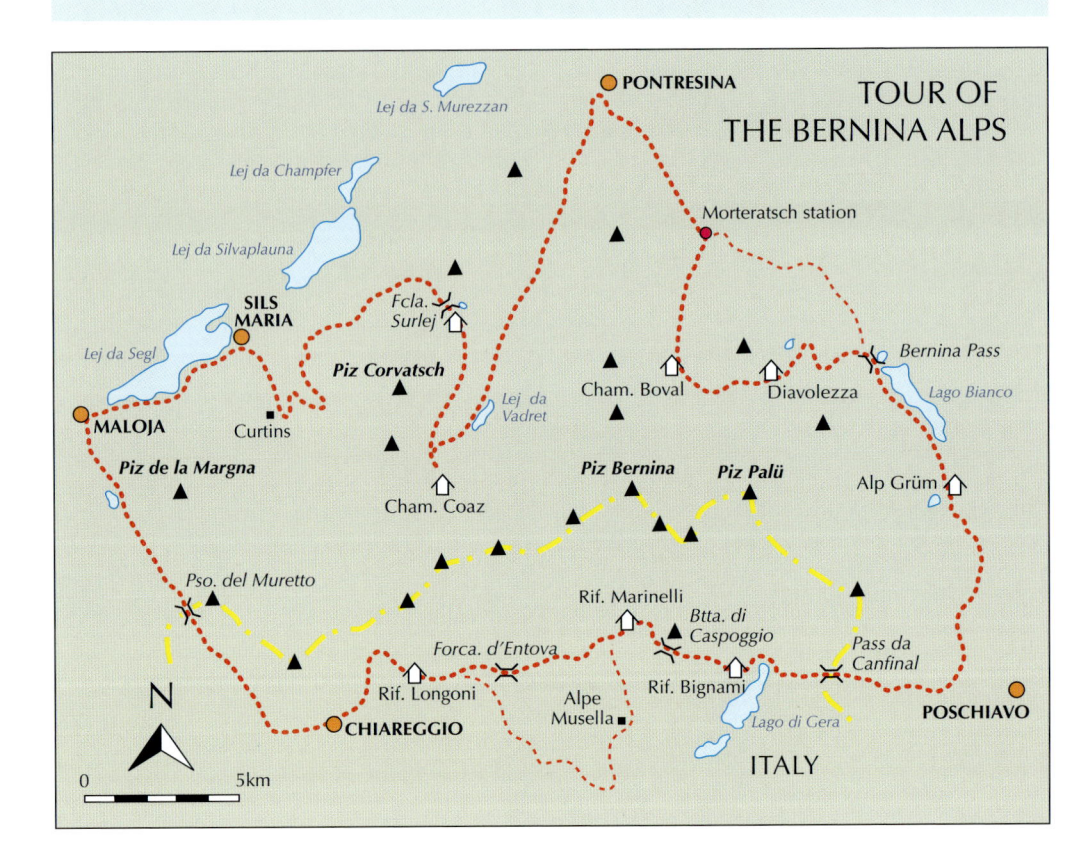

4:5 THE SWISS NATIONAL PARK

Lago di Poschiavo, a gem of a lake lying midway between Poschiavo and Campocologno on the Italian border.

4:5 THE SWISS NATIONAL PARK

Interrupted by the Ofen Pass road which runs from Zernez to Müstair, Switzerland's only national park lies almost entirely within the Lower Engadine (Engiadina Bassa) district, spreading north from Val Trupchun to the west bank of Val S-charl. With an area of only 172 square kilometres it's the second smallest of the 13 national parks in the alpine chain, but having been established in 1914 it's also the oldest, with strictly observed principles that guarantee nature's freedom from Man's interference. Everything here is protected, from the tiniest flower to the tallest tree, from lichens to bearded vultures, from the butterfly to the ibex. Visitors are welcome, indeed are encouraged, to walk the 21 marked trails that run throughout the park, but they're not allowed to stray

Val Cluozza in the heart of the National Park

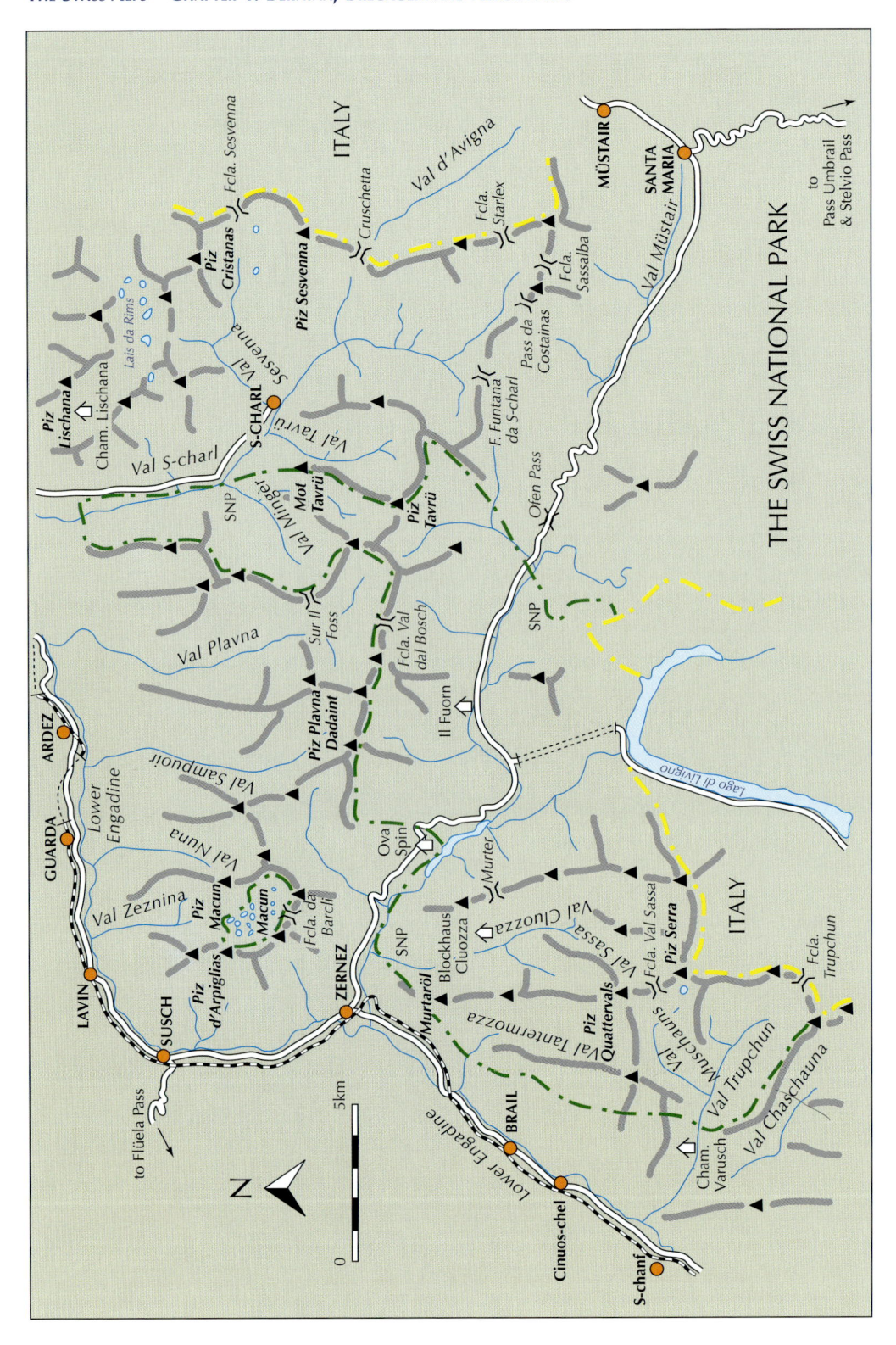

The Swiss Alps – Chapter 4: Bernina, Bregaglia and Albula Alps

from them, and regulations that prevent everything from picking berries to hunting, tree-felling or making unnecessary noise, have helped to achieve a pristine yet truly wild environment, with untamed forests growing up to 2300m, beautiful alpine meadows and abundant wildlife. Chamois, ibex, red and roe deer, large colonies of marmots, hares and foxes all benefit from protective measures that have been in place since the park's inception. Birdlife is well represented, with several species of owl and three of woodpecker; there are kestrels and golden eagles, grouse, partridge and capercaillie, skylarks, ravens, dippers and wrens, and nutcrackers, tree creepers and numerous tits.

The national park's headquarters (www.nationalpark.ch) are in **Zernez**, which sits at a junction of valleys, from where an hourly bus service heads east along the Ofen Pass road. A bus stop at each of the parking areas alongside the road coincides with a footpath that leads into one or more outlying valleys.

Camping and overnight bivouacs are forbidden inside the national park, but there's no shortage of accommodation around its rim, with hotels in most of the Engadine villages and in S-charl, campsites at Zernez, Scuol, and near the entrance to Val Susauna, a mountain hut in Val Trupchun and, on the park's boundary about 6km east of Zernez, dormitory places can be found at the Naturfreundehaus Ova Spin and at Wegerhaus Ova Spin. Within the park itself, about 8km west of the Ofen Pass, the old-fashioned Hotel Il Fuorn has standard rooms and dormitory places in a *matratzenlager* (tel 081 856 12 26). And deep within Val Cluozza at 1882m, some 3hrs walk from Zernez, hut-style lodging is to be had at the rustic **Blockhaus Cluozza** (Chamanna Cluozza). Owned by the national park authority, it has 70 places in beds and dormitories, and is fully staffed from late June until mid-October (tel 081 856 12 35).

Val Trupchun to Val S-charl

Accessible from S-chanf near the border between Upper and Lower Engadine, Val Trupchun is the most southerly of the national park's valleys. Partly wooded, it is headed by 3000m summits and flanked by other peaks that fall only a little short of that height. Its meadows are grazed by deer and chamois. Ibex roam the higher slopes, but small herds can also be seen sometimes on an early summer's morning at a natural salt lick near Alp Purcher. Close to the park's boundary, an hour's walk from S-chanf, stands a privately owned hut, the **Chamanna dal Parc Varusch**. With 40 places and restaurant service, it is open from June until the end of October (tel 081 854 31 22), and it makes a very fine base from which to explore, not only Val Trupchun, but also the neighbouring Val Chaschauna.

From the hut a short 10min walk leads into the park, where the path then continues upvalley to the one-time pig farm of Alp Purcher, soon after which it forks. One route breaks left into Val Müschauns in order to cross the 2857m **Fuorcla Val Sassa** on a cross-country trek to Blockhaus Cluozza; the other follows the north bank of the Ova da Trupchun to the head of the valley, where it then climbs the headwall to cross **Fuorcla Trupchun** (2782m) on the Swiss/Italian border. On the Italian flank the path swoops down to Livigno.

The Fuorcla Val Sassa route is part of a recommended three-day ☆ **tour of the Swiss National Park**. Passing between Piz Serra and Piz Quattervals, the highest of the national park's mountains at 3165m, walkers cross the *fuorcla* and descend through Val Sassa (the 'Valley of Stones') to reach **Blockhaus Cluozza** in 5½hrs from the Varusch Hut. Since it's not permitted to stray from marked trails, the ascent of **Piz Quattervals** from Fuorcla Val Sassa is forbidden. However, a route is allowed via the mountain's NW Ridge which is gained by way of Val Valletta, the blue-white waymarked trail being joined at Plan Valletta a short distance upstream from Blockhaus Cluozza. (Allow 8hrs for a summit-and-back round trip.)

Originally built in 1910, the modernised Cluozza Hut stands above the stream among larch trees, and is invariably busy throughout the summer opening period, so advanced booking is essential if you plan to spend a night there. Its most frequented approach route comes from Zernez. After crossing valley meadows southeast of the village, the trail comes to a plaque dedicated to Paul Sarasin, one of the founders of the national park movement in Switzerland, then climbs along the park's boundary as far as a junction. The left branch (heading south) is the one to take for Blockhaus Cluozza, while the alternative path continues up the mountain spur to gain the 2579m vantage point of **Murtaröl**, with its superb panoramic view which shows (among others) the sharply pointed

Piz Linard in the Silvretta Alps to the north, flanked by glacier-draped peaks.

From Blockhaus Cluozza, the next stage of the tour (or traverse) of the national park climbs eastward, at first through forest, then over open hillsides to gain the flat saddle of **Murter** (2545m) after about 2½hrs. On the east side of the ridge chamois and ibex can often be seen grazing, but it's necessary to keep to the marked way as you descend across the Plan dals Poms, then more steeply in zigzags to Plan Praspöl above the Spöl river, where one of a choice of routes will bring you to **Hotel Il Fuorn** on the Ofen Pass road.

The final stage of the national park traverse goes upvalley a short distance, before turning north into Val dal Bosch. At first narrow and wooded, the valley opens as you gain height, then steepens considerably on the final 500m to the 2677m pass of **Fuorcla Val dal Bosch**, across which runs the national park boundary. From here a retrospective view shows a glimpse of the Bernina Alps to the south, but to the north, and much nearer to hand, rise the so-called Engiadina Dolomites, with the perfectly formed pyramid of Piz Plavna Dadaint capturing one's imagination nearby. Over the pass and out of the park's jurisdiction, the trail sweeps down into a basin at the head of Val Plavna. Here the path splits. The easiest option goes all the way downvalley to Tarasp in the Lower Engadine, but the recommended route contours along the valley's east wall to re-enter the national park at the 2317m saddle of **Sur Il Foss**, and then descends through the lonely **Val Mingèr**, passing bizarre sandstone formations on the way into Val S-charl on the park's outer limit. A 45min walk upvalley leads to the tiny village of **S-charl** where there are three hotels: Gasthof Mayor, Landgasthof Crusch Alba and the Garni Chasa Sesvenna.

Cradled by mountains, but reached by postbus from Scuol, S-charl has a delightfully remote ambience. It nestles at a confluence of streams with the elegant Piz Cristanas standing proud to the northeast, and Piz Sesvenna to the east, the summit of the latter peak marking the Italian border. On either side of Piz Sesvenna walker's passes entice with the promise of long days of exercise, while to the west of Piz Cristanas, tucked on the far side of a mountain rim, the tarns of ◐ **Lais da Rims and Lajet da Lischana** lie scattered on a stony plateau. A path climbs to them from Alp Sesvenna through the Fora da l'Aua, and a continuing trail swings northwestward to reach the SAC's **Chamanna Lischana**, romantically built at 2500m on the west flank of Piz Lischana and with a view out across the Engadine. With 46 places, the hut is fully manned from late June until the end of October (www.lischanahuette.ch).

S-charl is without question a very fine walking centre, for in addition to the handful of outline routes mentioned above, there are plenty more options to consider. West of the village, for example, lies the entrance to **Val Tavrü**, where a broad path/track goes through spacious larch and pinewoods alongside the stream, then swings up to Alp Tavrü standing at 2121m on the valley's west flank. Above the alp a trail then mounts the walling ridge, before striking north along it to gain the summit viewpoint of ◐ **Mot Tavrü** at 2420m, just 2hrs from S-charl – a route for all mountain walkers.

Other possibilities lie at the head of Val S-charl, and on the way to it. One of these is the cross-border route which uses the 2296m saddle of ◐ **Cruschetta** (or S-charlsjoch) below Piz Sesvenna. On the Italian side of the pass the way descends through **Val d'Avigna**, at the bottom of which it's possible to make a return to Switzerland to the border town of Müstair (there's a postbus link with Zernez across the Ofen Pass); but a short way below the Cruschetta another path breaks to the north to make the ascent of **Piz Sesvenna** by a marked route all the way.

The upper reaches of **Val S-charl** consist of generously proportioned pasturelands, streams and boggy patches white with cotton grass. A few lonely alp buildings are all that inhabit these open spaces, but walker's trails cross three passes (**Fuorcla Funtana da S-charl**, **Pass da Costainas** and **Fuorcla Sassalba**), each leading to the Ofen Pass, or into various points east of that road pass in Val Müstair.

At the far western end of the Ofen Pass road, Zernez marks the start of a steeply climbing switchback route that makes the ascent of Munt Baselgia overlooking the confluence of the Spöl and Inn river valleys, reaching a 2945m high point that rewards with great views of the Bernina, Silvretta and Ortler Alps. From here an eastward traverse leads to the **Fuorcletta da Barcli** (2850m) in order to enter the lake-spattered ◐ **Macun cirque**, which became the latest addition to the Swiss National Park on 1 August 2000. This is a wild but scenic enclave of 3.6 square kilometres, a region of old glacial debris among which no less

4:5 THE SWISS NATIONAL PARK

S-charl and Val Sesvenna

than 23 lakes and pools lie trapped in hollows and scoops of moraine at around 2600m. A trail works through the rough basin heading north, then crossing the park boundary it passes between the guarding peaks of **Piz d'Arpiglias** and **Piz Macun**, and descends some 1200m to **Lavin**, the small unassuming village crammed on the north bank of the Inn directly below Piz Linard, highest of the Silvretta Alps (see 7:1).

ACCESS, BASES, MAPS AND GUIDES

Access

Averstal By minor road cutting south of the Hinterrhein's valley 15km from Thusis. Infrequent postbus service from Thusis to Avers-Juf. For Val Madris take the postbus to Avers Cröt and walk from there.

Engadine Valley Road access is via the Maloja Pass (in the south), Bernina and Ofen Passes (from the east), the Julier, Albula and Flüela Passes from the rest of Switzerland, and Austria by way of Martina (Martinsbruck) in the north. By rail, a frequent service comes from Chur to St Moritz via the Albula tunnel, and from St Moritz to Scuol. There's also a fast drive-on drive-off car-carrying service which uses the 19km long Vereina rail tunnel between Klosters and Sagliains (near Lavin).

Val Bregaglia By road either via the Maloja Pass or from Lake Como. There is no rail access, but postbuses run through the valley from the Engadine.

Val Bernina By both bus and rail from Samedan. The Bernina railway runs throughout the valley and descends the Bernina Pass to Val Poschiavo and Tirano.

Valley Bases
Averstal Avers-Juf, and limited accommodation in most hamlets
Engadine Maloja, St Moritz, Zernez, S-charl
Bregaglia Vicosoprano
Bernina Pontresina

Information
Graubünden Tourism, Alexanderstrasse 24, CH-7001 Chur (www.graubunden.co.uk)

Huts
More than a dozen huts (*Chamanna* in Romansch) belonging to the SAC or are privately owned, provide a useful overnight base for walks and climbs in the most popular areas.

Maps
The 1:120,000 sheet Graubünden, published by Kümmerly + Frey, is useful for overall planning purposes, but the same company also produce two Wanderkarten at 1:60,000 that are sufficient for most needs: Oberengadin and Unterengadin. The Swiss National Survey (Landeskarte der Schweiz) have the following sheets at 1:50,000 – 267 San Bernardino, 268 Julierpass, 258 Bergün/Bravuogn, 278 Monte Disgrazia, 249 Tarasp, 259 Ofenpass/Pass dal Fuorn, 269 Passo del Bernina

Walking and/or Trekking Guides
Walks in the Engadine by Kev Reynolds (Cicerone, 3rd edition 2019)

The Tour of the Bernina by Gillian Price (Cicerone 2015)

Walking in Switzerland by Clem Lindenmayer (Lonely Planet, 2nd edition 2001)

Alpinwandern Graubünden by Peter Donatsch and Paul Meinherz (SAC)

The Bernina Trek by Geoffrey Pocock (www.leisure-and-business.co.uk 2009)

Climbing Guides
Bernina and Bregaglia by Lindsay Griffin (Alpine Club, 1995)

Bündner Alpen 3 – Avers; San Bernardino to Septimer Pass (SAC)

Bündner Alpen 4 – Bregaglia and Monte Disgrazia (SAC)

Bündner Alpen 5 – Bernina Group and Val Poschiavo (SAC)

Bündner Alpen 6 – Septimer to the Flüela Pass (SAC)

Bündner Alpen 9 – Lower Engadine and Val Müstair (SAC)

Bündner Alpen 10 – Central Engadine and Val Poschiavo (SAC)

The Alpine 4000m Peaks by the Classic Routes by Richard Goedeke (Bâton Wicks, 2nd edition 2003)

The 4000m Peaks of the Alps by Martin Moran (Alpine Club, 2007)

Eastern Alps: the Classic Routes on the Highest Peaks by Dieter Seibert (Diadem, 1992)

Skitouring Guides
Alpine Ski Mountaineering: Volume 2 by Bill O'Connor (Cicerone, 2003)

Skitouren Graubünden (SAC)

See Also
The High Mountains of the Alps by Helmut Dumler and Willi P Burkhardt (Diadem, 1994)

Walking in the Alps by Kev Reynolds (Cicerone, 2nd edition 2005)

Walking in the Alps by J Hubert Walker (Oliver & Boyd, 1951)

Freie Sicht aufs Gipfelmeer by Marco Volken and Remo Kundert (SAC/Salvioni Edizioni, 2003)

Badile: Kathedrale aus Granit by Marco Volken (AS-Verlag, Zürich)

Piz Bernina: König der Ostalpen by Daniel Anker (AS-Verlag, Zürich)

Piz Palü: Dreiklang in Fels und Eis by Daniel Anker and Hans Philipp (AS-Verlag, Zürich)

Adventures of an Alpine Guide by Christian Klucker (John Murray, 1932)

Starlight and Storm by Gaston Rébuffet (Dent, 1956)

Fifty Years of Alpinism by Riccardo Cassin (Diadem, 1981)

Nanga Parbat Pilgrimage: The Lonely Challenge by Hermann Buhl (Bâton Wicks, 1998)

CHAPTER 5: BERNESE ALPS

Often referred to as the Bernese Oberland, the mountains extend along the north flank of the Rhône valley from Martigny to the Grimsel Pass.

BERNESE ALPS: CHAPTER SUMMARY

Location
North of the Pennine Alps, and stretching in an unbroken line of 112km from the low valley of the Rhône, south of Lac Léman, to the Grimsel Pass, this is the longest major range in the Alps. The Rhône valley forms its southern limit, but to the north the mountains fold away to minor summits before foothills spill into the Mittelland.

★ Highlights

🟢 Walks
- Tour des Muverans (5:1)
- Crossing of the Hohtürli (5:5)
- Faulhornweg (5:8)
- Tour of the Jungfrau Region (5:8)
- The Grosser Aletschgletscher (5:10)
- Lötschentaler Höhenweg (5:10)
- Alpine Pass Route (5:10)

🟣 Climbs
- Eiger North Face (5:8)
- Schreckhorn (5:8)
- Finsteraarhorn (5:8)
- Wetterhorn (5:8)
- Eldorado slabs (5:9)
- Aletschhorn via the Hasler Rib (5:10)

🟠 Summits for all
- Arpelistock (5:2)
- Wildstrubel (5:3)
- Bütlasse (5:6)

Contents

5:1 Alpes Vaudoises	296
Tour des Muverans (box)	299
Leysin	301
5:2 Les Diablerets to the Rawil Pass	301
The Lauenental	304
Ober Simmental	304
5:3 The Wildstrubel Massif	306
Engstligenalp	307
5:4 Kandersteg and the Gemmipass	308
Melchior Anderegg: The King of Guides (box)	309
5:5 Blüemlisalp and the Gasterntal	310
5:6 The Kiental	313
5:7 Lauterbrunnen Valley	316
Mürren	318
Wengen and Kleine Scheidegg	320
The Jungfraujoch	321
Climbs from the Guggi Hut	322
The Upper Valley	322
Climbs from the Rottal Hut	323
Climbs from the Schmadri Hut	324
UNESCO World Natural Heritage Site (box)	325
5:8 Grindelwald and the Lütschental	325
Tour of the Jungfrau Region (box)	327
The Grindelwald Basin	329
The Eiger	330
The 4000ers	332
The Wetterhorn	334
5:9 Haslital and Grimsel Pass	336
Urbachtal	338
Grimselsee	339
Grimsel Pass	340
5:10 The Southern Valleys	341
Fieschertal	341
The Aletsch Glacier	343
Lötschental	344
Leukerbad	348
Alpine Pass Route (box)	349
Access, Bases, Maps and Guides	351

◀ *Mürren, perched above the Lauterbrunnen valley*

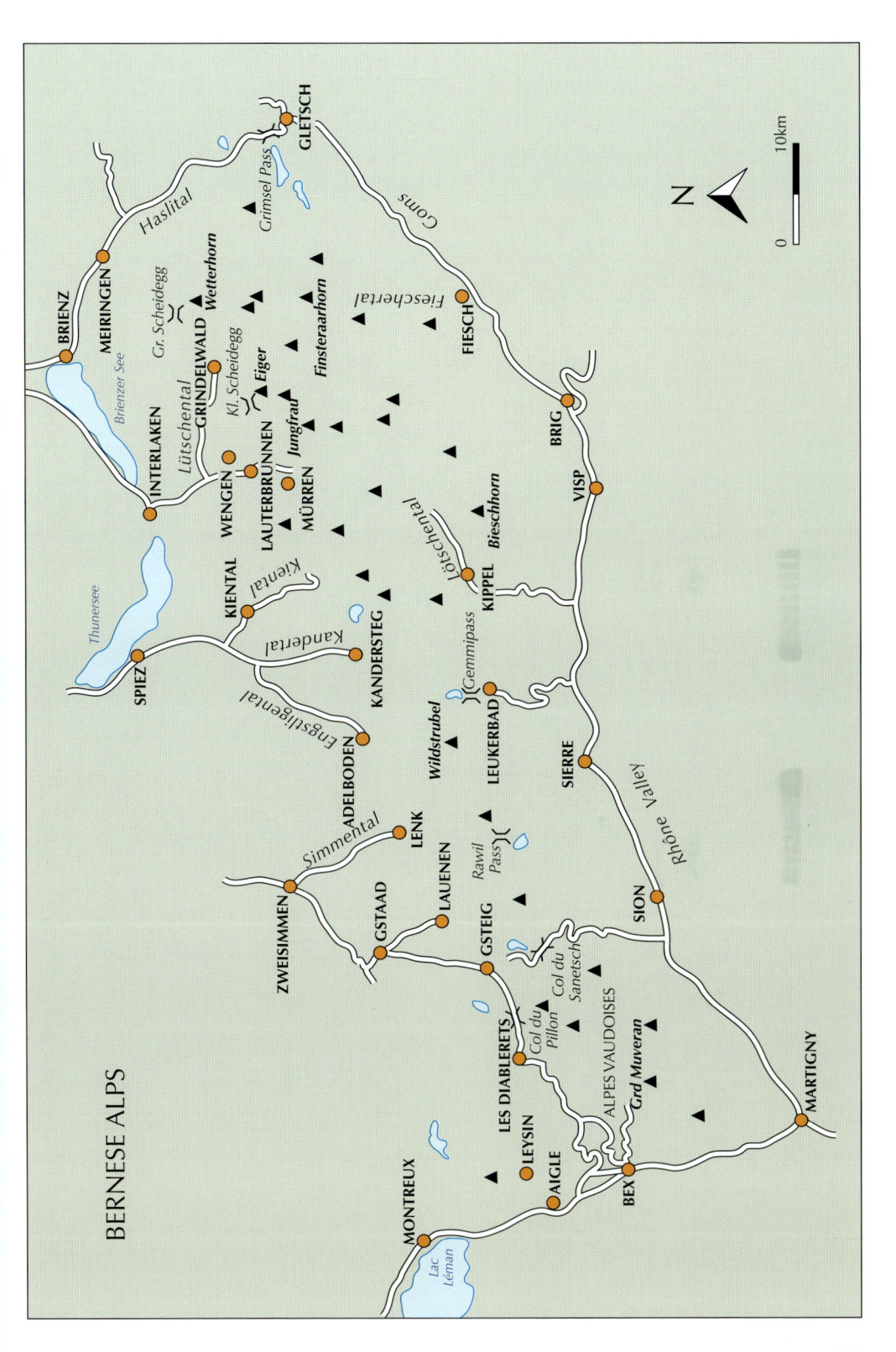

BERNESE ALPS

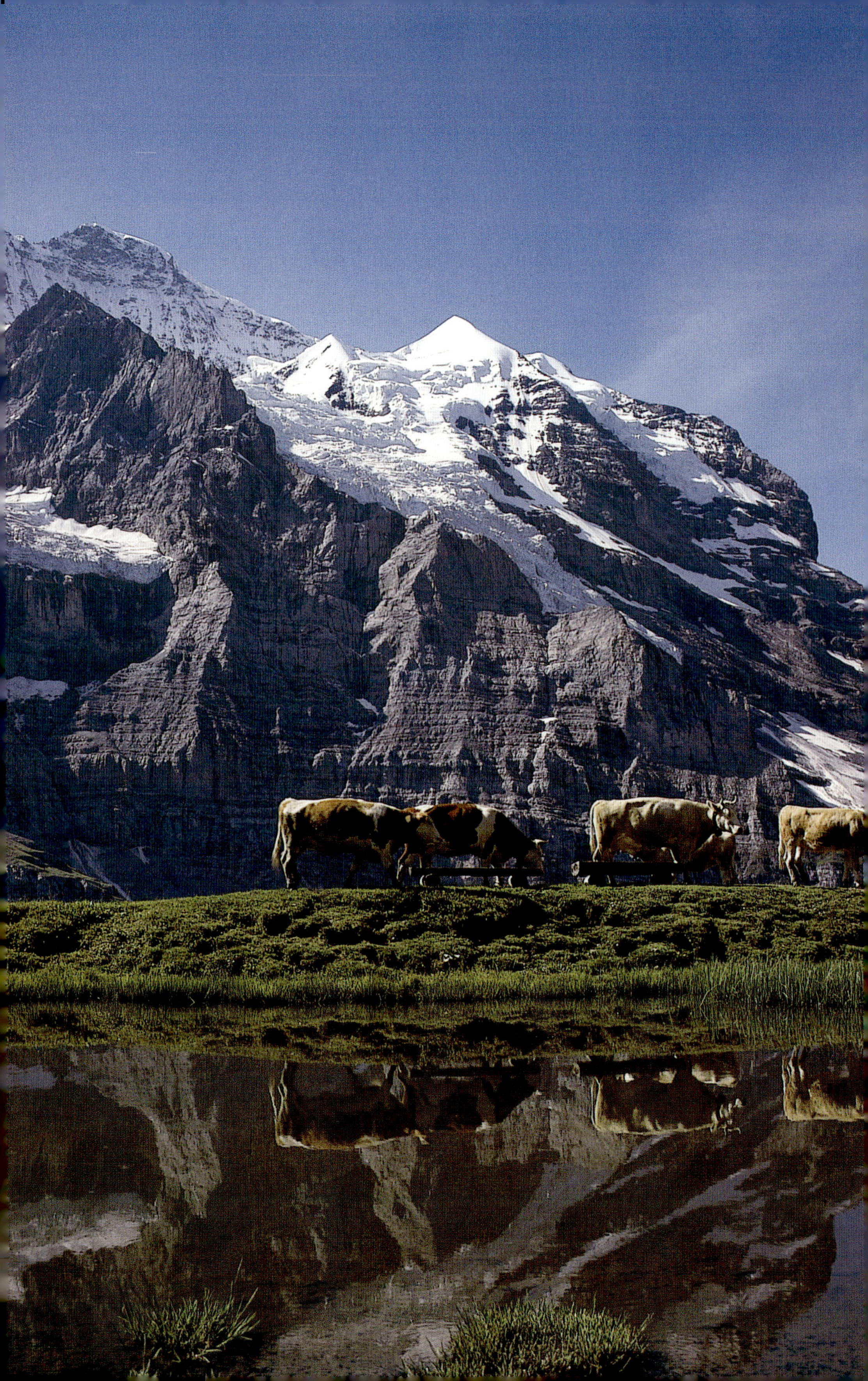

BERNESE ALPS: INTRODUCTION

No earthly object that I have seen approaches in grandeur to the stupendous mountain wall whose battlements overhang in mid-air the villages of Lauterbrunnen and Grindelwald.

Leslie Stephen, *The Playground of Europe*

In terms of altitude the Bernese Alps may be slightly inferior to the Pennine chain, but they are no less attractive or inspiring than their neighbours to the south, and their wealth of opportunities for the active walker, climber and ski-touring enthusiast is legendary. Containing eight 4000m peaks and many others of 3000m and more, the mountains have iconic appeal, especially those above Grindelwald, among which the ascent by Alfred Wills of the Wetterhorn in 1854 gave birth to the Golden Age of mountaineering. Among its many glaciers, that of the Grosser Aletsch is the longest ice sheet in Western Europe, which now lies at the heart of the first World Natural Heritage Site to be designated in the Alps by UNESCO.

Despite the region attracting some of the most turbulent weather conditions in all Switzerland, tourism has long played an important role in its economy, thanks to the unquestionable beauty of its landscapes. For the valleys are as diverse and romantically ordered as any in the alpine chain, and the popularity of Grindelwald, Wengen, Mürren, Kandersteg and Adelboden – to name but a few of its resorts – testifies to that beauty which seduces beyond the smart hotels and glossy brochures. And if the weather is at times not what the brochures might suggest, you need only look at the greenness of the valleys and the size of the glaciers to appreciate that they are as they are partly because of all that precipitation.

For convenience the range may be separated into two sections, east and west, with the dividing line being drawn across the Gemmipass south of Kandersteg. The western chain is a good district

The alp of Hinderer Wispile lies below Les Diablerets

◂ *The Jungfrau forms a backing to Kleine Scheidegg*

for first-season alpinists with plenty of low-altitude climbing, and it begins above and to the east of Evionnaz, between St-Maurice and Martigny in the Rhône valley, where the Dents de Morcles project from a ridge spreading up to the Grand Muveran, the first of the 3000m summits. Straddling the canton borders of Vaud and Valais, these peaks have their advocates, of course, but it's the complex massif of Les Diablerets that draws most attention here. Winter sports having given prominence to such resorts as Villars, Leysin, Château-d'Oex and Gstaad, it is skiing that also brings visitors to Les Diablerets (resort and mountain) in winter, with lifts and tows adding alien clutter to the northern slopes above Col du Pillon. In summer, however, there's modest climbing to be had and no shortage of trails to explore without the crowds.

Canton Vaud gives way to Canton Bern on the 3123m summit of the Oldenhorn, after which the ridge, which forms the watershed between the Rhône and the Rhine via its tributary the Aare, makes an arc around the Sanetsch basin before reaching the Arpelistock and Wildhorn overlooking the Lauenental. Both of these peaks rise above the apron-like Gelten glacier and would suit first-season alpinists, as would the 3243m Wildstrubel, noted for its Plaine Morte glacier plateau which that much-travelled mountain explorer Martin Conway reckoned to be one of the most remarkable sights in the Alps.

To the east of the Plaine Morte, from which it is separated by a ridge running from the Wildstrubel to the Rothorn by way of the Schneehorn, the Wildstrubel glacier drains into the Daubensee which lies in a long scoop of a valley culminating at the Gemmipass, an ancient pass known since at least the 13th century, and an obvious line of division between the western and eastern Bernese Alps.

Represented by the famous Eiger, Mönch and Jungfrau, the mountains east of the Gemmi are better known by far than their western counterparts, with their northern aspect being the true Bernese Oberland – an epithet sometimes wrongly attributed to the Bernese Alps as a whole. Angling northeast the range is much wider now, with three parallel ridges rising to an icy crown from which a chaos of glaciers – remnants of the massive ice sheet that once covered much of central Switzerland – mostly drain into the Rhône, while the virtually ice-free north flank plunges to pastures ringing with cowbells.

All of the 4000m peaks are gathered in this section of the chain, but many others ranged around and beyond them are every bit as appealing and challenging despite failing to reach that magical spot height, and here I think especially of Bietschhorn, Blüemlisalp, Gspaltenhorn, two Breithorns (Lauterbrunnen and Lötschentaler), Eiger and Wetterhorn. These defy denigration as bit-players, and would stand out in any mountain region.

So much for the mountains. Some of the valleys that flow between them are almost as dramatic in their appeal as the summits themselves. Take the Lauterbrunnental as a prime example. From its untamed upper reaches below the curious Lauterbrunnen Wetterhorn, to its confluence with the Lütschental at Zweilütschinen, the precipitous, waterfall-streaked walls and flat bed make this the perfect example of a glacier-cut valley. Wengen is perched upon its east flank, Mürren on its west, both giving unforgettable views of the Jungfrau, as graceful a mountain as any in the alpine chain. And on the other side of the Lauterbrunnental's headwall, the Lötschental conjures an image of how the Alps might have appeared to the Victorian pioneers who came here when virgin summits were ten-a-penny.

For the ambitious climber with an eye on epic routes, as for traditional mountaineers, walkers, ski tourers and dreamers, the Bernese Alps have plenty to offer.

5:1 ALPES VAUDOISES

This westernmost portion of the chain, spreading as far as Les Diablerets, is commonly known as Les Alpes Vaudoises, and rising directly from the low-lying Rhône, the mountains can appear much higher than they really are. When viewed from the Dents du Midi, for example, the cloud-piercing Dents de Morcles and Grand Muveran appear especially alluring, as they do from Gryon above Bex. This small group has much to offer both the mountain walker and the climber content with modest ascents and big views from his summits. As well as gaps between the mountains that enable fit walkers to cross from one side to the other, there's no shortage of huts and linking trails that remain high and therefore avoid the necessity of descending to the main valleys.

5:1 ALPES VAUDOISES

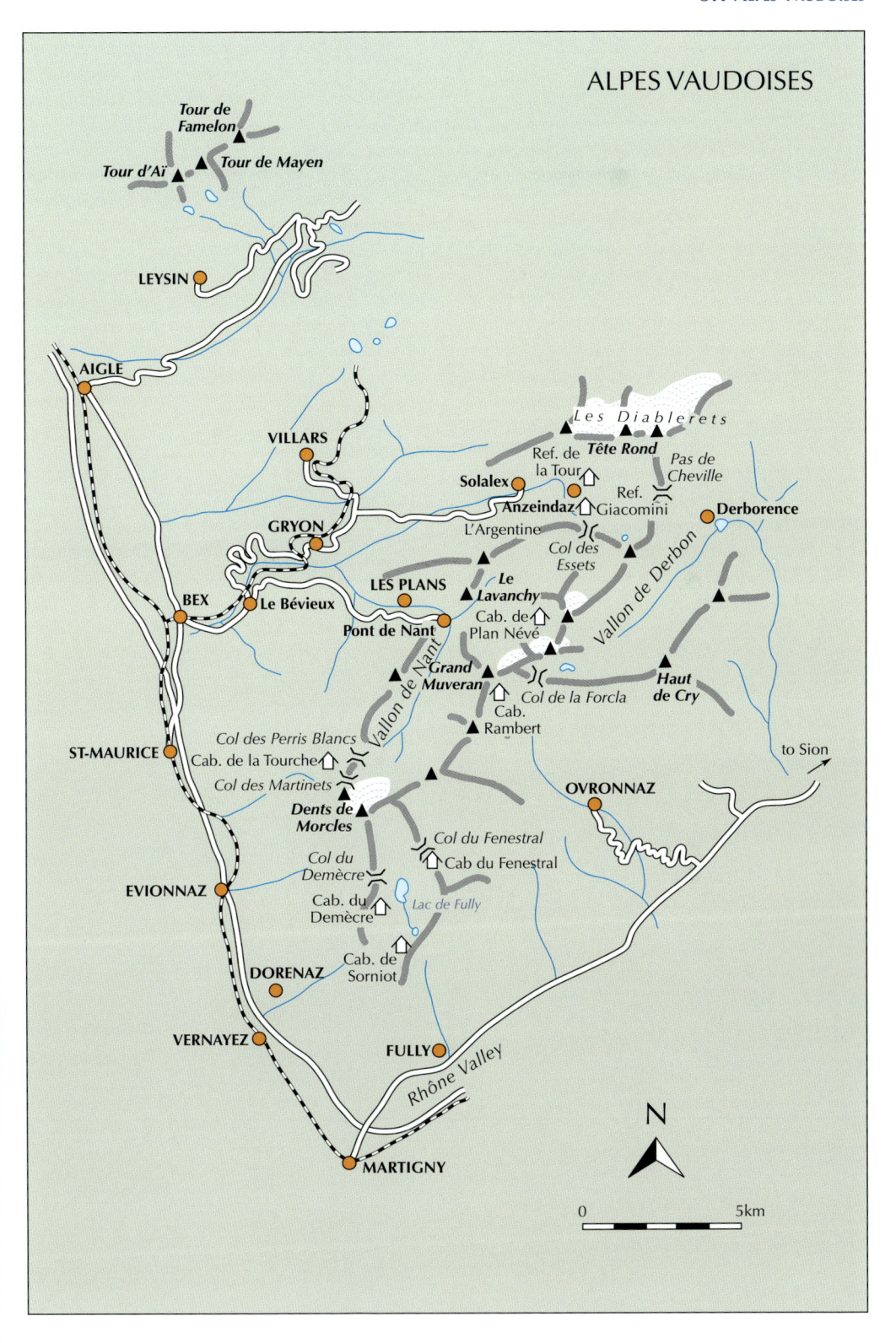

Although access is perfectly feasible from the southeast, there's no better way to discover the true nature of the district than by drifting in from the southern end of Lac Léman. Here, lying on the east side of the Rhône a few kilometres north of St-Maurice, the small town of **Bex** is noteworthy only for the fact that it has the last working salt mine in Switzerland nearby, and is linked with the ski resort of **Villars** by rack-railway. From the town a minor road climbs in 7km via **Le Bévieux** to **Les Plans**, or Les-Plans-sur-Bex to give its full title, a small village of timber chalets set in a lush green basin northwest of the Grand Muveran. The village also has a church, two restaurants, a food store and b&b accommodation at the Chalet Beausite, and is served by postbus from Bex. A narrow side road continues eastward through woods as far as **Pont de Nant** (1253m) at a confluence of valleys. It is here that the University of Lausanne has an alpine botanical garden containing around 2500 plant species from many of the world's mountain ranges, and an overnight could happily be spent at the Auberge Communale, from where several expeditions begin.

Rough pastures flanked by rock walls arouse the imagination, and built on a prominent site below the Tête à Pierre Grept east of Pont de Nant at 2262m, the **Cabane de Plan Névé** can be reached in 2½–3hrs. This climber's hut does not belong to the SAC, but is open to all with 35 places and a resident warden in July and August (www.montagne.ch/plan-neve.asp). Northeast of Pont de Nant the limestone slabs of **L'Argentine** are said to offer excellent climbing at a modest altitude, although most of the action is focused on the north side above the hamlet of **Solalex**. On the nearby 1498m **Le Lavanchy**, however, a short practice *via ferrata* offers a try-out for aspirants, while a trek heading northeast takes the walker beside the long Argentine wall and over **Col des Essets** (2029m) to the hamlet of **Anzeindaz** below Les Diablerets, where there are two huts: **Refuge Giacomini** at 1900m (80 places; tel 024 498 22 95) and **Refuge de la Tour** (70 places; tel 024 498 11 47) at 1880m.

Southeast of Pont de Nant the imposing dolomitic walls of the 3051m **Grand Muveran** erupt from the pastures, but its upper reaches are confused by Pointe des Encrenes which stands in front as if to shield its higher neighbour from too much attention. A fairly demanding 4½hr crossing of the

The Alpes Vaudoises, seen across the Rhône valley from the Dents du Midi

Muveran's SSW Ridge at the 2589m Frête de Saille (dangerous when coated with ice or snow) leads to **Cabane Rambert** on the south flank. Property of the Diablerets section of the SAC, it has 36 places and is fully staffed from mid-June to the end of September (www.cas-diablerets.ch). From here a roped scramble leads to the summit with its magnificent panoramic view of the Pennine Alps stretching from the Weissmies to Mont Blanc. The Vaud/Valais border runs across the Muveran summit and continues eastward before veering northeast towards Les Diablerets, while a secondary ridge extends eastward to the 2969m peak of **Haut de Cry** where J J Bennen, one of the great guides of the Golden Age, lost his life in an avalanche in 1864.

To the south of Pont de Nant the wildly romantic **Vallon de Nant** (a nature reserve) has the twin **Dents de Morcles** at its head. The 2936m Petite, and 2968m Grande Dent de Morcles project side by side from a headwall whose ridges splay out in four directions. On the more northerly of these, between the Pointe des Martinets and Pointe des Perris Blancs, the 2544m Col des Perris Blancs carries the route of the Tour des Muverans (see box) over the mountains from **Cabane de la Tourche**. Set 1000m above Morcles village, but less than 500m below the col, this SAC refuge has 60 places and is manned from June until the end of September (tel 079 471 98 56). A trail heads south from the hut, and passing below **Col des Martinets**, turns a spur running down from the Petite Dent de Morcles, and then an alternative path strikes up and across the precipitous West Face, partly on scree, but in places cut into the rock before the final slope leads to the summit of the ⊙ **Grande Dent de Morcles**. From here views are not only of neighbouring Vaudois peaks and ridges, but are especially fine to the south and east where the Pennine Alps stretch far off, while to the west the Dents du Midi rise in an outburst of rock from the Rhône valley. As R L G Irving once proclaimed, there is not a better view in the district.

The Dents de Morcles are well served with huts, for on the south flank and reached by steep trails from Fully near Martigny, **Cabane du Demècre** (tel 027 746 35 87), **Cabane de Sorniot** (or Sorgno; tel 027 746 24 26), and **Cabane du Fenestral** (tel 027 746 20 80) all provide overnight accommodation. Each of these belongs to Fully-based clubs, but as with SAC huts, they're open to all-comers.

The southeast flank of the district folds into a whole series of combes and minor valleys above the vineyards and orchards of the Rhône valley. It's all attractive country, with rock and scree above alpine meadows, then grass slopes that plunge to woodland, then onto terraced vineyards. A few roads and farm tracks make their tortuous way up these slopes, but waymarked trails are plentiful. Under the south wall of Les Diablerets, the tiny summer-only hamlet of **Derborence** (1449m) lies snug within a classic mountain cirque by the side of a shallow lake formed by an 18th-century rockfall that destroyed 40 chalets and blocked the Derbonne stream. Reached by road from Conthey, near Sion, Derborence has dormitory accommodation in the Auberge du Godet and the Refuge du Lac de Derborence (tel 027 346 14 28).

Almost 600m above Derborence to the northwest, the gentle ⊙ **Pas de Cheville** (2038m) carries a walker's route over the final gap in the mountains before the massif of Les Diablerets takes over. On the west side of the pass lies the scattered hamlet of **Anzeindaz** which, as we have already seen, may be reached by walkers coming from Pont de Nant across the Col des Essets. But it can also be reached by a minor road from Gryon which goes as far as Solalex, 2km west of, and 200m below, Anzeindaz.

★ TOUR DES MUVERANS

This four-day high-level circuit of the Muveran/Dents de Morcles massif covers a distance of a little over 50km, treks through a variety of landscapes, crosses several passes, and rewards with spectacular views of the Pennine Alps, Mont Blanc and the Dents du Midi. There's no shortage of accommodation, but it's a reasonably tough route with plenty of height gain and loss on some sections. Whilst it could as easily be started from Pont de Nant, the suggestion here is to begin at Derborence and to follow the route in a clockwise direction. For information visit www.tourdesmuverans.ch.

Day 1: From **Derborence** begin by heading southwest on a steady climb through the Vallon de Derbon. Beyond the alp of Six Long the way rises to the upper pastures of Pro Fleuri, and continues to a small reservoir at 2450m in the basin of La Forcla. Pass along the north shore of the lake, then

THE SWISS ALPS – CHAPTER 5: BERNESE ALPS

TOUR DES MUVERANS

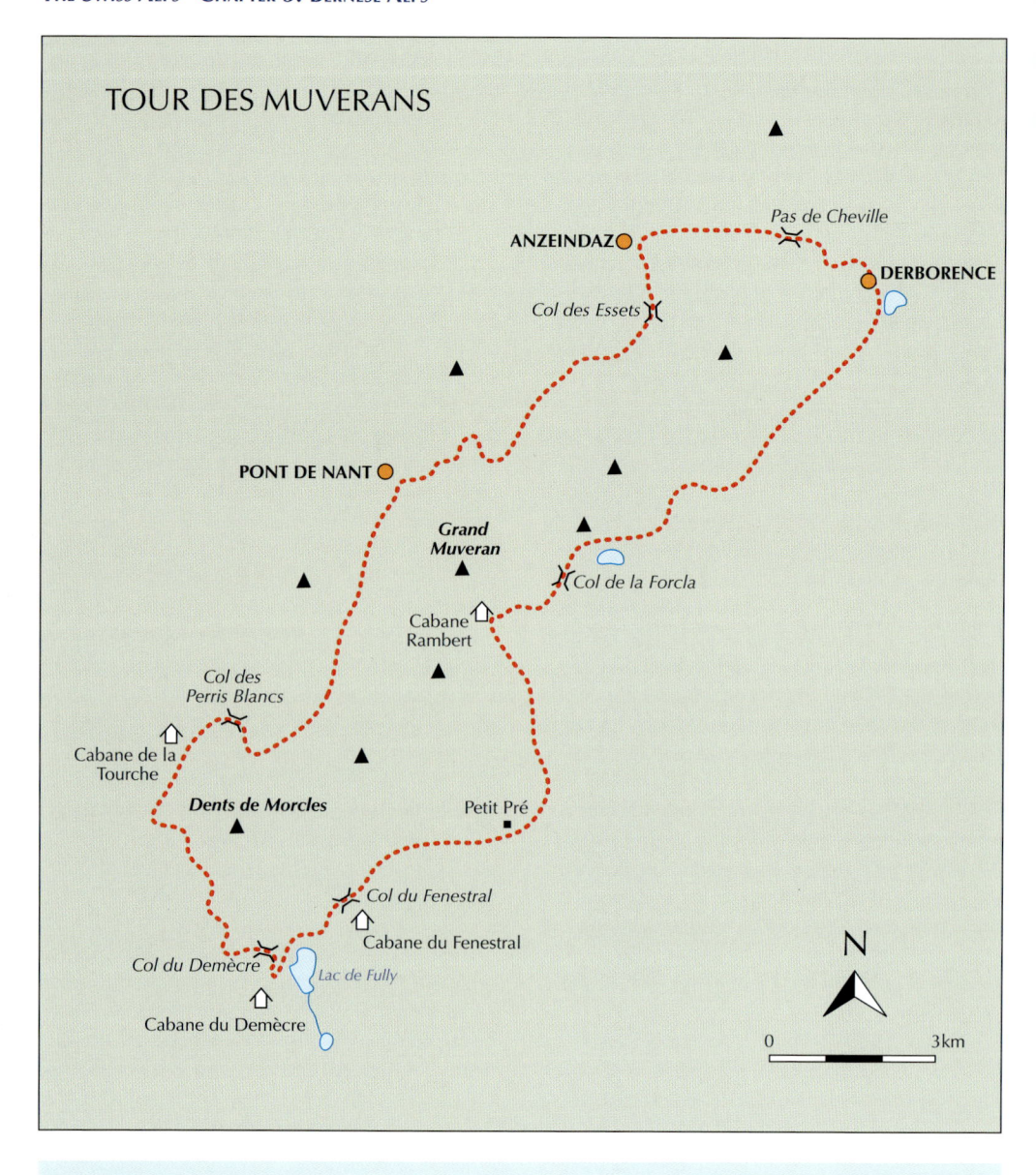

over glacial remnants to gain the 2612m **Col de la Forcla**. A steep descent on the south side leads to a traverse over scree, before a final steep pull brings you up to **Cabane Rambert**, about 5hrs from Derborence.

Day 2: With two cols on this next 5hr stage, the day begins with a steep 800m descent before heading south then southwest, rising across the hillside high above the Rhône to the buildings of **Petit Pré**. From here the route trends westward into the Euloi basin on the way to **Col du Fenestral** at 2453m. **Cabane du Fenestral** nearby enjoys a fine view onto Lac de Fully. On the western side of the hollow which contains the lake, **Cabane du Demècre** stands on the **Col du Demècre** at 2361m, and is gained about 1½hrs from the Fenestral hut.

Day 3: On occasion during the summer, the Swiss military use the country between Col du Demècre and Col des Perris Blancs for exercises, which may delay the start of this stage of the Tour des Muverans. From the col you turn a spur and head north then northwest along the west flank of the **Dents de Morcles**, with exciting views of the Dents du Midi across the Rhône valley. About 2½hrs into the trek **Cabane de la Tourche** is gained. From here the route swings to the east and climbs in another 45mins to **Col des Perris Blancs**. Vallon des Nants stretches to the northeast, and having descended into it, a trail leads past the Grand Muveran and brings you to **Pont de Nant** for overnight accommodation in the Auberge Communale.

Day 4: This concluding stage of the tour works a way northeast among pastures below L'Argentine, then up and over **Col des Essets** in order to gain the hamlet of **Anzeindaz**. It is here that you reach the northernmost point of the tour and head east on an easy approach to **Pas de Cheville** under the looming presence of Les Diablerets. Given decent conditions, tremendous views of the Pennine Alps gained from this final pass will no doubt delay your descent to **Derborence**.

Leysin

Before leaving the Alpes Vaudoises and looking at Les Diablerets, it's worth turning briefly to a small group of grey limestone mountains (the highest is Tour de Mayen at 2326m) stretching northeast above **Aigle** and then declining between Col des Mosses and Lac de l'Hongrin. With one-time health resort **Leysin** the main base, a choice of easy ascents and short but challenging rock climbs can be found on the Tour d'Aï, Tour de Mayen and Tour de Famelon, the southern slopes of the latter being protected as a nature reserve, while much of the country lying between the north side of the Tour d'Aï and Lac de l'Hongrin is a military zone with limited public access.

Spread across the south-facing slopes of the group, Leysin is a popular, if modest, ski resort and home of the highly respected International School of Mountaineering which was founded here in 1965 (www.alpin-ism.com). Resort facilities are good and accommodation plentiful, including a campsite open throughout the year. For information contact the tourist office (www.leyson.ch).

For rock climbers the 2331m ✪ **Tour d'Aï** is perhaps the most rewarding of the group, with sport climbs and an airy 150m *via ferrata* attracting attention. Easily reached from the Berneuse gondola lift below the WSW Face, numerous routes of between 70 and 150m have been created; most of these are at least partly protected. The nearby ✪ **Tour de Mayen** is noted for the south-facing 130m high cliff of Le Diamant, which soars above a small lake and also gives a fine selection of climbs in a splendid setting.

5:2 LES DIABLERETS TO THE RAWIL PASS

The sprawling massif of Les Diablerets dominates the Vaud/Bern border south of Col du Pillon. On the western side of the col, and almost 300m below it, lies the unassuming village of **Les Diablerets** spread across meadows facing the Creux de Champ, a cirque buttressed by the Culan in the west, and the Sex Rouge spur on the east. In *The Rough Guide to Switzerland* Matthew Teller considered the resort so tranquil that 'it's almost a shame to mark it on a map'. Served by the ASD railway from Aigle, and by bus from Gstaad, Les Diablerets has most facilities, a clutch of hotels and chalets and tourist information (www.alpes.ch/diablerets). Mechanical lifts on both sides of the valley suggest a concentration of downhill skiing, but in summer a number of tracks and trails give walkers plenty of scope. Some of the best skiing here takes place on the massif after which the resort takes its name, for lifts carry enthusiasts from Col du Pillon up to Sex Rouge on the north flank at almost 3000m.

Sex Rouge (2971m) and its easterly neighbour, the 3123m **Oldenhorn** (also known as the Becca d'Auden), form the northernmost horns of the Diablerets massif, most of whose summits range along the rim of the rapidly disappearing Tsanfleuron glacier plateau and the icy tributaries for which it was once known. The highest peak is the 3210m Sommet des Diablerets which overlooks the Pas de Cheville and, via a brief diversion to the southeast, the scene of the massive 18th-century landslips mentioned above in 5:1.

The Swiss Alps – Chapter 5: Bernese Alps

LES DIABLERETS TO RAWIL PASS

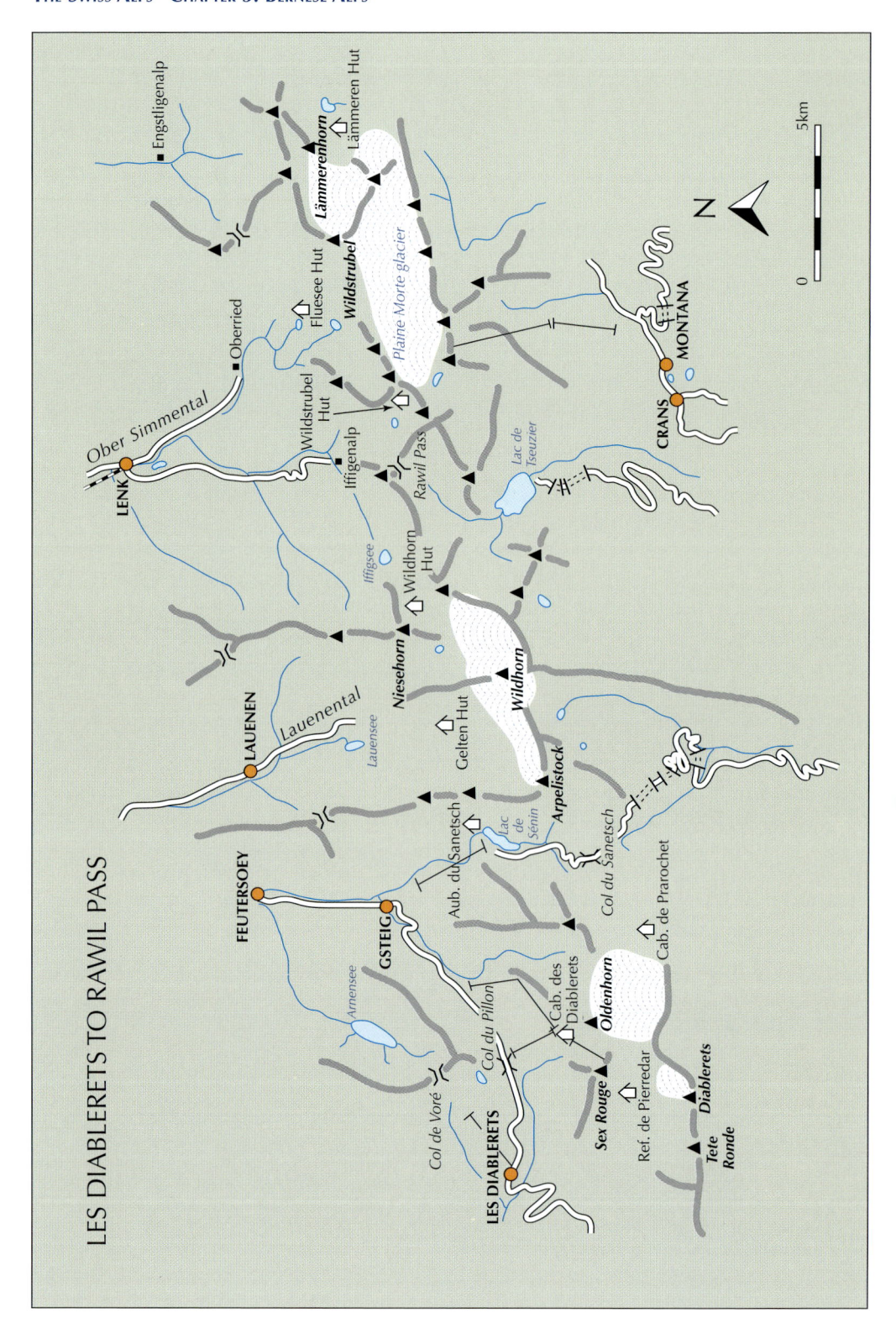

There are three huts: the SAC-owned **Cabane des Diablerets** at 2485m on the northern slopes by the ski lifts (80 places, manned mid-June to mid-October; www.cas-chaussy.ch); **Refuge de Pierredar** (2293m) which belongs to the Club de Pierredar and lies southwest of Sex Rouge (22 places, manned mid-June until end of September; tel 024 492 13 03), and **Cabane de Prarochet** which is found at 2555m on smooth slabs below the Tsanfleuron glacier, reached in a little under 2hrs from Col du Sanetsch. Property of the Savièse Ski Club, it has 44 places and is manned from the end of June until mid-September (tel 027 395 27 27).

First climbed by the prodigious 19th-century alpine explorer Gottlieb Studer, the *voie normale* on the **Sommet des Diablerets** makes a fine snowshoe ascent in winter starting from the top of the two-stage cable car on the Sex Rouge. The lack of snow and ice makes it a less attractive proposition in summer, although perhaps the more entertaining route is that which tackles the mountain from the Pierredar Hut and involves a *via ferrata* to gain the Prapio glacier, then chains and ladders to reach Col de Paprio and the Tsanfleuron glacier where the normal route is joined. Mont Blanc, the Pennine Alps and a mass of Bernese summits fill an extensive summit panorama.

On the east side of the massif the 2251m **Col du Sanetsch** carries a minor road over the mountains from Sion to the Lac de Sénin reservoir close to the Valais/Bern border (bus from Sion), from where a steep path descends to Gsteig. Overlooking the lake from the southwest a fairly extensive area of **limestone crags** stretching from Les Montons to the Gstellihorn offer sport on aid-protected routes up to 300m long, many of which were created by well-known local activists, the brothers Claude and Yves Remy. Accommodation in beds and dormitories is available at the **Auberge du Sanetsch** situated at the barrage.

Auberge du Sanetsch is not only a useful base for climbers drawn by the Montons crags, but it's also an obvious place from which to make the ascent of the 3035m ☆ **Arpelistock**, by an uncomplicated outing made memorable by a series of glorious views. By no means an eye-catching peak, its location at a junction of ridges above the Sanetsch basin makes the Arpelistock a commanding vantage point from which to survey the Pennine range to the south. From Lac de Sénin a good path is taken up to the Col du Sanetsch, where you then

Bereft of snow, Les Diablerets reveals its contorted strata (Photo: Alexandre Luczy)

mount the Arête de l'Arpille and follow the ridge all the way to the summit (about 3½hrs from the Auberge).

About 10km south of Gstaad, **Gsteig** straddles the Col du Pillon road northeast of the pass and below the Sénin lake. A tiny but attractive village, whose main features are the church, with its slender pointed steeple, and the nearby heavy-beamed 18th-century Hotel Bären, is dwarfed by the towering crags of the Diablerets massif. Served by the Gstaad to Les Diablerets postbus, Gsteig has just three hotels, but several chalets and holiday apartments, a campsite, and a general store. For tourist information tel 033 755 81 81.

To access the crags above Lac de Sénin from Gsteig, the Sanetschbahn cable car goes almost as far as the reservoir dam to save a lengthy walk, but those who are in Gsteig to walk rather than climb, will find a limited number of local routes, unless they are prepared to create itineraries based on the Alpine Pass Route (see box), for example, which passes through the village. One suggestion would be to head west along the APR as far as **Col de Voré** on the Bern/Vaud border, then head southwest to the lovely tree-enclosed ◯ **Lac Retaud** north of Col du Pillon. From the lake other linking paths and farm tracks lead back to Gsteig.

Perhaps of more interest to walkers would be a longer circuit which breaks away from the APR at the alp farm of Seeberg (about 3hrs from Gsteig), then drops down to the southern end of the ◯ **Arnensee**, at the far end of which trails strike off to the scattered village of **Feutersoey** on the road to Gstaad. A trail on the east side of the road returns to Gsteig.

The Lauenental
Heading northeast away from Gsteig, a path adopted by the Alpine Pass Route crosses the wooded Krinnen Pass on the way to the tranquil Lauenental. Lying about 6km southeast of Gstaad, the unpretentious little village of **Lauenen** (1241m) gazes upvalley to a splendid headwall running from Arpelistock to Wildhorn. A small glacial scarf hangs across it, and at mid-height the Geltenschuss waterfall sprays into a small meadowland protected as a nature reserve. It is an alluring scene. As a base, the village has a limited number of facilities, but it does have a post office, bank, two general stores, three hotels and tourist information (tel 033 765 91 81).

Out of the village a pleasant valley stroll leads to the reedy shores of the **Lauenensee**, from whose southern end a choice of paths continue to the ◯ **Gelten Hut** at 2003m. The more direct route (2hrs from the Lauenensee) climbs alongside the Geltenschuss, while a higher, and more varied trail mounts the east side of the valley and has one or two exposed sections on the flank of the Follhore before dropping down to the hut. Owned by the Saanen-based Oldenhorn section of the SAC, the Gelten Hut enjoys a scenic location on a lip overlooking the Rottal and Furggetäli, both of which drain the Gelten glacier. With 87 dormitory places it is fully staffed from mid-March until the end of April, and from the end of June until early October (www.geltenhuette.ch). From it the ◉ **Arpelistock** (see above) makes an obvious ascent by way of the west side of the Gelten glacier to gain the summit ridge a little north of the top, while the higher ◉ **Wildhorn**, though more frequently climbed from its eponymous hut, has a PD route via Col du Brotset and the SE Ridge. Both summits are popular with ski-touring parties.

East of the lower Lauenental, and beyond the minor indent of the Turnelsbach valley, the pastoral Turbach glen curves like a quotation mark between grass-covered foothills and, at its lower end, feeds into Gstaad. The 2000m hills and summits that fall away from the main chain in green rumpled folds make an enticing landscape for walkers, and as they're breached by easy passes such as Trüttlisberg, Stübleni and Tungel, it's tempting to wander across the grain of the land from one valley to the next. So it is by one of these routes that we move from the Lauenental to Ober Simmental, from Lauenen to Lenk, or from Gelten Hut to Wildhorn Hut.

Ober Simmental
The way from the Gelten Hut to the Wildhorn Hut makes an enjoyable half-day outing skirting across the lower, northern slopes of the **Niesehorn** a little south of the Tungelpass. On rounding the Niesehorn spur the **Iffigsee** comes into view 300m below, walled on its southeastern side by the Seeschnide cliffs that funnel a great sweep of screes to the lake's southern shore. Usually approached by a walk of 2½hrs or so from Iffigenalp, the **Wildhorn Hut** (2303m) stands on a rocky knoll above these screes in the midst of wild and desolate surroundings (www.cas-moleson.ch or www.wildhornhuette.ch). With 94 places, and

Base for climbs on Wildhorn and Arpelistock, the Gelten Hut stands at the head of the Lauenental

manned from mid-March until the end of April, and from late June until the end of September, the hut is owned by the Fribourg-based Moléson section of the SAC and is a popular base for climbs on the **Wildhorn** which rises to the southwest above the Tungel, Ténéhet and Audannes glaciers. First climbed in 1843, the mountain has two summits with only 1m difference in height between them, the higher of the two measuring 3257m. The normal route is a 3hr PD ascent from the hut via the Tungel glacier and NE flank, and it's also popular with ski mountaineers. Although it stands high above Sion, towards which it casts a long southerly ridge, the Wildhorn maintains an air of remoteness. Both flanks, north and south, are rocky. On the south side near the Col de la Selle, a bare plateau has been described as a petrified glacier. On the north side, as we have seen, a great scree tip falls between craggy ridges, yet these soon give way to gentle green crests and short transverse valleys grazed by cattle.

Casting roughly northeastward these transverse valleys filter down to the Ober Simmental whose uppermost village, **Lenk**, is an attractive but modest little resort served by train from Spiez. With plentiful accommodation and most facilities, including campsites, it makes a useful base for a walking holiday (for tourist information visit www.lenk-simmental.ch). Hillsides on both flanks of the valley carry a good number of signed paths, and a gondola lift to Betelberg southwest of the village adds to the possibilities.

Two roads project further upvalley beyond Lenk. One leads to the famed Simmenfälle at the foot of the Wildstrubel massif, the other, which has a timed one-way traffic control system above Färiche and is served by postbus, ends at the rustic, 100 year-old **Berghaus Iffigenalp**. Standing at the entrance to the Iffigtal at 1584m, it has 27 beds and makes an atmospheric centre from which to explore. The Iffigtal, of course, is used to approach the Wildhorn Hut, while a less used path heads northeast from the *berghaus* and crosses the high block of land topped by the Oberlaubhorn which divides the two upper stems of the Simmental.

But it is the imposing mountain wall that blocks all views south of Berghaus Iffigenalp that provides the most challenge. It is here that the somewhat desolate **Rawil Pass**, 854m above Iffigenalp, makes an obvious goal, for it has

THE SWISS ALPS – CHAPTER 5: BERNESE ALPS

long been used as a point of crossing from the Simmental to the Rhône. On the Rhône valley side of the pass the route descends to the dammed Lac de Tseuzier, trapped in a valley between Six des Eaux-Froides and the Wetzsteinhorn, from where a road descends to the world-famous ski resort of **Crans-Montana** (basking in what is claimed to be the sunniest plateau in the Alps) before continuing down to Sion.

5:3 THE WILDSTRUBEL MASSIF

The steeply climbing path from Iffigenalp to the Rawil Pass forks at 2278m, with the left branch leading to the SAC-owned **Wildstrubel Hut** (2791m). Standing on the west flank of the Weisshorn, one of the peaks that rims the Plaine Morte glacier, there are, in fact, two huts with a total of 70 places, fully staffed from mid-March until the end of April, and from late June until mid-October (www.wildstrubelhuette.ch). For the majority of hut visitors it will be the glacier plateau and ascent of the Wildstrubel that are the main interest here.

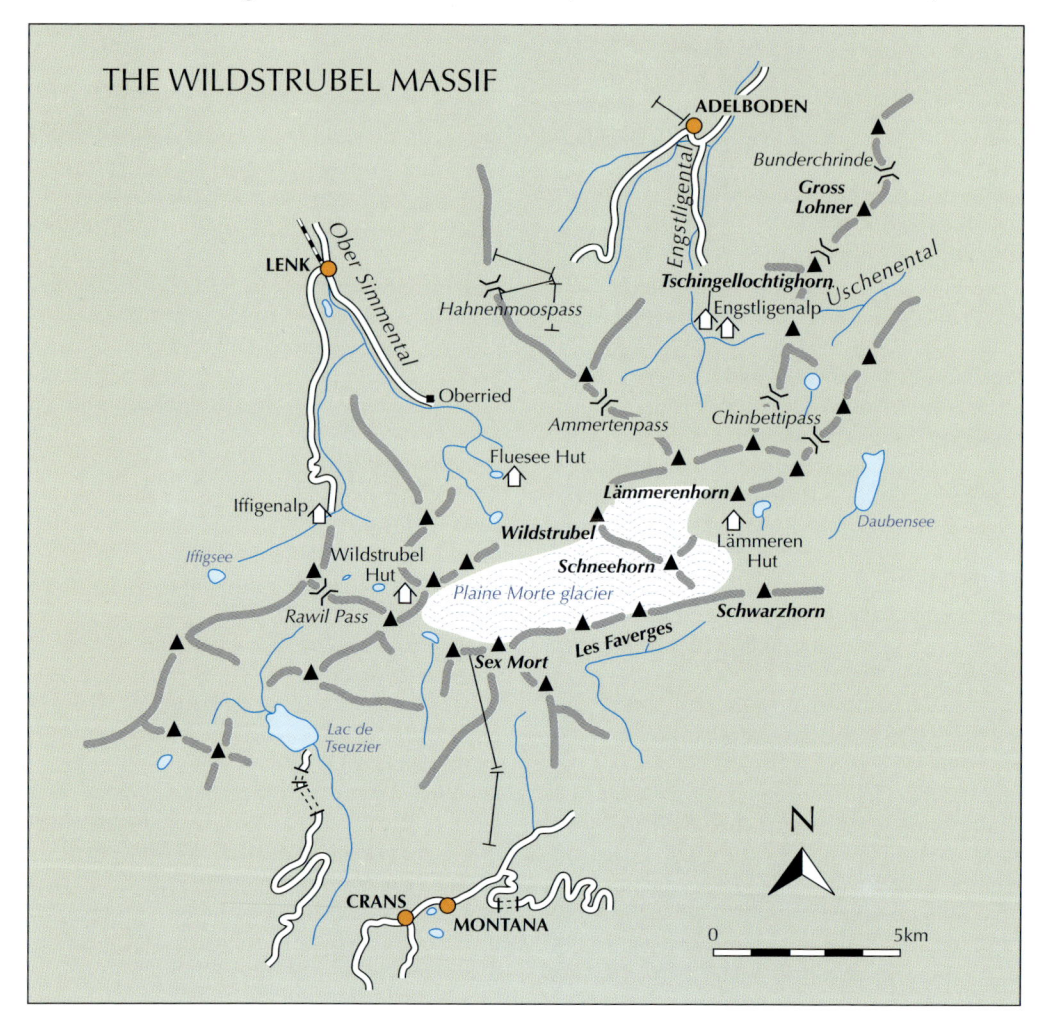

The Wildstrubel massif extends for about 13km from the Rawil Pass in the west to the Gemmipass in the east, with a number of summits above the 3000m elevation, and almost as many that don't quite make that height. But whilst this might suggest a series of crenellated ridges bristling with spires, reality is quite different. Truth is, the long ridges that support the massif are almost horizontal, with the main Wildstrubel summits (and there are three) varying only slightly in height. The peak rising directly from the Glacier de la Plaine Morte at the southwestern end of a curving ridge is named Wildstrubel on the map, but at 3243.5m it is exactly the same altitude as the so-called Mittlerer-Gipfel (or Mittelstrubel), while the Grossstrubel a little further east is barely inferior, for that measures a round 3243m.

Despite remaining hidden from the surrounding valleys, it is the **Glacier de la Plaine Morte** that gives the massif its character, contained as it is within a saucer-rim of ridges south and west of the named Wildstrubel summit. A cable car swings visitors from Les Barzettes above the Crans-Montana ski complex, to the Pointe de la Plaine Morte overlooking the glacier plateau at 2882m, so solitude is not to be expected. When he came here in 1894 during his famous high-level traverse of the Alps from Monte Viso to the Grossglockner, Martin Conway was impressed by the glacier. 'It is so large, so simple, so secluded,' he wrote. 'It seems like a portion of some strange world. Its effect of size is increased by the insignificance of the wall that surrounds it – enough to shut out all distant views and no more … The further we went the more profound was the solitude. Here a man might come and, setting up his tent for a week, learn what it is to be alone' (*The Alps from End to End*).

Whether starting from the Wildstrubel Hut or the cable car terminus, the ascent of the ☆ **Wildstrubel** involves little more than a trek across the glacier (in summer tracks are bulldozed across the ice to make the way safe), to a point immediately below the south flank where a path climbs 400m or so to the summit. This is the route taken by the first party to climb it in the mid-1850s, while the East Flank provides an ascent of similar ease via the Wildstrubel glacier, below which lies the **Lämmeren Hut** at the foot of the 2862m Lämmerenhorn. The usual approach to this hut is from the Gemmipass. Owned by the SAC's Angenstein section, it has 96 places and is fully staffed at Christmas and New Year, from late February until mid-May, and from the end of June until mid-October (www.laemmerenhuette.ch).

A third hut serves the Wildstrubel massif, albeit an unmanned hut with just 12 places. This, the single-storey **Fluesee Hut**, stands above and to the west of the little Flueseeli tarn below the northwest flank of the Wildstrubel at 2049m, and is gained by a path from the Oberreid roadhead by way of the thundering Simmenfälle, the rustic Gasthaus Rezliberg and the group of Siebenbrunnen cascades. From the hut a path continues southeastward, climbing without complication for a little under 800m to join the normal ascent route on the South Flank – 3hrs from hut to summit.

Engstligenalp

The near-horizontal crest of the Wildstrubel massif is seen to good effect from Engstligenalp, a large basin of flat pastureland which lies directly below and to the north of the Grossstrubel. This remarkable elevated basin once held a post-glacial lake, and is contained by the interlinking Ammertengrat and Rotstock ridges on the west, and craggy Engstligengrat on the east, while the southern end is walled by the Wildstrubel massif. Close to its northern outflow overnight accommodation can be found at Berghotel Enstligenalp, and Berghaus Bärtschi (www.engstligenalp.ch), both of which have dormitories as well as standard rooms.

The **Ammertenpass** at 2443m provides a way for walkers to cross the Ammertengrat, with an excessively steep descent on the west side that leads to the Simmenfälle at the head of the Ober Simmental, while the Engstligengrat and continuing Schedelsgrätli (north of the Tschingellochtighorn), have at least two crossings that lead either to the Gemmipass or into the Kandertal above Kandersteg. But north of the Engstligenalp hotels, and close to the cable car that swings visitors up from Unter dem Berg in the Engstligental, a thunderous waterfall drains the basin and pours in two cascades known as the **Engstligenfälle**, which has been classed as a Swiss national monument since 1948.

Four kilometres to the north **Adelboden** (1353m) lies on a south-facing slope above the confluence of the Allebach and Engstligenbach streams. A small family resort, as popular in winter as in summer, it can be reached by postbus from Frutigen (train from Thun and Spiez), has all facilities, plenty of hotels and apartments, two campsites and tourist information (www.adelboden.ch). The resort's ski area is mostly concentrated in the valley southwest of the town, some of its lifts feeding the **Hahnenmoosspass** which is on a summer walking route to Lenk.

This is all good walking country with an abundant network of trails, but among the more challenging routes are those that venture onto the flanks of the **Gross Lohner** which towers over the east side of the Engstligental. Though usually tackled in the opposite direction (east to west), the classic crossing here is via the rocky 2385m ◐ **Bunderchrinde** which takes walkers over the mountains to Kandersteg on an energetic but highly rewarding trek.

5:4 KANDERSTEG AND THE GEMMIPASS

Kandersteg (1176m) is the first of the real mountaineering centres on our eastward journey along the Bernese Alps, with access to peaks above the Gemmipass and the Gasterntal, on the Doldenhorn and the Blüemlisalp (5:5). A straggling, popular resort, but of no great size, it's the highest village in the Kandertal which cuts into the mountains south of Spiez, and has a railway station on the important trans-alpine line connecting the cantons of Bern and Valais via the Lötschberg Tunnel that emerges on the south side at Goppenstein. (The more recently completed Lötschberg Base Tunnel runs for 34.5km beneath the mountains from Frutigen to Raron near Visp.) Kandersteg's attractions are all mountain-based, and walkers, climbers and paragliders are well catered for. There's a range of accommodation, from low-priced pensions to the 5-star Royal Park Hotel. There are holiday apartments and chalets to rent, and a campsite below the Oeschinensee. Most other facilities will be found in the resort, which also has a useful tourist office (www.kandersteg.ch).

A little over 2km south of Kandersteg the Kandertal appears to be blocked by an abrupt 600m tree- and shrub-covered wall of rock, the only apparent continuation being the Klus gorge to the east through which the Kander escapes from the Gasterntal. But above and behind that abrupt wall there stretches the high and comparatively barren valley of Schwarzbach which ends at the Gemmipass. A track mounts the steep forested slopes out of the **Kandertal** to access that valley, but there's also a cable car from Eggeschwand that provides an effortless ascent to the **Sunnbüel** terminus, saving something like 3hrs of walking.

The natural appeal of the Schwarzbach valley is diminished only by the intrusion of pylons carrying power cables that march across the stark landscape. On the west it is flanked by the Üschenegrat, on the far side of which the Üschenental runs a parallel course and is headed by the Steghorn and Roter Totz, outliers of the Wildstrubel massif. But the east wall of the valley soars up to the Altels, a 3629m peak whose conspicuous triangular NW Face confronts the walker heading south beyond Sunnbüel across the Spittelmatte pastures. In 1895 a large section of the Altels glacier collapsed onto these pastures, burying six herdsmen and their cattle in a mass of ice that took five years to melt.

An hour's walk from Sunnbüel, and separated from the Spittelmatte pastures by a chaos of rocks, the old **Berghotel Schwarenbach** stands close to the Bern/Valais canton border at 2060m. This one-time customs house was built in 1742, but in its reincarnation as a mountain inn it has been patronised by a number of eminent guests, among them de Saussure and Mark Twain, and by climbers who choose it as a base from which to tackle such peaks as the Rinderhorn, Altels and Balmhorn. With standard rooms and 120 dormitory places, it's open from March until late October (tel 033 675 12 72).

Seen from certain points in the Kandertal the Altels and Balmhorn (unequal in height, but close enough to appear almost as a single peak with two summits linked by a fine snow crest) present an attractive and tempting North Face, and the two are often climbed in a single expedition from Berghotel Schwarenbach. At 3698m, the ◐ **Balmhorn** is the higher by 69m, and is noteworthy for the fact that when it was climbed in 1864, by Frank, Horace and Lucy Walker with the guides Jakob and Melchior Anderegg, it was the only occasion that an alpine first ascent was made by a joint effort of father, son and daughter. Their route by the SW Ridge, the so-called Zackengrat (which runs on to the Rinderhorn) is today graded PD, while the more challenging NW Ridge, connected to the **Altels**, is an AD outing along what is, in part, a narrow and corniced snow crest. Other routes, on the North Face and NE Ridge are tackled from the **Balmhorn Hut** approached from the Gasterntal (see 5:5).

Continuing upvalley beyond Schwarenbach, another 30mins or so brings you to the shallow **Daubensee**. Cupped amid limestone rocks, and drained by way of a subterranean channel into the Rhône valley, the lake has paths along both east and west shores, and one at the northwestern end which breaks out of the valley and goes by way of the Rote Chumme and **Chinbettipass** to the Engstligenalp (see 5:3). Another at the southwestern

5:4 KANDERSTEG AND THE GEMMIPASS

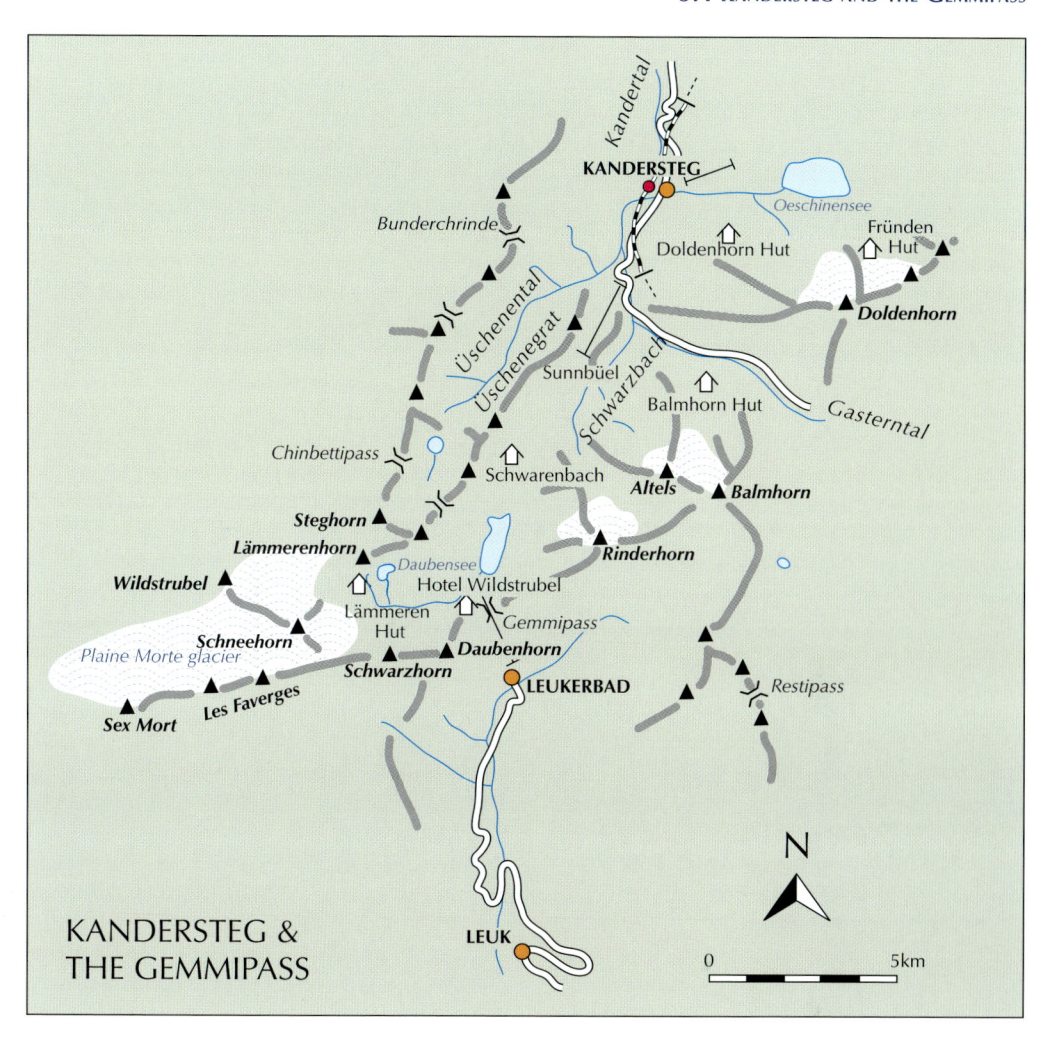

KANDERSTEG & THE GEMMIPASS

end of the lake veers away from the Gemmipass route and heads west through the little Lämmerntal to reach the **Lämmeren Hut** (5:3). But from the end of the lake the main paths here finally lead in about 10mins to **Hotel Wildstrubel** (tel 027 470 12 01) and the historic 2314m **Gemmipass**.

Known as long ago as 1250, the Gemmipass is noted for its alpine flora, which is especially rich here in June, for its panoramic view of the Pennine Alps to the south, and for the impressive path created between 1736 and 1741 up the precipitous wall on the southeast side of the pass. This veritable staircase was hewn in the rock, with the sharpest corners being protected by parapets, but a cable car rising from **Leukerbad** (5:10) makes an ascent (or descent) by this path today the preserve of the purist.

MELCHIOR ANDEREGG: THE KING OF GUIDES

By the time he led the Walker family on the first ascent of the Balmhorn, Melchior Anderegg was already established as one of the most sought-after guides of mountaineering's Golden Age. An Oberland man through and through, he was born in a tiny hamlet near Meiringen in 1828, where he became a gifted wood carver and the champion wrestler of the Haslital before his mountaineering abilities were properly 'discovered' in 1855 by Thomas Hinchliff, a prime mover in the formation of the Alpine Club. Aged 27, Melchior was by now 'tall and big-muscled', with an honest square-bearded face, and although Hinchliff was only a modest climber, he introduced the guide to Leslie Stephen who had more demanding work in mind. With Stephen Anderegg made a number of climbs, among them first ascents of Monte Disgrazia (in 1862), Zinalrothorn (1864), and Mont Mallet in 1871, but he also climbed with many of the other leading amateurs of the day, including Tuckett, Kennedy, A W Moore, and C E Mathews (who employed him for more than 20 seasons). Although a heavy, strong man, he was also gentle and with an unfailing courtesy which made him a favourite with the few early women climbers, of whom Lucy Walker was a good example. For two decades (from 1859 to 1879) he was regularly employed by her whenever she, or other members of the Walker family, visited the Alps. His principal climbs include first ascents of the Rimpfischhorn, Mont Blanc by the Bosses Ridge, and also by the Brenva Face, the Dent d'Hérens, Blüemlisalphorn, and Parrotspitze on Monte Rosa. In 1864 Melchior married Marguerite Metzener, and together they raised four daughters and eight sons, four of whom also became professional guides. Melchior's cousin Jakob often climbed with him (as he did on the Balmhorn), and although much more daring and with an equally fine record of ascents, his reputation was overshadowed by that of the man from Meiringen. Throughout his guiding career, wood-carving remained Melchior Anderegg's first love (he served for several seasons as 'carver-in-or-dinary' at the Schwarenbach inn) and examples of his work were exhibited in major galleries in London, yet it is for his record as a prudent mountaineer whose superb craftsmanship on rock, ice and snow made him stand out above most of his contemporaries (apart, perhaps, from Christian Almer), that his name is remembered in alpine circles. Credited with making no less than 14 first ascents of major peaks, his wonderful grace and ease of movement were legendary. As Ronald Clark makes clear in *The Early Alpine Guides*, Melchior was not only a great guide, but by his example he also made great guides, one of whom was Hans Jaun, another Oberland man and one of his protégés, who looked upon him with both admiration and respect, and called him 'the king of guides'.

5:5 BLÜEMLISALP AND THE GASTERNTAL

On the eastern side of the Kandertal, the first of the 'high' peaks of the Bernese Alps form a long wall stretching above and away from Kandersteg running northeastward from the Doldenhorn to Gspaltenhorn, after which it steadily subsides into the Lauterbrunnen valley. Midway along this wall the Blüemlisalp group sends out another ridge which curves northwest and west to enclose a deep 'well' in which lies the famed **Oeschinensee**, high on the list of must-see sites for Kandersteg visitors. A cable lift which begins at the village campsite makes short work of the 400m approach, although a steady hike along a service road which goes to two hotels overlooking the lake (both of which have dormitory accommodation as well as stand-ard rooms) could be taken by those who need the exercise – allow 1hr 15mins for this.

The oval-shaped Oeschinensee is one of the most beautiful of all mountain lakes in Switzerland, almost completely ringed by steep walls of rock and ice which culminate in 3000m summits, except on the north side that is, where the highest peak on the Oeschinengrat is the 2861m Dündenhorn. Exactly 1200m above the eastern shore, the cleft of the 2778m ○ ☆ **Hohtürli** makes a tough but rewarding crossing from the Kandertal to the Kiental (easier when taken in the opposite direction), while 56m above the pass the **Blüemlisalp Hut** is as popular with trekkers tackling the epic Alpine Pass Route (see box) as it is with climbers attempting routes on the snowy Morgenhorn, Wyssi Frau and Blüemlisalphorn which rise nearby.

At 3663m the ● **Blüemlisalphorn** is the highest summit above Kandersteg, with three ridges and a 500m North Face seen to good effect from the Blüemlisalp Hut, while the south side falls in precipices to the Kanderfirn. The normal route by way of the NW Ridge (4–5hrs from the hut) is one of Leslie Stephen's first ascents dating from 1860, and now graded AD. According to the Alpine Club guide, the glaciated face on view from the hut has an average angle of only 45°, but with sections of 70° and graded D, it makes a good introduction to north face climbing. But perhaps the best route here is a traverse of all three peaks, starting with

5:5 Blüemlisalp and the Gasterntal

BLÜEMLISALP & THE GASTERNTAL

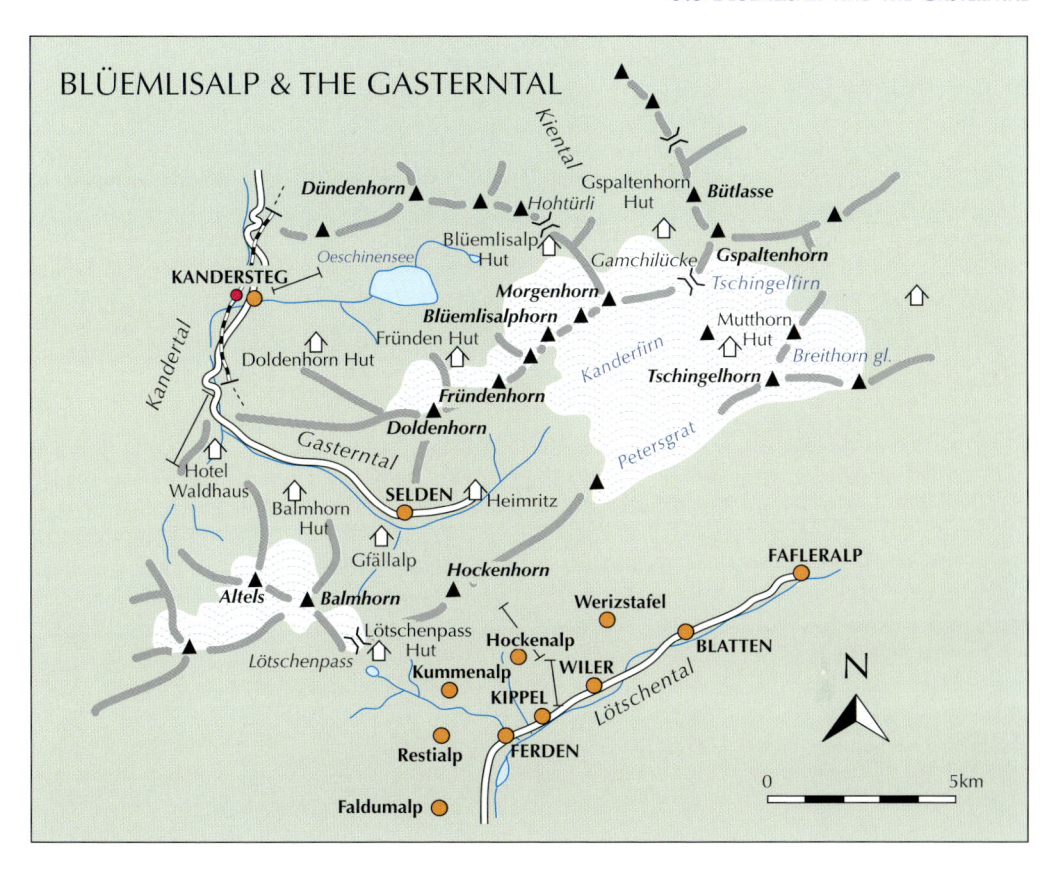

the Morgenhorn (by its NW Ridge), then along the WSW Ridge to the Wyssi Frau, which is connected to the Blüemlisalphorn by a magnificent narrow snow crest.

Peaks and glaciers of the Blüemlisalp massif

Rising directly above Kandersteg, the 3643m ❸ **Doldenhorn** makes its presence felt in a powerful way. It's a fine-looking peak with two summits, its north flank draped with snow and ice above the Oeschinensee, its south side raised on limestone walls above the Gasterntal. Situated on a prominent grassy meadow southeast of the village at 1915m, the **Doldenhorn Hut** is gained by a 2½hr walk. Owned by the Emmental section of the SAC, it has 40 places and is fully staffed in July and August and at weekends from April to the end of June, and also in September (www.doldenhornhuette.ch). From it the normal route (PD) via the mountain's NW Flank is reckoned to take from 5–6hrs. Several other routes on the Doldenhorn begin, not from the Doldenhorn Hut, but from the sturdy-looking **Fründen Hut** which occupies a spectacular site on a rocky bluff close to the Fründen glacier, some 980m above the Oeschinensee. Property of the Kandersteg-based Altels section of the SAC, it is reached in 3hrs from the lake, has 70 places, and is manned from late May until mid-October (www.sac-altels.ch). Apart from one or two routes on the ❸ **Fründenhorn** (3369m) which is the next peak along the wall to the northeast, the 650m North Face of the Doldenhorn is an obvious attraction from here. The route is mostly snow and ice, but with a grade III rock band which may be avoided (D/D+).

As was mentioned in 5:4 above, a short distance upvalley from Kandersteg the Kander torrent explodes out of the Klus gorge. A narrow road squeezes through the gorge to emerge in the wildly beautiful **Gasterntal**, a seemingly 'lost' world of multi-braided streams, waterfalls and soaring rock walls. In summer a daily minibus service runs from Kandersteg railway station as far as the two mountain inns at Selden. But a far better method of exploring the valley, of course, is to ignore the road and take a footpath which branches south after leaving the gorge, and within a few minutes brings you to **Hotel Waldhaus**. Set amid a crescent of woods, but looking upvalley, the hotel is open from June to October, and has both standard bedrooms and dormitory accommodation. Nearby there's an old dairy farm, but between the hotel and the farm another path breaks away and soon climbs beside the Schwarzbach on the way to the Gemmipass (4hrs from here).

Beyond Hotel Waldhaus a track continues into the Gasterntal, and where it crosses an open meadow a sign indicates the start of a path which climbs the steep south flank of the valley, using sections of fixed cable and ladders in places, to gain a glacial cirque in which the small **Balmhorn Hut** (1956m) enjoys a privileged view of the Balmhorn and Altels peaks which tower above it. Property of the Frutigen based Altels section of the SAC, the hut has just 26 places and is manned at weekends from the end of May until the end of September, and more permanently for about a month from mid-July (www.balmhornhuette.ch). The North Face of the ❸ **Balmhorn** is an obvious attraction from here (D-), as is the AD grade NE Ridge.

Whilst the continuing walk upvalley is a delight of streams, waterfalls, flower meadows and wooded areas, by far the majority of visitors to the Gasterntal take the minibus transport to **Selden**. This is hardly the hamlet referred to by some, for it consists of little more than a couple of modest mountain inns on the true right bank of the Kander; Gasthaus Steinbock, and Hotel Gasterntal-Selden, both of which have standard beds and dormitory accommodation, and plenty of atmosphere.

It is here, just below Gasthaus Steinbock, that a wooden suspension bridge spans the Kander torrent, taking a path steeply up the south flank of the valley alongside the Leilibach stream which cascades over a series of rock steps. Some 300m above the bridge the modest-sized **Berghaus Gfällalp** also has dormitory accommodation and a fine view towards the Kanderfirn glacier at the head of the valley. Above the *berghaus* the trail continues its steep zigzag climb with the snout of the Lötschengletscher appearing above a wall of crags. Eventually the way reaches this glacier and crosses along a line of marker poles to the right-bank lateral moraine, then resumes the ascent to the 2690m **Lötschenpass** and the privately owned **Lötschenpass Hut**, reached in about 4hrs from Selden. The hut has a splendid location, set upon glacier-smoothed rocks on the dividing ridge between Gasterntal and Lötschental, with an absorbing view of the Bietschhorn to the south, and the big face of the Balmhorn rising to the west. With 40 places, it is fully staffed from February until the end of April, and from June until the end of October (www.loetschenpass.ch).

The dividing ridge between the Gasterntal and Lötschental angles northeastwards above the hut, to eventually become the ice-covered and virtually featureless Petersgrat. On the way to the Petersgrat, the ridge is punctuated by several minor summits, the first of any note being the 3293m

The wildly attractive Gasterntal

◉ **Hockenhorn**, along whose SW Ridge a partially cairned ascent route leads in about 2hrs from the Lötschenpass Hut.

From the hut two paths descend into the **Lötschental**. The left branch angles across the hillside and descends eastward to Lauchernalp, while the right-hand option slopes gently down to a tarn, then more steeply to Kummenalp. Both of these alps, and the Lötschental itself, are visited in 5:10 below.

Back at Selden in the Gasterntal the track pushes on upvalley beyond the two inns, and terminates at **Berggasthaus Heimritz** that has beds and dormitory places, after which a footpath rises through a somewhat desolate region before coming to a natural rock garden, then crossing the Kander stream and working a way up to the **Kanderfirn**, the glacier that spreads over the Petersgrat and is a remnant of the great ice sheet that once covered much of the Bernese Alps. The northwest side of the Kanderfirn is flanked by bare cliffs that fall from the Blüemlisalp massif, and at the head of the glacier, the flat-topped Mutthorn rises between two icy saddles which connect the Kanderfirn with the Tschingelfirn, the latter draining into the upper reaches of the Lauterbrunnen valley.

Dominated by the double-peaked Tschingelhorn, the **Mutthorn Hut** is tucked at the base of crags on the east side of the Mutthorn at 2900m (4½hrs from Selden). A large and sturdy SAC hut with 100 dormitory places, it is fully manned for the brief summer season between the end of June and early September (www.mutthornhuette.ch), and is used as a base by climbers focused on the South Face and East Ridge of the ◉ **Morgenhorn**, various routes on the ◉ **Tschingelhorn**, and West Ridge of the ◉ **Lauterbrunnen Breithorn**. An easy crossing of the **Petersgrat** from here leads into the Lötschental; the Gamchilücke (between Morgenhorn and Gspaltenhorn) enables climbers to move on to the Gspaltenhorn Hut; while descent of the **Tschingelfirn** to the northeast is an obvious attraction for anyone planning to visit the Lauterbrunnen valley (5:7).

5:6 THE KIENTAL

Lying on the north side of the Gamchilücke, the Kiental is very different from the Gasterntal. An unassuming little valley, it has largely escaped the

THE SWISS ALPS – CHAPTER 5: BERNESE ALPS

THE KIENTAL

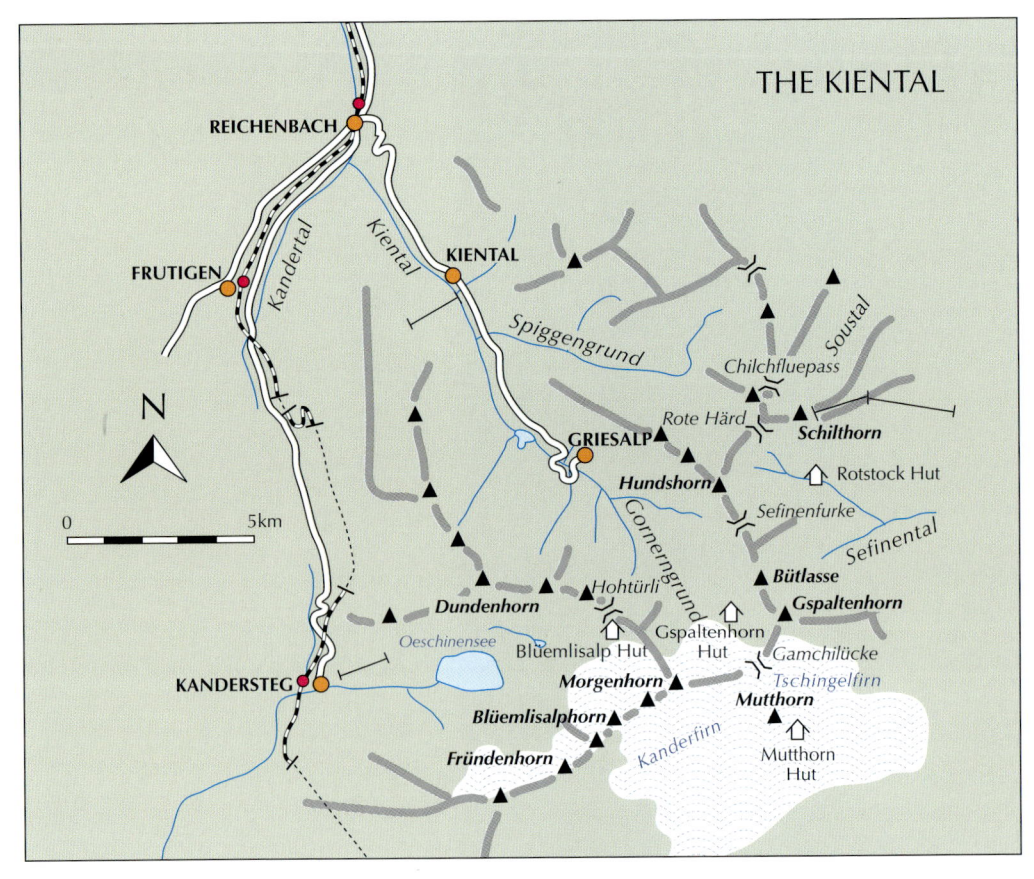

attention of most visitors to the Bernese Alps, and reserves its true identity for those of an independent nature. Gentle, pastoral and partly wooded in its lower reaches, but more wild and grand towards its head, the Kiental wears two faces, both of which are clearly defined not far from its entrance where the neat, low-lying farmland is in stark contrast to the great wall of snowpeaks of the Blüemlisalp massif that shimmers in the distance.

Flowing into the Frutigtal near Reichenbach, about 10km south of Spiez, the Kiental has a smattering of little hamlets, but only one real village which also shares its name with that of the valley. **Kiental** has a handful of hotels, a few shops, a chairlift and tourist information (www.kiental.ch). Lying midway through the valley in an unspoilt landscape of greenery, early Baedeker guides described it as 'charmingly situated, and well adapted for a stay of some time'.

Southeast of Kiental village, the valley subdivides into the **Spiggengrund** and **Gornerngrund**. The first of these digs roughly eastward into the mountains before rising under the 2833m Kilchfluh, a close neighbour of the Schilthorn above Mürren, while the more southerly stem, the Gornerngrund, is of greater interest to those in search of higher, more rugged and challenging terrain, for its headwall is composed of a ridge linking Morgenhorn and Gspaltenhorn via the Gamchilücke, from which flows the Gamchigletscher.

Outside Kiental village a toll road, served by the ubiquitous postbus, runs alongside a small lake, then corkscrews through a savagely steep defile that opens at the hamlet of **Griesalp** which, at 1407m, has rooms and dormitory accommodation at Berghaus Griesalp. Similar accommodation can also be found a short walk above the hamlet at Berggasthaus Golderli (www.golderli.ch). Despite its severely limited facilities, Griesalp would make an acceptable out-of-the-way base for a few days, for there are several good, if demanding, hikes to be made in the neighbourhood by strong walkers, although the main climbing interest is better served

The Gornerngrund, the upper Kiental, topped by the Blüemlisalp ▶

5:6 The Kiental

from a couple of mountain huts accessible by two of those hikes.

The **Blüemlisalp Hut** has already been mentioned in 5:5 as being approached from Kandersteg, but it's also reached in 4½hrs or so from Griesalp via the 2778m ⊙ **Hohtürli**. On the way to it the trail passes a couple of dairy farms, one of which offers beds and dormitory accommodation from June until mid-October at Berggasthof Enzian (tel 033 676 11 92). This is located on the west side of the upper valley at 1840m.

On the opposite, east, side of the Kiental more dairy farms are linked by another trail from Griesalp which climbs to the narrow, craggy pass of the ⊙ **Sefinenfurke**, midway between Hundshorn and Bütlasse. At 2612m this is a classic crossing used to reach Mürren and the Lauterbrunnen valley (5:7), but from it another path cuts to the south and after negotiating a shoulder, angles down and round the Trogegg spur of the Bütlasse to join a direct route from Griesalp on its final climb to the **Gspaltenhorn Hut**. Owned by the Bern section of the SAC, this traditional-looking hut stands in the midst of a rocky combe at 2455m on the west flank of the Gspaltenhorn (www.gspaltenhornhuette.ch). With 75 places, and manned from the end of June until early October, it is used by climbers tackling assorted routes on the Gspaltenhorn and Bütlasse, and for crossing the Gamchilücke to the Tschingel Pass and the Mutthorn Hut.

Though perhaps seen at its best from the Sefinental, which it blocks alongside the Gspaltenhorn, the 3192m ❸ ◈ ☆ **Bütlasse** nonetheless has a fine-looking south wall rising directly above the hut, and a West Ridge (above the South Face) along which an AD- route leads to the summit, while the *voie normale* from the Sefinenfurke enables conditioned mountain walkers to achieve a 3000m summit without undue difficulty in 2hrs from the pass. From the summit a rewarding panoramic view includes most of the major peaks of the Oberland.

Almost 250m higher than its neighbour, the ❸ **Gspaltenhorn** (3437m) is a distinctive rock peak whose daunting NE Face towers above the Sefinental, and whose extensive ESE Ridge (the Tschingelgrat) forms a crusty divide between the Sefinental and the upper reaches of the Lauterbrunnen valley. The normal route, via the NW Ridge which connects the mountain to the Bütlasse and by which it was first climbed in 1869, is a fairly short (4–4½hrs) AD- climb from the Gspaltenhorn Hut. But the well-known, multi-pinnacled Rote Zähne, or SW Ridge, is a TD route made famous by Geoffrey Winthrop Young who was in the first party to climb it (in 1914), along with Siegfried Herford and the guide Josef Knubel, who brought along 'a straight-backed young chamois-hunter' named Hans Brantschen to join them. Until then, it was considered to be the last great unclimbed ridge in the Alps, and more than a dozen years later, Young included an account of it in his autobiographical *On High Hills*. As for the 1600m NE Face, this is reputedly one of the highest and most remote in the Alps, and for steepness is comparable with the Eigerwand. There are several routes on it, and all of them are serious. Needless to say, the Gspaltenhorn Hut is no good as a base from which to attempt this face; instead a bivouac at the head of the **Sefinental** (5:7) is probably the best bet.

5:7 LAUTERBRUNNEN VALLEY

One of the most famous of all alpine valleys, the Lauterbrunnental challenges every superlative in the thesaurus. It is, quite simply, stunning. A deep U-shaped trench walled by immense cliffs laced by waterfalls and headed by a regiment of lofty summits, it repays a prolonged visit by all mountain lovers no matter what their interest or level of commitment.

With **Interlaken** to the north acting as a public transport hub, access by rail from almost anywhere in Switzerland is easy. From the station of Interlaken Ost, local trains head south to Wilderswil, then follow the Lütschine upstream to Zweilütschinen where the line divides; east to Grindelwald, south again to Lauterbrunnen. For a while forest crowds out any noteworthy views, but as the trees thin and the valley becomes less constricted, so the headwall mountains slowly reveal themselves.

Lauterbrunnen (795m) is as far as trains go within the valley itself, although a side line crawls up the eastern slope to Wengen and Kleine Scheidegg, with further options to Grindelwald or the spectacular and expensive Jungfraujoch. On the west side of the valley a cable car replaces an old funicular to transport visitors up the cliffs to Grütschalp, from where a brief train ride continues the journey along a natural shelf into Mürren which, like Wengen, is a traffic-free resort with much to reward a visit.

5:7 LAUTERBRUNNEN VALLEY

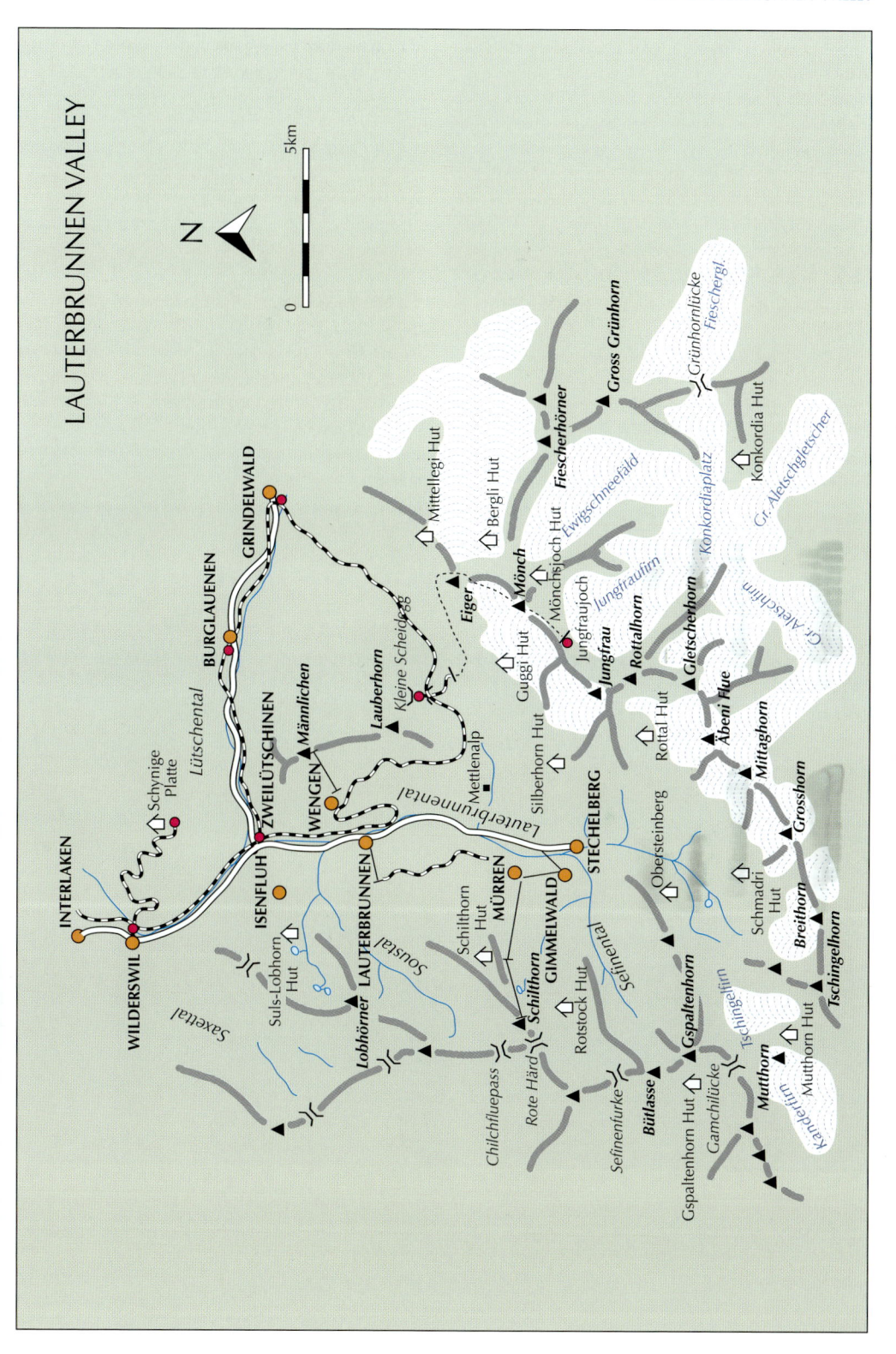

Lauterbrunnen itself has no obvious appeal apart from its location and views. Basically it's a one-street village lined with hotels and shops, two large campsites, which also provide dormitory accommodation, a busy railway station with adjacent multi-storey car park, and tourist information (www.lauterbrunnen-tourismus.ch). The exquisite Staubbach Falls spray over the walling cliffs into a meadow on the south side of the village, while on the northern side a steeply winding road claws its way up the valley's precipitous west flank to reach the isolated hamlet of **Isenfluh** at 1081m, above which the open pastures of Sulwald may be gained by cableway. There are also trails that fan out across the hillside, one of which climbs to the little timber-built **Suls-Lobhorn Hut** magically set upon a limestone-pitted meadow at 1955m, with a heart-stopping view of the Jungfrau, seen in a single glance from its lofty summit virtually to its roots more than 3200m below. The hut is owned by the Lauterbrunnen section of the SAC. It has just 24 places, so advanced booking is essential, and it's manned from July until mid-October (tel 079 656 53 20). Overlooking the hut from the southwest, the six limestone fingers of the 🌀 **Lobhörner** have a number of well-equipped routes at various grades, but it is the mountain walker who has the most options at his disposal when staying at this hut.

One rewarding walk descends from the hut to the dairy farm of Suls, then cuts along a heavily vegetated slope heading south, with views to Eiger, Mönch and Jungfrau, before turning into the pastoral **Soustal**, above which rise the Lobhörner pinnacles once more. At the head of the valley it's the Schilthorn that dominates, and although trails continue below it before crossing one of two passes (Chilchflüe and Rote Härd), the most popular walk here merely wanders across the valley's entrance, then turns the Marchegg spur on the way to Grütschalp or Mürren.

Mürren

Synonymous with downhill skiing (it is claimed the slalom was invented here in 1922), **Mürren** is one of the best known of Oberland resorts, an eyrie of a village perched 800m above the Lauterbrunnental in full view of the Jungfrau. But the Jungfrau is just one of many high peaks that jostle for attention in a widely sweeping

The glacier-carved Lauterbrunnen valley

panorama enjoyed from most of the hotels and chalets. It's a resort with all facilities, and a visit to the tourist office (www.wengen-muerren.ch) in the sports centre shows that little money is spared in its promotion. Skiers flock here in winter, with the 'Inferno' downhill race (a 2170m descent from the Schilthorn) being an annual fixture in February. But once the snow has gone, the flower-filled meadows are transformed into a walker's paradise.

Above and to the west of Mürren the 2970m **Schilthorn**, topped by the Piz Gloria revolving restaurant featured in the James Bond film *On Her Majesty's Secret Service*, is one of the region's must-visit viewpoints. Reached by cable car from **Stechelberg** in the bed of the valley via Gimmelwald and Mürren, the summit is undeniably touristy, but its position, standing back from the main range, makes it an unforgettable vantage point from which to study the central block of the Oberland wall.

Despite being accessible to anyone with the price of a cable car ticket, despite the crowds, and despite its having been reshaped and 'tamed', the **Schilthorn** can still repay a visit by those prepared to walk and indulge in a little assisted scrambling. A direct route from Mürren via the Kanonenrohr (below the **Schilthorn Hut**) and the mountain's East Ridge is merely a 4½hr slog through rather uninspiring scenery, but the West Ridge, gained at the **Rote Härd** saddle, provides an entertaining scramble assisted, in places, by sections of ladder, metal rungs and fixed cables. By continuing over the summit and down the East Ridge, then via the little Grauseeli tarn (an engaging spot with another breathtaking backdrop) followed by a descent through the pastures of Schiltalp and Blumental down to Mürren, a complete traverse of the mountain can be achieved by fit mountain walkers.

The best place from which to begin such a traverse is the Stechelberg Ski Club's **Rotstock Hut**, which stands on a bluff at 2039m, about 2–2½hrs to the west of Mürren on the way to the Sefinenfurke, the pass used as a link with Griesalp (see 5:6). This small traditional hut has 52 dormitory places and is fully staffed from June until the end of September (www.rotstockhuette.ch) and is used by walkers following the multi-day Tour of the Jungfrau Region (see box).

Eiger, Mönch and Jungfrau, seen from the outskirts of Mürren

With no shortage of walks to enjoy from a base in either Mürren or tiny **Gimmelwald** which lies nearly 300m below the resort, an active week could be happily spent on this west side of the Lauterbrunnen valley. But for those who enjoy the adrenalin rush inspired by extreme exposure, a spectacular ⓒ **via ferrata** replete with Himalayan-style suspension bridge, 60m Tyrolean traverse, rungs and ladders, has been created on the vertical cliffs below Mürren. Entered by a tunnel located near the village tennis courts, the route is a little over 2km long and, unusually for a *via ferrata*, it descends a total of 300m – grade K3. The Via Ferrata Mürren–Gimmelwald is open from mid-June until the end of October, and is free to use. Guides are also available for newcomers to the *via ferrata* experience; contact the Lauterbrunnen Valley Mountain Guides Office on tel 033 821 61 00 (www.klettersteig-muerren.ch).

Wengen and Kleine Scheidegg

On the east side of the valley directly above Lauterbrunnen at 1275m, **Wengen**, like Mürren, boasts of being a traffic-free resort with year-round appeal. Reached by trains bound for Kleine Scheidegg, it is perhaps best known as a ski resort which hosts the annual World Cup slalom and downhill races on the Lauberhorn. But unlike most winter resorts, Wengen is not cluttered with tows or chairlifts, for most of these are located either on the east flank of the Männlichen ridge, or above Kleine Scheidegg. A single cable car carries visitors above the village to Männlichen, and the only alien clutter is a barrier of avalanche fences that protect the resort, built on the steep slope just below the ridge. With around 30 hotels and pensions, and numerous chalets and apartments for rent, accommodation is plentiful, with everything from luxurious palace-style hotels at the upper end of the scale, to budget-priced dormitories – for a list contact the tourist office in the main street (www.wengen-muerren.ch).

In springtime and early summer alpine flowers replace the snowfields, and Wengen then becomes a focus for botanical holidays. Footpaths abound to provide walks of varying levels, and the scenery is first-rate. Most walkers will head towards the Jungfrau, which gives the impression of soaring above the resort, and those who find their way through the woods to Mettlenalp, Biglenalp or Wengernalp gain a powerful introduction to the Mönch as well as its better-known neighbour.

Kleine Scheidegg

Those with less inclination to walk, will take the train to **Kleine Scheidegg**, the tourist circus of a saddle on the ridge midway between Lauterbrunnen and Grindelwald, from which crowds gather to peer up at the Eiger, or to change trains for the final section of the journey to the Jungfraujoch. At 2061m Kleine Scheidegg is not the most tranquil of Oberland vantage points. With trains arriving there from three directions, it has become a major gathering ground for tourists, though it's neither resort nor mountain village. Kleine Scheidegg is not even a hamlet; just a group of buildings – the station which also has beds and dorms, a couple of hotels (www.scheidegg-hotels.ch), kiosks, and (often) an American Indian-style tepee. Five minutes' walk away, the aptly named Grindelwaldblick restaurant also has dormitory accommodation and fine views (www.grindelwaldblick.ch).

Depending on your background or ambition, arrival at Kleine Scheidegg will either excite you with its close proximity to the Eigerwand (see 5:8), appal you with its bedlam, or bewilder you with options. If you're a tourist collecting sites as well as sights, the next departure for the Jungfraujoch will be on your itinerary. If you're a skier (and it's winter) both sides of the ridge have slopes that attract. A walker? There's a broad trail heading north to the Männlichen viewpoint; another that goes south to Eigergletscher where the highly recommended Eiger Trail begins; yet more that sweep down to Wengen, to Wengernalp, Biglenalp and Mettlenalp; or east to Grindelwald. But if you're a climber having emerged from an apprenticeship and now hanker to step up a notch or two, the big black wall of the Eigerwand will get the adrenalin going (see 5:8). But despite its domineering presence, the Eiger is not the only mountain above Kleine Scheidegg that appeals, for the Mönch has its own undeniable attraction as, of course, does the Jungfrau.

The Jungfraujoch

R L G Irving once commented that commercialism had much to answer for in spoiling the Alps with its hotels, railways and its crowds, but pointed out that it also managed to focus the stream of tourists and 'enabled tens of thousands to look at things which it is good for a man to look at'. He added that climbers often abuse, but as often use, railways and *téléferiques* to reduce the time it takes to approach a hut or their chosen peak. He could have been thinking of the Jungfraujoch.

No matter what your view of such developments, the Jungfraujoch railway is a remarkable piece of 19th-century engineering which took 16 years to complete at a cost of 15 million Swiss francs. Rising almost 1400m from Kleine Scheidegg to the icy terminus at 3454m, it burrows through both Eiger and Mönch at a gradient of 1 in 4, and carries something like half a million visitors a year. It is at once the highest and most expensive railway in Europe.

Between Eigergletscher and the Jungfraujoch, the train stops twice. The Eigerwand viewing gallery enables tourists to peer down the lower slopes of the Eiger's North Face, and is from where a number of attempts to rescue injured climbers have been conducted. Eismeer is located much higher, at 3159m, and its windows look out across the cascading Fiescher glacier to the Schreckhorn and Lauteraarhorn. It is from here that climbers let themselves out through a tunnel (crampons often needed) to make their way to the Mittellegi Hut.

At the Jungfraujoch a lift takes visitors to the higher observation point of the Sphinx, with its outlook down the Jungfraufirn to the great confluence of glaciers at Konkordiaplatz, from where the Grosser Aletschgletscher is channelled far off through an avenue of attractive peaks. The name derives from a comment made by Victorian climber, the Revd John Hardy, who described this glacial crossroads as 'the Place de la Concorde of Nature: wherever you look there is a grand road and a lofty dome'. In winter and spring, skiers can enjoy an exhilarating run down to Konkordia and beyond, while ski-mountaineers have boundless opportunities to make both ascents and tours in this ice-bound heart of the Bernese Alps.

Accessed by an ever-increasing flight of metal ladders leading from the shrinking Konkordiaplatz icefield, the **Konkordia Hut** stands at 2850m at the foot of the Fülbärg (Faulberg) and makes a near-perfect base in a spectacular location. This large hut, owned by the Grindelwald section of the SAC, has 150 places and is fully staffed from March to the end of May, and from July to the end of September (www.konkordiahuette.ch).

Much closer to the Jungfraujoch, and reached by a hike of just 45mins, the privately owned **Mönchsjoch Hut** stands just above the Ober Mönchsjoch at 3657m, and also makes a convenient departure point for numerous ascents in summer. With places for 120, it is fully staffed in April and May, and from July until the end of September (www.moenchsjoch.ch). From here, ascents can be made of (among others) the ✦ **Mönch**, whose ordinary route via the SE Ridge takes only 2–3hrs; ✦ **Eiger** by the South Ridge (AD); the ✦ **Gross Fiescherhorn** by its NW Ridge (AD); and the ✦ **Jungfrau** via its long NE Ridge (D+), and by the SE Ridge from the Rottalsattel (PD).

Climbs from the Guggi Hut
For routes on the north side of the Mönch, Jungfrau and Jungfraujoch, the small, usually unmanned **Guggi Hut** is perched on a rock crest dividing the Eiger and Guggi glaciers, about 3hrs from the Eigergletscher station. Owned by the Interlaken section of the SAC, it has 30 dormitory places and self-catering facilities (www.sac-interlaken.ch).

From the hut the long Nollen Route (NW Buttress) on the 4107m ✦ **Mönch** is mostly PD with some very steep pitches and, depending on conditions, may be expected to take from 6 to 10hrs. On the mountain's NE Rib the 1921 Lauper Route enjoys a good reputation as one of the best mixed climbs in the district (TD), while the steep North Face between the two has a choice of routes, including a direct line put up during Christmas 1976 by Dick Renshaw and Dave Wilkinson. Their route (grade ED2), which had previously defeated several determined efforts, is affected by stonefall in summer, so is best avoided until winter or spring.

The original so-called 'ordinary' route on the ✦ **Jungfrau** from Kleine Scheidegg is the classic Guggi Route put up in 1865 by H B George and Sir George Young (father of Geoffrey Winthrop Young), with the guides Christian and Ulrich Almer and Hans Baumann. Once a popular ice climb it is now rarely in condition, but when it is, the Guggi Hut is usually adopted as the base, with the route (grade D) taking in the 3406m Schneehorn on the way. The scenery is magnificent throughout.

As for the ✦ **Jungfraujoch**, this is reached from the Guggi Hut by climbers via the Chielouwenen glacier; another D-grade route.

The Upper Valley
South of Lauterbrunnen the valley is flat-bedded and hemmed in by soaring cliffs. Meadows border the Lütschine, a footpath on one bank, the road on the other. There are groups of chalets, old dark-timbered Bernese farms and small hamlets. It rains a lot and often mist hangs for days at a time like a duvet over the river. No wonder everything is green and waterfalls so numerous. On the east side of the valley the famed Trümmelbach Falls, fed by the combined snowmelt from Eiger, Mönch and Jungfrau, corkscrew through the limestone wall near the hamlet of Sandbach, and emerge as a powerful torrent to join the slightly more placid Weisse Lütschine. On crags forming the south side of the Trümmelbach, a path has been created (at first little more than a shelf cut in the rock) that ascends this steep east wall of the valley to gain the tiny alp farm of Prechalp at 1320m, and continues above it, eventually coming to **Mettlenalp**, some 900m above the bed of the Lauterbrunnental.

At Sandbach there's a large campsite (Camping Breithorn), and a smaller, less formal one at Stechelberg. Between Sandbach and Stechelberg the cableway which serves Gimmelwald, Mürren and the Schilthorn rises out of the valley, giving a fine view of activists tackling the *via ferrata* mentioned above.

The public road ends at **Stechelberg**, a small village nestling at the foot of the Jungfrau. Served by postbus from Lauterbrunnen, the village consists of little more than a scattering of houses, a shop, post office, campsite, one hotel (the 30-bed Hotel Stechelberg, www.stechelberg.ch) and a former Naturfreundehaus, the welcoming, budget-priced Alpenhof run by Marc Jones and Diane Sifis (44 beds at b&b rates, or self-catering possible: www.alpenhof-stechelberg.ch).

Immediately to the west a narrow cleft, out of which bursts a tributary of the Lütschine, offers no hint whatsoever that behind it stretches the short but wildly attractive and mostly uninhabited ◐ **Sefinental**, blocked at its head by the great NE Face of the Gspaltenhorn and East Face of the Bütlasse (see 5:6). The south wall of the Sefinental, across which lies the head of the Lauterbrunnen valley, is formed by an extension of the Gspaltenhorn's Tschingelgrat, punctuated by the crown of rocks of the Ellstabhorn, although this, and the spires of the Ghudelhorn, remain unseen from the bed of the valley. A farm track projects for a short distance into the Sefinental, then forks. One branch cuts back on itself to make a lengthy slant up the northern hillside to reach Gimmelwald at about 1380m. The continuing track pushes further upstream before giving way to a path used by climbers aiming for a bivouac below the Gspaltenhorn, and by trekkers who soon break away on another trail which climbs the north flank of the valley to gain either the Rotstock Hut, or Mürren via Oberberg and Spielbodenalp.

Not far from where the farm track forks, a wooden bridge spans the Sefinen Lütschine. On the south side a trail climbs the brutally steep and heavily wooded lower slopes of the valley. Just short of the forest's upper reaches a minor path cuts off to the west, and leads in 15mins or so to the ⬤ **Busenalp**, a solitary building in a sublime location on a natural terrace high above the Sefinental, but looking directly at the west flank of the Jungfrau. Another path continues above the alp and rejoins the main trail at the Busengrat – the easternmost point of the dividing ridge between the Sefinental and upper (or inner) Lauterbrunnental. Once again the path forks, with the main trail turning the spur on its way to Obersteinberg, while the other, a minor offshoot, climbs very steeply straight up the grass ridge to gain the ⬤ **Tanzbödeli**, a surprisingly level meadow at 2095m that falls dramatically on three sides. From it one may enjoy a 360° panoramic view that includes all the summits along the Lauterbrunnental Wall.

Back at Stechelberg a footpath continues upvalley, but forks after about 8mins, with a minor but important trail cutting left which marks the start of the approach to the Silberhorn and Rottal Huts, both of which are used by climbers tackling different routes on the Jungfrau. The way to the **Silberhorn Hut** is long (6hrs), complicated and hazardous in inclement weather, and the hut itself is small (12 places) and without a resident guardian, so supplies must be carried (www.sac-lauterbrunnen.ch). Built upon the Rotbrättlücke saddle below the prominent Silberhorn at 2663m, it is owned by the Lauterbrunnen section of the SAC. The most obvious goal for climbers staying there is the 3695m **Silberhorn**, using the ridge (the Rotbrätt) directly above the hut (grade D) and continuing via the Guggi Route (see above) to the 4158m summit of the **Jungfrau**, although this is sometimes impractical due to changing glacier conditions.

Climbs from the Rottal Hut

The route to the **Rottal Hut** is not much shorter than that to the Silberhorn Hut, and it too mounts one or two difficult sections eased by fixed ropes or chains. Built by the Interlaken section of the SAC in a commanding position overlooking the glacial amphitheatre of the Rottal at 2755m (some 1845m above Stechelberg), the hut has 34 places, but is

The Rottal Hut

usually manned only at weekends from the end of June until mid-September (www.sac-interlaken.ch). A small herd of ibex can sometimes be seen grazing nearby. The Jungfrau rises above to the northeast. Its ridge then runs round via Rottalhorn and Louwihorn to the Gletscherhorn and Äbeni Flue. From the latter a spur effectively encloses the Rottal, forming an ice-filled bay.

From here the ❸ **Jungfrau** is climbed by way of the lengthy Inner Rottal Ridge. Dating from 1885, the route is mostly on rock and graded AD (III).

The Rottalhorn and Louwihorn are usually climbed from the east or south sides, but the 3983m ❸ **Gletscherhorn** has an impressive 1000m high NW Face on which the great Munich climber Willo Welzenbach put up the first route in 1932. Considered by some to be the finest and most difficult of his Lauterbrunnen Wall climbs, it is still graded TD+, although it is often out of condition nowadays. A more direct route was created by the rope of Etter, Reiss and Jaun in 1945 (TD+/ED1), while Rab Carrington and Alan Rouse pioneered a line to the right of this in 1972 (ED2), and five years later Phil Bartlett and Lindsay Griffin added one of their own to the left of the Welzenbach original (ED1).

The broad 900m North Face of the 3962m ❸ **Äbeni Flue** (formerly known as Ebnefluh) which blends into the Gletscherhorn, offers some fine climbs when its coating of snow and ice is in condition, although on the whole routes are a little less severe than those of its neighbour. The face received its first ascent as long ago as 1895 by C A McDonald, with Christian Jossi and Peter Bernet. Other lines followed, and in 1980 French ace Patrick Gabarrou with Pierre-Alain Steiner put up the hardest route on the face; a fairly direct line (grade TD) to the mountain's west summit. The North Ridge is also climbed from the Rottal Hut.

The ◯ **path from Stechelberg** crosses to the right-hand side of the river which, in the upper reaches of the valley is known as the Tschingel Lütschine (after the Tschingelhorn), and in about 45mins comes to Berghaus Trachsellauenen, set in a small meadow on the edge of woodland. This is the first of three rustic mountain inns located in the back-of-beyond upstream from Stechelberg, the other two standing at least 400m higher than Trachsellauenen on the northwest flank of the valley. Beyond the *berghaus* a path climbs first to Hotel Tschingelhorn, then continues to the charming **Berghotel Obersteinberg** whose rooms have neither electricity nor running water. Both the Tschingelhorn and Obersteinberg inns have standard rooms and dormitory accommodation, are open from June until the end of September, and enjoy splendid views across the valley to the head of the Lauterbrunnen Wall.

Upstream beyond Trachsellauenen, another trail recrosses to the true right bank of the Lütschine and works its way up to and above the dramatic Schmadribach Falls which pour over the lip of a rough, rock-littered meadow in which the drainage of several hanging glaciers unite. Above that meadow, and set close to a moraine rib between the Schmadri and Breithorn glaciers at 2262m, the small unmanned **Schmadri Hut** has an outlook of untamed grandeur. With just 14 places and self-catering facilities, it is owned by the Academic Alpine Club of Bern, and is useful as a base for climbs on the Mittaghorn, Grosshorn, and Lauterbrunnen Breithorn.

Climbs from the Schmadri Hut

The ❸ **Mittaghorn** (3892m) is the most easterly of these, and its steep north flank, though containing some challenging lines, has not received the same degree of attention that has been centred on the Gletscherhorn or Äbeni Flue, for example.

Directly above the hut the 3754m ❸ **Grosshorn** has a 1200m high North Face pioneered in 1932 by Welzenbach, Drexel and others from the Munich School, since when other lines and variations have been created in the TD/TD+ range of difficulty.

But it is the ❸ **Lauterbrunnen Breithorn** (3780m) that is the most attractive summit on the almost 10km length of the Lauterbrunnen Wall, and it's no surprise to discover that a wide selection of routes have been created on it, most of which can be tackled from the Schmadri Hut. The ENE Ridge is accessed from the Schmadrijoch to give a fine expedition on sound rock (grade D), but once again it was Willo Welzenbach who first climbed the North Face during his raid on the district in 1932. Now graded ED1, the rock is however, poor, making the route prone to objective dangers unless tackled in winter. The spurs on either side of the face are not subject to the same dangers and so are more popular than Welzenbach's route. The NNE Spur was climbed eight years before Welzenbach

UNESCO WORLD NATURAL HERITAGE SITE

In December 2001 the upper reaches of the Lauterbrunnen valley became part of the Jungfrau–Aletsch–Bietschhorn UNESCO World Natural Heritage Site, the first such site to be designated within the Alps in recognition of its unique landscape qualities. Covering an area of 824 square kilometres it includes mountains such as Wetterhorn, Schreckhorn, Finsteraarhorn, Eiger, Mönch, Jungfrau, Breithorn, Gspaltenhorn and the impressive Bietschhorn. Among its valleys, the upper Lauterbrunnental and neighbouring Sefinental are included, as is a large portion of the Lötschental to the south. Some 40 percent of the site is rock, but almost 50 percent is covered with ice, thanks largely to the 23km long Grosser Aletschgletscher, the Fieschergletscher, and the Petersgrat ice sheet which makes a convenient link between the two sides of the Oberland wall. (For further information visit www.swissworld.org)

stormed the central North Face, and is now graded TD, while the NNW Spur (also TD) is a recommended mixed climb.

In the meadow below the Schmadri Hut a path goes up to the little ☯ **Oberhornsee** tarn, a popular outing for guests staying at Obersteinberg, while another crosses the Schmadribach and makes its way directly to the Obersteinberg inn. At the head of the valley, though, glaciers hang on either side of the spur linking the Tschingelhorn and Lauterbrunnen Wetterhorn, and a route up the more northerly of these, the Tschingelfirn, leads to the **Mutthorn Hut**, beyond which lies the Kanderfirn and the ice sheet of the Petersgrat (see 5:5).

5:8 GRINDELWALD AND THE LÜTSCHENTAL

While the Lauterbrunnen valley flows from south to north, the neighbouring Lütschental drains westward out of Grindelwald's pastoral basin. The dramatic Lauterbrunnental is hemmed in by precipitous grey walls; the Lütschental is green,

Schynige Platte is one of the great alpine vantage points

The Swiss Alps — Chapter 5: Bernese Alps

Grindelwald & the Lütschental

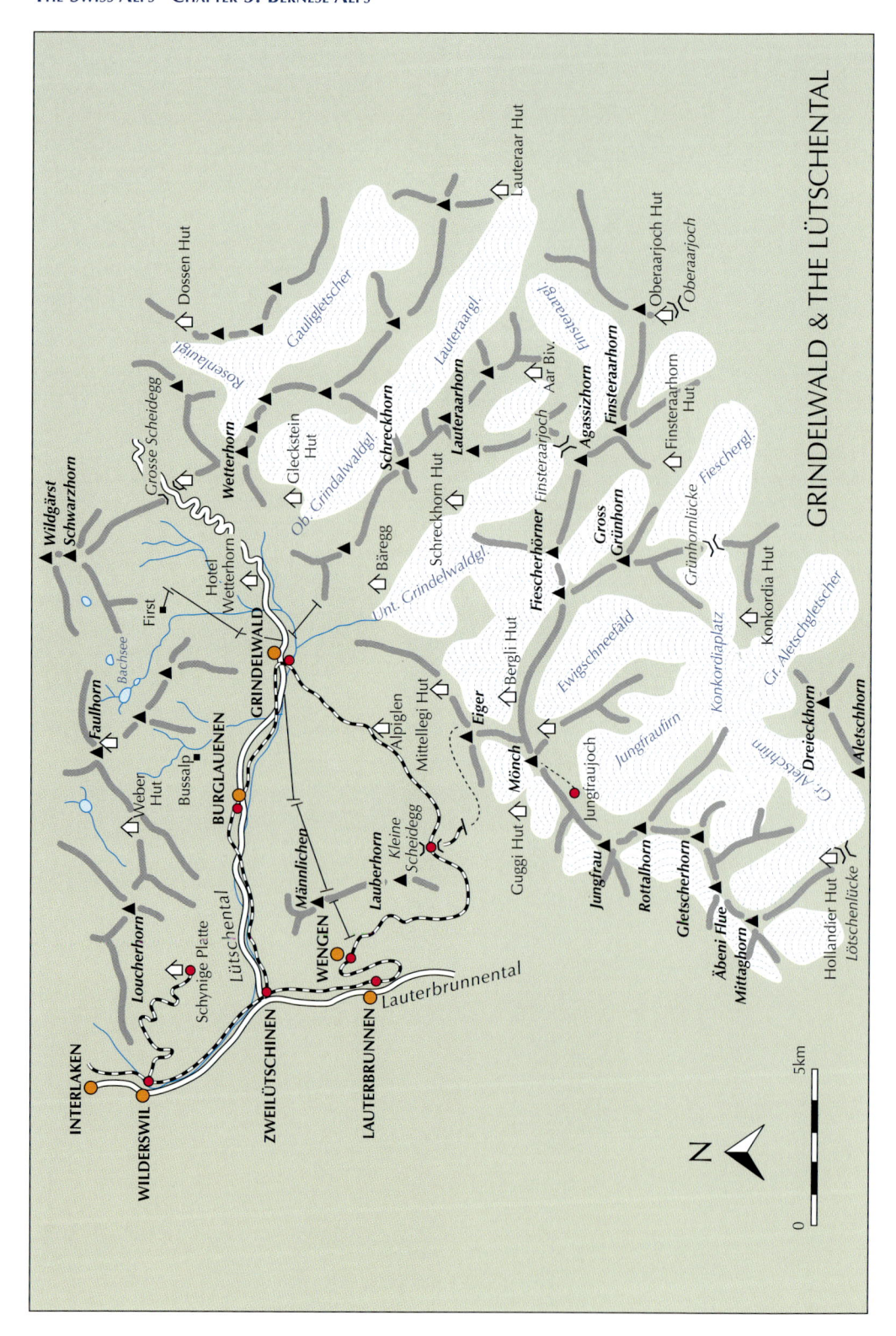

5:8 GRINDELWALD AND THE LÜTSCHENTAL

open and not at all intimidating. Villages in the Lauterbrunnental are necessarily small and closely contained, but 20km from Interlaken, Grindelwald sprawls across the hillside as though it has no boundaries.

The two valleys are therefore very different, but what unites them is the splendour of their mountains and, more prosaically, the railway that connects Lauterbrunnen with Grindelwald across the Kleine Scheidegg saddle, watched over by the looming presence of the Eiger.

There is another railway, of course, a direct line serving Grindelwald from Interlaken by way of Wilderswil and Zweilütschinen. But one should not ignore the old narrow-gauge cog railway, dating from 1893, that crawls up the abrupt eastern hillside above **Wilderswil** to arrive 50mins and 1403 vertical metres later at **Schynige Platte**, one of the truly great alpine vantage points from which to survey the central group of Oberland summits like an army officer with his crack troops lined up before him.

Schynige Platte marks the western end of a ridge system that effectively forms the north wall of the Lütschental. As well as being the terminus of the cog railway, it has a notable alpine garden and a *berghotel* at 1980m, open from May to October with 36 beds and spectacular views (www.schynigeplatte.ch). From the hotel, or the station just below it, a classic day's walk known as the ☼ ★ **Faulhornweg** traces a 15km route along this ridge, passing over easy saddles, skirting crags and crossing screes. The route visits the **Faulhorn** summit, and descends past the matchless Bachsee to finish at the First gondola lift station above Grindelwald. It is without question one of the most visually spectacular and rewarding hikes to be had anywhere in the Alps. In addition to the Schynige Platte *berghotel*, accommodation can be found along the route at the privately owned **Weber Hut** (Berghütte Männdlenen: www.

berghaus-maenndlenen.ch) set in a limestone cleft at 2344m, and reached 2½hrs along the trail, and at **Berghotel Faulhorn**, built just below the Faulhorn's 2681m summit. This is the oldest mountain hotel in Switzerland, with a view deemed worthy of a pull-out panorama in early Baedeker guides; it has both standard beds and dormitory places and is open from the end of June until mid-October (www.berghotel-faulhorn.ch). And finally, the gondola station, **Berghaus First** offers dormitory accommodation from mid-May until the end of October (tel 033 853 12 84).

The Faulhornweg may be the finest day walk in the hills above Grindelwald, the mountain landscape spread before it unrivalled, but the ridge system it traverses, this north wall of the Lütschental, has other prizes in store. Return from First to the Bachsee (Bachalpsee), and after you've had your fill of the heart-stopping sight of Wetterhorn, Schreckhorn and Finsteraarhorn thrown on their heads in the perfect stillness of the lake shortly after dawn, find a trail winding up the eastern slope into a secretive groove-like valley in which there lies the little Hagelsee (or Hagelseewli as some maps would have it), often with ice flows drifting in early summer. Beyond it lies another small lake, the Häxensee (Haxeseeli) below two modest peaks with stunning summit views. These are the 2891m ⊗ **Wildgärst** and, aided by ladders, the 2928m ⊗ **Schwarzhorn**, while a crossing of the ridge running southwest from the latter peak, gives an entertaining descent safeguarded by fixed chains into a scenic meadowland beside the Gemschberg.

Before leaving this north side of the Lütschental, it would also be worth looking at a multi-day trek that begins at Schynige Platte and makes a circuit of the Lütschental–Lauterbrunnental district. The Tour of the Jungfrau Region is a trek that deserves to become an alpine classic.

Finally, there's the exquisite pastureland of ☼ **Bussalp** spilling across a vast open basin

☼ ★ TOUR OF THE JUNGFRAU REGION

Making a highly scenic clockwise tour of the district, the TJR has several bad-weather alternatives and optional diversions that increase the opportunities for trekkers to experience the very best of the mountains over a course of 9–11 days. The route avoids all resorts and villages except tiny Stechelberg at the Lauterbrunnental roadhead, and Saxeten in the Saxettal on the final stage. For full details, see the Cicerone guidebook *Tour of the Jungfrau Region*.

Day 1: Beginning at **Schynige Platte** above Wilderswil, the first day follows the popular Faulhornweg, remaining above 2000m for much of the way, passing the **Weber Hut** and **Berghotel Faulhorn** before descending past the beautiful **Bachsee** and ending at **Berghaus First** to find dormitory accommodation at the gondola lift station.

Day 2: While the basic route is very short, cutting across the pastures of Alp Grindel to **Grosse Scheidegg**, then straight down to **Hotel Wetterhorn** (an easy 2½–3hrs), the preferred option breaks away from the main trail and goes up the lip of the Oberer Grindelwaldgletscher's gorge to the **Gleckstein Hut** with its view across the glacier's icefall to the Schreckhorn at the end of a 5hr day.

Day 3: Options again: the basic tour makes a 5hr direct route to Alpiglen, but a diversion to **Berghaus Bäregg** overlooking the Unterer Grindelwaldgletscher and the Fiescherwand glacial amphitheatre, is a highly recommended alternative. For those trekkers who spent the previous night at the Gleckstein Hut, this makes a natural follow-on, with the route being continued to Alpiglen next day.

Day 4: Assuming the previous stage ended at Bäregg, day four begins by returning down the east side of the Unterer Grindelwaldgletscher's gorge, and joining the main route where it crosses the mouth of the gorge at its narrowest point on a footbridge. Thereafter a trail is taken which climbs up and across rock slabs, into forest, then out to a high trail skirting the lower slopes of the Eiger to reach **Alpiglen**, where the rustic **Berghaus Alpiglen** offers atmospheric rooms and dormitory accommodation.

Day 5: A short stage is suggested here, for the TJR follows the Eiger Trail to Eigergletscher above Kleine Scheidegg, from where a host of opportunities for exploring the area become evident. **Kleine Scheidegg** has plenty of overnight accommodation, and for newcomers to the area, a wide range of day walks with excellent views.

Day 6: There's a loss of height of almost 1300 steep and knee-crunching metres between Eigergletscher and the bed of the Lauterbrunnen valley, but it's an interesting trail that follows the melt of the Eiger and Guggi glaciers all the way down to the Trümmelbach Falls. Initially on a moraine crest, then down forested slopes to Biglenalp and Mettlenalp, then via the secluded farm of Prechalp with bird's-eye views onto the rooftops of Lauterbrunnental chalets, the day ends at **Stechelberg**, the tiny roadhead village with a single hotel, and budget accommodation in the Alpenhof nearby.

Day 7: On this stage the Tour of the Jungfrau Region wanders to the head of the Lauterbrunnen valley, a wild region of waterfalls, old moraines and rough meadows rimmed by mountains of the fabled Lauterbrunnen Wall. At the end of an exhilarating day's trekking of 5–5½hrs, an overnight is spent in **Berghaus Obersteinberg**.

Day 8: Now heading north, the trek crosses the grassy Busengrat, descends steeply into the Sefinental, and after wandering towards the Gspaltenhorn's great NE Face, a climb of more than 850m brings you to the **Rotstock Hut** at 2039m.

Day 9: On this stage a scramble along the West Ridge of the **Schilthorn** is one of the highlights of the route. Descent by the East Ridge is not so inspiring, but it's a short descent that leads to the jade-green Grauseeli. Below this tarn the way drops steeply to Schiltalp, before coming to the **Blumental** above Mürren, where two pensions provide overnight lodging in a tranquil setting.

Day 10: The penultimate stage continues the northbound trend, among pastures, through woodland and via the Soustal to reach the **Suls-Lobhorn Hut** after 3½hrs of trekking. But such is the nature of the route, and the landscape it passes through, that these 3½hrs can easily be doubled.

Day 11: A little over 4hrs is all that's needed to reach the end of the trek in Wilderswil. At first a trail is taken across limestone-pitted meadows, then round a steep rocky slope that spills into the Sylertal, across the Bällehöchst ridge and down into the sweeping pastures of the **Bällenalp**. The Saxettal is then followed all the way down to **Wilderswil** to conclude a memorable tour.

5:8 GRINDELWALD AND THE LÜTSCHENTAL

TOUR OF THE JUNGFRAU REGION

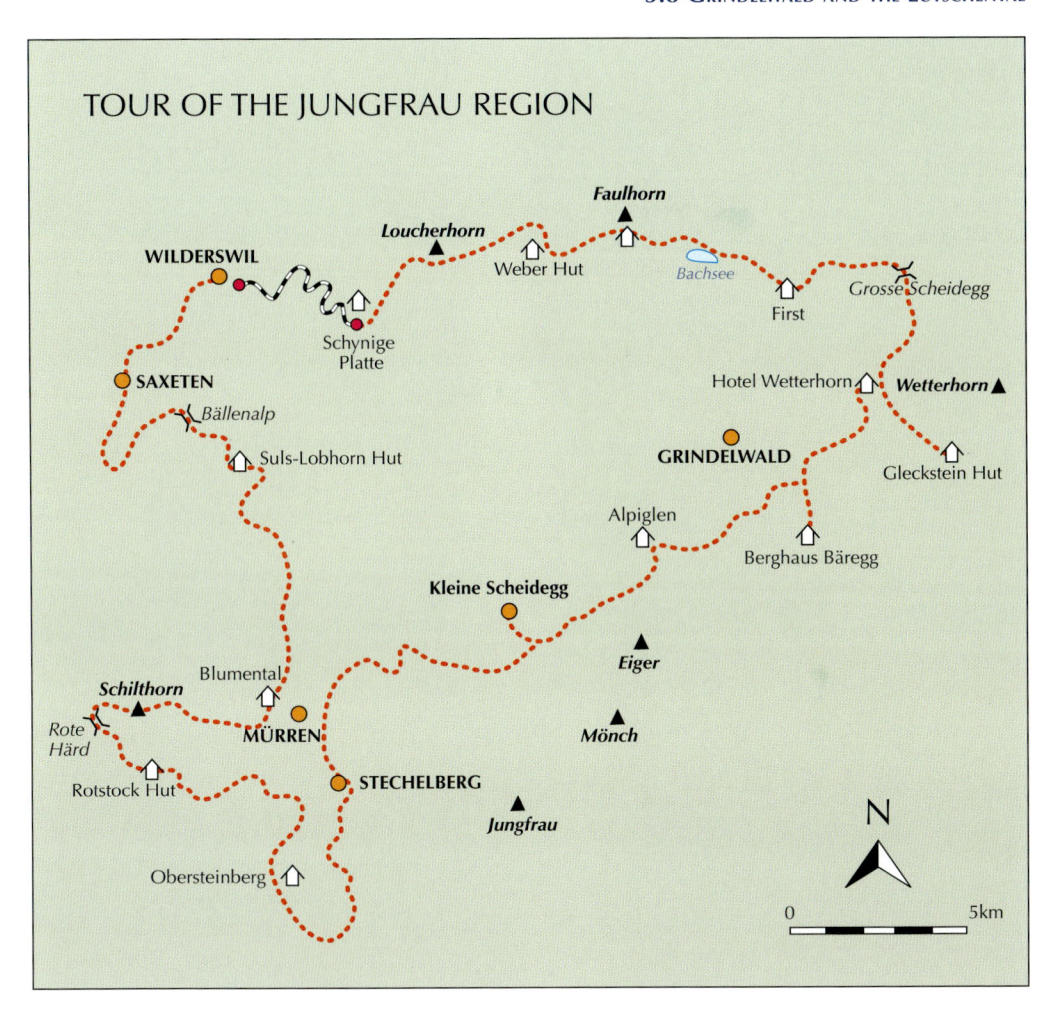

south of the Faulhorn. Buses come here from Grindelwald, and while many visitors barely stray from the restaurant at the bus terminus, paths climb up to the Faulhorn, cross over to the Bachsee, or work a way roughly eastward over yet more scenic green ridges with eye-watering views, to lead step by step deeper into a mountain wonderland.

The Grindelwald Basin

While Chamonix owes its popularity to Mont Blanc, and Zermatt to the Matterhorn, Grindelwald basks in the notoriety of the Eiger. But long before the Eiger became a mountaineering issue, Grindelwald was known as a glacier village, for it was the two major ice streams of the Upper (Oberer) and Lower (Unterer) Grindelwaldgletschers that first drew visitors to what in the late 18th century was little more than a collection of chalets, each with its own small garden adorned with cherry trees. 'In Grindelwald', writes Claire Elaine Engel in *Mountaineering in the Alps*, 'tourists used to ride to the snouts of the two glaciers and there eat strawberries while they listened to the roar of an Alpine horn, blown by a bearded native.' The mountains were of only secondary importance, and according to historian Ronald W Clark, it was the ascent of the Wetterhorn by Alfred Wills in 1854 that really made Grindelwald; the Eiger's attraction came much later.

All through the 18th century, and the early years of the 19th, **Grindelwald** was one of the three main resorts of the Alps (if such innocent villages could be so-called), the other two being Chamonix and Lauterbrunnen. While Lauterbrunnen has today been replaced in the hierarchy by Zermatt, St Moritz and several others, Grindelwald's fame as a

329

The glassy Bachsee mirrors Schreckhorn and Finsteraarhorn in its still waters

year-round resort has spread across the continents, its flourishing hotels, chalets and apartments lie scattered over the south- and west-facing hillsides, and construction cranes are a semi-permanent challenge to conservationists. Every day in every season, trains pull in at the station to spill their cargo of camera-clutching visitors into the streets and onto the various cableways that rise with a soft buzzing sound to select vantage points. Signs in Japanese rival those in German or English, for Grindelwald is very much a multi-cultural honeypot – with a mountain backdrop.

There's no shortage of accommodation of every standard, including campsites and hostels. Shops cater for all tastes; there are banks, restaurants, a mountain guides' bureau (www.grindelwaldsports.ch) and a large and well-resourced tourist office at the sports centre a short stroll from the bus station (www.grindelwald.ch).

Above the resort to north and east, service roads, farm tracks and footpaths angle across flower meadows in full view of the Wetterhorn, Grindelwald's 'home mountain'. In winter skiers carve their slaloms on the snowslopes served by the First gondola lift system.

Above Grindelwald to the northwest, it is the great pastoral basin of **Bussalp**, served by local bus, that is so rewarding for walkers. The Wetterhorn is hidden from view, and instead, it is the Eiger and mountains further west that draw the eye.

But on the other side of the Lütschental, on the slopes above Grund west and southwest of Grindelwald, an immense, almost unbroken sweep of meadowland rises to a ridge running from Männlichen to Kleine Scheidegg. This ridge effectively forms the Lütschental's west wall dividing the valley from that of Lauterbrunnen. Again, a gondola lift system swings across that meadowland which, in winter, is another paradise for downhill skiers, while some way south of the gondola, trains creep their way below the Eiger to gain the busy Kleine Scheidegg saddle. In summer, yet more paths, tracks and service roads entice the walker, with direct views of the Eiger, and retrospective views to Wetterhorn and Schreckhorn.

The Eiger
The 1901 edition of Baedeker's *Switzerland* devotes just one sentence to the mountain whose North Face alone has since inspired numerous books and at least half a dozen films. The tragic history of early attempts to scale the Eigerwand in the 1930s, with all the graphic horror of lifeless bodies left hanging in full view of the Kleine Scheidegg telescopes,

transformed a 3970m mountain (unknown to all but those who lived in its shadow, plus a few ambitious climbers) into a gruesome icon of misguided adventure. At least, that was how it was perceived by a public hungry for sensation, and the newspapers of the time had no qualms about feeding that hunger.

The Eiger is a big mountain, no doubt about it. It may not reach 4000m, but its northern wall is a truly massive piece of architecture, around 1800m high. Its bulk, which of course includes the Eigerwand, faces across the meadows towards Interlaken, and extends for almost 5km between the Klein Eiger above Eigergletscher Station, and the mouth of the Unterer Grindelwaldgletscher's gorge. By contrast the 800m SE Face is hidden from public scrutiny, overlooking the Fiescher glacier and an arctic world so different from the pastoral nature of Alpiglen at the foot of the north flank.

It was first climbed on 11 August 1858 by Charles Barrington, an amateur jockey who had once won the Irish Grand National. On a visit to Switzerland he arrived in Grindelwald in early August and engaged two well-known local guides, Christian Almer and Peter Bohren, for his first taste of mountaineering. On 6 August they climbed to the Strahlegg Pass, and three days later made the ascent of the Jungfrau from a bivouac in a cave on the Faulberg, returning to Grindelwald the same evening. Restless for more exercise Barrington asked what else there was to do. 'You could do the Matterhorn,' he was told, 'or the Eiger. Neither has been climbed as yet.'

The Matterhorn was a long and expensive way off. The Eiger was near at hand. So the Eiger it would be. 'I was surprised to see the families of the guides in a state of distraction at their departure for the ascent,' wrote Barrington later, 'and two elderly ladies came out and abused me for taking them to risk their lives.'

Arriving at Wengernalp at about midnight on the 10th, they snatched a few hours of sleep and at 3am set off by lantern light, their chosen route being more or less that which is taken as the *voie normale* today (AD). According to Barrington it was he, and not his guides, who took over the lead once they were on rock, and climbing well, they went straight up the crest of the West Ridge to reach the summit before midday. On the descent they twice escaped being overwhelmed by avalanches, and arrived back at Wengernalp four hours after leaving the summit. 'Thus ended my first and only visit to Switzerland,' he commented in a letter to the Alpine Club 25 years later. 'Not having money enough to try the Matterhorn, I went home.'

The Eiger's South Ridge (AD) was climbed in 1876, and in 1885 local guides managed to descend the narrow NE (Mittellegi) Ridge. However, this classic arête had to wait until 1921 before it received its first *ascent* by the young Japanese climber Yuko Maki with three Grindelwald guides, Fritz Amatter, Fritz Steuri senior and Samuel Brawand. Three years later Maki contributed 10,000 francs to the construction of a hut on the lower part of the ridge at 3355m, and this was replaced in 2001 by a new building capable of sleeping 36 in its dormitories. Reached by way of the Eismeer Station on the Jungfraujoch railway, the **Mittellegi Hut** is manned from June until the end of August (www.grindelwald.ch/mittellegi). From it the ridge itself (D) may be climbed in something like 4–5hrs.

In 1932 a Swiss team, comprising Hans Lauper and Alfred Zürcher, with the Valais guides Josef Knubel and Alexander Graven, achieved a fine ascent of the NE Face; a classic ice climb now known as the Lauper Route (TD+) which came to be used by some ambitious parties in order to reconnoitre the nearby Eigerwand. Five years later the SE Face was climbed by Eidenschink and Moeller (TD with many pitches of IV and V), thus completing all the major features of the mountain, save that of the 'rugged and precipitous' North Face.

The Eiger's North Face is a big dark amphitheatre of vertical rock rising from the sunlit pastures of Alpiglen. Said to be the largest continuously steep mountain wall in the Alps, its reputation today inspires both awe and respect in equal measure. When A W Moore made the third ascent of the mountain in 1864, he managed to look directly down the North Face whose steepness was such that he commented: 'A stone dropped from the edge would have fallen hundreds of feet before encountering any obstacle to its progress' (*The Alps in 1864*). Gaston Rébuffet described it as 'black, cold and joyless ... The face is ... hollowed like a sick man's chest, often veiled in mist or blotted out by clouds.' He wrote of the wall cracking with frost, and concluded that 'the Eiger is slowly breaking to pieces' (*Starlight and Storm*). It is indeed a face of shattered rock, both sombre and forbidding.

Between August 1935 and June 1938, four separate attempts by German, Austrian and Italian climbers were made to scale the Eigerwand, resulting in no less than eight fatalities. These deaths brought the mountain a savage notoriety which resulted in a decree by the Swiss government that banned all climbing on the wall. (The ban was later withdrawn, as it was clearly impossible to control.) But on 24 July 1938 the breakthrough came when Heinrich Harrer and Fritz Kasparek from Austria, and the Germans Andreas Heckmair and Ludwig Vörg, joined forces after having begun as separate ropes, and reached the summit after spending four days on the face. As Walt Unsworth says in Hold the Heights, 'It was a breakthrough as profound as the first ascent of the Matterhorn had been or the Brenva Spur but much more wide-reaching because it became the cornerstone of all modern mountaineering.'

In the 70-odd years since, the original ☆ **1938 Route** (ED2) has been repeated countless times, and on those rare occasions when the face is in condition, it's climbed almost on a daily basis. Apparently a large amount of gear has been left *in situ* with pegs and belay bolts especially in the lower section.

A number of other routes have also been created on the Eigerwand, but they are too numerous to mention here. The face has been climbed direct; winter ascents are common; it's often been tackled solo and, being something of an alpine showpiece, it has been treated to some extraordinarily fast ascents. On 20 April 2011, for example, 27-year-old Swiss climber Dani Arnold romped up the Heckmair route in 2hrs 28mins. Despite such achievements the North Face of the Eiger remains a serious undertaking, and a goal for all ambitious climbers as standards of alpinism soar. Yet the face itself has changed. In the hot summer of 2003 the White Spider (the well-named patch of frozen snow near the top of the wall) disappeared and the icefields were reduced to gravel, making it even more dangerous than normal. The fickle nature of Oberland weather, and the frequency and ferociousness of its storms add both to the aura of the face, and the need for luck as well as skill to complete an ascent in safety. March seems to be the preferred month on the face, but autumn is also favoured. (For details of selected routes on the Eiger, see the Alpine Club guide *Bernese Oberland* by Les Swindin.)

The 4000ers

South of Grindelwald, between the Eiger and Mättenberg, the Oberland wall is breached by the gorge of the Unterer Grindelwaldgletscher, which

The Finsteraarhorn from the Schreckhorn Hut

appears to be blocked at its far end by the ice-crusted face of the Fiescherhorn. That is almost, but not quite, the reality, for if you follow a path along the eastern lip of that gorge, you will come to ◐ **Berghaus Bäregg**, a modern timber-clad building perched on a prominent spur of land at 1775m, with an unrestricted view into a glacial cirque dominated by the Fiescherwand, around whose east flank tumbles another glacier separate from that which once filled the icy basin. That intruding glacier is the Ischmeer (Eismeer), whose corridor is flanked by 4000m peaks leading to the Agassizhorn, behind and above which rises the Finsteraarhorn, highest of the Bernese Alps. The 4km wide ◐ **Fiescherwand** is one of the great Oberland north faces. Around 1200m high, sections of the face are threatened by falling seracs, but many routes have been made on it since the first ascent in 1926 by the well-known Swiss climber Walter Amstutz, with Peter von Schumacher. The face is crowned by the tapering 4049m summit of the ◐ **Gross Fiescherhorn**, a popular goal for ski-mountaineers based at the Mönchsjoch Hut.

But what of **Berghaus Bäregg**? Opened in the summer of 2006 to replace Restaurant Stieregg, which disappeared the year before when the moraine meadow on which it stood collapsed, it is the latest in a list of mountain hostels to carry the Bäregg name. The first was built between 1856 and 1858 some way below the present *berghaus*, but was later destroyed by avalanche. In 1868 a second Bäregg hotel opened, but this too was destroyed in 1906, to be replaced the same year by Berghaus Bäregg Eismeer. Once again, this was demolished by an avalanche in 1940. Bergrestaurant Stieregg opened in 1954; a new name and a different site, about 100m beneath the present *berghaus* on an idyllic moraine meadow grazed by a handful of sheep. But climate change led to the melting of permafrost, the collapse of rock walls, shrinking glaciers and snowfields, and crumbling moraines. Stieregg's meadow shrank dramatically, until the restaurant building was finally undercut and destroyed in June 2005.

Berghaus Bäregg today is extremely popular with day visitors who walk up from the Pfingstegg cableway, but it also has 28 dormitory places and a full meals service for those wishing to stay overnight, and is open from June until October (www.baeregg.com). From it a path descends steeply, then continues along the eastern side of the glacial bowl, crosses avalanche runnels (some stonefall danger), scales the steep Rots Gufer rocks via fixed ladders, and about 3hrs from Bäregg, reaches the **Schreckhorn Hut**. Located at the foot of the peak after which it is named, on the east bank of the Obers Ischmeer glacier at 2529m, this is a modern hut with 90 places. Owned by the Basle section of the SAC, it is manned throughout July, August and September (www.sac-basel.ch) and makes a useful base for climbs on the Schreckhorn, Lauteraarhorn, Strahlegghorn and Agassizhorn, and for the crossing of cols such as the Strahleggpass, Finsteraarjoch, and Agassizjoch between Agassizhorn and Finsteraarhorn.

Translated as the 'Terror Peak', the 4087m ◐ ★ **Schreckhorn** is reckoned to be one of the most difficult of the Oberland 4000ers, whose first ascent was won in August 1861 by Leslie Stephen with the guides Peter and Christian Michel and Christian Kaufmann from Grindelwald. (Ulrich Kaufmann is often quoted as being on this climb instead of Christian, but in his account of the ascent which appeared in *The Playground of Europe*, Stephen is unambiguous when naming his guides.) Their route, which took in the Schreck Couloir up to the Schrecksattel, then by the ESE Ridge, became a variant of what was treated as the 'normal' route for the next 50 years, but has since fallen from favour. Instead, the mountain is most often climbed nowadays by the SW Ridge, on a route (D-) pioneered in 1902 by the unguided rope of John Wicks, Claude Wilson and Edward Bradby. The South Pillar (D+) has the reputation of being one of the best rock climbs in the Bernese Alps, about 600m long, and with pitches of IV and V. The North Face and NW Ridge also claim some fine routes, but are as often tackled from either a bivouac, or from the Gleckstein or Lauteraar Huts, the latter being a long way off. The Schreckhorn is in all respects a serious mountain with a reputation for attracting sudden storms – see Frank Smythe's *The Adventures of a Mountaineer* for a cautionary tale.

Near neighbour of the Schreckhorn, to which it is joined by a pinnacled ridge above the Schreck glacier, the ◐ **Lauteraarhorn** (4042m) has an incomparably better location, for it stands at the apex of three ridges above a great complex of icefields: the Lauteraar, Finsteraar, Strahlegg and Obers Ischmeer glaciers. And the summit view of the Finsteraarhorn is outstanding. Nestling at the foot of the Lauteraar Rothorn in a remote location near the confluence of the Strahlegg and Finsteraar glaciers, the **Aar Bivouac Hut** (2733m) provides easy access to the normal route (AD-) via a couloir on the South Face which leads to the SE Ridge (www.sac-pilatus.ch). This is the route by which the mountain was first climbed by a large party of glaciologists and their guides in 1842. The bivouac hut belongs to the Lucerne-based Pilatus section of the SAC, has room for 17, and is reached by a 7hr glacier trek from the Grimsel Pass. (Access from the Schreckhorn Hut involves crossing either the Finsteraarjoch or the Strahleggpass.) To climb the Lauteraarhorn from the Schreckhorn Hut, the most obvious route is by way of the SW Ridge (TD-) gained at the Strahleggpass, although there's loose rock to contend with.

The SW Ridge of the Lauteraarhorn connects with the 3461m **Strahlegghorn**, known more for its views than any climbing appeal. Then the ridge runs south and southeast to the Nasse Strahlegg at 3482m before disappearing into converging icefields. To the southwest lies the glacier pass of the **Finsteraarjoch**, beyond which stands the ③ **Agassizhorn**, named after Louis Agassiz, the leading Swiss scholar who conducted a famous series of studies from a base on the Unteraar glacier in the 1840s. Falling short of the magical 4000m mark by just 47m, the Agassizhorn presents a graceful 'fin' when seen from the north, but is dominated by the towering Finsteraarhorn which it imitates. Coolidge claimed the first ascent in 1872, attacking the peak via the Agassizjoch and the SE Ridge (F), but the NE Ridge from the Finsteraarjoch (TD) is considered a better route.

At 4273m the imposing ③ ☆ **Finsteraarhorn** is not only the highest of the Bernese Alps, but one of the most remote of the major alpine peaks. This remoteness both adds to its appeal, and deters all but the most resolute of climbers from making the long approach to it. Standing on a rocky promontory on the edge of the Fiescher glacier at 3048m, the large **Finsteraarhorn Hut** is most easily reached in a 5–6hr hike from the Jungfraujoch via the **Grünhornlücke**, but in springtime, when skis allow a relatively speedy access, it can be overcrowded, despite its 110 places. Owned by the Meiringen based Oberhasli section of the SAC, it is manned in April and May, and from July to the end of September (www.finsteraarhornhuette.ch). From the hut, the ordinary route via the SW Flank and NW Ridge, is said to be rather tedious at first, but from the Hugisattel it improves with an exposed scramble along the ridge – a PD route of 4–5hrs.

Across the upper Fiescher glacier west of the Finsteraarhorn, the ③ **Gross Grünhorn** is another attractive 4000er (4044m) tackled, depending on route, from either the Finsteraarhorn Hut (SE Face and East Pillar), Konkordia Hut (SW Ridge, by which it was first climbed in 1865), or the Mönchsjoch Hut for the North Ridge. It is the last of the 4000m peaks that can realistically be approached from Grindelwald, for the only one outstanding from the Oberland list is the **Aletschhorn**, which stands south of the Aletschfirn between the Hollandia Hut and the Mittelaletsch Bivouac Hut, and will be visited in 5:10.

The Wetterhorn

Towering over the Grosse Scheidegg saddle, and only lightly dusted with snow in summer, the Wetterhörner dominate the view from Grindelwald, with fearsome-looking rock walls and a prominent crown of three individual summits. The 3692m ③ ☆ **Wetterhorn**, formerly known as the Hasli Jungfrau, is the second highest but most conspicuous of the group (the Mittelhorn is 3704m), and both fame and appearance make it a clear and obvious objective for the first-time alpinist with an ambition to bag a big name.

Yet what is seen from Grindelwald is only part of the picture, for the Wetterhorn's eastern side is very different. From a distance, from Engstlenalp for instance, it displays creamy waves of snow and ice above a foreground of grey rock, but on closer inspection the Rosenlaui, and smaller Hengsteren glaciers, suggest a fairly straightforward approach, and it was from this eastern side that the mountain was first climbed in 1844 by Édouard Desor's guides Melchior Bannholzer and Johann Jaun of Meiringen. (Three days earlier Desor and his guides had made the first ascent of the 3689m Rosenhorn, the third of the Wetterhörner's summits.) To follow Bannholzer and Jaun's route today (PD) involves an initial glacier plod from a base at the SAC's **Dossen Hut** (2663m) above the right bank of the Rosenlaui glacier. Near the head of the glacier the Wellhornsattel leads onto the upper Hengstengletscher, and from the Wettersattel a final steep climb takes the route up the SSE Ridge to the summit.

By the time of Wills' ascent in 1854, which historians mark as the start of the so-called Golden

The Wetterhorn turns bronze with the alpenglow

Age of mountaineering, the Wetterhorn had already been climbed four or five times. Wills was not even the first amateur, for Louis Aggasiz was just one who had been up it a decade earlier, but the Victorian conceit which determined to claim the plums of early alpine peak-bagging for Britain – a form of Empire building that required the help of local guides rather than political and military backing – made Wills' climb (or perhaps his account of it in *Wanderings Among the High Alps*) a not-altogether-convincing argument to be considered one of these. And why this ascent is taken to be the start of alpinism as a sport is difficult to understand. The fact that a good many Swiss (and other nationalities) had been collecting summits without any scientific pretension for decades, was (and continues to be) conveniently glossed over.

Alfred Wills had enjoyed several visits to the Alps before he made his mark there. A lawyer who later became a distinguished High Court judge, a knight of the realm and an original member of the Alpine Club, he was 26 years old and newly married when he arrived in Grindelwald, where he was steered towards the Wetterhorn by local guide Ulrich Lauener, who assured him that the mountain had not been climbed from that side. Lauener, 'the most renowned guide of the Oberland' would surely have known the mountain's history, as would the second Grindelwald guide Peter Bohren, who knew the Wetterhorn better than anyone, for he had already climbed it twice, once in 1845, and on a second occasion a few weeks before Wills' arrival on the scene. But as Walt Unsworth suggests (in *Hold the Heights*), the purpose of this duplicity was perhaps to make the expedition more attractive to Wills, and to benefit himself and the other guides who would make up the party, including Auguste Balmat and Auguste Simond (nicknamed Sampson) from Chamonix.

Wills and most of the party left Grindelwald at 1:30pm on the afternoon of 16 September, and after passing Bohren's home, Lauener caught up with them, carrying a 3.5m mast and an iron 'flagge' intended for the summit. Before dusk they reached the Gleckstein cave where they made their bivouac, and resumed their ascent at 4.30am next morning. It was light by the time the Chrinnen glacier was reached. In less than an hour they were safely off the ice and working their way up small ledges and 'steep slopes covered with loose stones and schisty débris'. It was then that Wills experienced what he claimed was 'the worst bit of scrambling I ever did'. Later they were perturbed to see two chamois hunters also making for the summit carrying a fir tree (these turned out to be the guides Ulrich Kaufmann and Christian Almer, the latter having been on the mountain earlier that year with Peter Bohren). After an exchange of words, the two parties eventually joined forces; the summit was now about 240m above them, crowning a slope of snow and ice of increasing steepness. Lauener led the way, cutting steps that were enlarged by Simond, following as second man, and as he reached the final cornice, Lauener hacked at it with his axe. A section of the cornice collapsed. 'I see blue sky', he cried, and at 11.20am the summit was theirs.

'The whole world seemed to lie at my feet,' wrote Wills, and in a way it did, for as a consequence his name will be forever associated with mountaineering's Golden Age; by contrast, that of Stanhope Templeman Speer is almost completely unknown.

Speer was a young Scot and son of a doctor living in Interlaken, who made the first ascent of the **Mittelhorn** (highest of the Wetterhörner's summits) in July 1845, nine years before Wills' arrival in Grindelwald. Having learned that several attempts to climb the mountain from Grindelwald had failed, Speer went round to the Grimsel to make his attempt on the Wetterhörner's last unclimbed summit. One of his guides was Johann Jaun who had made the first ascent of both the Rosenhorn and Hasli Jungfrau the previous year. For their Mittelhorn ascent the party started from the Pavillon Dollfus overlooking the Unteraar glacier, and after reaching the summit by climbing on ice and snow almost all the way, they descended by the Rosenlaui glacier, thus making a complete traverse of the mountain. In November that year Speer published his report of the climb in the widely read *Athenaeum*, but despite having a small part in promoting mountaineering as a sport, his name and achievement were effectively eclipsed by those of Alfred Wills, who went on to become one of the first presidents of the Alpine Club.

Today, the route taken by Wills (the SW Flank) remains the most popular on the ☆ **Wetterhorn**, and is graded AD-. The **Gleckstein Hut** is used as the base for this and for several other routes, not only on the Wetterhörner, but also on the Bärglistock and Schreckhorn, and for the crossing of the Lauteraarsattel. Reached by a 3½hr trek from Hotel Wetterhorn along the east lip of the Oberer Grindelwald glacier's gorge, the hut stands on a prominent grassy shelf at 2317m. Property of the Burgdorf section of the SAC, it has 100 dormitory places and is usually manned from June until the end of October (www.gleckstein.ch). The original Gleckstein Hut was built in 1880, but the present building was constructed as a hotel in 1904 at a time when there were plans to create the world's first passenger cableway in four stages to the summit of the Wetterhorn, with an intermediate station nearby. In 1908 the first stage was completed (remains of the station can be seen from the approach path leading to the hut), but with the outbreak of the First World War the project was abandoned, and the hotel was taken over by the SAC in 1920 to replace their more modest hut.

5:9 HASLITAL AND GRIMSEL PASS

The road across the Grosse Scheidegg is closed to private vehicles, but buses use the pass for journeys between Grindelwald and Meiringen. On the 1962m saddle, immediately below the great walls of the **Scheideggwetterhorn**, the large **Berghotel Grosse Scheidegg** has about 50 dormitory places as well as standard hotel beds (www.scheidegg.ch.vu), and provides access to climbs on the north-facing cliffs. All routes on these are long (up to 1300m) and serious, some of which count among the most difficult in the Swiss Alps.

While walker's routes stay mainly on the left flank of the valley, the road snakes down into the Rosenlauital, and below Schwarzwaldalp passes through the rather gloomy, tree-crowded climbing centre of **Rosenlaui** where the massive building of **Hotel Rosenlaui** provides both standard beds and dormitory accommodation (www.rosenlaui.ch). It is here that the drainage of the Rosenlaui glacier thunders through a gorge, the Rosenlauischlucht, to swell the Rychen Bach stream, and is where the approach to the **Dossen Hut** begins. Crossing to the right bank of the glacier torrent, the way heads south, mounts a rock barrier with the aid of fixed cables and ladders, passes the **Rosenlaui Bivouac Hut** at 2330m (not open in summer: for information see www.sac-oberaargau.ch) and reaches the Dossen Hut about 4½hrs from Rosenlaui. The hut

5:9 Haslital and Grimsel Pass

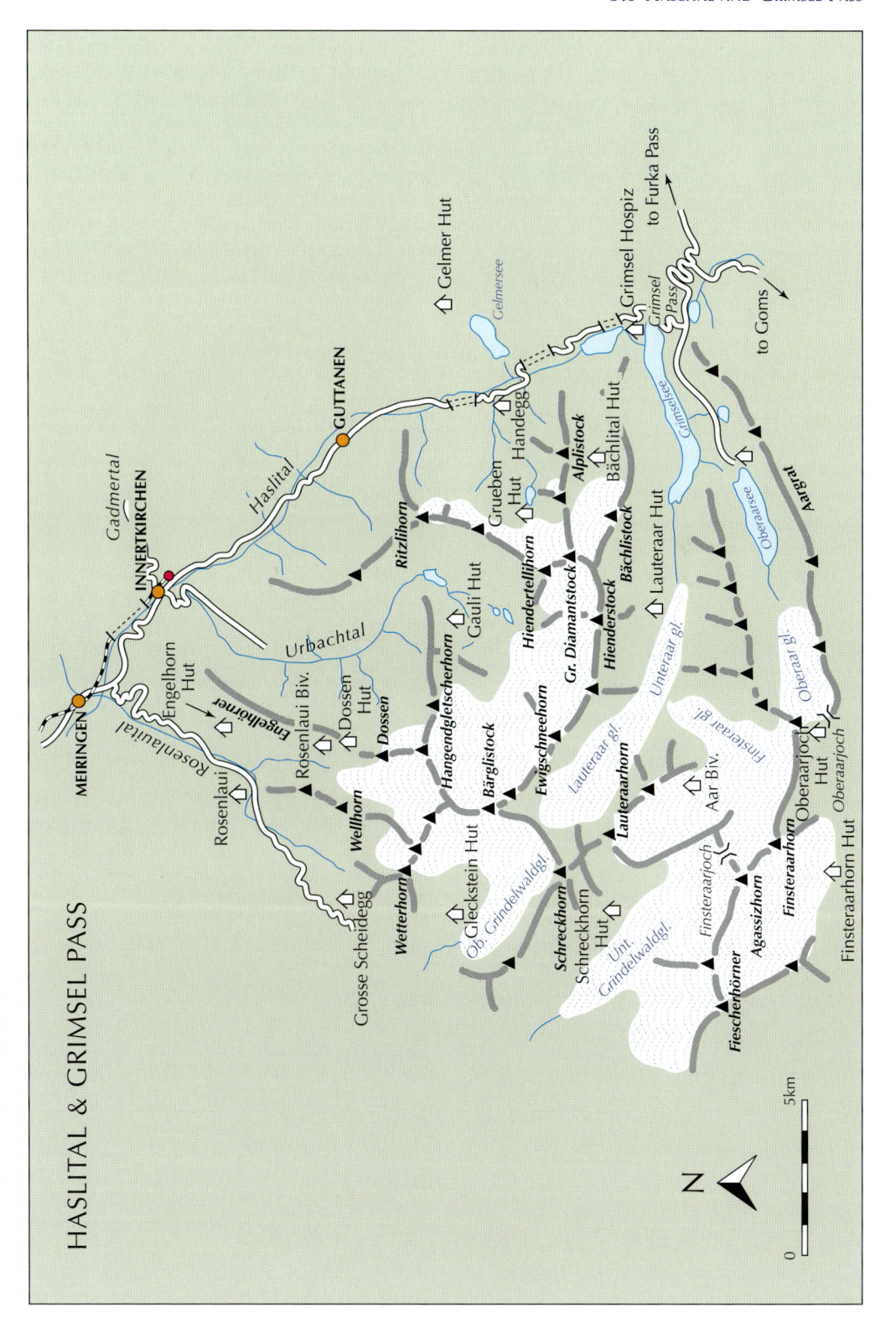

has 55 places and is manned from July to the end of September (www.dossenhuette.ch). As mentioned in 5:8, it's used by climbers tackling routes on the eastern side of the Wetterhörner, as well as on the nearby 3138m Dossen and the more distant Bärglistock.

A long ridge system projects northeast from the Dossen to form the divide between the Rosenlauital and Urbachtal. This ridge contains the well-known ● **Engelhörner** whose string of limestone peaks boast a number of well-established and fully equipped rock climbs, most of which are easily accessed from the **Engelhorn Hut** which belongs to the Academic Alpine Club of Bern. Reached in 1½hrs from Rosenlaui, it has 50 places and is partly manned from June until the end of October (www.aacb.ch). The Alpine Club guide *Bernese Oberland* lists literally dozens of climbs (with topos) on the Engelhörner and SE Face of the ● **Klein Wellhorn**, the latter perhaps better served from the Dossen Hut.

Meiringen lies in the lower Haslital at 595m, directly opposite the wooded entrance to the Rosenlauital and the famous Reichenbach Falls. Despite its modest size Meiringen is the main tourist centre of the Haslital, with access by train via Interlaken or Lucerne. It has all modern facilities, plenty of accommodation and a useful tourist office on the Bahnhofstrasse (www.alpenregion.ch). Below the resort the valley widens before spilling into the Brienzersee, but upstream it contracts and is squeezed by the Aareschlucht, through whose walls the railway is tunnelled before emerging at its terminus at Innertkirchen. On the steep right-hand wall of the valley, immediately above Meiringen and reached by cableway, several hamlets are scattered on the sunny terrace of the Hasliberg with views south towards the Wetterhorn.

With the Grimsel Pass at its head, the **Haslital** has been used as a major transit route for centuries, and when the old mule track was replaced by the specially engineered highway in 1895, some 300 horses were stabled in Meiringen to draw the post coaches along it. As early as 1211 the Bernese marched through the valley and over the Grimsel to invade the Valais, but in later years it was used in conjunction with the Griespass (see 3:3) for more peaceful trade with Italy. The Haslital also marks the eastern extent of the Bernese Alps, for the east wall of the valley, crowned by the Dammastock, belongs to the Central Swiss Alps.

After Meiringen, the Haslital's only other resort (if it can be so-called) is **Innertkirchen**, which lies in a grassy plain about 6km from its better-known neighbour, with the Gadmertal reaching up to the Sustenpass to the northeast, and the Urbachtal cutting to the south. With rail and bus transport from Brienz and Interlaken, in many ways it's more appealing to the active walker and climber than is Meiringen, and with about half a dozen hotels, a variety of chalets and holiday apartments to rent, it has sufficient accommodation, while two campsites have their own attraction (for tourist information see www.innertkirchen.ch).

Urbachtal

In its lower reaches the Urbachtal has something of a fjord-like quality about it – without the water, for it's flanked on the west by the imposing Engelhörner's wall, on the east by the Gallauistock, and to the south by the massive North Face of the Hangendgletscherhorn which appears to block the valley. Streaked with waterfalls, the Engelhörner's wall makes a powerful impression as you wander along the east bank of the Urbachwasser (a road goes part-way along the valley floor). There are neither villages nor hamlets here, just a handful of farm buildings and, at the end of a 5½hr trek, the ● **Gauli Hut** is remotely situated on a grassy alp at 2205m below the Hangendgletscherhorn, with the Ritzlihorn crowning the ridge on the other side of the valley to the northeast. Owned by the Bern section of the SAC, the hut has 65 dormitory places, and is usually manned from April until mid-October, with a period in June when it may be staffed only at weekends (www.gauli.ch). The scenic isolation of the hut makes it a worthwhile destination for hill walkers, but of course its main function is as a base for a variety of climbs.

Among these, the most obvious is the 3292m ● **Hangendgletscherhorn** whose SE and NW Ridges both offer AD climbs; the SE (Chamligrat) is said to be slightly easier than the NW Ridge. The ● **Bärglistock** (3656m) overlooks a complex of glaciers which fall away on all sides, but its North Ridge, rising from the Bärglijoch, is broken by a couple of gendarmes to give another AD climb. Meanwhile the 3329m ● **Ewigschneehorn** southwest of the hut is apparently included when making a traverse of the Urbachtal's headwall on the way to the Lauteraar Hut (PD).

The Unteraargletscher once fiilled the valley to the Grimselsee, but is now retreating to the heartland of the Bernese Alps

Grimselsee

About 15km from Innertkirchen the Grimsel road reaches 🚶 **Handegg** (1400m), noted for its hydro-electric station and (by climbers) for the quantity and quality of climbs to be had on the granite slabs that rise above the road. On the eastern side three groups give long routes, while above them the Gelmerhörner also has some noteworthy climbs and traverses, but as these properly belong to the chapter dealing with the Central Swiss Alps, we turn to the slabs on the west of the road where the 🚶 **Bügeleisen** crags provide climbs up to 150m in length – all routes have been equipped. Climbers using their own transport should park near the hydro station for a 10min approach. The nearest accommodation is at the Handegg Hotel.

It is from Handegg that a well-marked path heads west for a 3½hr hike leading to the **Grueben Hut** (2512m), which stands on a promontory nearly 200m above the Gruebensee and is backed by the Golegghorn. It belongs to the Academic Alpine Club of Basle, has 28 places and self-catering facilities, but no permanent warden (www.gruebenhuette.ch). From it the 3263m 🚶 **Ritzlihorn** is one attraction, as is the short but steep East Ridge of the 🚶 **Hiendertellihorn** (3179m) which rises out of the Grueben glacier (D). South of the hut the 🚶 **Gross Diamantstock** (3162m) is another whose East Ridge offers a quality climb of D- on firm granite.

On the south side of the ridge projecting eastward from the Gross Diamantstock, the **Bächlital Hut** stands at the foot of the 500m face of the 🚶 **Alplistock** (2878m), which offers some good rock scrambles and an AD+ traverse. Reached in 2hrs by a good path from the Räterischbodensee (400m below the Grimsel Pass), the hut, at 2328m, is owned by the SAC. It has 75 places and is fully staffed from mid-June until mid-October, and occasionally for the rest of the year (www.baechlitalhuette.ch).

The Bächlital is an interesting little valley closed at its western end by a headwall running from the Gross Diamantstock to Bächlistock, between which lies the Obri Bächli-Licken, a 3074m col used by climbers to get onto the SW Ridge of the 🚶 **Gross Diamantstock** (PD). The Bächli glacier fills the basin at the head of the valley, and ladders and fixed cables are used to reach the col from it. The 3247m 🚶 **Bächlistock** walls the southwestern end of this basin, and its fine granite ridge makes a rewarding traverse (AD+). Sometimes climbed from the Lauteraar Hut which stands above the Unteraargletscher on the other side of the ridge, the Bächlistock is the best-looking mountain hereabouts, whose prominent SE summit (3240m) was first climbed in 1888, while the higher NW peak had to wait another four years.

The **Grimsel Hospiz** stands above the dam blocking the Grimselsee that stretches back to the west. A very pleasant walk takes a path among clusters of alpenrose above the north shore of the lake, and towards its western end passes below the famed ❸ ☆ **Eldorado** slabs, reckoned to be among the finest granite cliffs in the Alps, with a rich variety of equipped routes providing climbs of around 500m. Facing south across the lake, and reached in 1½–2hrs from the Hospiz, the slabs become a suntrap on cloudless days.

The Grimselsee collects meltwater from the Unteraargletscher, the long tongue of ice (rubble-covered in its lower reaches) fed by the Finsteraar, Strahlegg and Lauteraar glaciers which gather above the SAC's Lauteraar Hut. It was on the Unteraargletscher that the geologist, Louis Agassiz, based his glacier studies in the 1840s, and for several summers slept on a strip of moraine in what became known as the Hôtel des Neuchâtelois. At first this was no more than a hollow beneath a huge boulder, with its entrance screened by a blanket. Later a rough cabin made of wood and canvas was added. This grew into a three-roomed building to house guides and workmen, with an additional bedroom for Agassiz and his companions.

The modern **Lauteraar Hut** stands high above the fast-receding glacier at 2393m on the site of the former Pavillon Dollfus, built by Daniel Dollfus-Ausset who was with Édouard Desor in 1844 on the first ascent of the Rosenhorn (lowest of the three Wetterhörner peaks – see 5:8). With a view southwest to the Finsteraarhorn, the hut belongs to the Zofingen section of the SAC. It has 50 places and a resident warden during July and August (www.haslihuetten.ch), and is reached in 4–4½hrs from the Grimsel Hospiz. Some of the finest summits of the Bernese Alps are climbed from here, including ❸ **Lauteraarhorn** and ❸ **Schreckhorn** – albeit after long approaches – while much nearer to hand there's the 3307m ❸ **Hienderstock** directly above the hut, and nearby ❸ **Bächlistock** whose ridge traverse has already been mentioned in relation to the Bächlital Hut.

West of the Lauteraar Hut, the Lauteraar and Finsteraar glaciers have their confluence below the Abschwunghorn which forms an eastern spur of the Lauteraar Rothörner. Tucked at the foot of the Rothörner's South Ridge, the small **Aar Bivouac Hut** is one of the most remote of all Swiss refuges (see 5:8). Unmanned and with a questionable water supply, it looks across the Strahlegg and Finsteraar glaciers at the great NE flank of the Finsteraarhorn and North Face of the Studerhorn.

Grimsel Pass

Connecting the Oberland with the upper Rhône valley, the Grimsel is one of the most frequented of Swiss passes. At 2165m it forms the border of cantons Bern and Valais (Wallis to German-speaking Swiss), and also has a link with Uri via the nearby Furka. Accommodation can be had at two hotels, the Grimselblick and Alpenrösli, and at least three buses cross daily between Meiringen and Oberwald from July to September. Almost 200m above the Grimselsee, the Totensee (lake of the dead) is a sullen tarn used, according to Baedeker, as a burial place during the bitter fighting which took place here in 1799 between the Austrians and French.

From the pass a single-track service road breaks to the west (a footpath soon cuts from it) heading for **Berghaus Oberaar** (2338m) at the eastern end of the Oberaarsee. Use of the road is controlled by traffic lights from 6am until 10pm. The milky Oberaarsee is flanked on its north by a ridge across which lies the Unteraargletscher, and on the south by the Aargrat which carries the Valais border high above the valley of Goms. The lake is fed by the Oberaar glacier which comes sweeping down from a headwall running from the Scheuchzerhorn to Oberaar-Rothorn via the Oberaarhorn and **Oberaarjoch**, the narrow 3216m pass that gives access to the glaciers and high peaks that gather at the icy heart of the Bernese Alps. Located 40m above the pass stands the **Oberaarjoch Hut**, a remote eyrie situated among rocks at 3256m (5hrs from Berghaus Oberaar; 6½hrs from the Grimsel Pass). Property of the Biel section of the SAC, it has 56 places, is staffed from mid-April until the end of May, and from July until the end of September (www.sac-biel.ch), and is frequently used by ski tourers in springtime.

Whether visited on ski in springtime, or on foot in summer, the Oberaarjoch Hut makes an obvious choice for a first night of a multi-day traverse of the central Bernese Alps from the Grimsel Pass to the Lötschental, created by linking the Oberaar, Studer, Fiescher, Grünegg, Aletsch and Lang glaciers by a series of interconnecting cols. Other huts along the route are the **Finsteraarhorn, Konkordia, Hollandia** and **Anen**. As there are numerous crevasses, it is a serious route, and participants should be equipped for and experienced in crevasse rescue techniques.

5:10 THE SOUTHERN VALLEYS

South of the Grimsel Pass the upper valley of the Rhône is known as **Goms**, a neat pastoral region with a string of unspoilt villages noted for their traditional wooden chalets and *mazots*. In winter the cross-country skiing is excellent, and a number of footpaths are cleared for walkers. In summer a whole network of trails provide endless opportunities for hikes of anything from a few hours to several days. Most of these are on the right flank, but the opposite, Lepontine, slope has its fair share also. But there's one path worth noting that heads south from the Furka Pass, for an hour's walk along it, passing below the Muttgletscher and Tällistock, leads to the 🟢 **Bidmergrat**, a vantage point *par excellence* from which to study the southeastern end of the Bernese Alps. Across the valley, the landscape appears almost Karakoram-like in its savagery: a wild complex of rocky peaks and glacial valleys, sufficient to excite the dreams of anyone with a taste for adventure. More than 1100m below cluster the toy-like houses of Oberwald, while other Goms villages and hamlets act as stepping stones for the imagination, pacing downvalley.

Fieschertal

On the journey through Goms down to the Rhône valley proper, **Fiesch** (1050m) is the first village of any size to be reached, and that only a modest resort in comparison with some of those in the Oberland. Accessible by train, and located at the entrance to the Fieschertal, it has most facilities, 10 hotels, numerous chalets and apartments, a campsite (open all year), and a tourist office (www.fiesch.ch).

The Märjelensee lies near the east bank of the Grosser Aletschgletscher

The Swiss Alps – Chapter 5: Bernese Alps

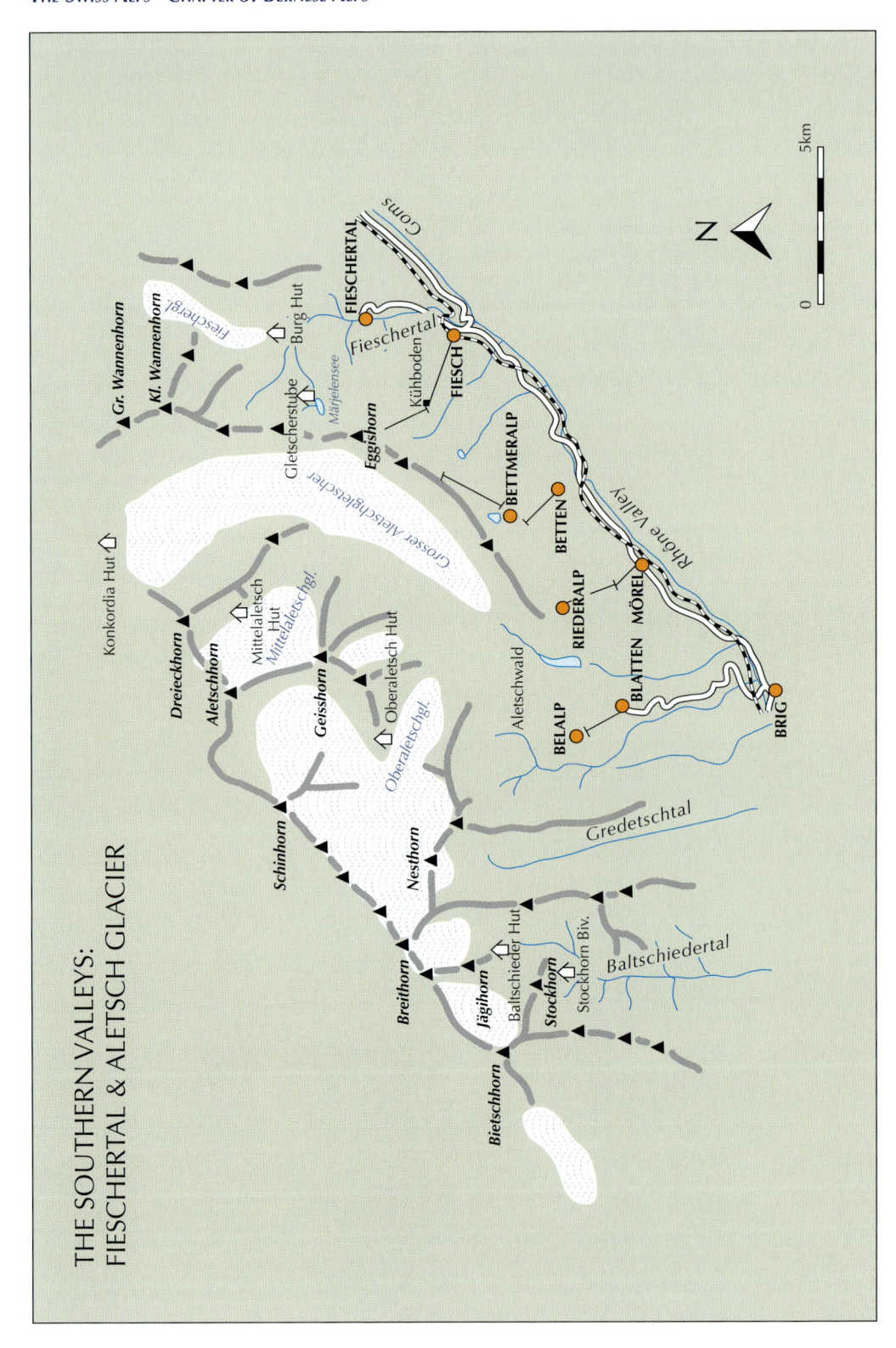

The Southern Valleys: Fieschertal & Aletsch Glacier

There's also cableway connection with **Kühboden** (Fiescheralp) and the Eggishorn high above the western side of the valley.

At the head of the valley, nestling among rock slabs at 1751m and overlooking a gorge created by the retreating Fieschergletscher, the privately owned ◯ **Burg Hut** makes an obvious destination for walkers, who can reach it in 1½–2hrs from the hamlet of **Fieschertal**. With just 32 dormitory places it is fully staffed from June until the middle of October (tel 027 971 40 27). A *klettergarten* nearby provides some entertaining climbs (see topos at the hut), while the nearest peak to consider is the 3707m ✪ **Klein Wannenhorn** (via the SE Face, SE Pillar and the ESE Ridge or Distelgrat), and the granite 'twins' of the ✪ **Wannenzwillinge** (not named on some maps) that protrude from the ridge running south of their higher neighbour. These twins are 3481m and 3432m, and both give good climbing on their respective east ridges. The ✪ **Gross Wannenhorn**, on the other hand, is a big mountain of 3906m, usually climbed from the Finsteraarhorn Hut, from where the ascent is almost entirely on snow.

Below the Burg Hut's *klettergarten* an alternative trail makes a long loop north before swinging back on itself, then heads southwest to reach the ◯ **Gletscherstube Märjela**, another privately owned hut lodged in a secluded valley at 2373m close to the famed **Märjelensee** (4½hrs from Fieschertal). This approach is one of the longest options, for a much shorter and easier walk to the hut, for activists choosing Fiesch as their holiday base, is to take the cable car to Kühboden (Fiescheralp) and follow a well-marked path that goes through a 1km-long tunnel opening just to the south of the Gletscherstube (1hr from Kühboden). The hut has 36 places and is fully staffed from July until the end of October (tel 027 971 47 83) and it makes an atmospheric lodging for a night or two.

The Märjelensee often has ice flows drifting across it in early summer. But sometimes the lake partially drains away through underground channels, leaving a cluster of pools rimmed with cotton grass. Even then it still creates a scene which R L G Irving reckoned 'cannot disappoint the highest expectations'.

The Aletsch Glacier

The **Grosser Aletschgletscher** lies just below to the west. Striped and herring-boned by medial moraines and crevasses, this longest of all alpine

Striped with moraine, the Grosser Aletschgletscher makes a long and gradual descent from Konkordiaplatz

glaciers is sufficient to impress both novice and old-hand alike, while peaks that wall it have an added dimension thanks to the icefields from which they emerge. Above and to the south of the Märjelensee the 2927m ⊙ **Eggishorn** is a much-sought-after vantage point. With the cable car swinging visitors to within a 20min walk of the summit, it looks out at a mountain scene as grand as any in the Alps, and grander than most. The Grosser Aletschgletscher is, of course, a natural focus, for it leads the eye along its highway through an avenue of peaks towards its distant catchment basin. But to the south and southwest too, across the Rhône valley the great summits of the Pennine Alps jostle for attention.

The **Konkordia Hut** can be reached from the Märjelensee by a traditional route along the central moraine of the Aletsch glacier, but most walkers will be content with tracing the path which eases along the glacier's east bank leading to ⊙ ☆ **Bettmeralp** or **Riederalp**, two small resorts at over 1900m accessible by cableways from the Rhône valley. The glacier-bank path is spectacular, and it's tempting to stop at regular intervals to take account of the arresting situation. On the far side of the glacier, the smaller **Mittelaletschgletscher** is receding into the valley it has carved below the dominant Aletschhorn and Dreieckhorn; further west it's the **Oberaletschgletscher** that has gouged a deep trench between Sparrhorn and Fusshorn. But glacial amphitheatres that create a swirl of mountains above and around that icestream, and its neighbour the Beichgletscher, remain a mystery that only the map unfolds. At almost any point along the path a backward view along the immense curve of the main Grosser Aletschgletscher is uplifting for all but the most hardened of cynics.

Just above and beyond the glacier's tongue, the **Aletschwald** nature reserve contains some of the oldest living trees in Switzerland, with many of the ancient Arolla pines thought to be more than 1000 years old. To the west is the 'supreme vantage-point' of **Belalp**, consisting of little more than a church, hotel and a few chalets on a green balcony at 2094m overlooking both the Aletsch glacier and the chain of the Pennine Alps. Visited by Ruskin in 1844, it was to Belalp that John Tyndall, the influential scientist and mountaineer, came first in 1858 and was so taken by it that he continued to visit almost every year for the next 32 years, establishing his summer home there in 1877 in the little Villa Lÿsgen. As Belalp grew in popularity, women guests for the famous hotel were carried up in a *chaise* carried by four porters. A cable car now makes the ascent from Blatten in about eight minutes. **Hotel Belalp** today has 36 beds and is open all year except May and November: www.hotelbelalp.ch.

Belalp is often taken as the starting point by climbers heading for the **Oberaletsch Hut**, which occupies a scenic location at 2640m overlooking the confluence of the Oberaletsch and Beich glaciers at the foot of a ridge running down from the Gross Fusshorn; about 4hrs from Belalp. Property of the Chasseral section of the SAC, it has 60 places and is manned in April and May, and from mid-June until mid-October (www.oberaletsch.ch). The hut is used as a base for climbs on many neighbourhood peaks, including Fusshorn, Geisshorn, Aletschhorn and Nesthorn.

Lötschental

Between the Grosser Aletschgletscher and the Lötschental, the southern wall of the Bernese Alps is scoured by a series of narrow, almost cleft-like valleys, the longest being the **Gredetschtal** and **Baltschiedertal**. The second of these lies almost due north of **Visp**, with the village of **Ausserberg** giving the most convenient access. The valley makes a clean northward slice through the mountains, kinks to the northeast then opens into two upper stems around which rise the Bietschhorn, Breitlauihorn and Lötschentaler Breithorn. At the end of a 6½hr approach from Ausserberg, the SAC's **Baltschieder Hut** (Baltschiederklause) stands on a rocky terrace at 2783m below the Jägihorn, which marks the end of the Breitlauihorn's South Ridge. With 76 places, and a warden from late June until the end of September, the hut makes a convenient base for climbs on all the surrounding peaks (www.rhone.ch). But there's also the **Stockhorn Bivouac Hut**, a futuristic, unmanned shelter with room for 18, located at 2598m near the foot of the Stockhorn's South Ridge, although it has no water supply, and it's not possible to make reservations, but is often overcrowded (www.sac-bluemlisalp.ch).

Whilst failing to top 4000m, the ⊙ **Bietschhorn** (3934m) is a big mountain which casts its metaphorical shadow over a large area. It has three principal ridges: a broad, multi-ribbed South Face overlooking the Bietschtal, a liberal coating of ice on its east flank and steep hanging glaciers on its northwest flank,

5:10 THE SOUTHERN VALLEYS

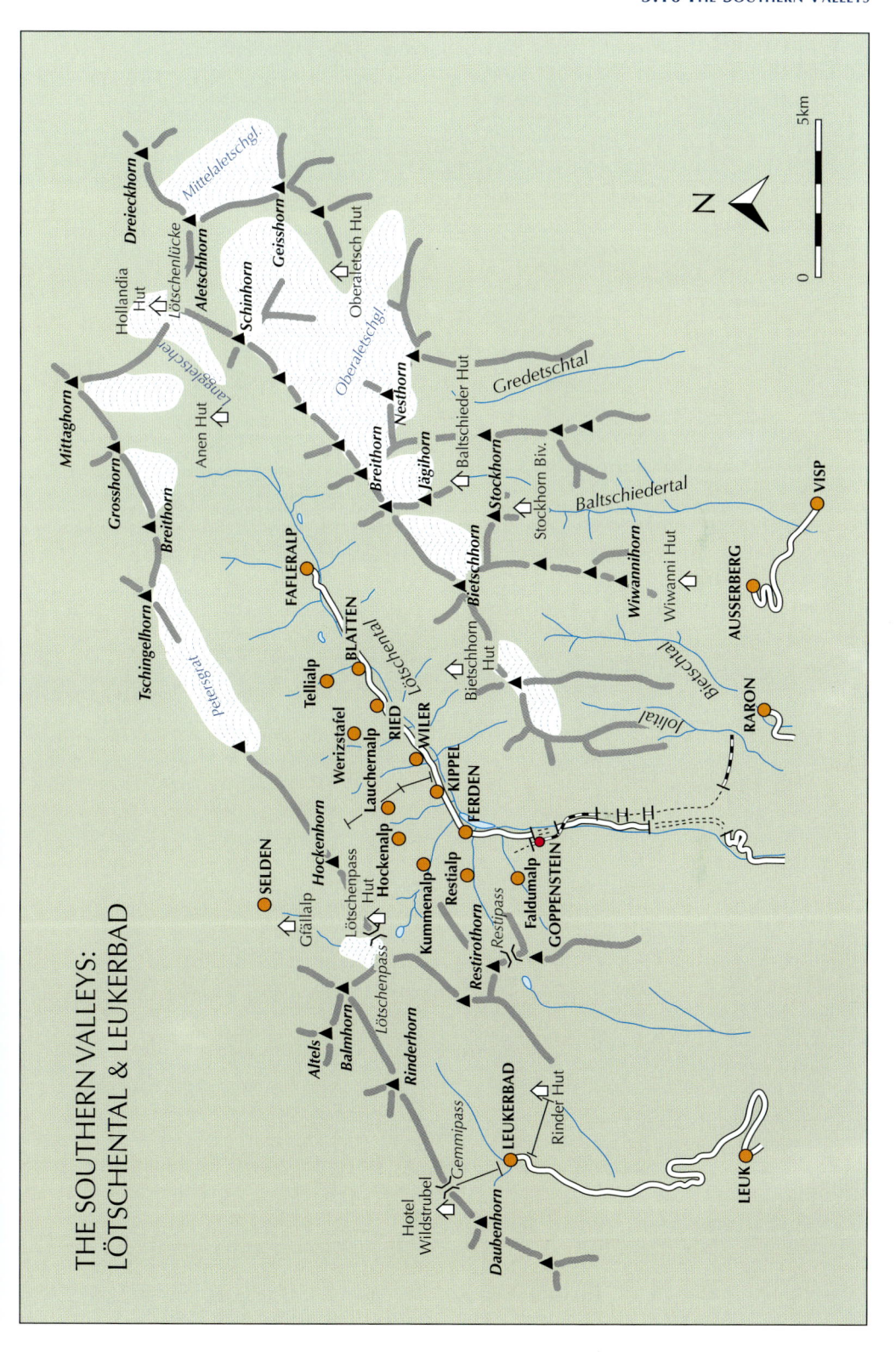

THE SOUTHERN VALLEYS:
LÖTSCHENTAL & LEUKERBAD

345

Seen from below the Lötschenpass, the Bietschhorn dominates all views

which falls into the Lötschental. First climbed in August 1859 by Leslie Stephen and his guides, their route began in the Lötschental and was made via the North Ridge (AD) – nowadays the Bietschhorn Hut is used, while the Baltschieder Hut is the best base for attempts on the SE Ridge (TD-) and East Rib (AD+).

The **Lötschentaler Breithorn** (3785m) is just 5m higher than its namesake on the Lauterbrunnen Wall (5:7), and whilst climbs on its north side are naturally based on the Lötschental, the Baltschieder Hut is used for climbs on the SE (Blanchet) Ridge, graded D, and a fine mixed route on the SW Ridge (PD+). The 3655m **Breitlauihorn** via the South Ridge (PD) is often included in an ascent of the Breithorn.

Both the Gredetschtal and Baltschiedertal are wild valleys, but so too is the **Bietschtal**, which falls from a vast cirque headed by the Bietschhorn, and spills into the Rhône valley at Raron. The Bietschtal has no hutted accommodation, but the privately owned **Wiwanni Hut** (2463m) stands on the south flank of the Wiwannihorn some 1400m above Ausserberg, midway between Bietschtal and Baltschiedertal. It has 34 places and is fully staffed from June until mid-October (www.wiwanni.ch). *Klettersteig* (via ferrata) fans are well provided for here, for there's not only the **Baltschieder Klettersteig** used on one of the approach routes,

but another has been created in the gorge at the entrance to the Bietschtal. A round trip to combine both these protected routes with a visit to the hut would make a good two-day outing.

But it is the **Lötschental** that wins most plaudits on this south side of the Bernese Alps. The longest of the inhabited valleys, it has a string of small, dark-timbered villages nestling among hay meadows, a collection of romantic alp hamlets on its north slope, the ice sheet of the Petersgrat crowning the ridge above those hamlets, the Langgletscher tapering into the upper valley from the snowy Lötschenlücke, the impressive Gletscherstafel Wall overlooking Fafleralp, and the matchless Bietschhorn towering head and shoulders above everything. And if these were not enough, the valley appears to be blocked at both ends, so that one is contained, cocoon-like, in a mountain sanctuary with few of the distractions of the 'outside world'.

Approached from the Rhône's valley through the once-forbidding, avalanche-prone narrows of the Quertalschlucht, the modern road is protected by tunnels and galleries. At **Goppenstein** trains emerge from the Lötschberg Tunnel whose northern end is near Kandersteg, but it is not until you reach **Ferden** that the Lötschental begins to reveal its true identity. The village, along with its neighbours **Kippel**, **Wiler**, **Ried** and **Blatten** all have accommodation, albeit rather limited in scope, as does **Fafleralp** at the road-head. On the hillside above Wiler, both **Lauchernalp** (reached by cableway from Wiler) and Fischbiel have chalets and apartments for rent; there are dormitories at Berghaus Lauchern, and also at Gasthaus Kummenalp, midway between Ferden and the Lötschenpass. (For details contact the Lötschentaler tourist office in Wiler, or visit www.loetschental.ch.)

While the standard means of approach to the valley are by road or rail, hill walkers, climbers and ski tourers have a choice of passes by which to enter the Lötschental. The ◯ **Lötschenpass** route from Kandersteg and the Gasterntal has been mentioned in 5:5 above. This is an excellent route, with the **Lötschenpass Hut** providing overnight accommodation or refreshments close to the actual pass. The Bietschhorn dominates views from here and for much of the descent to the valley, whether you choose to descend via Kummenalp or Lauchernalp.

West of Ferden the 2626m ◯ **Restipass** is another fine walker's route which begins at **Leukerbad**, above which the top station of the Torrent cableway at 2313m has 50 basic dormitory places in what is known as the **Rinder Hut** (www.torrent.ch). From here the pass, which lies between the Restirothorn and Locherspitza, is reached in 2½–3hrs. The saddle makes a tremendous vantage point with the Lötschental seen stretching directly ahead and some 1200m below, with the Bietschhorn again towering over the valley to the northeast, while a backward view shows the Pennine Alps blending into the Mont Blanc range. The steep descent to Ferden from the pass takes about 2½hrs via Restialp.

Then there's the glacial 🧗 **Lötschenlücke** (3178m) at the head of the valley, a classic crossing for climbers and ski tourers coming from Konkordiaplatz, for the pass forms a link between the Grosser Aletschfirn and the Langgletscher on the Lötschental flank. Perched above the pass at 3240m, the SAC-owned **Hollandia Hut** (also known as the Lötschen Hut) has 100 places and a resident guardian from mid-March until the end of May, and from mid-July to mid-September (www.hollandiahuette.ch).

A number of peaks are accessible from this hut, among them the coveted 🧗 ☆ **Aletschhorn**, the second highest summit in the Bernese Alps at 4195m, whose 4km-wide North Face is around 1000m high. Although the normal routes on the mountain are via the SW Rib (PD+) from the Oberaletsch Hut, or the SE Flank/NE Ridge from the Mittelaletsch Bivouac Hut, it is the Hasler Rib (AD+) on the North Face that attracts most attention here. Named after Gustav

The left-hand wall of the Lötschental is studied from the hillside below the Lötschenpass

Hasler who made the first winter ascent in January 1904 (it was first climbed in July 1873), the route is about 700m long, and is mostly free from objective dangers. Elsewhere the steep and heavily glaciated face holds a number of lines, some of which are menaced by falling ice.

On the Lötschental side of the Lötschenlücke, the privately owned **Anen Hut** has been built upon the lateral moraine of the Langgletscher at 2358m. Reached by a pleasant walk of 2½hrs from the Fafleralp roadhead, the present hut replaces the original which was destroyed by avalanche. Comfortable, and environmentally friendly, it is one of the ugliest of all Swiss huts. It has 50 places in its spacious dormitories, and is staffed at weekends from mid-March until mid-May, and throughout the period running from mid-June until mid-October (www.anenhuette.ch). Climbs on the Lauterbrunnen Breithorn and the Grosshorn are among the attractions faced by visitors to this hut.

But for walkers, there's one route above all others that makes a visit to the Lötschental a must. The ⊙ ☆ **Lötschentaler Höhenweg** runs along the true right flank of the valley at mid-height, linking no less than eight alp hamlets. It is better to begin this 18km hike at Ferden, which involves a 1½hr uphill walk to reach **Faldumalp**, a glorious collection of timber chalets, haybarns and a tiny chapel, perched some 660m above the road. From there the trail heads north and northeast, curving into minor valleys and combes, crossing streams, passing through stands of larch or pine and visiting other alps which more or less line the 2000m contour. Once again it is the Bietschhorn that demands most attention across the valley, although the mountain landscape is rewarding wherever you turn.

Before leaving the Lötschental, mention must be made of the **Bietschhorn Hut** which serves climbers following the original 1866 route on the Bietschhorn's North Ridge (AD). An old timber hut built by the Academic Alpine Club of Bern, it stands high above the valley at 2565m in a direct line for the Bietschjoch; about 3hrs from Blatten or Wiler. With just 26 places, it's fully manned for a very brief period in summer (mid-July to mid-August), and usually for a few weekends either side of the main season (www.aacb.ch).

Leukerbad

Backed by the precipitous grey cliffs of the Daubenhorn, the somewhat pretentious thermal spa resort of Leukerbad can seem a gloomy dead-end when the clouds hang low, for the town is cramped in a semi-circle of mountains. But when the sun shines it merits a visit, for there's much to do there.

Frequent buses twist up the valley narrows above **Leuk**, and climb above the Dala's gorge to reach **Leukerbad** at 1402m. It's an old resort, but the buildings are modern and hold little appeal for those who prefer smaller, more traditional mountain villages. To support the thermal baths there are plenty of hotels, but there's also a campsite, and budget accommodation available in dormitories and rooms at Torrentalp on the slopes of the Torrenthorn, served by cable car (for details check Leukerbad Tourismus www.leukerbad.ch). At the upper cable car station, there are 50 places in basic dormitories in the **Rinder Hut** (see above), from

The Lötschentaler Höhenweg passes through a string of alp hamlets

where an unbroken view south across the Rhône valley shows the range of the Pennine Alps stretching to the Mont Blanc massif.

If the view of the Pennine Alps is fine, so too is that of the Daubenhorn west of Leukerbad, while the Balmhorn blocks the head of the Dala's valley. Between Balmhorn and Daubenhorn there's the Rinderhorn, then comes the dip of the Gemmipass, with its cableway rising steeply out of Leukerbad to provide a less energetic ascent than that demanded by the ancient zigzag path created in the first half of the 18th century – see 5:4. From that path at 2030m, access is given to the longest *via ferrata* in Switzerland; the 1000m high **Ⓑ Daubenhorn Klettersteig** (grade ED). There are, in fact, two options here; a shorter route of about 350m, and the main one that takes about 8hrs to complete, finishing on the Gemmipass after crossing the 2941m summit of the Daubenhorn. Both are very exposed, need good dry conditions to attempt, and are open from July to October – weather permitting.

ALPINE PASS ROUTE

Before leaving the Bernese Alps, the multi-day Alpine Pass Route, mentioned several times in this chapter, deserves to be given at least a brief outline. One of the most challenging of alpine treks, the APR makes an east to west traverse across Switzerland, taking in no fewer than 16 passes during its 326km journey from Sargans to Montreux. Although it begins not far from the Liechtenstein border, a large part of this route crosses non-glacier passes in the Bernese Alps. For a full description and accommodation details, see the Cicerone guide *Alpine Pass Route*.

Days 1–2: From **Sargans** in the valley of the Rhine, the trek enters the Weisstannental heading southwest to its highest village, Weisstannen, and next day tackles the 2223m **Foopass** which takes the route into Canton Glarus (see 6:3). This is all pastoral countryside which continues beyond the pass on the descent to **Elm** in the Sernftal.

Days 3–4: These two stages are more demanding as the APR moves towards higher mountains. From Elm the way climbs to the 2261m **Richetlipass** with views of the Hausstock, then makes a steep descent to **Linthal**. From there an epic 32km stage (but with options to shorten it) crosses the Klausenpass en route to **Altdorf**.

Days 5–6: The **Surenenpass** and **Jochpass** are the physical highlights of these two stages which take the route to **Engelberg** and **Meiringen** on the edge of the Bernese Alps. Big mountain views spattered with tarns add much to the enjoyment.

Days 7–8: A long walk through the Rosenlauital leads to the Grosse Scheidegg below the Wetterhorn, with an easy stroll down to **Grindelwald**. Next day it's the turn of the Kleine Scheidegg, then down to Wengen and a sudden steep drop to **Lauterbrunnen** and its waterfalls.

Days 9–10: A very tough stage climbs out of the Lauterbrunnental to Mürren, continues to the 2612m Sefinenfurke, then plunges down to Griesalp. Day 10 is almost as tough, for it involves the crossing of the Hohtürli (2778m) below the Blüemlisalp, and a knee-crunching descent of 1600m to **Kandersteg** – but both days are magnificent.

Days 11–12: The rugged Bunderchrinde gives access to **Adelboden** on the first of these stages, but the Hahnenmoospass is gentle by comparison, providing an almost relaxing stage 12 which ends in the neat little resort of **Lenk**.

Days 13–14: Stage 13 has two passes, the Trüttlisberg and Krinnen, but despite this it is not overly demanding. But the next day, which takes the route from **Gsteig** to **Col des Mosses** is both long and reasonably tough, with two more passes along the way. The Alpes Vaudoises provide a backdrop.

Day 15: This final stage is 28km long, and although the big snow mountains have been left behind, there's nothing second-rate about the scenery. Col de Chaude, on a ridge between the Rochers de Naye and Pointe d'Aveneyre, gives an exciting view of the Lake of Geneva more than 1200m below, and the descent to **Montreux** on that lakeside seems endless – but immensely satisfying on arrival.

The Swiss Alps – Chapter 5: Bernese Alps

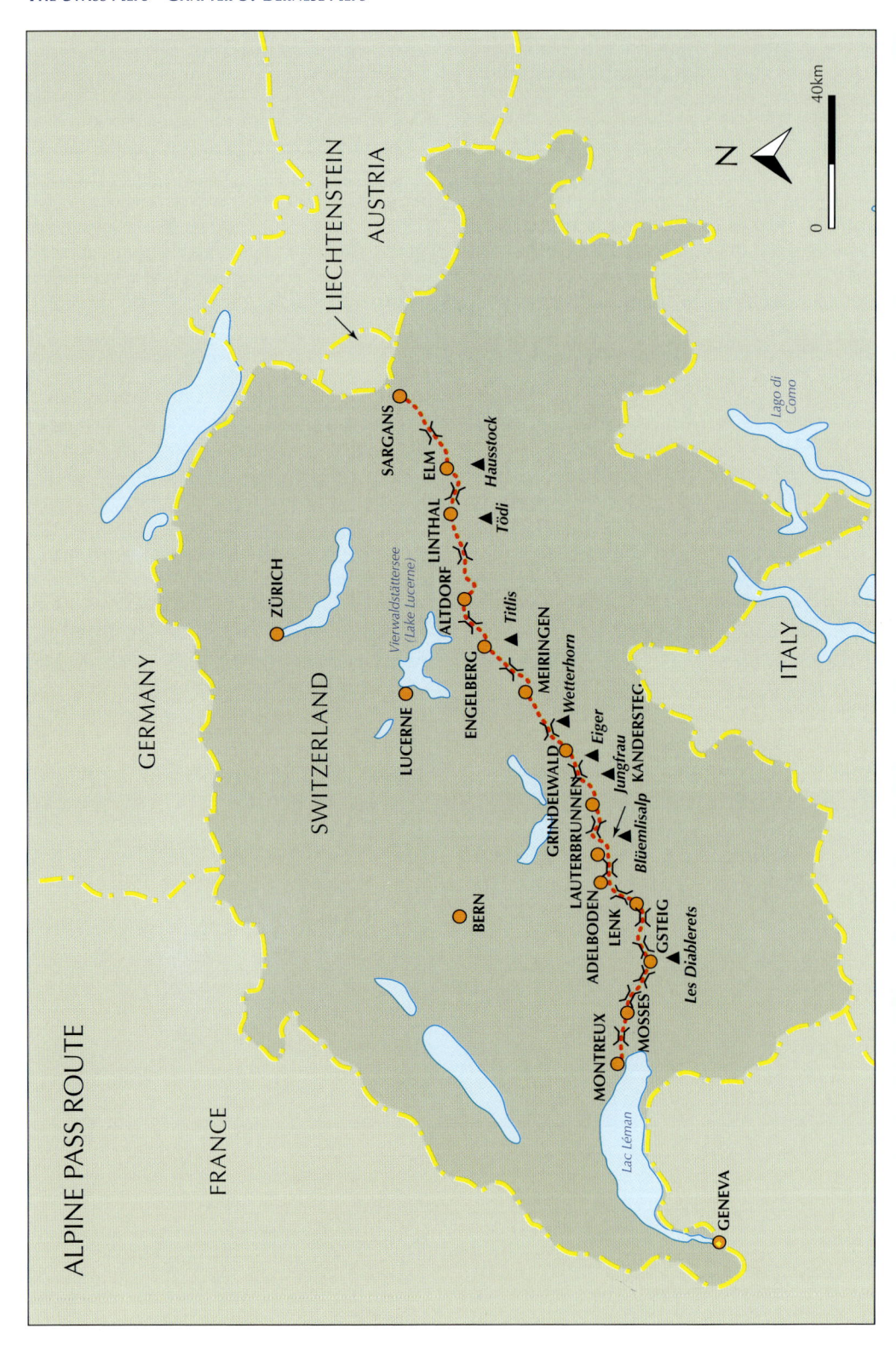

Alpine Pass Route

ACCESS, BASES, MAPS AND GUIDES

Access

Alpes Vaudoises A reasonable road cuts across the northern foothills between Aigle, on the Rhône south of Lac Léman, to Gsteig and Gstaad by way of Les Diablerets and Col du Pillon. Another climbs from Bex to Pont de Nant and Solalex. Aigle and Les Diablerets are connected by railway.

Lauenental The valley is served by postbus from Gstaad, which has mainline rail links.

Ober Simmental By railway to Lenk, then postbus service to Iffigenalp.

Engstligental Postbus service from Frutigen (mainline railway) to Adelboden.

Kandertal Mainline railway to Kandersteg; minibus service from Kandersteg to Selden in the Gasterntal.

Kiental Postbus from Reichenbach (railway from Spiez).

Lauterbrunnen Valley By train from Interlaken to Lauterbrunnen, then cableway and train to Mürren; train to Wengen, Kleine Scheidegg and Jungfraujoch; bus to Stechelberg.

Lütschental By train from Interlaken to Grindelwald.

Haslital and Grimsel Pass Train to Meiringen and Innertkirchen. Daily postbus service (several in summer only) between Meiringen and Andermatt over the Grimsel Pass.

Fieschertal Train from Brig to Fiesch.

Aletschgletscher Cable car from Fiesch to Kühboden (Fiescheralp); cable car from Betten for Bettmeralp, and from Mörel to Riederalp.

Lötschental By train to Goppenstein, then postbus to Fafleralp.

Leukerbad Postbus from Leuk (mainline railway) to Leukerbad.

Valley Bases

Alpes Vaudoises Pont de Nant, Leysin
Les Diablerets to Rawil Pass Les Diablerets, Gsteig, Leuenen, Lenk, Iffigenalp
Wildstrubel Massif Adelboden, Engstligenalp
Kandersteg and Gemmipass Kandersteg
Blüemlisalp and Gasterntal Kandersteg, Selden
Kiental Kiental, Griesalp
Lauterbrunnen Valley Lauterbrunnen, Mürren, Wengen, Kleine Scheidegg, Stechelberg
Lütschental Grindelwald, Alpiglen
Haslital and Grimsel Pass Meiringen, Innertkirchen
Fieschertal Fiesch
Lötschental Ferden, Kippel, Wiler, Blatten, Fafleralp
Leukerbad Leukerbad

Information

Destination Berner Oberland, Höhenweg 37, CH-3800 Interlaken (www.berneroberland.ch)

Huts

More than 70 huts and bivouacs are located within the region covered by this chapter. Most belong to individual club sections of the SAC, but several are privately owned but open to all.

Maps

The Swiss National Survey (LS) produce a series of maps at 1:50,000 to cover the Bernese Alps: 262 Rochers de Naye, 272 St Maurice, 263 Wildstrubel, 273 Montana, 254 Interlaken, 264 Jungfrau, 274 Visp, 255 Sustenpass, 265 Nufenenpass. For greater detail, the following 1:25,000 sheets are available: 1264, 1284, 1265, 1285, 1266, 1286, 1247, 1267, 1287, 1228, 1248, 1268, 1288, 1229, 1249, 1269, 1289, 1210, 1230, 1250. Kümmerly + Frey have a useful series of Wanderkarten at 1:60,000. These are: 824 Grand St Bernard–Dents du Midi–Les Diablerets, 805 Saanenland–Simmental–Frutigland, 18 Jungfrau Region, 327 Lötschental

Walking and/or Trekking Guides

The Bernese Oberland by Kev Reynolds (Cicerone, 4th edition 2015)

Walking in the Valais by Kev Reynolds (Cicerone, 3rd edition 2007) – for the southern valleys

Walking in Switzerland by Clem Lindemayer (Lonely Planet, 2nd edition 2001)

Swiss Alpine Pass Route – Via Alpina 1 by Kev Reynolds (Cicerone, 3rd edition 2017)

Tour of the Jungfrau Region by Kev Reynolds (Cicerone, 3rd edition 2018)

Trekking in the Alps by Kev Reynolds (Cicerone, 2011)

Alpinwandern: Rund um die Berner Alpen by Ueli Mosimann (SAC Verlag)

Climbing Guides

Bernese Oberland by Les Swindin (Alpine Club, 2003)

The 4000m Peaks of the Alps by Martin Moran (Alpine Club, 2007)

The Alpine 4000m Peaks by the Classic Routes by Richard Goedeke (Bâton Wicks, 2nd edition 2003)

Berner Alpen 1 – Sanetsch bis Gemmi (SAC)

Berner Alpen 2 – Gemmi bis Petersgrat (SAC)

Berner Alpen 3 – Bietschhorn, Lötschentaler etc (SAC)

Berner Alpen 4 – Tschingelhorn bis Finsteraarhorn (SAC)

Berner Alpen 5 – Von Grindelwald zur Grimsel (SAC)

Hochtouren Berner Alpen, Vom Sanetschpass zur Grimsel (SAC)

Skitouring Guides

Alpine Ski Mountaineering: Volume 2 by Bill O'Connor (Cicerone, 2003)

Skitouren Berner Alpen West (SAC)

Skitouren Berner Alpen Ost (SAC)

See Also

The High Mountains of the Alps by Helmut Dumler and Willi P Burkhardt (Diadem, 1994)

Walking in the Alps by Kev Reynolds (Cicerone, 2nd edition 2005)

Frei Sicht aufs Gipfelmeer by Marco Volken and Remo Kundert (SAC/Salvioni Edizioni, 2003)

Snowshoeing: Mont Blanc & the Western Alps by Hilary Sharp (Cicerone, 2002)

The White Spider by Heinrich Harrer (Rupert Hart-Davis, 1959)

The Beckoning Silence by Joe Simpson (Jonathan Cape, 2002)

The Adventures of a Mountaineer by Frank Smythe (Dent, 1940)

Eiger-Nordwand by Thomas Ulrich (AS-Verlag, Zürich)

Eiger: die Vertikale Arena by Daniel Anker (AS-Verlag, Zürich)

Bietschhorn: Erbe des Alpinisten by Daniel Anker and Marco Volken (AS-Verlag, Zürich)

Mönch: Mittelpunkt im Dreigestirn by Daniel Anker (AS-Verlag, Zürich)

Jungfrau: Zauberberg der Männer by Daniel Anker (AS-Verlag, Zürich)

Finsteraarhorn: Die einsame Spitze by Daniel Anker (AS-Verlag, Zürich)

L'Oberland Bernois: Les 100 Plus Belles Courses by Hans Gossen (Denöel, 1982)

Die schönsten Höhenwege im Berner Oberland by Rose Marie Kaune and Gerhard Bleyer (Bruckmann, Munich, 1988)

CHAPTER 6: CENTRAL SWISS ALPS

Mountain groups to the north and east of the Grimsel, Furka and Oberalp passes, including the Uri and Glarner Alps

CENTRAL SWISS ALPS: CHAPTER SUMMARY

Location
Extending northeast of the Bernese Alps and north of the Lepontines, these diverse groups are divided and outlined by major roads linked by passes such as the Grimsel, Furka, Susten, Oberalp and Klausen. In the north the mountains descend to the Vierwaldstättersee (Lake of Lucerne), while the eastern limit follows the Rhine to Sargans.

☆ Highlights

🟢 Walks
- Chelenalp Hut approach (6:1)
- Nepali Highway (6:1)
- Fürenalp balcony path (6:2)
- Surenenpass (6:2)

⬢ Climbs
- Salbitschijen (6:1)
- Dammastock (6:1)
- Tälli Klettersteig (6:2)

⬗ Summits for all
- Wissigstock (6:2)
- Schattig Wichel (Piz Giuv) (6:3)

Contents

6:1 Uri Alps – Dammastock Group 359
Voralptal 360
Göschenertal 361
Furkapass to Andermatt 364
Meiental 366
Gadmertal 367

6:2 North of the Sustenpass – Titlis Group 369
Gental 370
Melchtal 372
Engelbergtal 372
Titlis: A Playground for All Seasons (box) 375
Grosstal 376

6:3 Glarner Alps 378
Fellital and Etzlital 379
Maderanertal 381
Schächental 385
Urner Boden 389
Linth Tal 391
The Monk and the Mountain (box) 395
Klöntal 395
Sernftal 397
Suvorov and the Alpine Passes (box) 399

Access, Bases, Maps and Guides 401

◀ *The charming Chelenalptal*

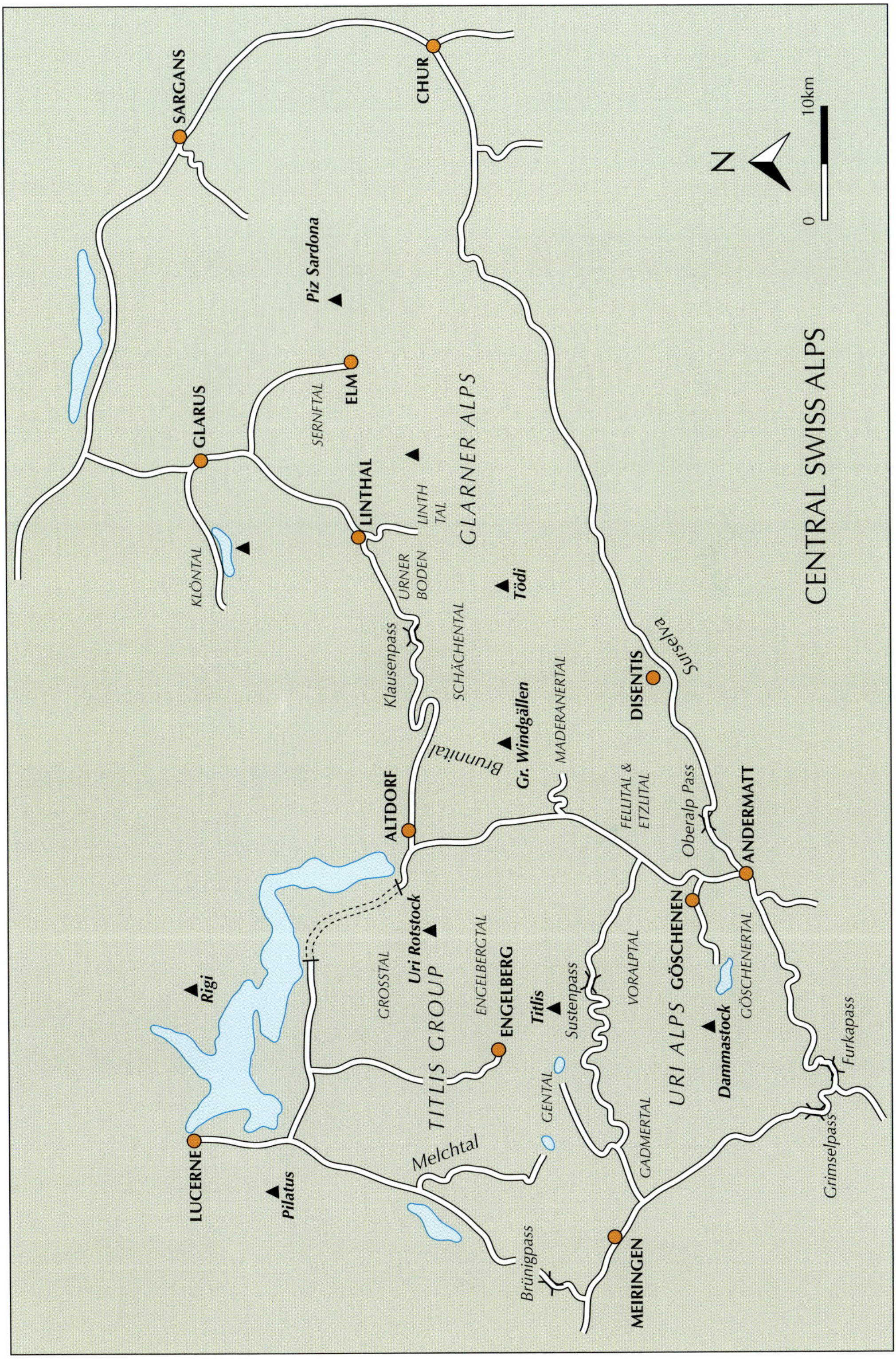
CENTRAL SWISS ALPS
N
0
10km
SARGANS
CHUR
Piz Sardona
GLARUS
ELM
SERNFTAL
GLARNER ALPS
LINTHAL
LINTH TAL
KLÖNTAL
URNER BODEN
Tödi
Klausenpass
SCHÄCHENTAL
Surselva
DISENTIS
MADERANERTAL
Gr. Windgällen
Brunnital
ALTDORF
FELLITAL & ETZLITAL
Oberalp Pass
ANDERMATT
GÖSCHENEN
GÖSCHENERTAL
Uri Rotstock
GROSSTAL
ENGELBERGTAL
TITLIS GROUP
ENGELBERG
Titlis
Sustenpass
VORALPTAL
URI ALPS
Dammastock
Furkapass
Grimselpass
GADMERTAL
GENTAL
Melchtal
Rigi
LUCERNE
Pilatus
MEIRINGEN
Brünigpass

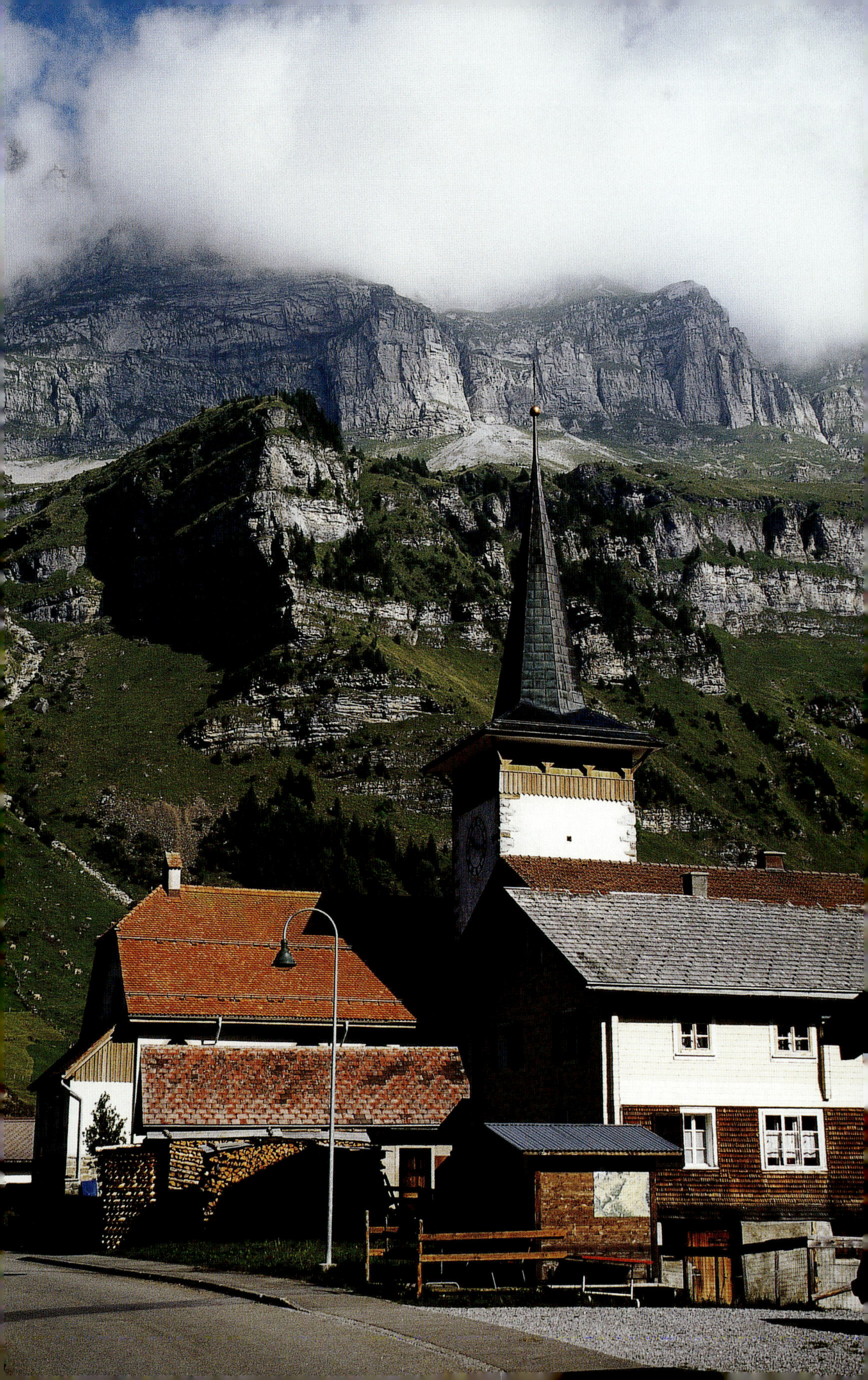

CENTRAL SWISS ALPS: INTRODUCTION

The whole area is scenically beautiful with the mountains forming excellent viewpoints.

Jeremy O Talbot, *Central Switzerland*

Viewed from the summit of Pilatus or the Rigi, both of which rise above the Lake of Lucerne, the Central Swiss Alps blend neatly into those of the Bernese Alps, with a line of white-capped peaks sometimes streaked at mid-height with mist from the lake. But unlike the Bernese or Pennine Alps, these mountains do not run in a convenient unbroken chain. Instead they consist of a cluster of individual groups of varying size and appeal, mostly confined within the cantons of Uri and Glarus. So far as the climber is concerned, the most important of these groups is also the smallest. With the Grimsel and Furka passes to the south, the Susten to the north and the gloomy Schöllenen gorge in the Reuss valley below Andermatt on the eastern side, the Uri Alps, crowned by the Dammastock, has the highest peaks and most challenging climbs on rock, snow and ice.

North of the Sustenpass lies the second group, in which the 3238m Titlis, complete with the world's first revolving gondola, towers over Engelberg and sends out a fine ridge of peaks spreading northeast from the Gross Spannort. A much shorter spur cuts south to the Fünffingerstöck above the Susten; another reaches southwest from the Titlis across the Wendenstöcke, effectively walling Engstlenalp and the Gental, while yet another ridge pushes northwestward over the Jochpass among lesser mountains and hills that ease down to the shores of the Vierwaldstättersee. West of this ridge lies the geographical heart of the country. Hard climbing exists on the south face of the Wendenstöcke and east face of the Titlis, with no shortage of good limestone to explore elsewhere.

The third group is by far the largest, forming an elongated block north of the Vorderrhein. Its

The Fünffingerstock at the head of the Meiental

◀ *Urnerboden village*

The Swiss Alps – Chapter 6: Central Swiss Alps

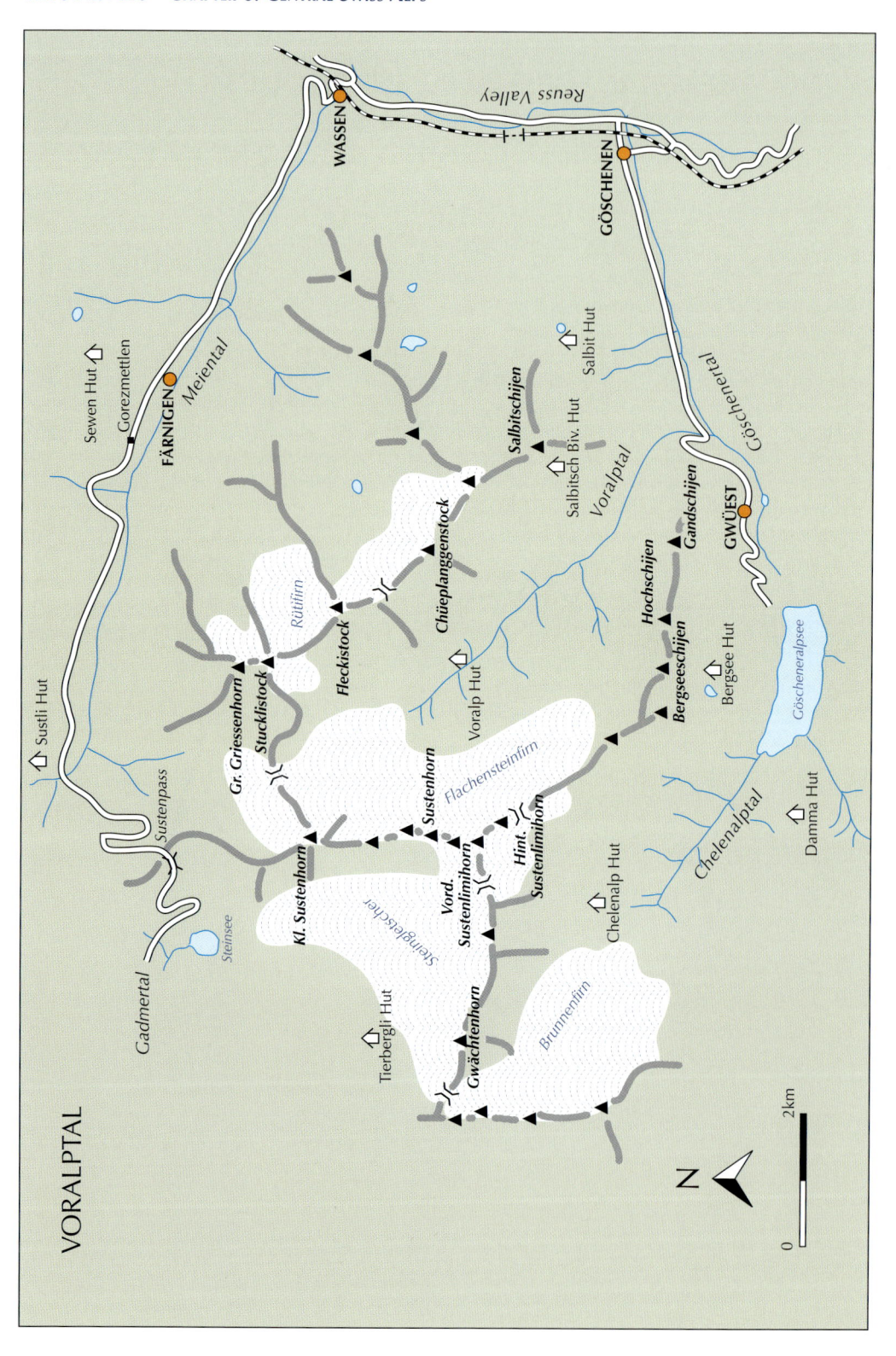

358

eastern end is traced by the Rhine between Chur and Sargans; the Andermatt to Altdorf road effectively marks its western extent, while the northern limit runs along the Schachental, Urner Boden and Linth valleys whose spectacular road links the first two by way of the 1948m Klausenpass. An assortment of valleys cuts into this block of mountains, whose highest and best-known summit is the 3614m Tödi, the so-called 'King of the Little Mountains' – one of the earliest of alpine snow peaks to be climbed.

Lower and less known to outsiders than the Bernese, Pennine or Bernina ranges, the Central Swiss Alps would repay the attention of an alpine novice with fairly easy snow and ice climbing, but there's no shortage of high-standard rock climbs and top-quality walking opportunities too. The Alpine Pass Route (5:10) strikes through the region from east to west, giving the long-distance hillwalker a unique view of some of its finest scenery. Access is good, with fast roads and efficient public transport links, and although there are few mountain resorts as such, and none to match those of the neighbouring Bernese Oberland, each group has its conveniently placed small towns and villages and a number of SAC huts, so finding suitable accommodation is rarely a problem.

6:1 URI ALPS: DAMMASTOCK GROUP

As part of the so-called Urner Oberland, this small and neatly defined group is sometimes referred to as the Eastern Bernese Alps, not simply for its close proximity to that chain, nor for the small section that lies within Canton Bern, but as much for its appearance. Glaciers, snowpeaks and challenging rock walls abound. But while the Bernese Alps are mostly limestone, the Dammastock group is largely composed of hard Aare granite that provides climbs of quality. Published in 1969 by West Col, the long out of print English-language mountaineering guide to the district (*Central Switzerland*) judged climbing here to be on a par with that of the Bregaglia and Mont Blanc ranges. Alan Blackshaw, in his classic handbook *Mountaineering*, also compared the climbing potential to that of the Chamonix Aiguilles, but on a smaller scale. Praise indeed.

But while the twin-peaked Dammastock dominates the group with its East Face overlooking

The Dammastock group overlooks the Göscheneralpsee

the Göschenertal, the much smaller Salbitschijen, guarding the Voralp tributary on the eastern edge of the district, commands respect on account of the five towers of its West Ridge, and its long, multi-pinnacled South Ridge, pioneered in 1935 and for a time considered one of the great alpine rock climbs. Like that of the Dammastock and its neighbours, climbing here is on excellent granite.

Access to the group is from the Gadmertal in the north where the Sustenpass road climbs from Innertkirchen; from the Meiental on the eastern side of the Susten; from valleys on the south side of the district linked by the Grimsel and Furka passes; and best of all, from the Reuss valley which neatly cuts along the eastern side of the mountains from where the Göschenertal holds the key to the district.

Entered at **Göschenen** (1106m), which has a station on the Gotthard line, the Göschenertal, with its Voralptal tributary, is arguably the finest and most dramatic of all those valleys in the Central Swiss Alps. Crowned by the Dammastock, the ice-plastered Winterberg massif forms a barricade at its western end; at its base lies the Göscheneralpsee reservoir where the valley road terminates, barely 10km from Göschenen. Göschenen itself has a few hotels, shops, a restaurant and tourist information (www.goeschenen.ch). Further upvalley the hamlet of **Gwüest** (1585m) has both a campsite and the Gasthaus Göscheneralp, with 12 beds and 25 dormitory places, and at the eastern end of the reservoir the Berggasthaus Dammagletscher also has both dormitories and standard rooms.

Voralptal

About 4km from Göschenen the Voralptal cuts into the north flank of the Göschenertal. This narrow and unspoilt side valley is hemmed in by ridges emanating from the Fleckistock on the east and Sustenhorn on the west, while its entrance is guarded by the famous Salbitschijen on one side and the lesser-known crags of the ❸ **Gandschijen** (2388m) on the other, where a number of modern bolt-protected routes of exceptional quality can be found on its 200m south-facing wall.

Though considerably higher than the Gandschijen, at just 2981m the ❸ ☆ **Salbitschijen** is dwarfed by its valley neighbours, most of which rise another 300–500m above it. But neither Fleckistock nor Sustenhorn can match the Salbitschijen's tremendous south, east and west ridges with their much-sought-after top-quality routes. The East Ridge is said to be the easiest; the pinnacled South Ridge is known for the 1935 classic pioneered by Alfred and Otto Amstad with Guido Masetto, which provides sustained climbing (D: Va) comparable to the South Ridge of the Moine in the Mont Blanc range; while the West Ridge, with its five individual towers, gives an exhilarating traverse (ED) and a number of 300–450m protected routes on the south or southeast face of some of those towers.

Below the West Ridge at 2400m the **Salbitsch Bivouac Hut** enables a short approach to be made to some of the best climbs, but the 60-place **Salbit Hut** below the East Ridge is the main accommodation option here. Reached by a stiff 2½hr climb from Ulmi, the hut stands 900m above the Göschenertal at 2105m. Owned by the SAC's Lindenberg section, it is fully staffed from mid-June until mid-October (www.salbit.ch).

Deep within the Voralptal, about 2½hrs from the bus stop at Wiggen, the SAC (Section Uto) has another hut, set at 2126m in the valley's wild upper reaches, midway between the Sustenhorn and Fleckistock. Dating from 1891, the original **Voralp Hut** was destroyed by avalanche in 1988. The present building has just 40 places, but is staffed between mid-March and mid-April, and from mid-June until the end of September (www.voralphuette.ch).

Above this hut the Stucklistock to the north, and Fleckistock and Winterberg to northeast and east, should appeal to any alpinist who enjoys impressive rock scenery and fairly straightforward routes. Their northeast flanks fall steeply into the Meiental where there's no suitable hut, so climbs from that valley inevitably involve a longer approach. The Voralp Hut therefore is the obvious base.

Apart from the subsidiary peaks of the Klein and Gross Griessenhorn which look down on the Grossalp (on the eastern side of the Sustenpass), the ❸ **Stucklistock** (3313m) is the northernmost summit on the left bank of the Voralptal. An elegant rock peak boasting a number of routes, it is probably best known for the classic ridge traverse to the 3417m ❸ **Fleckistock**, which usually leads over the summit of the latter to the **Flüelücke**, before descending to the Voralp Hut. Also known as the Rot Stock, the Fleckistock is the highest on the Voralptal's northeast wall. First climbed in 1864, it's an impressive peak whose rock is said to be generally good, and the southwest rib which rises directly above the hut provides an obvious route (II) to the summit.

The deep cleft of the Flüelücke cuts into the ridge running from the Fleckistock to the 3167m Winterberg, the lower of the two-summit 🏃 **Chüeplanggenstock** whose higher peak is at 3208m. The mountain's NW Ridge, which connects with the Fleckistock via the Flüelücke, gives a rewarding traverse (III) first achieved in 1896.

West of the Voralp Hut, the 3503m 🏃 **Sustenhorn** is one of the most popular peaks of the district. The highest point on a ridge aligned from north to south, the east and west flanks are glaciated, which makes it a good choice for mixed rock and ice climbs, and for ski mountaineering. In addition to the Voralp Hut, two other SAC huts are located close enough to offer a choice of routes from the west and the south: the **Tierbergli**, approached from the Sustenpass road, and the **Chelenalp Hut**, which stands high in the Chelenalptal above the Göscheneralpsee. (Details of both these huts will be found below.) A north–south traverse of the Sustenhorn has a good reputation and is recommended.

At the northern end of the Sustenhorn ridge, the rock peak of the 🏃 **Klein Sustenhorn** (3318m) has some fairly long and interesting routes to consider from a base at the Voralp Hut, including the East Wall (II) which leads to the 3308m South Summit, and the more difficult East Ridge (V+) first climbed in 1962 by M Betschart and F Auf der Mauer. A south–north ridge traverse from the Sustenhorn is another fine objective here.

South of the Sustenhorn the ridge kinks to the southwest on the 3316m summit of the **Vorder Sustenlimihorn**, while the continuing ridge that carries the west wall of the Voralptal angles more to the southeast over the summit of the **Hinter Sustenlimihorn** (3194m). A traverse of this latter ridge linking the two summits is another recommended outing of moderate difficulty. Meanwhile, the southwest angling ridge kinks again, first west then northwest to enclose the head of the Chelenalptal, which to all intents and purposes may be taken as the upper reaches of the Göschenertal.

Göschenertal

As mentioned above, the Göschenertal road terminates at the large Göscheneralpsee reservoir at

Tiny pools reflect neighbouring peaks in the Göschenertal

THE SWISS ALPS – CHAPTER 6: CENTRAL SWISS ALPS

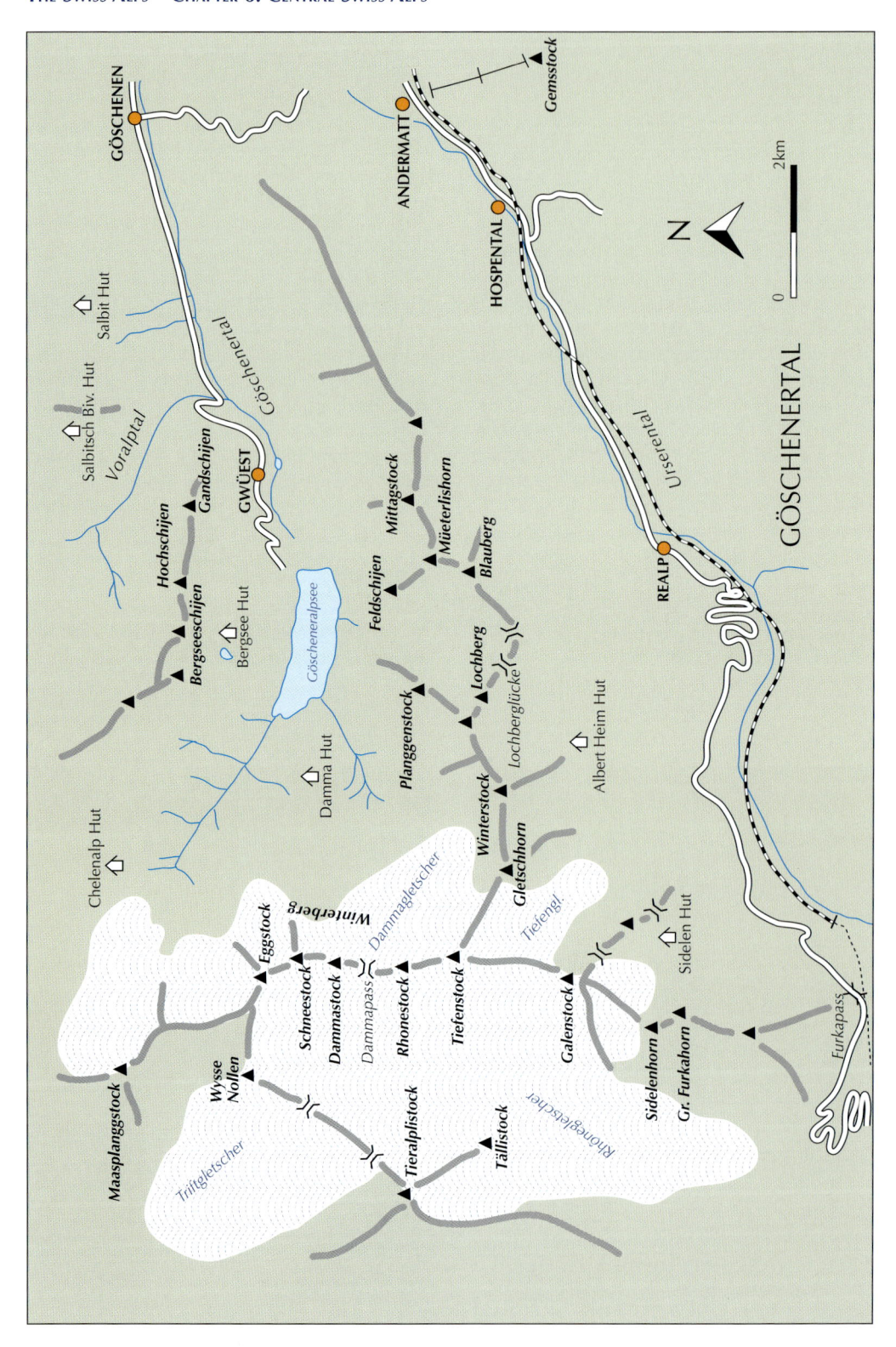

6:1 Uri Alps: Dammastock Group

1797m. At the far end of the lake the glacier-hung peaks of the Dammastock group create a formidable wall, rising from boulder tips and old moraine debris slashed with riotous streams, while exciting prospects for climbers will be found also on both north and south flanks of the valley overlooking the lake. On the northern slopes alpenrose and tiny pools lead to rock peaks that guard the Voralptal, and 500m or so above the Göscheneralpsee, the **Bergsee Hut** (2370m) is perfectly situated to serve as a base for climbs on the Bergseeschijen and Hochschijen. Property of the Basel-based Angenstein section of the SAC, it has 70 places and is fully staffed from June until the end of October (www.bergsee.ch).

Known for its perfect rock, the 2816m **Bergseeschijen** has a number of excellent climbs to consider at a variety of grades. High on the list will be the steep South Wall (IV/V); others will be found on the East Wall where in 1967 Borer, Wymann and Walther pioneered a much-respected route (VI, A3) which has a prominent roof barrier to contend with. Just to the east of this stands the rock peak of **Hochschijen** (2634m), and between the two a blue-white marked alpine route links the Bergsee and Voralp Huts by way of the Horefellistock.

Another blue-white trail connects the Bergsee Hut with the Chelenalp Hut by remaining high above the Chelenalptal (or Kehlenalptal), although the standard route of approach to the **Chelenalp Hut** remains close to the valley stream, weaving among marmot burrows and clumps of alpenrose until, after passing the tiny building of Hinter Röti, the trail angles up to a large granite slab, then climbs steeply to gain the hut with its truly spectacular view.

At 2350m the **Chelenalp Hut** has one of the finest outlooks of any in the Central Swiss Alps, for it sits within a magnificent cirque of bold peaks, icefalls and glaciers crowned by the Hinter Tierberg and Gwächtenhorn – neither of which will mean much to anyone who has not seen them at close quarters, but memorable to those who cut their alpine teeth on them. Reached in 3–3½hrs from the Göscheneralpsee, the hut belongs to the Aarau section of the SAC, has 65 places and is fully staffed from mid-June until mid-October (www.chelenalp.ch). The hut's location, and the walk to reach it, are both highly recommended.

Climbs from the hut naturally include the **Sustenlimihorn** which rises directly above it, the **Gwächtenhorn** by its SSW ridge, and

The trail to the Chelenalp Hut

individual summits of the ● **Tierberg** group on the opposite side of the valley, although these latter peaks are more often tackled from the Trift Hut which nestles at the foot of the Hinter Tierberg's west wall (see the Gadmertal section below).

The whole of the Chelenalptal's west wall is taken up by the Winterberg massif, which extends southward to include the Dammastock group, the main focus of attention hereabouts. The 23-bed **Damma Hut** (2439m) serves as the climber's base. Easily reached in 3hrs from the Göscherneralpsee roadhead, it enjoys an outlook almost as spectacular as that of the Chelenalp, for it looks directly onto the enticing East Wall of the Dammastock and its smear of glacier from which thrusts the rock band that carries a ridge 1000m or so above the hut. Fully manned from July until mid-September, the Damma Hut is owned by the Lucerne-based Pilatus section of the SAC (www.sac-pilatus.ch).

The 3630m ● ☆ **Dammastock** is the highest mountain in the Central Swiss Alps. The mighty Rhône rises on its west flank, where popular ski ascents are made from the old Belvedere hotel on the Furkapass road. It was from this side that the mountain was first climbed on 28 July 1864 by A Hoffmann-Burckhardt, with Andreas von Weissenfluh and Johann Fischer. The South Ridge offers a short and easy climb from the 3501m **Dammapass**, while it is the East Rib above the Dammagletscher that offers more challenging climbs.

North of the Dammastock the ● **Schneestock** (3608m) provides a few climbs of a serious nature. Its first ascent (by the North Ridge) was made on the same day and by the same team who climbed the Dammastock. A little further to the north comes the **Eggstock** (3556m) and, standing back to the west and overlooking the Trift Hut, the 3398m snow peak of the **Wysse Nollen** (Wissnollen). Von Weissenfluh was involved in pioneering routes on each of these peaks, while in the 1930s Alfred Amstad and Guido Masetto (who were active throughout the Uri Alps) climbed what was considered for a long time the best and most difficult route on the Schneestock via the East Edge (V).

South of the Dammastock, beyond the Dammapass, comes the 3589m **Rhonestock**, followed by the ● **Tiefenstock** standing at a junction of ridges. The main ridge, aligned from north to south, carries the cantonal boundary which continues southward across the Galenstock and Grosse Furkahorn to the Furkapass, while the southeast ridge leads to the Gletschhorn before easing eastward to form the south flank of the Göschenertal. At 3515m the Tiefenstock rises above three glaciers: the Damma, Tiefen and Rhône, and is served not only by the Damma Hut, but also by the Albert Heim Hut (details below) above Realp, which is the choice of climbers aiming for the 350m South Wall of this fine rock peak, while anything from the north will be tackled from the Damma Hut.

The south side of the Göschenertal features a number of summits worth considering, as well as the rock climber's playground of the ● **Feldschijen**, which stands above the shore of the Göscheneralpsee and positively bristles with towers and pinnacles noted for the quality of their rock and quantity of routes. In the walling ridge above and to the southwest of the Feldschijen, the ◐ **Lochberglücke** is a pass of about 2815m which provides a direct route between the Göschenertal and the Albert Heim Hut.

Furkapass to Andermatt
Drained by the Furkareuss, the south side of the Dammastock district of the Uri Alps is known as the Urserental, a U-shaped valley once described by D H Lawrence as 'raw and flat'. Raw it may be, but it's only flat between Realp and Andermatt, for above Realp the road climbs 900m to the bleak Furkapass, one of the highest road passes in Europe at 2429m (the railway tunnels beneath it). Given reasonable weather views from the pass are extensive, but paths on either side and south of the road give even better prospects; that on the western side leading to the Bidmergrat (see 5:10) reveals a vast section of the Bernese Alps as well as the Rhône glacier, while the trail on the eastern side rises to a group of small lakes and rewards with a panoramic view of both the Uri and Glarner Alps.

On the northern side of the road, a short distance from the actual pass, a marked trail breaks away to the **Sidelen Hut** (2708m), a comparatively new building owned by the Alpine Sports School of Andermatt. With 30 places, it's staffed from late June until early October (tel 041 887 02 33) and is conveniently placed for climbs on the Grosse Furkahorn, Galenstock and the Grosse and Kleine Bielenhorn (formerly known as the Büelenhorn) which tower over it. The hut is also on the so-called ◐ ☆ **Nepali Highway**, a scenic trail linking the Albert Heim, Sidelen and Rotondo Huts.

First climbed in 1845 via its south ridge by a seven-man team that included members of the party which, the previous year, had climbed the lowest of the three Wetterhörner above Grindelwald (see 5:8), the 🔵 **Galenstock** (3586m) is one of the most prominent mountains of the district, its East Face defined by three rock ribs, the most northerly of which runs from the Tiefen glacier to the summit. Though not unduly difficult (II) in some seasons it may be overhung by a massive cornice. The SE Rib, gained by way of the Ober Bielenlücke, is a grade IV+ rock route first climbed in 1901 but is still rewarding. Other routes will be evident on the South and SE Walls, and on the South and North Ridges, the latter being the standard route of ascent pioneered in 1902 by Charles and Paul Montadon. The South Ridge, or Galengrat, prickles with summits, while the Sidelengrat continues the ridge between the Grosse and Kleine Furkahorn. Despite having obvious appeal, the West Ridge above the Rhône glacier appears to have been the last to be climbed, waiting until September 1999 for its first recorded ascent. This was made by Dutch climber Gerard van Sprang, who climbed the ridge directly to the summit in 3½hrs; the 480m route is graded AD with sections of II and IV.

The **Albert Heim Hut** is the traditional base for most climbs on those peaks that form the northwest wall of the upper Urserental. Standing on a rocky outcrop below the Winterstock, about 1½hrs from Hotel Tiefenbach on the Furkapass road (or 3hrs from Realp), the present building replaces the original hut dating from 1918. Owned by the Zürich-based Uto section of the SAC, it has 80 dormitory places and is fully staffed from mid-June until mid-October (www.albert-heim-huette-sac.ch).

The 3203m triple-headed 🔵 **Winterstock** is an obvious attraction to the rock specialist, for it boasts an impressive number of both wall and ridge climbs at a variety of grades. Again, Alfred Amstad and Guido Masetto were active here in the 1930s on the South Wall of the West Summit, while the 1000m long SE Ridge (VI) leading to the South Summit was pioneered by Max Niederman and Werner Sieber in 1965 and quickly gained a reputation as the most difficult route of that group of mountains south of the Göscheneralpsee.

East of the Winterstock the 3040m **Lochberg** does not have the same appeal, but it offers an easy scramble from the Lochberglücke (in 1½hrs), and another from the Winterlücke (40mins) in the ridge connecting the two peaks. The SW Wall, on the other hand, provides sustained climbing of grade IV/V.

For mountain walkers the 🟢 **path** linking the Sidelen and Albert Heim huts with Andermatt makes a rewarding two-day excursion. Beginning on the eastern side of the Furkapass it climbs for less than 300m to the Sidelen Hut, then works a more challenging way (a blue-white alpine route) to the Albert Heim Hut and continues high above the valley bed until, above Hospental, it slopes directly down to Andermatt.

With the Furkapass in one direction, Oberalp in another, St Gotthard to the south and the Reuss valley to the north, **Andermatt** stands at a strategic crossroads at 1436m. The fast and efficient transalpine motorway and rail line both avoid the town by burrowing through lengthy tunnels, but the narrow-gauge Furka–Oberalp Railway (built in 1926) uses Andermatt's station which is located 400m north of the town centre. The tourist office (www.andermatt.ch) provides details of accommodation, most of which will be found on or near the attractive main street, the Gotthardstrasse. A campsite is located beside the Furka road on the western edge of town. Nearby a cableway rises over 1400m to the **Gemsstock** (2961m), the finest viewpoint hereabouts for non-active visitors. In winter numerous red and black runs draw skiers to its slopes.

Northeast and east of the Gemsstock the Unteralptal provides walkers with ways to gain access to the Lepontine Alps (see Chapter 3) above Airolo. The Vermigel and unmanned Wildenmatten Huts are both situated high in this valley, with passes in the region of 2600–2700m by which to cross the Lepontine ridge.

Below Andermatt the Reuss drains northward, to eventually empty into the Vierwaldstättersee near Altdorf. East of its grim gorge the Glarus (Glarner) Alps will be explored later in this chapter, while the Dammastock group of the Uri Alps, as we have already discovered, is most conveniently reached by way of Göschenen and its valley, a short distance downstream from Andermatt. But go beyond Göschenen and 9km from Andermatt you come to **Wassen** at 916m, where a side road loops its way up and into the Meiental which cuts into the mountains on the west bank of the Reuss.

Meiental

This delightful valley carries the Sustenpass road and effectively marks the northeastern limit of the Dammastock district. There are no resort villages and few tourist facilities, just a scattering of small hamlets and farms set amid pastures. A short way inside the valley ruins of the old Meienschanz redoubt date from 1712 when it was built to defend Uri from the Bernese; but it was destroyed by the French in 1799.

Without huts to facilitate access, outlying peaks of the Dammastock district remain largely unvisited from the Meiental, although both the Sewen and Sustli Huts extend opportunities on the valley's north flank for walkers and climbers. After passing above the hamlet of **Färnigen** the **Sewen Hut** (2150m) is reached by two paths; the first from Gorezmettlen in a little under 2hrs, the other from a hairpin above Gorezmettlen in 1½hrs. An attractive, traditional hut with 60 places, it lies immediately below the Sewenstock and is wardened from mid-June until mid-October (www.sewenhuette.ch).

The hairpin bend above Gorezmettlen spans a stream draining the seductive little valley of Chlialp, at whose head rises a cirque topped by the Chli (or Klein) Spannort, a peak visited from the Engelbergtal in 6:2. The Chlialptal is a wildly attractive little valley that is well worth wandering into, whether or not you have designs on any of the summits that rim its headwall.

Continuing its way to the Sustenpass, the road now angles above the Meienreuss with the aptly named Fünffingerstock seducing from a ridge to the west. Shortly after the old road rejoins the present highway it curves sharply over another stream dashing from the northern heights. This is known as Chli Sustli (the Sustenbrüggli bus stop with car park and a café), from where a path strikes steeply up the hillside for 350m to gain the **Sustli Hut** at 2257m. There are, in fact, two routes from Chli Sustli, one of which is a mini *klettersteig* created to the right of the standard hut approach.

Built by the SAC's Zug-based Rossberg section, the Sustli Hut can sleep 83 in its dormitories and is fully staffed from July to the end of October (www.sustlihuette.ch). From it a blue-white alpine route swings round the hillside to pass beneath the **Fünffingerstock** on its way to the Sustenpass.

The gentle Meiental

Gadmertal

Breaching a watershed, the actual road pass is bored through a 325m tunnel at 2224m. It's an austere site when clouds restrict views, but on a good day there's much to lift the spirits with the Steingletscher hanging from the Gwächtenhorn and Sustenhorn to the south, the little Steinsee 300m below the pass; Fünffingerstock to the north and a fine run of ridges which flank the road as it descends westward into the Gadmertal in Canton Bern. The Wetterhorn can also be seen ahead.

Immediately above the pass to the south stands the sharp and rocky **Sustenspitz**, which just falls short of the 3000m mark. Said to be a fine viewpoint, it may be climbed directly from the pass in 2–3hrs via either the northeast or northwest ridges. Neither route is more demanding than grade II, but for a good overview of the district the ascent is considered worthwhile.

Below the Sustenpass the Steingletscher Hotel is built on a hairpin at 1865m not far from the **Steinsee**. From it a path heads south to the **Tierbergli Hut** (2795m) in 3½hrs. Standing in the midst of imposing glacial scenery below the Gwächtenhorn, this sturdy-looking hut, which belongs to the Baselland section of the SAC, has 70 dormitory places, is partly wardened from March until the end of June, but is fully staffed from July until the end of September (www.tierbergli.ch). A number of peaks above it vie for attention: the **Sustenhorn** is one, its southwest flank and south ridge being especially popular, not only in summer with first-season alpinists, but for ski-aided ascents in late spring when the route can sometimes become crowded. West of the hut the 2900m **Giglistock** also makes a popular ski ascent, while the **Sustenlimi**, a 3089m pass located between Rot Stock (Fleckistock) and Vorder Sustenlimihorn, is often used by parties moving from the Tierbergli Hut to the Chelenalp Hut.

Built between 1938 and 1945, the motor road continues down from Hotel Steingletscher in a series of hairpins that underscore a masterpiece of engineering. The Gschletter bend at 1638m projects as a belvedere overlooking the Gadmertal. Above the viewpoint the South Face of the **Wendenstöcke** will surely have a climber's fingers itching, for the wall contains a wealth of

The Gwächtenhorn, on show from the Sustenpass

The Swiss Alps – Chapter 6: Central Swiss Alps

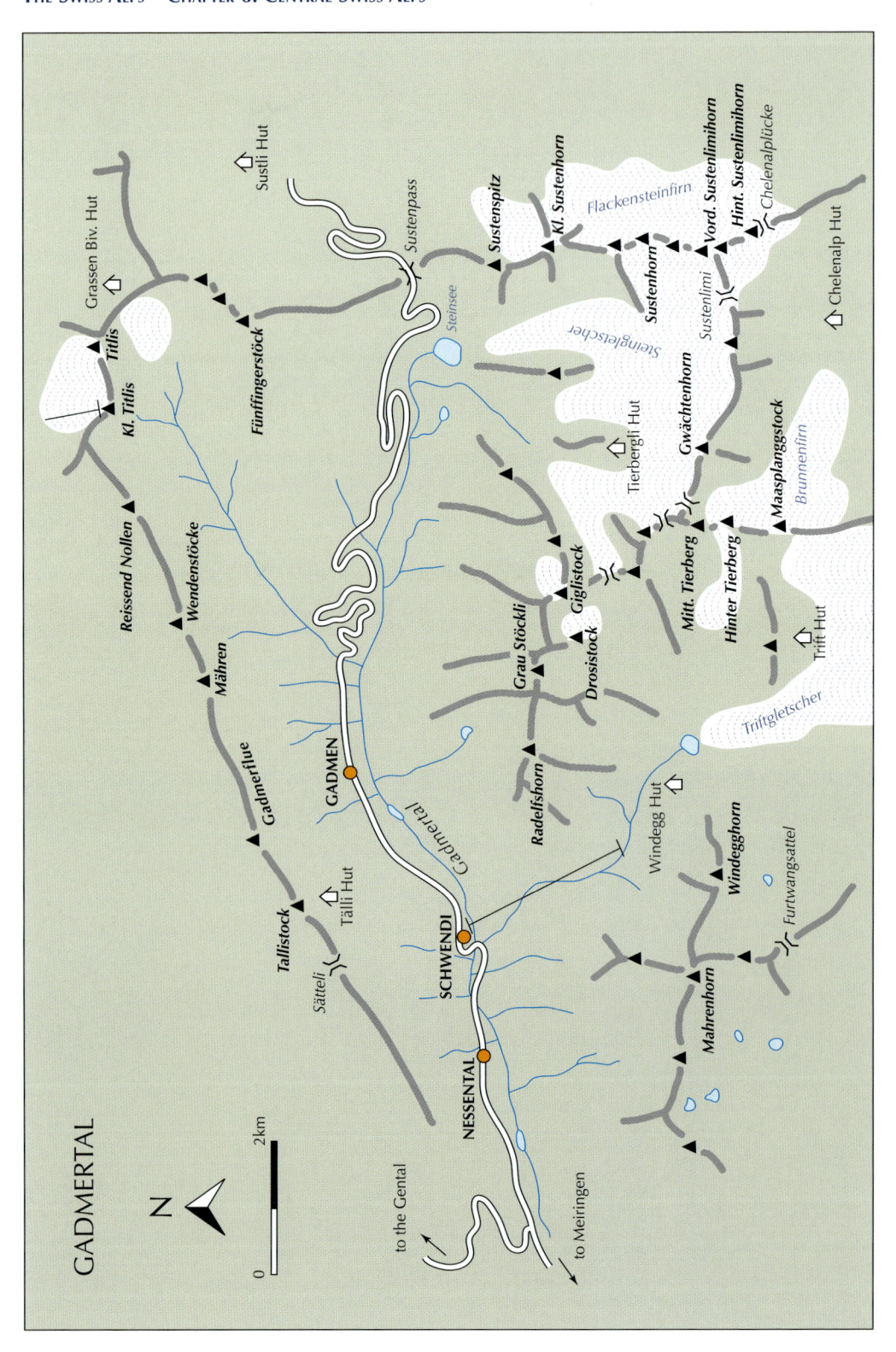

368

routes, many of which were created by the ubiquitous Remy brothers. A path leaves the road here, and cuts away to sweep round the little valley of the Wendenwasser before heading west across the slope below Wendenstöcke and **Gadmerflue**, eventually reaching the **Tälli Hut** (1726m) built at the foot of the ● **Tällistock**, which sports some good introductory bolted routes up to 400m long.

Not an SAC hut, the Tälli Hut is owned by the Haslital mountain guides, has 26 places and is occasionally wardened in June and October, fully staffed from July until the end of September, but closed in winter (www.taellihuette.ch). Apart from its proximity to some exciting climbs, a little west of the hut there's a saddle in the Gadmerflue ridge that allows a crossing from Gadmen to Engstlenalp at the head of the lovely Gental (see 6:2). Of additional interest to hut visitors, however, is the ● ☆ **Tälli-Klettersteig**, claimed to be Switzerland's first *via ferrata*. Created by the Haslital guides to mark their association's centenary, it uses 1300m of cable to ascend around 600m of near-vertical limestone, and gains the Gadmerflue ridge near the Horlaui Pillar.

With its old wooden chalets **Gadmen** is the valley's principal village, beyond which the descent eases before slipping down to **Nessental**. Between the two the Triftwasser drains the Trift glacier which begins high up on the Tieralplistock. Two SAC huts are located on the way to, or close by, this glacier. The **Windegg Hut** (1887m) can be reached by a stiff 3hr hike from the Susten road, or by cable car from Schwendi to Underi Trift, followed by a walk of about 1½hrs. The property of the SAC's Bern section, it has 48 places and a guardian in the main summer months of mid-June until the end of September, and when conditions allow, is partly wardened between March and May (www.windegghuette.ch). An interesting route connects the hut with Guttanen in the upper Haslital (5:9). Heading south, it goes along the Windegg ridge before cutting into the little Trifttälli to pass alongside a tarn, then climbs over rock and scree to gain the 2568m ● **Furtwangsattel** from which a splendid view of the Bernese Alps is won. Guttanen lies more than 1500m below, so a knee-crunching descent is guaranteed. Allow 5–6hrs from start to finish.

From the Windegg Hut a new route has been created to connect with the **Trift Hut**, using a 102m long suspension bridge to cross a ravine at the outflow of the Triftsee (www.trift.ch) below the retreating Trift glacier. Beyond the bridge a blue-white alpine route, taking 3hrs to the hut at 2520m, is only recommended for experienced mountain walkers. Also owned by the SAC's Bern section, the Trift Hut has just 40 places. Useful as a base for ski ascents of peaks at the head of the Trift glacier's basin, it is staffed from mid-March until mid-May, and from July until the end of September (www.trifthuette.ch).

The main peak at the head of the Trift glacier is the ● **Tieralplistock** (3383m), an easy snowpeak with three summits most often climbed from the popular **Gelmer Hut** above Handegg on the Grimselpass road. But above the Trift Hut, the 3447m ● **Hinter Tierberg** makes an obvious goal, as does the imposing rock peak of the ● **Maasplanggstock** (3401m), which stands on the ridge south of the Tierberg. This ridge, starting from the northerly Maasplanggjoch (at the top of a steep snow gully) offers an interesting climb (II/III), finishing with a descent by way of the South Ridge and the deep gap of the south Maasplanggjoch.

Back in the Gadmertal the road descends past walnut and fruit trees with views opening into the Urbachtal, until entering Innertkirchen (see 5:9), about 6km upstream of Meiringen. To the left (southeast) the road climbs through the upper Haslital to the Grimsel and Furka Passes, thereby closing the circle around the Dammastock group. To the right (northwest) the road pushes beyond the Aare's gorge to reach Meiringen, Brienz and the Brienzersee. But if we turn back into the Gadmertal, after passing through Wiler a minor road enters the Gental, at the head of which lies the Engstlenalp in the second of our districts of the Central Swiss Alps.

6:2 NORTH OF THE SUSTENPASS: TITLIS GROUP

Though larger in extent than the Dammastock group, mountains north of the Sustenpass are not so neatly defined as their neighbours, but spread along ridge systems largely emanating from the Titlis, which forms a lynchpin for the district. Here, huge limestone towers and pinnacles have been favourably compared to Dolomite walls with Verdon rock, from which great views are won of the Oberland. Ridges that spread northeast round the upper Engelbergtal twist in a confusion of glacier-carved cirques from which a whole series of small valleys make an untidy, but wildly romantic geography, and virtually all the high land drains into the Lake of Lucerne (Vierwaldstättersee). There are few glaciers left; bare rock peaks project from some of the highest ridges, others appear to have been planed clean, a few of the lower spurs contain broad grassy levels. And for all their proximity to some of Switzerland's busiest towns, all but the most accessible of valleys are surprisingly free from large numbers of visitors. In the heart of the region at the foot of the Titlis Engelberg is an exception as the one resort town that makes an impact, with a string of cableways serving a comparatively small ski area. Other lifts occur on the western outskirts above Meiringen, and at the head of the Grosse Melchtal where a high plateau appeals to cross-country skiers in winter, and walkers in summer.

A rough outline of the district may be drawn on the west by the road crossing the Brünigpass on the way to Lucerne, by the Sustenpass road to the south, the Reuss valley between Wassen and Altdorf to the east, and the arthritic curves of the Vierwaldstättersee spreading across the northern limits.

Gental

Having approached the Titlis group from the south, the U-shaped Gental makes an obvious route of access, but motorists need to be aware that the road is a toll road, with tolls payable 4km from the entrance, which is found midway between Wiler and Nessental on the Sustenpass route. Served by bus from Meiringen and Innertkirchen, the valley slices northeastward between the Gadmerflue–Wendenstöcke ridge to one side, and an extensive wooded wall on the other. Walkers on the Alpine Pass Route (5:10) grow familiar with the latter on a choice of trails, while the rocky Wendenstöcke side appears to be much more forbidding and has more appeal to climbers.

A small settlement reservoir lies in the lower reaches of the valley on the way to the cheesemakers' chalets at Gentalhütten, also known as Alp Gental, and at **Schwarzental** (1369m) an old dairy farm built in 1799, has been converted to a restaurant with dormitory accommodation (tel 033 975 12 40). A picturesque series of cascades burst from the limestone cliffs nearby.

Above Schwarzental the road climbs with the aid of a few hairpins before terminating on the edge of the **Engstlenalp** at 1834m. This broad open pasture at the head of the Gental was celebrated by Professor John Tyndall, the scientist, pioneering mountaineer and Vice President of the Alpine Club, as 'one of the most charming

The Engstlensee at the head of the Gental

6:2 NORTH OF THE SUSTENPASS: TITLIS GROUP

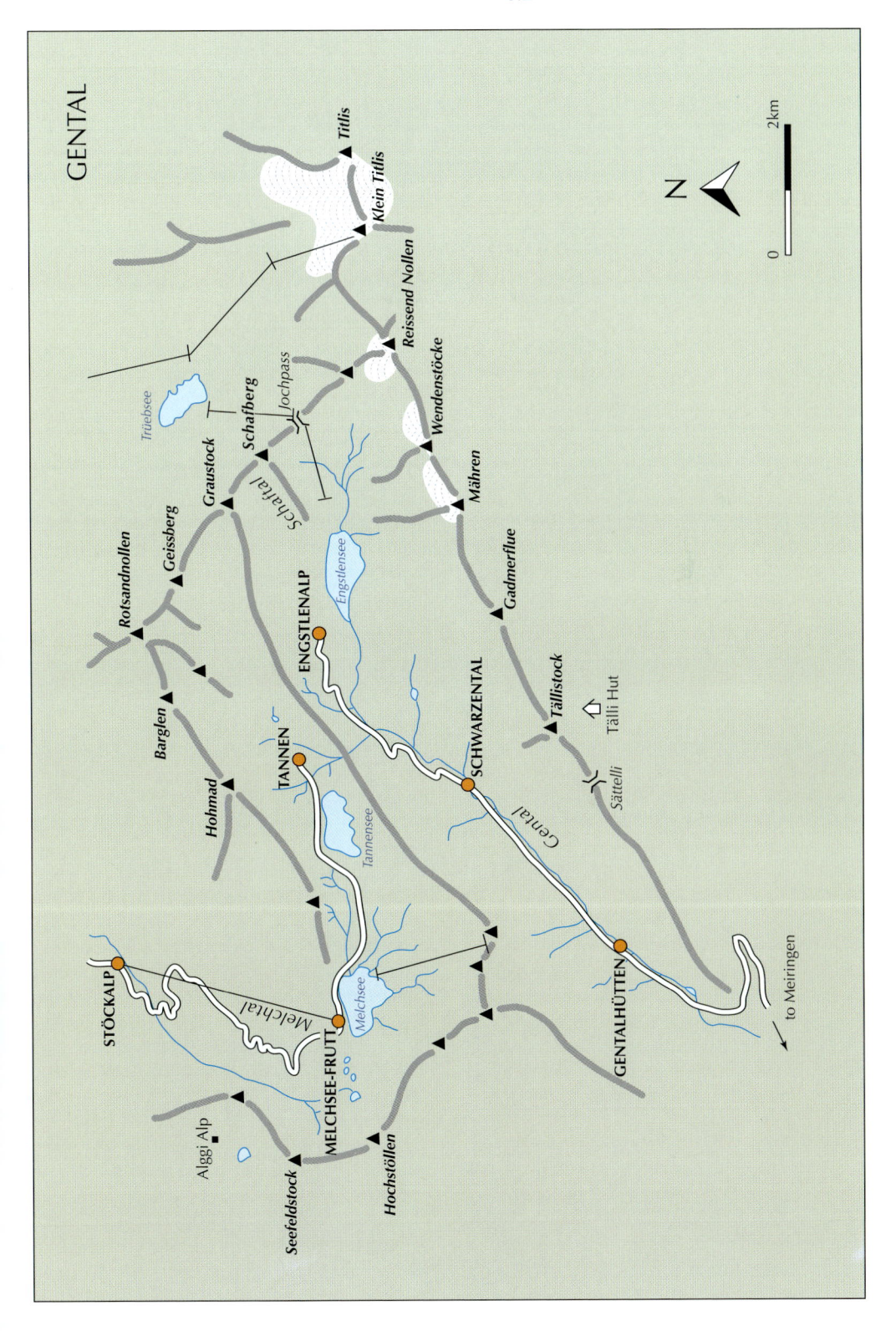

spots in the Alps'. With its view of the Wetterhorn and Schreckhorn to the west, its clutch of timber barns and chalets, and the clear, blue-green Engstlensee walled by the ice-topped slabs of the Wendenstöcke whose ridge rises over the Reissend Nollen to the Titlis, Tyndall's comments are easy to understand. What was true in 1866 is largely true today. The lake is popular with anglers, there are several rewarding walks to be had in the vicinity, and with 60 beds and 60 dormitory places, Hotel Engstlenalp (www.engstlenalp.ch) makes an obvious base for a short stay.

Among the recommended ○ **walks** from here, one crosses the low crest to the west of the hotel to visit the Melchsee plateau with its lakes and flower meadows; another (adopted by the Alpine Pass Route) goes along the right flank of the valley to the tiny alp hamlet of Baumgarten, and continues all the way to Meiringen; while a third skirts the north shore of the Engstlensee and, ignoring a chairlift, climbs to the 2207m **Jochpass**. On this somewhat cluttered pass the Berghaus Jochpass has both standard beds and dormitory places, and is open from June to the end of September (www.jochpass.ch). Another cableway descends on the north side of the pass to the **Trüebsee**, set in a basin at the foot of the Titlis, but for *via ferrata* fans, the ⓑ ☆ **Graustock Klettersteig** mounts the left-hand ridge above the Jochpass to the 2522m Schafberg, and continues to the summit of the Graustock at 2662m (allow 3hrs from the Jochpass). Descent is usually made below the SW Ridge to gain the **Schaftal** above Engstlenalp.

Melchtal

Northwest of Engstlensee there are two valleys named Melchtal: Kleine and Grosse, the two divided by a long ridge. The first of these lies on the very west of the district where it falls from the Hochstöllen and drains down to the southern end of the Sarner See. Near the head of this valley, on the east flank below the Seefeldstock, lies the **Alggi Alp** (1636m), noted as being at the geographical centre of Switzerland.

The Grosse Melchtal, usually referred to simply as the Melchtal, also empties its river (the Melchaa) into the Sarner lake, but at its northern end. As its name suggests, it's a longer, more important valley than its neighbour, and for most of its length the Melchtal is both narrow and steep. Although its west wall never quite tops 3000m it appears much higher than it really is, for the bed of the valley invariably lies more than 1000m below its crest. The right-hand wall comes from the Titlis via the Jochpass, and also fails to reach the 3000m height. Nevertheless, the Melchsee plateau at its head, which can be reached by cableway from Stöckalp, gives every impression of a high mountain basin of grass and water in which two small lakeside resort villages give plenty of accommodation options (www.melchsee-frutt.ch). **Melchsee-Frutt** lies at 1902m, while **Tannen** overlooks the Tannensee at 1974m.

A line of low crags make a *klettergarten* above the north shore of the Melchsee, with numerous short ⓢ **sport climbs** to enjoy. But the main focus of interest here is the range of easy walks in summer, and the potential for cross-country skiing in winter. The southern lip of the plateau gives views into and along the Gental; the three lakes of **Melchsee**, **Tannensee** and **Engstlensee** attract family walkers, while one of the most interesting outings is the 2½hr walk to Alggi Alp from Melchsee-Frutt. From there you could either continue down through the Klein Melchtal, or return to Melchsee-Frutt via Stöckalp and its cableway.

Meanwhile the right-hand wall of the Melchtal contains several ○ **walker's passes** that lead to Engelberg; among them are the 2171m Juchli (south of the Nünalphorn), the Bocki (2204m) which lies between Nünalphorn and Widderfeldstock, and the 1742m Storegg Pass which gives a 6hr crossing from Melchtal village.

Engelbergtal

By far the longest of the valleys in the Titlis region of the Central Swiss Alps, the Engelbergtal is entered by road off the A2 motorway that skirts the south side of the Vierwaldstättersee near Stans, and along with the railway from Lucerne, it follows the Engelberger Aa all the way to Engelberg. At Dallenwil several cableways rise on both sides of the valley; further south Wolfenschiessen is a small resort village where a side road climbs steeply southeastward to Oberrickenbach below the Bannalpsee reservoir at the foot of the Walenstöcke.

Between Dörfli and Grafenort the Falenbach waterfall is seen to the right (west). By now the valley has narrowed and with the Walenstöcke towering on the left, and the Widderfeldstock crags above on the right, the road climbs with a few hairpins until curving at last to gain a view of the Spannort pinnacles on the final approach to

6:2 NORTH OF THE SUSTENPASS: TITLIS GROUP

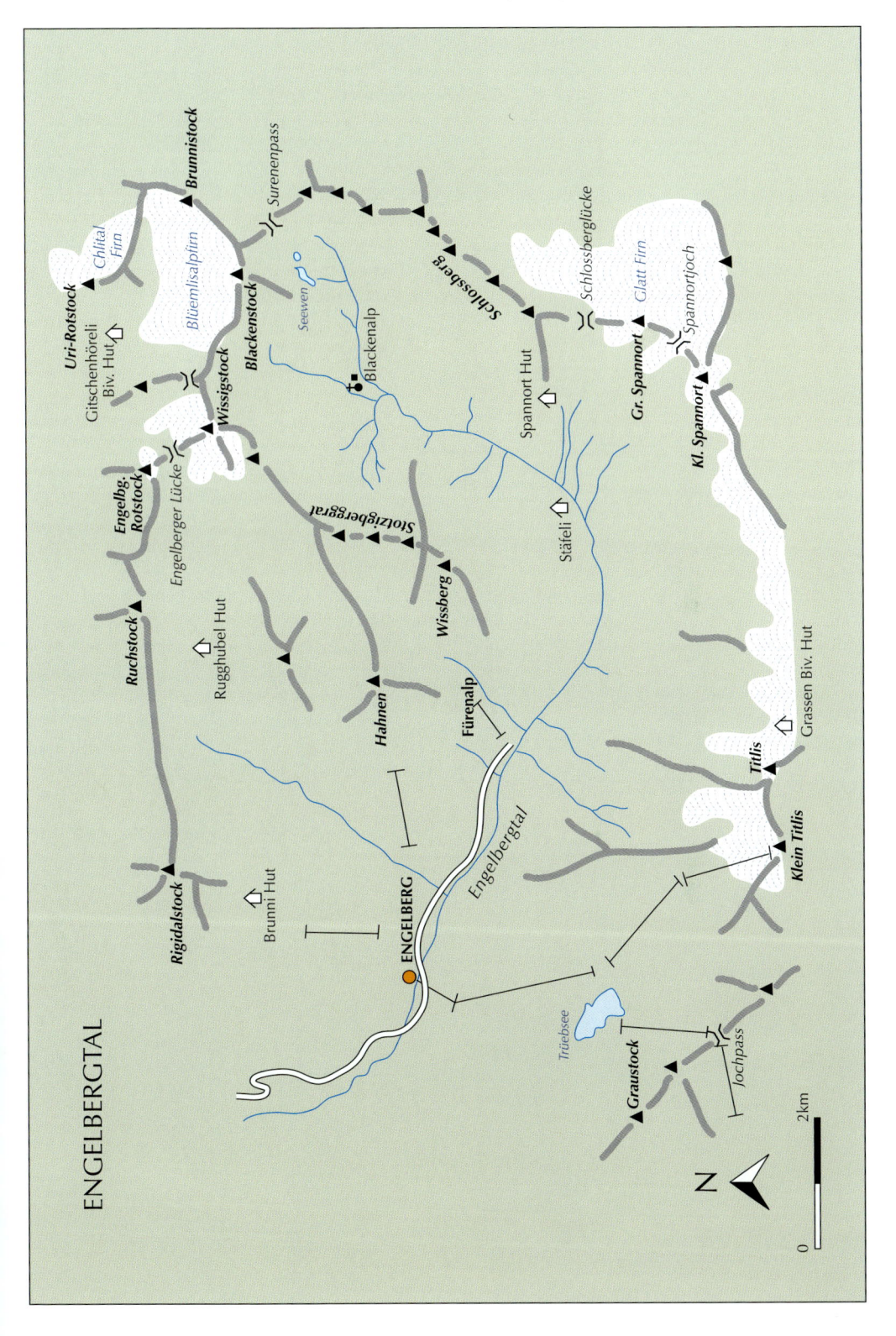

Engelberg (1004m), which lies in an enclave of Canton Obwalden about 20km from Stans.

Built around a large Benedictine abbey thought to have been founded in about 1120, Engelberg developed into a low-key mountaineering centre in the early years of the 20th century. In 1901 Baedeker described it as 'loftily and prettily situated', since when it has become Central Switzerland's main ski attraction. That being said, it remains little more than a large village mostly contained within a grid of streets north of the railway station and west of the *kloster* (monastery). The tourist office is located in a sports complex on Klosterstrasse (www.engelberg.ch) where information on dozens of hotels and other accommodation can be obtained. Engelberg also has a youth hostel, and a 5-star campsite southeast of the village. There's no shortage of shops, cafés, restaurants and banks, a mountain guides office, and a wealth of walking opportunities nearby.

The north flank of the valley offers the best walking, for views from its high trails are dominated by the Titlis, but often have the pinnacles of the Spannörter as an additional attraction. The Ristis cableway makes short work of a 600m ascent immediately above the village, and from there a number of trails entice to various destinations. A 45min walk leads to the **Brunni Hut** (1860m) at the foot of the Rigidalstock. A noted viewpoint, this 40-place hut is owned by the local Engelberg section of the SAC and is fully staffed throughout the year (www.brunnihuette.ch). One of the local attractions is the *klettersteig* ascent of the 2594m ⓑ **Rigidalstock**.

A longer walk from the Ristis cableway heads northeast on a high trail with far-reaching views, and in 2½hrs reaches the large ◯ **Rugghubel Hut** (2290m), set amid a great arc of mountains. Owned by the Stans-based Titlis section of the SAC, it has 100 places and is manned from June until the end of October (www.rugghubel.ch). A trail continues beyond the hut, climbing to the **Engelberger Lücke** on the ridge connecting the **Engelberger Rotstock** and Wissigstock, then cuts along the ridge to make the ascent of the 2887m ◯ ☆ **Wissigstock**, which commands a panoramic view of the region. Allow 3hrs for this from the Rugghubel Hut.

The ◯ ☆ **Fürenalp** balcony is also rewarding. Reached by cable car, or by the dramatic ⓑ **Fürenwand Klettersteig** – or via a longish trail from Hinter Horbis in a tributary valley northeast of Engelberg – an excellent day's outing can be had by following a good path from Fürenalp upvalley to Stalden (1630m) in view of the Stauber waterfall, then on to Blackenalp in the bed of a magnificent cirque of abrupt mountains, before returning downvalley all the way to Engelberg (5hrs from Fürenalp).

At 1773m the tiny white chapel and rustic alp farm (with dormitory accommodation) of

Blackenalp near the head of the Engelbergtal

6:2 North of the Sustenpass: Titlis Group

TITLIS: A PLAYGROUND FOR ALL SEASONS

At 3238m Titlis is undisputed king of the district, with its shining crown of ice and snow and vertiginous limestone walls. The date of its first ascent by Ignaz Herz, J E Waser and two monks from the local monastery varies between 1739 and 1744, but it is generally considered to be the first of Switzerland's major snow mountains to be climbed. In the 19th century several Alpine Club pioneers served part of their mountaineering apprenticeship on its slopes, but it has since suffered the indignity of lacing by cableways as far as the **Klein Titlis**, leaving all and sundry to make the final 200m of ascent to the summit in 40 minutes or so without too much effort (www.titlis.ch).

A revolving gondola, the Rotair, carries visitors to the Klein Titlis at 3028m to discover the ubiquitous souvenir stands, a bar and an ice grotto. Views are outstanding – especially from the true summit, where the alpine chain stretches from the Austrian Tyrol to the snow giants of France. The summit glacier enables summer skiing and snowboarding to take place, but in winter the mountain becomes a true playground; not only on its upper slopes, but in the Trüebsee basin where cross-country skiing comes into its own.

The tourist circus is concentrated on the north and northwest flanks of the Titlis, leaving the massive walls of the isolated **SE Pillar** and **East Face** to the attention of dedicated rock specialists. In July 2004 Markus Dorftleitner and Stefan Glowacz completed a celebrated 13-pitch sport route on the latter after two years of preparation. *Last Exit Titlis* has no pitch graded lower than 6c, and the hardest was claimed to be 8b. This was later refined to 8a+ by Ines Papert and Ueli Steck who made the second ascent two months later. Remains of the Firnalpeli glacier lie beneath the face, with a climber's path working up the moraine to reach the **Grassen Bivouac Hut** at 2647m on the Tierberg (4½hrs from Herrenrüti).

The great East Face of the Titlis

Blackenalp are among the highest buildings in the Engelbergtal. Encircled by pastures that end abruptly at the foot of soaring rock walls, the scenery is exquisite. But even better is to be found by taking the trail that climbs roughly eastward to the 2291m **Surenenpass** southeast of the Blackenstock. Crossed in the opposite direction by walkers on the Alpine Pass Route, the pass is a classic vantage point

375

from which to study the elegant shape of the Titlis that appears as a great bastion of rock, snow and ice far beyond a foreground in which the Seewen lakes sparkle in their basin of pasture.

After the Titlis, the two Spannort peaks are the most eye-catching of all mountains in the Engelberg valley. Where the walling ridge curves northeastward, they soar above pasture and scree with more than a passing likeness to the Dolomites. A 2hr walk from the farm restaurant of **Stäfeli** (or 4hrs from Engelberg) leads to the small **Spannort Hut**, set on the slopes of the Gross Spannort at 1956m. A perfect base for climbs on the two peaks, the hut has just 40 places, is occasionally manned in June, September and some of October each year, but fully wardened in July and August (www.spannorthuette.ch).

The ❸ **Gross Spannort** (3198m) is the more northerly of the two summits, and is separated from the 3140m ❸ **Chli (or Klein) Spannort** by the glacial **Spannortjoch**. On the north side of the Gross Spannort the 2627m **Schlossberglücke** gives access to the Glatt Firn glacier which hangs below the east side of the peaks and offers a way round to the Spannortjoch where the normal route of ascent by the South Ridge (I/II) of the Gross Spannort begins. Baedeker summed it up as being 'highly interesting, but toilsome'. The lower peak is also climbed from the Spannortjoch by a slightly more difficult route than that of its neighbour, and the two are often achieved in the same day.

Grosstal

At its farthest point from Lucerne, the Vierwaldstättersee projects a long watery finger south towards Flüelen and the Reuss valley near Altdorf. Known as the Urnersee, this stem of the lake plays an important part in the Swiss psyche, for it was on the west bank Rütli meadow that the founding fathers of the Swiss Confederation gathered in August 1291 to swear an oath to defend the liberties of the three forest cantons surrounding the lake (Uri, Schwyz and Unterwalden), against tyrannical Habsburg rule. The meadow has since attained great significance, and become almost a site of pilgrimage for the patriotic Swiss. To celebrate the Confederation's 700th anniversary in 1991, the 35km ◐ **Swiss Path** was created as a tour of the Urnersee from Rütli to Brunnen, making an easy and scenic two-day walk (see *Central Switzerland: a Walker's Guide*).

If you follow the shoreline south of Rütli to the **Isleten** promontory where the Isitaler Bach enters the lake, then turn upstream on a narrow road, you will come to the village of **Isenthal** (771m), set at a confluence of valleys divided by a ridge extending from the Uri-Rotstock. Served by postbus from Flüelen, Isenthal has hotel accommodation, but more simple lodging is to be found further upvalley. To the south lies the **Chlital** (or Kleintal) in which there's a hut at **Musenalp** (1486m); to the west the **Grosstal** soon makes a steady southward curve with the road ending at **St Jakob**. Continue on a logging road until a path breaks away to mount the east flank of the valley and you'll reach **Biwaldalp** at 1694m where there's another chalet with accommodation (tel 041 878 11 62). Further still, at 2380m below the West Face of the Uri-Rotstock, the 15-place **Gitschenhöreli bivouac hut** is owned by the Infanger family from the Biwaldalp chalet, from whom the key should be collected.

Popular with local climbers, but little visited by others, the ❸ **Uri-Rotstock** is an attractive rust-tinted peak of 2928m that makes its presence felt over a large part of the surrounding country, and is the main reason for visiting either the wild and seemingly remote Grosstal or neighbouring Chlital. To quote from Baedeker: 'The mountain-group which culminates in the Uri-Rotstock and the Brunnistock is, like the Titlis, almost perpendicular on the E and SE sides (towards the Gitschen-Thal and Surenen), and is composed of gigantic and fantastically contorted limestone rocks.'

Winter ski ascents are not uncommon, but check the precise route and current conditions at Isenthal in order to avoid avalanche danger. The normal summer route from St Jakob via Biwaldalp and the Gitschenhöreli bivouac skirts the South Face to Point 2740m, followed by an easy ascent of the SE Ridge. Alternatively, climb directly from the bivouac hut, taking extra care when the rock is wet (II) to an obvious saddle at 2826m, then head north up the ridge to the summit (5–6hrs from St Jakob). The North Ridge is said to offer pleasant climbing (III). Starting from Biwaldalp this first takes in the North Ridge of the 2830m subsidiary peak (**Schlieren**) and continues along the connecting ridge to the Uri-Rotstock. Yet another route, this one starting from Musenalp in the Chlital, follows a path to the **Chlital Firn**, above which the 2826m saddle on the South Ridge is gained, from where the normal route is followed to the top.

6:2 NORTH OF THE SUSTENPASS: TITLIS GROUP

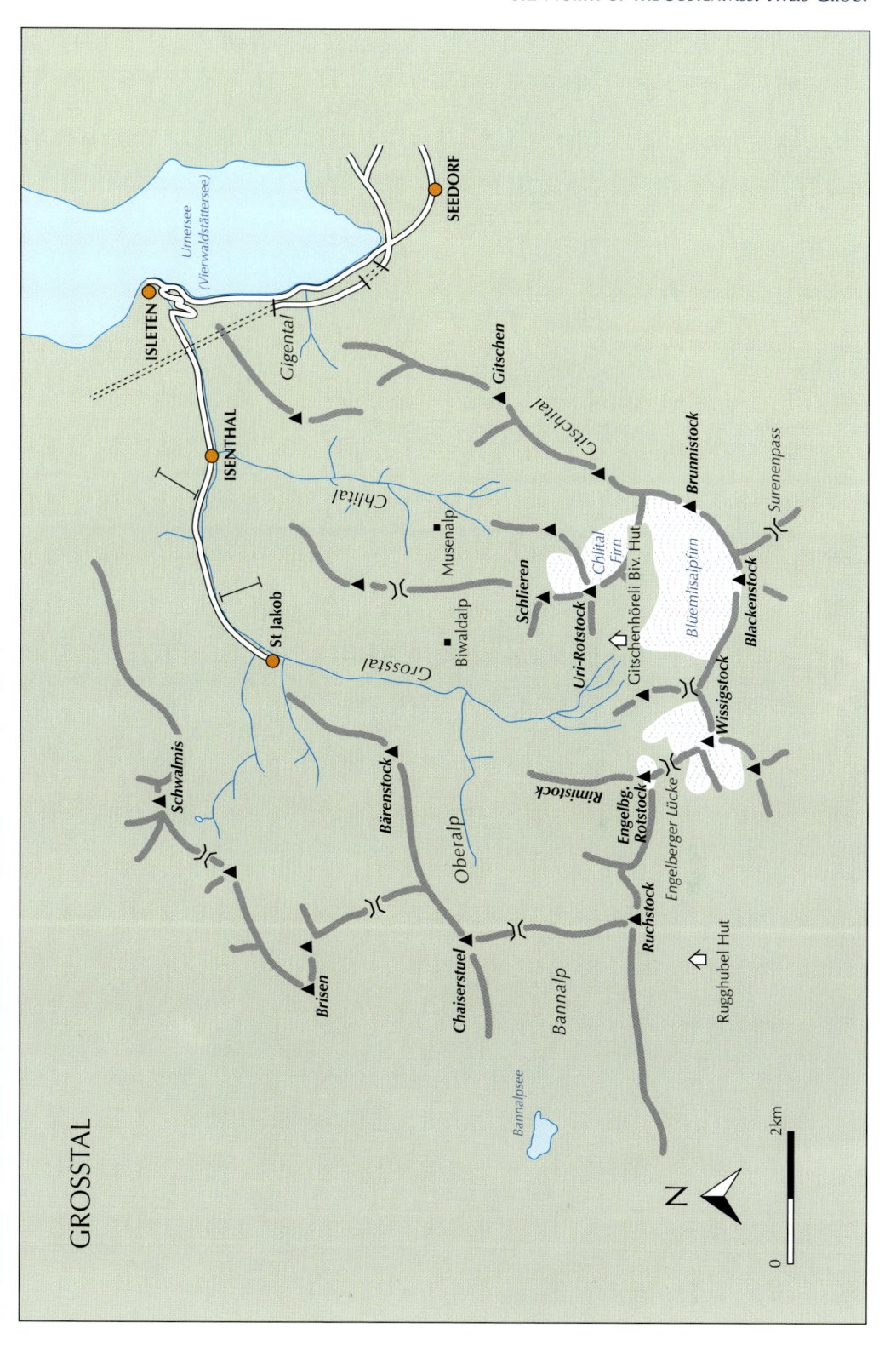

THE SWISS ALPS – CHAPTER 6: CENTRAL SWISS ALPS

Although the climbing here may not be as challenging or exciting as on many other peaks of the Central Swiss Alps, the Uri-Rotstock's summit panorama is said to be 'exceedingly grand' (Baedeker again). To the east a long band of mountains stretches from the Säntis to Bernina; to the west can be seen the chain of the Bernese Alps; while 2500m below lies the Vierwaldstättersee backed by Rigi and Pilatus.

6:3 GLARNER ALPS

Least known of all districts of the Central Swiss Alps, the Glarner Alps (the Alps of Canton Glarus and its neighbours) have undoubted attractions, yet they fail to entice in any substantial numbers active climbers or walkers from outside Switzerland. Perhaps that is to their benefit – or at least to the benefit of those who do find themselves drawn there, for it's possible to wander the valleys, cross their passes and scramble on some of their peaks in splendid isolation; a rarity in the more celebrated regions of the Bernese or Pennine Alps. Road passes such as the Oberalp and Klausen somehow do not have the cachet of Furka or Grimsel, yet the valleys they lead to are as interesting and scenically arresting as any, and some of their villages and hamlets are rich in both history and culture.

The region is not confined to Canton Glarus though, for Uri and Schwyz claim the western fringe, Graubünden edges the south and the south-eastern corner, and St Gallen takes a large slice of the eastern side. But with Glarus at the centre of the district, the Glarner Alps seems a reasonable umbrella title for the massifs that lie within this block.

If any mountain could be considered an icon of the district, it would have to be the Tödi, which claims an important part in mountaineering's history, thanks to the dedication of Placidus à Spescha, a Benedictine monk from the monastery at nearby Disentis who, in the early years of the 19th century, made at least five attempts to climb it. The great alpine historian, W A B Coolidge, named à Spescha as one of the founders of alpinism, but as Walt Unsworth pointed out (in *Hold the Heights*), 'It was the monk's misfortune to live in a remote part of Switzerland where the peaks have never been popular…' Popular or no, many of the peaks in this 'remote part of Switzerland' are worth

The Glarner Alps, viewed from the Surenenpass

visiting, as are the valleys that divide them, and the passes that unite them.

Fellital and Etzlital

Our examination of the district begins in the west, where access is gained from the **Reuss valley** below Göschenen and Wassen. Roughly midway between Wassen and Amsteg the Felli Bach drains into the Reuss near the village of **Gurtnellen**. But while Gurtnellen sits up on the west bank of the Reuss, the Felli Bach's valley, the **Fellital**, slices through the east bank mountains. Noted for its crystals, this small tributary valley is narrow and wooded in its lower reaches, but widens slightly as it extends southward and rises to a headwall breached by the 2478m **Fellilücke**, an easy saddle 400m above the **Oberalp Pass** (mentioned in 3:9). Beginning at the Oberalp, a recommended day's walk crosses the Fellilücke and descends through the Fellital all the way to Gurtnellen in about 6½hrs. A few simple alp huts are used by local goatherds, and at 1475m on the edge of woodland, the SAC has the neat stone-built **Tresch Hut** for an overnight base. It's a small hut with just 40 places and is open throughout the year but fully manned only in July and August (www.treschhuette.ch).

On the east wall of the Fellital a fine cirque is rimmed by the spires and jagged ridges of the Sunnig and Schattig Wichel, while north of these the ridge dips to the **Portilücke** (2506m), a pass crossed by a trail connecting the Tresch Hut with the **Etzli Hut** in 3½hrs. Built at 2052m high in the **Etzlital** which lies parallel with the Fellital, the Etzli Hut belongs to the Thurgau section of the SAC (www.etzlihuette.ch). Much larger than the Tresch Hut, it has 75 places and is staffed in the spring ski-touring season (mid-February to the end of April) and in summer from mid-June until mid-October. The normal approach route is from Bristen in the Maderanertal in 4hrs.

From the hut an ascent of the 3096m **Schattig Wichel** (otherwise known as Piz Giuv) is a recommended outing without technical difficulty that rewards with a very fine view of the Dammastock group and the distant Titlis. Allow 4–4½hrs from hut to summit.

Below the Etzli Hut there's a four-way crossing of trails. To the south, one climbs briefly to the 2487m **Mittelplatten**, then descends through Val Mila to Rueras in the Vorderrhein's valley; to the east another rises through the Chrüzlital hanging valley, crosses the **Chrüzlipass** (2347m) and then

Above the Oberalp Pass the 2478m Fellilücke gives access to the Fellital

The Swiss Alps – Chapter 6: Central Swiss Alps

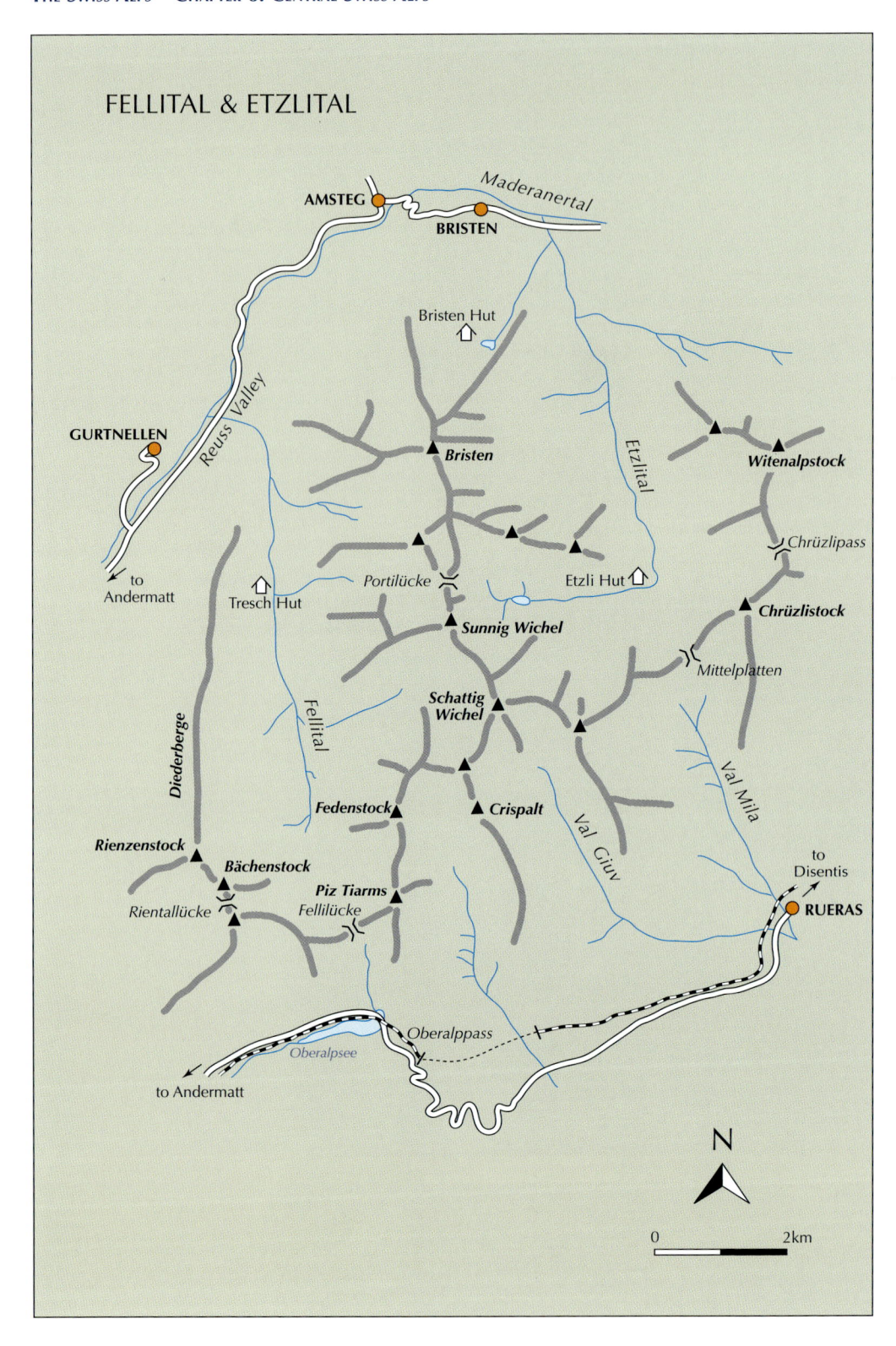

FELLITAL & ETZLITAL

380

The Tresch Hut, in the lower Fellital

eases through Val Strem to Sedrun, a short distance below Rueras; while to the north a way crosses and recrosses the Etzli Bach as it flows down to its confluence with the milky Chärstelenbach in the **Maderanertal**.

Several groups of alp buildings add a pastoral touch to the otherwise wild Etzlital, and from one of these, Vorder Etzliboden, an alternative path strikes up the left-hand hillside, and after mounting over 800m, turns a spur to find the Bristensee tarn with the ○ **Bristen Hut** close by at 2140m. Reached in 3hrs from Vorder Etzliboden, or 4hrs from Bristen, this tiny non-SAC hut has just 14 places and is partly manned from mid-June until mid-October (www.maderanertal.ch). From it the ascent of the 3073m pyramid-shaped ⊗ **Bristen** (also known as the Bristenstock), highest summit on the ridge that separates the Fellital and Etzlital, makes an obvious goal. The first recorded ascent was made in 1823, and the normal route (F) is via the NE Ridge. In recent years this has become popular with local skiers as a winter ascent.

Maderanertal

Although the Fellital and Etzlital flow in parallel lines, only the first of these feeds directly into the Reuss, for the Etzlital leads to the charming Maderanertal, a real gem of a valley whose main route of access is from Amsteg in a gloomy curve of the Reuss valley. A postbus service grinds its way up the steep and narrow road above a gorge to reach **Bristen**, the little community that takes its name from the mountain at whose foot it lies at a modest 770m. With limited facilities for tourists, it does have *gasthaus* and dormitory accommodation and is the only real village base here (www.maderanertal.ch). At Platten, 2km further along the metalled road, a cableway carries visitors up the north slope to **Golzern** (1423m) where *gasthaus* accommodation is also available, and yet further upvalley another *gasthaus* is found at **Legni**, while at **Balmenegg** (1349m) a large Victorian-era one-time SAC hotel is now known as Hotel Maderanertal (www.hotel-maderanertal.ch). In its hey-day the hotel had its own barbershop and butcher, a ladies' salon, a library and reading room with German and English newspapers. There was also a bowling alley, while the church next door held services in English during the summer.

Today the Maderanertal remains remarkably unspoilt and relatively unknown to the vast majority of visitors who flock to the Swiss Alps, yet its scenic beauty is hard to beat. The

Grosse Windgällen and Grosse Ruchen dominate the north side of the valley, with Bristen and Oberalpstock being the main peaks on the south side. But it is a glimpse of the Hüfifirn glacier flanked by the Schärhorn and 3256m Grosse Düssi (or Düssistock) at the head of the valley that holds your attention, plus the waterfalls that spray down the steep hillsides, and these – and the number of walks and climbs to be made – ensure that the Maderanertal is difficult to leave.

One of the most rewarding of ◯ **day walks** begins by taking the cableway to Golzern, beyond whose small lake a narrow path slants across meadows and through patches of woodland with the Grosse Düssi seen ahead. After almost 2hrs a large cairn is reached below the Windgällen Hut. Beyond the cairn the trail leads to Alp Stafel, then continues across open slopes with streams and waterfalls and magnificent scenery, to the Tritt viewpoint. After this the way descends in zigzags towards the head of the valley, before reaching Balmenegg and returning to Platten along an easy track (5½–6hrs).

The ◯ **Windgällen Hut** is worth visiting for the approach walk alone, whether or not you plan to spend a night there. Standing on a high shelf of meadow on the north side of the valley at 2032m, its setting is idyllic. There are in fact two buildings with a total of 89 places. Owned by the Academic Alpine Club of Zürich (AACZ), the hut is fully staffed from June until the end of October (www.windgaellenhuette.ch) and is a good base for climbers tackling the Kleine and Grosse Windgällen peaks that rise above it, and also for access to a ◉ **Klettergarten** 20mins away – information and topos are available at the hut.

The grey limestone peak of the ◉ **Grosse Windgällen** (3188m) holds a number of ascent routes, most of which start at the Windgällen Hut. The standard route centres on the East Face which rises above the last remnants of the Stäfelfirn where a gully leads to the summit (4hrs from the hut); the SE Face is also popular. The South Face is the most challenging (VI), while the long West Ridge offers climbing up to grade IV. The big North Face overlooks the Brunnital (see below) and is usually approached from there as the Windgällen Hut is too far removed from the action. West of the hut the neighbouring 2986m **Kleine Windgällen** is less demanding than its big

Cascades in the Maderanertal

6:3 GLARNER ALPS

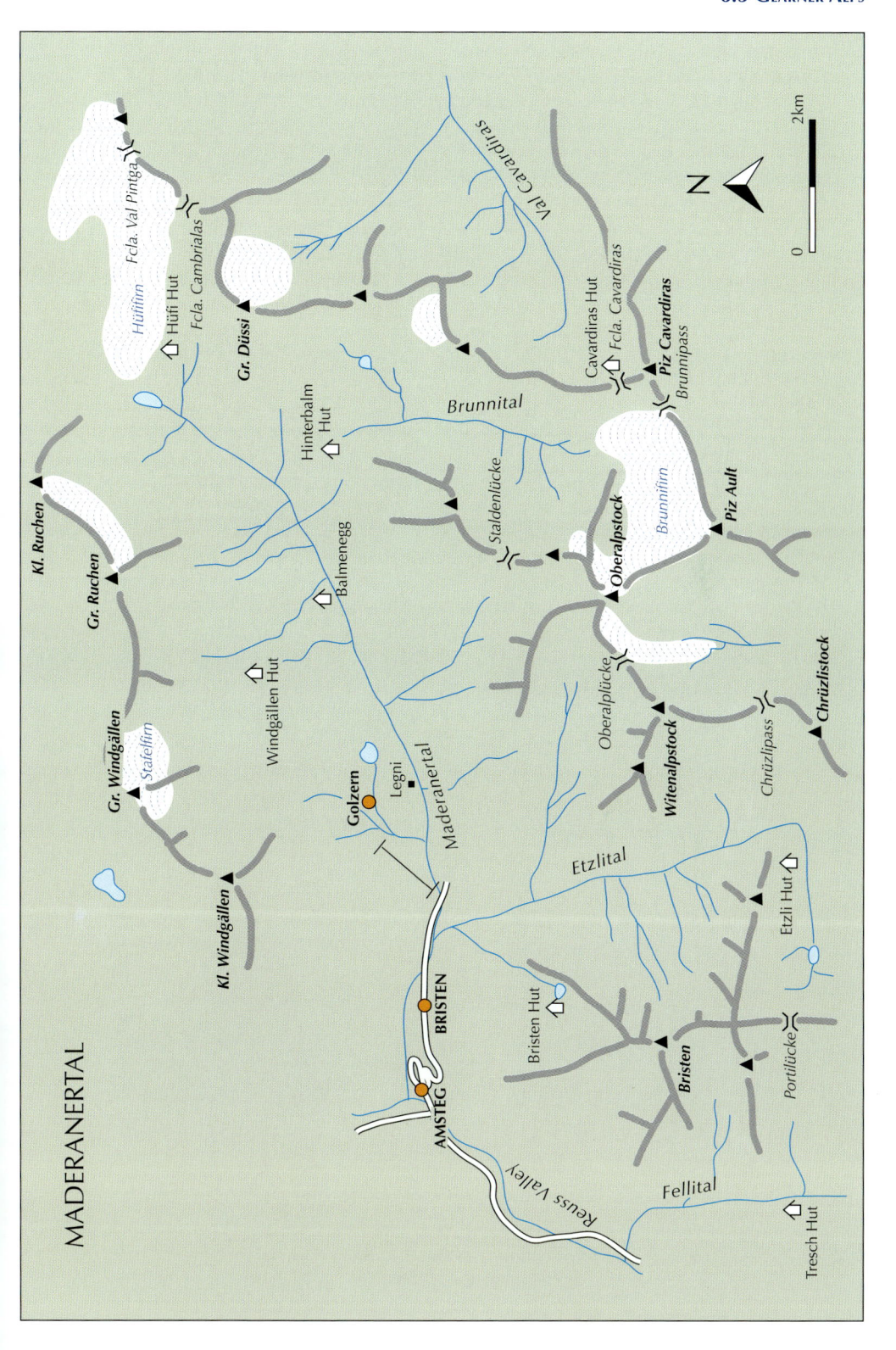

brother, but makes a splendid vantage point from which to survey the district.

At the head of the Maderanertal the **Hüfi Hut** is perched on a rock ledge overlooking the Hüfifirn glacier at 2334m. Reached by a 5hr walk with a height gain of more than 1500m from Bristen, this SAC hut belongs to the Pilatus section of Lucerne, has 60 places and is fully staffed from mid-June until October (www.hueffipaul.ch). In addition to climbs on the 3256m 🯄 **Grosse Düssi** that rises directly above it, a 3hr glacier hike takes roped parties up the **Hüfifirn** to the wedge-shaped **Planura Hut** (2947m) standing at the head of the glacier south of the Hüfipass (see Schächental map). Financed by a Zürich tycoon, this hut occupies a wonderfully scenic location, and is used by climbers for routes on the Tödi and Clariden, but is of more value to mountain walkers with glacier experience when making a hut-to-hut tour. It has places for 60 and a guardian in April and May to cater for ski touring parties, and from July to the end of September (www.sac-toedi.ch/huetten). The standard approach to this hut from the Klausenpass at the head of the Schächental is via the 3031m Chammlijoch and Hüfifirn, and takes about 5hrs.

Reached directly from the Maderanertal, the shingle-faced **Hinterbalm Hut** (1817m) is found near the mouth of the little valley of the Brunnibach which lies below the west flank of the Grosse Düssi, and is gained by a walk of about 4hrs from Bristen. Privately owned, the hut faces west down the Maderanertal to the distant summit of the Titlis. Fully staffed from June until mid-October, it has dormitory places for 45 (www.top-of-uri.ch) and serves as a base for climbs on the Grosse Düssi, Fruttstock, Tschingelstöcke and Oberalpstock, among others.

The Brunnital valley that rises south of the hut is noted for its waterfalls, alpine flora and for the herds of ibex and chamois that roam there. The headwall contains the retreating Brunnifirn glacier cradled between Oberalpstock and Piz Cavardiras, and on its eastern side the **Fuorcla da Cavardiras** gives access to the **Camona da Cavardiras** at 2649m.

Since the pass marks the cantonal boundary, the Cavardiras Hut stands in Graubünden, but is owned by the Winterthur section of the SAC. With 70 dormitory places, it makes a tremendous vantage point, and being just a 3hr hike from the Hinterbalm Hut (but 6½hrs from Disentis via Vals Russein and Cavardiras) it is an obvious attraction for mountain

The 3256m Grosse Düssi stands in a prominent position at the head of the Maderanertal

The Oberalpstock

walkers as well as for climbers. The hut is fully staffed from early July until mid-September (www.cavardiras.ch). The highest of the nearby peaks is the 3328m ❂ **Oberalpstock**, and quite naturally is the main focus of attention, with the normal route (F) tackling the southeast flank via the Brunnifirn. This is also the standard route for ski ascents.

Schächental

The Reuss escapes its gorge-like restrictions north of Amsteg and enters a broad, flat-bottomed section of valley beyond Erstfeld. Between Attinghausen and Altdorf this valley reaches its widest point, thanks to its confluence with the Schächental, a long tributary flowing from the east, with the Klausenpass at its head. There is no railway through the steep, V-shaped Schächental, but a postbus service operates between Altdorf and Linthal which lies on the eastern side of the pass. Several small villages line the road, and the northern slopes are dotted with clusters of alp farms and tiny hamlets. A few ski lifts lace the slope above Spiringen.

About 12km before the road begins its winding ascent to the Klausenpass, the unassuming village of **Unterschächen** (995m) nestles below the Schächentaler Windgällen whose 2764m summit is the highest point on the valley's north walling ridge. But south of the village the alluring Brunnital (not to be confused with the valley of the same name that feeds into the Maderanertal) is headed by the Grosse Windgällen and Grosse Ruchen, across both of which lies the Maderanertal.

Unterschächen makes a low-key mountaineering centre, a base for walkers and a staging post along the Alpine Pass Route, with a handful of modest hotels and *gasthäuser* (some offering dormitory accommodation), a few shops, a bank and post office (www.unterschaechen.ch).

The **Brunnital** is well worth a visit. Flanked by steep rock walls dashed by slender waterfalls, it shares an affinity with Lauterbrunnen's valley, albeit on a smaller scale. Woodland and meadow clothe the valley bed; groups of alp buildings nestle on shelves of pasture at mid-height, and a little under 2hrs from Unterschächen, girdled by a magnificent cirque of mountains, the tiny summer-only hamlet of **Brunnialp** has a restaurant and a chapel set among a few trees. Above it soar the great north-facing cliffs of the Windgällen–Ruchen massif. It's an impressive scene.

Alp farm in the Brunnital

With paths on both flanks, and in the valley bed, the Brunnital has plenty to offer walkers. One of the more demanding of its trails climbs steeply westward above the hamlet into the hanging valley of the **Griesstal**. At Vorder Griesstal another path breaks away to the south to cross the ● **Seewligrat** at 2245m. This pass lies along the Rot Grat, on the south side of which the **Seewlisee** tarn gleams below the west flank of the Grosse Windgällen. A long, knee-punishing descent continues the route from the lake down to Silenen in the Reuss valley. For climbers attracted to the 1000m high North Face of the ❸ **Grosse Windgällen** (IV), the Seewlisee meadows make a decent pre-climb bivvy site.

Between Unterschächen and the Klausenpass the attractive two-part hamlet of ● **Äsch** (1234m) is reached by an easy walk along a track. The main reason to visit this hamlet is to see at close quarters the huge waterfall that explodes from the steep slope behind a cluster of chalets. Clouds of spray drift in the breeze, and the powerful thunder of water on rock can be heard long before you see it. A continuation of the path climbs steeply to the Klausenpass in tight zigzags against a cliff face, but another recommended trail breaks away from the Klausenpass route to ascend the south slope above the waterfall to visit **Nideralp** and Wannenalp (cable car down to Ribi near Unterschächen), then turns into the Brunnital with several descent options.

Above Unterschächen the road climbs in long loops from which a wall of cliffs can be seen to the south culminating in the snow-capped Clariden appearing alongside the 3214m Chammliberg. At the final hairpin before the pass (Ober Balm) a track eases away from the road heading west. From it a path climbs to the **Ruosalper Chulm**, a 2178m saddle in the ridge below the ❸ **Schächentaler Windgällen**. To make a scrambling ascent of this interesting limestone peak (II), bear left at the saddle and mount a series of karst terraces, crossing a secondary summit before reaching the main peak, about 3½hrs from the Klausenpass road.

At the misnamed Klausenpasshöhe, about 1km short of the actual pass, there's a hotel with both standard beds and dormitory places (www.klausenpasshoehe.ch), while the **Klausenpass** proper has a refreshment kiosk, public toilets, a bus stop and a tiny chapel. As soon as the pass reopens at the end of winter, ski-touring enthusiasts arrive to make the ascent of the 3268m

6:3 Glarner Alps

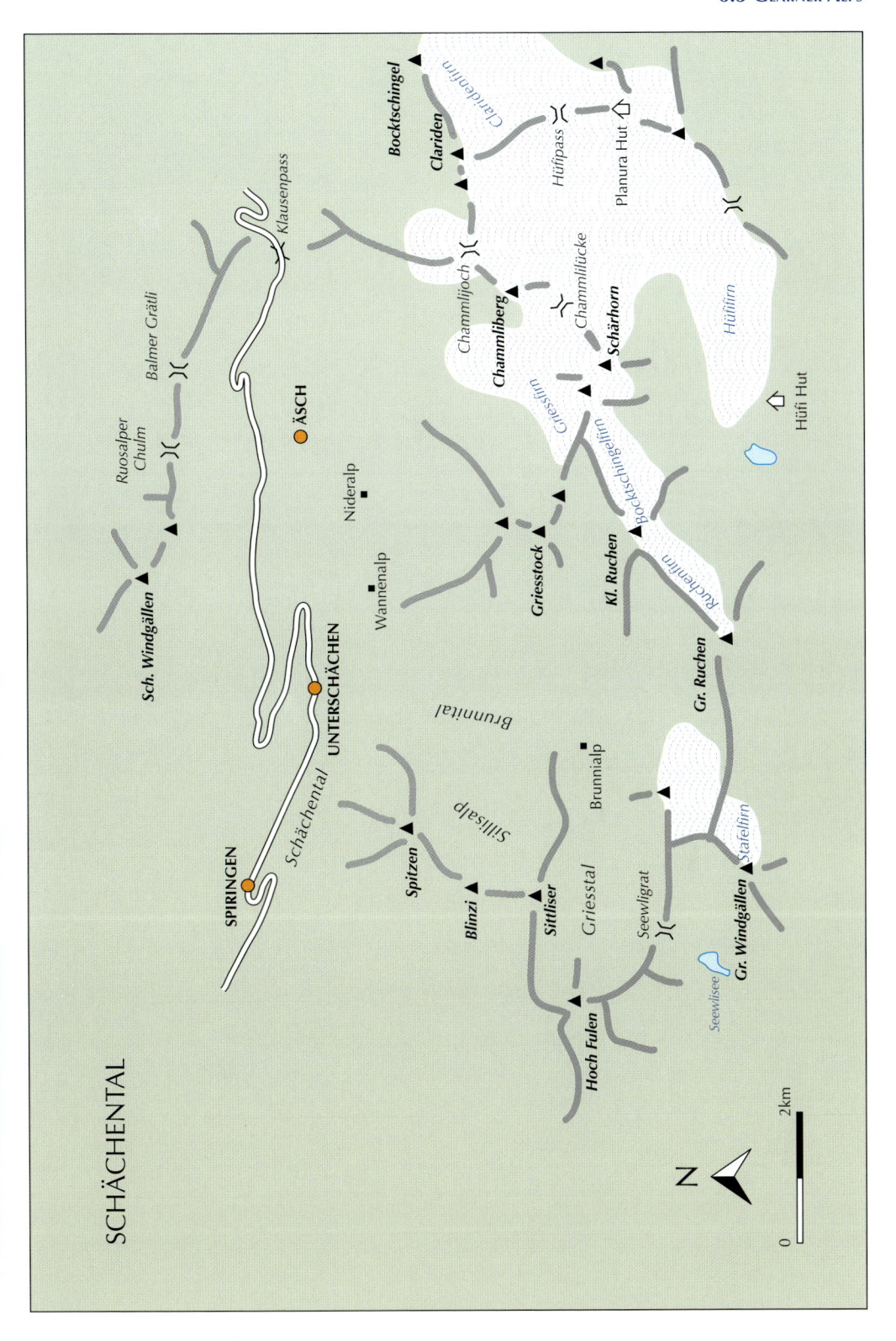

SCHÄCHENTAL

THE SWISS ALPS – CHAPTER 6: CENTRAL SWISS ALPS

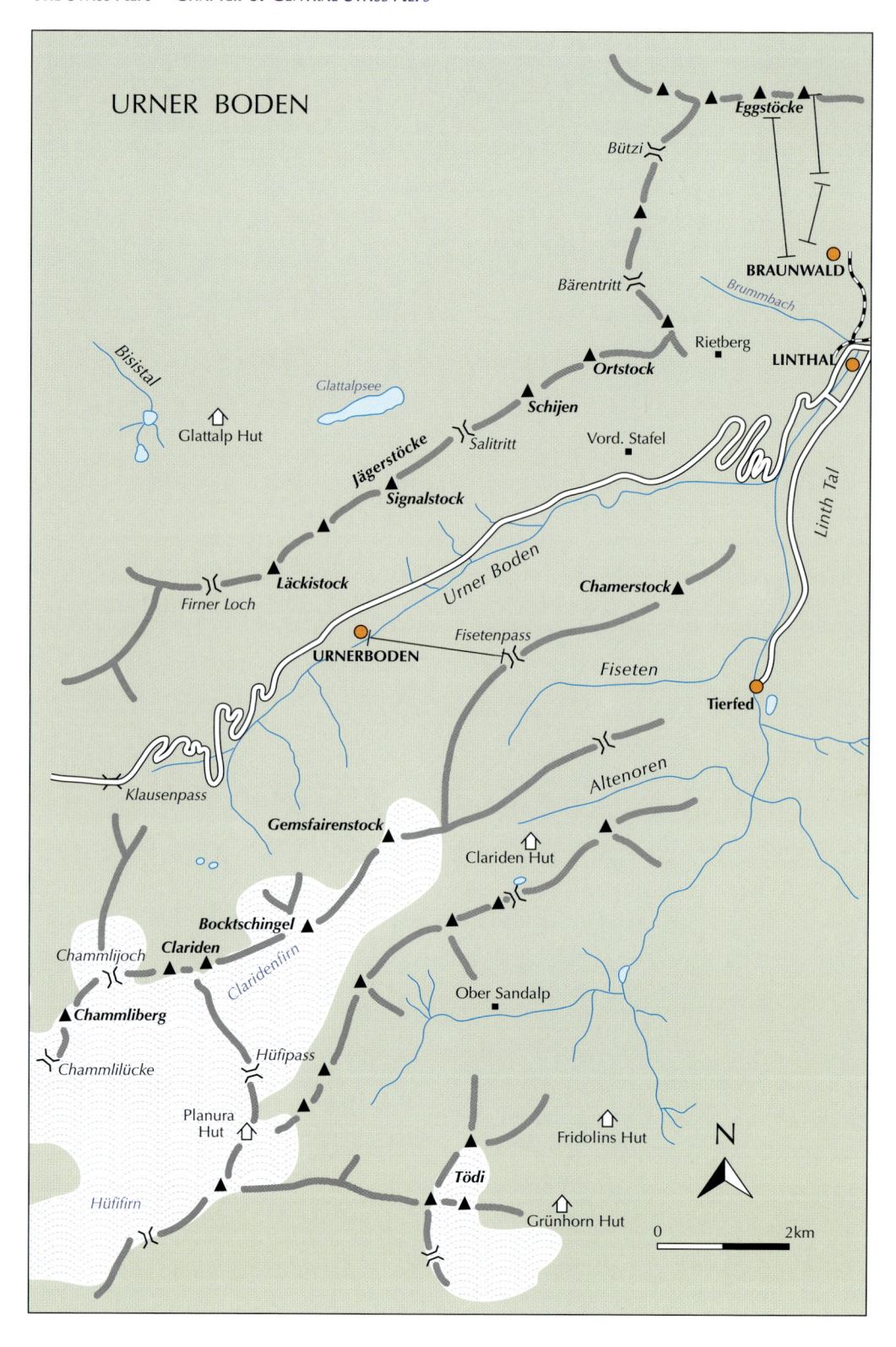

388

Urnerboden with Clariden towering behind

⊙ **Clariden** which overlooks the pass from the south. Though not a difficult ascent under good conditions via the Rau Stöckli and Tierälpligrat, the narrow Eiswand, gained about 2hrs above the Klausenpass, has a certain notoriety, claiming a number of victims who have misjudged the way in mist and skied over the edge. A summer ascent by the same route (finishing along the West Ridge) is considered much less hazardous, while the almost 1000m high North Face above the alp buildings of Vorfrutt on the Urner Boden side of the pass, is in a different league of difficulty.

Urner Boden

At 1948m the Klausenpass is one of the nicest of alpine road passes, its comparatively modest altitude lending it a much more welcoming atmosphere than some of the higher, more celebrated – but infinitely more bleak and forbidding – crossings. And the view northeast into the beautiful U-shaped valley of Urner Boden is exquisite.

Flanked by the long Jägerstöcke ridge on one side, and the Clariden–Gemsfairenstock connecting ridge that gradually subsides into forest on the other, the broad flat-bottomed valley of Urner Boden was

The Firner Loch is a 2248m pass in the Jägerstöcke ridge

clearly gouged out by glacial action, leaving behind a rich, well-watered grassland grazed in summer by as many as 1200 cows. This is Switzerland's largest alp, on which groups of herdsmen's huts and milking sheds provide a human dimension, while **Urnerboden**, the only village between the Klausenpass and Linthal in the main Linth Tal, is gathered round a square just off the road at the foot of the pass at 1372m (www.urnerboden.ch). The valley's accommodation is limited to just three *gasthäuser* with dormitory places, one of which is located in Urnerboden village. The boundary between Cantons Uri and Glarus runs across the lower valley, which may be why the village is politically aligned, not with Linthal in Glarus, but with Spirigen, many kilometres away on the far side of the Klausenpass in Canton Uri.

In winter the flat valley is perfect for cross-country skiing, but it also boasts opportunities for challenging water-ice climbs on its steep walls, and ski mountaineering to some of its summits. In summer there's no shortage of rock climbing to be enjoyed, as well as several easy peaks that would appeal to first-season alpinists.

The valley's headwall is located a little south of the Klausenpass road where streams draining the north flank of the Clariden form a cascade that pours down the Chlus rocks. Clariden and Gemsfairenstock are by far the highest summits, but the line of limestone peaks on the valley's north flank consist of individual turrets, spires, slabs and chimneys, all with more than a nod of familiarity with the Dolomites. Not that these features are immediately recognisable from the valley floor; it's only when you venture onto its mid-height, flower-rich terrace that the diverse nature of the **Jägerstöcke** is revealed. At its western end the rocky little pass of **Firner Loch** (2248m) gives access to the delightful Bisistal and the **Glattalp Hut** built on that valley's right flank at 1892m (see *Central Switzerland: a Walker's Guide*).

On the south side of the Urner Boden valley a cable car carries visitors from Urnerboden village to the **Fisetenpass**, northeast of the Gemsfairenstock at 2036m. This is a very popular viewpoint and a gathering place for numerous trails, one of which follows the Fisetengrat northeastward for less than an hour to reach the ◯ **Chamerstock**, a noted vantage point with a 360° panorama. Another heads in the opposite direction and, remaining high above the valley, eventually arrives at the ◯ **Klausenpass** after about 3½hrs. A third trail beginning at the Fisetenpass curves round the headwall of the Fiseten hanging valley, crosses the ridge spur on the far side, then heads southwest to reach the SAC's **Clariden Hut** after about 3hrs. Built on the Altenorenstock plateau in view of steep rock walls, the hut has 77 places, is fully staffed from mid-March until mid-May, and from July until the end of September, serving as an overnight base for ski-touring parties in springtime, and for climbers in summer (www.sac-bachtel.ch).

The 2972m ⛰ **Gemsfairenstock** is the nearest attraction. Given reasonable conditions the mountain can be climbed on ski in winter and spring, although summer ascents are naturally far more numerous. The normal route from the hut tackles the mountain from the south to reach a 2848m col on the West Ridge where an easy scramble leads to the summit. It can also be climbed from the Fisetenpass by following a good path heading southwest below Ober Orthalden, then climbing south on scree and rock to the tiny Langfirn glacier which takes the route directly to the summit cross.

⛰ **Clariden** (see above) is another natural goal for climbers and ski tourers based overnight at the Clariden Hut, the standard route (winter and summer) being via the Claridenfirn glacier leading to a saddle just short of the summit.

Linth Tal

East of the canton boundary the road descends from Urner Boden for more than 600m via numerous hairpins into the Linth Tal, the longest valley in the Glarner Alps. Formed by various tributaries draining the Tödi massif, the Linth flows roughly northward through Linthal, Schwanden, Glarus and the small industrial town of Näfels, beyond which it enters the Walensee west of the Churfirsten range.

The main village, so far as mountain activity is concerned, is **Linthal** (663m), which is also the terminus of the railway in the upper Linth valley. Yet despite having plenty of hotels and budget-priced dormitory accommodation, a supermarket, bank and post office, it has a more business-like atmosphere than that of a resort centred on tourism (www.linthal-rueti.ch).

A funicular climbs the north flank of the valley above Linthal to reach the traffic-free resort of **Braunwald** at 1256m. Built on a large natural shelf 600m above the valley floor, backed by the shapely limestone towers of the Eggstöcke and with views towards the Tödi range, the setting is idyllic. As the only true resort of the Linth Tal it has a large amount of accommodation ranging from a popular backpacker's hostel to 3- and 4-star hotels (www.braunwald.ch).

The south wall of the 2449m ⛰ **Eggstöcke** makes a fine *klettergarten* with more than 40 routes to choose from. Cableways from the village reduce the effort to reach the foot of these climbs, and with Berghaus Gumen close by, it's possible to climb almost from the bedroom (www.gumen.ch). The Eggstöcke is also host to a three-stage 🅶 **Klettersteig** that takes in the summits of the Leiteregg (2310m), Vorder Eggstock (2449m), Mittler Eggstock (2420m) and the 2456m Hinter Eggstock (see Urner Boden map). For information see www.klettersteige.ch.

A path skirts below the Eggstöcke to cross a line of cliffs at **Bützi**, beyond which will be found the largest karst plateau in Switzerland. Across this desert of white limestone a walker's route eventually leads to the Bisistal. Another eases along the eastern edge of the karst heading south to the **Barentritt** crossing, where it joins another path that rises southwestward to the 2395m Furggele and continues down to the **Glattalpsee** and the Glattalp Hut.

But the 🟢 **classic walk** from Braunwald is one that is used as a variant by trekkers following the Alpine Pass Route. It leaves the resort on a road heading west towards Unter Stafel, then by a track across the Brummbach. The way continues to the alp of Rietberg and along a trail to Vorder Stafel above the valley of Urner Boden, where it then descends into the valley proper to finish at Urnerboden village in about 3½hrs.

Back in the Linth valley, the Tödi range needs to be visited. To achieve this, take a road heading south for 5km out of Linthal as far as **Tierfed** (805m) and Hotel Tödi. Apart from this being the trailhead for a northerly approach to the Tödi, there's also a small cable car which carries visitors up to Ober Baumgarten (1860m). A trail then climbs to the **Muttsee Hut** built on a high plateau backed by screes and bare cliffs south of the Muttsee at 2501m (2½hrs from the cable car, or 5hrs from Tierfed). The property of the Winterthur section of the SAC, the hut has 65 places and is fully manned from mid-June until mid-October (www.muttseehuette.ch).

Above the hut to the east, the Muttenstock ridge forms part of the Hausstock massif. Between Muttenstock and Hausstock, the 3107m ⛰ **Ruchi**

The Swiss Alps – Chapter 6: Central Swiss Alps

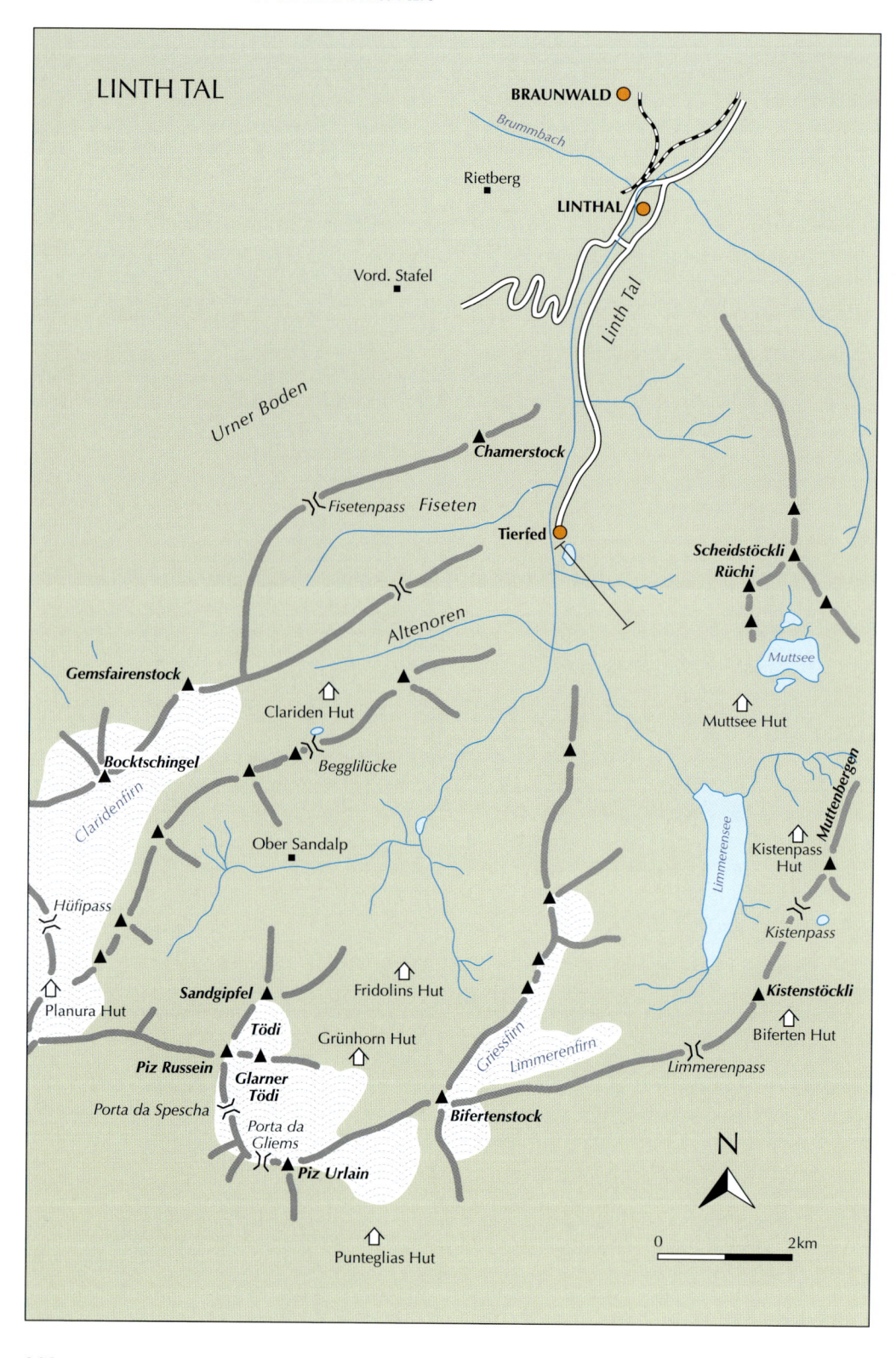

LINTH TAL

provides a fairly undemanding 2hr ascent from the hut on a trail that cuts across slopes of shale and scree with fine views of the Tödi. Another option is to make a traverse of the massif, linking the Ruchi with the ❸ **Hausstock** summit at 3158m, then continue along the latter's SE Ridge to the Panixerpass where there's the small, unmanned **Panixerpass Hut** above the Sernftal with places for 14; self-catering only (information from the tourist office in Elm: tel 055 642 60 67). It would be possible to spend a night there, and next day take a path heading roughly southwest across the south flank of the Hausstock, with the Pigniu reservoir far below, and eventually reach either the **Biferten Hut** (see below) or **Kistenpass Hut** to complete a challenging circuit of the massif. Other paths from the Panixerpass Hut descend either to Elm in the north (see below), or south to the Vorderrhein's valley.

Tucked against crags of the Muttenbergen high above the Limmerensee and north of the pass after which it is named, the tiny **Kistenpass Hut** (2714m) is reached in just 1½hrs from the Muttsee Hut. Also owned by the SAC's Winterthur section, this 16-place bivouac hut is closed except during the main summer period (July to mid-October) when for a few weeks in July and August there's a guardian in residence to provide meals (tel 079 480 41 18).

But despite its various alternative attractions, the primary aim of visitors to the upper Linth valley is, naturally, the famed Tödi, once described as a huge rampart of rock topped by a glacier (*The Outdoor Traveler's Guide: The Alps*). Although glimpsed from several outlying districts, it is not at first evident from Tierfed, for the southward view is somewhat dominated by the rock peak of the Vorderer Selbsanft, below which the Linthschlucht, the defile carrying the main approach route, is reckoned to be one of the finest gorges in the Swiss Alps.

At first a farm track is flanked by woodland, then it goes through a short tunnel before reaching the celebrated Pantenbrügge, with the original narrow bridge seen immediately below it. Other paths veer away from the track; one strikes left for Baumgarten and the Muttsee Hut; another leads to the Clariden and Planura Huts.

Imposing scenery lifts the spirits as you emerge from the gorge to enter a mountain sanctuary of green pastures flanked by rock walls to right and left, while the magnificent ice-crowned Tödi appears directly ahead, its full glory on display from the valley pasture of its roots to its creamy head. The highest of the Glarner Alps, it is a great block of a mountain. 'Even on the easiest routes,' announced Herbert Maeder in *The Mountains of Switzerland*, 'ascents are exhausting, because of the great difference in height to be covered.'

At the cattle sheds of Vorder Sand (1256m) water bursts from a hole in the right-hand rock face; then the track climbs and twists over a great boulder tip, the result of a major rockfall from the Zuetribistock, and once this has been crossed you come to the upper pastures and a small settlement reservoir at Hinter Sandalp. Here the way forks, with the right branch climbing 600m to the chalets of ❍ **Ober Sandalp** (1937m), gained in about 3½hrs from Tierfed. The situation here is quite magnificent, but the best views are said to be had about 30mins beyond the chalets on the way up to the **Planura Hut** standing on the edge of the Hüfifirn glacier (see above).

The left-hand option from Hinter Sandalp climbs roughly southward up a hanging valley watered by the Biferten Bach under the NW Wall of the Bifertenstock. Eight hundred metres above the alp the **Fridolins Hut** (2111m) is well placed for climbs on both the Bifertenstock and the Tödi, and provides overnight accommodation for 60 in its dormitories. Owned by the Glarus-based Tödi section of the SAC, the hut is reached in about 4–4½hrs from Tierfed, and has a guardian during April and May, and from July until the end of August (www.fridolinshuette.ch).

About 300m and less than an hour's walk above it stands the historic little **Grünhorn Hut** at 2448m. Dating from 1863 it was the first to be built by members of the Swiss Alpine Club, formed earlier that year, but with just eight places it is little more than a basic shelter, and anyone planning to spend a night there should carry food and a stove.

The Grünhorn Hut nestles at the foot of the NW Wall of the ❸ **Bifertenstock** which, at 3421m, is the second highest of the Glarner Alps after the Tödi. Also known as Piz Durschin, it stands astride the Glarus/Graubünden border with small glaciers on both sides. A popular mountain in both spring and summer, it has routes of varying difficulty on all flanks, but was first climbed in 1863 (by Roth, Sand and Raillard with H Elmer) via the so-called Bänderweg which runs along the south side of the lengthy NE Ridge. Overlooking the Limmerensee the NE Wall is an impressive feature on which the Eisnase is said to be a difficult ice route and one

The NE Face of the Tödi

of the finest climbs of its kind in the Glarner Alps, while other lines attract on the banded south side of the mountain above Val Frisal.

The normal route takes the line of the first ascent, starting from the **Biferten Hut** which stands 250m below the Muot da Rubi (Kistenstöckli) on the Graubünden (southeast) side of the mountain at 2482m. The property of the Academic Alpine Club of Basel (AACB), the hut has 24 places, is sometimes manned between mid-June and the end of September (www.biferten.ch), and it can be reached in 2hrs from the Muttsee Hut, or 4hrs from Breil/Brigels in the Vorderrhein's valley.

West of the Bifertenstock, and 200m higher than its neighbour, the 3614m 🚶 **Tödi** is by far the most dominant peak hereabouts, but its shape and appearance are markedly different from whichever side it is examined. Forever associated with Placidus à Spescha (see *The Monk and the Mountain* box), it's a big bold mountain daubed with tiny glaciers and crowned by three distinct summits, all of which can be climbed in the same expedition. But according to Herbert Maeder the rock is mostly fragile and often covered with ice. The main peak is known as **Piz Russein**; the 3586m **Glarner Tödi** stands a little to the east of that; while north of the main summit the **Sandgipfel** (3390m) is most evident on the approach from Linthal.

Four huts serve a number of different routes. To the west there's the Planura Hut; east and northeast the Grünhorn and Fridolins Huts; and to the southeast the **Punteglias Hut** (Camona da Punteglias), a 42-place SAC-owned building with a guardian from July until the end of September (www.punteglias.ch). Standing at an altitude of 2311m in Val Punteglias, about 3½–4hrs from Trun in the Vorderrhein's valley, it gives access to the Tödi via the 3260m glacier pass of **Porta da Gliems**.

The first ascent of the Tödi was made from the south, but the majority of routes are found on the north and west flanks, including the *voie normale* from the Fridolins Hut which uses the Biferten glacier for ski ascents as well as summer climbs. The long North Ridge gives a mixture of rock and ice (IV); the Rötifirn couloir (V) on the NE Face is another long and varied mixed climb; the NW Wall rising above the Sandfirn holds several routes accessible from both the Fridolins and Planura Huts, and the SW Face also offers a variety of climbs approached from the Planura Hut.

THE MONK AND THE MOUNTAIN

For ever linked with the Tödi, the climbs and explorations of Placidus à Spescha earned him recognition as one of the founders of alpinism. Born in 1752 at Trun at the foot of the mountain, he received a good education and after taking Holy Orders as a young man, entered the Benedictine monastery at nearby Disentis. He later developed a passion for geology and botany at Einsiedeln, and when posted to the hospice on the Lukmanier Pass in his early thirties, saw the mountains of the Glarner Alps to the north with fresh eyes, and decided that their exploration would become his life's work. Between 1788 and 1824 Spescha is credited with making more than 30 ascents, often alone, drawing summit panoramas, collecting rocks and minerals, and calculating the movement of glaciers. In the study of nature he claimed to have found a better understanding of God, but this set him at odds with some of his fellow monks who became vindictive and set about destroying his character.

From Disentis his first ascent is thought to have been of nearby Piz Ault (3027m) with its close view of the Oberalpstock, which he also climbed. He also made several attempts on the Tödi, and successful ascents of Cristallina (2912m), Piz Urlaun (3359m), Rheinwaldhorn (3402m), Güferhorn (3383m), and many more. But these were difficult times, for in 1799 the French army swept into Central and Eastern Switzerland and burned the Disentis monastery to the ground. The French were replaced by the Austrians who took Spescha and held him hostage in Innsbruck from September 1799 until February 1801. Surprisingly this turned out to be in his favour, for while there he was allowed to study at the Academy, was given leave to climb the neighbouring peaks of Patscherkofel and Rosskopf, and wrote a book on mountaineering techniques.

Returning to his home valley he moved from parish to parish as a priest, and resumed his efforts to win the Tödi with a single-minded dedication that would later be reflected in Whymper's focus on the Matterhorn. But unlike Whymper, Placidus à Spescha failed to set foot on the summit of his ambition. His final attempt was made on 1 September 1824 in the company of his servant, Carli Cogenard, and two chamois hunters, August Bisquolm and Placidus Curschellas. Now aged 72 he was exhausted by the time they reached the gap in the ridge that now bears his name, the Porta da Spescha, so he remained behind with Cogenard. There he watched with satisfaction as the two chamois hunters continued to the summit. Spescha died six years later, having been responsible for opening the unfashionable Glarner, Lepontine and Adula Alps, and in so doing becoming, without question, one of the first true mountaineers.

Klöntal

About 16km north of Linthal **Glarus** (489m) is the capital of this small mountain canton which, to outsiders, must be one of the least known of all. It's a busy little industrial town with all services, overlooked from the southwest by the **Glärnisch** massif whose highest point is 2914m, and whose bulk effectively forms the southern wall of the Klöntal, a small but attractive valley lying west of the town and served by local bus.

The main feature is the fjord-like **Klöntaler See**, a long artificial lake with a campsite and *gasthaus* at either end, the south side rising steeply to rock peaks of the Glärnischer Ruchen which are especially striking when seen from the north shore; a footpath skirts the south side of the lake among trees. At the western end, a scattered hamlet of chalets marks the entrance to the tributary valley of Rossmatter Tal, through which a path heads south to **Chäseren**, then climbs 1100m to reach the large, 120-bed **Glärnisch Hut** in 3½–4hrs from the lakeside. Standing at 1990m below a shrinking *firn* the hut is owned by the local Glarus-based Tödi section of the SAC and is fully manned from July until mid-October, and at weekends in June and late October (www.glhuette.ch). The ascent of the 2904m ❸ **Vrenelisgärtli** at the head of the Glärnischfirn is a popular outing from here. But there are several other summits of the massif to climb too, all of which provide wide-ranging views of the Alps of Central and Eastern Switzerland.

A little above Chäseren the path to the Glärnisch Hut forks, with the right branch leading to the karst plateau west of the Eggstock mentioned above, but with several options that continue to Braunwald, to the Glattalp Hut, into the Bisistal, or to the Muotatal.

The Swiss Alps – Chapter 6: Central Swiss Alps

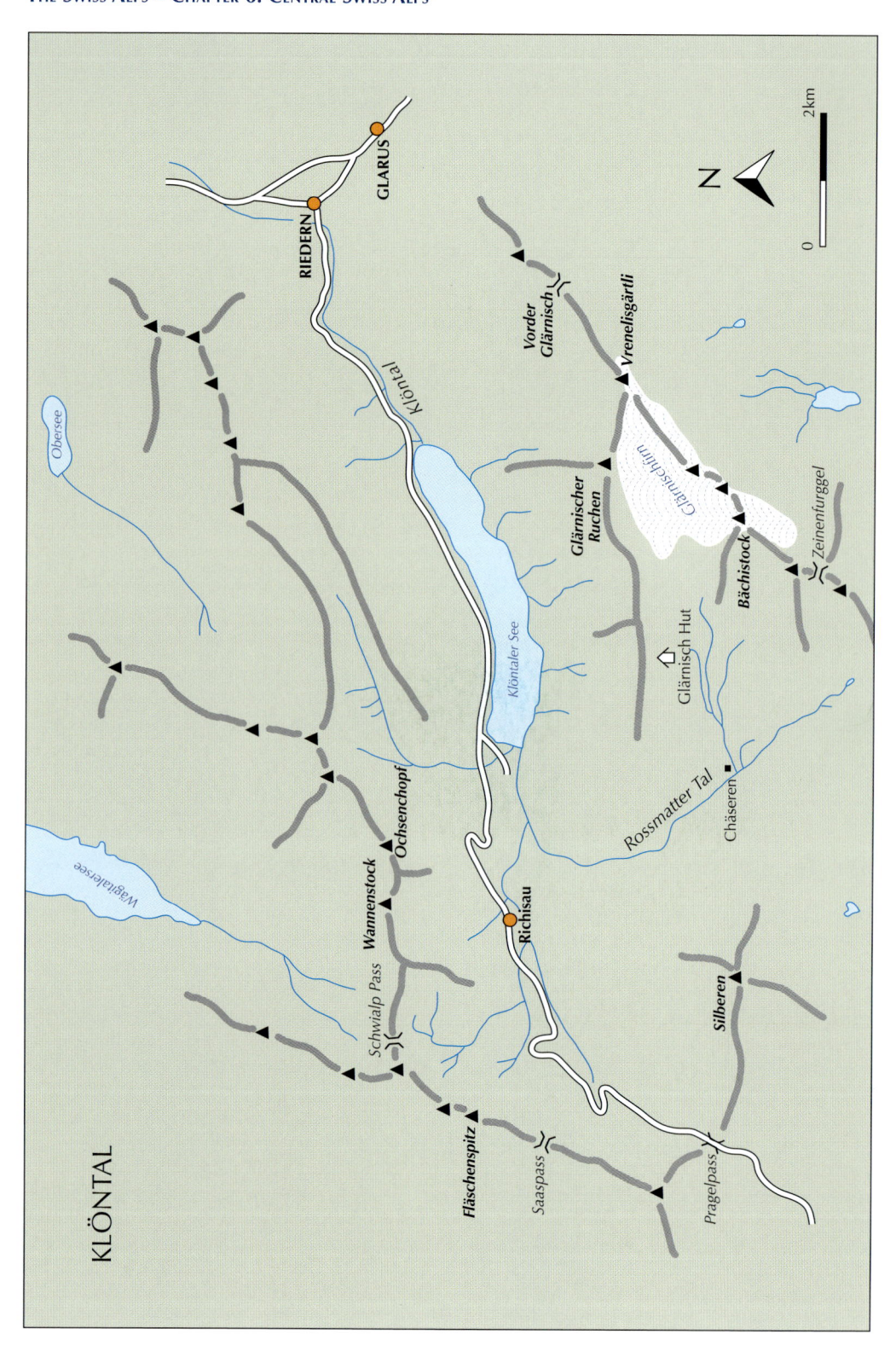

The Klöntal valley road continues as far as **Richisau** where there's a *gasthaus* with a range of accommodation options at 1103m. This occupies a neat and pretty scene with flower meadows and groups of trees, backed by Wannenstock and Ochsenchopf to the north, and Silberen to the south, and is the turning point for the bus service. The continuing road is closed to unauthorised vehicles, but the historic **Pragel Pass** (1550m) is another 2–2½hrs walk from here, with a further 2hrs to reach the Muotatal. Heading southeast from Richisau a trail goes through woodland to enter the **Rossmatter Tal**, while another aims north over the **Schwialp Pass** to the large **Wägitalersee** (4hrs), and yet another trail works a way northeast to the Obersee lake in 4½–5hrs, thereby suggesting that Richisau would make a peaceful and very pleasant out-of-the-way base for a few days of a walking holiday.

Sernftal

The final valley under review here is the Sernftal, which lies to the east of the Linth Tal, and whose river rises on the northeast flank of the Hausstock. Gathering run-off from the Panixer Pass, Piz Segnas and Piz Sardona into a single stream near Elm, it then flows north and west to join the Linth at Schwanden, 5km south of Glarus. A footpath which remains in the valley to accompany the river between Schwanden and Elm is known as the Suworowweg, named after the Russian general who in 1799 led his retreating army towards the Panixer Pass (see box 'Suvorov and the Alpine Passes').

In its lower reaches the Sernftal is tightly constricted and heavily wooded, but the valley opens to meadows between Matt and Elm. At **Engi Vorderdorf** (770m) it is joined from the north by the Mülibach tributary. On the opposite side of the valley there's a 30m high *klettergarten* with about 40 routes ideal for newcomers to practise on (www.engi.ch).

More compact than Engi, **Matt** is the next village, situated a short distance upstream at 826m. This too is located at the entrance to a tributary valley, the **Chrauchtal** that cuts into the mountains to the east. Footpaths and farm tracks abound on the hillsides above the village, and a small cable car takes walkers up to Weissenberge (Wissenberg) at 1257m to take advantage of these mostly easy trails. But there's more of a challenge to be found in the walling ridge of the Chrauchtal, where the 2189m ⬤ **Risetenpass** leads into the neighbouring Weisstannental which eventually spills out of the mountains near Sargans.

Elm (977m) is the most important Sernftal community, a summer and winter resort and mountaineering centre, but tiny by comparison with most resorts in this book. Standing just 14km from Schwanden it's an attractive, historic village with around half a dozen hotels and *gasthäuser*, a number of rustic chalets to rent, a few shops, restaurants, a cash machine, and the valley's tourist office (www.elm.ch). The buildings are neat and decked with flowers in summer; there's a 15th-century church and a sturdy, thick-walled house in which General Suvorov spent a night in October 1799 before leading his troops across the Panixer Pass in a blizzard. On the west side of the valley a gondola lift serves **Ampächli** at 1480m for skiing in winter, and summer walking on the steep grass slopes.

Near the entrance to the Raminertal, which cuts into the mountains to the east of Elm, the Tschingenalp cableway rises to Nideren at 1480m, from where one route mounts the southern slope to reach the **Martinsmad Hut** in 1½hrs (3hrs from Elm). Standing at 2002m below the little glacier draped across the face of the Glarner Vorab, this SAC hut has 64 places, is fully staffed in July and August, and at weekends in June, September and October (www.sac-randen.ch). From the hut a blue and white blazed alpine trail crosses the canton boundary wall at the 2760m ⬤ **Grisonsattel**, and descends on the far side to Flims (see 3:9).

Another trail beginning at Nideren climbs to the 2627m ⬤ **Pass dil Segnas** below Piz Segnas. South of this pass the renowned **Martinsloch** is a natural hole in the rock, some 17m high by 19m wide, through which the sun beams onto Elm's church tower on two days of the year (12 or 13 March and 30 September or 1 October). Northeast of Pass dil Segnas the 3099m summit of ⬤ **Piz Segnas** can be gained by a straightforward route (F) on the east side of the ridge.

Piz Segnas and Piz Sardona are the highest and most dominant mountains that rim the Raminertal east of Elm, and their broad connecting ridge carries the canton border northwards. Northwest of Piz Sardona the saddle of the ⬤ **Foopass** (2223m) enables trekkers to cross this border ridge on the second stage of the Alpine Pass Route (5:10) between Weisstannen and Elm, descending into the Raminertal via the alp buildings of Raminer Matt and Mittler Stafel. But when it leaves Elm, the APR

THE SWISS ALPS – CHAPTER 6: CENTRAL SWISS ALPS

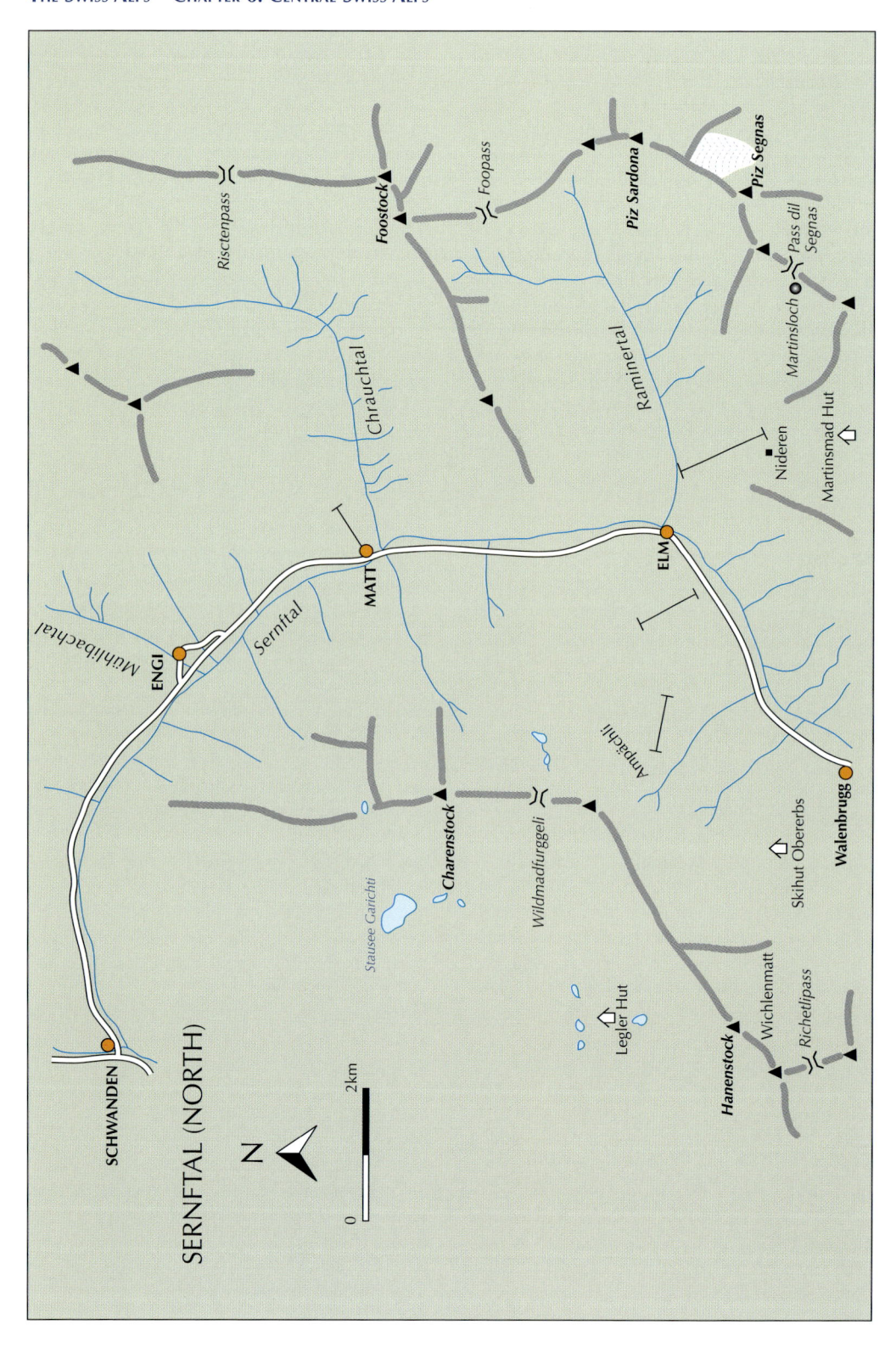

SERNFTAL (NORTH)

398

SUVOROV AND THE ALPINE PASSES

In the closing years of the 18th century Napoleon's vision of a united Europe brought warfare to the Alps of Central Switzerland, with battles being fought in one of the toughest of all environments.

The enigmatic 70-year-old Russian General Alexander Vasilyevich Suvorov, known for living with his men and sleeping on a truss of hay, was called out of retirement in Moscow and sent to Italy to help the Austrians in their opposition to the French. In quick succession he oversaw victories on the Adda, at Trebbia and Novi, and was then ordered north to the mountains of Switzerland. In September 1799 he set off with 21,000 men, passing through Bellinzona and Airolo and then climbing the St Gotthard Pass, where he found the hospice to be occupied by French troops who made a tactical withdrawal to Andermatt. The French then entered the Schöllenen gorge in the Reuss valley where they prepared to meet Suvorov's army.

For three days the battle in the gorge was ferocious, but then the French retreated downstream, destroying the Devil's Bridge on the way. Suvorov took up the chase, marching down the Reuss valley to Flüelen on the shores of the Lake of Lucerne. As the French had seized all the boats, the Russians turned to the east, crossed the 2073m Chinzig Chulm (Kinzigkulm Pass), then marched down the Muotatal to outflank the opposition. But the French barred the way with a strong force, and pushed Suvorov back into the mountains. There he crossed the Pragel Pass and went down to Glarus where the French were waiting once more. Weakened by a long campaign, the Russians were now forced into the Sernftal where they spent a night in Elm, and next day started for the Panixer Pass.

By now it was October and the weather turned bad. There was deep snow and no marked route, and the descent in a blizzard above Alp di Pigniu saw many battle-weary soldiers and their pack horses fall to their deaths. But Suvorov led over 14,000 of his men to safety, and five days later they crossed into Austria to join the remnants of General Korsakoff's army at Feldkirch.

heads southwest along the Sernftal before mounting the western hillside to the Wichlenmatt basin and tackling the narrow saddle of the ◯ **Richetlipass** (2261m) north of the snowy Hausstock. From the

The SE Face of the Hausstock towers over the Pigniu lake

The Swiss Alps – Chapter 6: Central Swiss Alps

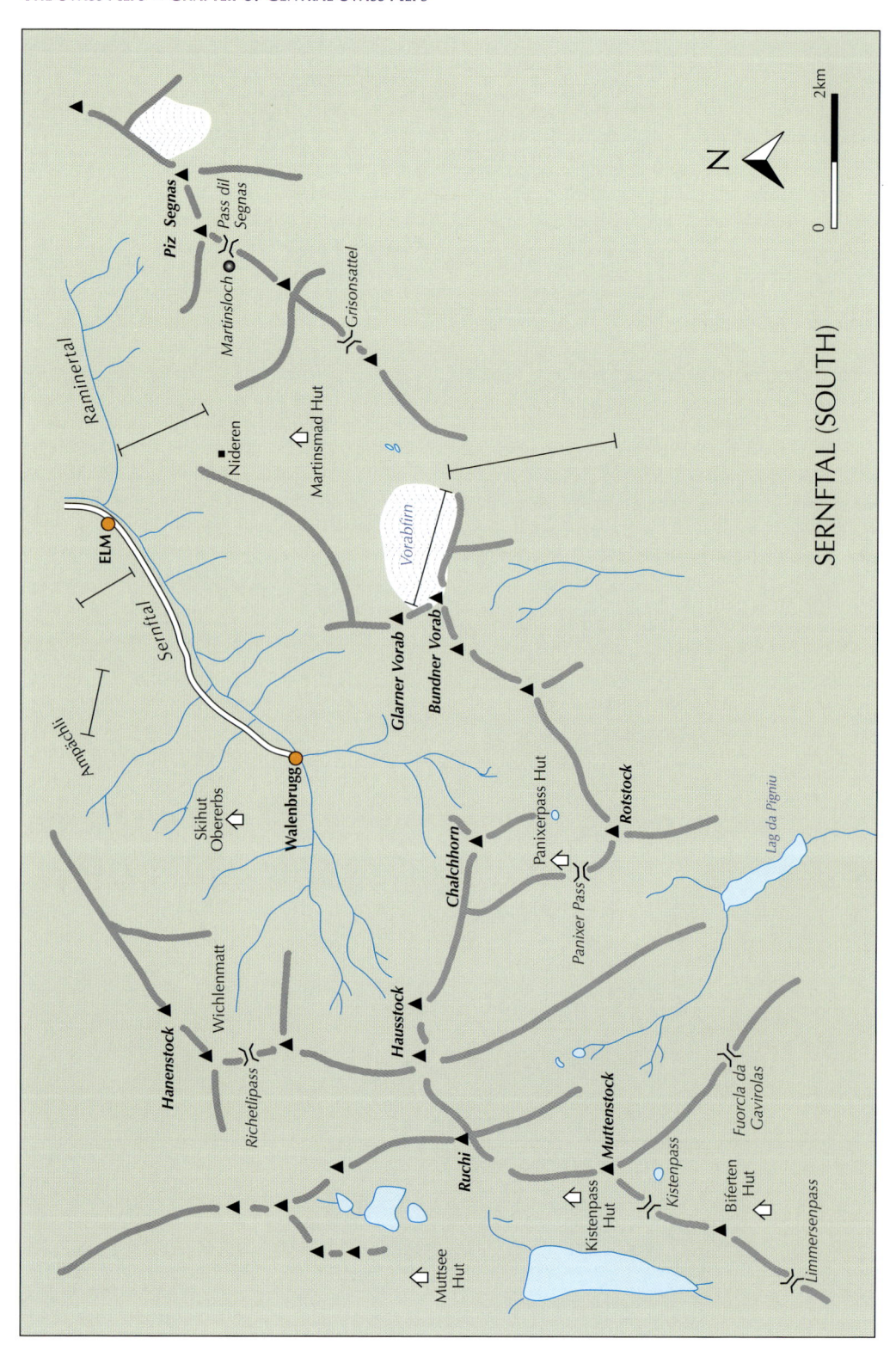

SERNFTAL (SOUTH)

pass the route descends to Linthal at the end of a fairly tough day's trekking.

One Sunday in September 1881 tragedy struck Elm when a steep 500m rock buttress that for years had been quarried for slate broke away from the Tschingelhorn and fell on the village, killing 114 local people – their names are listed on a plaque in the church.

The upper valley west of **Walenbrugg** is part of a military training area with firing ranges, although most of the time access is given for walkers and climbers aiming for the ○ **Panixer Pass** or the ⊕ **Hausstock** via the steep-walled southern stem – beware of avalanche risk in winter. Lying between the Chalchhorn to the right and Rotstock to the left, the pass is 1100m above Walenbrugg, and it will take a good 3hrs to reach. As mentioned above, the small 14-place **Panixerpass Hut** is located at 2407m, but as it's unmanned, anyone planning to spend a night there will need to carry provisions (check current facilities at the Elm tourist office). It's a base for climbing the 3158m Hausstock by a mixed rock and ice route in 3½–4hrs, or for crossing the mountains from north to south, with a long descent through Val da Pigniu to Rueun in the valley of the Vorderrhein. Wedged at the head of Val da Pigniu a dammed lake, **Lag da Pigniu**, lies in a gloriously impressive cleft below the Hausstock's south-facing walls from which waterfalls tumble from great heights; a magnificent sight.

ACCESS, BASES, MAPS AND GUIDES

Access

Göschenertal By train from Lucerne or Zürich (Gotthard line) to Göschenen. By road, take the Gotthard motorway to the Göschenen exit.

Engelbergtal By train from Lucerne to Engelberg. By road, take the A2 motorway south of Lucerne to the Stans exit.

Grosstal By bus from Altdorf or Flüelen to Isenthal. By lake ferry from Lucerne to Isleten, then bus to Isenthal. By car, take the Gotthard motorway to Altdorf, then follow signs to Seedorf and Iselten.

Maderanertal By train from Lucerne or Zürich to Erstfeld, then bus to Amsteg; change buses for Bristen. By road, take the Gotthard motorway to the Amsteg exit, then by narrow road to Bristen.

Schächental By bus or car along the Klausenpass road east of Altdorf.

Urner Boden Buses run across the Klausenpass (closed in winter) between Linthal and Altdorf.

Linth Tal By train from Zürich via Glarus to Linthal. By car, take the A3 motorway from Zürich, leave it at the Näfels/Glaris exit and follow the Linth upstream.

Klöntal By bus or car from Glarus as far as Richisau.

Sernftal By car or Glarner bus from Schwanden to Elm.

Valley Bases

Göschenertal Göschenen
Melchtal Melchsee-Frutt
Engelbergtal Engelberg
Maderanertal Bristen
Schächental Unterschächen
Urner Boden Urnerboden
Linth Tal Linthal, Braunwald
Klöntal Richisau
Sernftal Elm

Information

Glarnerland Tourismus, CH-8750 Glarus (www.glarnerland.ch)

Huts

A number of SAC huts, including the oldest in the country, give access to most districts. Details are given in the main chapter text.

Maps

The Kümmerly + Frey 1:60,000 Wanderkarte series has three sheets of use to mountain walkers and climbers visiting the Central Swiss Alps: No 11 Vierwaldstättersee, No 12 Glarnerland Walensee, and No 19 Gotthard

The Swiss National Survey (Landeskarte der Schweiz) cover the same area at 1:50,000 with 236 Lachen, 245 Stans, 246 Klausenpass, 247 Sardona, 255 Sustenpass, 256 Disentis, and 23 sheets at 1:25,000

Walking and/or Trekking Guides

Alpine Pass Route by Kev Reynolds (Cicerone, 2nd edition 2008)

The Bernese Alps by Kev Reynolds (Cicerone, 3rd edition 2008) – for Gental only

Central Switzerland: a Walker's Guide by Kev Reynolds (Cicerone, 1993)

Trekking in the Alps by Kev Reynolds (Cicerone, 2011)

Walking in Switzerland by Clem Lindenmayer (Lonely Planet, 2nd edition 2001)

Alpinwandern Zentralschweiz – Glarus–Alpstein (SAC)

Climbing Guides

Bernese Oberland by Les Swindin (AC, 2003) – for routes on Salbitschijen

Central Switzerland by Jeremy Talbot (West Col, 1969) for the Dammastock group

Glarner Alpen (SAC)

Urner Alpen Ost (1) (SAC}

Urner Alpen (2) – Göscheneralp – Furka – Grimsel (SAC)

Urner Alpen (3) – Vom Susten zum Urirotstock (SAC}

Klettersteig Schweiz by Iris Kürschner (Rother, 2004)

Schweiz Plaisir by Jürg von Kanel (Filidor) – topo guide, includes Salbitschijen

Skitouring Guides

Alpine Skitouren 2: Graubünden (SAC)

Alpine Skitouren 5: Glarus–St Gallen–Appenzell (SAC)

Alpine Skitouren Zentralschweiz – Tessin (SAC)

See Also

Walking in the Alps by Kev Reynolds (Cicerone, 2nd edition 2005)

The Outdoor Traveler's Guide: The Alps by Marcia R Lieberman (Stewart, Tabori & Chang, New York, 1991)

Freie Sicht aufs Gipfelmeer by Marco Volken and Remo Kundert (Salvioni Edizioni, Bellinzona, 2003)

Tödi: Sehnsucht und Traum by Emil Zopfi (AS-Verlag, Zürich)

CHAPTER 7: SILVRETTA AND RÄTIKON ALPS

The Northern Bündner Alps of eastern Switzerland. The mountains border Austria and Liechtenstein, but also include the Säntis and Churfirsten in the Alpstein range.

SILVRETTA AND RÄTIKON ALPS: CHAPTER SUMMARY

Location
North of the Albula Alps, and spreading west and northwest of the Lower Engadine as far as the Alpstein massif of cantons St Gallen and Appenzell west of the Rhine. The main range straddles the borders of Austria and Liechtenstein, the southern limit being the Flüela Pass. Scuol in the Lower Engadine, and Klosters in the Prättigau, are the main resorts, with Appenzell and Wildhaus serving the Säntis.

Highlights

🚶 Walks
- Vereinapass – Berghaus Vereina to Lavin (7:2)
- Tour of the Silvretta (7:2)
- Prättigauer Höhenweg (7:2 and 7:3)
- Carschina Hut to Schesaplana Hut (7:3)
- Tour of the Rätikon (7:3)

🧗 Climbs
- Piz Buin (7:1)
- Sulzfluh Klettersteig (7:3)
- Schweizereck – sport climbs (7:3)
- Kirchlispitzen – sport climbs (7:3)

⛰ Summits for all
- Flüela Wisshorn (7:1)
- Tällispitz (7:2)
- Sulzfluh (7:3)
- Schesaplana (7:3)
- Säntis (7:4)

Contents

7:1 Silvretta Alps – Lower Engadine 408

7:2 Silvretta Alps – Prättigau 413
Vereinatal 415
Val Sardasca 416
Tour of the Silvretta (box) 418
Schlappintal 419

7:3 Rätikon Alps 420
St Antöniental 420
Tour of the Rätikon (box) 424
The Western Rätikon 426
Prättigauer Höhenweg (box) 429

7:4 The Alpstein Massif 429
Säntis: King of the Appenzeller Alps (box) 432
Churfirsten 433

Access, Bases, Maps and Guides 435

◀ *Piz Buin, mirrored in a pool below the Furcletta*

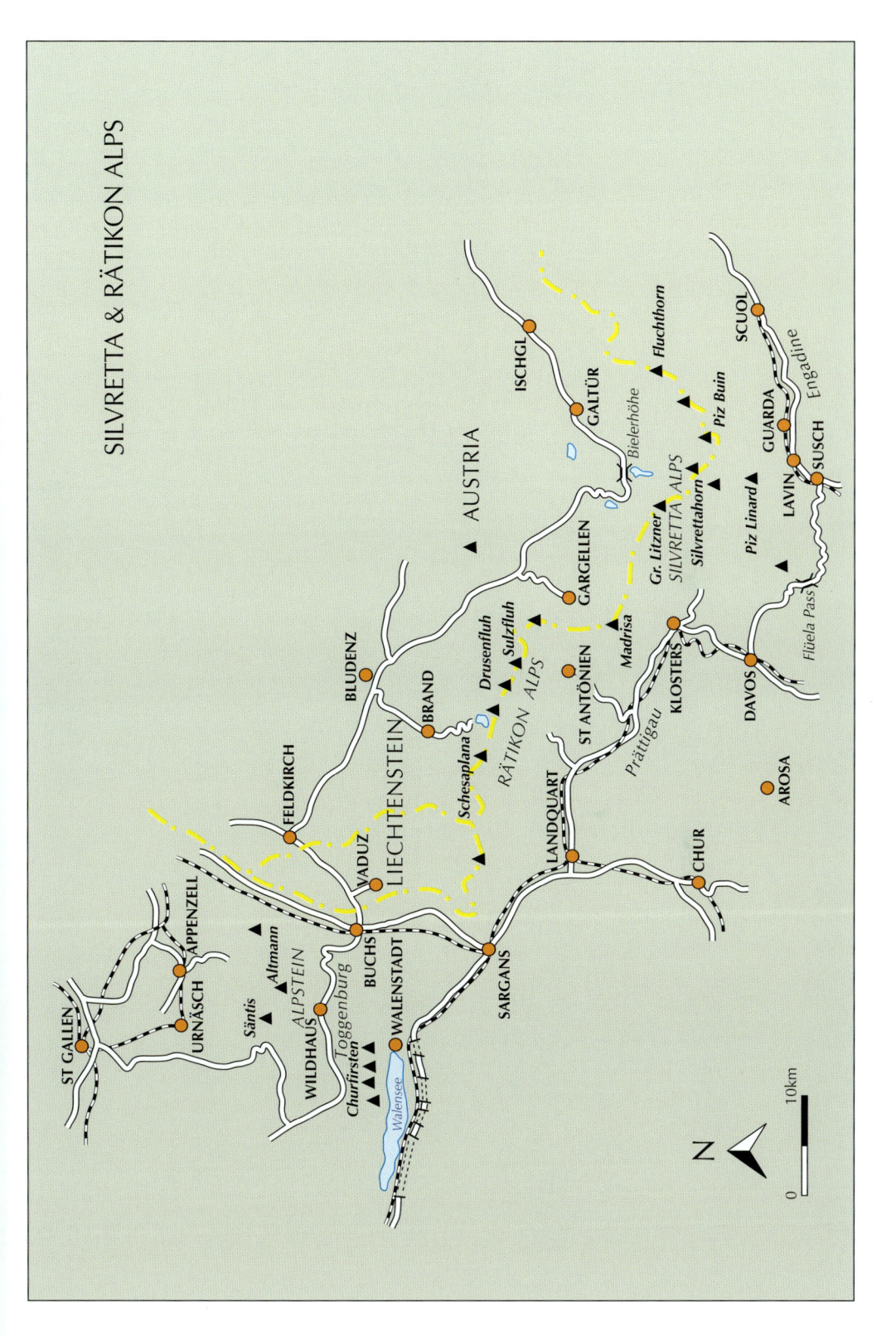

SILVRETTA & RÄTIKON ALPS

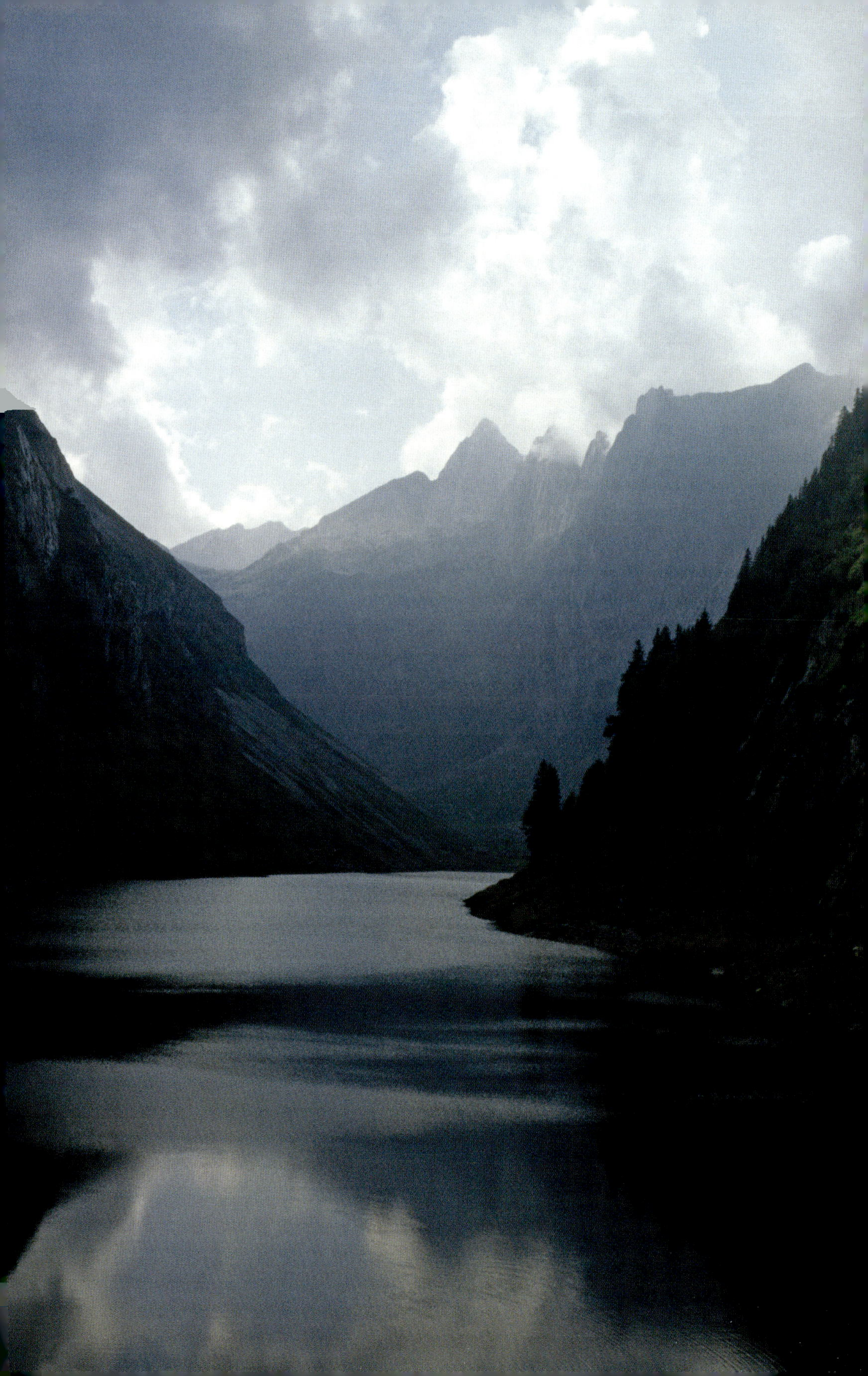

SILVRETTA AND RÄTIKON ALPS: INTRODUCTION

This is a region of straightforward mountaineering. Indeed, it is country for experienced mountain walkers and those climbers who prefer shorter routes with less exacting glaciers than those in the Western Alps.

Jeff Williams, *Silvretta Alps*

Divided by the exquisite St Antöniental, these neighbouring districts form part of the Northern Bündner Alps, the mountains of Canton Graubünden. Geologically and scenically very different from one another, the Silvretta range is crystalline and truly alpine in appearance, with small glaciers and snowfields. The Rätikon mountains, on the other hand, are limestone and, in places, almost dolomitic in their block-like stature with clusters of bizarre spires, towers and turrets, vast screes and a host of natural rock gardens at their feet.

The Austrian provinces of Vorarlberg and Tyrol have less than an equal share of the Silvretta Alps, but make perhaps a greater claim to popularity than the Swiss side of the chain. Their highest summits barely reach 3400m, and provide climbs of a traditional nature. Well supplied with huts on both sides of the border, and smeared with fairly 'innocent' glaciers, routes are mostly short and of a standard to favour the first-time alpinist. It's also a district that would appeal to the experienced hillwalker with opportunities to create adventurous hut-to-hut tours, while several of their villages are among the most attractive in all Switzerland: Guarda, Ardez and Ftan being foremost among them. With no customs formalities to consider,

Piz Buin and the Tuoi Hut (Photo: Linda Reynolds)

◂ *The moody Fälensee below the Kreuzberge*

cross-border treks are worth tackling, for there are several passes accessible to anyone with sufficient energy and an inquisitive nature. Passes and valleys will be as important as peaks.

Spanning both sides of the Swiss/Austrian border and spilling into Liechtenstein, the Rätikon Alps have a dramatic beauty quite unrelated to that of the Silvretta. It's a much more narrow chain than its neighbour, mostly confined to a single strip of mountains broken in several places to provide easy access from one side to the other. Modern-style hard climbing has a rich pedigree here, for a number of vertical walls of compact limestone give quality routes of 200–300m in a setting of great beauty. Those that face south out to the Prättigau valley which runs from Klosters to Landquart, boast literally scores of routes, and the 450m *klettersteig* developed on the SE face of the Sulzfluh above the St Antöniental is reckoned to be one of the country's most exciting via ferratas.

None of these Rätikon peaks tops 3000m, while the Alpstein massif west of the Rhine has the 2502m Säntis as its loftiest summit. This too is a limestone district. Much loved by natives of Appenzell and St Gallen for whom it is a distinctive totem, the Säntis is something of a bastion of the pre-Alps, with a summit panorama that encompasses a large part of eastern Switzerland as well as the Austrian and German border country.

Downhill skiing, with all its paraphernalia of lifts and tows, has left the Silvretta and Rätikon largely unscathed, despite the close proximity of Davos and Klosters, but ski mountaineers have a wonderland to explore in late winter and early springtime. The majority of ski tours are, however, made on the Austrian slopes of the Silvretta, although there's still a fair amount of potential to exploit on the Swiss flank, especially in Val Sardasca and the Vereinatal above Klosters.

The whole area is accessible by public transport. The Rhaetian Railway runs from Landquart to Klosters through the lovely green valley of Prättigau, and has a link with the Lower Engadine via the 19km long Vereina Tunnel, said to be the world's longest narrow-gauge rail tunnel. The Lower Engadine has rail access as far east as Scuol, and reliable bus services elsewhere. For Säntis and the Alpstein massif a narrow-gauge railway runs between St Gallen and Appenzell, while buses serve the Toggenburg valley which lies between the Alpstein massif and the Churfirsten ridge.

7:1 SILVRETTA ALPS: LOWER ENGADINE

From the Flüela Pass to the Samnaun group (the latter sandwiched between the Silvretta and the Austrian Tyrol) the Lower Engadine is walled to the north by some of the highest peaks of the district, including Piz Linard, the loftiest of them all, together with Piz Buin (third highest), Dreiländerspitz and Augstenberg. Only the tiniest of remnant glaciers remain on these south-facing slopes, and little of the Silvretta's appeal can be gauged from the Engadine itself – the one exception being that of Piz Linard, whose cone-like outline is seen to powerful effect from the Inn's valley south of Susch.

Closed to traffic in winter the 2383m **Flüela Pass** is the only road linking the southeast and southwest flanks of the Silvretta Alps. About six times a day from late June until mid-October a postbus service runs across the pass between Davos Platz and **Susch**, a small Engadine village of cobbled streets, sgraffitied houses and the ruined hilltop keep of Chaschinas. On the pass and overlooking the Schottensee stands the Flüela Hospiz which has dormitory accommodation as well as standard hotel rooms. On the east side of the pass Val Susasca descends to the Inn; to the south rise outlying peaks of the Albula Alps (4:2), while the northern side marks the start of the Silvretta range, with the 3085m ⊗ ☆ **Flüela Wisshorn** (or Weisshorn) overlooking the pass itself. The most appealing aspect of this popular mountain is that which is seen from Berghaus Vereina (7:2) and the Jöritjal, with the standard route tackling its NW Ridge from the Winterlücke – an hour's scramble from pass to summit. But the shortest approach to the Winterlücke is from the Wägerhaus north of the Flüela Pass, where there's a bus stop and car park.

Midway between the Flüela Pass and Susch the tributary of Val Fless offers a walker's route over the ⊙ **Flesspass** (2453m) to Berghaus Vereina and, eventually, to Klosters. The way divides at Alp Fless Dadaint where an alternative trail heads west to cross the **Jöriflesspass** (2561m) where the Flüela Wisshorn's NE Ridge dips to a saddle before rising to the Muttelhorn. Over this pass the cluster of milky lakes known as the Jöriseen add a sparkle below the Wisshorn's North Face. These lakes, however, are usually visited by walkers from a base at Berghaus Vereina.

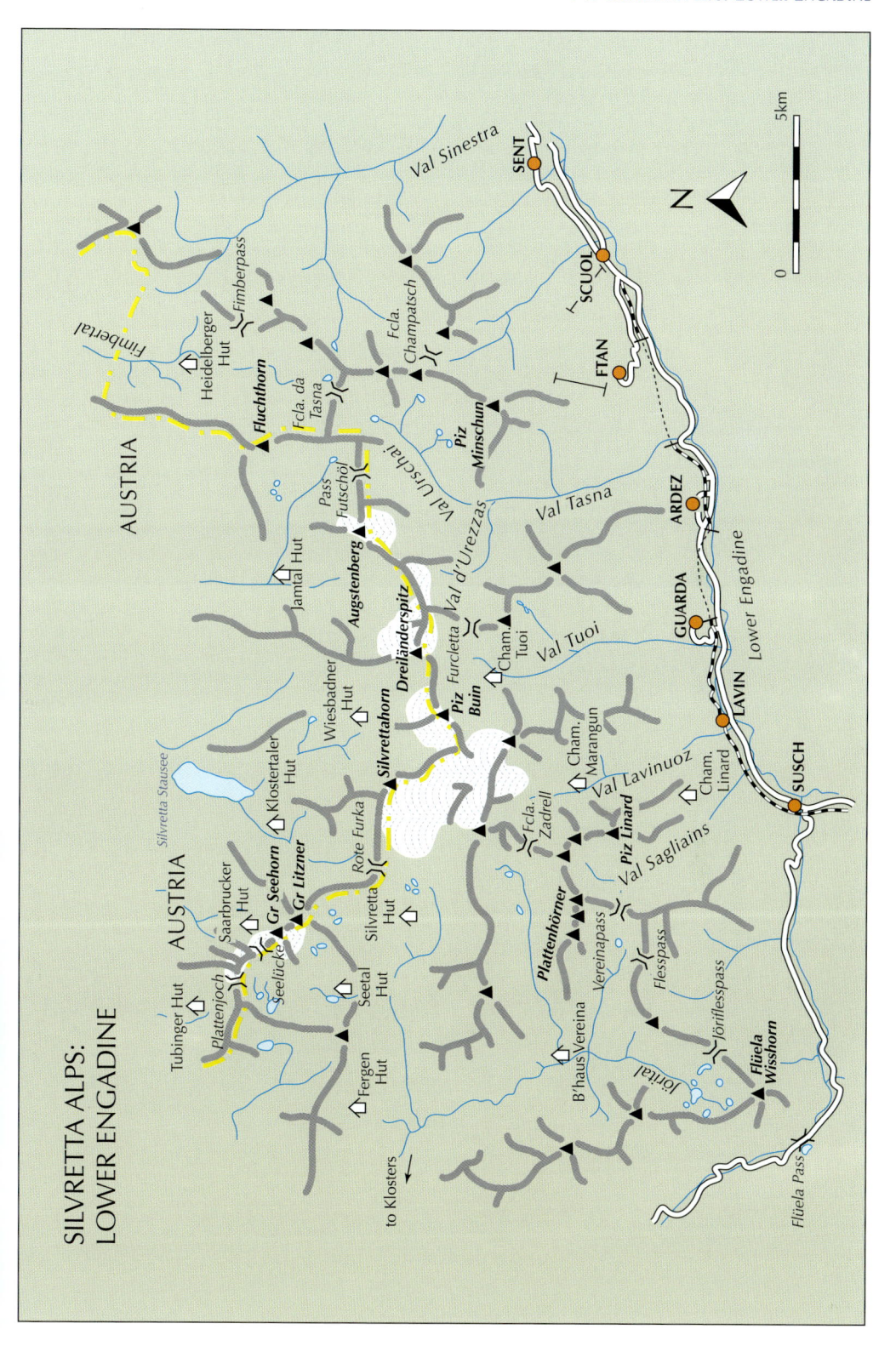

7:1 SILVRETTA ALPS: LOWER ENGADINE

A little over 3km from Susch in the Lower Engadine **Lavin** (1412m) squats directly below Piz Linard. An unpretentious village, it boasts two hotels, low-priced dormitory accommodation at the Chasa Fliana, and beds in several other establishments. There's a railway station, a bakery, a small supermarket and tourist information available at the post office (www.lavin.ch).

As mentioned above 🛈 **Piz Linard** (3411m) is the highest of the Silvretta Alps. Seen from the Engadine it appears as a gracefully tapered cone, but viewed from east or west it presents a very different profile, and its reputation for loose rock is well founded. Helmets are advised for all would-be summiteers. First climbed via the South Face in 1835 by Oswald Heer and Johann Madutz (just six days after the two had made the first ascent of Piz Palü's East Summit – see 4:4), the original route is graded no more than F-, but stonefall danger should not be underestimated (allow 3½–4hrs from the Linard Hut).

As a base for climbers **Chamanna dal Linard** (2327m) is a small, old-style SAC hut located on an open site below the mountain's South Face at the head of a stiff approach through woods. With sleeping places for just 41, and a warden in residence from July until mid-September, it is reached in 2½–3hrs from Lavin (www.alpinist.ch). To access peaks other than Piz Linard from the hut would entail the crossing of Fuorcla da Glims on Linard's SW Ridge, and descending into Val Sagliains, the head of which is enclosed by the four-peaked Plattenhörner, Piz Zadrell and Piz Sagliains, the last named being attached to Piz Linard across the Fuorcla dal Linard. The cirque created by these peaks is extremely attractive, while its western wall contains the 2585m saddle of the 🟢 ☆ **Vereinapass**, a well-used walker's pass connecting the Lower Engadine with Berghaus Vereina and Klosters (see 7:2).

Val Sagliains runs along the western flank of Piz Linard; **Val Lavinuoz** drains the eastern side. Both are accessible from Lavin, with roads or farm tracks easing into their lower reaches. That in Val Sagliains soon gives way to a narrow path that squeezes through rampant vegetation on the west bank of the Sagliains torrent, while the farm track in Val Lavinuoz continues deep into its valley where the unmanned **Chamanna Marangun** (owned by the Lavin Gemeinde) offers simple accommodation for a dozen people at 2025m.

Val Sagliains drains the west side of Piz Linard

Guarda, an old Romansch village at the foot of the Silvretta Alps

Reached by a walk of about 2½hrs from Lavin, the single-storey stone-built hut is located on an alp between two streams, and it makes a useful stopover (assuming you remember to take your own food) for the trek to Berghaus Vereina via the 2752m ◯ **Fuorcla Zadrell**. This straightforward pass is named after one of those indomitable alpine priests, Father Jon Clos Zadrell, who would think nothing of striding across it after preaching in Lavin in the morning, to conduct a service in Klosters later on the same day.

The Marangun Hut is too far north to be of use to walkers following the long distance ◯ **Via Engiadina** trail that explores the lower Val Lavinuoz before curving round the Munt da las Muojas and pushing into Val Tuoi. This is a very fine and highly scenic trail, but by taking it the walker ignores the splendours of **Guarda**, surely one of the most perfect of Swiss villages with its extensive views along and across the Engadine, its cobbled alleys, fountains and centuries-old weathered buildings beautifully decorated with traditional sgraffiti, family coats of arms above doorways, and boxes of geraniums at the windows (www.engadin.net/guarda).

Val Tuoi stretches north of the village, with a track leading all the way from Guarda to Chamanna Tuoi below Piz Buin. The valley is a delight, and in early summer the meadows are so rich in wild flowers there's barely room for a blade of grass to intrude. The buildings of Alp Suot sit just above the left bank of the stream midway between Guarda and the valley's headwall, and it is here that the Via Engiadina crosses by footbridge then climbs the east flank hillside before turning south away from the mountains. That is a shame, for ☆ **Piz Buin** dominates every view and casts its personality over the whole valley. From the terrace at the Tuoi Hut it is a towering presence, deflecting attention from its neighbours. There are, in fact, two peaks: Piz Buin Grond (3312m) and Pitschen (or Klein Piz Buin) at 3256m, the former being the most celebrated and probably most frequently climbed of all Silvretta summits, whose first ascent was made on 14 July 1865 (the day of Whymper's ascent of the Matterhorn) by Johann Jakob Weilenmann, Joseph Anton Specht, Franz Pöll and J Pfitscher.

Piz Buin – main peak right, Klein Piz Buin on left

From the south Piz Buin is a distinguished pear-shaped rock peak seen to be leaning slightly to the right. Viewed from the east it is even more impressive; a graceful pyramid with what appears to be a slab face tapering to grooves and gullies. But it is the Austrian aspect that is most familiar, for the northern slopes garland the mountain with glacier and snowfield and it is these ramps of snow and ice that provide the normal route of ascent (F) from the Wiesbadener Hut. To tackle this route from the Tuoi Hut involves first crossing the old trade route of the Fuorcla Vermunt between Piz Buin and Dreiländerspitz. Although difficult to believe when viewed from the Tuoi Hut, until the early 17th century a mule track crossed Fuorcla Vermunt, but this was destroyed by the Swiss in 1622. By appearances the Swiss flank of Piz Buin above Val Tuoi is far more challenging to climb than the Austrian side, and is the preserve of the rock specialist.

The SAC's **Chamanna Tuoi** (2250m) makes a comfortable base for walks and climbs in and around Val Tuoi. With 95 places and excellent facilities, the hut is staffed at Christmas and New Year, from mid-February until mid-May, and from July until the middle of October (www.tuoi.ch). Immediately behind the hut a trail rises to the 2735m Furcletta (in 1½hrs), but after 15mins or so, another breaks off to the right to visit the little tarn of **Lai Blau**, then continues southward for a return to Guarda. The **Furcletta** route is somewhat tortuous towards the pass for it involves a scramble over a chaotic shamble of rocks and boulders, but the descent into Val d'Urezzas on the eastern side, though initially steep, leads eventually to the gentle Val Tasna which opens into the Engadine above Ardez.

Where Val d'Urezzas meets Val Tasna, another path heads northeast through Val Urschai for a cross-border route via **Pass Futschöl** to the Jamtal Hut in Austria. All this is splendid trekking country, wild and barely inhabited and immensely rewarding to explore on foot.

Val Tasna's east wall is crowned by the 3068m **Piz Minschun**. Though not particularly attractive, and noted for its loose screes, Piz Minschun nonetheless makes a popular ascent for hillwalkers based in the Lower Engadine, most of whom take advantage of the gondola lift from Scuol to Motta Naluns in order to ease the first 900m of ascent. From the upper gondola station the climb takes about 3hrs to the summit on a path which tackles the mountain's SW Ridge. Summit views are said to be spectacular and worth the effort of reaching the top.

Scuol (1243m) is the most important resort in the Lower Engadine and the terminus of the valley's railway. A thermal spa and low-key ski centre, it has more than 20 hotels of all grades, plenty of holiday apartments and, a rarity in these parts, a campsite on the south side of the Inn. There's no shortage of shops, restaurants and banks and the village has a well-stocked tourist office (www.scuol.ch). To the south Val S-charl (4:5) entices towards the Engiadina Dolomites and edges the national park, but a short distance downstream along the Engadine valley, between Sent and Ramosch, the final tributary in this corner of the Silvretta Alps is **Val Sinestra** which virtually divides the Silvretta from the small Samnaun group.

Heading north through Val Sinestra a narrow service road leads to the Kurhaus hotel, beyond which a way continues to the group of buildings of Zuort (one of which is a restaurant) at a confluence of streams at 1711m. To the west Val Laver takes a trail into a no-man's-land of mountains with ◓ **Fuorcla Champatsch** (2730m) at its head. The trail crosses this saddle and descends through Scuol's ski grounds back to the Engadine to conclude a long day's hike. But perhaps of more interest is the route which pushes north of Zuort, for this leads to the chalets of Griosch, then entices into Val Chöglias for a crossing of the 2608m ◓ **Fimberpass** (also known as the Cuolmen d'Fenga). The main reason for making this trek is to visit the **Heidelberger Hut**, which sits amid stream-cut pastures in the upper reaches of the Fimbertal (Val Fenga) at 2264m. Despite being on Swiss soil, for the border makes a curious kink here and instead of following a ridge it cuts directly across the valley, the Heidelberger Hut belongs to the DAV (German Alpine Club), is usually approached from Ischgl in Austria's Paznauntal, and payment for accommodation and meals is made, not in Swiss francs, but in Euros. Originally built in 1889, but enlarged in the late 1970s, it has places for more than 150 in beds and dormitories, and is fully staffed from January until the end of April, and from July to the end of September (www.alpenverein-heidelberg.de). Experienced trekkers who visit this hut and prefer an alternative route by which to return to the Lower Engadine, could use the 2835m **Fuorcla da Tasna** which leads into Val Urschai and, eventually, into Val Tasna – a long and, in places, trackless route for which at least 7hrs should be set aside to walk from the hut to Ardez.

7:2 SILVRETTA ALPS: PRÄTTIGAU

Flowing southeast to northwest from Klosters to Landquart, the Prättigau (appropriately translated as Meadow Valley) is a lush pastoral swathe drained by the Landquart river whose first tributaries rise among the Silvretta mountains. It is these mountains on the right flank of the valley with which we are concerned in this section. The Swiss/Austrian border traces the crestline of these mountains, whose alignment, stretching roughly northwest from Piz Buin, makes a sudden northward kink by the 2826m Madrisa, only to resume its northwesterly course above the St Antöniental where the Silvretta's crystalline rock is exchanged for Rätikon limestone.

Like that of the Lower Engadine described in 7:1, little of the Silvretta's grandeur can be seen from the green bed of the Prättigau. It's all very pleasant country, of course; impressive and uplifting hills and mountains that provide a backdrop to neat villages lining the river's bank. But the real grandeur of the Silvretta can only be truly appreciated after penetrating the intervening valleys and entering their heartland. No better gateway for this will be found than the small town of Klosters.

Originally a monastic settlement, as its name would imply, **Klosters** is the main springboard from which activity on the Silvretta Alps west of the Flüela Pass depends. Despite being linked with Davos in one of the most popular ski circuses in the Alps, its ambience is more likely to appeal to the sensibilities of the walking fraternity than that of its neighbour, while its location at the top end of the long and narrow Prättigau, and at the mouth of the Sardasca and Schlappin tributaries, gives it a head start over the comparatively snooty bustle of Davos. And despite being noted as the favoured winter resort of the British royals, in summer there are times when Klosters seems almost deserted; its chalets promoting a village-like atmosphere.

It's a two-part resort: **Klosters Platz** at 1206m is the hub containing the main railway station and most of the hotels; **Klosters Dorf** (1124m) lies 2km to the north and is much smaller, with the Schlappintal opening directly behind it. Dorf also has a railway station, but the main tourist office is in Platz (www.klosters.ch) in the Alte Bahnhofstrasse. There's no shortage of accommodation or other facilities, including a climbing

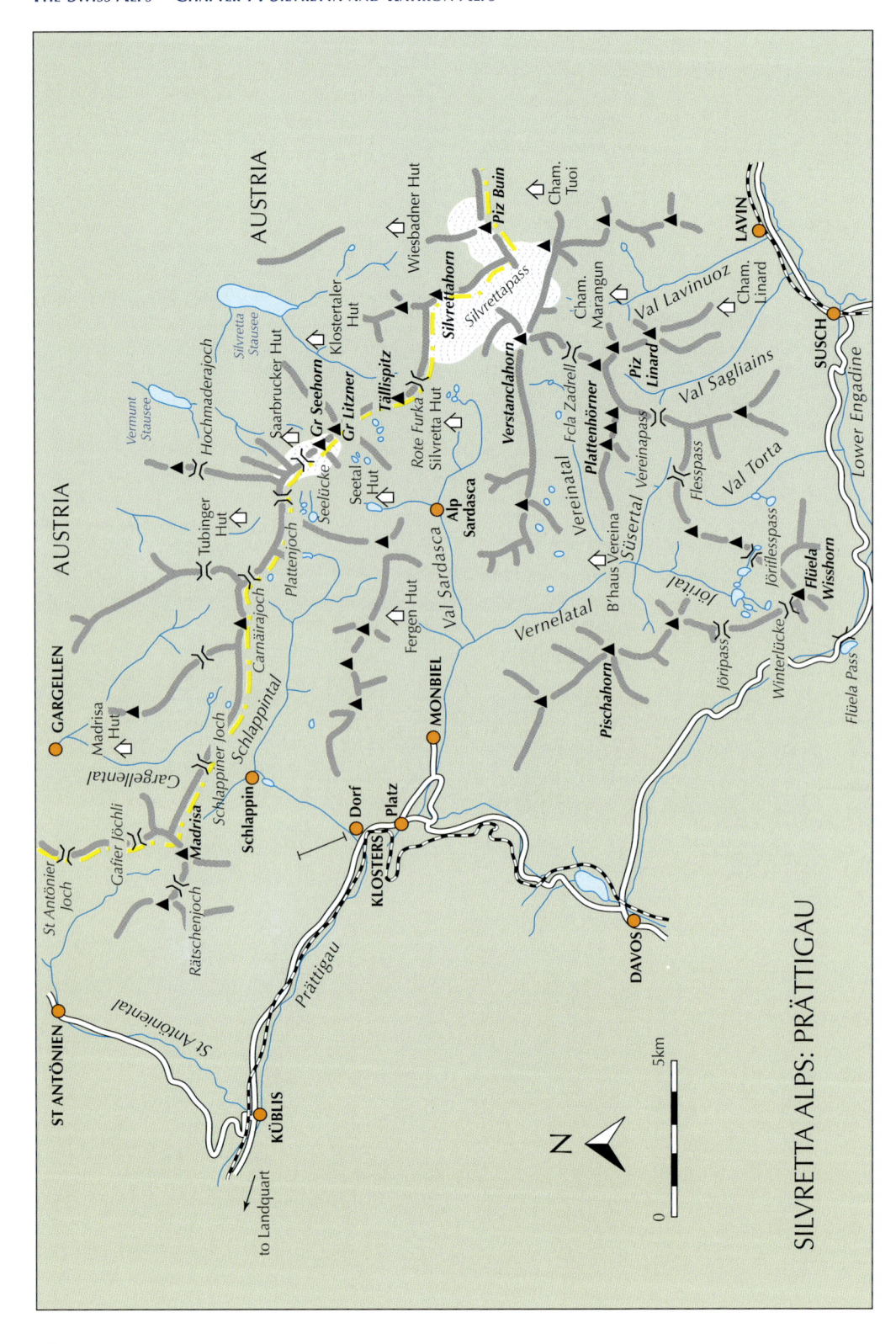

The Swiss Alps – Chapter 7: Silvretta and Rätikon Alps

414

school – Bergsteigerschule Silvretta (tel 081 422 36 36) – and visitors staying overnight in the resort are handed a guest card with which to claim free local transport as well as discounts on cableways and a range of activities. Among lower-priced options for accommodation, a youth hostel stands above the village.

Despite Klosters' reputation as a winter resort, the Silvretta range is not overwhelmed with cableways. Most of these are located on the south side of the valley on the slopes of the Weissfluh, the one exception being the gondola lift from Klosters Dorf to a point below the Madrisa at 1887m which, in summer, marks the start of the delightful **Prättigauer Höhenweg**, described below.

East of Klosters Platz **Val Sardasca** is the main route into the Silvretta Alps for walkers, trekkers and climbers. With the small village of **Monbiel** at its entrance, it's a beautiful valley of meadow and woodland, a few alp farms and lively streams. Local buses journey only as far as Monbiel where the public road ends, but a minibus taxi service operates several times a day during summer as far as Alp Sardasca, about 12km from Klosters railway station (check times and fares at the tourist office).

Alp Sardasca lies at the head of the valley, from where trails climb east to the Silvretta Hut, and north to the tiny Seetal Hut, both of which will be visited later in this chapter.

Vereinatal

About 3km from Monbiel the valley forks. Alp Novai nestles above the confluence of the Verstancla and Vereina streams with spacious woods of Arolla pine lining the hillside. The dirt road leading to Alp Sardasca continues roughly eastward, but another breaks to the south behind the farm to snake up through a gorge before emerging in the **Vereinatal**. This route is also served by minibus taxi (5–6 times a day from Sport Gotschna in Klosters) which goes as far as Berghaus Vereina.

Built in the early 1930s **Berghaus Vereina** stands on a rocky bluff at 1943m marking the junction of the Vernela and Vereina valleys. A comfortable, privately owned inn-like building with 50 dormitory places and restaurant service, it's open from late June until mid-October (tel 081 422 12 16). Unlike SAC huts, there is no winter room. The minibus taxi (Vereina Bus) from Klosters is operated by the *berghaus* owners, and reservations can be

Berghaus Vereina, a mountain inn with atmosphere

made by telephone either via the *berghaus* or by phoning Sport Gotschna (tel 081 422 11 97) in Klosters.

Berghaus Vereina makes a very fine base for walkers wishing to concentrate on this southern corner of the Silvretta Alps, for there are three valleys to explore nearby, and at least six passes and a handful of summits to tempt the more adventurous. West of the *berghaus*, for example, the 2979m **Pischahorn** has a marked route to the summit, while 6km to the south the 3085m **Flüela Wisshorn** (7:1) is by far the most appealing mountain on show, although this is more frequently climbed from the Flüela Pass (see 7:1).

Of the many tempting walks, the easiest is probably the signed **Vereina Rundweg**, but the most popular must surely be that which heads south through the Jöntal to visit the cluster of **Jörisee lakes** that lie below the Wisshorn. The highest of these is reached in about 2–2½hrs, and following a hard or late winter, ice flows can bring an arctic appearance to the area well into summer.

But it is the close proximity of so many passes that makes Berghaus Vereina of particular interest to hillwalkers with a love of trekking, for numerous possibilities arise from study of the relevant maps. The passes, and their ultimate destinations, are listed below, the first three being reached through the Jöntal that extends the Vereinatal south towards the Jörisee lakes and the Flüela Wisshorn.

- The **Jöriflüelafurgga** (2725m), or Jöripass, is located northwest of the lower Jörisee lakes on the west wall of the valley. Over the pass a trail swings south to descend (easily at first, then more steeply) to the Wägerhus bus stop and car park on the Davos side of the Flüela Pass; 4½–5hrs from the hut.
- The 2787m **Winterlücke** lies northwest of the Flüela Wisshorn and is the easiest and most popular of the crossings between the Berghaus Vereina and the Flüela Pass, making a crossing of around 5hrs. The Winterlücke is also used by climbers making the normal ascent of the Wisshorn (see 7:1).
- Southeast of the Jörisee lakes the 2561m **Jöriflesspass** is also an easy crossing, although longer than the previous two because it descends through Val Fless before joining the Flüela Pass road about 5km west of Susch.
- To the east of Berghaus Vereina the Vernelatal rises to a headwall topped by the impressive rock pyramid of the Verstanclahorn and the Chapütschin (or Schwarzkopf). Southwest of the latter peak lies the 2752m **Fuorcla Zadrell**, a lonely but straightforward crossing that descends into Val Lavinuoz on the east side of Piz Linard. As mentioned in 7:1 there's an unmanned hut high in this valley (Chamanna Marangun) from which a track leads all the way to Lavin in the Lower Engadine.
- A short distance from Berghaus Vereina, a path on the east side of the main valley curves southeastward into the uninhabited Süsertal. Towards the head of this tributary, at the top of a steepish climb, the trail forks. The right branch heads south then southwest beyond a few tarns to cross the **Flesspass** at 2453m (1½hrs from the hut). Beyond the pass the way eases through Val Torta to Alp Fless Dadaint where it is then joined by the trail from the Jöriflesspass for the continuing descent to the Flüela road west of Susch.
- The alternative route near the head of the Süsertal rises a little farther north-northeast to gain the 2585m **Vereinapass**, a popular and long-used saddle gained in about 2½hrs from Berghaus Vereina. The West Face of Piz Linard towers over the descent into Val Sagliains where the continuing route follows the right bank of the Sagliains torrent most of the way to Lavin or Susch.

Val Sardasca

As we have seen, a dirt road extends beyond Monbiel above Klosters Platz all the way through Val Sardasca to Alp Sardasca. On the northern hillside, 800m above the river and almost opposite Alp Novai where the road to Berghaus Vereina breaks away, the Prättigau section of the SAC maintains the unmanned **Fergen Hut** at 2141m (www.sac-praettigau.ch). Accessed by a steeply twisting path from the Schwendi chalets, the hut is gained in about 3hrs from Monbiel. With 24 places and self-catering facilities, it lies below the Fergenhörner across whose shoulder a route makes its way into the head of the Schlappintal, where an alternative trail breaks to the east over another ridge to enter the upper reaches of the Seetal.

The Seetal rises immediately to the north of Alp Sardasca. Narrow and steep-walled in its lower third, a turquoise lake lies in its middle section with the **Seetal Hut** nearby (see below), while the upper reaches open to a broad basin of lakes, pools, streams and patches of old snow at around 2500m. A small glacier tapers into this basin from a scoop between the Chlein (3031m) and **Gross Seehorn** (3121m), the latter peak standing astride the Swiss/Austrian border that forms the Seetal's headwall. The frontier ridge continues east of the Gross Seehorn to the spiky finger of the 3109m **Gross Litzner**, a superb pinnacle that, together with the Gross Seehorn, makes a very fine east–west traverse (PD). Thanks to the close proximity of the DAV's Saarbrucker Hut, climbs on these peaks are almost always tackled from the Austrian flank, but the first-ever combined traverse of the Gross Seehorn and Gross Litzner was made from Alp Sardasca by Ludwig Norman-Neruda and Christian Klucker on 24 July 1890, in the same season during which the pair made first ascents of Piz Scerscen (NW Face), Liskamm (NE Face), Piz Roseg (NE Face) and the first Wellenkuppe–Gabelhorn traverse.

This is magnificent wild country. In the headwall two passes give opportunities for cross-border treks. The 2772m **Seelücke** is a glacier saddle lying northwest of the Gross Seehorn, and is useful for climbers based at the **Saarbrucker Hut** on the Austrian side, who have plans for tackling routes on the Seehorn peaks. The **Plattenjoch**, on the other hand, is a rocky pass at 2728m. Gained by a steep scrambly path (fixed cables in several places) from the Seetal, the northern, Austrian, side has the last remnants of the Plattengletscher draped just below it. A small emergency hut is tucked against the Austrian flank just above the pass to the east, while the **Tübinger Hut** can be seen 500m or so below. The Plattenjoch is often used by walkers and climbers as a shortcut between the Tübinger and Saarbrucker Huts, but with the dramatic shrinkage of the Kromer glacier which forms part of the route, it is becoming more difficult and hazardous to access.

Descent of the Seetal is of knee-crunching severity, with almost 1100m height difference between the Plattenjoch and Alp Sardasca. But the variety of vegetation and splendour of the scenery give it added meaning. The apparently barren upper reaches are speckled with alpine flowers; alpenroses splash the middle section above and either side of the Seetal lake with pink and scarlet blooms, while the path in its lower levels is almost swamped with a rampant vegetation.

Just below the lake, and tucked against a huge boulder at 2065m, the **Seetal Hut** is a simple, tiny wooden building with places for 16 – at least, that's the official number. Currently manned from July to the end of September, the hut was built by the Swiss army during the war, but it now belongs to the St Gallen section of the SAC (www.sac-stgallen.ch). From Alp Sardasca it may be reached by a very steep path in about 1½hrs.

At 1646m **Alp Sardasca** marks the end of the motorable track and is where the minibus taxi from Klosters terminates its journey. As a working farm there's no accommodation for visitors, but self-service refreshments are often available. By the side of the alp building a sign directs the way to the Silvretta Hut which stands 700m above and to the east of the alp, and is reached in about 2hrs by a well-made path.

Located above the Medjibach at 2341m with a view to the Silvrettahorn, the **Silvretta Hut** stands at the very heart of the Silvretta Alps. The original hut stood higher up the valley, and when it was built in 1865 it was only the third to be provided by the Swiss Alpine Club, founded just two years earlier. The present building dates from 1904, but has been enlarged and modernised several times since. Today it has places for 75, and is fully staffed from mid-February until early May, and from mid-June until mid-October (www.silvrettahuette.ch).

Glacier shrinkage is clearly evident here, and a nature trail has been created around the area between the hut and the Silvretta glacier to show the effects on landscape and vegetation. A collection of post-glacial lakes add lustre to the scene, and ibex are often sighted. At the head of the glacier the 3244m ❸ **Silvrettahorn** straddles the Swiss-Austrian border. First climbed in 1865 by J Jacot, with the guides Jegen and Schlegel (the trio also made the first ascent of the Gross Litzner in the same season), its most impressive side looks onto the Wiesbadener Hut. A frequently climbed peak, its normal route is only graded F, and summit views are extensive.

But perhaps the most impressive peak to interest the climber based on the Silvretta Hut, is the 3298m ❾ **Verstanclahorn**. Aptly described by Jeff Williams in the West Col guide as a 'three-sided pyramidal rock peak', the fin-like profile of the 3058m secondary summit known as the Verstanclachöpf is also seen from the hut, apparently dwarfing its higher neighbour. Williams

TOUR OF THE SILVRETTA

With a number of non-technical passes connecting so many Silvretta valleys, a tour of the district could be made by experienced walkers using the following outline. It's a fairly tough trek which calls for a degree of scrambling ability and a good head for heights, but as all the huts are manned in summer, it's possible to trek in a lightweight fashion.

Day 1: Either walk from **Klosters**, or take the Vereina Bus taxi to **Berghaus Vereina** (1943m) where the first night is spent.

Day 2: Follow the signed trail into the Süsertal and at its head climb to the 2585m **Vereinapass**. This is gained in about 2½hrs from the *berghaus*. Descend into Val Sagliains and follow a trail downstream until joining a motorable track which leads to **Lavin** (1412m) in the Lower Engadine – a trek of 5–6hrs.

Day 3: On the eastern outskirts of Lavin a track climbs north into Val Lavinuoz. This is used by the long-distance Via Engiadina, a route that eventually curves round the hillside of **Munt da las Muojas** and enters Val Tuoi some way below the Tuoi Hut. An alternative to the Via Engiadina is to follow a good track all the way to **Guarda**, then directly north on another track which pushes through Val Tuoi as far as **Chamanna Tuoi** at 2250m below Piz Buin.

Day 4: This is a demanding day's trek with two passes to cross. The first is the 2735m **Furcletta**, gained in 1½hrs from the hut, the last uphill section being over a chaotic slope of rocks and boulders. Descent into Val d'Urezzas is steep but straightforward, although the way downvalley to its confluence with Val Tasna needs concentration to keep to the route. From Alp Urezzas branch northeast into Val Urschai where a trail loops up the left-hand slope before turning into a wild and rocky hanging valley, at whose head lies the **Pass Fütschol** (2768m) on the Swiss-Austrian border. Descend the northern slope to spend a night in the large **Jamtal Hut** at 2165m.

Day 5: The west wall of the Jamtal is steep and craggy, and after descending from the hut a path picks its way northwestward to the 2965m **Getschnerscharte**, followed by descent into the Bieltal. On reaching the valley stream, cross and immediately climb the opposite slope to gain the easy **Radsattel** (2652m), then head south to the **Wiesbadener Hut** (2443m), with its close view of Piz Buin.

Day 6: Follow the hut's service track all the way to the **Silvretta reservoir** (Silvretta Stausee), and keep to its western side. Shortly before reaching the Bielerhöhe cut left to pass the Madlener Haus and find a narrow path leading into the lower reaches of the Kromertal. From the track which cuts through the valley to the Saarbrucker Hut, cross onto another path that climbs to the **Hochmaderajoch** (2505m), on the west side of which the trail weaves a route through rocky terrain and eventually brings you to the **Tübinger Hut** at 2191m.

Day 7: A steep and direct route climbs from the Tübinger Hut to the 2728m **Plattenjoch** on the frontier ridge. Descent into Switzerland is fairly precipitous at first, with fixed cables and chains to safeguard the way, but it eases lower down as you enter a basin running with streams. This in turn leads to another steep descent and a narrow trail which passes the tiny **Seetal Hut** and continues to Alp Sardasca at the head of Val Sardasca (about 4hrs from the Tübinger Hut). A track then leads all the way down to **Klosters** (in another 3hrs) to complete the circuit. Alternatively, call for a taxi to collect you.

---

claims that there are no easy ways up and the peak is rarely climbed, which adds to its appeal, of course. Jacot and Brosi, with Jegen and Jann as their guides, made the first ascent in 1866, a year after Jacot and Jegen had been together on the Silvrettahorn and Gross Litzner. The NW Ridge,

reached by way of the Verstanclagletscher, is considered the best route (AD).

The frontier ridge forms the north and east rim of the glacier, but at the Egghorn it angles southeastward to link with Piz Buin above Val Tuoi (7:1). South of the Egghorn the broad glacier saddle of the

7:2 SILVRETTA ALPS: PRÄTTIGAU

TOUR OF THE SILVRETTA

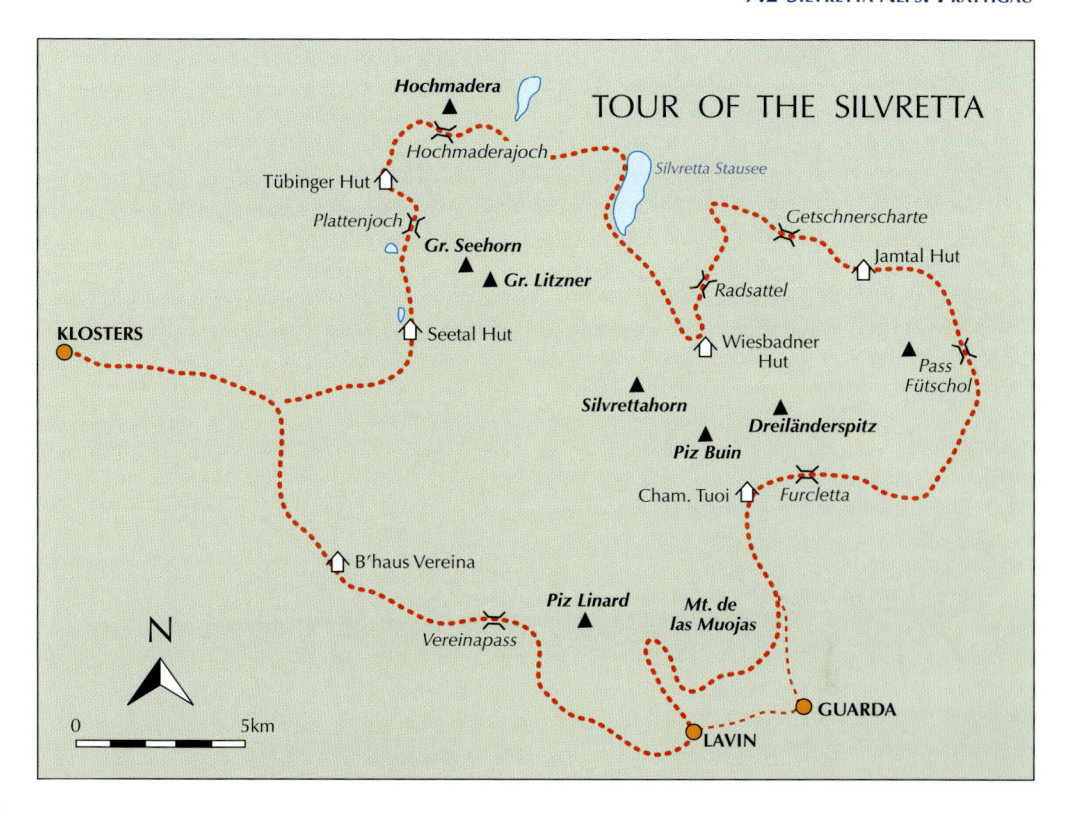

Silvrettapass (3003m) provides a convenient crossing from the Silvretta Hut to the Tuoi Hut. Crevasses demand caution on both sides of the pass, while the steep descent of a rock rib into the head of Val Tuoi can be problematic.

By contrast the path to the much frequented 🍀 **Rote Furka** now avoids the shrinking glacier altogether. Located northeast of the Silvretta Hut, this 2688m pass is regularly used in summer by parties moving between the hut and the Bielerhöhe or Saarbrucker Hut via the Klostertal on the Austrian side of the border. Incidentally, it is worth pointing out that the large **Klostertaler Hut** which stands above the right bank of the Klostertaler Bach, is unmanned, so provisions need to be carried should a night be planned there.

From the Rote Furke an 'alpine route' (blue-white waymarks) follows the ridge northwest to the 2843m summit of the ⛰ ☆ **Tällispitz**, a splendid vantage point from which to study the central Silvretta Alps and much more. The waymarked route continues west of the summit, then descends back to the Silvretta Hut to conclude an entertaining circuit.

Schlappintal

Behind Klosters Dorf the Schlappintal provides a direct way into the mountains. A little over 3km from the village, at the head of the gorge-like Schlappintobel, a small lake is an obvious attraction, beyond which stand the Schlappin chalets where the valley makes an abrupt right-angle turn. Two *gasthofs* provide accommodation with standard beds and dormitories in a romantic setting. Here the valley is wedged between frontier mountains to the north, and to the south a 2800m ridge across which lies Val Sardasca. A few alp farms line the stream, the highest being Inner Säss at 2026m, from where several walking options arise. One of these aims roughly northward to cross the 2489m **Carnäirajoch** into the rocky head of Austria's Garneratal where the **Tübinger Hut** occupies a prominent position east of the pass. Two routes cross the Schlappintal headwall into the upper Seetal, while yet another crosses the south wall of the valley below the Fergenhörner and visits the unmanned **Fergen Hut** before continuing down into Val Sardasca.

But perhaps the route most frequently used is that which continues north of the Schlappin chalets

419

to gain the 🔄 **Schlappiner Joch** (2202m), an old pass on the frontier ridge (1½hrs from Schlappin), beyond which descent is made into the Gargellental that feeds down to the Montafon valley. **Gargellen** is a small resort with a variety of accommodation, but note that the DAV's **Madrisa Hut** which lies between the pass and the village is unmanned and the key only available from Gargellen.

On the Austrian side of the mountains, the **Gargellental** is the longest of the Montafon's tributaries, and its west wall is breached by at least four passes that carry cross-border trails. Not surprisingly it has a long history of travellers and locals crossing between Prättigau and Montafon. In late winter and spring organised ski-mountaineering tours make cross-border raids, and in summer hikers are attracted by prospects of moving from one country to the other and back again.

The mountain that unites Klosters and Gargellen is the 2826m ⬆ **Madrisa** (also known as the Madrisahorn), a triangular rock peak visible from both resorts, although the summit is on the Swiss side of the frontier ridge immediately above Schlappin. The ascent from Schlappin is steep but not unduly difficult, and the summit panorama is said to be far reaching. From it the alignment of the Silvretta chain makes its abrupt northward turn with the western slopes falling into the St Antöniental.

The first breach in the ridge north of Madrisa is the **Gafier Jöchli** (2415m). Not only does a route cross the border here and descend to a chairlift coming from Gargellen, but another trail heads north along the ridge which rises gradually towards the 2515m Gargäller Kopf, before skirting round the peak on the Swiss flank and rejoining the ridge at the **St Antönier Joch**, a popular crossing of 2379m which links St Antönien and Gargellen. From it, and from the trail that continues roughly northward on the Swiss flank all the way to the 2354m **Plasseggenpass**, splendid views are to be had of the big south-facing walls of the Sulzfluh and the Rätikon range spreading off to the west beyond the tranquil St Antöniental.

Two fine 🔄 **walks**, promoted locally, link Klosters and the Schlappintal with St Antönien. The Madrisa gondola lift is recommended to ease the initial climb above Klosters Dorf, for the top station on the Saaser Alp is at an elevation of 1887m, from which both trails begin. The first of these, and the higher option which takes around 5hrs, is a narrow path that strikes uphill into the flower meadows of Chüecalanda to gain the noted viewpoint of the **Rätschenjoch** below the Madrisa's NW Ridge at 2602m. From here the Bundner Alps above Davos are seen to the south, while the Schesaplana, highest of the Rätikon Alps, calls for attention in the northwest. This is the high point of the walk, for the path now eases below the frontier ridge, and after the trail to the Gafier Jöchli breaks away, it sweeps round to the northwest and, with tremendous views all the way, follows the Gafier Bach down to the road a short distance upstream of St Antönien.

The second walk from the Madrisa lift to St Antönien forms the first stage of the multi-day 🔄 ☆ **Prättigauer Höhenweg**. Taking a lower course than the previous route, it is still a very scenic 4hr outing that strays through alpine meadows with haybarns, remote chalets and fine views throughout. From the Madrisabahn top station a short uphill stroll along the path used by the previous route soon reaches the junction with the *höhenweg* at 1937m. The way now contours along the hillside almost 1000m above the river, skirts below the Saaser Calanda and turning a spur overlooks the St Antöniental. With the pale limestone wall of the Rätikon Alps directly ahead, but several kilometres away, the descent to St Antönien leads across the Aschariner Alp, crosses the Alpbach stream and arrives in the village a short distance from the church.

7:3 RÄTIKON ALPS

Little of the Rätikon mountains may be seen from the Prättigau valley, for a range of high hills mostly blocks them from view, except for an occasional brief glimpse that may be had through one of the tributary valleys that suggest ways of approach. The best of these is the St Antöniental whose upper reaches mark the division between the Rätikon and Silvretta Alps. **Küblis** lies at its entrance at a lowly 810m. With a few shops, restaurants, banks and hotels, the village is on the Landquart to Klosters railway line and has postbus connections with St Antönien.

St Antöniental

The road loops up the hillside to Luzein and Pany before slipping into the St Antöniental proper. The valley is narrow, steep-walled and wooded in its lower reaches, but after passing through St Antönien

St Antönien, a small but attractive village at the foot of the Rätikon mountains

Ascharina with a hint of good things to come, it opens out at **St Antönien Platz** (commonly referred to simply as St Antönien), a small but attractive village flanking the road at 1420m, about 11km from Küblis. Formerly avalanche-prone, most of the buildings have been tucked into or against the northern slope, and a barrier of protective fences has been erected high above on the face of the Chüenihorn. Although tiny, the village has a few shops, including a small supermarket, a tourist office (www.st-antoenien.ch), a restaurant or two and a handful of hotels and *gasthäuser* with low-priced dormitory accommodation. Some bus routes terminate here, a few continue a short distance beyond.

With plenty of footpaths striking away from the village, and lots of climbing opportunities at the head of the valley, St Antönien serves as a base for activists with their own transport (there's a fairly large parking area near the head of the road south of Partnun). Most walks, however, involve mounting the steep hillsides directly above the village, one of the best of which leads to the shallow **Carschinasee** at 2180m (in 2½hrs), with a continuation to the **Carschina Hut** at the foot of the Sulzfluh in a further 40mins. First climbed in 1782 (by J B Catani and L Pool) the Sulzfluh is an impressive block of limestone whose summit cross, seen from the approach to the hut, is at 2817m.

Out of St Antönien the road continues upvalley for another 5km as far as **Partnun**, a hamlet at 1763m where Berghaus Sulzfluh (www.sulzfluh.ch) and Berghaus Alpenrösli (www.berghaus-alpenroesli.ch) are located below the SE Face of the Sulzfluh. Both establishments have beds and dormitory places and are set among fine walking country, with routes that lead to the **Partnunsee** tarn and several passes on the frontier ridge, as well as providing access to dozens of mostly short sport climbs on the **Gruoben/Grüenwändli Klettergarten** between the Grüenfürggli and Tilisunafürggli, and a variety of routes on the **Schijenflue** and Chlein Venedig.

Gained by a walk from Partnun which goes via the Partnunsee and crosses either the 2319m Grüenfürggli or 2226m Tilisunafürggli, the Austrian Alpine Club's **Tilisuna Hut** lies just across the border. From the hut a popular and highly recommended walker's route climbs the ☆ **Sulzfluh** (2817m) by way of a large area of limestone pavement.

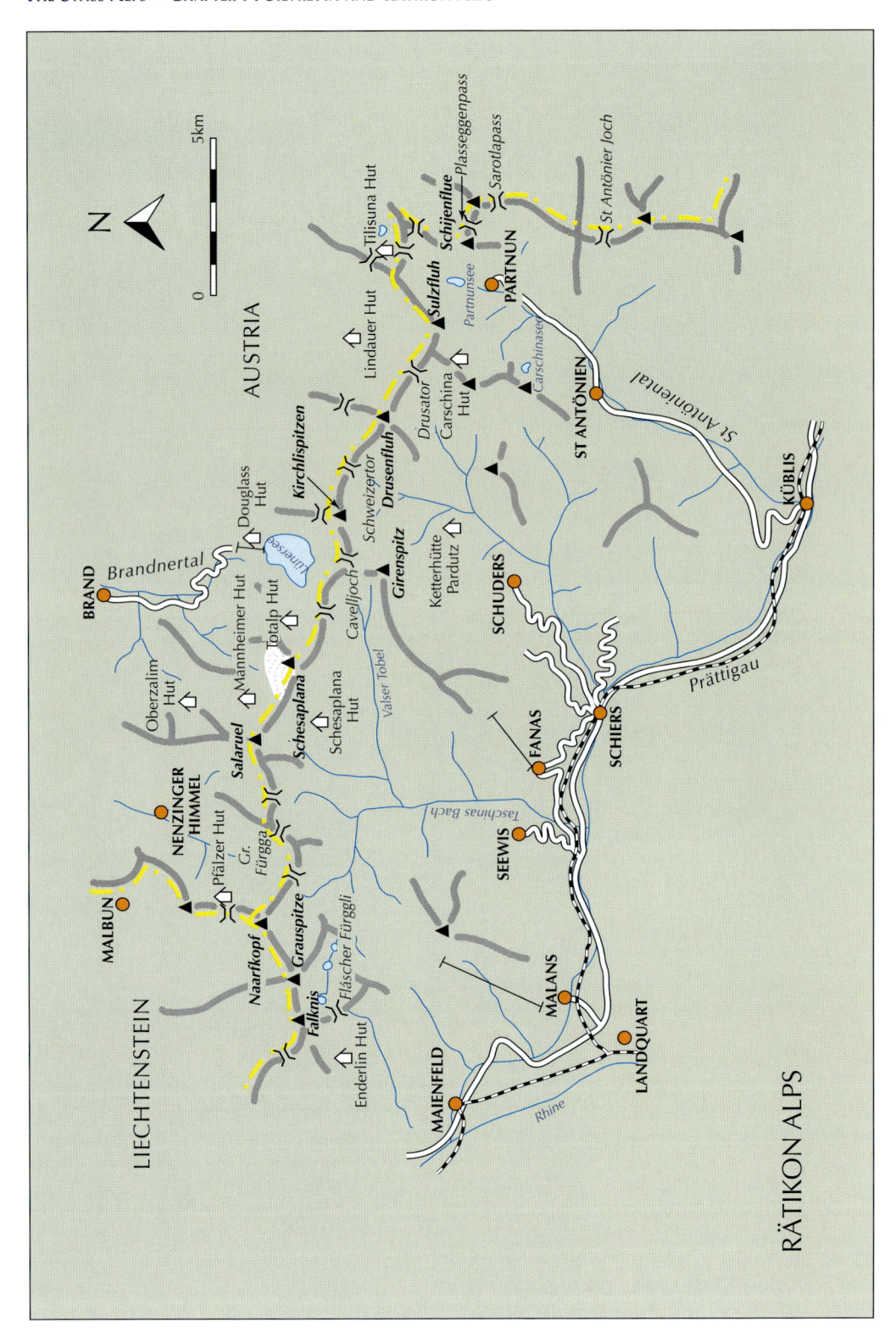

The Swiss Alps – Chapter 7: Silvretta and Rätikon Alps

The Carschina Hut, dwarfed by walls of the Sulzfluh

A short distance above Partnun's Alpenrösli *berghaus* a bridge spans the stream coming down from the Partnunsee. On the west side of the bridge a narrow path strikes up a steep grass slope towards the Sulzfluh whose wall grows both in bulk and challenge the closer you draw to it. At a junction below the SE Face one trail breaks towards the head of the valley, while the left branch continues to the SAC's **Carschina Hut** at 2236m. With 85 places, this comfortable hut is fully staffed from mid-June until the middle of October (www.carschinahuette.ch). Sometimes spelt Garschina, it has a direct view across the screes to the Sulzfluh's South Face, so it makes a perfect base for climbs on that face, as well as for some of the hardest routes which are to be found on the mountain's southwest flank. The hut is also handy for the 🄑 ⭐ **Sulzfluh Klettersteig**. The start of this *via ferrata* is found nearby at around 2360m, which gives a 450m height difference to the summit, and 2½–3hrs of protected climbing in magnificent surroundings (see www.klettersteigsulzfluh.ch).

A few paces along the track below the hut the Carschinafurgga saddle gathers several trails. One heads south to the Carschinasee, another winds down to the St Antöniental, yet another crosses the saddle and works towards the limestone block of the **Drusenfluh** (2830m). Confined between the Drusator at its southeastern end, and the deep gash of the Schweizertor to the northwest, this massif appears from a distance to be a single flat-topped mountain, but on closer acquaintance it reveals a number of individual towers and turrets, with splinters and pinnacles of rock standing below or projecting from it. Seen from the Austrian flank (gained by crossing the 2342m **Drusator** en route to the Lindauer Hut), the mountain is best known for the Drei Türm – a popular *klettergarten* with over 60 routes. Although the Swiss side would surely repay the close attention of rock climbers, the north flank has won most of the plaudits here.

But if rock climbing is not your scene, the trail that sweeps across the screes, spurs and small grasslands at the foot of the Drusenfluh on the Swiss flank is not only scenically uplifting, but weaves its way among a host of exquisite natural rock gardens that in early summer splash both colour and fragrance across the landscape. The full day's walk from the 🄒 ⭐ **Carschina Hut to the Schesaplana Hut**, adopted by the Prättigauer

The Drusenfluh

Höhenweg mentioned in 7:2, is worth every adjective heaped upon it.

At the western end of the Drusenfluh block overlooking the great U-shaped cleft of the Schweizertor, the SW Face of the ☆ **Schweizereck** holds some quality sport climbs that give 6–9 pitch routes of up to 350m, among them Austrian Beat Kammerlander's classic New Age (8a) which dates from 1988.

West of the Schweizertor the precipitous 2.5km long wall of the multi-summited ☆ **Kirchlispitzen** towers above the trail to the Schesaplana Hut. With in excess of 50 routes to consider, this playground is home to Pardutzerweg (8-), Galadriel (8-) and Kammerlander's The Endless Story which, when it was climbed in 1991, was claimed to be the hardest in the Alps, with five pitches of 6c to 7a+, three of 7c, two of 8a, and one of 8b+.

The normal approach to climbs on the Kirchlispitzen and Schweizereck is via **Schiers** in the Prättigau, from where a motorable track rises along the true right flank of the Schraubach's valley and passes through **Schuders** before terminating some way below the Schweizertor. An unmanned climber's hut, **Kletterhütte Pardutz** provides self-catering accommodation. Owned by the Rätikon Kletterclub, it has 24 places, and advanced booking is essential (www.kcr-online.ch).

☆ TOUR OF THE RÄTIKON

Before continuing into the Western Rätikon, it is worth giving an outline of a circular tour of the district. This itinerary joins the Rätikon Höhenweg Sud (which makes a traverse of the Swiss side of the mountains) with the better-known Rätikon Höhenweg Nord on the Austrian flank, thereby creating a superb six-day loop trek.

Day 1: The tour begins in **St Antönien** at 1420m and makes a gruelling ascent of the steep west flank of the St Antöniental to reach the picturesque Carschinasee, which lies some 700m above where you started. Since it will take less than an hour to reach the Carschina Hut from there, it's tempting to spend a lazy hour or two enjoying the lake, its flowers and views before moving on. Shortly after leaving the lake the Sulzfluh is revealed, and it seems to grow in stature as you draw nearer. The **Carschina Hut** stands below the mountain's South Face at 2236m, and it will have taken just a morning's walk to get there.

Day 2: A longer, and in some ways a more demanding stage than Day 1 takes the route northwestward below the great limestone walls of the Drusenfluh and Kirchlispitzen through a magical region that could be described as Nature's own alpine garden. (This section is identical to that of the Prättigauer Höhenweg described below.) Several options are available for crossing into Austria along the way, but the tour described here remains on the Swiss slope as far as the **Schesaplana Hut** at 1908m.

Day 3: Strong walkers with scrambling ability and a good head for heights could climb the **Schesaplana** on the Swiss-Austrian border and descend to the **Totalp Hut** to make a challenging day's trek. Another option would be to backtrack towards the east and climb a very steep path to cross the airy 2378m **Gamsluggen** for a direct route to the Totalp Hut or, as recommended here, reverse yesterday's route as far as the **Cavelljoch**, then descend into Austria to spend the night at the **Douglass Hut** (1976m) at the northern end of the Lünersee reservoir (tel 05559 206).

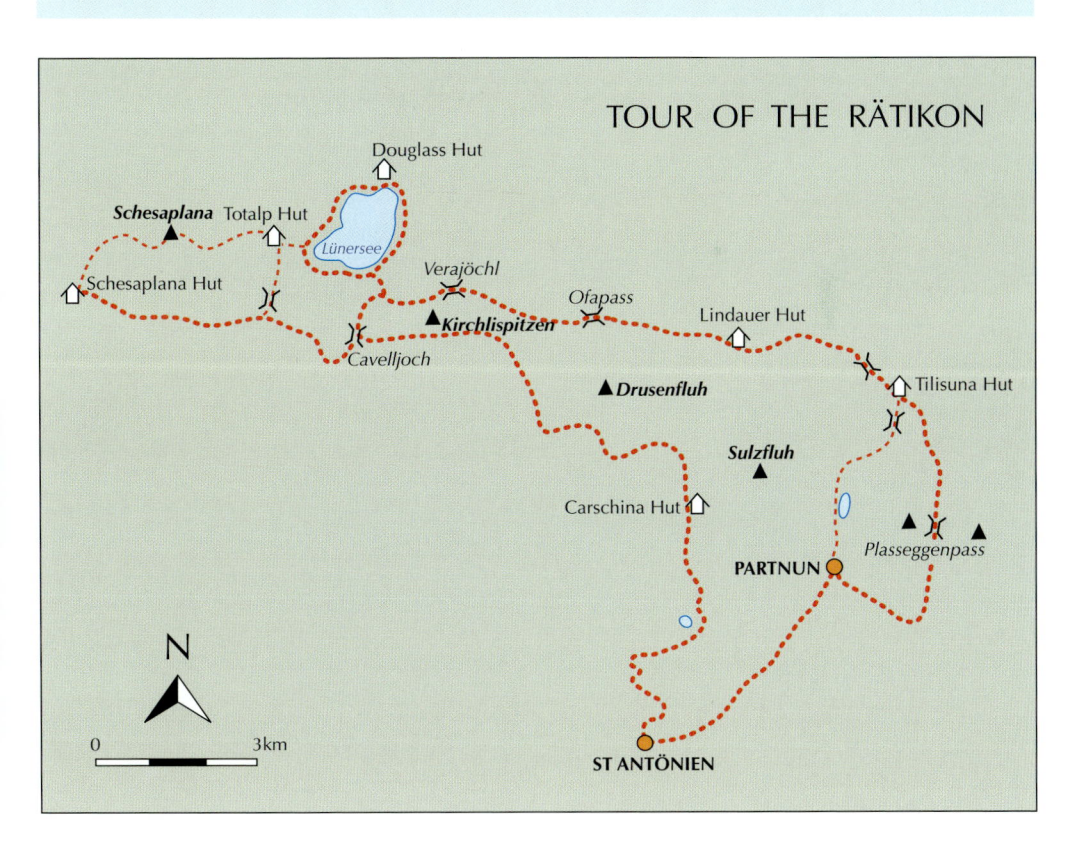

Day 4: In Austria throughout this stage, the Rätikon Höhenweg Nord returns the tour to the southern end of the Lünersee, skirts below the Cavelljoch and climbs to the **Verajöchl** at 2330m. It then descends to the great cleft of the Schweizertor, through which you have a fine view south to the distant ranges of the Bündner Alps, before climbing easily to the **Ofapass** (2291m). From the pass the bustling **Lindauer Hut** (1744m) may be detected nestling among trees in the valley ahead. It will take another

hour or so to reach it (for reservations tel 0664 5033456). The hut has a very pleasant outlook with the Sulzfluh and Drei Türm of the Drusenfluh on show as well as a fine alpine garden.

Day 5: The Tilisuna Hut is the destination for this stage of the trek, and once again it remains in Austria and will only take a morning to walk there via the steep Bilkengrat which leads to a saddle on a spur pushing north from the Sulzfluh. Unseen from here, the **Tilisuna Hut** lies below and to the south of this saddle at 2211m (tel 0664 1107969), and as you should arrive there by midday, it would be worth making the easy but rewarding ascent of the **Sulzfluh** in the afternoon – given decent conditions, that is.

Day 6: Several passes are easily accessible from the Tilisuna Hut, offering ways back into Switzerland. Probably the most direct of these is the **Tilisunafürggli** to the south which has a trail descending to the Partnunsee at the head of the St Antöniental. But perhaps the best, albeit longest, option is to continue on the Höhenweg Nord to the 2354m **Plasseggenpass**, and descend south and west through a hanging valley at the foot of which lies **Partnun**. From there join the Prättigauer Höhenweg as it descends through meadows on the west bank of the river on the return to **St Antönien**.

Fixed chains on an exposed section of the Gamsluggen

The Western Rätikon

From the Schweizertor the walker's route used by the Prättigauer Höhenweg rises under the soaring Kirchlispitzen crags to gain a grassy shoulder, then cuts across the broad scree apron that falls from the South Face of the mountain, and arrives at the **Cavelljoch** (2239m) on the Austrian border. This fine saddle marks the western extent of the Kirchlispitzen wall and offers contrasting views. Below to the north lies the Lünersee reservoir, beyond which stretches the Brandnertal, but south of the *joch* green hillsides fall away to the Schaubach's valley, while a short and rather exposed continuation of the path leads to yet another saddle on a spur whose highest point is the 2394m **Girenspitz**, on whose west side lies the Valser Tobel overlooked by the ☆ **Schesaplana**.

This is the highest of the Rätikon Alps at 2964m. First climbed in 1730 it's a mountain that wears several different faces. The Swiss flank is a long broken wall of steep limestone. The Austrian side above the **Totalp Hut** is made up of rocky ribs separating scoops and basins that collect snow and hold onto it well into summer, while the NW Face falls into the only glacial remnant west of the Silvretta range. Looking onto the Brandner glacier is the DAV's **Mannheimer Hut**, from which a route leads to the SW Ridge, where it is joined by the direct route from the Schesaplana Hut on the Swiss side of the mountain. This Swiss route is a scramble of about 3½hrs from hut to cross-marked summit, but the standard route from the Totalp Hut is the easiest and most popular option, and on a fine summer's day it records scores of ascents.

A challenging 2hr linking route between the Totalp and Schesaplana Huts crosses the frontier ridge south of the Totalp Hut at the 2378m **Gamsluggen**, a narrow section of ridge with a very steep descent on the Swiss side, the upper sections of this being along narrow ledges protected by fixed chains, and with considerable exposure.

The **Schesaplana Hut** consists of two main buildings set on a slope of pasture below the steep crags of its eponymous peak at 1908m. Owned by the Pfannenstiel section of the SAC, it's a busy hut with 90 dormitory places and a full meals service when manned, which is usually from June until mid-October (www.schesaplana-huette.ch). From it there's a clear view of the final section of the Rätikon ridge as it spreads westward before falling to the Rhine's confluence with the Seez near Sargans.

As far as the 2570m Naarfkopf that ridge carries the border with Austria, after which it is Liechtenstein that shares the crest with Switzerland. The tiny Principality of Liechtenstein is said to be the world's sixth smallest country, but per capita must surely be one of the richest. The Rhine forms its western boundary, while Austria marks its eastern (and longest) border. The Rätikon mountains spread into and across the Principality, whose valleys are divided by a series of ridges and spurs, and whose highest peak is the **Grauspitze** (2599m) with its summit straddling the Swiss border. Liechtenstein has just two mountain refuges: the 80-bed **Pfälzer Hut** (www.alpenverein.li) which sits on the Bettlerjoch at 2108m, and is reached by an entertaining walk of about 3–3½hrs from the Schesaplana Hut, and the Gafadura Hut located north of the Drei Schwestern at 1428m. With 55 places, it is reached by a walk of about 1½hrs from Planken (for information email: liechtensteiner@alpenverein.li).

Liechtenstein has one small ski resort at **Malbun** (1600m), and various cross-country ski routes heading out from Steg which lies some way below Malbun. A number of walking trails and tracks head up into the mountains from both places, a few of which take advantage of accessible cols to cross into either Austria or Switzerland. One favoured route links Malbun with the Schesaplana Hut by way of the Pfälzer Hut (where a tempting path mounts the ridge to the south to gain the summit of the ☆ **Naarfkopf**), followed by an exposed section on the Austrian side of the mountains where the path is tucked against steep crags with fixed cable safeguards, then across two bands of pink limestone towards the Barthumeljoch. The Schesaplana route passes just below this saddle, but it's worth straying to it to enjoy views onto the Maienfelder Alp on the Swiss flank, before sweeping round to the 2359m **Gross Furgga** from which the Schesaplana Hut can be seen.

The final stage of the Prättigauer Höhenweg leaves the Schesaplana Hut initially heading west, instead of making a direct descent towards the main Prättigau valley where the route ends. Contouring round the upper slopes of the **Valser Tobel**, it changes direction at the Stürfis chalets on the Maienfelder Alp, cutting back and descending now to the Canibach, which it then crosses and heads south along the true right flank of the valley as far as **Seewis** (947m), from where it's possible to catch a bus into the main valley below.

The Maienfelder Alp west of the Stürfis chalets has a string of three lakes in the little Fläscher Tal directly below the Grauspitze. These lakes feed a stream that flows eastward to join the Canibach, but above and to the west of the upper lake the **Fläscher Fürggli** (2247m) marks a junction of trails. One of these goes up onto the Rätikon crest at the 2452m **Mazorakopf** and the higher ☆ **Falknis** (2562m) – the latter a noted viewpoint from which not only is the full length of the Rätikon Alps on show, but also the Rhine's valley stretching from Chur to the Bodensee. The other trail at the

The Swiss Alps – Chapter 7: Silvretta and Rätikon Alps

The Rätikon Alps, seen from the slopes of Schesaplana

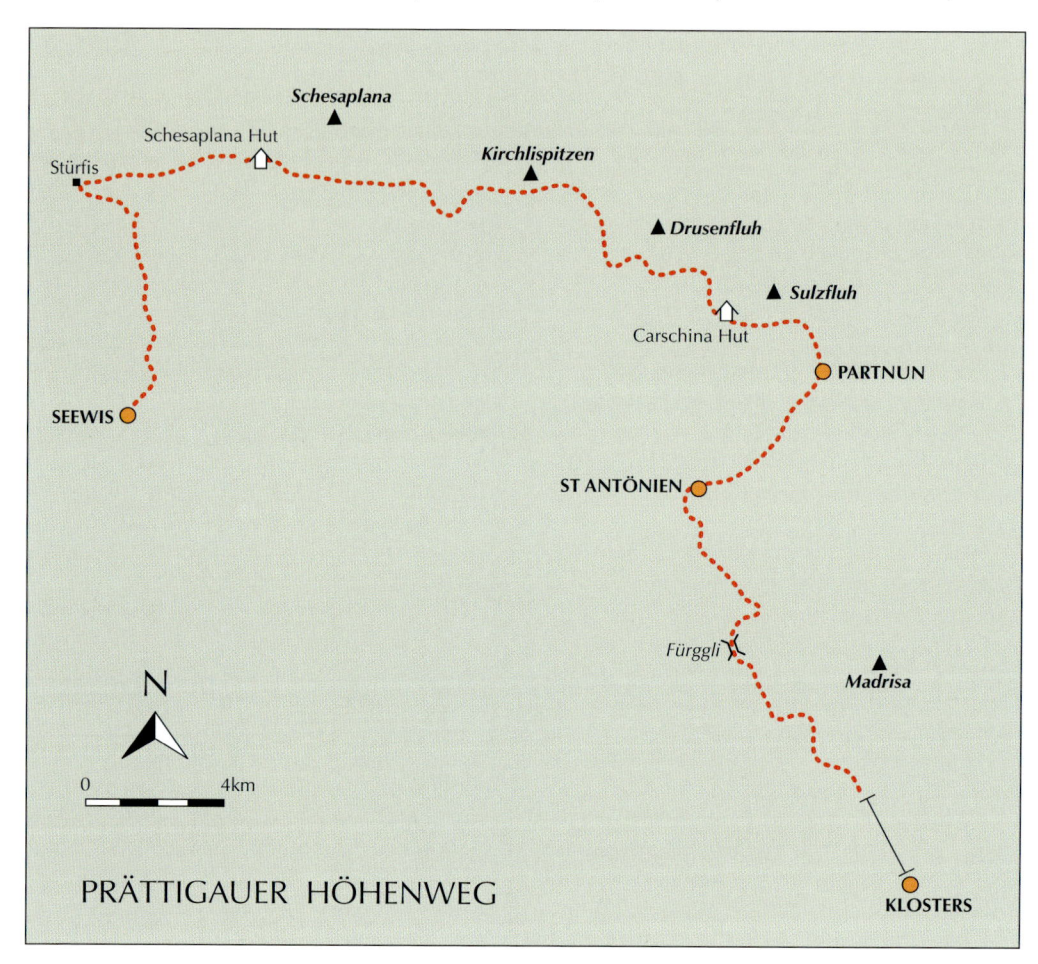

PRÄTTIGAUER HÖHENWEG

⚑ ☆ PRÄTTIGAUER HÖHENWEG

Making a 68km traverse of the Rätikon's south side, this four-day trek is a scenic trail with a few steep ascents and descents, but no major difficulties. Signed and waymarked throughout it begins on the edge of the Silvretta range above Klosters and culminates at Seewis towards the western end of the Prättigau valley.

Day 1: Take the Madrisabahn gondola lift from **Klosters Dorf** to the upper station at Untersäss on the Saaser Alp and go up the slope a short way to pick up the *höhenweg* heading roughly west then northwest. Passing below the Saaser Calanda, the path veers more to the north to cross the **Fürggli** saddle at 2255m, before descending into the Aschariner Alp. The way then swoops down into the St Antöniental to spend a night in **St Antönien** (1420m).

Day 2: The first kilometre or so of this stage goes upvalley alongside the road, before taking a rising footpath through a series of meadows and light woodland as far as **Partnun** at the roadhead. It then climbs a very steep hillside heading northwest towards the base of the Sulzfluh, before easing along another path which breaks to the left on the way to the **Carschina Hut** (2236m).

Day 3: This is a magnificent, if rather energetic, stage that follows an undulating course below the Drusenfluh, Kirchlispitzen and outliers of the Schesaplana massif, crossing grass slopes and screes, and weaving among beautiful rock gardens. The physical high point of the day is a 2297m saddle southwest of the Cavelljoch, after which the trail enters a pastoral landscape below the long ridge system that supports the Schesaplana. Overnight is spent in the SAC's **Schesaplana Hut** at 1908m.

Day 4: The final stage of the *höhenweg* begins by contouring round the head of the Stägertobel valley and continuing westward to the chalets of **Stürfis**. The way then swings round to the east, descends to the Canibach, and keeps to the west side of its valley on a long walk south as far as **Seewis** (947m). This village has a bus link with the Prättigau valley.

Fläscher Fürggli breaks to the south and southwest on a descent to the often unmanned, timber-built **Enderlin Hut** standing among trees at 1498m. This hut has 40 places, is the property of the Piz Sol section of the SAC (based in Buchs on the Rhine west of Liechtenstein) and when staffed has meals provision – but check first (www.sac-piz-sol.ch). A trail descends steeply from the hut, eventually spilling out to **Maienfeld** where novelist Johanna Spyri based her children's story *Heidi*. The tourist authority milks the connection for all its worth, and has even named the district Heidiland – cringeworthy or cute? Take your pick. At least the Rätikon Alps can rise above it all.

7:4 THE ALPSTEIN MASSIF

The mainline railway from Zürich to Landquart or Chur at first runs alongside the crowded shoreline of the Zürichsee, after which there's a stretch of countryside before a second lake attracts attention out of the left-hand window. Though considerably shorter than the Zürichsee, the Walensee is a much more impressive lake, for on its far side mountains rise in dramatic fashion to produce a fjord-like appearance, and as the train makes progress above its southern shore, so that sheer mountain wall to the north displays an extraordinary wave-like crest. This is the Churfirsten, an outlier of the Alpstein massif.

The Alpstein is a compact group of limestone mountains whose modest height appears much more impressive than it really is, since the peaks tower over verdant hills and low-lying valleys with traditional farms, grazing cattle and orchards of fruit trees. Consisting of three parallel ridges aligned roughly southwest to northeast, their intervening valleys contain attractive alpine meadows and lakes. Huts and mountain inns are plentiful, the district is criss-crossed by numerous walking trails, and there's no shortage of good climbing to be had, especially on the Altmann, southeast of the Säntis, and the Kreuzberg overlooking the Rhine valley. But it is the **Säntis** that attracts most visitor attention here, thanks not only to cable-car access from **Schwägalp** (www.saentisabahn.ch) where there's also a 3-star *berghotel* at the

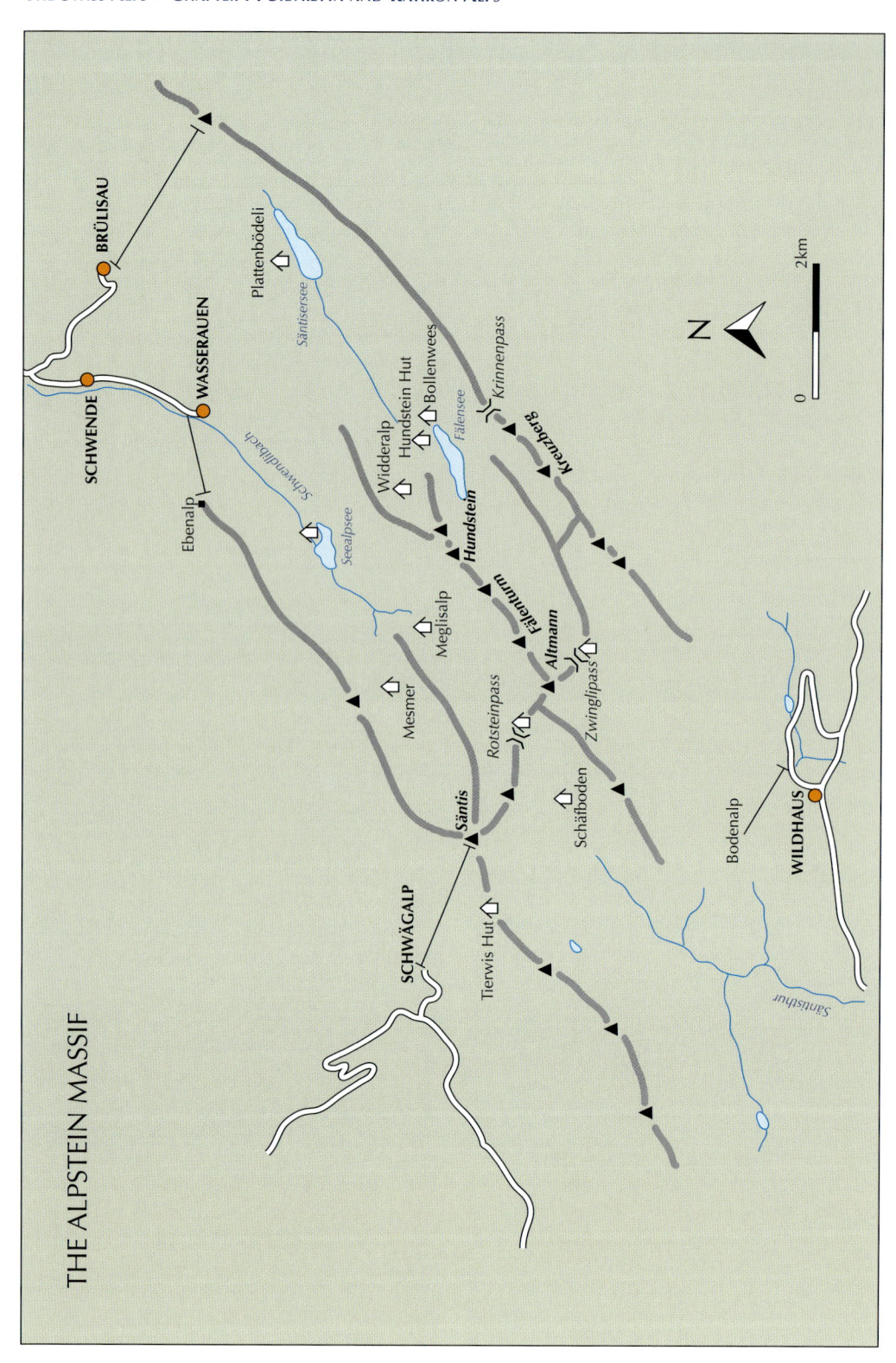

THE SWISS ALPS – CHAPTER 7: SILVRETTA AND RÄTIKON ALPS

THE ALPSTEIN MASSIF

430

Seealpsee with the distant Säntis

western foot of the mountain, but to the various walker's trails that approach from virtually every direction.

Effectively cut off from the Rätikon mountains by the flat-bottomed trench of the Rhine's valley which runs roughly northward from Sargans to the Bodensee (Lake Constance), access to the Alpstein is easy enough by public transport, for the district is almost completely ringed by railway lines, with bus services filling the gaps. To the north St Gallen is the terminus of a main line from Zürich, with branch lines pushing their tentacles closer to the mountains, one of which terminates at Urnäsch for connections with the Schwägalp bus, while Appenzell (www.appenzell.ch), the village-sized capital of the half-canton of Appenzell-Innerhoden, is the place to aim for on the northern side of the range. From here, **Wasserauen** (train) and **Brülisau** (postbus) are the main trailheads for walks into the heart of the district, while **Ebenalp** (cable car from Wasserauen) has easy access to a line of crags for numerous sport climbs, as well as many fine walks. For a southern approach Buchs, about 10km north of Sargans, has rail connections not only with Zürich, but also with the Austrian state railway system. From it buses climb 600m up the Werdenberg hills to Wildhaus in the upper Toggenburg (Thur valley).

Wildhaus (1090m) is without question the best centre on this side of the Alpstein, although Unterwasser and Alt St Johann further downvalley are also popular. A modest little resort with just a handful of hotels, a campsite, bank, a few shops and tourist information (www.toggenburg.org), Wildhaus's location between the Alpstein and Churfirsten makes it an obvious choice. Low-key skiing is practised on the Churfirsten slopes to the south, but long distance walking routes such as the 87km Toggenburger Höhenweg and 115km Rheintal Höhenweg touch on the village, yet it is the Säntis that not surprisingly forms the main summer attraction for active visitors.

⛰ ★ SÄNTIS: KING OF THE APPENZELLER ALPS

In alpine terms the 2502m Säntis is a pretentious dwarf, yet it is without doubt the best-known mountain of northeastern Switzerland, and a much-loved local icon with impressive rock walls, a variety of ridges and a justifiably famous summit panorama. Crowning the most westerly of the three extensive ridges of the Alpstein massif, it is said that on the proverbial clear day the Säntis is visible from as far away as Neuchâtel, while summit views apparently include the Zugspitze in Germany, Monte Rosa above Zermatt, and the Jungfrau. Sadly, a monstrous red and white banded telecommunications tower rises from what must be the most cluttered summit in the Alps, on which there's also a restaurant, art gallery, cable car station and the Berghaus Säntis (www.berggasthaus-saentis.ch). A weather station was built there in 1879.

Despite the summit clutter and the inevitable crowds who visit by cable car from Schwägalp, the mountain is worth ascending. There are many routes to choose from, and from whichever side the mountain is approached a rewarding day out can be guaranteed. The following selection should be suitable for all experienced hillwalkers, and on most, if not all approaches, huts or inns offer refreshments and accommodation.

From Wildhaus (1090m) in the south at least three routes are worth considering: one of which makes for the West Ridge at 2085m before heading for the summit; the most direct and steepest route takes a narrow path a short way above Berghaus Schäfboden (4–4½hrs); and a third tackles the classic Lisengrat (exposed but protected) from the Rotsteinpass where there's another hut (4½–5hrs from Wildhaus to summit).

From the Schwägalp cable car station at 1352m (reached by a spur off the St Johann to Urnäsch road), the dramatically impressive West Wall of the mountain has a route aided by ladders and protective ropes, which tops a ridge near the **Tierwis Hut** (Berggasthaus Tierwis: www.tierwis.ch) at 2085m, then cuts along the flank to a point where the ridge is regained for a final steep climb (more fixed ropes) to the summit – about 3hrs from Schwägalp.

From Wasserauen railway station (868m) northeast of the Säntis, an easy and very popular route begins by walking through the valley of the Schwendlibach to the Seealpsee, where there's accommodation, continues on a track to Seealp, then begins the ascent proper via Berghaus Mesmer, Fälalp and the Wagenlücke (5–5½hrs).

At the eastern end of the exposed but protected Lisengrat (known locally as the Grützi Weg because of the frequent greetings from walkers who tackle it), the 2120m saddle of the Rotsteinpass gives access to the **Altmann**, at 2436m the third highest of the Alpstein summits and a focus for a number of climbing opportunities. The privately owned **Berggasthaus Rotsteinpass** makes a useful base. With 90 places, the hut is often open from January to the end of March, and from mid-June until the end of October (www.rotsteinpass.ch). There's also a hut on the 1999m Zwinglipass, below the southeast flank of the Altmann, which is easily accessible from Wildhaus in less than 3hrs. The **Zwinglipass Hut** is owned by the Toggenburg section of the SAC, it has 42 places and is manned from mid July until the middle of August, and occasionally staffed at other periods between May and the end of October, but note that apart from soup meals are not provided. There are, of course, self-catering facilities (info: tel 071 988 02).

First climbed in 1825, the ❾ **Altmann** is noted for its comparatively big South Face which has numerous routes created on the limestone slabs, among them the mountain's first grade 8, the five-pitch Allegro ma non Troppo put up in 1987 by Christof and Markus Meier, and the six-pitch Schnodernasenweg (grade 7) dating from 1983 (Ruedi Abderhalden, Peter Diener and Thomas Utelli).

With access from the Rotsteinpass via the Altmannsattel, the very popular but easy normal route focuses on the north flank, but more challenging climbs will be found on the NW Buttress where some good modern routes exist – see *Kletterführer Alpstein* for guidance (published in German). The Altmann chain spreads northeastwards over the Fälenturm, Rotturm and Hundstein to culminate in

The Kreuzberge, seen from the Saxenlücke

the 2058m Widderalpstöck, thereby extending the range of climbing opportunities, while the easternmost crest of the Alpstein is noted for the eight turrets of the ragged 🚶 **Kreuzberge**. Here the rock is mostly excellent, with a huge variety of routes to choose from, and airy views into the Rhine's valley 1600m below the summits are said to be spectacular. Berggasthaus accommodation is plentiful to allow for fairly short approach walks.

Churfirsten

Writing in the 1901 edition of his guide to Switzerland, Baedeker described the Walensee as being 'hardly inferior to the Lake of Lucerne in grandeur. The N bank' he continued, 'consists of precipices, 2000' to 3000' high, above which rise the barren peaks of the Curfirsten (sic).' These peaks are anything but barren when viewed from the Toggenburg valley, for their north flank is a long sweep of pastureland dotted with farm buildings and criss-crossed with marked trails. In winter it becomes a ski playground with cableways rising above Wildhaus, Unterwasser and Alt St Johann. Even the 'precipices' above the Walensee are not quite what Baedeker suggested, for the south facing wall of the Churfirsten rises in tiers, between which a road snakes its way from Walenstadt to Walenstadtberg and continues heading west among farms, holiday homes and a restaurant lodged midway between the lake and the summits. However, the upper rock walls are impressively steep and make an obvious attraction for climbers.

The Churfirsten chain consists of seven individual peaks running more or less in an east to west alignment: **Chäserrugg** (2262m), **Hinderugg**, the highest at 2306m, **Schibenstoll** (2234m), **Zuestoll** (2235m), **Brisi** (2279m), **Frümsel** (2263m) and **Selun** (2205m). After Selun the chain curves to the southwest where four further peaks continue the line: **Wart** (2068m), **Schären** (2171m), **Nägeliberg** (2163m) and lastly, the **Leistchamm** (2101m). Each of the main summits can be reached by walkers coming from the north, but the south side, with its magnificent rock strata, remains the preserve of the climber, for whom the most obvious base is the little town of **Walenstadt** (www.walenstadt.ch) which lies at the eastern end of the Walensee and has a station on the Zürich to Sargans railway line.

🚶 **Brisi** has the highest and broadest face of all the Churfirsten, with routes up to 500m in

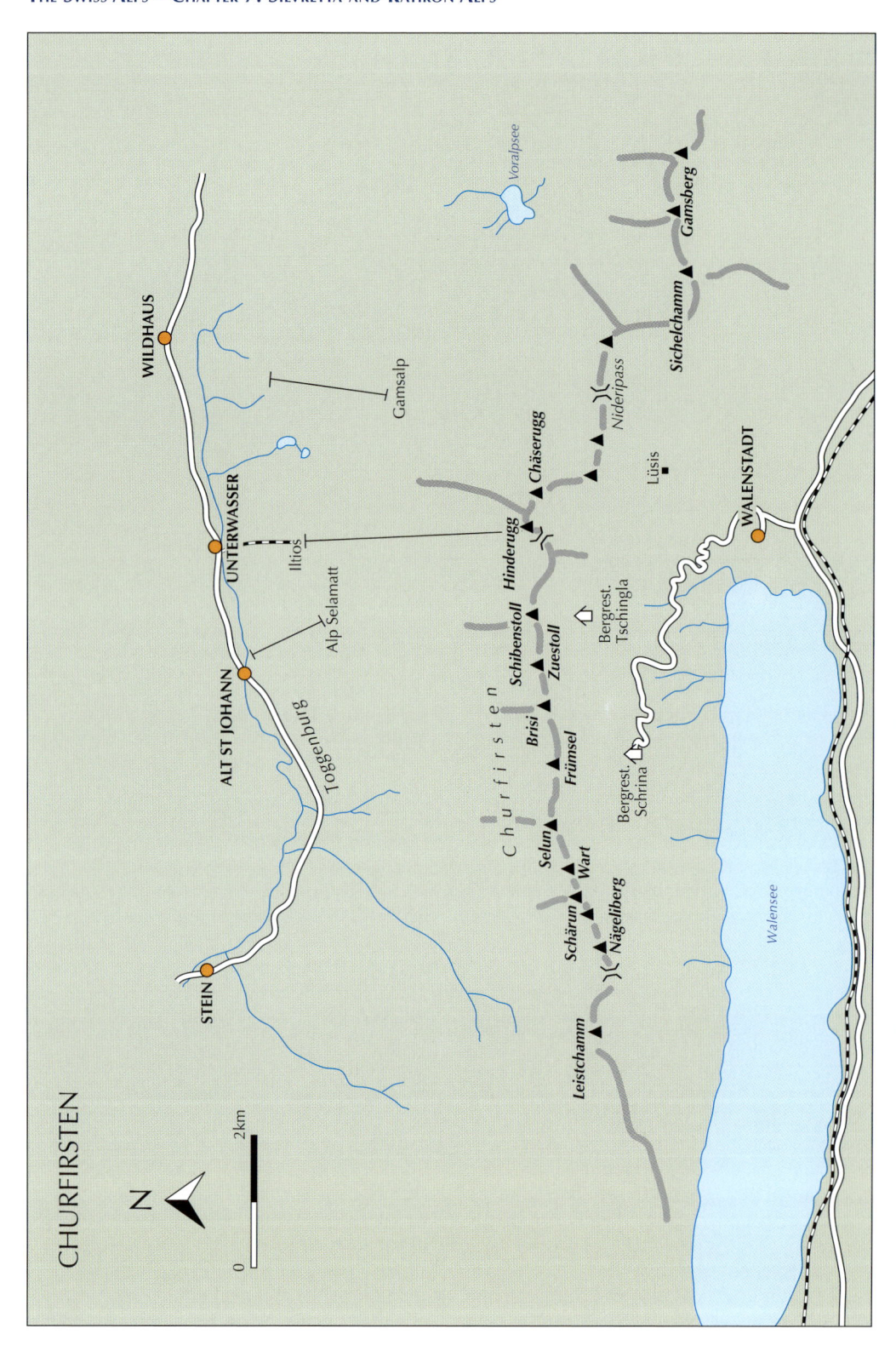

The Swiss Alps – Chapter 7: Silvretta and Rätikon Alps

Churfirsten

length. Access is via the Walenstadtberg road, where you continue to a point about 1km beyond **Bergrestaurant Schrina**. There a signed path climbs the Schrina ridge and heads eastward along a balcony, first under the Frümsel, then Brisi, whose intricate face overhangs in places.

A popular ◯ **circular walking tour** high above the Walensee follows much the same route taken by climbers heading for the Brisi face, after which it continues eastward on an undulating trail to another mountain restaurant at Alp Tschingla at the foot of the Schibenstoll. **Bergrestaurant Tschingla** (1536m) also provides overnight accommodation in dormitories and standard rooms, and is open from June to late September. From there the route gradually descends southeastward with fine views all the way, to the attractive hamlet of **Lüsis** at 1272m where there's another restaurant, before making the steep descent to Walenstadt (about 5hrs from the Knoblisbüel bus stop beyond Walenstadtberg).

Very few paths cross the Churfirsten, but at the very eastern end of the chain two connecting passes, the 1946m Sattel, and the **Nideripass** at 1839m, provide a means by which to create a ◯ **north–south crossing** from Wildhaus to Walenstadt in 5–6hrs. The Toggenburg side is somewhat cluttered with ski lifts and pistes, but between the two passes there's a very fine stretch of tilted limestone pavement cut by ribs and fissures in which ferns and alpenroses find anchorage, and the descent to Walenstadt is steep and demanding.

ACCESS, BASES, MAPS AND GUIDES

Access

Lower Engadine Road access (not winter) via the Flüela Pass links the valley with Prättigau. All-year access is straightforward from the Upper Engadine, or from the Austrian Tyrol (Landeck to Martinsbruck/Scuol). A fast drive-on drive-off car-carrying train uses the Vereina rail tunnel from Klosters to Sagliains near Lavin. A narrow-gauge railway connects the Upper Engadine (St Moritz, Pontresina etc) with the Lower Engadine as far as Scuol.

Prättigau By road the valley is entered from the Swiss motorway system at Landquart. Landquart is also the rail junction where the main line from Zürich is exchanged for the Rhaetian railway's narrow-gauge route to Davos via Klosters.

St Antöniental By road from Küblis in the Prättigau. Nearest railway station in Küblis; bus service from Küblis to St Antönien.

Toggenburg The upper valley (Wildhaus) is served by bus from Buchs in the Rhine's valley. Nearest mainline railway station is at Buchs (trains from Zürich, and Austria via Feldkirch). The lower Toggenburg valley has rail access as far as Nesslau, on a line from Wil (between Winterthur and St Gallen).

Valley Bases

Lower Engadine Lavin, Guarda, Scuol
Prättigau Klosters
St Antöniental St Antönien, Partnun
Toggenburg Wildhaus, Unterwasser, Alt St Johann

Information

Graubünden Tourism, Alexanderstrasse 24, CH-7001 Chur (www.graubunden.co.uk)

Prättigau Tourismus, Sand 151, CH-7214 Grüsch (www.praettigau.info)

Rätikon climbing information: www.raetikon.ch

St Gallen Tourism, Bahnhofplatz 1a, St Gallen (www.st.gallen-bodensee.ch www.ostschweiz-i.ch)

Appenzell Tourism, Hauptgasse 4, Appenzell (www.appenzell.ch)

Huts

A number of manned and unmanned huts are strategically placed throughout the Silvretta, Rätikon and Alpstein districts; most belong to the SAC, but a few are privately owned. There are also plenty of Austrian and German Alpine Club huts that provide useful accommodation with good facilities for activists crossing the border – but remember to take Euros for payment.

Maps

For planning purposes the 1:120,000 sheet Graubünden published by Kümmerly + Frey shows the whole area covered by this chapter, except for Alpstein. K+F also produce three sheets at 1:60,000 with major walking routes and huts picked out in red: No 7 St Gallen–Appenzellerland; No 13 Davos–Arosa; No 14 Unterengadin

The Swiss National Survey (Landeskarte der Schweiz) cover the same area at 1:50,000 with 227 Appenzell, 237 Walenstadt, 238 Montafon, 248 Prättigau, 249 Tarasp, and 14 sheets at 1:25,000

Walking and/or Trekking Guides

Trekking in the Alps by Kev Reynolds (Cicerone, 2011)
Walks in the Engadine (for the Lower Engadine section of the Silvretta Alps) by Kev Reynolds (Cicerone, 3rd edition 2019)
Trekking in the Silvretta & Rätikon Alps by Kev Reynolds (Cicerone 2014)
Alpinwandern Graubünden (SAC)
Alpinwandern Zentralschweiz – Glarus–Alpstein (SAC)

Climbing Guides

Silvretta Alps by Jeff Williams (West Col, 1995)
Bundner Alpen 7: Rätikon (SAC)
Bundner Alpen 8: Silvretta und Samnaun (SAC)
Säntis – Churfirsten, von Appenzell zum Walensee (SAC)
Kletterführer Rätikon by Vital Eggenberger (SAC, 1988)
Rätikon Sud by Mario Luginbühl (Panico Verlag, 2008)
Kletterführer Alpstein by Werner Küng (SAC)
Kletterführer Churfirsten – Alvierkette–Fläscherkette by Thomas Wälti (SAC)

Skitouring Guides

Alpine Skitouren 5: Glarus–St Gallen–Appenzell (SAC)

See Also

Freie Sicht aufs Gipfelmeer by Marco Volken and Remo Kundert (Salvioni Edizioni, Bellinzona, 2003)
Walking in the Alps by Kev Reynolds (Cicerone, 2nd edition 2005)
Walking in Switzerland by Clem Lindenmayer (Lonely Planet, 2nd edition 2001)

APPENDIX A
Glossary of Alpine Terms

(Rom) Romansch, (It) Italian, (Ger) German and otherwise terms are from French, if italic, or standard English.

ablation valley	the trough between moraine bank and mountain	dormitorio	(It) dormitory
alp	mountain pasture	dortoir	(Fr) dormitory
alp hut	summer dwelling of a mountain farmer	fels	(Ger) rock
		fenêtre	a narrow gap in a ridge (French for 'window')
aiguille	a pointed mountain (French for needle)	firn	(Ger) a snowfield
alpine zone	area above the treeline	föhn	a warm, dry wind from the south
arête	a sharply defined mountain ridge	furka	a col; usually referring to a frequently used crossing point
bach	(Ger) stream or river	gendarme	a prominent rock finger or tower on a ridge
bergschrund	the crevasse separating the upper section of a glacier from the mountain's rock	ghiacciaio	(It) glacier
		gletscher	(Ger) glacier
bergweg	mountain path	gross	large
bisse	an irrigation channel, typically found in the Valais	haute route	a high-level route among mountains
buvette	a simple mountain restaurant	höhenweg	a high mountain trail (often multi-day in length)
brèche	a gap or notch in a ridge		
cabane	(Fr) mountain hut/refuge	hütte	(Ger) mountain hut/refuge
camona	(Rom) see cabane	icefall	a broken section of glacier
chamanna	(Rom) see cabane	joch	see col
cirque	a corrie; mountain amphitheatre	karst	a section of fairly level limestone; limestone 'pavement'
chli	small – see also klein(e)	klamm	(Ger) a gorge
col	a pass or saddle, usually between two mountains	klein(e)	small – see also chli
		klettergarten	sport/rock climbing area, often by a hut
cornice	a lip of snow or ice projecting from the crest of a ridge	klettersteig	(Ger) an artificial climbing 'path' consisting of metal rungs, ladders, and/or footplates, protected by fixed cables, ropes or chains (see also via ferrata)
couloir	a gully		
crevasse	a deep crack or cleft in the ice of a glacier		
doline	a subterranean cavern or hole in a karst (limestone) region, formed by water seepage	lücke	(Ger) a high and rocky pass

massenlager	(Ger) dormitory		*scharte*	(Ger) a rocky pass
matratzenlager	(Ger) see massenlager		*schlucht*	(Ger) a gorge
moraine	a bank of debris, including rock and soil, deposited by a glacier		scree	a slope of small shattered rocks
			see	(Ger) lake
névé	the snowfield that feeds a glacier; a type of snow that has been partly frozen, then melted and compacted		serac	an ice tower often found in icefalls
			spalte	(Ger) crevasse
piz, pizzo	Italian for mountain peak or summit		*touristenlager*	(Ger) dormitory
			vadret	glacier
refuge	(Fr) mountain hut		*verglas*	a thin coating of ice on rock
rifugio	(It) see refuge		*via ferrata*	see *klettersteig*
rognon	a large section of rock protruding from a glacier			

APPENDIX B
Selective Bibliography

Note Guidebooks for walkers, trekkers, climbers and ski tourers are listed in the Introduction.

General tourist guides
Blue Guide to Switzerland by Ian Robertson (A&C Black, 1989)
Green Guide to Switzerland (Michelin Travel Publications, 2000)
Switzerland by Damien Simonis et al (Lonely Planet, 4th edition 2003)
The Rough Guide to Switzerland by Matthew Teller (Rough Guides, 4th edition 2010)

Instruction
Alpine Climbing (Crowood Press, 1995) by John Barry
Mountaineering: from Hill Walking to Alpine Climbing by Alan Blackshaw (Penguin, 1970)
On Snow and Rock by Gaston Rébuffat (Kaye & Ward, 1971)

Mountains and mountaineering
Adventures of an Alpine Guide by Christian Klucker (John Murray, 1932)
Alpine Points of View by Kev Reynolds (Cicerone, 2004)
Alps 4000 by Martin Moran (David & Charles, 1994)
Collins Guide to Mountains and Mountaineering by John Cleare (Collins, 1979)
Early Travellers in the Alps by Gavin de Beer (Sidgwick & Jackson, 1930)
Fifty Years of Alpinism by Riccardo Cassin (Diadem, 1981)
Hold the Heights: the Foundations of Mountaineering by Walt Unsworth (Hodder & Stoughton, 1993)
How the English Made the Alps by Jim Ring (John Murray, 2000)
I Chose to Climb by Chris Bonington (Victor Gollancz, 1966)
In Monte Viso's Horizon by Will McLewin (Ernest Press, 1992)
Killing Dragons: the Conquest of the Alps by Fergus Fleming (Granta Books, 2000)
Matterhorn Centenary by Arnold Lunn (Allen & Unwin, 1965)
Men and the Matterhorn by Gaston Rébuffat (Kaye & Ward, 1973)
Men, Myths and Mountains by Ronald W Clark (Weidenfeld & Nicolson, 1976)
Mountaineering in the Alps by Claire Elaine Engel (Allen & Unwin, 1971)
On High Hills by Geoffrey Winthrop Young (Methuen, 1927)
Scrambles Amongst the Alps in the years 1860–69 by Edward Whymper (John Murray, 1871, and numerous editions since)
Starlight and Storm by Gaston Rébuffat (Kaye & Ward, 1968)
Summits and Secrets by Kurt Diemburger (Allen & Unwin, 1971)
The Alpine Journal (Alpine Club, 1864 to present date)
The Alps by R L G Irving (Batsford, 1939)
The Alps by Ronald W Clark (Weidenfeld & Nicolson, 1973)
The Alps from End to End by Martin Conway (Constable, 1905)
The Alps in 1864 by A W Moore (Blackwell, 1939)
The Early Alpine Guides by Ronald W Clark (Phoenix, 1949)
The Eiger by Dougal Haston (Cassell, 1974)
The High Mountains of the Alps by Helmut Dumler and Willi P Burkhardt (Diadem, 1993)
The Mountains of Europe by Kev Reynolds (Oxford Illustrated Press, 1990)
The Mountains of Switzerland by Herbert Maeder (Allen & Unwin, 1968)
The Playground of Europe by Leslie Stephen (Longmans, 1871/Blackwell, 1936)
The Swiss and their Mountains by Arnold Lunn (Allen & Unwin, 1963)
The Victorian Mountaineers by Ronald W Clark (Batsford, 1953)
The White Spider by Heinrich Harrer (Hart-Davis, 1959)
Unjustifiable Risk? by Simon Thompson (Cicerone, 2010)
Wanderings Among the High Alps by Alfred Wills (Blackwell, 1939)
When the Alps Cast their Spell by Trevor Braham (The In Pinn, 2004)
World Atlas of Mountaineering by Wilfrid Noyce and Ian McMorrin (Thomas Nelson, 1969)

Mountain walking
Trekking in the Alps by Kev Reynolds (Cicerone, 2011)
Walking in the Alps by J Hubert Walker (Oliver & Boyd, 1951)
Walking in the Alps by Kev Reynolds (Cicerone, 2nd edition 2005)

APPENDIX C
Index of maps

AREA COVERED	PAGE
The Swiss Alps	7
Chapter 1: Chablais Alps	**51**
Val de Morgins	53
Val d'Illiez	55
Tour des Dents Blanches	58
Tour des Dents du Midi	62
Vallon de Susanfe	64
Rhône Valley Approaches	66
Vallée du Trient	69
Tour du Ruan	71
Tour de la Vallée du Trient	78
Chapter 2: Pennine Alps	**84**
Val Ferret	87
Walker's Haute Route	91
Val d'Entremont	97
Tour des Combins	99
Val de Bagnes	103
Tour du Val de Bagnes	104
The Classic Haute Route	114
Val de Nendaz	115
Val d'Hérémence	117
Val d'Hérens	121
Tour du Val d'Hérens	123
Val de Moiry	133
Val d'Anniviers	138
Tour du Val d'Anniviers	140
Turtmanntal	147
Mattertal	150
Tour of the Matterhorn	161

AREA COVERED	PAGE
Saastal	169
Tour of Monte Rosa	177
Simplon Pass	180
Chapter 3: Lepontine and Adula Alps	**185**
Simplon Pass East	189
Binntal	192
Val Bedretto	195
Valle Leventina	201
Val Verzasca	206
Valle Maggia	210
Valle di Blenio	218
Tour of Valle di Blenio	223
Vals Calanca and Mesolcina	225
The Northern Valleys	230
Chapter 4: Bernina, Bregaglia and Albula Alps	**241**
Val Madris and the Averstal	245
Engadine Valley: Left Bank Maloja Pass to Albula Pass	249
Engadine Valley: Left Bank Albula Pass to Flüela Pass	255
Val Bregaglia	257
Bernina Alps	271
Tour of the Bernina Alps	284
Swiss National Park	286
Chapter 5: Bernese Alps	**293**
Alpes Vaudoises	297
Tour des Muverans	300
Les Diablerets to Rawil Pass	302
The Wildstrubel Massif	306

Appendix C – Index of maps

AREA COVERED	PAGE
Kandersteg and the Gemmipass	309
Blüemlisalp and the Gasterntal	311
The Kiental	314
Lauterbrunnen Valley	317
Grindelwald and the Lütschental	326
Tour of the Jungfrau Region	329
Haslital and Grimsel Pass	337
The Southern Valleys: Fieschertal and Aletsch Glacier	342
The Southern Valleys: Lötschental and Leukerbad	345
Alpine Pass Route	350
Chapter 6: Central Swiss Alps	**355**
Uri Alps: Voralptal	358
Göschenertal	362
Gadmertal	368
Gental	371
Engelbergtal	373
Grosstal	377

AREA COVERED	PAGE
Fellital and Etzlital	380
Maderanertal	383
Schächental	387
Urner Boden	388
Linth Tal	392
Klöntal	396
Sernftal (North)	398
Sernftal (South)	400
Chapter 7: Silvretta and Rätikon Alps	**405**
Silvretta Alps: Lower Engadine	409
Silvretta Alps: Prättigau	414
Tour of the Silvretta	419
Rätikon Alps	422
Tour of the Rätikon	425
Prättigauer Höhenweg	428
Alpstein Massif	430
Churfirsten	434

APPENDIX D

The Swiss 4000m peaks

In 1994 a UIAA committee produced a list of 82 alpine summits of 4000m, 49 of which are located in the Swiss Alps. The original tally recorded and climbed by Austrian climber Karl Blodig (1859–1956) gave 76 summits, while Richard Goedeke, in the second edition of *The Alpine 4000m Peaks by the Classic Routes* (Bâton Wicks, 2003) identified no less than 150 main summits and 'tops', thus continuing a long tradition of debate and controversy among the mountaineering community. Without wishing to intrude on this debate, the following table of 4000m peaks in the Swiss Alps is based on the official UIAA list.

BERNINA ALPS
The most easterly of the 4000ers, Piz Bernina crowns the Swiss-Italian border in Canton Graubünden (Grisons), the culminating point on a ridge dividing Vals Roseg and Morteratsch south of Pontresina. Although only one summit exceeds 4000m, several of its neighbours fall short by less than 100m.
Guidebook: Bernina and Bregaglia by Lindsay Griffin (Alpine Club, 1995)

Piz Bernina (4049m)
First ascent: 1850 by Johann Coaz, with Jon and Lorenz Ragut Tscharner
Valley base: Pontresina
Huts: Chamanna da Boval (2495m), Chamanna da Tschierva (2583m), Rifugio Marco e Rosa (3599m)
Maps: LS 1277 Piz Bernina 1:25,000; LS 268 Julierpass 1:50,000
See: Chapter 4:4

BERNESE ALPS
Nine individual 4000m peaks cluster at the eastern end of the Bernese chain, rising above a complex glacier system which, in some areas, is reminiscent of the Karakoram. Not surprisingly 19th-century glaciologists were among the pioneers who explored here, making some of the first ascents, or contributing to them. Only three of the Bernese 4000ers were won by British mountaineers.
Guidebook: Bernese Oberland by Les Swindin (Alpine Club, 2003)

Aletschhorn (4195m)
First ascent: 1859 by Francis Fox Tuckett with J J Bennen, Victor Tairraz and Peter Bohren
Valley base: Fiesch or Grindelwald
Huts: Oberaletsch Hut (2640m), Mittelaletsch Bivouac Hut (3013m), Hollandia Hut (3240m), Konkordia Hut (2850m)
Maps: LS 1269 Aletschgletscher 1:25,000; LS 5004 Berner Oberland 1:50,000
See: Chapter 5:10

Finsteraarhorn (4273m)
First ascent: 1829 by Jakob Leuthold and Johann Währen (geologist Franz Joseph Hugi remained just below the summit)
Valley base: Fiesch
Huts: Finsteraarhorn Hut (3048m), Oberaarjoch Hut (3256m), Aar Bivouac Hut (2733m)
Maps: LS 1249 Finsteraarhorn 1:25,000; LS 5004 Berner Oberland 1:50,000
See: Chapter 5:8

Gross Fiescherhorn (4049m) and Hinter Fiescherhorn (4025m)
First ascent: (Gross Fiescherhorn): 1862 by A W Moore and Revd Hereford Brooke George with Christian Almer and Ulrich Kaufmann
First ascent: (Hinter Fiescherhorn): 1864 by Edmund von Fellenberg with Peter Inäbnit and Ulrich Kaufmann
Valley base: Grindelwald
Huts: Mönchsjoch Hut (3657m), Konkordia Hut (2850m), Finsteraarhorn Hut (3048m)
Maps: LS 1249 Finsteraarhorn 1:25,000; LS 5004 Berner Oberland 1:50,000
See: Chapter 5:8

Gross Grünhorn (4044m)
First ascent: 1865 by Edmund von Fellenberg with Peter Egger, Peter Michel and Peter Inäbnit
Valley base: Grindelwald or Fiesch
Huts: Mönchsjoch Hut (3657m), Konkordia Hut (2850m), Finsteraarhorn Hut (3048m)
Maps: LS 1249 Finsteraarhorn, 1269 Aletschgletscher 1:25,000; LS 5004 Berner Oberland 1:50,000
See: Chapter 5:8

Jungfrau (4158m)
First ascent: 1811 by Johann and Hieronymus Meyer with Aloys Volker and Joseph Bortes
Valley base: Grindelwald, Wengen, Lauterbrunnen, Stechelberg
Huts: Mönchsjoch Hut (3657m), Silberhorn Hut (2663m), Rottal Hut (2755m)
Maps: LS 1249 Finsteraarhorn 1:25,000; LS 5004 Berner Oberland 1:50,000
See: Chapter 5:7

Lauteraarhorn (4042m)
First ascent: 1842 by Arnold Escher, Eduard Desor and Christian Girard, with Melchior Bannholzer, Jakob Leuthold, Johann Madutz, Fahner and D Brigger
Valley base: Grimsel Hospiz
Huts: Aar Bivouac Hut (2733m), Lauteraar Hut (2393m), Schreckhorn Hut (2529m)
Maps: LS 1229 Grindelwald; 1249 Finsteraarhorn; 1250 Ulrichen 1:25,000; LS 5004 Berner Oberland 1:50,000
See: Chapter 5:8

Mönch (4099m)
First ascent: 1857 by Siegmund Porges with Christian Almer and Ulrich and Christian Kaufmann
Valley base: Grindelwald
Huts: Mönchsjoch Hut (3657m); Guggi Hut (2791m)
Maps: LS 1249 Finsteraarhorn 1:25,000; LS 5004 Berner Oberland 1:50,000
See: Chapter 5:7

Schreckhorn (4078m)
First ascent: 1861 by Leslie Stephen with Christian and Peter Michel and Ulrich Kaufmann
Valley base: Grindelwald
Huts: Schreckhorn Hut (2529m), Gleckstein Hut (2317m)
Maps: LS 1229 Grindelwald; 1249 Finsteraarhorn; 1250 Ulrichen 1:25,000; LS 5004 Berner Oberland 1:50,000
See: Chapter 5:8

PENNINE ALPS

Between the isolated Grand Combin in the west and Weissmies above the Saastal in the east, the Pennine Alps of Canton Valais (Wallis) gather the greatest number of 4000m peaks in the alpine chain. The majority of these form a horseshoe on three sides of the Mattertal, including such significant summits as Weisshorn, Zinalrothorn, Ober Gabelhorn, Dent Blanche, Dent d'Hérens, Matterhorn, Breithorn, Monte Rosa, Alphubel, Täschhorn and Dom. Zinal, Zermatt, Saas Fee and Saas Grund are the main centres, and the scenery is spectacular throughout.

Guidebooks: Valais Alps West by Lindsay Griffin (Alpine Club, 1998); Valais Alps East by Les Swindin and Peter Fleming (Alpine Club, 1999)

Allalinhorn (4027m)
First ascent: 1856 by Edward Levi Ames with Johann Josef Imboden and Franz Josef Andenmatten
Valley base: Saas Fee or Täsch
Huts: Brittania Hut (3030m), Täsch Hut (2701m)
Maps: LS 1329 Saas 1:25,000; LS 5006 Matterhorn–Mischabel 1:50,000
See: Chapter 2:11

Alphubel (4206m)
First ascent: 1860 by Leslie Stephen
Valley base: Täsch or Saas Fee
Huts: Täsch Hut (2701m), Mischabeljoch Bivouac Hut (3847m)
Maps: LS 1328 Randa 1:25,000; LS 5006 Matterhorn–Mischabel 1:50,000
See: Chapter 2:11

Bishorn (4159m)
First ascent: 1884 by G S Barnes and Revd R Chessyre-Walker with Joseph Imboden and J M Chanton
Valley base: Zinal or Gruben
Huts: Cabane de Tracuit (3256m), Turtmann Hut (2519m)
Maps: LS 1328 Randa 1:25,000; LS 5006 Matterhorn–Mischabel 1:50,000
See: Chapter 2:8

Breithorn (4164m), Breithorn Central (4159m), Breithorn West (4139m)
First ascent: 1813 by Henri Maynard with Joseph-Marie Couttet, Jean Gras, Jean-Baptiste and Jean-Jacques Erin
Valley base: Zermatt
Huts: Gandegg Hut (3029m), Rifugio del Teodulo (3317m), Rifugio Testa Grigia (3479m)
Maps: LS 1348 Zermatt 1:25,000; LS 5006 Matterhorn–Mischabel 1:50,000
See: Chapter 2:10

Castor (4226m)
First ascent: 1861 by William Mathews and F W Jacomb with Michel Croz
Valley base: Zermatt
Huts: Monte Rosa Hut (2795m)
Maps: LS 1348 Zermatt 1:25,000; LS 5006 Matterhorn–Mischabel 1:50,000
See: Chapter 2:10

Dent Blanche (4356m)
First ascent: 1862 by T S Kennedy and William Wigram with J B Croz and Johann Krönig
Valley base: Les Haudères, Ferpècle, Zinal or Zermatt

Huts: Cabane de la Dent Blanche (3507m), Bivouac au Col de la Dent Blanche (3540m), Cabane du Mountet (2886m), Schönbiel Hut (2694m)
Maps: LS 1327 Evolène and 1347 Matterhorn 1:25,000; LS 5006 Matterhorn–Mischabel 1:50,000
See: Chapters 2:6 and 2:8

Dent d'Hèrens (4171m)
First ascent: 1863 by William Hall, Florence Crauford Grove, Reginald MacDonald and Montagu Woodmass with Melchior Anderegg, Peter Perren and Jean-Pierre Cachat
Valley base: Zermatt
Huts: Schönbiel Hut (2694m)
Maps: LS 1347 Matterhorn 1:25,000; LS 5006 Matterhorn–Mischabel 1:50,000
See: Chapter 2:10

Dom (4545m)
First ascent: 1858 by Revd J Llewellyn-Davies with Johann Zumtaugwald, Johann Krönig and Hieronymus Brantschen
Valley base: Randa or Saas Fee
Huts: Dom Hut (2940m), Mischabeljoch Bivouac Hut (3847m)
Maps: LS 1328 Randa 1:25,000; LS 5006 Matterhorn–Mischabel 1:50,000
See: Chapter 2:10

Dürrenhorn (Dirruhorn: 4035m)
First ascent: 1879 by A F Mummery and William Penhall with Alexander Burgener and Ferdinand Imseng
Valley base: Grächen, Gasenried, St Niklaus or Randa
Huts: Dom Hut (2940m), Bordier Hut (2886m), Mischabel Hut (3329m)
Maps: LS 1328 Randa 1:25,000; LS 5006 Matterhorn–Mischabel 1:50,000
See: Chapter 2:10

Grand Combin: Combin de Grafeneire (4314m), Combin de Valsory (4184m), Combin de la Tsessette (4141m)
First ascent: 1859 (Combin de Grafeneire) by Charles St-Clair Deville, Daniel, Emmanuel and Gaspard Balleys and Basile Dorsaz
Valley base: Fionnay or Bourg-St-Pierre
Huts: Cabane de Panossière (2645m), Cabane de Valsorey (3030m)
Maps: LS 1345 Orsières, 1346 Chanrion 1:25,000; LS 5003 Mont Blanc–Grand Combin 1:50,000
See: Chapter 2:2 and 2:3

Hobärghorn (4219m)
First ascent: 1869 by R B Heathcote with Franz Biner, Peter Perren and Peter Taugwalder Jnr
Valley base: Saas Fee, Grächen, Gasenried or Randa
Huts: Dom Hut (2940m), Bordier Hut (2886m), Mischabel Hut (3329m)
Maps: LS 1328 Randa 1:25,000; 5006 Matterhorn–Mischabel 1:50,000
See: Chapter 2:10

Lagginhorn (4010m)
First ascent: 1856 by Edward Ames and three companions, with Johann-Joseph Imseng and Franz Joseph Andenmatten and three other guides
Valley base: Saas Grund or Simplon Dorf
Huts: Weissmies Hut (2726m), Bergrestaurant Hohsaas (3100m), Laggin Bivouac Hut (2428m)

Maps: LS 1329 Saas 1:25,000; LS 5006 Matterhorn–Mischabel 1:50,000
See: Chapter 2:11

Lenzspitze (4294m)
First ascent: 1870 by Clinton Dent with Alexander and Franz Burgener
Valley base: Saas Fee or Randa
Huts: Mischabel Hut (3329m), Dom Hut (2940m)
Maps: LS 1328 Randa 1:25,000; LS 5006 Matterhorn–Mischabel 1:50,000
See: Chapter 2:11

Liskamm (E 4527m: W 4479m)
First ascent: 1861 by W E Hall, J F Hardy, J Hudson, C Pilkington, A C Ramsey, T Rennison, F Sibson and R M Stephenson with J Cachet, F Lochmatter, K Herr, J and P Perren and S Zumtaugwald
Valley base: Zermatt
Huts: Monte Rosa Hut (2795m)
Maps: LS 1348 Zermatt 1:25,000; LS 5006 Matterhorn–Mischabel 1:50,000
See: Chapter 2:10

Matterhorn (4477m)
First ascent: 1865 by Edward Whymper, Lord Francis Douglas, Revd Charles Hudson and Douglas Hadow, with Michel Croz and Peter Taugwalder (father and son)
Valley base: Zermatt
Huts: Hörnli Hut (3260m), Solvay Hut (4003m)
Maps: LS 1347 Matterhorn, 1348 Zermatt 1:25,000; LS 5006 Matterhorn–Mischabel 1:50,000
See: Chapter 2:10

Monte Rosa: Dufourspitze (4634m), Nordend (4609m), Zumsteinspitze (4563m), Signalkuppe (4554m), Parrotspitze (4432m), Ludwigshöhe (4341m), Schwarzhorn (4322m), Piramide Vincent (4215m), Punta Giordani (4046m)
First ascent: 1855 (Dufourspitze) by Revd Charles Hudson, John Birkbeck, Edward Stephenson, James and Christopher Smyth, with Ulrich Lauener and Johann and Matthias Zumtaugwald
Valley base: Zermatt
Huts: Monte Rosa Hut (2795m), Rifugio Regina Margherita (4554m)
Maps: LS 1348 Zermatt 1:25,000; LS 5006 Matterhorn–Mischabel 1:50,000
See: Chapter 2:10

Nadelhorn (4327m)
First ascent: 1858 by Joseph Zimmermann, Alois Supersaxo and Baptiste Epiney with Franz Andermatten
Valley base: Saas Fee, Grächen, Gasenried or Randa
Huts: Mischabel Hut (3329m), Dom Hut (2940m), Bordier Hut (2886m)
Maps: LS 1328 Randa 1:25,000; LS 5006 Matterhorn–Mischabel 1:50,000
See: Chapter 2:10

Ober Gabelhorn (4063)
First ascent: 1865 by A W Moore and Horace Walker, with Jakob Anderegg
Valley base: Zermatt or Zinal
Huts: Rothorn Hut (3198m), Cabane du Mountet (2886m), Arben Bivouac Hut (3224m)
Maps: LS 1327 Evolène, 1348 Zermatt 1:25,000; LS 5006 Matterhorn–Mischabel 1:50,000
See: Chapter 2:8 and 2:10

Appendix D – The Swiss 4000m peaks

Pollux (4091m)
First ascent: 1864 by Jules Jacot with Peter Taugwalder Snr and Joseph-Maria Perren
Valley base: Zermatt
Huts: Monte Rosa Hut (2795m)
Maps: LS 1348 Zermatt 1:25,000; LS 5006 Matterhorn–Mischabel 1:50,000
See: Chapter 2:10

Rimpfischhorn (4199m)
First ascent: 1859 by Leslie Stephen and Robert Living, with Melchior Anderegg and Johan Zumtaugwald
Valley base: Zermatt, Täsch or Saas Fee
Huts: Berghütte Fluhalp (2616m), Täsch Hut (2701m), Britannia Hut (3030m)
Maps: LS 1348 Zermatt 1:25,000; LS 5006 Matterhorn–Mischabel 1:50,000
See: Chapter 2:10 and 2:11

Stecknadelhorn (4241m)
First ascent: 1887 by Oscar Eckenstein with Matthias Zurbriggen
Valley base: Grächen, Gasenried, Randa or Saas Fee
Huts: Mischabel Hut (3329m), Dom Hut (2940m), Bordier Hut (2886m)
Maps: LS 1328 Randa 1:25,000; LS 5006 Matterhorn–Mischabel 1:50,000
See: Chapter 2:10

Strahlhorn (4190m)
First ascent: 1854 by James, Christopher and Edmund Smyth with Franz Joseph Andenmatten and Ulrich Lauener
Valley base: Saas Fee or Zermatt
Huts: Britannia Hut (3030m), Berghütte Fluhalp (2616m)
Maps: LS 1348 Zermatt, 1328 Randa 1:25,000; LS 5006 Matterhorn–Mischabel 1:50,000
See: Chapter 2:11

Täschhorn (4490m)
First ascent: 1862 by Revd John Llewellyn-Davies and Revd J W Hayward with Johann and Stephan Zumtaugwald
Valley base: Täsch, Randa or Saas Fee
Huts: Täsch Hut (2701m), Dom Hut (2940m), Mischabeljoch Bivouac Hut (3847m)
Maps: LS 1328 Randa 1:25,000; LS 5006 Matterhorn–Mischabel 1:50,000
See: Chapter 2:10 and 2:11

Weisshorn (4506m)
First ascent: 1861 by John Tyndall with J J Bennen and Ulrich Wenger
Valley base: Randa or Zinal
Huts: Weisshorn Hut (2932m), Schalijoch Bivouac Hut (3786m), Cabane d'Ar Pitetta (2786m)
Maps: LS 1328 Randa 1:25,000; LS 5006 Matterhorn–Mischabel 1:50,000
See: Chapter 2:8 and 2:10

Weissmies (4023m)
First ascent: 1855 by Peter Joseph Zurbriggen and Jakob Christian Häuser
Valley base: Saas Grund or Saas Almagell
Huts: Weissmies Hut (2726m), Bergrestaurant Hohsaas (3100m), Almageller Hut (2984m)

Maps: LS 1329 Saas 1:25,000; LS 5006 Matterhorn–Mischabel 1:50,000
See: Chapter 2:11

Zinalrothorn (4221m)
First ascent: 1864 by Leslie Stephen and Florence Crauford Grove, with Melchior and Jakob Anderegg
Valley base: Zermatt or Zinal
Huts: Rothorn Hut (3198m), Cabane du Mountet (2886m)
Maps: LS 1327 Evolène, 1328 Randa, 1348 Zermatt 1:25,000; LS 5006 Matterhorn–Mischabel 1:50,000
See: Chapter 2:8 and 2:10

THE 4000M PEAKS IN PRINT

Guidebooks devoted to the 4000ers are Richard Goedeke's *The Alpine 4000m Peaks by the Classic Routes* (Bâton Wicks, 2nd edition 2003) and *The 4000m Peaks of the Alps* by Martin Moran (Alpine Club, 2007).

The High Mountains of the Alps by Helmut Dumler and Willi P Burkhardt (Diadem, 1994) is a lavishly illustrated coffee table book. Trevor Braham's *When the Alps Cast their Spell* (The In Pinn, 2004) is a highly readable account of early 4000m ascents and those who pioneered them, but Will McLewin's *In Monte Viso's Horizon* (Ernest Press, 1992) and Martin Moran's *Alps 4000* (David & Charles, 1994) are both personal narrative accounts of climbing all of these summits.

INDEX

A

Aar Bivouac Hut 334, 340, 442, 443
Aare 296, 359, 369
Äbeni Flue 324
Acquarossa 220, 238
Adelboden 295, 307, 349, 351
Adlerpass 167, 175
Adula Alps 11, 13, 13, 18, 184, 187, 188, 189, 205, 217, 220, 222, 224, 229, 231, 232, 234, 236,
Agassizhorn 333, 334
Ago di Sciora 263
Agra, Val d' 207
Agro 207
Aigle 56, 301
Aiguille d'Argentière 93
Aiguille de la Tsa 126, 128
Aiguille du Chardonnet 93
Aiguille du Croissant 109
Aiguille du Tour 67, 75, 79, 92
Aiguilles Dorées 67, 92, 93
Aiguilles Rouges d'Arolla 119, 128, 129, 131
Airolo 188, 197, 200, 202, 203, 204, 216, 238, 365, 399
Albert Heim Hut 364, 365
Albigna, Val 264, 265, 267, 270
Albrunhorn 193
Albrunpass 193
Albula
    Albula Alps 13, 14, 40, 229, 231, 243, 251, 252, 254, 256, 270
    Albula Pass 251, 252, 256, 440
Aletschgletscher 344, 442, 443
Aletschhorn 180, 190, 292, 334, 344, 347, 442
Aletschwald 344
Alggi Alp 372
Allalinhorn 155, 156, 173, 174, 175, 444
Almagelleralp 168, 178
Almageller Hut 170, 178, 179, 447
Almagellertal 179
Alnasca 207
Alpes Vaudoises 90, 296, 301, 349, 351, 440
Alp Grüm 283, 284
Alphubel 155, 156, 173, 175, 444

Alpiglen 18, 328, 331
Alpine Pass Route (APR) 292, 304, 310, 349, 359, 370, 372, 375, 385, 391, 397, 441
Alp Sardasca 415, 416, 417, 418
Alpstein 15, 404, 408, 429, 431, 432
Altdorf 349, 359, 365, 370, 376, 385
Altels 308, 312
Altmann 15, 432
Alt St Johann 431, 433
Am Bach 247
Ambra, Val d' 209
Ammertenpass 307
Andermatt 200, 237, 357, 359, 364, 365, 399
Anen Hut 348
Anniviers, Val d' 89, 130, 132, 137, 139, 148, 160, 181, 440
Antabia, Val d' 214, 215
Antigorio, Valle 211, 238
Anzano 219
Anzeindaz 298, 299, 301
Appenzell 404, 408, 431
Ardez 407, 412, 413
Argentine 298, 301
Arolla 86, 89, 113, 114, 120, 122, 124, 125, 126, 127, 128, 129, 160, 181, 228, 274, 344, 415
    Arolla Val d' 125, 129
Arpelistock 292, 296, 303, 304
Arpette, Val d' 76, 79, 86, 88, 90, 114
Äsch 386
Ascona 211
Augio 226
Augstenberg 408
Ausserberg 344, 346
Ausserbinn 191
Ausserferrera 246
Avegno 211
Avers Cresta 246
Avers Cröt 246
Avers Juppa 247
Avers Pürt 247
Averstal 244, 246, 248, 440

B

Bächlistock 339, 340
Bächlital Hut 339, 340
Bachsee 327, 328
Badus Hut 237
Bagnes, Val de 86, 89, 98, 100, 101, 103, 106, 108, 109, 111, 113, 114, 120, 181, 440
Balfrin 152, 153, 168, 174, 176
Balmhorn 308, 309, 312, 349
    Balmhorn Hut 308, 312
Baltschieder Hut 344, 346
Baltschiedertal 344, 346
Bäregg 328, 333
Bärglistock 336, 338
Barme 56, 57, 58, 59
Barone, Passo 205, 209
Barrhorn 148, 151, 153
Basòdino 184, 188, 196, 199, 212, 214, 215, 216
Bättelmatthorn 196
Bavona, Val 199, 212, 214, 215, 216
Bec d'Epicoune 113
Bedretto 188, 194, 197, 199, 238
    Bedretto Val 188, 194, 196, 197, 199, 200, 205, 216, 217, 238, 440
Belalp 344
Bella Tola 82, 139, 146, 148
Bellavista 270, 278, 280, 281
Bellinzona 80, 188, 196, 197, 220, 229, 238, 399, 402, 28
Bergalgapass 246, 247, 248
Bergalgatal 247
Berghaus Gfällalp 312
Berghaus Vereina 404, 408, 410, 411, 415, 416, 418
Berghütte Längfluh 173, 175
Bergsee Hut 363
Bergseeschijen 363
Berisal 179, 191
Bernese Alps 11, 14, 18, 18, 40, 66, 73, 92, 101, 107, 129, 132, 137, 170, 180, 187, 188, 190, 191, 194, 196, 215, 243, 295, 296, 308, 310, 313, 314, 321, 333, 334, 338, 340, 341, 344, 346, 347, 349, 351

449

Bernina
  Bernina Alps 11, 13, 18, 240,
    243, 244, 248, 251, 252, 253,
    267, 269, 270, 273, 274, 275,
    276, 277, 278, 279, 280, 281,
    282, 283, 284, 288, 289, 290,
    359, 378
  Bernina Val 252, 270, 273, 274,
    278, 281, 283, 284, 289
Besso 141, 142, 144, 145
Bettmeralp 344
Bever 252, 284
  Bever Val 251, 252
Bex 296, 298
Biasca 188, 217, 220, 224, 238
Bidmergrat 341, 364
Bietschhorn 137, 168, 296, 312,
  325, 344, 346, 347, 348
  Bietschhorn Hut 346, 348
Bietschtal 344, 346
Biferten Hut 393, 394
Bifertenstock 393, 394
Bignasco 211, 212, 214, 215, 216,
  238
Binn 191, 192, 193, 238
Binntal 188, 191, 192, 193, 194,
  238, 440
  Binntal Hut 193, 194
Bishorn 143, 145, 146, 148, 153,
  444
Bisistal 390, 391, 395
Bivio 248, 251, 258
Bivouac au Col de la Dent Blanche
  130, 445
Blackenalp 374, 375
Blatten 166, 344, 346, 348, 351
Blaunca 251
Blenio, Valle di 184, 188, 189, 200,
  203, 217, 219, 220, 221, 223,
  224, 226, 233, 236, 238, 440
Blinnenhorn 188, 193, 194, 196,
  197
Blockhaus Cluozza 287, 288
Blüemlisalp 296, 308, 310, 313,
  314, 316, 349, 351, 441
  Blüemlisalp Hut 310, 316
Blüemlisalphorn 310
Blumental 319, 328
Bonavau 57, 58, 61, 62, 64
Bondasca, Val 246, 256, 258, 259,
  261, 263, 264, 265, 269

Bondo 246, 258, 261
Bordier Hut 152, 153, 445, 446, 447
Bortelhorn 179, 191
Bortel Hut 191
Bosch, Fuorcla Val dal 288
Bosco Gurin 211, 214, 238
Bosco, Valle di 211, 214
Bouquetins 127, 128, 132, 134,
  135, 144
Bourg-St-Pierre 88, 98, 100, 101,
  102, 114, 181, 445
Boval, Fuorcla da 274, 279
Braunwald 391, 395
Bregaglia
  Bregaglia Alps 244, 18, 262, 263,
    265, 267, 269, 270, 273
  Bregaglia Val 246, 248, 250, 251,
    256, 258, 259, 263, 264, 267,
    281, 282, 440
Breithorn 157, 164, 166, 167, 190,
  313, 322, 324, 325, 344, 346,
  348, 444
  Breithorn Lauterbrunnen 295,
    296, 310, 313, 316, 318, 320,
    321, 322, 323, 324, 325, 327,
    328, 329, 330, 346, 348, 349,
    351, 385, 441, 443
  Breithorn Lötschentaler 292, 296,
    344, 346, 347, 348
Breithornpass 190
Breitlauihorn 344, 346
Breitstock 229
Breuil-Cervinia 162, 167
Bricola 130
Brienz 338, 369
Brig 102, 179, 181, 189, 191
Brione 207, 208, 209, 238
Brisi 433, 435
Bristen 379, 381, 382, 384
  Bristen Hut 381
Bristenstock 381
Britannia Hut 156, 163, 173, 174,
  175, 447
Broglio 215
  Broglio Val 212, 215
Brülisau 431
Brunegghorn 146, 148, 153
Brünigpass 370
Brunnialp 385
Brunni Hut 374
Brunnital 382, 384, 385, 386

Bruschghorn 232
Buchs 429, 431
Buffalora, Pass de 226, 227
Bunderchrinde 308, 349
Bundner Alps 420
Burg Hut 343
Busenalp 323
Bussalp 327, 330
Bütlasse 292, 316, 322

C
Cabane Bella Tola 89, 139, 146
Cabane Brunet 98, 105, 106, 108,
  109, 110
Cabane Champillon 100
Cabane d'Antème 60, 64
Cabane d'Ar Pitetta 142, 447
Cabane de Bertol 127, 128
Cabane de Chanrion 100, 104, 105,
  112, 114
Cabane de la Dent Blanche 130,
  166, 445
Cabane de la Maye 94
Cabane de l'A Neuve 94
Cabane de la Tourche 299, 301
Cabane de la Tsa 126, 128
Cabane de Louvie 105, 107, 108,
  116
Cabane de Moiry 89, 132, 134,
  139, 142
Cabane de Panossière 100, 106, 108,
  109, 110, 445
Cabane de Plan Névé 298
Cabane de Prafleuri 89, 116, 119
Cabane de Prarochet 303
Cabane des Aiguilles Rouges 125,
  128
Cabane de Saleina 93
Cabane des Becs de Bosson 125, 135
Cabane des Diablerets 303
Cabane des Dix 89, 120, 124, 128
Cabane de Sorebois 142
Cabane de Sorniot 299
Cabane de Susanfe 58, 60, 61, 62,
  64, 65, 70, 72, 74
Cabane des Vignettes 114, 127
Cabane de Tracuit 143, 444
Cabane de Valsorey 101, 110, 114,
  445
Cabane d'Illhorn 137, 139, 146
Cabane d'Orny 90, 92, 93

Index

Cabane du Col de Mille 98, 101, 105, 106
Cabane du Demècre 299, 300
Cabane du Fenestral 299, 300
Cabane du Mont Fort 89, 105, 106, 107, 108, 116
Cabane du Petit Mountet 139, 142
Cabane du Trient 77, 88, 92, 114
Cabane du Vélan 101
Cabane Glacier de Tortin 116
Cabane Mountet 130
Cabane Rambert 299, 300
Cabbiola 227
Cacciabella Pass 263
Cadabi, Passo dei 220, 229
Cadlimo
    Cadlimo Bocchetta di 200
    Cadlimo Val 200, 202, 203, 221, 237
Cairasca, Valle 190
Calanca, Val 219, 224, 226, 227, 229, 238
Calnegia, Val 211, 213, 214
Cam
    Cam Pass da 240, 258
    Cam Val da 258, 282, 283
Camadra, Valle 189, 217, 221, 222
Camona da Cavardiras 384
Camona da Maighels 237
Camona da Medel 236
Camona da Punteglias 394
Camona da Terri 222, 234
Campala, Bocchetta della 209
Campo 188, 205, 211, 214, 216, 221, 234, 235, 236
    Campo Blenio 189, 220, 221, 234, 235, 236
    Campo Valle di 211, 221, 224
Campolungo, Passo 204, 216
Camp, Val da 282, 283
Canaltal 233, 234
Canaria, Val 200
Canfinal, Pass da 283, 284
Cantun, Passo dal 266
Capanna Adula 220, 224
Capanna Basòdino 196, 199, 214, 215, 216
Capanna Borgna 207
Capanna Boverina 221, 224
Capanna Buffalora 226, 229
Capanna Cadagno 202, 203, 221

Capanna Cadlimo 200, 202, 221
Capanna Campo Tencia 205
Capanna Cognora 209
Capanna Corno-Gries 196
Capanna Cristallina 199, 216
Capanna da l'Albigna 265
Capanna del Forno 268
Capanna di Sciora 262, 264
Capanna Dötra 224
Capanna Efra 209
Capanna Garzonera 204
Capanna Grossalp 211
Capanna Leit 204, 205, 216
Capanna Miralago 227
Capanna Motterascio 222, 224, 233
Capanna Osola 208
Capanna Piansecco 197
Capanna Prodör 203
Capanna Quarnei 220, 224, 229
Capanna Sasc Furä 261
Capanna Scaletta 222, 224, 235
Capanna Sovèltra 215
Capanna Tremorgio 204, 216
Carassino, Val di 220, 224
Carecchio, Val 207
Carnäirajoch 419
Carschina Hut 404, 421, 423, 425, 429
Carschinasee 421, 423, 424
Casaccia 240, 248, 251, 258, 264
Casnil Pass 266
Cassinello, Val 199
Castasegna 246, 256, 258, 259
Castor 157, 164, 444
Cavanna, Passo di 199
Cavegna, Passo della 211
Cavelljoch 425, 426, 429
Cavergno 212
Cavloc, Lägh da 267, 284
Cazzola, Passo 214
Celerina 252, 256
Cerentino 211
Cevio 211, 238
Chablais Alps 12, 49, 52, 56, 75
Chamanna Coaz 274, 277
Chamanna da Boval 278, 442
Chamanna da Grialetsch 256
Chamanna dal Linard 410
Chamanna dal Parc Varusch 287
Chamanna da Tschierva 274, 275, 442

Chamanna d'Es-cha 253
Chamanna digl Kesch 256
Chamanna Jenatsch 251
Chamanna Lischana 288
Chamanna Marangun 410, 416
Chamanna Iuoi 411, 412, 418
Chamerstock 390
Chammliberg 386
Chamona d'Ela 251
Chamonix 54, 67, 68, 73, 75, 88, 89, 113, 119, 126, 156, 205, 243, 262, 329, 335, 359
Champagna, Fuorcla 281
Champéry 53, 56, 57, 12, 60, 61, 64, 65
Champex 76, 77, 86, 87, 88, 89, 90, 114, 181
Champfer 248, 252
Chandolin 137, 141, 146
Chants 253, 256
Chaschauna, Val 287
Châtelard, Le 52, 67, 73, 77
Chaude, Col de 349
Chelenalp Hut 354, 361, 363, 367
Chelenalptal 361, 363, 364
Cheville, Pas de 299, 301
Chèvres, Pas de 89, 120, 124, 128
Chiareggio 269, 284
Chindonne 62, 64
Chinzig Chulm 399
Chironico 205, 209
    Chironico Val 205, 209
Chüebodenhorn 197
Chüeplanggenstock 361
Chur 229, 232, 238, 252, 274, 278, 359, 427, 429
Churfirsten 391, 408, 429, 431, 433, 435, 441
Cima dal Cantun 265, 266
Cima dal Largh 267
Cima della Bondasca 264, 265
Cima di Castello 264, 265, 270
Cima di Rosso 269
Cima di Val Bona 269
Cima di Vazzeda 269
Cimalmotto 211
Cinuos-chel 254
Clariden 15, 386, 389, 390, 391, 393
    Clariden Hut 391
Classic Haute Route (Mt Blanc to Matterhorn ski tour) 113, 440

451

Clocher des Planereuses
  Clocher des Planereuses Grande 93
  Clocher des Planereuses Petite 93
Cocco
  Cocco Passo del 208
  Cocco Val 208, 215
Colombe, Passo 203, 221
Combin de Corbassière 109, 110
Combin de Grafeneire 101, 109, 110, 445
Combin de la Tsessette 109, 110, 112, 445
Combin de Valsorey 101, 109, 110
Corn da Tinizong 251
Corne du Sorebois 135, 137
Corno
  Corno Passo del 194, 196
  Corno Val 196
Cristallina 184, 188, 199, 203, 211, 212, 214, 216, 221, 236, 395
  Cristallina Massif 199
  Cristallina Passo di 184, 199, 200
  Cristallina Piz 199, 236
Cruina, Alpe di 196, 197
Cruschetta 288
Curaglia 235, 236
Curciusa, Val 228, 229
Curnera, Val 237
Curtins 272, 283
Cusie 219

D

Dagro 219, 224
Dalpe 204, 205
Damma Hut 364
Dammastock 338, 357, 359, 360, 363, 364, 365, 14, 366, 369, 26, 379
Dangio 220
Daubenhorn 348, 349
Daubensee 296, 308
Davos 244, 256, 408, 413, 416, 420, 39
Dent Blanche 13, 59, 82, 85, 122, 129, 130, 132, 135, 142, 143, 144, 149, 157, 166, 444
Dent de Morcles 53, 67, 299
Dent de Rosses 135
Dent de Tsalion 128
Dent d'Hérens 130, 135, 157, 159, 165, 310, 444

Dents Blanches 52, 54, 56, 57, 58, 59, 64
Dents du Midi 12, 50, 52, 53, 54, 56, 58, 59, 60, 61, 62, 64, 65, 67, 68, 69, 70, 79, 90, 101, 105, 106, 108, 296, 299, 301
Derborence 299, 301
Devero, Valle 191, 193
Diablerets, Les 14, 137, 296, 298, 299, 301, 304, 351
Diavolezza 278, 279, 280, 281, 282, 283
Diesrut, Pass 234
Disentis 221, 232, 234, 235, 236, 238, 378, 384, 395
Doldenhorn 148, 308, 310, 312
  Doldenhorn Hut 312
Dom 13, 85, 145, 151, 153, 154, 155, 173, 174, 176, 444, 445, 446, 447
  Dom Hut 154, 445, 446, 447
Domodossola 102, 179, 181, 194
Dongio 220
Dossen Hut 334, 336, 338
Dreieckhorn 344
Dreiländerspitz 408, 412
Drei Türm 423, 426
Drusator 423
Drusenfluh 423, 424, 425, 426, 429
Duana
  Duana Pass da la 246, 248, 258
  Duana Val da la 248, 258
Dufourspitze 154, 157, 163, 167, 446
Dündenhorn 310
Dürrenhorn 153, 445
Düssi, Grosse 382, 384

E

Ecandies, Col des 88, 90, 114
Efra, Val d' 209
Eggishorn 343, 344
Eggstock 364, 391, 395
Eggstöcke 391
Eiger 11, 14, 18, 31, 33, 296, 318, 321, 322, 327, 329, 330, 331, 332
Eldorado 292, 340
Elm 349, 393, 397, 399, 401
Emosson, Lac d' 52, 64, 70, 72, 73, 74, 75, 79
Enderlin Hut 429

Engadine Valley 248, 289, 440
Engelberg 15, 349, 370, 372, 374, 376
Engelbergtal 366, 369, 372, 375, 441
Engelhörner 338
Engelhorn Hut 338
Engi 397
Engstlenalp 334, 357, 369, 370, 372
Engstligenalp 307, 308, 351
Engstligenfälle 307
Engstligental 307, 308
Entremont, Val d' 86, 96, 97, 98, 100, 101, 102, 103, 114, 181, 440
Ernen 191
Essets, Col des 298, 299, 301
Etzli Hut 379
Europa Hut 90, 152, 154, 160, 176
Europaweg 82, 90, 152, 153, 154, 156, 160, 176
  Europaweg Hut 155
Euseigne 116, 119, 120
Evolène 120, 122, 124, 125, 132, 181, 445, 446, 448
Ewigschneehorn 338

F

Fafleralp 346, 347, 348, 351
Fain, Val da 281
Faldumalp 348
Falknis 427
Fallerfurgga 248
Faulhorn 327, 328
Faulhornweg 292, 327, 328
Fedoz
  Fedoz Fuorcla da 272
  Fedoz Val 270, 272
Feldschijen 364
Fellilücke 379
Fellital 379, 381, 441
Fenestral, Col du 300
Fenêtre d'Arpette 76, 77, 88, 89, 90
Fenêtre de Durand 100, 113
Fenêtre de Ferret 86, 96
Ferden 346, 347, 348, 351
Fergen Hut 416, 419
Ferpècle 125, 129, 130, 131, 444
Ferrera, Val 244, 246
Ferret 86, 93, 95, 96
  Ferret Grand Col 86, 95, 96
  Ferret Petit Col 82, 95

452

Ferret Val 86, 92, 93, 94, 95, 97, 181, 440
Feutersoey 304
Fex Crasta 272
Fiesch 191, 341, 343, 351, 442, 443
Fiescherhorn 14, 322, 333, 443
Fieschertal 341, 343, 351, 441
Fiescherwand 31, 333
Filisur 244, 251, 256
Fimberpass 413
Fimbertal 413
Finhaut 53, 67, 68, 70, 73, 75
Finsteraarhorn 14, 43, 148, 292, 325, 327, 333, 334, 340, 341, 343, 442, 443
    Finsteraarhorn Hut 334, 343, 442, 443
Fionnay 108, 109, 111, 181, 445
Fisetenpass 390, 391
Fläscher Fürggli 427
Fleckistock 360, 361, 367
Flesspass 408, 416
Fless, Val 408, 416
Fletschhorn 148, 168, 170, 174, 179, 180, 181, 190
Flims 232, 238, 32
Flüela Pass 244, 254, 256, 404, 408, 413, 416, 440
Flüela Wisshorn 404, 408, 416
Flüelen 376, 399
Flüelücke 360, 361
Fluesee Hut 307
Fluhalp 158, 163, 167, 175, 447
Foopass 349, 397
Forcellina 240, 248
Forclaz, Col de la 67, 76, 77, 79, 89, 90
Formazza, Val 184, 194, 196, 214
Forno
    Forno Sella del 269
    Forno Val 258, 267, 269, 270
Foroglio 213, 214
Frasco 209
Fridolins Hut 393, 394
Fründenhorn 312
Fründen Hut 312
Frutigen 26, 308, 312
Frutigtal 314
Ftan 407
Fünffingerstock 357, 366
Funtauna, Val 256

Fuorcla Champatsch 413
Fuorcla Pischa 253, 281
Fuorcla Vermunt 412
Fuorcla Zadrell 411, 416
Furcletta 412, 418
Fürenalp 354, 374
Fürenwand Klettersteig 374
Furkapass 14, 32, 364, 365
Furtwangsattel 369
Fusio 204, 215, 216, 238

G
Gadmen 369
Gadmerflue 369
Gadmertal 338, 360, 364, 367, 369, 441
Gafadura Hut 427
Gafier Jöchli 420
Gagnone, Passo del 209
Galenstock 364, 365
Gamchilücke 313, 314, 316
Gamsluggen 425, 426, 427
Gana Negra, Passo di 221, 224
Gandegg Hut 162, 164, 176, 444
Gandschijen 360
Gargellen 420
Gasenried 90, 152, 153, 154, 160, 445, 446, 447
Gasterntal 308, 310, 312, 313, 347, 351, 441
Gauli Hut 338
Gelmer Hut 369
Gelten Hut 304
Gemmipass 14, 295, 296, 306, 307, 308, 309, 312, 349, 351
Gemsfairenstock 390, 391
Geneva 12, 18, 19, 20, 20, 32
Gental 357, 369, 370, 372, 402, 441
Georgy Hut 281
Gerenpass 197
Gerra 209, 213
Ghirone 221, 222
Giglistock 367
Gimmelwald 319, 322
Giübin 200
Glarner Alps 11, 15, 231, 237, 378, 391, 393
Glärnisch Hut 395
Glärnisch massif 395
Glarus 349, 357, 365, 378, 390, 391, 393, 395, 397, 399

Glattalp Hut 390, 391, 395
Gleckstein Hut 328, 336, 443
Gletscherhorn 247, 324
Gletscherstube Märjela 343
Goglio 193
Golzern 381, 382
Goms 340, 341
Gondo 179, 180
Goppenstein 308, 346
Gordevio 211
Gordola 206
Gornergrat 115, 157, 158, 163
Göschenen 360, 365, 379
Göschenertal 360, 361, 364, 14
Grächen 90, 151, 152, 176, 181, 445, 446, 447
Grand Combin 67, 82, 85, 90, 98, 100, 101, 102, 105, 107, 108, 109, 110, 131, 146, 444, 445
Grand Cornier 128, 131, 132, 134, 135, 142, 143
Grande Fourche 93
Grande Lui 94
Grandes Dents 126, 128, 130
Grand Muveran 296, 298, 301
Grand St Bernard, Col du 82, 86, 96, 97, 100, 102
Grand Tavé 82, 109
Gran Paradiso 96, 113, 129
Grassen Bivouac Hut 375
Grauspitze 427
Graustock Klettersteig 372
Gredetschtal 344, 346
Greina, Passo della 217, 221, 222, 224, 235
Grevasalvas 251
    Grevasalvas Fuorcla 251
Griesalp 314, 316, 319, 349, 351
Grieshorn 197
Griespass 184, 194, 196, 338
Griessee 188, 194, 196
Grimentz 131, 132, 135, 137, 141, 181
Grimsel Pass 292, 334, 336, 338, 339, 340, 341, 351, 441
Grindelwald 11, 14, 31, 32, 39, 126, 205, 295, 316, 321, 325, 327, 329, 330, 331, 332, 333, 334, 335, 336, 349, 351, 365, 441, 442, 443
Grisonsattel 397

453

Grono 229
Gross Bigerhorn 153
Gross Diamantstock 339
Grosser Aletschgletscher 14, 292, 321, 343, 344
Grosse Scheidegg 328, 334, 336, 349
Gross Grünhorn 334, 443
Grosshorn 324, 348
Gross Litzner 417, 418
Grosstal 376, 441
Gruben 89, 146, 147, 148, 149, 160, 181, 444
Grueben Hut 339
Grünhorn Hut 393
Grünhornlücke 334
Gspaltenhorn 296, 310, 313, 314, 316, 322, 325, 328
  Gspaltenhorn Hut 313, 316
Gspon Höhenweg 82, 168
Gstaad 296, 301, 304
Gsteig 303, 304, 349, 351
Guarda 407, 411, 412, 418
Güferhorn 229, 233, 234, 395
Guggi Hut 322, 443
Guriner Furka 211
Guttanen 369
Gwächtenhorn 363, 367
Gwüest 360

H

Hahnenmoospass 307, 349
Handegg 339, 369
Hasliberg 338
Haslital 309, 336, 338, 351, 369, 441
Hausstock 349, 391, 397, 399, 401
Haut de Cry 299
Haute Cime 50, 59, 60, 61, 64, 65, 70
Heidelberger Hut 413
Heiligkreuz 191, 193
Helsenhorn 191
Hendar Furggu 211
Hérémence 115, 116, 119, 120, 122, 124, 128, 181, 440
Hérens, Val d' 116, 120, 125, 126, 129, 131, 132, 160, 181, 440
Hienderstock 340
Hiendertellihorn 339
Hinterbalm Hut 384

Hinterrhein 220, 229, 231, 232, 238, 244, 246, 248
Hochschijen 363
Hockenhorn 313
Höhenweg 82, 149, 152, 168, 176, 351, 424, 425, 426, 431
Hohsandhorn 193, 194
Hohsandjoch 194
Hohtürli 292, 310, 316, 349
Hörnli Hut 159, 167, 446
Hotel Weisshorn 89, 139, 146, 160
Hübschhorn 190

I

Iffigenalp 304, 305, 306, 351
Ilanz 232, 234
Il Chapütschin 272, 273, 274, 277, 278
Il Fuorn 287, 288
Illhorn 137, 139
Illiez, Val d' 52, 53, 54, 56, 59, 60, 61, 64, 66, 440
Ils Dschimels 277
Imfeld 192, 193
Innerferrera 246, 247
Innertkirchen 338, 339, 351, 360, 369, 370
Interlaken 316, 322, 323, 327, 331, 336, 338, 351
Isenfluh 318
Isenthal 376
Isola 270

J

Jamtal Hut 412, 418
Jegihorn 172
Jochpass 349, 357, 372
Joderhorn 179
Jöriflesspass 408, 416
Jöriflüelafurgga 416
Jörital 408, 416
Juf 240, 248
Julier Pass 244, 247, 248, 251, 252, 258
Jungen 90, 149, 151, 160
Jungfrau 11, 14, 296, 318, 320, 321, 322, 323, 324, 325, 331, 334, 336, 351
Jungfraujoch 316, 321, 322, 331, 334

K

Kandersteg 295, 307, 308, 310, 312, 316, 346, 347, 349, 351, 441
Kandertal 307, 308, 310
Kiental 310, 313, 314, 316, 351, 441
Kinhut 154, 155
Kippel 346, 351
Kirchlispitzen 15, 404, 424, 425, 426
Klausenpass 349, 359, 384, 385, 386, 389, 390
Kleine Scheidegg 316, 320, 321, 322, 327, 328, 330, 349, 351
Klein Matterhorn 157, 164, 167, 176
Klein Wellhorn 338
Kletterhütte Pardutz 424
Klöntal 395, 397, 441
Klöntaler See 395
Klösters 39
Konkordia Hut 321, 334, 344, 442, 443
Konkordiaplatz 321, 347
Kreuzberge 15
Kriegalppass 191
Krinnen Pass 304
Küblis 420, 421
Kühboden 343
Kummenalp 313, 347

L

La Fiamma 240, 265
La Fouly 86, 92, 93, 94, 95, 181
Laggin Bivouac Hut 181, 445
Lagginhorn 168, 170, 179, 181, 445
Lago Nero, Passo del 199, 216
La Gouille 125, 160
Lai Blau 412
Lais da Rims 288
Lämmeren Hut 307, 309
Landquart 408, 413, 420, 429
Langgletscher 346, 347, 348
Länta Hut 220, 233
La Punt 244, 251, 252, 281
Largè, Val 226
La Ruinette 113, 120
La Sage 89, 125, 130, 131, 132, 160
La Sella 277
Lauberhorn 320
Lauenen 304
Lauenental 296, 304
Lauteraarhorn 321, 333, 334, 340, 443

INDEX

Lauteraar Hut 333, 338, 340, 443
Lauterbrunnen 295, 296, 310, 313, 316, 318, 320, 321, 322, 323, 324, 325, 327, 328, 329, 330, 346, 348, 349, 351, 385, 441, 443
   Lauterbrunnen Valley (Lauterbrunnental) 296, 316, 318, 322, 323, 325, 327, 328, 349
   Lauterbrunnen Wetterhorn 74, 292, 295, 296, 325, 327, 328, 329, 330, 334, 335, 336, 338, 349, 367, 372
Lavaz, Val 234
Lavertezzo 207, 238
Lavin 289, 404, 410, 416, 418
Lavinuoz, Val 410, 411, 416, 418
Lavizzara, Val 204, 208, 209, 212, 215, 216, 217
Le Catogne 90
Le Châble 89, 105, 106, 108, 181
Le Chargeur 116, 119, 120, 124
Leit, Passo di 205
Lei, Valle di 246
Lengtal 191
Lenk 304, 305, 307, 349, 351
Lenzspitze 151, 153, 173, 176, 446
Le Peuty 67, 76, 77
Lepontine Alps 46, 179, 184, 189, 190, 13, 211, 212, 217, 236, 237
Les Haudères 86, 89, 122, 124, 125, 129, 130, 131, 160, 181, 444
Les Plans 298
Leuk 348
Leukerbad 309, 347, 348, 349, 351, 441
Leventina, Valle 188, 200, 202, 203, 205, 207, 217, 238, 440
Leysin 38, 296, 301
Liddes 96, 101, 142
Liechtenstein 15, 349, 408, 427, 429
Limmerensee 393
Linard Hut.
   See Chamanna dal Linard
Lindauer Hut 423, 425
Linthal 349, 385, 390, 391, 394, 395, 401
Linth Tal 390, 391, 397, 441
Lisengrat 432
Liskamm 157, 164, 417, 446
Lobhörner 318

Locarno 205, 211, 214, 216
Lochberg 365
Lochberglücke 364, 365
Lötschberg Tunnel 308, 346
Lötschenlücke 346, 347, 348
Lötschenpass 312, 313, 347
   Lötschenpass Hut 312, 313, 347
Lötschental 296, 312, 313, 325, 341, 344, 346, 347, 348, 351, 441
Lötschentaler Höhenweg 292, 348
Lourtier 108
Louvie, Col de 89, 107, 116
Lower Engadine 46, 250, 252, 278, 285, 287, 288, 404, 408, 410, 412, 413, 416, 418, 436
Lucerne 338, 354, 357, 370, 372, 376, 384, 399, 433
   Lucerne Lake (Vierwaldstättersee) 354, 357, 365, 370, 372, 376, 378
Lukmanier Pass 184, 188, 189, 199, 200, 203, 217, 221, 223, 224, 235, 236, 395
Lumnezia, Val 232, 234, 238
Lunghin, Lägh dal 250, 251
Lütschental 296, 325, 327, 329, 330, 351, 441

M

Maasplanggstock 369
Macun cirque 288
Maderanertal 379, 381, 384, 385, 441
Madone 204, 207, 213
Madone di Formazöö 213
Madra 219
   Madra Val 219
Madrano 200
Madrisa 413, 415, 420
   Madrisa Hut 420
Madris, Val 244, 246, 440
Madulain 14, 254
Maggia 196, 206, 211, 212, 215
   Maggia Valle 188, 199, 208, 211, 212, 215, 238, 440
Maienfeld 429
Maienfelder Alp 427
Maighels, Val 237
Malbun 427
Maloja 240, 243, 248, 250, 251, 252, 256, 258, 267, 269, 270,

283, 284, 289, 440
   Maloja Pass 240, 243, 251, 256, 258, 289, 440
Malvaglia 219, 220, 223, 224
   Malvaglia Val 219, 220, 224, 229
Mannheimer Hut 427
Männlichen 320, 321, 330
Marangun Hut. See Chamanna Marangun
Märjelensee 343, 344
Marmorera, Lai da 247
Maroz, Val 248, 258
Martigny 50, 52, 67, 68, 73, 77, 86, 97, 102, 105, 112, 147, 296, 299
Martinets, Col des 299
Martinsloch 397
Martinsmad Hut 397
Matt 170, 397
Mättenberg 332
Matterhorn 11, 13, 18, 31, 40, 72, 85, 90, 113, 115, 119, 135, 145, 149, 156, 157, 158, 159, 162, 164, 165, 166, 167, 176, 251, 329, 331, 332, 395, 411
Mattertal 18, 31, 89, 90, 145, 148, 149, 151, 152, 153, 154, 155, 157, 160, 167, 168, 174, 175, 176, 181, 182
Mattwaldhorn 170
Mauvoisin 100, 103, 105, 108, 109, 110, 111, 112
Mazorakopf 427
Medels 231, 236
Medel, Val 235, 236
Meiental 360, 365, 366
Meiringen 309, 334, 336, 338, 340, 349, 351, 369, 370, 372
Melchsee-Frutt 372
Melchtal 370, 372
Mello, Valle di 256, 265, 268, 269
Menzonio 215
Mera, Val 282
Mesocco 226, 227
Mesolcina, Valle 189, 226, 227, 228, 229, 238
Mettelhorn 82, 160
Mex 61, 62, 67
Mingèr, Val 288
Minor, Val 282
Mischabel 148, 153, 154, 155, 170, 173, 175, 176, 178, 445, 446, 447

455

Mischabel Hut 173, 176, 445, 446, 447
Mischabeljoch Bivouac Hut 173, 444, 445, 447
Mittaghorn 172, 174, 193, 324
Mittelaletsch Bivouac Hut 334, 347, 442
Mittelhorn 334, 336
Mittellegi Hut 321, 331
Mittlenbärg Hut 194
Mittlenbergpass 194
Moiry, Val de 89, 131, 132, 135, 137, 139, 141, 143, 181, 440
Monbiel 415, 416
Mönch 11, 14, 296, 318, 320, 321, 322
Mönchsjoch Hut 321, 333, 334, 443
Mont Avril 113, 114
Mont Blanc 12, 13, 40, 52, 54, 59, 61, 67, 68, 72, 73, 74, 75, 76, 77, 79, 82, 86, 87, 89, 92, 93, 95, 96, 98, 100, 101, 102, 106, 107, 113, 116, 119, 120, 129, 131, 146, 166, 299, 11, 303, 329, 347, 349
Mont Blanc de Cheilon 82, 89, 116, 119, 120, 129, 131
Mont Brulé 101, 106, 114, 127, 128
Mont Collon 126, 127, 128, 160
Mont de l'Etoile 129
Mont Dolent 94, 95, 96, 98
Mont Durand 114, 157
Monte del Forno 268
Monte di San Carlo 215
Monte Disgrazia 265, 267, 269, 273, 284, 290, 310
Monte Leone 170, 180, 184, 190, 191, 194, 13
 Monte Leone Hut 191
Monte Moro Pass 176, 178, 179, 189
Monte Rosa 85, 120, 128, 145, 148, 154, 157, 158, 159, 163, 164, 167, 176, 178, 281, 310, 432, 444, 446, 13
 Monte Rosa Hut 158, 163, 164, 444, 446, 447
Monte Rosso 268
Monte Sissone 269
Monte Zucchero 208, 215
Mont Gelé 106, 107, 116
Monthey 53, 56, 66
Montreux 52, 349

Mont Ruan 52, 54, 58, 64, 65, 72, 73, 74, 90
Mont Vélan 97, 98, 101
Morasco, Valle di 196
Morcles 296, 299, 301
Morgenhorn 310, 311, 313, 314
Morgins 12, 53, 54, 56
 Morgins Val de 53, 54, 56, 440
Morteratsch, Val 278, 283
Mot Tavrü 288
Mügaia, Bocchetta di 208, 209
Munt Baselgia 288
Munt Pers 278, 280
Muotatal 395, 397, 399
Muottas Muragl 281
Muragl, Fuorcla 281
Muretto
 Muretto Passo del 267, 269, 272, 284
 Muretto Val 267
Mürren 14, 40, 295, 296, 314, 316, 318, 319, 320, 322, 323, 328
Murtaröl 287
Murter 288
Müstair 240, 244, 285, 288
 Müstair Val 240, 288
Mutthorn 313, 316, 325
 Mutthorn Hut 313, 316, 325
Muttsee Hut 391, 393, 394

N

Naarfkopf 427
Nadelhorn 151, 153, 173, 174, 176, 446
Nalps, Val 237
Nante 217
Narèt, Passo del 199, 217
Nendaz 106, 116, 181
 Nendaz Val de 115, 116, 181, 440
Nepali Highway 354, 364
Nessental 369, 370
Niemet, Val 246
Nufenen 187, 188, 194, 196, 205, 229
 Nufenen Pass 188, 194, 196, 205

O

Oberaarjoch Hut 340, 341, 442
Oberaletsch Hut 344, 347, 442
Oberalp Pass 32, 184, 231, 235, 236, 237, 238, 252

Oberalpstock 15, 237, 382, 384, 385
Ober Gabelhorn 18, 82, 85, 113, 142, 144, 157, 166, 176, 444
Oberhornsee 325
Obersteinberg 323, 324, 325, 328
Oeschinensee 308, 310, 312
Ofapass 425
Ofenhorn 13, 188, 192, 193, 194, 196
Ofen Pass 240, 244, 285, 287, 288
Ofental 179
Oldenhorn 296, 301, 304
Olivone 217, 220, 221, 224, 238
Onsernone, Valle 211
Orgels, Pass digis 251
Orsières 86, 92, 95, 97, 101, 114, 181, 445
Ortler Alps 288
Osco 203
Ossasco 197, 199, 200, 217
Osura, Val d' 207, 208, 209
Otanes, Col des 100, 106, 109

P

Panixer Pass 397, 399, 401
Panixerpass Hut 393, 401
Partnun 421, 423, 426, 429
Partnunsee 421, 423, 426
Pass Bernina 11, 13, 18, 240, 243, 244, 248, 251, 252, 253, 267, 269, 270, 273, 274, 275, 276, 277, 278, 279, 280, 281, 282, 283, 284, 288, 289, 290
Pass Futschöl 412
Passit
 Passit Passo di 226
 Passit Val di 226
Passo di 184, 188, 194, 196, 197, 199, 200, 205, 209, 211, 215, 221, 224, 226
Peccia 199, 211, 215, 216, 217
 Peccia Val di 216, 217
Pennine Alps 13, 18, 52, 53, 59, 67, 76, 82, 85, 86, 89, 103, 130, 135, 137, 146, 149, 168, 170, 175, 176, 179, 180, 189, 190, 252, 292, 299, 301, 303, 309, 344, 347, 349, 357, 378
Pesciüm 197, 203, 204
Petersgrat 312, 313, 325, 346
Petit Col Ferret 82, 95

Index

Petit Combin 98, 109, 110
Pfälzer Hut 427
Pianaccio, Passo 211
Piano di Peccia 216
Pian San Giacomo 227, 228
Piatto, Passo di 205, 209
Pierre Avoi 106
Pigne d'Arolla 82, 113, 114, 120, 127, 128, 131
Pigne de la Lé 128, 134
Pigniu, Val da 401
Pilatus 334, 357, 364, 378, 384
Pillon, Col du 296, 301, 304
Pincascia, Val 207
Piora
    Piora Tour of Val 184
    Piora Val 200, 202, 203, 221
Piotta 202, 207
Pischahorn 416
Piumogna, Val 204, 205
Piz Albana 252
Piz Argient 278
Piz Ault 395
Piz Bacun 266, 267
Piz Badile 14, 240, 256, 261, 262, 269, 281
Piz Bernina 13, 240, 243, 253, 270, 273, 275, 277, 278, 279, 281, 283, 442
Piz Blaisun 253
Piz Blas 200
Piz Boval 274, 278, 279
Piz Buin 404, 408, 411, 412, 413, 418
Piz Cacciabella 258, 264, 265
Piz Calderas 252
Piz Cambrena 280, 282
Piz Casnil 258, 266, 267
Piz Corbet 227
Piz Corvatsch 272, 273, 278
Piz d'Agnel 251
Piz da las Coluonnas 251
Piz dal Märc 246
Piz d'Ela 251
Piz de la Margna 250, 270, 272, 281
Piz del Largè 226
Piz d'Err 251, 252
Piz Duan 248, 258
Piz Fora 272
Piz Frachiccio 265
Piz Gallagiun 240, 246

Piz Glüschaint 270, 272, 274, 277
Piz Grevasalvas 251
Piz Grialetsch 243, 256
Piz Jenatsch 252
Piz Julier 252
Piz Kesch 14, 240, 243, 252, 253, 256
Piz Lagalb 281, 282
Piz Lagrev 251
Piz Languard 240, 281
Piz Linard 280, 288, 289, 408, 410, 416
Piz Lischana 288
Piz Lunghin 240, 250
Piz Medel 221, 222, 224, 235, 236
Piz Minschun 412
Piz Moesola 229
Piz Morteratsch 273, 274, 275, 279
Piz Nair 252
Piz Ot 252
Piz Palü 11, 240, 243, 270, 275, 277, 278, 279, 280, 281, 283
Piz Plavna Dadaint 288
Piz Quattervals 287
Piz Radönt 256
Piz Roseg 243, 270, 273, 275, 276, 277, 417
Piz Russein 394
Piz Sardona 397
Piz Scerscen 273, 276, 277, 417
Piz Segnas 397
Piz Sella 276, 277, 278
Piz Sesvenna 288
Piz Surlej 274
Piz Taneda 202
Piz Terri 184, 189, 222, 224, 234, 235
Piz Tgietschen 189, 234
Piz Tremoggia 272
Piz Trovat 278, 280
Piz Uccello 229
Piz Urlaun 395
Piz Vadret 243, 256
Pizzi Gemelli 261, 262, 263
Pizzo Barone 205, 209
Pizzo Campolungo 204, 205
Pizzo Campo Tencia 184, 203, 204, 205, 212, 215
Pizzo Castello 216
Pizzo Cengalo 262
Pizzo Centrale 200
Pizzo Cramorino 220

Pizzo del Prévat 204
Pizzo del Sole 203
Pizzo di Sassello 204
Pizzo di Zocco 265
Pizzo Forca 220
Pizzo Forno 205
Pizzo Gararesc 199
Pizzo Penca 205
Pizzo Pesciora 197
Pizzo Rotondo 197, 199
Pizzo Tambo 184, 229, 231
Pizzo Trubinasca 261
Piz Zupò 278
Plaine Morte 296, 14, 306, 307
Planura Hut 384, 393, 394
Plasseggenpass 420, 426
Plattans, Val 236
Plattenjoch 417, 418
Plaun la Greina 184, 222, 224, 234, 235
Pointe de Bricola 132, 135
Pointe des Ecandies 88, 90
Pointe des Genevois 126, 128
Pointe de Vouasson 122, 129
Pointe de Zinal 144, 157, 166
Pointe d'Orny 67, 76, 77, 88, 92
Pointe d'Otemma 113
Pointe du Drone 103
Pointes de Mourti 135
Pollux 157, 164, 447
Poncione del Laghetto 205
Poncione di Braga 216
Poncione di Ruino 197
Poncione Sambuco 204
Pont de Nant 298, 299, 301, 351
Pontresina 11, 13, 240, 250, 252, 262, 273, 274, 276, 278, 281, 283
Porta, Val della 207
Portes du Soleil 53, 54, 56
Portjengrat 167, 179
Poschiavo 244, 278, 283, 284
    Poschiavo Val 252, 270, 274, 282, 283, 284
Prafleuri, Col de 89, 116
Pralong 116, 122, 181
Prato 209, 215, 216, 238
    Prato Val di 215
Prättigau 404, 408, 413, 416, 420, 424, 427, 429, 441
Prättigauer Höhenweg 404, 415, 420, 424, 425, 426, 427, 429, 441

Praz de Fort 93
Predèlp, Passo 203
Promontogno 258, 259, 261, 269
Punta da l'Albigna 266
Punta Pioda di Sciora 263
Punta Rasica 270
Punteglias Hut. *See* Camona da Punteglias
Puzzatsch 234

Q
Quadrella, Passo 211

R
Randa 31, 151, 153, 154, 155, 157, 181, 444, 445, 446, 447
Rappenhorn 193, 194
Raron 308, 346
Rätikon Alps 15, 407, 408, 420, 427, 441
Rätschenjoch 420
Ravais-ch-Sur, Lai da 256
Rawil Pass 301, 305, 306, 351, 440
Realp 197, 199, 364, 365
Redorta
    Redorta Passo di 184, 215
    Redorta Val 209
Refuge de Bostan-Tornay 58
Refuge de Chalin 60, 67
Refuge de Chésery 54
Refuge de la Gentiane la Barma 119
Refuge de la Tour 298
Refuge de la Vogealle 58, 72
Refuge de Pierredar 303
Refuge des Bouquetins 127
Refuge des Dents du Midi 60, 70
Refuge des Ecoulaies 119
Refuge de St Laurent 116
Refuge du Col de Balme 75
Refuge du Lac de Derborence 299
Refuge du Plan du Jeu 102
Refuge Giacomini 298
Refuge-Igloo des Pantalons Blancs 120
Refuge Les Grands 76, 79
Refuge Vieux Emosson 72, 74, 75, 79
Restipass 347
Reuss 15, 357, 360, 365, 370, 376, 379, 381, 385, 386, 399
Rheinquellhorn 229
Rheinwald 229, 231, 232, 233, 238

Rheinwaldhorn 13, 184, 189, 194, 203, 205, 219, 220, 224, 229, 233
Rhine 197, 200, 220, 237, 250, 296, 349, 354, 359, 404, 408, 427, 429, 431, 433
Rhône Valley 66, 440
Richetlipass 349, 399
Richisau 397
Riederalp 344
Riedmatten, Col de 89, 120, 124, 128
Riffelhorn 163
Rifugio Barone 205, 209
Rifugio Bignami 283, 284
Rifugio Ganan 226
Rifugio Gaspare Oberto 176, 178
Rifugio Longoni 284
Rifugio Marinelli 284
Rifugio Pian Grand 227
Rifugio Piano delle Creste 214
Rifugio Poncione di Braga 216
Rifugio Saoseo 282
Rifugio Sponda 205
Rigi 357, 378
Rigidalstock 374
Rimpfischhorn 155, 156, 157, 158, 163, 167, 175, 310, 447
Rinderhorn 308, 349
Rinder Hut 347, 348
Risetenpass 397
Ritterpass 191
Ritzhörner 197
Ritzlihorn 338, 339
Roc de la Vache 143
Rocher de Barme 57
Rochers de Naye 18, 349
Roda, Val da 246, 248
Rognoi, Bocchetta di 207
Ronco 197, 238
Rosablanche 107, 115, 116, 119, 131
Roseg
    Roseg Porta da 276
    Roseg Val 270, 272, 273, 274, 277, 278, 283
Rosenhorn 334, 336, 340
Rosenlaui 334, 336, 338
    Rosenlaui Bivouac Hut 336
Rosenlauital 336, 338, 349
Rossa 224, 226, 238
Rote Furka 419

Rothorn 139, 143, 145, 149, 157, 166, 296, 333, 446, 448
Rotondo Hut 197, 364
Rotsteinpass 432
Rotstock Hut 319, 323, 328
Rottal Hut 323, 324, 443
Roveredo 224, 227, 238
Ruchen, Grosse 382, 385
Rueras 379
Rugghubel Hut 374

S
Saarbrucker Hut 417, 418, 419
Saas Almagell 172, 174, 176, 179, 181, 447
Saas Balen 168
Saas Fee 13, 40, 86, 115, 137, 152, 156, 163, 167, 170, 172, 173, 174, 175, 176, 181, 444, 445, 446, 447
Saas Grund 168, 170, 174, 176, 179, 181, 444, 445, 447
Saastal 18, 148, 149, 152, 167, 168, 170, 174, 175, 176, 178, 179, 181, 182, 189, 440
Safienberg 232
Safiental 232, 238
Sagliains, Val 410, 416, 418
Salanfe
    Salanfe Auberge de 60, 61, 62, 69, 70, 72, 79
    Salanfe Lac de 60, 62, 68, 70
Salbit Hut 360
Salbitschijen 354, 360, 14, 402
Salvan 67, 68, 79
Sambuco, Val 215, 216, 217
Samedan 244, 252, 281, 289
Samnaun 408, 413
San Bernardino 187, 224, 226, 227, 228, 229, 238, 290
    San Bernardino Passo del 229
San Carlo 214, 216
Sandalp 393
Sandgipfel 394
Sanetsch, Col du 303
San Giacomo
    San Giacomo Passo di 184, 188, 194, 196, 215
    San Giacomo Valle 227, 231, 246
Santa Domenica 224
Santa Maria 189, 202, 221, 229, 244

Santa Maria Valle 203, 217, 220, 221, 223, 224, 236
Säntis 378, 404, 408, 15, 429, 431, 432
Sardasca, Val 408, 415, 416, 418, 419
Sargans 349, 354, 359, 397, 427, 431, 433
Sarsura, Val 251
Sassa
   Sassa Fuorcla Val 287
Sassello, Passo 204, 217
Sasseneire 125, 132, 135
Sassiglion, Forca di 283
Sasso Nero, Passo del 199, 216, 217
Savognin 251
Scalettapass 256
Schächental 384, 385, 441
Schalihorn 132, 142, 157
S-chanf 250, 287
S-charl 240, 287, 288
   S-charl Val 285, 287, 288, 413
Schattig Wichel 354, 379
Scheideggwetterhorn 336
Schesaplana 15, 404, 420, 423, 424, 425, 427
   Schesaplana Hut 404, 423, 424, 425, 427, 429
Schiers 424
Schijenflue 421
Schilthorn 314, 318, 319, 322, 328
   Schilthorn Hut 319
Schinhorn 193
Schlappiner Joch 420
Schlappintal 413, 416, 419, 420
Schmadri Hut 324, 325
Schneehorn 296, 322
Schneestock 364
Schöllenen gorge 357, 399
Schönbiel Hut 130, 144, 159, 165, 166, 445
Schreckhorn 14, 292, 321, 325, 327, 328, 330, 333, 336, 340, 372, 443
   Schreckhorn Hut 333, 334, 443
Schuders 424
Schwägalp 429, 431, 432
Schwanden 391, 397
Schwarenbach 308, 310
Schwarzental 370
Schwarzhorn 82, 137, 148, 256, 327, 446

Schweizereck 404, 424
Schweizertor 423, 424, 425, 426
Schynige Platte 327, 328, 329
Sciora
   Sciora Dadent 263, 265
   Sciora Dafora (Sciora di Fuori) 263, 264
Scopi 221
Scuol 252, 287, 288, 404, 408, 412, 413
Sedrun 236, 237, 238, 381
Seehorn 417
   Seehorn Chlein 419
   Seehorn Gross 417, 419
Seelücke 417
Seetalhorn 152
Seetal Hut 415, 416, 417, 418
Seewis 427, 429
Sefinenfurke 316, 319, 349
Sefinental 316, 322, 323, 325, 328
Segantini Hut 281
Selden 312, 313, 351
Selma 224
Sembrancher 86, 103, 105, 112
Sentier des Chamois 82, 89, 105, 107, 109
Sentiero Alpino Calanca 184, 229
Sentiero Panoramico 240, 258
Septimer Pass 248, 250, 258
Sernftal 349, 393, 397, 399, 441
Sertig Pass 256
Sewen Hut 366
Sex de Marinda 135
Sex Rouge 301, 303
Sidelen Hut 364, 365
Sierre 132, 137, 139, 141, 148
Silberhorn 323, 443
   Silberhorn Hut 323, 443
Sils
   Sils Baselgia 248
   Sils Maria 272, 283
Silvaplana 244, 248, 252, 272
Silvretta Alps 26, 288, 289, 407, 408, 410, 413, 415, 416, 417, 419, 420, 436, 441
Silvrettahorn 417, 418
Silvretta Hut 415, 417, 418, 419
Silvrettapass 418
Simmenfalle 305, 307
Simmental 304, 305, 306, 307
Simplon Pass 13, 82, 147, 170, 172,

179, 180, 181, 182, 184, 188, 189, 190, 191, 238
Sinestra, Val 413
Sion 20, 106, 109, 116, 120, 124, 125, 303, 305, 306
Siviez 116, 181
Soazza 227
Soglio 240, 246, 256, 258, 259
Soi, Val 220
Solalex 298, 299
Sole, Passo del 203
Sonlerto 214
Sonogno 205, 207, 208, 209, 215, 238
Soreda, Passo de 233
Sornico 215
Spannort
   Spannort Gross 357, 376
   Spannort Hut 376
Spazzacaldeira 265
Spiez 305, 307, 308, 314
Spiringen 385
Splügen 13, 184, 187, 188, 189, 228, 229, 231, 232, 238
   Splügen Pass 184, 13, 231
Stalden 149, 168, 174, 374
Stallerberg 248
Stampa 258
St Antönien 407, 408, 413, 420, 421, 423, 424, 426, 429
St Antöniental 407, 408, 413, 420, 423, 424, 426, 429
St Antönier Joch 420
Starlera, Val 247
Stechelberg 319, 322, 323, 324, 327, 328, 351, 443
Steg 157, 162, 167, 427
Stelvio Pass 240
St Gallen 256, 378, 404, 408, 417, 431
St Gotthard Pass 188, 200, 217, 399
St-Luc 137, 141
St-Maurice 52, 61, 67, 296, 298
St Moritz 40, 244, 248, 250, 14, 252, 273, 274
St Niklaus 90, 148, 149, 151, 153, 160, 174, 181, 445
Stockhorn Bivouac Hut 344
Storegg Pass 372
Strahlegghorn 333, 334
Strahleggpass 333, 334

459

Strahlhorn 156, 157, 163, 167, 175, 447
St-Rhémy 100
Stucklistock 360
Studerhorn 340
Suls-Lobhorn Hut 318, 328
Sulzfluh 15, 404, 408, 420, 421, 423, 425, 426
    Sulzfluh Klettersteig 404, 423
Sumvitg 234
    Sumvitg Val 234, 236
Surenenpass 349, 354, 375
Surettahorn 231, 246
Sur Il Foss 288
Surlej 252, 272, 273, 274
    Surlej Fuorcla 240, 273, 274, 283
Surselva 32, 221, 231, 232, 234, 238
Susanfe, Vallon de 64, 72, 74, 440
Susauna, Val 254, 287
Susch 244, 408, 410, 416
Süsertal 416, 418
Sustenhorn 360, 361, 367
Sustenlimi 367
Sustenlimihorn 361, 363, 367
Sustenpass 14, 338, 351, 360, 361, 366, 367, 369, 370
Sustenspitz 367
Sustli Hut 366
Swiss National Park 46, 240, 278, 285, 287, 288
Swiss Path 376

T
Täli 247
Tälli Hut 369
Tällispitz 404, 419
Tällistock 341, 369
Tannen 372
Tanzbödeli 323
Tarasp 288, 290
Täsch 153, 155, 156, 157, 163, 173, 174, 175, 181, 444, 447
    Täsch Hut 155, 156, 157, 163, 173, 175, 444, 447
Täschalp 90, 152, 155, 167
Täschhorn 156, 173, 175, 176, 444, 447
Tenero 207
Tenigerbad 234
Termine
    Termine Passo 220, 224

Termine Val 203, 221
Tête Blanche 130, 131, 157
Tête de Valpelline 157, 165
Thalkirch 232
Theodulpass 32, 157, 162, 167
Thun 307
Thusis 229, 231, 244, 246
Ticino 13, 18, 43, 148, 187, 188, 191, 194, 196, 197, 199, 18, 200, 205, 211, 214, 215, 217, 221, 235
Tiefencastel 244
Tiefenstock 364
Tieralplistock 369
Tierberg 363, 364, 369, 375
Tierbergli Hut 367
Tierfed 391, 393
Tierwis Hut 432
Tilisunafürggli 421, 426
Tilisuna Hut 421, 426
Tinizong 251
Titlis 14, 357, 369, 370, 372, 374, 375, 376, 379, 384
Tochuhorn 189
Tödi 15, 252, 281, 359, 378, 384, 391, 393, 394, 395
Toggenburg 408, 431, 432, 433, 435
Toggenburger Höhenweg 431
Tomülpass 232
Topali Hut 151
Torrone
    Torrone Centrale 269
    Torrone Occidentale 269
    Torrone Orientale 269
Torta, Val 199, 200, 217, 416
Tosa Falls 192, 194, 215
Totalp Hut 425, 427
Tour d'Aï 301
Tour de Famelon 301
Tour de la Vallée du Trient 50, 78, 79, 440
Tour de Mayen 301
Tour des Combins 82, 98, 101, 106, 108, 113, 440
Tour des Dents Blanches 50, 58, 440
Tour des Dents du Midi 50, 58, 61, 62, 64, 67, 71, 440
Tour des Muverans 292, 299, 301, 440
Tour des Portes du Soleil 54, 57
Tour du Mont Blanc 67, 75, 79, 86

Tour du Ruan 50, 70, 71, 72, 74, 75, 79, 440
Tour du Val d'Anniviers 82, 137, 139, 141, 440
Tour du Val de Bagnes 82, 105, 106, 108, 109, 440
Tour du Val d'Hérens 122, 124, 125, 440
Tour of Monte Rosa 82, 174, 176, 440
Tour of the Bernina Alps 240, 283, 440
Tour of the Jungfrau Region 292, 319, 327, 328, 441
Tour of the Matterhorn 82, 127, 154, 160, 176, 440
Tour of the Rätikon 404, 424, 441
Tour of the Silvretta 404, 418, 441
Tour of the Swiss National Park 240
Tour of Valle di Blenio 184, 223, 440
Tour Sallière 50, 61, 64, 65, 69, 70, 72, 74, 90
Tresch Hut 379
Tresculmine, Passo di 226
Trient 52, 67, 76, 77, 79, 87, 88, 89, 90, 92, 114
    Trient Gorges du 53, 68, 73, 75
    Trient Vallée du 50, 53, 67, 68, 73, 75, 77, 79, 440
Trift Hut 364, 369
Troistorrents 53, 56
Trubinasca
    Trubinasca Passo della 261
    Trubinasca Vallun da 261
Trümmelbach Falls 322, 328
Trun 234, 394, 395
Trupchun
    Trupchun Fuorcla 287
    Trupchun Val 285, 287
Tschingelhorn 313, 324, 325, 401
Tschingel Pass 316
Tübinger Hut 417, 418, 419
Tuoi, Val 411, 412, 418
Turtmann Hut 145, 148, 444
Turtmanntal 89, 139, 145, 146, 147, 148, 149, 160, 181, 182, 440

U
Uffiern, Pass d' 224
UNESCO World Natural Heritage Site 325

Unteraargletscher 340
Unterschächen 385, 386
Unterwasser 431, 433
Urbachtal 338, 369
Urezzas, Val d' 412, 418
Uri Alps 357, 359, 364, 365, 441
Uri-Rotstock 15, 376, 378
Urnäsch 431, 432
Urnerboden 390, 391
Urner Boden 359, 389, 390, 391, 441
Urnersee 376
Urschai, Val 412, 413, 418
Üschenental 308

V
Valbella 226
Valle Maggia, Bocchetta di 215
Vals 115, 116, 120, 188, 199, 207, 211, 224, 232, 238, 270, 272, 384, 440, 442
Valsertal 220, 232, 233, 234, 238
Valtellina 267, 282, 283
Vegorness, Val 205, 209
Vella 234, 238
Venett, Passo 204
Verajöchl 425
Verbier 40, 86, 88, 13, 104, 105, 106, 115, 116
Vercorin 139, 141
Vereinapass 404, 410, 416, 418
Vereinatal 408, 415, 416
Vergeletto 211
Verstanclahorn 416, 417
Verzasca, Val 205, 206, 207, 209, 211, 215, 238, 440
Via Engiadina 250, 411, 418
Vial, Colle 262
Via Splüga 231
Vicosoprano 258, 264, 267
Vierwaldstättersee 354, 357, 365, 370, 372, 376, 378
Vieux Emosson, Lac du 72, 74, 75, 79
Vignun, Val 228
Villa 122, 125, 131, 132, 160, 199, 344
Villars 296, 298
Viola, Val 282, 283
Visp 148, 149, 168, 238, 308, 344, 351

Vissoie 137, 141
Vogeljoch 229
Vogorno 207, 209
Voralp Hut 360, 361, 363
Voralptal 360, 361, 363, 441
Vorarlberg 407
Vorderrhein 187, 229, 231, 232, 234, 235, 236, 237, 357, 379, 393, 394, 401
Voré, Col de 304
Vrenelisgärtli 395
Vrin 232, 234, 238

W
Walensee 391, 429, 433, 435
Walenstadt 433, 435
Wandfluehorn 130
Wannenhorn
    Wannenhorn Gross 343
    Wannenhorn Klein 343
Wannenzwillinge 343
Wasenhorn 179, 184, 191
Wassen 365, 370, 379
Wasserauen 431, 432
Weber Hut 327, 328
Weisshorn 13, 82, 85, 132, 135, 139, 142, 143, 145, 146, 147, 148, 151, 153, 154, 157, 191, 306, 408, 444, 447
    Weisshorn Hut 145, 153, 154, 447
Weissmies 82, 148, 167, 170, 172, 179, 299, 444, 445, 447
    Weissmies Hut 170, 172, 179, 445, 447
Weisstannen 349, 397
Weisstannental 349, 397
Wellenkuppe 157
Wendenstöcke 357, 367, 370, 372
Wengen 14, 40, 295, 296, 316, 320, 321, 349
Wetterhorn 74, 292, 295, 296, 325, 327, 328, 329, 330, 334, 335, 336, 338, 349, 367, 372
Wiesbadener Hut 412, 417, 418
Wildenmatten Hut 365
Wilderswil 316, 327, 328
Wildgärst 327
Wildhaus 404, 431, 432, 433, 435
Wildhorn 14, 137, 304, 305
    Wildhorn Hut 304, 305

Wildstrubel 14, 137, 292, 296, 305, 306, 307, 308, 309, 351
    Wildstrubel Hut 306, 307
Wiler 346, 348, 351, 369, 370
Windegg Hut 369
Windgällen 382, 386
    Windgällen Grosse 15, 382, 385, 386
    Windgällen Kleine 382
    Windgällen Schächentaler 385, 386
Winterberg 360, 361, 364
Winterlücke 365, 408, 416
Winterstock 365
Wissberg 247
Wissigstock 354, 374
Witenwasserenstock 197
Wiwannihorn 346
Wiwanni Hut 346
Wolfenschiessen 372
Wysse Nollen 364
Wyssi Frau 310, 311

Z
Zadrell, Fuorcla 411, 416
Zapporthorn 224, 226, 229
Zapport Hut 220, 229
Zermatt 11, 13, 34, 40, 67, 75, 82, 86, 88, 89, 90, 104, 113, 115, 119, 126, 130, 131, 137, 152, 153, 154, 155, 156, 157, 158, 159, 160, 162, 163, 164, 165, 166, 167, 174, 176, 181, 188, 252, 329, 432, 444, 445, 446, 447
Zernez 244, 251, 285, 287, 288
Zervreilahorn 233, 234
Zinal 82, 86, 89, 128, 131, 135, 137, 139, 141, 142, 143, 144, 145, 146, 160, 181, 444, 446, 447, 448
    Zinal Val de 141, 142, 144, 145, 166
Zinalrothorn 82, 85, 141, 142, 145, 147, 157, 160, 166, 310, 444, 448
Zuoz 14
Zweilütschinen 296, 316, 327
Zwinglipass Hut 432

LISTING OF INTERNATIONAL CICERONE GUIDES

INTERNATIONAL CHALLENGES, COLLECTIONS AND ACTIVITIES
Canyoning in the Alps
Europe's High Points
The Via Francigena Canterbury to Rome – Part 2

AFRICA
Kilimanjaro
The High Atlas
Walking in the Drakensberg
Walks and Scrambles in the Moroccan Anti-Atlas

ALPS CROSS-BORDER ROUTES
100 Hut Walks in the Alps
Alpine Ski Mountaineering Vol 1 – Western Alps
Alpine Ski Mountaineering Vol 2 – Central and Eastern Alps
Chamonix to Zermatt
The Karnischer Hohenweg
The Tour of the Bernina
Tour of Monte Rosa
Tour of the Matterhorn
Trail Running – Chamonix and the Mont Blanc region
Trekking in the Alps
Trekking in the Silvretta and Ratikon Alps
Trekking Munich to Venice
Trekking the Tour of Mont Blanc
Walking in the Alps

PYRENEES AND FRANCE/SPAIN CROSS-BORDER ROUTES
Shorter Treks in the Pyrenees
The GR10 Trail
The GR11 Trail
The Pyrenean Haute Route
The Pyrenees
Walks and Climbs in the Pyrenees

AUSTRIA
Innsbruck Mountain Adventures
The Adlerweg
Trekking in Austria's Hohe Tauern
Trekking in the Stubai Alps
Trekking in the Zillertal Alps
Walking in Austria
Walking in the Salzkammergut: the Austrian Lake District

EASTERN EUROPE
The Danube Cycleway Vol 2
The High Tatras
The Mountains of Romania
Walking in Bulgaria's National Parks
Walking in Hungary

FRANCE, BELGIUM AND LUXEMBOURG
Chamonix Mountain Adventures
Cycle Touring in France
Cycling London to Paris
Cycling the Canal de la Garonne
Cycling the Canal du Midi
Mont Blanc Walks
Mountain Adventures in the Maurienne
Short Treks on Corsica
The GR20 Corsica
The GR5 Trail
The GR5 Trail – Benelux and Lorraine
The GR5 Trail – Vosges and Jura
The Grand Traverse of the Massif Central
The Loire Cycle Route
The Moselle Cycle Route
The River Rhone Cycle Route
The Robert Louis Stevenson Trail
The Way of St James – Le Puy to the Pyrenees
Tour of the Queyras
Trekking the Robert Louis Stevenson Trail
Vanoise Ski Touring
Via Ferratas of the French Alps
Walking in Corsica
Walking in Provence – East
Walking in Provence – West
Walking in the Ardennes
Walking in the Auvergne
Walking in the Briançonnais
Walking in the Dordogne
Walking in the Haute Savoie: North
Walking in the Haute Savoie: South

GERMANY
Hiking and Cycling in the Black Forest
The Danube Cycleway Vol 1
The Rhine Cycle Route
The Westweg
Walking in the Bavarian Alps

HIMALAYA
Annapurna
Everest: A Trekker's Guide
The Mount Kailash Trek
Trekking in Bhutan
Trekking in Ladakh
Trekking in the Himalaya

IRELAND
The Wild Atlantic Way and Western Ireland

ITALY
Italy's Sibillini National Park
Shorter Walks in the Dolomites
Ski Touring and Snowshoeing in the Dolomites
The Way of St Francis
Trekking in the Apennines
Trekking in the Dolomites
Trekking the Giants' Trail: Alta Via 1 through the Italian Pennine Alps
Via Ferratas of the Italian Dolomites Vols 1&2
Walking and Trekking in the Gran Paradiso
Walking in Abruzzo
Walking in Italy's Cinque Terre
Walking in Italy's Stelvio National Park
Walking in Sardinia
Walking in Sicily
Walking in the Dolomites
Walking in Tuscany
Walking in Umbria
Walking Lake Como and Maggiore
Walking Lake Garda and Iseo
Walking on the Amalfi Coast
Walking the Via Francigena Pilgrim Route – Part 3
Walks and Treks in the Maritime Alps

JAPAN, ASIA AND AUSTRALIA
Hiking and Trekking in the Japan Alps and Mount Fuji
Hiking the Overland Track
Japan's Kumano Kodo Pilgrimage
Trekking in Tajikistan

MEDITERRANEAN
The High Mountains of Crete
Trekking in Greece
Treks and Climbs in Wadi Rum, Jordan
Walking and Trekking in Zagori
Walking and Trekking on Corfu
Walking in Cyprus
Walking on Malta
Walking on the Greek Islands – the Cyclades

NORTH AMERICA
The John Muir Trail
The Pacific Crest Trail

SOUTH AMERICA
Aconcagua and the Southern Andes
Hiking and Biking Peru's Inca Trails
Torres del Paine

SCANDINAVIA, ICELAND AND GREENLAND
Trekking in Greenland – The Arctic Circle Trail
Trekking in Southern Norway
Trekking the Kungsleden
Walking and Trekking in Iceland
Walking in Norway

SLOVENIA, CROATIA, MONTENEGRO AND ALBANIA
Mountain Biking in Slovenia
The Islands of Croatia
The Julian Alps of Slovenia
The Mountains of Montenegro
The Peaks of the Balkans Trail
The Slovene Mountain Trail
Walking in Slovenia: The Karavanke
Walks and Treks in Croatia

SPAIN AND PORTUGAL
Camino de Santiago: Camino Frances
Coastal Walks in Andalucia
Cycle Touring in Spain
Cycling the Camino de Santiago
Mountain Walking in Mallorca
Mountain Walking in Southern Catalunya
Portugal's Rota Vicentina
Spain's Sendero Historico: The GR1
The Andalucian Coast to Coast Walk

The Camino del Norte and
  Camino Primitivo
The Camino Ingles and Ruta do Mar
The Camino Portugues
The Mountains of Nerja
The Mountains of Ronda
  and Grazalema
The Sierras of Extremadura
Trekking in Mallorca
Trekking in the Canary Islands
Walking and Trekking in the
  Sierra Nevada
Walking in Andalucia
Walking in Menorca
Walking in Portugal
Walking in the Algarve
Walking in the Cordillera Cantabrica
Walking on Gran Canaria
Walking on La Gomera and
  El Hierro
Walking on La Palma
Walking on Lanzarote and
  Fuerteventura
Walking on Madeira
Walking on Tenerife
Walking on the Azores
Walking on the Costa Blanca
Walking the Camino dos Faros

SWITZERLAND
Switzerland's Jura Crest Trail
The Swiss Alpine Pass Route –
  Via Alpina Route 1
The Swiss Alps
Tour of the Jungfrau Region
Walking in the Bernese Oberland
Walking in the Engadine – Switzerland
Walking in the Valais

TECHNIQUES
Fastpacking
Geocaching in the UK
Map and Compass
Outdoor Photography
Polar Exploration
The Mountain Hut Book

MINI GUIDES
Alpine Flowers
Navigation
Pocket First Aid and Wilderness
  Medicine
Snow

MOUNTAIN LITERATURE
8000 metres
A Walk in the Clouds
Abode of the Gods
Fifty Years of Adventure
The Pennine Way – the Path, the
  People, the Journey
Unjustifiable Risk?

For full information on all our guides,
and to order books and eBooks, visit our
website:
www.cicerone.co.uk.

Explore the world with Cicerone

walking • trekking • mountaineering • climbing • mountain biking • cycling • via ferratas • scrambling • trail running • skills and techniques

For over 50 years, Cicerone have built up an outstanding collection of nearly 400 guides, inspiring all sorts of amazing experiences.

www.cicerone.co.uk – where adventures begin

- Our **website** is a treasure-trove for every outdoor adventurer. You can buy books or read inspiring articles and trip reports, get technical advice, check for updates, and view videos, photographs and mapping for routes and treks.

- **Register this book** or any other Cicerone guide in your member's library on our website and you can choose to automatically access updates and GPX files for your books, if available.

- Our **fortnightly newsletters** will update you on new publications and articles and keep you informed of other news and events. You can also follow us on Facebook, Twitter and Instagram.

We hope you have enjoyed using this guidebook. If you have any comments you would like to share, please contact us using the form on our website or via email, so that we can provide the best experience for future customers.

CICERONE

Juniper House, Murley Moss Business Village, Oxenholme Road, Kendal LA9 7RL

info@cicerone.co.uk   cicerone.co.uk